EVERYMAN, I will go with thee,

and be thy guide,

In thy most need to go by thy side

EDWARD GIBBON

Born 27th April 1737 at Putney. Educated at Westminster School, Oxford, and privately at Lausanne. Toured Italy, 1764–5, and conceived the plan of his 'History'. Settled in London in 1772 and sat in Parliament from 1774 to 1783. Lived in Lausanne, 1784–93, and died in London 16th January 1794.

EDWARD GIBBON

Decline and Fall of the Roman Empire

IN SIX VOLUMES · VOLUME SIX

INTRODUCTION BY
CHRISTOPHER DAWSON

DENT: LONDON, MELBOURNE AND TORONTO
EVERYMAN'S LIBRARY
DUTTON: NEW YORK

No. 476 Hardback ISBN 0 460 00476 X
No. 1476 Paperback ISBN 0 460 01476 5

CONTENTS

CHAP.   PAGE

LVII. The Turks of the House of Seljuk—Their Revolt against Mahmud, Conqueror of Hindostan—Togrul subdues Persia, and protects the Caliphs—Defeat and Captivity of the Emperor Romanus Diogenes by Alp Arslan—Power and Magnificence of Malek Shah—Conquest of Asia Minor and Syria—State and Oppression of Jerusalem   1

LVIII. Origin and Numbers of the First Crusade—Characters of the Latin Princes—Their March to Constantinople—Policy of the Greek Emperor Alexius—Conquest of Nice, Antioch, and Jerusalem, by the Franks—Deliverance of the Holy Sepulchre—Godfrey of Bouillon, First King of Jerusalem 33

LIX. Preservation of the Greek Empire—Numbers, Passage, and Event of the Second and Third Crusades—St. Bernard—Reign of Saladin in Egypt and Syria—His Conquest of Jerusalem—Naval Crusades—Richard the First of England—Pope Innocent the Third; and the Fourth and Fifth Crusades—The Emperor Frederic the Second—Louis the Ninth of France; and the two last Crusades—Expulsion of the Latins or Franks by the Mamalukes 93

LX. Schism of the Greeks and Latins—State of Constantinople—Revolt of the Bulgarians—Isaac Angelus dethroned by his Brother Alexius—Origin of the Fourth Crusade—Alliance of the French and Venetians with the Son of Isaac—Their Naval Expedition to Constantinople—The two Sieges and Final Conquest of the City 134

LXI. Partition of the Empire by the French and Venetians—Five Latin Emperors of the Houses of Flanders and Courtenay—Their Wars against the Bulgarians and Greeks—Weakness and Poverty of the Latin Empire—Recovery of Constantinople by the Greeks—General Consequences of the Crusades 178

LXII. The Greek Emperors of Nice and Constantinople—Elevation and Reign of Michael Palæologus—His false Union with the Pope and the Latin Church—Hostile Designs of Charles of Anjou—Revolt of Sicily—Revolutions and present State of Athens 216

LXIII. Civil Wars, and Ruin of the Greek Empire—Reigns of Andronicus the Elder and Younger, and John Palæologus—Regency, Revolt, Reign, and Abdication of John Cantacuzene—Establishment of a Genoese Colony at Pera or Galata . . . 247

viii Gibbon's Decline and Fall of Rome

CHAP.   PAGE

LXIV. Conquests of Zingis Khan and the Moguls from China to Poland—Escape of Constantinople and the Greeks—Origin of the Ottoman Turks in Bithynia—Reigns and Victories of Othman, Orchan, Amurath the First, and Bajazet the First—Foundation and Progress of the Turkish Monarchy in Asia and Europe—Danger of Constantinople and the Greek Empire . . . 273

LXV. Elevation of Timour or Tamerlane to the Throne of Samarcand—His Conquests in Persia, Georgia, Tartary, Russia, India, Syria, and Anatolia—His Turkish War—Defeat and Captivity of Bajazet—Death of Timour—Civil War of the Sons of Bajazet—Restoration of the Turkish Monarchy by Mohammed the First—Siege of Constantinople by Amurath the Second . . 308

LXVI. Applications of the Eastern Emperors to the Popes—Visits to the West of John the First, Manuel, and John the Second, Palæologus—Union of the Greek and Latin Churches promoted by the Council of Basil, and concluded at Ferrara and Florence—State of Literature at Constantinople—Its Revival in Italy by the Greek Fugitives—Curiosity and Emulation of the Latins 346

LXVII. Schism of the Greeks and Latins—Reign and Character of Amurath the Second—Crusade of Ladislaus, King of Hungary—His Defeat and Death 392

LXVIII. Reign and Character of Mohammed the Second—Siege, Assault, and Final Conquest of Constantinople by the Turks—Death of Constantine Palæologus—Servitude of the Greeks—Extinction of the Roman Empire in the East—Consternation of Europe—Conquests and Death of Mohammed the Second 417

LXIX. State of Rome from the Twelfth Century—Temporal Dominion of the Popes—Seditions of the City—Political Heresy of Arnold of Brescia—Restoration of the Republic—The Senators—Pride of the Romans—Their Wars—They are deprived of the Election and Presence of the Popes, who retire to Avignon—The Jubilee—Noble Families of Rome—Feud of the Colonna and Ursini . 461

LXX. Character and Coronation of Petrarch—Restoration of the Freedom and Government of Rome by the Tribune Rienzi—His Virtues and Vices, his Expulsion and Death—Return of the Popes from Avignon—Great Schism of the West—Reunion of the Latin Church—Last Struggles of Roman Liberty—Statutes of Rome—Final Settlement of the Ecclesiastical State . . 503

LXXI. Prospect of the Ruins of Rome in the Fifteenth Century—Four Causes of Decay and Destruction—Example of the Coliseum—Renovation of the City—Conclusion of the whole Work . 547

Index 571

THE
HISTORY OF THE DECLINE AND FALL
OF THE
ROMAN EMPIRE

CHAPTER LVII

The Turks of the House of Seljuk—Their Revolt against Mahmud, Con-
queror of Hindostan—Togrul subdues Persia, and protects the
Caliphs—Defeat and Captivity of the Emperor Romanus Diogenes by
Alp Arslan—Power and Magnificence of Malek Shah—Conquest of
Asia Minor and Syria—State and Oppression of Jerusalem—Pil-
grimages to the Holy Sepulchre

FROM the isle of Sicily the reader must transport himself beyond
the Caspian Sea to the original seat of the Turks or Turkmans,
against whom the first crusade was principally directed. Their
Scythian empire of the sixth century was long since dissolved,
but the name was still famous among the Greeks and Orientals,
and the fragments of the nation, each a powerful and independent
people, were scattered over the desert from China to the Oxus
and the Danube: the colony of Hungarians was admitted into
the republic of Europe, and the thrones of Asia were occupied by
slaves and soldiers of Turkish extraction. While Apulia and
Sicily were subdued by the Norman lance, a swarm of these
northern shepherds overspread the kingdoms of Persia; their
princes of the race of Seljuk erected a splendid and solid empire
from Samarcand to the confines of Greece and Egypt, and the
Turks have maintained their dominion in Asia Minor till the
victorious crescent has been planted on the dome of St. Sophia.

One of the greatest of the Turkish princes was Mamood or
Mahmud,[1] the Gaznevide, who reigned in the eastern provinces
of Persia one thousand years after the birth of Christ. His

[1] I am indebted for his character and history to D'Herbelot (Bibliothèque
Orientale, *Mahmud*, p. 533-537), M. de Guignes (Histoire des Huns, tom.
iii. p. 155-173), and our countryman Colonel Alexander Dow (vol. i. p. 23-
83). In the two first volumes of his History of Hindostan he styles himself the translator of the Persian Ferishta; but in his florid text it is not
easy to distinguish the version and the original.

father Sebectagi was the slave of the slave of the slave of the
commander of the faithful.   But in this descent of servitude
the first degree was merely titular, since it was filled by the
sovereign of Transoxiana and Chorasan, who still paid a nominal
allegiance to the caliph of Bagdad.   The second rank was that
of a minister of state, a lieutenant of the Samanides,[1] who broke,
by his revolt, the bonds of political slavery.   But the third step
was a state of real and domestic servitude in the family of that
rebel, from which Sebectagi, by his courage and dexterity,
ascended to the supreme command of the city and province of
Gazna,[2] as the son-in-law and successor of his grateful master.
The falling dynasty of the Samanides was at first protected,
and at last overthrown, by their servants, and, in the public
disorders, the fortune of Mahmud continually increased.   For
him the title of *Sultan*[3] was first invented; and his kingdom
was enlarged from Transoxiana to the neighbourhood of Ispahan,
from the shores of the Caspian to the mouth of the Indus.   But
the principal source of his fame and riches was the holy war
which he waged against the Gentoos of Hindostan.   In this
foreign narrative I may not consume a page, and a volume would
scarcely suffice to recapitulate the battles and sieges of his
twelve expeditions.   Never was the Musulman hero dismayed
by the inclemency of the seasons, the height of the mountains,

[1] The dynasty of the Samanides continued 125 years, A.D. 874-999,
under ten princes.   See their succession and ruin in the Tables of M. de
Guignes (Hist. des Huns, tom. i. p. 404-406).   They were followed by the
Gaznevides, A.D. 999-1183 (see tom. i. p. 239, 240).   His division of nations
often disturbs the series of time and place

[2] Gaznah hortos non habet: est emporium et domicilium mercaturæ
Indicæ. Abulfedæ Geograph. Reiske, tab. xxiii. p. 349; D'Herbelot,
p. 364.   It has not been visited by any modern traveller.

[3] By the ambassador of the caliph of Bagdad, who employed an Arabian
or Chaldaic word that signifies *lord* and *master* (D'Herbelot, p. 825).   It
is interpreted Αὐτοκράτωρ, Βασιλεὺς Βασιλέων, by the Byzantine writers of
the eleventh century; and the name (Σουλτανὸς, Soldanus) is familiarly
employed in the Greek and Latin languages, after it had passed from the
Gaznevides to the Seljukides, and other emirs of Asia and Egypt.
Ducange (Dissertation xvi. sur Joinville, p. 238-240, Gloss. Græc. et Latin.)
labours to find the title of Sultan in the ancient kingdom of Persia: but
his proofs are mere shadows; a proper name in the Themes of Constantine
(ii. 11 [tom. iii. p. 61, ed. Bonn]), an anticipation of Zonaras, etc., and a
medal of Kai Khosrou, not (as he believes) the Sassanide of the sixth, but
the Seljukide of Iconium of the thirteenth century (De Guignes, Hist. des
Huns, tom. i. p. 246).

[It is uncertain when the title " sultan " was first used, but it seems, at
all events, to have been anterior to the time of Mahmud.   It is mentioned
by Halebi under the reign of Motawaccel in the ninth century, but according to Ibn Chaldun it was first assumed by the Bowides.   Vambery thinks
that the name of one of the sons of the Hungarian chief Arpad, Ζαλτας or
Zoltan, was really his designation of rank—sultan.—O. S.]

the breadth of the rivers, the barrenness of the desert, the multitudes of the enemy, or the formidable array of their elephants
of war.[1]   The sultan of Gazna surpassed the limits of the conquests of Alexander; after a march of three months, over the
hills of Cashmir and Thibet, he reached the famous city of
Kinoge,[2] on the Upper Ganges, and, in a naval combat on one of
the branches of the Indus, he fought and vanquished four thousand boats of the natives. Delhi, Lahor, and Multan were
compelled to open their gates; the fertile kingdom of Guzarat
attracted his ambition and tempted his stay; and his avarice
indulged the fruitless project of discovering the golden and
aromatic isles of the Southern Ocean. On the payment of a
tribute the *rajahs* preserved their dominions, the people their
lives and fortunes: but to the religion of Hindostan the zealous
Musulman was cruel and inexorable; many hundred temples
or pagodas were levelled with the ground, many thousand idols
were demolished, and the servants of the prophet were stimulated and rewarded by the precious materials of which they were
composed. The pagoda of Sumnat was situate on the promontory of Guzarat, in the neighbourhood of Diu, one of the last
remaining possessions of the Portuguese.[3]   It was endowed
with the revenue of two thousand villages; two thousand
Brahmins were consecrated to the service of the deity, whom
they washed each morning and evening in water from the distant
Ganges; the subordinate ministers consisted of three hundred
musicians, three hundred barbers, and five hundred dancing
girls, conspicuous for their birth or beauty. Three sides of the
temple were protected by the ocean, the narrow isthmus was
fortified by a natural or artificial precipice, and the city and

[1] Ferishta (apud Dow, Hist. of Hindostan, vol. i. p. 49) mentions the
report of a *gun* in the Indian army. But as I am slow in believing this
premature (A.D. 1008) use of artillery, I must desire to scrutinise first the
text and then the authority of Ferishta, who lived in the Mogul court in
the last century.
  [Milman says in his edition, " This passage is differently written in the
various MSS. I have seen; and in some the word *tope*, gun, has been
written for *nupth*, naphtha, and *toofung*, musket, for *khudung*, arrow. But
no Persian or Arabic history speaks of gunpowder before the time usually
assigned for its invention (A.D. 1317), long after which it was first applied
to the purposes of war. Briggs' *Ferishta*."—O. S.]
  [2] Kinoge, or Canouge (the old Palimbothra), is marked in latitude
27° 3′, longitude 80° 13′. See D'Anville (Antiquité de l'Inde, p. 60-62),
corrected by the local knowledge of Major Rennell (in his excellent Memoir
on his Map of Hindostan, p. 37-43): 300 jewellers, 30,000 shops for the
areca nut, 60,000 bands of musicians, etc. (Abulfed. Geograph. tab. xv.
p. 274; Dow, vol. i. p. 16), will allow an ample deduction.
  [3] The idolaters of Europe, says Ferishta (Dow, vol. i. p. 66).   Consul
Abulfeda (p 272) and Rennell's Map of Hindostan.

adjacent country were peopled by a nation of fanatics. They confessed the sins and the punishment of Kinoge and Delhi; but if the impious stranger should presume to approach *their* holy precincts, he would surely be overwhelmed by a blast of the divine vengeance. By this challenge the faith of Mahmud was animated to a personal trial of the strength of this Indian deity. Fifty thousand of his worshippers were pierced by the spear of the Moslems; the walls were scaled, the sanctuary was profaned, and the conqueror aimed a blow of his iron mace at the head of the idol. The trembling Brahmins are said to have offered ten millions sterling for his ransom; and it was urged by the wisest counsellors that the destruction of a stone image would not change the hearts of the Gentoos, and that such a sum might be dedicated to the relief of the true believers. " Your reasons," replied the sultan, " are specious and strong; but never in the eyes of posterity shall Mahmud appear as a merchant of idols." He repeated his blows, and a treasure of pearls and rubies, concealed in the belly of the statue, explained in some degree the devout prodigality of the Brahmins. The fragments of the idol were distributed to Gazna, Mecca, and Medina. Bagdad listened to the edifying tale, and Mahmud was saluted by the caliph with the title of guardian of the fortune and faith of Mohammed.

From the paths of blood, and such is the history of nations, I cannot refuse to turn aside to gather some flowers of science or virtue. The name of Mahmud the Gaznevide is still venerable in the East: his subjects enjoyed the blessings of prosperity and peace; his vices were concealed by the veil of religion; and two familiar examples will testify his justice and magnanimity. I. As he sat in the divan, an unhappy subject bowed before the throne to accuse the insolence of a Turkish soldier who had driven him from his house and bed. " Suspend your clamours," said Mahmud; " inform me of his next visit, and ourself in person will judge and punish the offender." The sultan followed his guide, invested the house with his guards, and, extinguishing the torches, pronounced the death of the criminal, who had been seized in the act of rapine and adultery. After the execution of his sentence the lights were rekindled, Mahmud fell prostrate in prayer, and, rising from the ground, demanded some homely fare, which he devoured with the voraciousness of hunger. The poor man, whose injury he had avenged, was unable to suppress his astonishment and curiosity; and the courteous monarch condescended to explain the motives of this singular behaviour. " I had reason to suspect that none, except one of my sons,

could dare to perpetrate such an outrage; and I extinguished
the lights that my justice might be blind and inexorable. My
prayer was a thanksgiving on the discovery of the offender; and
so painful was my anxiety, that I had passed three days without
food since the first moment of your complaint." II. The sultan
of Gazna had declared war against the dynasty of the Bowides,
the sovereigns of the western Persia; he was disarmed by an
epistle of the sultana mother, and delayed his invasion till the
manhood of her son.[1] " During the life of my husband," said
the artful regent, " I was ever apprehensive of your ambition:
he was a prince and a soldier worthy of your arms.   He is now
no more; his sceptre has passed to a woman and a child, and you
dare not attack their infancy and weakness.   How inglorious
would be your conquest, how shameful your defeat! and yet
the event of war is in the hand of the Almighty."   Avarice was
the only defect that tarnished the illustrious character of
Mahmud; and never has that passion been more richly satiated.
The Orientals exceed the measure of credibility in the account of
millions of gold and silver, such as the avidity of man has never
accumulated; in the magnitude of pearls, diamonds, and rubies,
such as have never been produced by the workmanship of
nature.[2]   Yet the soil of Hindostan is impregnated with precious
minerals: her trade, in every age, has attracted the gold and
silver of the world; and her virgin spoils were rifled by the first
of the Mohammedan conquerors.   His behaviour, in the last days
of his life, evinces the vanity of these possessions, so laboriously
won, so dangerously held, and so inevitably lost.   He surveyed
the vast and various chambers of the treasury of Gazna; burst
into tears; and again closed the doors, without bestowing any
portion of the wealth which he could no longer hope to preserve.
The following day he reviewed the state of his military force; one
hundred thousand foot, fifty-five thousand horse, and thirteen
hundred elephants of battle.[3]   He again wept the instability

[1] D'Herbelot, Bibliothèque Orientale, p. 527.   Yet these letters,
apophthegms, etc., are rarely the language of the heart, or the motives of
public action.

[2] For instance, a ruby of four hundred and fifty miskals (Dow, vol. i.
p. 53), or six pounds three ounces: the largest in the treasury of Delhi
weighed seventeen miskals (Voyages de Tavernier, partie ii. p. 280).   It
is true that in the East all coloured stones are called rubies (p. 355), and
that Tavernier saw three larger and more precious among the jewels de
notre grand roi, le plus puissant et plus magnifique de tous les rois de la
terre (p. 376).

[3] Dow, vol. i. p. 65.   The sovereign of Kinoge is said to have possessed
2500 elephants (Abulfed. Geograph. tab. xv. p. 274).   From these Indian
stories the reader may correct a note in my first volume; or from that
note he may correct these stories.

of human greatness; and his grief was embittered by the hostile
progress of the Turkmans, whom he had introduced into the
heart of his Persian kingdom.

In the modern depopulation of Asia the regular operation of
government and agriculture is confined to the neighbourhood of
cities, and the distant country is abandoned to the pastoral
tribes of Arabs, Curds, and *Turkmans*.[1] Of the last-mentioned
people, two considerable branches extend on either side of the
Caspian Sea: the western colony can muster forty thousand
soldiers; the eastern, less obvious to the traveller, but more
strong and populous, has increased to the number of one hundred
thousand families. In the midst of civilised nations they preserve the manners of the Scythian desert, remove their encamp-
ments with the change of seasons, and feed their cattle among
the ruins of palaces and temples. Their flocks and herds are
their only riches; their tents, either black or white, according
to the colour of the banner, are covered with felt, and of a
circular form; their winter apparel is a sheepskin; a robe of
cloth or cotton their summer garment: the features of the men
are harsh and ferocious; the countenance of their women is soft
and pleasing. Their wandering life maintains the spirit and
exercise of arms; they fight on horseback; and their courage is
displayed in frequent contests with each other and with their
neighbours. For the licence of pasture they pay a slight tribute
to the sovereign of the land; but the domestic jurisdiction is in
the hands of the chiefs and elders. The first emigration of the
Eastern Turkmans, the most ancient of their race, may be
ascribed to the tenth century of the Christian era.[2] In the
decline of the caliphs, and the weakness of their lieutenants, the
barrier of the Jaxartes was often violated: in each invasion,
after the victory or retreat of their countrymen, some wandering
tribe, embracing the Mohammedan faith, obtained a free encampment in the spacious plains and pleasant climate of Transoxiana
and Carizme. The Turkish slaves who aspired to the throne
encouraged these emigrations, which recruited their armies,

[1] See a just and natural picture of these pastoral manners, in the history
of William Archbishop of Tyre (l. i. c. vii. in the Gesta Dei per Francos,
p. 633, 634), and a valuable note by the editor of the Histoire Généalogique
des Tatars, p. 535-538.

[2] The first emigrations of the Turkmans, and doubtful origin of the
Seljukians, may be traced in the laborious History of the Huns, by M. de
Guignes (tom. i. Tables Chronologiques, l. v. tom. iii. l. vii. ix. x.), and the
Bibliothèque Orientale of D'Herbelot (p. 799-802, 897-901), Elmacin (Hist.
Saracen. p. 331-333 [4to ed., Lugd. B., 1625]), and Abulpharagius (Dynast
p. 221, 222).

awed their subjects and rivals, and protected the frontier against
the wilder natives of Turkestan; and this policy was abused by
Mahmud the Gaznevide beyond the example of former times.
He was admonished of his error by a chief of the race of Seljuk,
who dwelt in the territory of Bochara. The sultan had inquired
what supply of men he could furnish for military service. "If
you send," replied Ismael, "one of these arrows into our camp,
fifty thousand of your servants will mount on horseback."
"And if that number," continued Mahmud, "should not be
sufficient?" "Send this second arrow to the horde of Balik, and
you will find fifty thousand more." "But," said the Gaznevide,
dissembling his anxiety, "if I should stand in need of the whole
force of your kindred tribes?" "Despatch my bow," was the
last reply of Ismael, "and, as it is circulated around, the
summons will be obeyed by two hundred thousand horse."
The apprehension of such formidable friendship induced Mahmud
to transport the most obnoxious tribes into the heart of Chorasan,
where they would be separated from their brethren by the river
Oxus, and enclosed on all sides by the walls of obedient cities.
But the face of the country was an object of temptation rather
than terror; and the vigour of government was relaxed by the
absence and death of the sultan of Gazna. The shepherds were
converted into robbers; the bands of robbers were collected into
an army of conquerors: as far as Ispahan and the Tigris Persia
was afflicted by their predatory inroads; and the Turkmans
were not ashamed or afraid to measure their courage and numbers
with the proudest sovereigns of Asia. Massoud, the son and
successor of Mahmud, had too long neglected the advice of his
wisest Omrahs. "Your enemies," they repeatedly urged,
"were in their origin a swarm of ants; they are now little
snakes; and, unless they be instantly crushed, they will acquire
the venom and magnitude of serpents." After some alterna-
tives of truce and hostility, after the repulse or partial success
of his lieutenants, the sultan marched in person against the
Turkmans, who attacked him on all sides with barbarous shouts
and irregular onset. "Massoud," says the Persian historian,[1]
"plunged singly to oppose the torrent of gleaming arms, ex-
hibiting such acts of gigantic force and valour as never king had
before displayed. A few of his friends, roused by his words
and actions, and that innate honour which inspires the brave,

---

[1] Dow, Hist. of Hindostan, vol. i. p. 89, 95-98. I have copied this
passage as a specimen of the Persian manner; but I suspect that, by some
odd fatality, the style of Ferishta has been improved by that of Ossian.

seconded their lord so well, that, wheresoever he turned his fatal
sword, the enemies were mowed down or retreated before him.
But now, when victory seemed to blow on his standard, misfortune was active behind it; for when he looked round he beheld
almost his whole army, excepting that body he commanded in
person, devouring the paths of flight." The Gaznevide was
abandoned by the cowardice or treachery of some generals of
Turkish race; and this memorable day of Zendecan [1] founded in
Persia the dynasty of the shepherd kings.[2]

The victorious Turkmans immediately proceeded to the
election of a king; and, if the probable tale of a Latin historian [3]
deserves any credit, they determined by lot the choice of their
new master. A number of arrows were successively inscribed
with the name of a tribe, a family, and a candidate; they were
drawn from the bundle by the hand of a child, and the important
prize was obtained by Togrul Beg, the son of Michael, the son of
Seljuk, whose surname was immortalised in the greatness of his
posterity. The sultan Mahmud, who valued himself on his skill
in national genealogy, professed his ignorance of the family of
Seljuk; yet the father of that race appears to have been a chief
of power and renown.[4] For a daring intrusion into the harem
of his prince, Seljuk was banished from Turkestan: with a
numerous tribe of his friends and vassals he passed the Jaxártes,
encamped in the neighbourhood of Samarcand, embraced the
religion of Mohammed, and acquired the crown of martyrdom
in a war against the infidels. His age, of a hundred and seven

[1] The Zendekan of D'Herbelot (p. 1028), the Dindaka of Dow (vol. i.
p. 97), is probably the Dandanekan of Abulfeda (Geograph. p. 345, Reiske),
a small town of Chorasan, two days' journey from Marû, and renowned
through the East for the production and manufacture of cotton.

[2] The Byzantine historians (Cedrenus, tom. ii. p. 766, 767 [p. 566, *sq.*,
ed. Bonn]; Zonaras, tom. ii. p. 255 [l. xvii. c. 25]; Nicephorus Bryennius,
p. 21 [p. 26, ed. Bonn]) have confounded in this revolution the truth of
time and place, of names and persons, of causes and events. The ignorance
and errors of these Greeks (which I shall not stop to unravel) may inspire
some distrust of the story of Cyaxares and Cyrus, as it is told by their most
eloquent predecessors.

[3] Willerm. Tyr. l. i. c. 7, p. 633. [In Gesta Dei per Franc. tom. i. fol.
Hanov. 1611.] The divination by arrows is ancient and famous in the
East.

[4] D'Herbelot, p. 801. Yet after the fortune of his posterity, Seljuk
became the thirty-fourth in lineal descent from the great Afrasiab emperor
of Touran (p. 800). The Tartar pedigree of the house of Zingis gave a
different cast to flattery and fable; and the historian Mirkhond derives the
Seljukides from Alankavah, the virgin mother (p. 801, col. 2). If they be
the same as the *Zalzuts* of Abulghazi Bahadur Khan (Hist. Généalogique,
p. 148), we quote in their favour the most weighty evidence of a Tartar
prince himself, the descendant of Zingis, Alankavah, or Alancu, and Oguz
Khan.

years, surpassed the life of his son, and Seljuk adopted the care
of his two grandsons, Togrul and Jaafar, the eldest of whom, at
the age of forty-five, was invested with the title of Sultan in the
royal city of Nishabur. The blind determination of chance was
justified by the virtues of the successful candidate. It would be
superfluous to praise the valour of a Turk; and the ambition of
Togrul [1] was equal to his valour. By his arms the Gaznevides
were expelled from the eastern kingdoms of Persia, and gradually driven to the banks of the Indus, in search of a softer and
more wealthy conquest. In the West he annihilated the dynasty
of the Bowides; and the sceptre of Irak passed from the Persian
to the Turkish nation. The princes who had felt, or who feared,
the Seljukian arrows bowed their heads in the dust; by the conquest of Aderbijan, or Media, he approached the Roman confines; and the shepherd presumed to despatch an ambassador,
or herald, to demand the tribute and obedience of the emperor
of Constantinople. [2] In his own dominions Togrul was the
father of his soldiers and people; by a firm and equal administration Persia was relieved from the evils of anarchy; and the same
hands which had been imbrued in blood became the guardians of
justice and the public peace. The more rustic, perhaps the
wisest, portion of the Turkmans [3] continued to dwell in the tents
of their ancestors; and, from the Oxus to the Euphrates, these
military colonies were protected and propagated by their native
princes. But the Turks of the court and city were refined by
business and softened by pleasure: they imitated the dress, language, and manners of Persia; and the royal palaces of Nishabur
and Rei displayed the order and magnificence of a great
monarchy. The most deserving of the Arabians and Persians
were promoted to the honours of the state; and the whole body
of the Turkish nation embraced with fervour and sincerity the
religion of Mohammed. The northern swarms of barbarians

[1] By a slight corruption Togrul Beg is the Tangroli-pix of the Greeks.
His reign and character are faithfully exhibited by D'Herbelot (Bibliothèque Orientale, p. 1027, 1028) and De Guignes (Hist. des Huns, tom. iii.
p. 189-201).

[2] Cedrenus, tom. ii. p. 774, 775 [p. 580, *sq.*, ed. Bonn]; Zonaras, tom. ii.
p. 257 [l. xvii. c. 25]. With their usual knowledge of Oriental affairs, they
describe the ambassador as a *sherif*, who, like the syncellus of the patriarch,
was the vicar and successor of the caliph.

[3] From William of Tyre I have borrowed this distinction of Turks and
Turkmans, which at least is popular and convenient. The names are the
same, and the addition of *man* is of the same import in the Persic and
Teutonic idioms. Few critics will adopt the etymology of James de Vitry
(Hist. Hierosol. l. i. c. 11, p. 1061 [Gesta Dei p. Franc.]), of Turcomani,
quasi *Turci* et *Comani*, a mixed people.

who overspread both Europe and Asia have been irreconcilably
separated by the consequences of a similar conduct. Among
the Moslems, as among the Christians, their vague and local
traditions have yielded to the reason and authority of the prevailing system, to the fame of antiquity, and the consent of
nations. But the triumph of the Koran is more pure and meritorious as it was not assisted by any visible splendour of worship
which might allure the pagans by some resemblance of idolatry.
The first of the Seljukian sultans was conspicuous by his zeal
and faith; each day he repeated the five prayers which are
enjoined to the true believers; of each week the two first days
were consecrated by an extraordinary fast; and in every city a
mosch was completed before Togrul presumed to lay the foundations of a palace.[1]

With the belief of the Koran, the son of Seljuk imbibed a
lively reverence for the successor of the prophet. But that
sublime character was still disputed by the caliphs of Bagdad
and Egypt, and each of the rivals was solicitous to prove his title
in the judgment of the strong, though illiterate, barbarians.
Mahmud the Gaznevide had declared himself in favour of the
line of Abbas; and had treated with indignity the robe of honour
which was presented by the Fatimite ambassador. Yet the
ungrateful Hashemite had changed with the change of fortune;
he applauded the victory of Zendecan, and named the Seljukian
sultan his temporal vicegerent over the Moslem world. As
Togrul executed and enlarged this important trust, he was
called to the deliverance of the caliph Cayem, and obeyed the
holy summons, which gave a new kingdom to his arms.[2] In the
palace of Bagdad the commander of the faithful still slumbered,
a venerable phantom. His servant or master, the prince of the
Bowides, could no longer protect him from the insolence of
meaner tyrants; and the Euphrates and Tigris were oppressed
by the revolt of the Turkish and Arabian emirs. The presence
of a conqueror was implored as a blessing; and the transient
mischiefs of fire and sword were excused as the sharp but salutary
remedies which alone could restore the health of the republic.
At the head of an irresistible force the sultan of Persia marched
from Hamadan: the proud were crushed, the prostrate were
spared; the prince of the Bowides disappeared; the heads of the

---

[1] Hist. Générale des Huns, tom. iii. p. 165, 166, 167. M. de Guignes
quotes Abulmahasen, an historian of Egypt.

[2] Consult the Bibliothèque Orientale, in the articles of the *Abbassides*,
Caher, and *Caiem*, and the Annals of Elmacin and Abulpharagius.

most obstinate rebels were laid at the feet of Togrul; and he inflicted a lesson of obedience on the people of Mosul and Bagdad. After the chastisement of the guilty, and the restoration of peace, the royal shepherd accepted the reward of his labours; and a solemn comedy represented the triumph of religious prejudice over barbarian power.[1] The Turkish sultan embarked on the Tigris, landed at the gate of Racca, and made his public entry on horseback. At the palace-gate he respectfully dismounted, and walked on foot, preceded by his emirs without arms. The caliph was seated behind his black veil: the black garment of the Abbassides was cast over his shoulders, and he held in his hand the staff of the apostle of God. The conqueror of the East kissed the ground, stood some time in a modest posture, and was led towards the throne by the vizir and an interpreter. After Togrul had seated himself on another throne his commission was publicly read, which declared him the temporal lieutenant of the vicar of the prophet. He was successively invested with seven robes of honour, and presented with seven slaves, the natives of the seven climates of the Arabian empire. His mystic veil was perfumed with musk; two crowns were placed on his head; two scimitars were girded to his side, as the symbols of a double reign over the East and West. After this inauguration the sultan was prevented from prostrating himself a second time; but he twice kissed the hand of the commander of the faithful, and his titles were proclaimed by the voice of heralds and the applause of the Moslems. In a second visit to Bagdad the Seljukian prince again rescued the caliph from his enemies; and devoutly, on foot, led the bridle of his mule from the prison to the palace. Their alliance was cemented by the marriage of Togrul's sister with the successor of the prophet. Without reluctance he had introduced a Turkish virgin into his harem; but Cayem proudly refused his daughter to the sultan, disdained to mingle the blood of the Hashemites with the blood of a Scythian shepherd; and protracted the negotiation many months, till the gradual diminution of his revenue admonished him that he was still in the hands of a master. The royal nuptials were followed by the death of Togrul himself;[2] as he

[1] For this curious ceremony I am indebted to M. de Guignes (tom. iii. p. 197, 198), and that learned author is obliged to Bondari, who composed in Arabic the history of the Seljukides (tom. v. p. 365). I am ignorant of his age, country, and character.

[2] Eodem anno (A.H. 455) obiit princeps Togrulbecus . . . rex fuit clemens, prudens, et peritus regnandi, cujus terror corda mortalium invaserat, ita ut obedirent ei reges atque ad ipsum scriberent. Elmacin, Hist. Saracen. p. 342, vers. Erpenii [4to ed.].

left no children, his nephew Alp Arslan succeeded to the title
and prerogatives of sultan; and his name, after that of the
caliph, was pronounced in the public prayers of the Moslems.
Yet in this revolution the Abbassides acquired a larger measure
of liberty and power. On the throne of Asia the Turkish
monarchs were less jealous of the domestic administration of
Bagdad; and the commanders of the faithful were relieved from
the ignominious vexations to which they had been exposed by
the presence and poverty of the Persian dynasty.

Since the fall of the caliphs, the discord and degeneracy of the
Saracens respected the Asiatic provinces of Rome; which, by
the victories of Nicephorus, Zimisces, and Basil, had been extended as far as Antioch and the eastern boundaries of Armenia.
Twenty-five years after the death of Basil, his successors were
suddenly assaulted by an unknown race of barbarians, who
united the Scythian valour with the fanaticism of new proselytes,
and the art and riches of a powerful monarchy.[1] The myriads of
Turkish horse overspread a frontier of six hundred miles from
Tauris to Arzeroum, and the blood of one hundred and thirty
thousand Christians was a grateful sacrifice to the Arabian
prophet. Yet the arms of Togrul did not make any deep or
lasting impression on the Greek empire. The torrent rolled
away from the open country; the sultan retired without glory
or success from the siege of an Armenian city; the obscure
hostilities were continued or suspended with a vicissitude of
events; and the bravery of the Macedonian legions renewed the
fame of the conqueror of Asia.[2] The name of Alp Arslan, the
valiant lion, is expressive of the popular idea of the perfection
of man; and the successor of Togrul displayed the fierceness and
generosity of the royal animal. He passed the Euphrates at
the head of the Turkish cavalry, and entered Cæsarea, the
metropolis of Cappadocia, to which he had been attracted by
the fame and wealth of the temple of St. Basil. The solid

---

[1] For these wars of the Turks and Romans, see in general the Byzantine
histories of Zonaras and Cedrenus, Scylitzes the continuator of Cedrenus
and Nicephorus Bryennius Cæsar. The two first of these were monks, the
two latter statesmen; yet such were the Greeks, that the difference of
style and character is scarcely discernible. For the Orientals, I draw as
usual on the wealth of D'Herbelot (see titles of the first Seljukides) and
the accuracy of De Guignes (Hist. des Huns, tom. iii. l. x.).

[2] Ἐφέρετο γὰρ ἐν Τούρκοις λόγος, ὡς εἴη πεπρωμένον καταστραφῆναι τὸ
Τούρκων γένος ὑπὸ τῆς τοιαύτης δυνάμεως, ὁποίαν ὁ Μακεδὼν Ἀλέξανδρος ἔχων
κατεστρέψατο Πέρσας. Cedrenus, tom. ii. p. 791 [p. 611, ed. Bonn]. The
credulity of the vulgar is always probable; and the Turks had learned
from the Arabs the history or legend of Escander Dulcarnein (D'Herbelot,
p. 317, etc.).

structure resisted the destroyer: but he carried away the doors
of the shrine incrusted with gold and pearls, and profaned the
relics of the tutelar saint, whose mortal frailties were now covered
by the venerable rust of antiquity. The final conquest of
Armenia and Georgia was achieved by Alp Arslan. In Armenia,
the title of a kingdom, and the spirit of a nation, were annihilated:
the artificial fortifications were yielded by the mercenaries of
Constantinople; by strangers without faith, veterans without
pay or arms, and recruits without experience or discipline.
The loss of this important frontier was the news of a day: and
the Catholics were neither surprised nor displeased that a people
so deeply infected with the Nestorian and Eutychian errors had
been delivered by Christ and his mother into the hands of the
infidels.[1] The woods and valleys of Mount Caucasus were more
strenuously defended by the native Georgians,[2] or Iberians: but
the Turkish sultan and his son Malek were indefatigable in this
holy war: their captives were compelled to promise a spiritual,
as well as temporal, obedience; and, instead of their collars and
bracelets, an iron horse-shoe, a badge of ignominy, was imposed
on the infidels who still adhered to the worship of their fathers.
The change, however, was not sincere or universal; and, through
ages of servitude, the Georgians have maintained the succession
of their princes and bishops. But a race of men whom Nature
has cast in her most perfect mould is degraded by poverty,
ignorance, and vice; their profession, and still more their practice, of Christianity is an empty name; and if they have emerged
from heresy, it is only because they are too illiterate to remember
a metaphysical creed.[3]

The false or genuine magnanimity of Mahmud the Gaznevide

[1] Οἱ τὴν Ἰβηρίαν καὶ Μεσοποταμίαν, καὶ τὴν παρακειμένην οἰκοῦσιν Ἀρμενίαν
καὶ οἱ τὴν Ἰουδαϊκὴν τοῦ Νεστορίου καὶ τῶν Ἀκεφάλων θρησκεύουσιν αἵρεσιν
(Scylitzes, ad calcem Cedreni, tom. ii. p. 834 [p. 687, ed. Bonn], whose
ambiguous construction shall not tempt me to suspect that he confounded
the Nestorian and Monophysite heresies). He familiarly talks of the μῆνις,
χόλος, ὀργὴ, Θεοῦ, qualities, as I should apprehend, very foreign to the
perfect Being; but his bigotry is forced to confess that they were soon
afterwards discharged on the orthodox Romans.

[2] Had the name of Georgians been known to the Greeks (Stritter,
Memoriæ Byzant. tom. iv. *Iberica*), I should derive it from their agriculture, as the Σκυθαί γεωργοί of Herodotus (l. iv. c. 18, p. 289, edit. Wessel-
ing). But it appears only since the crusades, among the Latins (Jac. a
Vitriaco, Hist. Hierosol. c. 79, p. 1095) and Orientals (D'Herbelot, p. 407),
and was devoutly borrowed from St. George of Cappadocia.

[3] Mosheim, Institut. Hist. Eccles. p. 632. See, in Chardin's Travels
(tom. i. p. 171-174), the manners and religion of this handsome but worthless nation See the pedigree of their princes from Adam to the present
century, in the Tables of M. de Guignes (tom. i. p. 433-438).

was not imitated by Alp Arslan; and he attacked without scruple
the Greek empress Eudocia and her children. His alarming
progress compelled her to give herself and her sceptre to the hand
of a soldier; and Romanus Diogenes was invested with the
Imperial purple. His patriotism, and perhaps his pride, urged
him from Constantinople within two months after his accession;
and the next campaign he most scandalously took the field
during the holy festival of Easter. In the palace, Diogenes was
no more than the husband of Eudocia: in the camp, he was the
emperor of the Romans, and he sustained that character with
feeble resources and invincible courage. By his spirit and success, the soldiers were taught to act, the subjects to hope, and
the enemies to fear. The Turks had penetrated into the heart
of Phrygia; but the sultan himself had resigned to his emirs the
prosecution of the war; and their numerous detachments were
scattered over Asia in the security of conquest. Laden with
spoil, and careless of discipline, they were separately surprised
and defeated by the Greeks: the activity of the emperor seemed
to multiply his presence; and while they heard of his expedition
to Antioch, the enemy felt his sword on the hills of Trebizond.
In three laborious campaigns the Turks were driven beyond the
Euphrates: in the fourth and last, Romanus undertook the
deliverance of Armenia. The desolation of the land obliged
him to transport a supply of two months' provisions; and he
marched forwards to the siege of Malazkerd,[1] an important
fortress in the midway between the modern cities of Arzeroum
and Van. His army amounted, at the least, to one hundred
thousand men. The troops of Constantinople were reinforced
by the disorderly multitudes of Phrygia and Cappadocia; but
the real strength was composed of the subjects and allies of
Europe, the legions of Macedonia, and the squadrons of Bulgaria; the Uzi, a Moldavian horde, who were themselves of the
Turkish race;[2] and, above all, the mercenary and adventurous

[1] This city is mentioned by Constantine Porphyrogenitus (de Administrat. Imperii, l. ii. c. 44, p. 119 [tom. iii. p. 192, ed. Bonn]) and the Byzantines of the eleventh century, under the name of Mantzikierte, and by
some is confounded with Theodosiopolis; but Delisle, in his notes and
maps, has very properly fixed the situation. Abulfeda (Geograph. tab.
xviii. p. 310) describes Malasgerd as a small town, built with black stone,
supplied with water, without trees, etc.

[2] The Uzi of the Greeks (Stritter, Memor. Byzant., tom. iii. p. 923-948)
are the Gozz of the Orientals (Hist. des Huns, tom. ii. p. 522; tom. iii.
p. 133, etc.). They appear on the Danube and the Volga, in Armenia,
Syria, and Chorasan, and the name seems to have been extended to the
whole Turkman race.
[The Uzi were the people who were afterwards called Cumani or Comani

bands of French and Normans. Their lances were commanded
by the valiant Ursel of Baliol, the kinsman or father of the
Scottish kings,[1] and were allowed to excel in the exercise of arms,
or, according to the Greek style, in the practice of the Pyrrhic
dance.

On the report of this bold invasion, which threatened his
hereditary dominions, Alp Arslan flew to the scene of action at
the head of forty thousand horse.[2]   His rapid and skilful evolutions distressed and dismayed the superior numbers of the
Greeks; and in the defeat of Basilacius, one of their principal
generals, he displayed the first example of his valour and
clemency. The imprudence of the emperor had separated his
forces after the reduction of Malazkerd.   It was in vain that he
attempted to recall the mercenary Franks: they refused to
obey his summons; he disdained to await their return: the
desertion of the Uzi filled his mind with anxiety and suspicion;
and against the most salutary advice he rushed forwards to
speedy and decisive action.   Had he listened to the fair pro-
posals of the sultan, Romanus might have secured a retreat,
perhaps a peace; but in these overtures he supposed the fear or
weakness of the enemy, and his answer was conceived in the
tone of insult and defiance.   " If the barbarian wishes for peace,
let him evacuate the ground which he occupies for the encampment of the Romans, and surrender his city and palace of Rei as
a pledge of his sincerity."   Alp Arslan smiled at the vanity of
the demand, but he wept the death of so many faithful Moslems;
and after a devout prayer, proclaimed a free permission to all
who were desirous of retiring from the field.   With his own
hands he tied up his horse's tail, exchanged his bow and arrows

by the Byzantine writers. They were a Turkish race, allied in some
respects to the Patzinaks. They are mentioned by Constantine Porphyrogenitus as living in his time beyond the Khazars and the Patzinaks.
They first appeared in Russia in 1055. Then they drove the Patzinaks
out of Atelkuzu, the land of which the latter had formerly dispossessed
the Hungarians into Wallachia.—O. S.]

[1] Urselius [Ursellus] (the Russelius of Zonaras) is distinguished by
Jeffrey Malaterra (l. ii. c. 33) among the Norman conquerors of Sicily,
and with the surname of *Baliol :* and our own historians will tell how the
Baliols came from Normandy to Durham, built Bernard's castle on the
Tees, married an heiress of Scotland, etc.   Ducange (Not. ad Nicephor.
Bryennium, l. ii. No. 4) has laboured the subject in honour of the President
de Bailleul, whose father had exchanged the sword for the gown.

[2] Elmacin (p. 343, 344) assigns this probable number which is reduced
by Abulpharagius to 15,000 (p. 227), and by D'Herbelot (p. 102) to 12,000
horse.   But the same Elmacin gives 300,000 men to the emperor, of whom
Abulpharagius says, Cum centum hominum millibus, multisque equis et
magnâ pompâ instructus.   The Greeks abstain from any definition of
numbers.

for a mace and scimitar, clothed himself in a white garment, perfumed his body with musk, and declared that, if he were vanquished, that spot should be the place of his burial.[1] The sultan himself had affected to cast away his missile weapons; but his hopes of victory were placed in the arrows of the Turkish cavalry, whose squadrons were loosely distributed in the form of a crescent. Instead of the successive lines and reserves of the Grecian tactics, Romanus led his army in a single and solid phalanx, and pressed with vigour and impatience the artful and yielding resistance of the barbarians. In this desultory and fruitless combat he wasted the greater part of a summer's day, till prudence and fatigue compelled him to return to his camp. But a retreat is always perilous in the face of an active foe; and no sooner had the standard been turned to the rear than the phalanx was broken by the base cowardice, or the baser jealousy, of Andronicus, a rival prince, who disgraced his birth and the purple of the Cæsars.[2] The Turkish squadrons poured a cloud of arrows on this moment of confusion and lassitude; and the horns of their formidable crescent were closed in the rear of the Greeks. In the destruction of the army and pillage of the camp, it would be needless to mention the number of the slain or captives. The Byzantine writers deplore the loss of an inestimable pearl: they forget to mention, that in this fatal day the Asiatic provinces of Rome were irretrievably sacrificed.

As long as a hope survived, Romanus attempted to rally and save the relics of his army. When the centre, the Imperial station, was left naked on all sides, and encompassed by the victorious Turks, he still, with desperate courage, maintained the fight till the close of day, at the head of the brave and faithful subjects who adhered to his standard. They fell around him; his horse was slain; the emperor was wounded; yet he stood alone and intrepid till he was oppressed and bound by the strength of multitudes. The glory of this illustrious prize was disputed by a slave and a soldier; a slave who had seen him on the throne of Constantinople, and a soldier whose extreme deformity had been excused on the promise of some signal service. De-

[1] The Byzantine writers do not speak so distinctly of the presence of the sultan; he committed his forces to a eunuch, had retired to a distance, etc. Is it ignorance, or jealousy, or truth?

[2] He was the son of the Cæsar John Ducas, brother of the emperor Constantine (Ducange, Fam. Byzant. p. 165). Nicephorus Bryennius applauds his virtues and extenuates his faults (l. i. p. 30, 38 [p. 41, 54, ed. Bonn]; l. ii. p. 53 [p. 76, ed. Bonn]). Yet he owns his enmity to Romanus, οὐ πανὺ δὲ φιλίως ἔχων πρὸς Βασιλέα. Scylitzes speaks more explicitly of his treason.

spoiled of his arms, his jewels, and his purple, Romanus spent a
dreary and perilous night on the field of battle, amidst a disorderly crowd of the meaner barbarians. In the morning the
royal captive was presented to Alp Arslan, who doubted of his
fortune, till the identity of the person was ascertained by the
report of his ambassadors, and by the more pathetic evidence of
Basilacius, who embraced with tears the feet of his unhappy
sovereign. The successor of Constantine, in a plebeian habit,
was led into the Turkish divan and commanded to kiss the
ground before the lord of Asia. He reluctantly obeyed; and
Alp Arslan, starting from his throne, is said to have planted his
foot on the neck of the Roman emperor.[1] But the fact is
doubtful; and if, in this moment of insolence, the sultan complied with the national custom, the rest of his conduct has
extorted the praise of his bigoted foes, and may afford a lesson to
the most civilised ages. He instantly raised the royal captive
from the ground; and thrice clasping his hand with tender
sympathy, assured him that his life and dignity should be
inviolate in the hands of a prince who had learned to respect
the majesty of his equals and the vicissitudes of fortune. From
the divan Romanus was conducted to an adjacent tent, where
he was served with pomp and reverence by the officers of the
sultan, who, twice each day, seated him in the place of honour at
his own table. In a free and familiar conversation of eight days,
not a word, not a look, of insult escaped from the conqueror;
but he severely censured the unworthy subjects who had
deserted their valiant prince in the hour of danger, and gently
admonished his antagonist of some errors which he had committed in the management of the war. In the preliminaries of
negotiation Alp Arslan asked him what treatment he expected
to receive, and the calm indifference of the emperor displays the
freedom of his mind. " If you are cruel," said he, " you will
take my life; if you listen to pride, you will drag me at your
chariot wheels; if you consult your interest, you will accept
a ransom and restore me to my country." " And what," continued the sultan, " would have been your own behaviour had
fortune smiled on your arms? " The reply of the Greek betrays
a sentiment which prudence, and even gratitude, should have
taught him to suppress. " Had I vanquished," he fiercely said,
" I would have inflicted on thy body many a stripe." The
Turkish conqueror smiled at the insolence of his captive;

[1] This circumstance, which we read and doubt in Scylitzes and Constantine Manasses, is more prudently omitted by Nicephorus and Zonaras.

observed that the Christian law inculcated the love of enemies and forgiveness of injuries; and nobly declared that he would not imitate an example which he condemned. After mature deliberation, Alp Arslan dictated the terms of liberty and peace, a ransom of a million, an annual tribute of three hundred and sixty thousand pieces of gold,[1] the marriage of the royal children, and the deliverance of all the Moslems who were in the power of the Greeks. Romanus, with a sigh, subscribed this treaty, so disgraceful to the majesty of the empire: he was immediately invested with a Turkish robe of honour; his nobles and patricians were restored to their sovereign; and the sultan, after a courteous embrace, dismissed him with rich presents and a military guard. No sooner did he reach the confines of the empire than he was informed that the palace and provinces had disclaimed their allegiance to a captive; a sum of two hundred thousand pieces was painfully collected; and the fallen monarch transmitted this part of his ransom, with a sad confession of his impotence and disgrace. The generosity, or perhaps the ambition, of the sultan prepared to espouse the cause of his ally; but his designs were prevented by the defeat, imprisonment, and death of Romanus Diogenes.[2]

In the treaty of peace it does not appear that Alp Arslan extorted any province or city from the captive emperor; and his revenge was satisfied with the trophies of his victory, and the spoils of Anatolia, from Antioch to the Black Sea. The fairest part of Asia was subject to his laws: twelve hundred princes, or the sons of princes, stood before his throne; and two hundred thousand soldiers marched under his banners. The sultan disdained to pursue the fugitive Greeks; but he meditated the more glorious conquest of Turkestan, the original seat of the house of Seljuk. He moved from Bagdad to the banks of the Oxus; a bridge was thrown over the river; and twenty days were con-

---

[1] The ransom and tribute are attested by reason and the Orientals. The other Greeks are modestly silent; but Nicephorus Bryennius dares to affirm that the terms were οὐκ ἀνάξιας Ῥωμαίων [p. 44, ed. Bonn], and that the emperor would have preferred death to a shameful treaty.

[2] The defeat and captivity of Romanus Diogenes may be found in John Scylitzes ad calcem Cedreni, tom. ii. p. 835-843 [p. 689-704, ed. Bonn]; Zonaras, tom. ii. p. 281-284 [l. xvii. c. 13-15]; Nicephorus Bryennius, l. i. p. 25-32 [p. 33-44, ed. Bonn]; Glycas, p. 325-327 [p. 607-611, ed. Bonn]; Constantine Manasses, p. 134 [v. 6594, p. 280, ed. Bonn]; Elmacin, Hist. Saracen. p. 343, 344; Abulpharag. Dynast. p. 227; D'Herbelot, p. 102, 103; De Guignes, tom. iii. p. 207-211. Besides my old acquaintance Elmacin and Abulpharagius, the historian of the Huns has consulted Abulfeda, and his epitomiser Benschounah, a Chronicle of the Caliphs, by Soyouthi, Abulmahasen of Egypt, and Novairi of Africa.

sumed in the passage of his troops. But the progress of the great king was retarded by the governor of Berzem; and Joseph the Carizmian presumed to defend his fortress against the powers of the East. When he was produced a captive in the royal tent, the sultan, instead of praising his valour, severely reproached his obstinate folly; and the insolent replies of the rebel provoked a sentence, that he should be fastened to four stakes and left to expire in that painful situation. At this command the desperate Carizmian, drawing a dagger, rushed headlong towards the throne: the guards raised their battle-axes; their zeal was checked by Alp Arslan, the most skilful archer of the age: he drew his bow, but his foot slipped, the arrow glanced aside, and he received in his breast the dagger of Joseph, who was instantly cut in pieces. The wound was mortal; and the Turkish prince bequeathed a dying admonition to the pride of kings. " In my youth," said Alp Arslan, " I was advised by a sage to humble myself before God; to distrust my own strength; and never to despise the most contemptible foe. I have neglected these lessons; and my neglect has been deservedly punished. Yesterday, as from an eminence I beheld the numbers, the discipline, and the spirit of my armies, the earth seemed to tremble under my feet; and I said in my heart, Surely thou art the king of the world, the greatest and most invincible of warriors. These armies are no longer mine; and, in the confidence of my personal strength, I now fall by the hand of an assassin." [1] Alp Arslan possessed the virtues of a Turk and a Musulman; his voice and stature commanded the reverence of mankind; his face was shaded with long whiskers; and his ample turban was fashioned in the shape of a crown. The remains of the sultan were deposited in the tomb of the Seljukian dynasty; and the passenger might read and meditate this useful inscription: [2] " O YE WHO HAVE SEEN THE GLORY OF ALP ARSLAN EXALTED TO THE HEAVENS, REPAIR TO MARU, AND YOU WILL BEHOLD IT BURIED IN THE DUST." The annihilation of the inscription, and the tomb itself, more forcibly proclaims the instability of human greatness.

During the life of Alp Arslan his eldest son had been acknow-

---

[1] This interesting death is told by D'Herbelot (p. 103, 104) and M. de Guignes (tom. iii. p. 212, 213), from their Oriental writers; but neither of them have transfused the spirit of Elmacin (Hist. Saracen. p. 344, 345).

[2] A critic of high renown (the late Dr. Johnson), who has severely scrutinised the epitaphs of Pope, might cavil in this sublime inscription at the words " repair to Maru," since the reader must already be at Maru before he could peruse the inscription.

ledged as the future sultan of the Turks. On his father's death
the inheritance was disputed by an uncle, a cousin, and a
brother: they drew their scimitars and assembled their followers;
and the triple victory of Malek Shah [1] established his own
reputation and the right of primogeniture. In every age, and
more especially in Asia, the thirst of power has inspired the
same passions and occasioned the same disorders; but, from
the long series of civil war, it would not be easy to extract a
sentiment more pure and magnanimous than is contained in a
saying of the Turkish prince. On the eve of the battle he performed his devotions at Thous, before the tomb of the Imam
Riza. As the sultan rose from the ground he asked his vizir,
Nizam, who had knelt beside him, what had been the object of
his secret petition: "That your arms may be crowned with
victory," was the prudent, and most probably the sincere,
answer of the minister. "For my part," replied the generous
Malek, "I implored the Lord of hosts that he would take from
me my life and crown, if my brother be more worthy than myself
to reign over the Moslems." The favourable judgment of
Heaven was ratified by the caliph; and for the first time the
sacred title of Commander of the Faithful was communicated to
a barbarian. But this barbarian, by his personal merit and the
extent of his empire, was the greatest prince of his age. After
the settlement of Persia and Syria he marched at the head of
innumerable armies to achieve the conquest of Turkestan,
which had been undertaken by his father. In his passage of the
Oxus the boatmen, who had been employed in transporting some
troops, complained that their payment was assigned on the
revenues of Antioch. The sultan frowned at this preposterous
choice; but he smiled at the artful flattery of his vizir. "It
was not to postpone their reward that I selected those remote
places, but to leave a memorial to posterity, that, under your
reign, Antioch and the Oxus were subject to the same sovereign."
But this description of his limits was unjust and parsimonious:
beyond the Oxus he reduced to his obedience the cities of
Bochara, Carizme, and Samarcand, and crushed each rebellious
slave or independent savage who dared to resist. Malek passed
the Sihon or Jaxartes, the last boundary of Persian civilisation:
the hordes of Turkestan yielded to his supremacy: his name was

---

[1] The Bibliothèque Orientale has given the text of the reign of Malek
(p. 542, 543, 544, 654, 655); and the Histoire Générale des Huns (tom. iii.
p. 214-224) has added the usual measure of repetition, emendation, and
supplement. Without those two learned Frenchmen I should be blind
indeed in the Eastern world.

inserted on the coins and in the prayers of Cashgar, a Tartar
kingdom on the extreme borders of China.   From the Chinese
frontier he stretched his immediate jurisdiction or feudatory
sway to the west and south, as far as the mountains of Georgia,
the neighbourhood of Constantinople, the holy city of Jerusalem,
and the spicy groves of Arabia Felix.   Instead of resigning himself to the luxury of his harem, the shepherd king, both in peace
and war, was in action and in the field.   By the perpetual
motion of the royal camp each province was successively blessed
with his presence; and he is said to have perambulated twelve
times the wide extent of his dominions, which surpassed the
Asiatic reign of Cyrus and the caliphs.   Of these expeditions
the most pious and splendid was the pilgrimage of Mecca: the
freedom and safety of the caravans were protected by his arms;
the citizens and pilgrims were enriched by the profusion of his
alms; and the desert was cheered by the places of relief and
refreshment which he instituted for the use of his brethren.
Hunting was the pleasure, and even the passion, of the sultan,
and his train consisted of forty-seven thousand horses; but
after the massacre of a Turkish chase, for each piece of game he
bestowed a piece of gold on the poor, a slight atonement, at the
expense of the people, for the cost and mischief of the amusement
of kings.   In the peaceful prosperity of his reign the cities of
Asia were adorned with palaces and hospitals, with moschs and
colleges: few departed from his divan without reward, and
none without justice.   The language and literature of Persia
revived under the house of Seljuk;[1] and if Malek emulated the
liberality of a Turk less potent than himself,[2] his palace might
resound with the songs of a hundred poets.   The sultan bestowed
a more serious and learned care on the reformation of the
calendar, which was effected by a general assembly of the
astronomers of the East.   By a law of the prophet the Moslems
are confined to the irregular course of the lunar months; in
Persia, since the age of Zoroaster, the revolution of the sun has
been known and celebrated as an annual festival;[3] but after the

[1] See an excellent discourse at the end of Sir William Jones's History of
Nadir Shah, and the articles of the poets Amak, Anvari, Raschidi, etc., in
the Bibliothèque Orientale.

[2] His name was Kheder Khan.   Four bags were placed round his sofa,
and, as he listened to the song, he cast handfuls of gold and silver to the
poets (D'Herbelot, p. 107).   All this may be true; but I do not understand how he could reign in Transoxiana in the time of Malek Shah, and
much less how Keder could surpass him in power and pomp.   I suspect
that the beginning, not the end, of the eleventh century is the true era of
his reign.

[3] See Chardin, Voyages en Perse, tom. ii. p. 235.

fall of the Magian empire, the intercalation had been neglected; the fractions of minutes and hours were multiplied into days; and the date of the spring was removed from the sign of Aries to that of Pisces. The reign of Malek was illustrated by the *Gelalæan* era; and all errors, either past or future, were corrected by a computation of time, which surpasses the Julian, and approaches the accuracy of the Gregorian, style.[1]

In a period when Europe was plunged in the deepest barbarism, the light and splendour of Asia may be ascribed to the docility rather than the knowledge of the Turkish conquerors. An ample share of their wisdom and virtue is due to a Persian vizir, who ruled the empire under the reigns of Alp Arslan and his son. Nizam, one of the most illustrious ministers of the East, was honoured by the caliph as an oracle of religion and science; he was trusted by the sultan as the faithful vicegerent of his power and justice.[2] After an administration of thirty years, the fame of the vizir, his wealth, and even his services, were transformed into crimes. He was overthrown by the insidious arts of a woman and a rival; and his fall was hastened by a rash declaration, that his cap and inkhorn, the badges of his office, were connected by the divine decree with the throne and diadem of the sultan. At the age of ninety-three years the venerable statesman was dismissed by his master, accused by his enemies, and murdered by a fanatic: the last words of Nizam attested his innocence, and the remainder of Malek's life was short and inglorious. From Ispahan, the scene of this disgraceful transaction, the sultan moved to Bagdad, with the design of transplanting the caliph, and of fixing his own residence in the capital of the Moslem world. The feeble successor of Mohammed obtained a respite of ten days; and before the expiration of the term the barbarian was summoned by the angel of death. His ambassadors at Constantinople had asked in marriage a Roman princess; but the proposal was decently eluded, and the daughter of Alexius, who might herself have been the victim, expresses her

---

[1] The Gelalæan era (Gelaleddin, Glory of the Faith, was one of the names or titles of Malek Shah) is fixed to the fifteenth of March, A.H. 471—A.D. 1079. Dr. Hyde has produced the original testimonies of the Persians and Arabians (de Religione veterum Persarum, c. 16, p. 200-211).

[2] [Nizám-al-Mulk, the vizier of Malek Shah, was himself a writer and left the *Siasset Nameh* or *Book of Government*, which has been published with a translation by Schefer. As Mr. Stanley Lane Poole says in his *Saladin*, it casts a flood of light on the events of the time, and shows us how the Seljuks were already changing under the influence of Iranian civilisation and Islamism.—O. S.]

abhorrence of this unnatural conjunction.[1] The daughter of the sultan was bestowed on the caliph Moctadi, with the imperious condition that, renouncing the society of his wives and con- cubines, he should for ever confine himself to this honourable alliance.

The greatness and unity of the Turkish empire expired in the person of Malek Shah. His vacant throne was disputed by his brother and his four sons; and, after a series of civil wars, the treaty which reconciled the surviving candidates confirmed a lasting separation in the *Persian* dynasty, the eldest and principal branch of the house of Seljuk. The three younger dynasties were those of *Kerman,* of *Syria,* and of *Roum :* the first of these commanded an extensive, though obscure,[2] dominion on the shores of the Indian Ocean;[3] the second expelled the Arabian princes of Aleppo and Damascus; and the third, our peculiar care, invaded the Roman provinces of Asia Minor. The generous policy of Malek contributed to their elevation: he allowed the princes of his blood, even those whom he had vanquished in the field, to seek new kingdoms worthy of their ambition; nor was he displeased that they should draw away the more ardent spirits who might have disturbed the tranquillity of his reign. As the supreme head of his family and nation, the great sultan of Persia commanded the obedience and tribute of his royal brethren: the thrones of Kerman and Nice, of Aleppo and Damascus, the Atabeks and emirs of Syria and Mesopotamia, erected their standards under the shadow of his sceptre:[4] and the hordes of Turkmans overspread the plains of the Western Asia. After the death of Malek the bands of union and subordination were relaxed and finally dissolved: the indulgence of the house of Seljuk in- vested their slaves with the inheritance of kingdoms; and, in the

---

[1] She speaks of this Persian royalty as ἀπάσης κακοδαιμονέστερον πενίας. Anna Comnena was only nine years old at the end of the reign of Malek Shah (A.D. 1092), and when she speaks of his assassination she confounds the sultan with the vizir (Alexias, l. vi. p. 177, 178 [tom. i. p. 314-317, ed. Bonn]).

[2] So obscure, that the industry of M. de Guignes could only copy (tom i. p. 244; tom. iii. part i. p. 269, etc.) the history, or rather list, of the Sel- jukides of Kerman, in Bibliothèque Orientale. They were extinguished before the end of the twelfth century.

[3] Tavernier, perhaps the only traveller who has visited Kerman, describes the capital as a great ruinous village, twenty-five days' journey from Ispahan, and twenty-seven from Ormus, in the midst of a fertile country (Voyages en Turquie et en Perse, p. 107, 110).

[4] It appears from Anna Comnena that the Turks of Asia Minor obeyed the signet and chiauss of the great sultan (Alexias, l. vi. p. 170 [tom. i. p. 302, ed. Bonn]), and that the two sons of Soliman were detained in his court (p. 180 [p. 319, *ib.*]).

Oriental style, a crowd of princes arose from the dust of their feet.[1]

A prince of the royal line, Cutulmish, the son of Izrail, the son of Seljuk, had fallen in a battle against Alp Arslan: and the humane victor had dropped a tear over his grave. His five sons, strong in arms, ambitious of power, and eager for revenge, unsheathed their scimitars against the son of Alp Arslan. The two armies expected the signal, when the caliph, forgetful of the majesty which secluded him from vulgar eyes, interposed his venerable mediation. "Instead of shedding the blood of your brethren, your brethren both in descent and faith, unite your forces in a holy war against the Greeks, the enemies of God and his apostle." They listened to his voice; the sultan embraced his rebellious kinsmen; and the eldest, the valiant Soliman, accepted the royal standard, which gave him the free conquest and hereditary command of the provinces of the Roman empire, from Arzeroum to Constantinople and the unknown regions of the West.[2] Accompanied by his four brothers, he passed the Euphrates: the Turkish camp was soon seated in the neighbourhood of Kutaieh in Phrygia; and his flying cavalry laid waste the country as far as the Hellespont and the Black Sea. Since the decline of the empire the peninsula of Asia Minor had been exposed to the transient though destructive inroads of the Persians and Saracens; but the fruits of a lasting conquest were reserved for the Turkish sultan; and his arms were introduced by the Greeks, who aspired to reign on the ruins of their country. Since the captivity of Romanus, six years the feeble son of Eudocia had trembled under the weight of the Imperial crown, till the provinces of the East and West were lost in the same month by a double rebellion: of either chief Nicephorus was the common name; but the surnames of Bryennius and Botoniates distinguish the European and Asiatic candidates. Their reasons, or rather their promises, were weighed in the divan; and, after some hesitation, Soliman declared himself in favour of Botoniates, opened a free passage to his troops in their march from Antioch to Nice, and joined the banner of the crescent to that of the

---

[1] This expression is quoted by Petit de la Croix (Vie de Gengiscan, p. 161) from some poet, most probably a Persian.

[2] On the conquest of Asia Minor, M. de Guignes has derived no assistance from the Turkish or Arabian writers, who produce a naked list of the Seljukides of Roum. The Greeks are unwilling to expose their shame, and we must extort some hints from Scylitzes (p. 860, 863 [p. 731, 736, ed. Bonn]), Nicephorus Bryennius (p. 88, 91, 92, etc., 103, 104 [p. 130, 136, sqq., 158 sqq., ed. Bonn]), and Anna Comnena (Alexias, p. 91, 92, etc., 168, etc. [tom. i. p. 169, sqq., 299, sqq., ed. Bonn]).

cross. After his ally had ascended the throne of Constantinople, the sultan was hospitably entertained in the suburb of
Chrysopolis or Scutari; and a body of two thousand Turks was
transported into Europe, to whose dexterity and courage the new
emperor was indebted for the defeat and captivity of his rival
Bryennius. But the conquest of Europe was dearly purchased
by the sacrifice of Asia; Constantinople was deprived of the
obedience and revenue of the provinces beyond the Bosphorus
and Hellespont; and the regular progress of the Turks, who
fortified the passes of the rivers and mountains, left not a hope of
their retreat or expulsion. Another candidate implored the aid
of the sultan: Melissenus, in his purple robes and red buskins,
attended the motions of the Turkish camp; and the desponding
cities were tempted by the summons of a Roman prince, who
immediately surrendered them into the hands of the barbarians.
These acquisitions were confirmed by a treaty of peace with the
emperor Alexius; his fear of Robert compelled him to seek the
friendship of Soliman; and it was not till after the sultan's death
that he extended as far as Nicomedia, about sixty miles from
Constantinople, the eastern boundary of the Roman world.
Trebizond alone, defended on either side by the sea and mountains, preserved at the extremity of the Euxine the ancient
character of a Greek colony, and the future destiny of a Christian
empire.

Since the first conquests of the caliphs, the establishment of
the Turks in Anatolia or Asia Minor was the most deplorable loss
which the church and empire had sustained. By the propagation of the Moslem faith, Soliman deserved the name of *Gazi*, a
holy champion; and his new kingdom of the Romans, or of
Roum, was added to the tables of Oriental geography. It is
described as extending from the Euphrates to Constantinople,
from the Black Sea to the confines of Syria; pregnant with mines
of silver and iron, of alum and copper, fruitful in corn and wine,
and productive of cattle and excellent horses.[1] The wealth of
Lydia, the arts of the Greeks, the splendour of the Augustan age,
existed only in books and ruins, which were equally obscure in
the eyes of the Scythian conquerors. Yet in the present decay
Anatolia still contains *some* wealthy and populous cities; and,
under the Byzantine empire, they were far more flourishing in
numbers, size, and opulence. By the choice of the sultan, Nice,

---

[1] Such is the description of Roum by Haiton, the Armenian, whose
Tartar history may be found in the collections of Ramusio and Bergeron
(see Abulfeda, Geograph. climat. xvii. p. 301-305).

the metropolis of Bithynia, was preferred for his palace and
fortress: the seat of the Seljukian dynasty of Roum was planted
one hundred miles from Constantinople; and the divinity of
Christ was denied and derided in the same temple in which it had
been pronounced by the first general synod of the Catholics. The
unity of God, and the mission of Mohammed, were preached in
the moschs; the Arabian learning was taught in the schools; the
Cadhis judged according to the law of the Koran; the Turkish
manners and language prevailed in the cities; and Turkman
camps were scattered over the plains and mountains of Anatolia.
On the hard conditions of tribute and servitude, the Greek
Christians might enjoy the exercise of their religion; but their
most holy churches were profaned, their priests and bishops were
insulted,[1] they were compelled to suffer the triumph of the *pagans*
and the apostacy of their brethren, many thousand children were
marked by the knife of circumcision, and many thousand captives
were devoted to the service or the pleasures of their masters.[2]
After the loss of Asia, Antioch still maintained her primitive
allegiance to Christ and Cæsar; but the solitary province was
separated from all Roman aid, and surrounded on all sides by the
Mohammedan powers. The despair of Philaretus the governor
prepared the sacrifice of his religion and loyalty, had not his
guilt been prevented by his son, who hastened to the Nicene
palace, and offered to deliver this valuable prize into the hands of
Soliman. The ambitious sultan mounted on horseback, and in
twelve nights (for he reposed in the day) performed a march of
six hundred miles. Antioch was oppressed by the speed and
secrecy of his enterprise; and the dependent cities, as far as
Laodicea and the confines of Aleppo,[3] obeyed the example of the
metropolis. From Laodicea to the Thracian Bosphorus, or arm
of St. George, the conquests and reign of Soliman extended thirty

---

[1] Dicit eos quendam abusione Sodomitica intervertisse episcopum
(Guibert. Abbat. Hist. Hierosol. l. i. p. 468). It is odd enough that we
should find a parallel passage of the same people in the present age. " Il
n'est point d'horreur que ces Turcs n'aient commis; et semblables aux
soldats effrénés, qui dans le sac d'une ville, non contens de disposer de
tout à leur gré, prétendent encore aux succès les moins désirables, quel-
ques Sipahis ont porté leurs attentats sur la personne du vieux rabbi de
la synagogue, et celle de l'Archevêque Grec." (Mémoires du Baron de
Tott, tom. ii. p. 193.)

[2] The emperor, or abbot, describe the scenes of a Turkish camp as if
they had been present. Matres correptæ in conspectû filiarum multi-
pliciter repetitis diversorum coitibus vexabantur (is that the true reading?); cum filiæ assistentes carmina præcinere saltando cogerentur. Mox
eadem passio ad filias, etc.

[3] See Antioch, and the death of Soliman, in Anna Comnena (Alexias,
l. vi. p. 168, 169 [tom. i. p. 299-301, ed. Bonn]), with the notes of Ducange.

days' journey in length, and in breadth about ten or fifteen, between the rocks of Lycia and the Black Sea.[1] The Turkish ignorance of navigation protected for a while the inglorious safety of the emperor; but no sooner had a fleet of two hundred ships been constructed by the hands of the captive Greeks, than Alexius trembled behind the walls of his capital. His plaintive epistles were dispersed over Europe to excite the compassion of the Latins, and to paint the danger, the weakness, and the riches of the city of Constantine.[2]

But the most interesting conquest of the Seljukian Turks was that of Jerusalem,[3] which soon became the theatre of nations. In their capitulation with Omar, the inhabitants had stipulated the assurance of their religion and property, but the articles were interpreted by a master against whom it was dangerous to dispute; and in the four hundred years of the reign of the caliphs the political climate of Jerusalem was exposed to the vicissitudes of storms and sunshine.[4] By the increase of proselytes and population the Mohammedans might excuse their usurpation of three-fourths of the city: but a peculiar quarter was reserved for the patriarch with his clergy and people; a tribute of two pieces of gold was the price of protection; and the sepulchre of Christ, with the church of the Resurrection, was still left in the hands of his votaries. Of these votaries the most numerous and respectable portion were strangers to Jerusalem; the pilgrimages to the Holy Land had been stimulated, rather than suppressed, by the conquest of the Arabs; and the enthusiasm which had always prompted these perilous journeys was nourished by the congenial passions of grief and indignation. A crowd of pilgrims from the

---

[1] William of Tyre (l. i. c. 9, 10, p. 635) gives the most authentic and deplorable account of these Turkish conquests.

[2] In his epistle to the count of Flanders, Alexius seems to fall too low beneath his character and dignity; yet it is approved by Ducange (Not. ad Alexiad. p. 335, etc.), and paraphrased by the Abbot Guibert, a contemporary historian. The Greek text no longer exists; and each translator and scribe might say with Guibert (p. 475), verbis vestita meis—a privilege of most indefinite latitude.

[3] Our best fund for the history of Jerusalem from Heraclius to the crusades is contained in two large and original passages of William archbishop of Tyre (l. i. c. 1-10; l. xviii. c. 5, 6), the principal author of the Gesta Dei per Francos. M. de Guignes has composed a very learned Mémoire sur le Commerce des François dans le Levant avant les Croisades, etc. (Mém. de l'Académie des Inscriptions, tom. xxxvii. p. 467-500.)

[4] Secundum Dominorum dispositionem plerumque lucida plerumque nubila recepit intervalla, et ægrotantis more temporum præsentium gravabatur aut respirabat qualitate (l. i. c. 3, p. 630). The Latinity of William of Tyre is by no means contemptible; but in his account of 490 years, from the loss to the recovery of Jerusalem, he exceeds the true account by thirty years.

East and West continued to visit the holy sepulchre and the
adjacent sanctuaries, more especially at the festival of Easter;
and the Greeks and Latins, the Nestorians and Jacobites, the
Copts and Abyssinians, the Armenians and Georgians, maintained the chapels, the clergy, and the poor of their respective
communions. The harmony of prayer in so many various
tongues, the worship of so many nations in the common temple
of their religion, might have afforded a spectacle of edification
and peace; but the zeal of the Christian sects was embittered by
hatred and revenge; and in the kingdom of a suffering Messiah,
who had pardoned his enemies, they aspired to command and
persecute their spiritual brethren. The pre-eminence was
asserted by the spirit and numbers of the Franks, and the greatness of Charlemagne [1] protected both the Latin pilgrims and the
Catholics of the East. The poverty of Carthage, Alexandria,
and Jerusalem was relieved by the alms of that pious emperor,
and many monasteries of Palestine were founded or restored by
his liberal devotion. Harun Alrashid, the greatest of the Abbassides, esteemed in his Christian brother a similar supremacy of
genius and power: their friendship was cemented by a frequent
intercourse of gifts and embassies; and the caliph, without
resigning the substantial dominion, presented the emperor with
the keys of the holy sepulchre, and perhaps of the city of
Jerusalem. In the decline of the Carlovingian monarchy the
republic of Amalphi promoted the interest of trade and religion
in the East. Her vessels transported the Latin pilgrims to the
coasts of Egypt and Palestine, and deserved, by their useful
imports, the favour and alliance of the Fatimite caliphs: [2] an
annual fair was instituted on Mount Calvary; and the Italian
merchants founded the convent and hospital of St. John of Jerusalem, the cradle of the monastic and military order which has
since reigned in the isles of Rhodes and of Malta. Had the
Christian pilgrims been content to revere the tomb of a prophet,
the disciples of Mohammed, instead of blaming, would have
imitated, their piety; but these rigid *Unitarians* were scandalised
by a worship which represents the birth, death, and resurrection

[1] For the transactions of Charlemagne with the Holy Land, see Egin-
hard (de Vitâ Caroli Magni, c. 16, p. 79-82), Constantine Porphyrogenitus
(de Administratione Imperii, l. ii. c. 26, p. 80 [tom. iii. p. 115, ed. Bonn]),
and Pagi (Critica, tom. iii. A.D. 800, No. 13, 14, 15).

[2] The caliph granted his privileges, Amalphitanis viris amicis et utilium
introductoribus (Gesta Dei, p. 934 [Willerm. Tyr. lib. xviii. c. 5]). The
trade of Venice to Egypt and Palestine cannot produce so old a title, unless
we adopt the laughable translation of a Frenchman who mistook the two
factions of the circus (Veneti et Prasini) for the Venetians and Parisians.

of a God; the Catholic images were branded with the name of idols; and the Moslems smiled with indignation [1] at the miraculous flame which was kindled on the eve of Easter in the holy sepulchre.[2] This pious fraud, first devised in the ninth century,[3] was devoutly cherished by the Latin crusaders, and is annually repeated by the clergy of the Greek, Armenian, and Coptic sects,[4] who impose on the credulous spectators [5] for their own benefit and that of their tyrants. In every age a principle of toleration has been fortified by a sense of interest, and the revenue of the prince and his emir was increased each year by the expense and tribute of so many thousand strangers.

The revolution which transferred the sceptre from the Abbassides to the Fatimites was a benefit rather than an injury to the Holy Land. A sovereign resident in Egypt was more sensible of the importance of Christian trade; and the emirs of Palestine were less remote from the justice and power of the throne. But the third of these Fatimite caliphs was the famous Hakem,[6] a frantic youth, who was delivered by his impiety and despotism from the fear either of God or man, and whose reign was a wild mixture of vice and folly. Regardless of the most ancient customs of Egypt, he imposed on the women an absolute confinement; the restraint excited the clamours of both sexes; their clamours provoked his fury; a part of Old Cairo was delivered to the flames, and the guards and citizens were engaged many days in a bloody conflict. At first the caliph declared himself a zealous Musulman, the founder or benefactor of moschs

---

[1] An Arabic chronicle of Jerusalem (apud Asseman. Biblioth. Orient. tom. i. p. 628, tom. iv. p. 368) attests the unbelief of the caliph and the historian; yet Cantacuzene presumes to appeal to the Mohammedans themselves for the truth of this perpetual miracle.

[2] In his Dissertations on Ecclesiastical History the learned Mosheim has separately discussed this pretended miracle (tom. ii. p. 214-306), de lumine sancti sepulchri.

[3] William of Malmesbury (l. iv. c. ii. p. 209) quotes the Itinerary of the monk Bernard, an eye-witness, who visited Jerusalem A.D. 870. The miracle is confirmed by another pilgrim some years older; and Mosheim ascribes the invention to the Franks soon after the decease of Charlemagne.

[4] Our travellers, Sandys (p. 134), Thevenot (p. 621-627), Maundrell (p. 94, 95), etc., describe this extravagant farce. The Catholics are puzzled to decide *when* the miracle ended and the trick began.

[5] The Orientals themselves confess the fraud, and plead necessity and edification (Mémoires du Chevalier D'Arvieux, tom. ii. p. 140; Joseph Abudacni, Hist. Copt. c. 20); but I will not attempt, with Mosheim. to explain the mode. Our travellers have failed with the blood of St. Januarius at Naples.

[6] See D'Herbelot (Biblioth. Orientale, p. 411), Renaudot (Hist. Patriarch. Alex. p. 390, 397, 400, 401), Elmacin (Hist. Saracen. p. 321-323), and Marei (p. 384-386), an historian of Egypt, translated by Reiske from Arabic into German, and verbally interpreted to me by a friend.

and colleges: twelve hundred and ninety copies of the Koran
were transcribed at his expense in letters of gold, and his edict
extirpated the vineyards of the Upper Egypt. But his vanity
was soon flattered by the hope of introducing a new religion;
he aspired above the fame of a prophet, and styled himself the
visible image of the Most High God, who, after nine apparitions
on earth, was at length manifest in his royal person. At the
name of Hakem, the lord of the living and the dead, every knee
was bent in religious adoration; his mysteries were performed
on a mountain near Cairo; sixteen thousand converts had
signed his profession of faith; and at the present hour a free and
warlike people, the Druses of Mount Libanus, are persuaded of
the life and divinity of a madman and tyrant.[1] In his divine
character Hakem hated the Jews and Christians, as the servants
of his rivals, while some remains of prejudice or prudence still
pleaded in favour of the law of Mohammed. Both in Egypt
and Palestine his cruel and wanton persecution made some
martyrs and many apostates; the common rights and special
privileges of the sectaries were equally disregarded, and a general
interdict was laid on the devotion of strangers and natives. The
temple of the Christian world, the church of the Resurrection,
was demolished to its foundations; the luminous prodigy of
Easter was interrupted; and much profane labour was exhausted to destroy the cave in the rock which properly constitutes the holy sepulchre. At the report of this sacrilege the
nations of Europe were astonished and afflicted; but, instead of
arming in the defence of the Holy Land, they contented themselves with burning or banishing the Jews, as the secret advisers
of the impious barbarian.[2] Yet the calamities of Jerusalem
were in some measure alleviated by the inconstancy or repentance of Hakem himself; and the royal mandate was sealed for

[1] The religion of the Druses is concealed by their ignorance and
hypocrisy. Their secret doctrines are confined to the elect who profess
a contemplative life; and the vulgar Druses, the most indifferent of men,
occasionally conform to the worship of the Mohammedans and Christians
of their neighbourhood. The little that is, or deserves to be known, may
be seen in the industrious Niebuhr (Voyages, tom. ii. p. 354-357), and the
second volume of the recent and instructive Travels of M. de Volney.

[The religion of the Druses has been fully examined in the erudite work
of M. Silvestre de Sacy, two vols., Paris, 1838. This has been largely
superseded by a very able treatise by the Rev. W. Ewing, M.A., of Edinburgh, *Arab and Druse at Home* (Jack, Edinburgh, 1907). The account
of Hakem Biamr-Allah enables us to correct several errors in the account
which Gibbon gives. This man has been revered by the Druses as their
spiritual leader for upwards of 800 years.—O. S.]

[2] See Glaber, l. iii. c. 7, and the Annals of Baronius and Pagi, A.D. 1009.

the restitution of the churches when the tyrant was assassinated by the emissaries of his sister. The succeeding caliphs resumed the maxims of religion and policy: a free toleration was again granted; with the pious aid of the emperor of Constantinople the holy sepulchre arose from its ruins; and, after a short abstinence, the pilgrims returned with an increase of appetite to the spiritual feast.[1] In the sea-voyage of Palestine the dangers were frequent, and the opportunities rare; but the conversion of Hungary opened a safe communication between Germany and Greece. The charity of St. Stephen, the apostle of his kingdom, relieved and conducted his itinerant brethren; [2] and from Belgrade to Antioch they traversed fifteen hundred miles of a Christian empire. Among the Franks the zeal of pilgrimage prevailed beyond the example of former times, and the roads were covered with multitudes of either sex and of every rank, who professed their contempt of life so soon as they should have kissed the tomb of their Redeemer. Princes and prelates abandoned the care of their dominions, and the numbers of these pious caravans were a prelude to the armies which marched in the ensuing age under the banner of the cross. About thirty years before the first crusade, the archbishop of Mentz, with the bishops of Utrecht, Bamberg, and Ratisbon, undertook this laborious journey from the Rhine to the Jordan, and the multitude of their followers amounted to seven thousand persons.

At Constantinople they were hospitably entertained by the emperor, but the ostentation of their wealth provoked the assault of the wild Arabs; they drew their swords with scrupulous reluctance, and sustained a siege in the village of Capernaum till they were rescued by the venal protection of the Fatimite emir. After visiting the holy places they embarked for Italy, but only a remnant of two thousand arrived in safety in their native land. Ingulphus, a secretary of William the Conqueror, was a companion of this pilgrimage; he observes that they sallied from Normandy thirty stout and well-appointed horse-

---

[1] Per idem tempus ex universo orbe tam innumerabilis multitudo cœpit confluere ad sepulchrum Salvatoris Hierosolymis, quantum nullus hominum prius sperare poterat. Ordo inferioris plebis . . . mediocres . . . reges et comites . . . præsules . . . mulieres multæ nobiles cum paupueriori-bus. . . . Pluribus enim erat mentis desiderium mori priusquam ad propria reverterentur (Glaber, l. iv. c. 6; Bouquet, Historians of France, tom. x. p. 50).

[2] Glaber, l. iii. c. 1. Kartona (Hist. Critic. Regum Hungariæ, tom. i. p. 304-311) examines whether St. Stephen founded a monastery at Jerusalem.

men; but that they repassed the Alps twenty miserable palmers, with the staff in their hand, and the wallet at their back.[1]

After the defeat of the Romans the tranquillity of the Fatimite caliphs was invaded by the Turks.[2] One of the lieutenants of Malek Shah, Atsiz the Carizmian, marched into Syria at the head of a powerful army, and reduced Damascus by famine and the sword. Hems, and the other cities of the province, acknowledged the caliph of Bagdad and the sultan of Persia; and the victorious emir advanced without resistance to the banks of the Nile: the Fatimite was preparing to fly into the heart of Africa; but the negroes of his guard and the inhabitants of Cairo made a desperate sally, and repulsed the Turk from the confines of Egypt. In his retreat he indulged the licence of slaughter and rapine: the judge and notaries of Jerusalem were invited to his camp; and their execution was followed by the massacre of three thousand citizens. The cruelty or the defeat of Atsiz was soon punished by the sultan Toucush, the brother of Malek Shah, who, with a higher title and more formidable powers, asserted the dominion of Syria and Palestine. The house of Seljuk reigned about twenty years in Jerusalem;[3] but the hereditary command of the holy city and territory was intrusted or abandoned to the emir Ortok, the chief of a tribe of Turkmans, whose children, after their expulsion from Palestine, formed two dynasties on the borders of Armenia and Assyria.[4] The Oriental Christians and the Latin pilgrims deplored a revolution which, instead of the regular government and old alliance of the caliphs, imposed on their necks the iron yoke of the strangers of the North.[5] In his court and camp the great sultan had adopted

---

[1] Baronius (A.D. 1064, No. 43-56) has transcribed the greater part of the original narratives of Ingulphus, Marianus, and Lambertus.

[2] See Elmacin (Hist. Saracen. p. 349, 350) and Abulpharagius (Dynast. p. 237, vers. Pocock). M. de Guignes (Hist. des Huns, tom. iii. part i. p. 215, 216) adds the testimonies, or rather the names, of Abulfeda and Novairi.

[3] From the expedition of Isar Atsiz (A.H. 469—A.D. 1076) to the expulsion of the Ortokides (A.D. 1096). Yet William of Tyre (l. i. c. 6, p. 633) asserts that Jerusalem was thirty-eight years in the hands of the Turks; and an Arabic chronicle, quoted by Pagi (tom. iv. p. 202), supposes that the city was reduced by a Carizmian general to the obedience of the caliph of Bagdad, A.H. 463—A.D. 1070. These early dates are not very compatible with the general history of Asia; and I am sure that, as late as A.D. 1064, the regnum Babylonicum (of Cairo) still prevailed in Palestine (Baronius, A.D. 1064, No. 56).

[4] De Guignes, Hist. des Huns, tom. i. p. 249-252.

[5] Willerm. Tyr. l. i. c. 8, p. 634, who strives hard to magnify the Christian grievances. The Turks exacted an *aureus* from each pilgrim! The *caphar* of the Franks is now fourteen dollars: and Europe does not complain of this voluntary tax.

in some degree the arts and manners of Persia; but the body of the Turkish nation, and more especially the pastoral tribes, still breathed the fierceness of the desert. From Nice to Jerusalem the western countries of Asia were a scene of foreign and domestic hostility; and the shepherds of Palestine, who held a precarious sway on a doubtful frontier, had neither leisure nor capacity to await the slow profits of commercial and religious freedom. The pilgrims, who, through innumerable perils, had reached the gates of Jerusalem, were the victims of private rapine or public oppression, and often sunk under the pressure of famine and disease, before they were permitted to salute the holy sepulchre. A spirit of native barbarism, or recent zeal, prompted the Turkmans to insult the clergy of every sect: the patriarch was dragged by the hair along the pavement and cast into a dungeon, to extort a ransom from the sympathy of his flock; and the divine worship in the church of the Resurrection was often disturbed by the savage rudeness of its masters. The pathetic tale excited the millions of the West to march under the standard of the cross to the relief of the Holy Land; and yet how trifling is the sum of these accumulated evils, if compared with the single act of the sacrilege of Hakem, which had been so patiently endured by the Latin Christians! A slighter provocation inflamed the more irascible temper of their descendants: a new spirit had arisen of religious chivalry and papal dominion; a nerve was touched of exquisite feeling; and the sensation vibrated to the heart of Europe.

CHAPTER LVIII

Origin and Numbers of the First Crusade—Characters of the Latin Princes —Their March to Constantinople—Policy of the Greek Emperor Alexius—Conquest of Nice, Antioch, and Jerusalem, by the Franks— Deliverance of the Holy Sepulchre—Godfrey of Bouillon, First King of Jerusalem—Institutions of the French or Latin Kingdom

ABOUT twenty years after the conquest of Jerusalem by the Turks, the holy sepulchre was visited by a hermit of the name of Peter, a native of Amiens, in the province of Picardy [1] in France.

---

[1] Whimsical enough is the origin of the name of *Picards*, and from thence of *Picardie*, which does not date earlier than A.D. 1200. It was an academical joke, an epithet first applied to the quarrelsome humour of those students, in the University of Paris, who came from the frontier of France and Flanders (Valesii Notitia Galliarum, p. 447; Longuerue, Description de la France, p. 54).

His resentment and sympathy were excited by his own injuries and the oppression of the Christian name; he mingled his tears with those of the patriarch, and earnestly inquired if no hopes of relief could be entertained from the Greek emperors of the East. The patriarch exposed the vices and weakness of the successors of Constantine. " I will rouse," exclaimed the hermit, " the martial nations of Europe in your cause;" and Europe was obedient to the call of the hermit. The astonished patriarch dismissed him with epistles of credit and complaint; and no sooner did he land at Bari than Peter hastened to kiss the feet of the Roman pontiff. His stature was small, his appearance contemptible; but his eye was keen and lively, and he possessed that vehemence of speech which seldom fails to impart the persuasion of the soul.[1] He was born of a gentleman's family (for we must now adopt a modern idiom), and his military service was under the neighbouring counts of Boulogne, the heroes of the first crusade. But he soon relinquished the sword and the world; and if it be true that his wife, however noble, was aged and ugly, he might withdraw with the less reluctance from her bed to a convent, and at length to a hermitage. In this austere solitude his body was emaciated, his fancy was inflamed; whatever he wished, he believed; whatever he believed, he *saw* in dreams and revelations. From Jerusalem the pilgrim returned an accomplished fanatic; but as he excelled in the popular madness of the times, Pope Urban the Second received him as a prophet, applauded his glorious design, promised to support it in a general council, and encouraged him to proclaim the deliverance of the Holy Land. Invigorated by the approbation of the pontiff, his zealous missionary traversed, with speed and success, the provinces of Italy and France. His diet was abstemious, his prayers long and fervent, and the alms which he received with one hand, he distributed with the other: his head was bare, his feet naked, his meagre body was wrapped in a coarse garment; he bore and displayed a weighty crucifix; and the ass on which he rode was sanctified, in the public eye, by the service of the man of God. He preached to innumerable crowds in the churches, the streets, and the highways: the hermit entered with equal confidence the palace and the cottage; and the people,

---

[1] William of Tyre (l. i. c. 11, p. 637, 638) thus describes the hermit: Pusillus, persona contemptibilis, vivacis ingenii, et oculum habens perspicacem gratumque, et sponte fluens ei non deerat eloquium. See Albert Aquensis, p. 185; Guibert, p. 482 [l. ii. c. 8]; Anna Comnena in Alexiad. l. x. p. 284, etc., with Ducange's notes, p. 349.

for all was people, was impetuously moved by his call to repentance and arms. When he painted the sufferings of the natives
and pilgrims of Palestine, every heart was melted to compassion;
every breast glowed with indignation when he challenged the
warriors of the age to defend their brethren, and rescue their
Saviour: his ignorance of art and language was compensated
by sighs, and tears, and ejaculations; and Peter supplied the
deficiency of reason by loud and frequent appeals to Christ and
his mother, to the saints and angels of paradise, with whom he
had personally conversed. The most perfect orator of Athens
might have envied the success of his eloquence: the rustic
enthusiast inspired the passions which he felt, and Christendom
expected with impatience the counsels and decrees of the
supreme pontiff.

The magnanimous spirit of Gregory the Seventh had already
embraced the design of arming Europe against Asia; the
ardour of his zeal and ambition still breathes in his epistles;
from either side of the Alps fifty thousand Catholics had enlisted
under the banner of St. Peter; [1] and his successor reveals *his*
intention of marching at their head against the impious sectaries
of Mohammed. But the glory or reproach of executing, though
not in person, this holy enterprise, was reserved for Urban the
Second, [2] the most faithful of his disciples. He undertook the
conquest of the East, whilst the larger portion of Rome was
possessed and fortified by his rival Guibert of Ravenna, who
contended with Urban for the name and honours of the pontificate. He attempted to unite the powers of the West, at a time
when the princes were separated from the church, and the people
from their princes, by the excommunication which himself and
his predecessors had thundered against the emperor and the
king of France. Philip the First of France supported with
patience the censures which he had provoked by his scandalous
life and adulterous marriage. Henry the Fourth of Germany
asserted the right of investitures, the prerogative of confirming
his bishops by the delivery of the ring and crosier. But the
emperor's party was crushed in Italy by the arms of the Normans
and the countess Mathilda; and the long quarrel had been
recently envenomed by the revolt of his son Conrad and the

[1] Ultra quinquaginta millia, si me possunt in expeditione pro duce et
pontifice habere, armatâ manû volunt in inimicos Dei insurgere et ad
sepulchrum Domini ipso ducente pervenire (Gregor. VII. epist. ii. 31, in
tom. xii. p. 322, concil.).

[2] See the original lives of Urban II. by Pandulphus Pisanus and
Bernardus Guido, in Muratori, Rer. Ital. Script. tom. iii. pars i. p. 352, 353.

shame of his wife,[1] who, in the synods of Constance and Placentia, confessed the manifold prostitutions to which she had been exposed by a husband regardless of her honour and his own.[2] So popular was the cause of Urban, so weighty was his influence, that the council which he summoned at Placentia [3] was composed of two hundred bishops of Italy, France, Burgundy, Swabia, and Bavaria. Four thousand of the clergy and thirty thousand of the laity attended this important meeting; and, as the most spacious cathedral would have been inadequate to the multitude, the session of seven days was held in a plain adjacent to the city. The ambassadors of the Greek emperor, Alexius Comnenus, were introduced to plead the distress of their sovereign, and the danger of Constantinople, which was divided only by a narrow sea from the victorious Turks, the common enemies of the Christian name. In their suppliant address they flattered the pride of the Latin princes; and, appealing at once to their policy and religion, exhorted them to repel the barbarians on the confines of Asia, rather than to expect them in the heart of Europe. At the sad tale of the misery and perils of their Eastern brethren the assembly burst into tears: the most eager champions declared their readiness to march; and the Greek ambassadors were dismissed with the assurance of a speedy and powerful succour. The relief of Constantinople was included in the larger and most distant project of the deliverance of Jerusalem; but the prudent Urban adjourned the final decision to a second synod, which he proposed to celebrate in some city of France in the autumn of the same year. The short delay would propagate the flame of enthusiasm; and his firmest hope was in a

[1] She is known by the different names of Praxes, Eupræcia, Eufrasia, and Adelais; and was the daughter of a Russian prince, and the widow of a margrave of Brandenburg. Struv. Corpus Hist. Germanicæ, p. 340.

[2] Henricus odio eam cœpit habere: ideo incarceravit eam, et concessit ut plerique vim ei inferrent; immo filium hortans ut eam subagitaret (Dodechin, Continuat. Marian. Scot. apud Baron. A.D. 1093, No. 4). In the synod of Constance she is described by Bertholdus, rerum inspector: quæ se tantas et tam inauditas fornicationum spurcitias, et a tantis passam fuisse conquesta est, etc.; and again at Placentia: satis misericorditer suscepit, eo quòd ipsam tantas spurcitias non tam commisisse quam invitam pertulisse pro certo cognoverit papa cum sanctâ synodo. Apud Baron. A.D. 1093, No. 4, 1094, No. 3. A rare subject for the infallible decision of a pope and council. These abominations are repugnant to every principle of human nature, which is not altered by a dispute about rings and crosiers. Yet it should seem that the wretched woman was tempted by the priests to relate or subscribe some infamous stories of herself and her husband.

[3] See the narrative and acts of the synod of Placentia, Concil. tom. xii. p. 821, etc.

nation of soldiers [1] still proud of the pre-eminence of their name,
and ambitious to emulate their hero Charlemagne,[2] who, in the
popular romance of Turpin,[3] had achieved the conquest of the
Holy Land. A latent motive of affection or vanity might
influence the choice of Urban: he was himself a native of France,
a monk of Clugny, and the first of his countrymen who ascended
the throne of St. Peter. The pope had illustrated his family and
province; nor is there perhaps a more exquisite gratification
than to revisit, in a conspicuous dignity, the humble and
laborious scenes of our youth.

It may occasion some surprise that the Roman pontiff should
erect, in the heart of France, the tribunal from whence he hurled
his anathemas against the king; but our surprise will vanish so
soon as we form a just estimate of a king of France of the eleventh
century.[4] Philip the First was the great-grandson of Hugh
Capet, the founder of the present race, who, in the decline of
Charlemagne's posterity, added the regal title to his patrimonial
estates of Paris and Orleans. In this narrow compass he was
possessed of wealth and jurisdiction; but in the rest of France
Hugh and his first descendants were no more than the feudal lords
of about sixty dukes and counts, of independent and hereditary
power,[5] who disdained the control of laws and legal assemblies,
and whose disregard of their sovereign was revenged by the disobedience of their inferior vassals. At Clermont, in the terri-

[1] Guibert, himself a Frenchman, praises the piety and valour of the
French nation, the author and example of the crusades: Gens nobilis,
prudens, bellicosa, dapsilis et nitida. . . . Quos enim Britones, *Anglos*,
Ligures, si bonis eos moribus videamus, non illico *Francos homines* appel-
lemus? (p. 478 [l. ii. c. 1]). He owns, however, that the vivacity of the
French degenerates into petulance [justius æquo feroces—S.] among
foreigners (p. 483 [l. ii. c. 10]) and vain loquaciousness (p. 502 [l. iv c. 9]).

[2] Per viam quam jamdudum Carolus Magnus mirificus rex Francorum
aptari fecit usque C. P. (Gesta Francorum, p. 1; Robert. Monach. Hist.
Hieros. l. i. p. 33), etc.

[3] John Tilpinus, or Turpinus, was Archbishop of Rheims, A.D. 773.
After the year 1000 this romance was composed in his name, by a monk of
the borders of France and Spain; and such was the idea of ecclesiastical
merit, that he describes himself as a fighting and drinking priest! Yet
the book of lies was pronounced authentic by Pope Calixtus II. (A.D. 1122),
and is respectfully quoted by the abbot Suger, in the great Chronicles of
St. Denys (Fabric. Biblioth. Latin. medii Ævi, edit. Mansi, tom. iv. p. 161).

[4] See Etat de la France, by the Count de Boulainvilliers, tom. i. p. 180-
182, and the second volume of the Observations sur l'Histoire de France,
by the Abbé de Mably.

[5] In the provinces to the south of the Loire, the first *Capetians* were
scarcely allowed a feudal supremacy. On all sides, Normandy, Bretagne,
Aquitain, Burgundy, Lorraine, and Flanders, contracted the name and
limits of the *proper* France. See Hadrian Vales. Notitia Galliarum.

tories of the count of Auvergne,[1] the pope might brave with
impunity the resentment of Philip; and the council which he
convened in that city was not less numerous or respectable than
the synod of Placentia.[2] Besides his court and council of Roman
cardinals, he was supported by thirteen archbishops and two
hundred and twenty-five bishops; the number of mitred prelates
was computed at four hundred; and the fathers of the church
were blessed by the saints and enlightened by the doctors of the
age. From the adjacent kingdoms a martial train of lords and
knights of power and renown attended the council,[3] in high
expectation of its resolves; and such was the ardour of zeal and
curiosity, that the city was filled, and many thousands, in the
month of November, erected their tents or huts in the open field.
A session of eight days produced some useful or edifying canons
for the reformation of manners; a severe censure was pronounced
against the licence of private war; the Truce of God [4] was confirmed, a suspension of hostilities during four days of the week;
women and priests were placed under the safeguard of the church;
and a protection of three years was extended to husbandmen
and merchants, the defenceless victims of military rapine.   But
a law, however venerable be the sanction, cannot suddenly
transform the temper of the times; and the benevolent efforts
of Urban deserve the less praise, since he laboured to appease
some domestic quarrels that he might spread the flames of war
from the Atlantic to the Euphrates. From the synod of
Placentia the rumour of his great design had gone forth among
the nations: the clergy on their return had preached in every
diocese the merit and glory of the deliverance of the Holy Land;
and when the pope ascended a lofty scaffold in the market-place
of Clermont, his eloquence was addressed to a well-prepared and
impatient audience. His topics were obvious, his exhortation
was vehement, his success inevitable. The orator was interrupted by the shout of thousands, who with one voice, and in

[1] These counts, a younger branch of the dukes of Aquitain, were at
length despoiled of the greatest part of their country by Philip Augustus.
The bishops of Clermont gradually became princes of the city. Mélanges
tirés d'une Grande Bibliothèque, tom. xxxvi. p. 288, etc.
[2] See the Acts of the Council of Clermont, Concil. tom. xii. p. 829, etc.
[3] Confluxerant ad concilium e multis regionibus, viri potentes, et honorati,
innumeri, quamvis cingulo laicalis militiæ superbi (Baldric, an eye-witness,
p. 86-88; Robert. Mon. p. 31, 32; Will. Tyr. i. 14, 15, p. 639-641; Guibert,
p. 478-480 [l. ii. c. 2-4]; Fulcher. Carnot. p. 382).
[4] The Truce of God (Treva, or Treuga Dei) was first invented in Aquitain,
A.D. 1032; blamed by some bishops as an occasion of perjury, and rejected
by the Normans as contrary to their privileges (Ducange, Gloss. Latin.
tom. vi. p. 682-685).

their rustic idiom, exclaimed aloud, "God wills it, God wills it!"[1] "It is indeed the will of God," replied the pope; "and let this memorable word, the inspiration surely of the Holy Spirit, be for ever adopted as your cry of battle, to animate the devotion and courage of the champions of Christ. His cross is the symbol of your salvation; wear it, a red, a bloody cross, as an external mark, on your breasts or shoulders, as a pledge of your sacred and irrevocable engagement." The proposal was joyfully accepted; great numbers, both of the clergy and laity, impressed on their garments the sign of the cross,[2] and solicited the pope to march at their head. This dangerous honour was declined by the more prudent successor of Gregory, who alleged the schism of the church, and the duties of his pastoral office, recommending to the faithful, who were disqualified by sex or profession, by age or infirmity, to aid with their prayers and alms the personal service of their robust brethren. The name and powers of his legate he devolved on Adhemar, bishop of Puy, the first who had received the cross at his hands. The foremost of the temporal chiefs was Raymond, count of Toulouse, whose ambassadors in the council excused the absence, and pledged the honour, of their master. After the confession and absolution of their sins, the champions of the cross were dismissed with a superfluous admonition to invite their countrymen and friends; and their departure for the Holy Land was fixed to the festival of the Assumption, the fifteenth of August, of the ensuing year.[3]

[1] *Deus vult, Deus vult!* was the pure acclamation of the clergy who understood Latin (Robert. Mon. l. i. p. 32). By the illiterate laity, who spoke the *Provincial* or *Limousin* idiom, it was corrupted to *Deus lo volt*, or *Diex el volt*. See Chron. Casinense, l. iv. c. 11, p. 497, in Muratori, Script. Rerum Ital. tom. iv., and Ducange (Dissertat. xi. p. 207, sur Joinville, and Gloss. Latin. tom. ii. p. 690), who, in his preface, produces a very difficult specimen of the dialect of Rovergue, A.D. 1100, very near, both in time and place, to the Council of Clermont (p. 15, 16).

[2] Most commonly on their shoulders, in gold, or silk, or cloth, sewed on their garments. In the first crusade all were red; in the third the French alone preserved that colour, while green crosses were adopted by the Flemings, and white by the English (Ducange, tom. ii. p. 651). Yet in England the red ever appears the favourite, and, as it were, the national colour of our military ensigns and uniforms.

[3] Bongarsius, who has published the original writers of the crusades, adopts, with much complacency, the fanatic title of Guibertus, Gesta DEI per Francos; though some critics propose to read Gesta *Diaboli* per Francos (Hanoviæ, 1611, two vols. in folio). I shall briefly enumerate, as they stand in this collection, the authors whom I have used for the first crusade. I. Gesta Francorum. II. Robertus Monachus. III. Baldricus. IV. Raimundus de Agiles. V. Albertus Aquensis. VI. Fulcherius Carnotensis. VII. Guibertus. VIII. Willielmus Tyriensis. Muratori has given us, IX. Radulphus Cadomensis de Gestis Tancredi (Script. Rer. Ital. tom. v. p. 285-333), and, X. Bernardus Thesaurarius de Acquisitione

So familiar, and as it were so natural to man, is the practice of violence, that our indulgence allows the slightest provocation, the most disputable right, as a sufficient ground of national hostility. But the name and nature of a *holy war* demands a more rigorous scutiny; nor can we hastily believe that the servants of the Prince of Peace would unsheathe the sword of destruction unless the motive were pure, the quarrel legitimate, and the necessity inevitable. The policy of an action may be determined from the tardy lessons of experience; but before we act, our conscience should be satisfied of the justice and propriety of our enterprise. In the age of the crusades, the Christians, both of the East and West, were persuaded of their lawfulness and merit; their arguments are clouded by the perpetual abuse of Scripture and rhetoric; but they seem to insist on the right of natural and religious defence, their peculiar title to the Holy Land, and the impiety of their Pagan and Mohammedan foes.[1] I. The right of a just defence may fairly include our civil and spiritual allies: it depends on the existence of danger; and that danger must be estimated by the twofold consideration of the malice and the power of our enemies. A pernicious tenet has been imputed to the Mohammedans, the duty of *extirpating* all other religions by the sword. This charge of ignorance and bigotry is refuted by the Koran, by the history of the Musulman conquerors, and by their public and legal toleration of the Christian worship. But it cannot be denied that the Oriental churches are depressed under their iron yoke; that, in peace and war, they assert a divine and indefeasible claim of universal empire; and that, in their orthodox creed, the unbelieving nations are continually threatened with the loss of religion or liberty. In the eleventh century the victorious arms of the Turks presented a real and urgent apprehension of these losses. They had subdued in less than thirty years the kingdoms

Terræ Sanctæ (tom. vii. p. 664-848). The last of these was unknown to a late French historian, who has given a large and critical list of the writers of the crusades (Esprit des Croisades, tom. i. p. 13-141), and most of whose judgments my own experience will allow me to ratify. It was late before I could obtain a sight of the French historians collected by Duchesne. I. Petri Tudebodi Sacerdotis Sivracensis Historia de Hierosolymitano Itinere (tom. iv. p. 773-815) has been transfused into the first anonymous writer of Bongarsius. II. The Metrical History of the First Crusade, in seven books (p. 890-912), is of small value or account.

[1] If the reader will turn to the first scene of the First Part of Henry the Fourth, he will see in the text of Shakspeare the natural feelings of enthusiasm; and in the notes of Dr. Johnson the workings of a bigoted, though vigorous, mind, greedy of every pretence to hate and persecute those who dissent from his creed.

of Asia, as far as Jerusalem and the Hellespont; and the Greek empire tottered on the verge of destruction.   Besides an honest sympathy for their brethren, the Latins had a right and interest in the support of Constantinople, the most important barrier of the West; and the privilege of defence must reach to prevent, as well as to repel, an impending assault.   But this salutary purpose might have been accomplished by a moderate succour; and our calmer reason must disclaim the innumerable hosts and remote operations which overwhelmed Asia and depopulated Europe.   II. Palestine could add nothing to the strength or safety of the Latins; and fanaticism alone could pretend to justify the conquest of that distant and narrow province.   The Christians affirmed that their inalienable title to the promised land had been sealed by the blood of their divine Saviour; it was their right and duty to rescue their inheritance from the unjust possessors, who profaned his sepulchre, and oppressed the pilgrimage of his disciples.   Vainly would it be alleged that the pre-eminence of Jerusalem and the sanctity of Palestine have been abolished with the Mosaic law; that the God of the Christians is not a local deity, and that the recovery of Bethlehem or Calvary, his cradle or his tomb, will not atone for the violation of the moral precepts of the Gospel.   Such arguments glance aside from the leaden shield of superstition; and the religious mind will not easily relinquish its hold on the sacred ground of mystery and miracle.   III. But the holy wars which have been waged in every climate of the globe, from Egypt to Livonia, and from Peru to Hindostan, require the support of some more general and flexible tenet.   It has been often supposed, and sometimes affirmed, that a difference of religion is a worthy cause of hostility; that obstinate unbelievers may be slain or subdued by the champions of the cross; and that grace is the sole fountain of dominion as well as of mercy.   Above four hundred years before the first crusade, the eastern and western provinces of the Roman empire had been acquired about the same time, and in the same manner, by the barbarians of Germany and Arabia.   Time and treaties had legitimated the conquests of the *Christian* Franks; but in the eyes of their subjects and neighbours the Mohammedan princes were still tyrants and usurpers, who, by the arms of war or rebellion, might be lawfully driven from their unlawful possession.[1]

[1] The sixth Discourse of Fleury on Ecclesiastical History (p. 223-261) contains an accurate and rational view of the causes and effects of the crusades.

As the manners of the Christians were relaxed, their discipline of penance [1] was enforced; and with the multiplication of sins the remedies were multiplied. In the primitive church a voluntary and open confession prepared the work of atonement. In the middle ages the bishops and priests interrogated the criminal, compelled him to account for his thoughts, words, and actions, and prescribed the terms of his reconciliation with God. But as this discretionary power might alternately be abused by indulgence and tyranny, a rule of discipline was framed to inform and regulate the spiritual judges. This mode of legislation was invented by the Greeks; their *penitentials* [2] were translated, or imitated, in the Latin church; and in the time of Charlemagne the clergy of every diocese were provided with a code, which they prudently concealed from the knowledge of the vulgar. In this dangerous estimate of crimes and punishments each case was supposed, each difference was remarked, by the experience or penetration of the monks; some sins are enumerated which innocence could not have suspected, and others which reason cannot believe; and the more ordinary offences of fornication and adultery, of perjury and sacrilege, of rapine and murder, were expiated by a penance which, according to the various circumstances, was prolonged from forty days to seven years. During this term of mortification the patient was healed, the criminal was absolved, by a salutary regimen of fasts and prayers: the disorder of his dress was expressive of grief and remorse; and he humbly abstained from all the business and pleasure of social life. But the rigid execution of these laws would have depopulated the palace, the camp, and the city; the barbarians of the West believed and trembled; but nature often rebelled against principle; and the magistrate laboured without effect to enforce the jurisdiction of the priest. A literal accomplishment of penance was indeed impracticable: the guilt of adultery was multiplied by daily repetition; that of homicide might involve the massacre of a whole people; each act was separately numbered; and, in those times of anarchy

[1] The penance, indulgences, etc., of the middle ages are amply discussed by Muratori (Antiquitat. Italiæ medii Ævi, tom. v. dissert. lxviii. p. 709-768) and by M. Chais (Lettres sur les Jubilés et les Indulgences, tom. ii. lettres 21 and 22, p. 478-556), with this difference, that the abuses of superstition are mildly, perhaps faintly, exposed by the learned Italian, and peevishly magnified by the Dutch minister.

[2] Schmidt (Histoire des Allemands, tom. ii. p. 211-220, 452-462) gives an abstract of the Penitential of Rhegino in the ninth, and of Burchard in the tenth, century. In one year five-and-thirty murders were perpetrated at Worms.

and vice, a modest sinner might easily incur a debt of three hundred years. His insolvency was relieved by a commutation or *indulgence :* a year of penance was appreciated at twenty-six *solidi* [1] of silver, about four pounds sterling, for the rich; at three solidi, or nine shillings, for the indigent: and these alms were soon appropriated to the use of the church, which derived from the redemption of sins an inexhaustible source of opulence and dominion. A debt of three hundred years, or twelve hundred pounds, was enough to impoverish a plentiful fortune; the scarcity of gold and silver was supplied by the alienation of land; and the princely donations of Pepin and Charlemagne are expressly given for the *remedy* of their soul. It is a maxim of the civil law, that whosoever cannot pay with his purse must pay with his body; and the practice of flagellation was adopted by the monks—a cheap though painful equivalent. By a fantastic arithmetic, a year of penance was taxed at three thousand lashes; [2] and such was the skill and patience of a famous hermit, St. Dominic of the Iron Cuirass,[3] that in six days he could discharge an entire century by a whipping of three hundred thousand stripes. His example was followed by many penitents of both sexes; and as a vicarious sacrifice was accepted, a sturdy disciplinarian might expiate on his own back the sins of his benefactors.[4] These compensations of the purse and the person introduced, in the eleventh century, a more honourable mode of satisfaction. The merit of military service against the Saracens of Africa and Spain and been allowed by the predecessors of Urban the Second. In the council of Clermont, that pope proclaimed a *plenary indulgence* to those who should enlist under the banner of the cross; the absolution of *all* their sins, and a full receipt for *all* that might be due of canonical penance.[5]

---

[1] Till the twelfth century we may support the clear account of twelve *denarii*, or pence, to the *solidus*, or shilling; and twenty *solidi* to the pound weight of silver, about the pound sterling. Our money is diminished to a third, and the French to a fiftieth, of this primitive standard.

[2] Each century of lashes was sanctified with the recital of a psalm; and the whole Psalter, with the accompaniment of 15,000 stripes, was equivalent to five years.

[3] The Life and Achievements of St. Dominic Loricatus was composed by his friend and admirer, Peter Damianus. See Fleury, Hist. Ecclés. tom. xiii. p. 96-104; Baronius, A.D. 1056, No. 7, who observes, from Damianus, how fashionable, even among ladies of quality (sublimis generis), this expiation (purgatorii genus) was grown.

[4] At a quarter, or even half, a rial a lash, Sancho Panza was a cheaper, and possibly not a more dishonest, workman. I remember in Père Labat (Voyages en Italie, tom. vii. p. 16-29) a very lively picture of the *dexterity* of one of these artists.

[5] Quicunque pro solâ devotione, non pro honoris vel pecuniæ adeptione, ad liberandam ecclesiam Dei Jerusalem profectus fuerit, iter illud pro

The cold philosophy of modern times is incapable of feeling the impression that was made on a sinful and fanatic world. At the voice of their pastor, the robber, the incendiary, the homicide, arose by thousands to redeem their souls by repeating on the infidels the same deeds which they had exercised against their Christian brethren; and the terms of atonement were eagerly embraced by offenders of every rank and denomination. None were pure; none were exempt from the guilt and penalty of sin; and those who were the least amenable to the justice of God and the church were the best entitled to the temporal and eternal recompense of their pious courage. If they fell, the spirit of the Latin clergy did not hesitate to adorn their tomb with the crown of martyrdom;[1] and should they survive, they could expect without impatience the delay and increase of their heavenly reward. They offered their blood to the Son of God, who had laid down his life for their salvation: they took up the cross, and entered with confidence into the way of the Lord. His providence would watch over their safety; perhaps his visible and miraculous power would smooth the difficulties of their holy enterprise. The cloud and pillar of Jehovah had marched before the Israelites into the promised land. Might not the Christians more reasonably hope that the rivers would open for their passage; that the walls of the strongest cities would fall at the sound of their trumpets; and that the sun would be arrested in his mid-career to allow them time for the destruction of the infidels?

Of the chiefs and soldiers who marched to the holy sepulchre, I will dare to affirm that *all* were prompted by the spirit of enthusiasm, the belief of merit, the hope of reward, and the assurance of divine aid. But I am equally persuaded that in *many* it was not the sole, that in *some* it was not the leading, principle of action. The use and abuse of religion are feeble to stem, they are strong and irresistible to impel, the stream of national manners. Against the private wars of the barbarians, their bloody tournaments, licentious loves, and judicial duels, the popes and synods might ineffectually thunder. It is a more easy task to provoke the metaphysical disputes of the Greeks,

omni pœnitentia reputetur.   Canon. Concil. Claromont. ii. p. 829 Guibert styles it novum salutis genus (p. 471 [l. i. c. 1], and is almost philosophical on the subject.

[1] Such at least was the belief of the crusaders, and such is the uniform style of the historians (Esprit des Croisades, tom. iii. p. 477); but the prayers for the repose of their souls are inconsistent in orthodox theology with the merits of martyrdom.

to drive into the cloister the victims of anarchy or despotism,
to sanctify the patience of slaves and cowards, or to assume the
merit of the humanity and benevolence of modern Christians.
War and exercise were the reigning passions of the Franks or
Latins; they were enjoined, as a penance, to gratify those
passions, to visit distant lands, and to draw their swords against
the nations of the East. Their victory, or even their attempt,
would immortalise the names of the intrepid heroes of the cross;
and the purest piety could not be insensible to the most splendid
prospect of military glory. In the petty quarrels of Europe
they shed the blood of their friends and countrymen for the
acquisition, perhaps, of a castle or a village. They could march
with alacrity against the distant and hostile nations who were
devoted to their arms; their fancy already grasped the golden
sceptres of Asia; and the conquest of Apulia and Sicily by the
Normans might exalt to royalty the hopes of the most private
adventurer. Christendom, in her rudest state, must have
yielded to the climate and cultivation of the Mohammedan
countries; and their natural and artificial wealth had been
magnified by the tales of pilgrims and the gifts of an imperfect
commerce. The vulgar, both the great and small, were taught
to believe every wonder, of lands flowing with milk and honey,
of mines and treasures, of gold and diamonds, of palaces of
marble and jasper, and of odoriferous groves of cinnamon and
frankincense. In this earthly paradise each warrior depended
on his sword to carve a plenteous and honourable establishment,
which he measured only by the extent of his wishes.[1] Their
vassals and soldiers trusted their fortunes to God and their
master: the spoils of a Turkish emir might enrich the meanest
follower of the camp; and the flavour of the wines, the beauty
of the Grecian women,[2] were temptations more adapted to the
nature, than to the profession, of the champions of the cross.
The love of freedom was a powerful incitement to the multitudes
who were oppressed by feudal or ecclesiastical tyranny. Under
this holy sign, the peasants and burghers, who were attached to

[1] The same hopes were displayed in the letters of the adventurers ad
animandos qui in Francia resederant. Hugh de Reiteste could boast that
his share amounted to one abbey and ten castles, of the yearly value of
1500 marks, and that he should acquire a hundred castles by the conquest of Aleppo (Guibert, p. 554, 555 [l. vii. c. 35]).
[2] In his genuine or fictitious letter to the Count of Flanders, Alexius
mingles with the danger of the church, and the relics of saints, the auri et
argenti amor, and pulcherrimarum fœminarum voluptas (p. 476 [l. i. c. 4]);
as if, says the indignant Guibert, the Greek women were handsomer than
those of France.

the servitude of the glebe, might escape from a haughty lord, and transplant themselves and their families to a land of liberty. The monk might release himself from the discipline of his convent, the debtor might suspend the accumulation of usury and the pursuit of his creditors, and outlaws and malefactors of every cast might continue to brave the laws and elude the punishment of their crimes.[1]

These motives were potent and numerous: when we have singly computed their weight on the mind of each individual, we must add the infinite series, the multiplying powers of example and fashion. The first proselytes became the warmest and most effectual missionaries of the cross: among their friends and countrymen they preached the duty, the merit, and the recompense of their holy vow, and the most reluctant hearers were insensibly drawn within the whirlpool of persuasion and authority. The martial youths were fired by the reproach or suspicion of cowardice; the opportunity of visiting with an army the sepulchre of Christ was embraced by the old and infirm, by women and children, who consulted rather their zeal than their strength; and those who in the evening had derided the folly of their companions were the most eager, the ensuing day, to tread in their footsteps. The ignorance which magnified the hopes, diminished the perils, of the enterprise. Since the Turkish conquest, the paths of pilgrimage were obliterated; the chiefs themselves had an imperfect notion of the length of the way and the state of their enemies; and such was the stupidity of the people, that, at the sight of the first city or castle beyond the limits of their knowledge, they were ready to ask whether that was not the Jerusalem, the term and object of their labours. Yet the more prudent of the crusaders, who were not sure that they should be fed from heaven with a shower of quails or manna, provided themselves with those precious metals which, in every country, are the representatives of every commodity. To defray, according to their rank, the expenses of the road, princes alienated their provinces, nobles their lands and castles, peasants their cattle and the instruments of husbandry. The value of property was depreciated by the eager competition of multitudes; while the price of arms and horses was raised to an exorbitant height by the wants and impatience of the buyers.[2]

[1] See the privileges of the *Crucesignati*—freedom from debt, usury, injury, secular justice, etc. The pope was their perpetual guardian (Ducange, tom. ii. p. 651, 652).

[2] Guibert (p. 481 [l. ii. c. 6]) paints in lively colours this general emotion. He was one of the few contemporaries who had genius enough to feel the

Those who remained at home, with sense and money, were enriched by the epidemical disease: the sovereigns acquired at a cheap rate the domains of their vassals, and the ecclesiastical purchasers completed the payment by the assurance of their prayers. The cross, which was commonly sewed on the garment, in cloth or silk, was inscribed by some zealots on their skin: an hot iron, or indelible liquor, was applied to perpetuate the mark; and a crafty monk, who showed the miraculous impression on his breast, was repaid with the popular veneration and the richest benefices of Palestine.[1]

The fifteenth of August had been fixed in the council of Clermont for the departure of the pilgrims; but the day was anticipated by the thoughtless and needy crowd of plebeians; and I shall briefly despatch the calamities which they inflicted and suffered before I enter on the more serious and successful enterprise of the chiefs. Early in the spring, from the confines of France and Lorraine, above sixty thousand of the populace of both sexes flocked round the first missionary of the crusade, and pressed him, with clamorous importunity, to lead them to the holy sepulchre. The hermit, assuming the character, without the talents or authority, of a general, impelled or obeyed the forward impulse of his votaries along the banks of the Rhine and Danube. Their wants and numbers soon compelled them to separate, and his lieutenant, Walter the Penniless, a valiant though needy soldier, conducted a vanguard of pilgrims, whose condition may be determined from the proportion of eight horsemen to fifteen thousand foot. The example and footsteps of Peter were closely pursued by another fanatic, the monk Godescal, whose sermons had swept away fifteen or twenty thousand peasants from the villages of Germany. Their rear was again pressed by a herd of two hundred thousand, the most stupid and savage refuse of the people, who mingled with their devotion a brutal licence of rapine, prostitution, and drunkenness. Some counts and gentlemen, at the head of three thousand horse, attended the motions of the multitude to partake in the spoil: but their genuine leaders (may we credit such folly?) were a goose and a goat, who were carried in the front, and to whom these worthy Christians ascribed an infusion of the divine spirit.[2] Of these, and of other bands of enthusiasts, the

astonishing scenes that were passing before their eyes. Erat itaque videre miraculum, caro omnes emere, atque vili vendere, etc.

[1] Some instances of these *stigmata* are given in the Esprit des Croisades (tom. iii. p. 169, etc.) from authors whom I have not seen.

[2] Fuit et aliud scelus detestabile in hac congregatione pedestris populi

first and most easy warfare was against the Jews, the murderers of the Son of God. In the trading cities of the Moselle and the Rhine their colonies were numerous and rich, and they enjoyed, under the protection of the emperor and the bishops, the free exercise of their religion.[1] At Verdun, Trèves, Mentz, Spires, Worms, many thousands of that unhappy people were pillaged and massacred,[2] nor had they felt a more bloody stroke since the persecution of Hadrian. A remnant was saved by the firmness of their bishops, who accepted a feigned and transient conversion; but the more obstinate Jews opposed their fanaticism to the fanaticism of the Christians, barricadoed their houses, and, precipitating themselves, their families, and their wealth into the rivers or the flames, disappointed the malice, or at least the avarice, of their implacable foes.[3]

Between the frontiers of Austria and the seat of the Byzantine monarchy the crusaders were compelled to traverse an interval of six hundred miles, the wild and desolate countries of Hungary [4] and Bulgaria. The soil is fruitful, and intersected with rivers; but it was then covered with morasses and forests, which spread

stulti et vesanæ levitatis . . anserem quendam divino spiritû asserebant afflatum, et capellam non minus eodem repletam, et has sibi duces [hujus] secundæ viæ fecerant, etc. (Albert. Aquensis, l. i. c. 31, p. 196). Had these peasants founded an empire, they might have introduced, as in Egypt, the worship of animals, which their philosophic descendants would have glossed over with some specious and subtle allegory.

[1] Benjamin of Tudela describes the state of his Jewish brethren from Cologne along the Rhine: they were rich, generous, learned, hospitable, and lived in the eager hope of the Messiah (Voyage, tom. i. p. 243-245, par Baratier). In seventy years (he wrote about A.D. 1170) they had recovered from these massacres.

[In connection with the terrible massacres which the Jews underwent, Benjamin of Tudela says that they had established themselves in Germany towards the fourth century. An edict of Constantine, addressed to the decurions of Cologne, shows that they were then very numerous in that city, a fact which is confirmed by the large number of tombstones engraved with Hebrew characters.—O. S.]

[2] These massacres and depredations on the Jews, which were renewed at each crusade, are coolly related. It is true that St. Bernard (Epist. 363, tom. i. p. 329 [p. 328, ed. Bened.]) admonishes the Oriental Franks, non sunt persequendi Judæi, non sunt trucidandi. The contrary doctrine had been preached by a rival monk.

[This is one of those silly witticisms as pointless as they are puerile in which Gibbon at times indulges. As Milman says, " It is an unjust sarcasm against St. Bernard, for he stood above all rivalry of the kind." He was a man of rare humility, as well as of rare self-sacrifice.—O. S.]

[3] [The persecution of the Jews became so violent in Germany that the bishops of various dioceses, such as Worms, Trèves, Mentz, and Spires, opened their palaces as asylums for the Jews of their dioceses. In this connection cf. Browning, Holy Cross Day.—O. S.]

[4] See the contemporary description of Hungary in Otho of Frisingen, l. i. c. 31, in Muratori, Script. Rerum Italicarum, tom. vi. p. 665, 666.

to a boundless extent whenever man has ceased to exercise his
dominion over the earth. Both nations had imbibed the rudiments of Christianity: the Hungarians were ruled by their native
princes, the Bulgarians by a lieutenant of the Greek emperor;
but, on the slightest provocation, their ferocious nature was rekindled, and ample provocation was afforded by the disorders of
the first pilgrims. Agriculture must have been unskilful and
languid among a people whose cities were built of reeds and
timber, which were deserted in the summer season for the tents
of hunters and shepherds. A scanty supply of provisions was
rudely demanded, forcibly seized, and greedily consumed, and
on the first quarrel the crusaders gave a loose to indignation and
revenge. But their ignorance of the country, of war, and of
discipline exposed them to every snare. The Greek præfect of
Bulgaria commanded a regular force; at the trumpet of the
Hungarian king, the eighth or the tenth of his martial subjects
bent their bows and mounted on horseback; their policy was
insidious, and their retaliation on these pious robbers was unrelenting and bloody.[1] About a third of the naked fugitives,
and the hermit Peter was of the number, escaped to the Thracian
mountains; and the emperor, who respected the pilgrimage and
succour of the Latins, conducted them by secure and easy
journeys to Constantinople, and advised them to await the
arrival of their brethren. For a while they remembered their
faults and losses, but no sooner were they revived by the
hospitable entertainment, than their venom was again inflamed;
they stung their benefactor, and neither gardens, nor palaces,
nor churches, were safe from their depredations. For his own
safety, Alexius allured them to pass over to the Asiatic side of
the Bosphorus; but their blind impetuosity soon urged them
to desert the station which he had assigned, and to rush headlong against the Turks, who occupied the road of Jerusalem.

[1] The old Hungarians, without excepting Turotzius, are ill-informed of
the first crusade, which they involve in a single passage. Katona, like
ourselves, can only quote the writers of France; but he compares with
local science the ancient and modern geography. *Ante portam Cyperon*
is Sopron or Poson; *Mallevilla*, Zemlin; *Fluvius Maroe*, Savus; *Lintax*,
Leith; *Mesebroch*, or *Merseburg*, Ouar, or Moson; *Tollenburg*, Pragg (de
Regibus Hungariæ, tom. iii. p. 19-53).
[The narrative of the first march is very incorrect, as Milman says.
The first party were under the command of Walter de Pexejo and Walter
the Penniless. They passed safe through Hungary, the kingdom of Calmany, but were attacked in Bulgaria. Peter the Hermit followed with
20,000 men, passed through Hungary, but seeing the clothing of sixteen
crusaders on the walls of Semlin, he attacked the city. He then marched
to Nissa, where at first he was hospitably received; but an accidental
quarrel taking place, he suffered a great defeat.—O. S.]

The hermit, conscious of his shame, had withdrawn from the camp to Constantinople; and his lieutenant, Walter the Penniless, who was worthy of a better command, attempted without success to introduce some order and prudence among the herd of savages. They separated in quest of prey, and themselves fell an easy prey to the arts of the sultan. By a rumour that their foremost companions were rioting in the spoils of his capital, Soliman tempted the main body to descend into the plain of Nice: they were overwhelmed by the Turkish arrows, and a pyramid of bones [1] informed their companions of the place of their defeat. Of the first crusaders, three hundred thousand had already perished before a single city was rescued from the infidels, before their graver and more noble brethren had completed the preparations of their enterprise.[2]

[1] Anna Comnena (Alexias, l. x. p. 287) describes this ὀστῶν κολωνὸς as a mountain ὑψηλὸν καὶ βάθος καὶ πλάτος ἀξιολογώτατον. In the siege of Nice such were used by the Franks themselves as the materials of a wall.

[This is a mistake of Gibbon's to say that Soliman tempted the main body to descend into the plain of Nice, for Soliman had been killed in 1086 in a battle against Toutouch, brother of Malek Shah, between Aleppo and Antioch. It was Soliman's son David, surnamed Kilidge-Arslan, the " Sword of the Lion," who succeeded in 1092 and reigned till 1100. His kingdom extended from the Orontes to the Euphrates, and as far as the Bosphorus.—O. S.]

[2] To save time and space, I shall represent, in a short table, the

	The Crowd.	The Chiefs.	The Road to Constantinople.	Alexius.	Nice and Asia Minor.
I. Gesta Francorum . .	p. 1, 2.	p. 2.	p. 2, 3.	p. 4, 5.	p. 5-7.
II. Robertus Monachus .	p. 33, 34.	p. 35, 36.	p. 36, 37.	p. 37, 38.	p. 39-45.
III. Baldricus .	p. 89.	—	p. 91-93.	p. 91-94.	p. 94-101.
IV. Raimundus de Agiles .	—	—	p. 139, 140.	p. 140, 141.	p. 142.
V. Albertus Aquensis	l. i. c. 7-31.	l. ii. c. 1-8.	l. ii. c. 9-19.	{ l. ii. c. 20-43; l. iii. c. 1-4. }
VI. Fulcherius Carnotensis .	p. 384.	—	p. 385, 386.	p. 386.	p. 387-389.
VII. Guibertus .	p. 482, 485.	—	p. 485, 489.	p. 485-490.	p. 491-493, 498.
VIII. Willermus Tyrensis . .	l. i. c. 18-30.	l. i. c. 17.	{ l. ii. c. 1-4, 13, 17, 22. }	l. ii. c. 5-23.	{ l. iii. c. 1-12; l. iv. c. 13-25. }
IX. Radulphus Cadomensis .	—	c. 1-3, 15	c. 4-7, 17.	{ c. 8-13, 18, 19. }	c. 14-16, 21-47.
X. Bernardus Thesaurarius	c. 7-11.	—	c. 11-20.	c. 11-20.	c. 21-25.

None of the great sovereigns of Europe embarked their persons in the first crusade. The emperor Henry the Fourth was not disposed to obey the summons of the pope; Philip the First of France was occupied by his pleasures; William Rufus of England by a recent conquest; the kings of Spain were engaged in a domestic war against the Moors; and the northern monarchs of Scotland, Denmark,[1] Sweden, and Poland were yet strangers to the passions and interests of the South. The religious ardour was more strongly felt by the princes of the second order, who held an important place in the feudal system. Their situation will naturally cast under four distinct heads the review of their names and characters; but I may escape some needless repetition, by observing at once that courage and the exercise of arms are the common attribute of these Christian adventurers. I. The first rank both in war and council is justly due to Godfrey of Bouillon; and happy would it have been for the crusaders, if they had trusted themselves to the sole conduct of that accomplished hero, a worthy representative of Charlemagne, from whom he was descended in the female line. His father was of

[1] The author of the Esprit des Croisades has doubted, and might have disbelieved, the crusade and tragic death of Prince Sueno, with 1500 or 15,000 Danes, who was cut off by Sultan Soliman in Cappadocia, but who still lives in the poem of Tasso (tom. iv. p. 111-115).

particular references to the great events of the first crusade.

Edessa.	Antioch.	The Battle.	The Holy Lance.	Conquest of Jerusalem.
—	p. 9-15.	p. 15-22.	p. 18-20.	p. 26-29.
—	p. 45-55.	p. 56-66.	p. 61, 62.	p. 74-81.
—	p. 101, 111.	p. 111-122.	p. 116-119.	p. 130-138.
—	p. 142-149.	p. 149-155.	p. 150, 152, 156.	p. 173-183.
{ l. iii. c. 5-32; l. iv. 9, 12; l. v. 15-22. }	{ l. iii. c. 33-66; iv. 1-26. }	l. iv. c. 7-56.	l. iv. c. 43.	{ l. v. c. 45, 46; l. vi. c. 1-50. }
p. 389, 390.	p. 390-392.	p. 392-395.	p. 392.	p. 396-400.
p. 496, 497.	p. 498, 506, 512.	p. 512-523.	p. 520, 530, 533	p. 523-537.
l. iv. c. 1-6.	{ l. iv. 9-24; l. v. 1-23. }	l. vi. c. 1-23.	l. vi. c. 14.	{ l. vii. c. 1-25; l. viii. c. 1-24. }
—	c. 48-71.	c. 72-91.	c. 100-109.	c. 111-138.
c. c. 26.	c. 27-38.	c. 39-52.	c. 45.	c. 54-77.

the noble race of the counts of Boulogne: Brabant, the lower province of Lorraine,[1] was the inheritance of his mother; and by the emperor's bounty he was himself invested with that ducal title, which has been improperly transferred to his lordship of Bouillon in the Ardennes.[2]   In the service of Henry the Fourth he bore the great standard of the empire, and pierced with his lance the breast of Rodolph, the rebel king: Godfrey was the first who ascended the walls of Rome; and his sickness, his vow, perhaps his remorse for bearing arms against the pope, confirmed an early resolution of visiting the holy sepulchre, not as a pilgrim, but a deliverer.   His valour was matured by prudence and moderation; his piety, though blind, was sincere; and, in the tumult of a camp, he practised the real and fictitious virtues of a convent.   Superior to the private factions of the chiefs, he reserved his enmity for the enemies of Christ; and though he gained a kingdom by the attempt, his pure and disinterested zeal was acknowledged by his rivals.   Godfrey of Bouillon[3] was accompanied by his two brothers, by Eustace the elder, who had succeeded to the county of Boulogne, and by the younger, Baldwin, a character of more ambiguous virtue.   The duke of Lorraine was alike celebrated on either side of the Rhine: from his birth and education, he was equally conversant with the French and Teutonic languages: the barons of France, Germany, and Lorriane assembled their vassals; and the confederate force that marched under his banner was composed of fourscore thousand foot and about ten thousand horse.   II. In the parliament that was held at Paris, in the king's presence, about two months after the council of Clermont, Hugh, count of Vermandois, was the most conspicuous of the princes who assumed the cross.   But the appellation of *the Great* was applied, not so much to his merit or possessions (though neither were

[1] The fragments of the kingdoms of Lotharingia, or Lorraine, were broken into the two duchies, of the Moselle, and of the Meuse: the first has preserved its name, which, in the latter, has been changed into that of Brabant (Vales. Notit. Gall. p. 283-288).

[Lotharingia or Lothringen, in the reign of Otto I., had been divided into the Upper and Lower Duchies, which were re-united under Conrad II. by Duke Gozelo.   On his death, however, they were again divided between his two sons.—O. S.]

[2] See, in the Description of France, by the Abbé de Longuerue, the articles of *Boulogne*, part i. p. 54; *Brabant*, part ii. p. 47, 48; *Bouillon*, p. 134.   On his departure Godfrey sold or pawned Bouillon to the church for 1300 marks.

[3] See the family character of Godfrey in William of Tyre, l. ix. c. 5-8; his previous design in Guibert (p. 485 [l. ii. c. 12]); his sickness and vow in Bernard.   Thesaur. (c. 78).

contemptible), as to the royal birth of the brother of the king of France.[1] Robert, duke of Normandy, was the eldest son of William the Conqueror; but on his father's death he was deprived of the kingdom of England, by his own indolence and the activity of his brother Rufus. The worth of Robert was degraded by an excessive levity and easiness of temper: his cheerfulness seduced him to the indulgence of pleasure; his profuse liberality impoverished the prince and people; his indiscriminate clemency multiplied the number of offenders; and the amiable qualities of a private man became the essential defects of a sovereign. For the trifling sum of ten thousand marks he mortgaged Normandy during his absence to the English usurper;[2] but his engagement and behaviour in the holy war announced in Robert a reformation of manners, and restored him in some degree to the public esteem. Another Robert was count of Flanders, a royal province, which, in this century, gave three queens to the thrones of France, England, and Denmark: he was surnamed the Sword and Lance of the Christians; but in the exploits of a soldier he sometimes forgot the duties of a general. Stephen, count of Chartres, of Blois, and of Troyes, was one of the richest princes of the age; and the number of his castles has been compared to the three hundred and sixty-five days of the year. His mind was improved by literature; and, in the council of the chiefs, the eloquent Stephen[3] was chosen to discharge the office of their president. These four were the principal leaders of the French, the Normans, and the pilgrims of the British isles: but the list of the barons who were possessed of three or four towns would exceed, says a contemporary, the catalogue of the Trojan war.[4] III. In the south of France the command was assumed by Adhemar, bishop of Puy, the pope's legate, and by Raymond count of St. Giles and Toulouse, who

---

[1] Anna Comnena supposes that Hugh was proud of his nobility, riches, and power (l. x. p. 288): the two last articles appear more equivocal; but an εὐγενεία, which seven hundred years ago was famous in the palace of Constantinople, attests the ancient dignity of the Capetian family of France.

[2] Will. Gemeticensis, l. vii. c. 7, p. 672, 673, in Camden. Normanicis [ed. Frankf. 1603]. He pawned the duchy for one hundredth part of the present yearly revenue. Ten thousand marks may be equal to five hundred thousand livres, and Normandy annually yields fifty-seven millions to the king (Necker, Administration des Finances, tom. i. p. 287).

[3] His original letter to his wife is inserted in the Spicilegium of Dom. Luc. d'Acheri, tom. iv., and quoted in the Esprit des Croisades, tom. i. p. 63.

[4] Unius enim, duûm, trium seu quatuor oppidorum dominos quis numeret? quorum tanta fuit copia, ut vix totidem Trojana obsidio coegisse putetur. (Ever the lively and interesting Guibert, p. 486 [l. ii. c. 17]).

added the prouder titles of duke of Narbonne and marquis of
Provence. The former was a respectable prelate, alike qualified
for this world and the next. The latter was a veteran warrior,
who had fought against the Saracens of Spain, and who consecrated his declining age, not only to the deliverance, but to the
perpetual service, of the holy sepulchre. His experience and
riches gave him a strong ascendant in the Christian camp, whose
distress he was often able, and sometimes willing, to relieve.
But it was easier for him to extort the praise of the Infidels than
to preserve the love of his subjects and associates. His eminent
qualities were clouded by a temper, haughty, envious, and
obstinate; and, though he resigned an ample patrimony for the
cause of God, his piety, in the public opinion, was not exempt
from avarice and ambition.[1] A mercantile, rather than a martial,
spirit prevailed among his *provincials*,[2] a common name, which
included the natives of Auvergne and Languedoc,[3] the vassals of
the kingdom of Burgundy or Arles. From the adjacent frontier
of Spain he drew a band of hardy adventurers; as he marched
through Lombardy, a crowd of Italians flocked to his standard,
and his united force consisted of one hundred thousand horse
and foot. If Raymond was the first to enlist and the last to
depart, the delay may be excused by the greatness of his preparation and the promise of an everlasting farewell. IV. The
name of Bohemond, the son of Robert Guiscard, was already
famous by his double victory over the Greek emperor: but his
father's will had reduced him to the principality of Tarentum,
and the remembrance of his Eastern trophies, till he was
awakened by the rumour and passage of the French pilgrims.
It is in the person of this Norman chief that we may seek for
the coolest policy and ambition, with a small allay of religious
fanaticism. His conduct may justify a belief that he had secretly
directed the design of the pope, which he affected to second with
astonishment and zeal: at the siege of Amalphi his example and

---

[1] It is singular enough that Raymond of St. Giles, a second character in
the genuine history of the crusades, should shine as the first of heroes in
the writings of the Greeks (Anna Comnen. Alexiad. l. x. xi.) and the
Arabians (Longueruana, p. 129).

[2] Omnes de Burgundiâ, et Alverniâ, et Vasconiâ, et Gothi (of *Languedoc*), provinciales appellabantur, cæteri vero Francigenæ; et hoc in exer-
citu; inter hostes autem Franci dicebantur. Raymond de Agiles, p. 144.

[3] The town of his birth, or first appanage, was consecrated to St.
Ægidius, whose name, as early as the first crusade, was corrupted by the
French into St. Gilles, or St. Giles. It is situate in the Lower Languedoc,
between Nismes and the Rhône, and still boasts a collegiate church of the
foundation of Raymond (Mélanges tirés d'une Grande Bibliothèque, tom.
xxxvii. p. 51).

discourse inflamed the passions of a confederate army; he instantly tore his garment to supply crosses for the numerous candidates, and prepared to visit Constantinople and Asia at the head of ten thousand horse and twenty thousand foot. Several princes of the Norman race accompanied this veteran general; and his cousin Tancred [1] was the partner, rather than the servant, of the war. In the accomplished character of Tancred we discover all the virtues of a perfect knight, [2] the true spirit of chivalry, which inspired the generous sentiments and social offices of man far better than the base philosophy, or the baser religion, of the times.

Between the age of Charlemagne and that of the crusades, a revolution had taken place among the Spaniards, the Normans, and the French, which was gradually extended to the rest of Europe. The service of the infantry was degraded to the plebeians; the cavalry formed the strength of the armies; and the honourable name of *miles*, or soldier, was confined to the gentlemen [3] who served on horseback, and were invested with the character of knighthood. The dukes and counts, who had usurped the rights of sovereignty, divided the provinces among their faithful barons: the barons distributed among their vassals the fiefs or benefices of their jurisdiction; and these military tenants, the peers of each other and of their lord, composed the noble or equestrian order, which disdained to conceive the peasant or burgher as of the same species with themselves. The dignity of their birth was preserved by pure and equal alliances;

[1] The mother of Tancred was Emma, sister of the great Robert Guiscard; his father, the marquis Odo the Good. It is singular enough that the family and country of so illustrious a person should be unknown; but Muratori reasonably conjectures that he was an Italian, and perhaps of the race of the marquises of Montferrat in Piedmont (Script. tom. v. p. 281, 282).

[2] To gratify the childish vanity of the house of Este, Tasso has inserted in his poem, and in the first crusade, a fabulous hero, the brave and amorous Rinaldo (x. 75, xvii. 66-94). He might borrow his name from a Rinaldo, with the Aquila bianca Estense, who vanquished, as the standard-bearer of the Roman church, the emperor Frederic I. (Storia Imperiale di Ricobaldo, in Muratori Script. Ital. tom. ix. p. 360; Ariosto, Orlando Furioso, iii. 30). But, 1. The distance of sixty years between the youth of the two Rinaldos destroys their identity. 2. The Storia Imperiale is a forgery of the Conte Boyardo, at the end of the fifteenth century (Muratori, p. 281-289). 3. This Rinaldo, and his exploits, are not less chimerical than the hero of Tasso (Muratori, Antichità Estense, tom. i. p. 350).

[3] Of the words *gentilis, gentilhomme, gentleman*, two etymologies are produced: 1. From the barbarians of the fifth century, the soldiers, and at length the conquerors, of the Roman empire, who were vain of their foreign nobility; and, 2. From the sense of the civilians, who consider *gentilis* as synonymous with *ingenuus*. Selden inclines to the first, but the latter is more pure, as well as probable.

their sons alone, who could produce four quarters or lines of ancestry, without spot or reproach, might legally pretend to the honour of knighthood; but a valiant plebeian was sometimes enriched and ennobled by the sword, and became the father of a new race. A single knight could impart, according to his judgment, the character which he received; and the warlike sovereigns of Europe derived more glory from this personal distinction than from the lustre of their diadem. This ceremony, of which some traces may be found in Tacitus and the woods of Germany,[1] was in its origin simple and profane: the candidate, after some previous trial, was invested with the sword and spurs; and his cheek or shoulder was touched with a slight blow, as an emblem of the last affront which it was lawful for him to endure. But superstition mingled in every public and private action of life: in the holy wars it sanctified the profession of arms; and the order of chivalry was assimilated in its rights and privileges to the sacred orders of priesthood. The bath and white garment of the novice were an indecent copy of the regeneration of baptism: his sword, which he offered on the altar, was blessed by the ministers of religion: his solemn reception was preceded by fasts and vigils; and he was created a knight in the name of God, of St. George, and of St. Michael the archangel. He swore to accomplish the duties of his profession; and education, example, and the public opinion were the inviolable guardians of his oath. As the champion of God and the ladies (I blush to unite such discordant names), he devoted himself to speak the truth; to maintain the right; to protect the distressed; to practise *courtesy*, a virtue less familiar to the ancients; to pursue the infidels; to despise the allurements of ease and safety; and to vindicate in every perilous adventure the honour of his character. The abuse of the same spirit provoked the illiterate knight to disdain the arts of industry and peace; to esteem himself the sole judge and avenger of his own injuries; and proudly to neglect the laws of civil society and military discipline. Yet the benefits of this institution, to refine the temper of barbarians, and to infuse some principles of faith, justice, and humanity, were strongly felt, and have been often observed. The asperity of national prejudice was softened; and the community of religion and arms spread a similar colour and generous emulation over the face of Christendom. Abroad in enterprise and pilgrimage, at home in martial exercise, the warriors of every country were perpetually associated; and impartial taste

[1] Framea scutoque juvenem ornant. Tacitus, Germania, c. 13.

must prefer a Gothic tournament to the Olympic games of classic antiquity.[1] Instead of the naked spectacles which corrupted the manners of the Greeks, and banished from the stadium the virgins and matrons, the pompous decoration of the lists was crowned with the presence of chaste and high-born beauty, from whose hands the conqueror received the prize of his dexterity and courage. The skill and strength that were exerted in wrestling and boxing bear a distant and doubtful relation to the merit of a soldier; but the tournaments, as they were invented in France, and eagerly adopted both in the East and West, presented a lively image of the business of the field. The single combats, the general skirmish, the defence of a pass, or castle, were rehearsed as in actual service; and the contest, both in real and mimic war, was decided by the superior management of the horse and lance. The lance was the proper and peculiar weapon of the knight: his horse was of a large and heavy breed; but this charger, till he was roused by the approaching danger, was usually led by an attendant, and he quietly rode a pad or palfrey of a more easy pace. His helmet and sword, his greaves and buckler, it would be superfluous to describe; but I may remark, that, at the period of the crusades, the armour was less ponderous than in later times; and that, instead of a massy cuirass, his breast was defended by a hauberk or coat of mail. When their long lances were fixed in the rest, the warriors furiously spurred their horses against the foe; and the light cavalry of the Turks and Arabs could seldom stand against the direct and impetuous weight of their charge. Each knight was attended to the field by his faithful squire, a youth of equal birth and similar hopes; he was followed by his archers and men-at-arms, and four, or five, or six soldiers, were computed as the furniture of a complete *lance*. In the expeditions to the neighbouring kingdoms or the Holy Land, the duties of the feudal tenure no longer subsisted; the voluntary service of the knights and their followers was either prompted by zeal or attachment, or purchased with rewards and promises; and the numbers of each squadron were measured by the power, the wealth, and the fame of each independent chieftain. They were distinguished by his banner, his armorial coat, and his cry of war; and the most ancient families of Europe must seek in these achievements the origin and proof

[1] The athletic exercises, particularly the cestus and pancratium, were condemned by Lycurgus, Philopœmen, and Galen, a lawgiver, a general, and a physician. Against their authority and reasons, the reader may weigh the apology of Lucian, in the character of Solon. See West on the Olympic Games, in his Pindar, vol. ii. p. 86-96, 245-248.

C 476

of their nobility. In this rapid portrait of chivalry I have been urged to anticipate on the story of the crusades, at once an effect and a cause of this memorable institution.[1]

Such were the troops, and such the leaders, who assumed the cross for the deliverance of the holy sepulchre. As soon as they were relieved by the absence of the plebeian multitude, they encouraged each other, by interviews and messages, to accomplish their vow, and hasten their departure. Their wives and sisters were desirous of partaking the danger and merit of the pilgrimage: their portable treasures were conveyed in bars of silver and gold; and the princes and barons were attended by their equipage of hounds and hawks to amuse their leisure and to supply their table. The difficulty of procuring subsistence for so many myriads of men and horses engaged them to separate their forces: their choice or situation determined the road; and it was agreed to meet in the neighbourhood of Constantinople, and from thence to begin their operations against the Turks. From the banks of the Meuse and the Moselle, Godfrey of Bouillon followed the direct way of Germany, Hungary, and Bulgaria; and, as long as he exercised the sole command, every step afforded some proof of his prudence and virtue. On the confines of Hungary he was stopped three weeks by a Christian people, to whom the name, or at least the abuse, of the cross was justly odious. The Hungarians still smarted with the wounds which they had received from the first pilgrims: in their turn they had abused the right of defence and retaliation; and they had reason to apprehend a severe revenge from a hero of the same nation, and who was engaged in the same cause. But, after weighing the motives and the events, the virtuous duke was content to pity the crimes and misfortunes of his worthless brethren; and his twelve deputies, the messengers of peace, requested in his name a free passage and an equal market. To remove their suspicions, Godfrey trusted himself, and afterwards his brother, to the faith of Carloman, king of Hungary, who treated them with a simple but hospitable entertainment:[2]

[1] On the curious subjects of knighthood, knights-service, nobility, arms, cry of war, banners, and tournaments, an ample fund of information may be sought in Selden (Opera, tom. iii. part i.; Titles of Honour, part ii. c. 1, 3, 5, 8), Ducange (Gloss. Latin. tom. iv. p. 398-412, etc.), Dissertations sur Joinville (i. vi.-xii. p. 127-142, p. 165-222), and M. de St. Palaye (Mémoires sur la Chevalerie).

[2] [Carloman (or Calmany) demanded the brother of Godfrey de Bouillon as hostage, but Count Baldwin refused the humiliating submission. Godfrey shamed him into this sacrifice for the common good by offering to surrender himself.—O. S.]

the treaty was sanctified by their common Gospel; and a proclamation, under pain of death, restrained the animosity and
licence of the Latin soldiers. From Austria to Belgrade, they
traversed the plains of Hungary, without enduring or offering
an injury; and the proximity of Carloman, who hovered on
their flanks with his numerous cavalry, was a precaution not
less useful for their safety than for his own. They reached the
banks of the Save; and no sooner had they passed the river
than the king of Hungary restored the hostages, and saluted
their departure with the fairest wishes for the success of their
enterprise. With the same conduct and discipline Godfrey
pervaded the woods of Bulgaria and the frontiers of Thrace;
and might congratulate himself that he had almost reached the
first term of his pilgrimage without drawing his sword against
a Christian adversary. After an easy and pleasant journey
through Lombardy, from Turin to Aquileia, Raymond and his
provincials marched forty days through the savage country of
Dalmatia [1] and Sclavonia. The weather was a perpetual fog;
the land was mountainous and desolate; the natives were either
fugitive or hostile: loose in their religion and government, they
refused to furnish provisions or guides; murdered the stragglers;
and exercised by night and day the vigilance of the count, who
derived more security from the punishment of some captive
robbers than from his interview and treaty with the prince of
Scodra.[2] His march between Durazzo and Constantinople was
harassed, without being stopped, by the peasants and soldiers
of the Greek emperor; and the same faint and ambiguous
hostility was prepared for the remaining chiefs, who passed the
Adriatic from the coast of Italy. Bohemond had arms and
vessels, and foresight and discipline; and his name was not
forgotten in the provinces of Epirus and Thessaly. Whatever
obstacles he encountered were surmounted by his military
conduct and the valour of Tancred; and if the Norman prince

[1] The Familiæ Dalmaticæ of Ducange are meagre and imperfect; the
national historians are recent and fabulous, the Greeks remote and careless. In the year 1104 Coloman reduced the maritime country as far as
Trau and Salona (Katona, Hist. Crit. tom. iii. p. 195-207).

[2] Scodras appears in Livy as the capital and fortress of Gentius king of
the Illyrians, arx munitissima, afterwards a Roman colony (Cellarius, tom.
i. p. 393, 394). It is now called Iscodar, or Scutari (D'Anville, Géographie
Ancienne, tom. i. p. 164). The sanjiak (now a pasha) of Scutari, or Schen-
deire, was the eighth under the Beglerbeg of Romania, and furnished 600
soldiers on a revenue of 78,787 rix-dollars (Marsigli, Stato Militare del
Imperio Ottomano, p. 128).

affected to spare the Greeks, he gorged his soldiers with the full plunder of an heretical castle.[1] The nobles of France pressed forwards with the vain and thoughtless ardour of which their nation has been sometimes accused. From the Alps to Apulia the march of Hugh the Great, of the two Roberts, and of Stephen of Chartres, through a wealthy country, and amidst the applauding Catholics, was a devout or triumphant progress: they kissed the feet of the Roman pontiff; and the golden standard of St. Peter was delivered to the brother of the French monarch.[2] But in this visit of piety and pleasure they neglected to secure the season and the means of their embarkation: the winter was insensibly lost: their troops were scattered and corrupted in the towns of Italy. They separately accomplished their passage, regardless of safety or dignity; and within nine months from the feast of the Assumption, the day appointed by Urban, all the Latin princes had reached Constantinople. But the count of Vermandois was produced as a captive; his foremost vessels were scattered by a tempest; and his person, against the law of nations, was detained by the lieutenants of Alexius. Yet the arrival of Hugh had been announced by four-and-twenty knights in golden armour, who commanded the emperor to revere the general of the Latin Christians, the brother of the king of kings.[3]

In some Oriental tale I have read the fable of a shepherd who was ruined by the accomplishment of his own wishes: he had prayed for water; the Ganges was turned into his grounds, and his flock and cottage were swept away by the inundation. Such was the fortune, or at least the apprehension, of the Greek emperor Alexius Comnenus, whose name has already appeared in this history, and whose conduct is so differently represented

---

[1] In Pelagonia castrum hæreticûm . . . spoliatum cum suis habitatoribus igne combussere. *Nec id eis injuriâ contigit :* quia illorum detestabilis sermo et [ut] cancer serpebat, jamque circumjacentes regiones suo pravo dogmate fœdaverat (Robert. Mon. p. 36, 37). After coolly relating the fact, the archbishop Baldric adds, as a praise, Omnes siquidem illi viatores, Judæos, hæreticos, Saracenos æqualiter habent exosos; quos omnes appellant inimicos Dei (p. 92).

[2] Ἀναλαβόμενος ἀπὸ Ῥώμης τὴν χρυσῆν τοῦ Ἁγίου Πέτρου σημαίαν (Alexiad. l. x. p. 288).

[3] Ὁ Βασιλεὺς τῶν βασιλέων, καὶ ἀρχηγὸς τοῦ Φραγγίκου στρατεύματος ἅπαν-τος [Alexiad. l. x. p. 288]. This Oriental pomp is extravagant in a count of Vermandois; but the patriot Ducange repeats with much complacency (Not. ad Alexiad. p. 352, 353; Dissert. xxvii. sur Joinville, p. 315) the passages of Matthew Paris (A.D. 1254) and Froissard (vol. iv. p. 201) which style the king of France rex regum, and chef de tous les rois Chrétiens.

by his daughter Anna,[1] and by the Latin writers.[2] In the
council of Placentia his ambassadors had solicited a moderate
succour, perhaps of ten thousand soldiers; but he was astonished
by the approach of so many potent chiefs and fanatic nations.
The emperor fluctuated between hope and fear, between timidity
and courage; but in the crooked policy which he mistook for
wisdom, I cannot believe, I cannot discern, that he maliciously
conspired against the life or honour of the French heroes. The
promiscuous multitudes of Peter the Hermit were savage beasts,
alike destitute of humanity and reason: nor was it possible for
Alexius to prevent or deplore their destruction. The troops of
Godfrey and his peers were less contemptible, but not less
suspicious, to the Greek emperor. Their motives *might* be pure
and pious; but he was equally alarmed by his knowledge of the
ambitious Bohemond, and his ignorance of the Transalpine
chiefs: the courage of the French was blind and headstrong;
they might be tempted by the luxury and wealth of Greece, and
elated by the view and opinion of their invincible strength; and
Jerusalem might be forgotten in the prospect of Constantinople.
After a long march and painful abstinence, the troops of Godfrey
encamped in the plains of Thrace; they heard with indignation
that their brother, the count of Vermandois, was imprisoned by
the Greeks; and their reluctant duke was compelled to indulge
them in some freedom of retaliation and rapine. They were
appeased by the submission of Alexius: he promised to supply
their camp; and as they refused, in the midst of winter, to pass
the Bosphorus, their quarters were assigned among the gardens
and palaces on the shores of that narrow sea. But an incurable
jealousy still rankled in the minds of the two nations, who
despised each other as slaves and barbarians. Ignorance is the
ground of suspicion, and suspicion was inflamed into daily
provocations: prejudice is blind, hunger is deaf; and Alexius
is accused of a design to starve or assault the Latins in a

---

[1] Anna Comnena was born the 1st of December, A.D. 1083, indiction vii.
(Alexiad. l. vi. p. 166, 167 [ed. Par.; tom. i. p. 295, 296, ed. Bonn.]) At
thirteen, the time of the first crusade, she was nubile, and perhaps married
to the younger Nicephorus Bryennius, whom she fondly styles τὸν ἐμὸν
Καίσαρα (l. x. p. 295, 296). Some moderns have *imagined* that her enmity
to Bohemond was the fruit of disappointed love. In the transactions of
Constantinople and Nice her partial accounts (Alex. l. x. xi. p. 283-317)
may be opposed to the partiality of the Latins, but in their subsequent
exploits she is brief and ignorant.

[2] In their views of the character and conduct of Alexius, Maimbourg has
favoured the *Catholic* Franks, and Voltaire has been partial to the *schismatic* Greeks. The prejudice of a philosopher is less excusable than that
of a Jesuit.

dangerous post, on all sides encompassed with the waters.[1]
Godfrey sounded his trumpets, burst the net, overspread the
plain, and insulted the suburbs: but the gates of Constantinople
were strongly fortified; the ramparts were lined with archers;
and after a doubtful conflict, both parties listened to the voice
of peace and religion. The gifts and promises of the emperor
insensibly soothed the fierce spirit of the Western strangers; as
a Christian warrior, he rekindled their zeal for the prosecution
of their holy enterprise, which he engaged to second with his
troops and treasures. On the return of spring, Godfrey was
persuaded to occupy a pleasant and plentiful camp in Asia;
and no sooner had he passed the Bosphorus than the Greek
vessels were suddenly recalled to the opposite shore. The same
policy was repeated with the succeeding chiefs, who were swayed
by the example, and weakened by the departure, of their foremost companions. By his skill and diligence Alexius prevented
the union of any two of the confederate armies at the same
moment under the walls of Constantinople; and before the
feast of the Pentecost not a Latin pilgrim was left on the coast
of Europe.

The same arms which threatened Europe might deliver Asia,
and repel the Turks from the neighbouring shores of the
Bosphorus and Hellespont. The fair provinces from Nice to
Antioch were the recent patrimony of the Roman emperor; and
his ancient and perpetual claim still embraced the kingdoms of
Syria and Egypt. In his enthusiasm, Alexius indulged, or
affected, the ambitious hope of leading his new allies to subvert
the thrones of the East; but the calmer dictates of reason and
temper dissuaded him from exposing his royal person to the
faith of unknown and lawless barbarians. His prudence, or his
pride, was content with extorting from the French princes an
oath of homage and fidelity, and a solemn promise that they
would either restore, or hold, their Asiatic conquests, as the
humble and loyal vassals of the Roman empire. Their independent spirit was fired at the mention of this foreign and
voluntary servitude: they successively yielded to the dexterous
application of gifts and flattery; and the first proselytes became
the most eloquent and effectual missionaries to multiply the

[1] Between the Black Sea, the Bosphorus, and the river Barbyses, which
is deep in summer, and runs fifteen miles through a flat meadow. Its
communication with Europe and Constantinople is by the stone bridge of
the *Blachernæ*, which in successive ages was restored by Justinian and
Basil (Gyllius de Bosphoro Thracio, l. ii. c. 3; Ducange, C. P. Christiana,
l. iv. c. 2, p. 179).

companions of their shame. The pride of Hugh of Vermandois
was soothed by the honours of his captivity; and in the brother
of the French king the example of submission was prevalent and
weighty.   In the mind of Godfrey of Bouillon every human consideration was subordinate to the glory of God and the success
of the crusade.   He had firmly resisted the temptations of
Bohemond and Raymond, who urged the attack and conquest
of Constantinople.   Alexius esteemed his virtues, deservedly
named him the champion of the empire, and dignified his homage
with the filial name and the rights of adoption.[1]   The hateful
Bohemond was received as a true and ancient ally; and if the
emperor reminded him of former hostilities, it was only to praise
the valour that he had displayed, and the glory that he had
acquired, in the fields of Durazzo and Larissa.   The son of
Guiscard was lodged, and entertained, and served with Imperial
pomp: one day, as he passed through the gallery of the palace,
a door was carelessly left open to expose a pile of gold and silver,
of silk and gems, of curious and costly furniture, that was heaped
in seeming disorder from the floor to the roof of the chamber.
" What conquests," exclaimed the ambitious miser, " might
not be achieved by the possession of such a treasure? "—" It
is your own," replied a Greek attendant, who watched the
motions of his soul; and Bohemond, after some hesitation,
condescended to accept this magnificent present.   The Norman
was flattered by the assurance of an independent principality;
and Alexius eluded, rather than denied, his daring demand of
the office of great domestic, or general of the East.   The two
Roberts, the son of the conqueror of England, and the kinsman
of three queens,[2] bowed in their turn before the Byzantine
throne.   A private letter of Stephen of Chartres attests his
admiration of the emperor, the most excellent and liberal of
men, who taught him to believe that he was a favourite, and
promised to educate and establish his youngest son.   In his
southern province, the count of St. Giles and Toulouse faintly
recognised the supremacy of the king of France, a prince of a
foreign nation and language.   At the head of a hundred thousand men, he declared that he was the soldier and servant of

---

[1] There were two sorts of adoption, the one by arms, the other by introducing the son between the shirt and skin of his father. Ducange (sur
Joinville, diss. xxii. p. 270) supposes Godfrey's adoption to have been of
the latter sort.

[2] After his return Robert of Flanders became the *man* of the king of
England, for a pension of four hundred marks. See the first act in Rymer's
Fœdera.

Christ alone, and that the Greek might be satisfied with an equal treaty of alliance and friendship. His obstinate resistance enhanced the value and the price of his submission; and he shone, says the princess Anna, among the barbarians, as the sun amidst the stars of heaven. His disgust of the noise and insolence of the French, his suspicions of the designs of Bohemond, the emperor imparted to his faithful Raymond; and that aged statesman might clearly discern, that, however false in friendship, he was sincere in his enmity.[1] The spirit of chivalry was last subdued in the person of Tancred; and none could deem themselves dishonoured by the imitation of that gallant knight. He disdained the gold and flattery of the Greek monarch; assaulted in his presence an insolent patrician; escaped to Asia in the habit of a private soldier; and yielded with a sigh to the authority of Bohemond, and the interest of the Christian cause. The best and most ostensible reason was the impossibility of passing the sea and accomplishing their vow without the licence and the vessels of Alexius; but they cherished a secret hope, that, as soon as they trod the continent of Asia, their swords would obliterate their shame, and dissolve the engagement, which on his side might not be very faithfully performed. The ceremony of their homage was grateful to a people who had long since considered pride as the substitute of power. High on his throne the emperor sat mute and immovable: his majesty was adored by the Latin princes; and they submitted to kiss either his feet or his knees, an indignity which their own writers are ashamed to confess, and unable to deny.[2]

Private or public interest suppressed the murmurs of the dukes and counts; but a French baron (he is supposed to be Robert of Paris[3]) presumed to ascend the throne, and to place

[1] Sensit vetus regnandi, falsos in amore, odia non fingere. Tacit. [Ann. vi. 44].

[2] The proud historians of the crusades slide and stumble over this humiliating step. Yet, since the heroes knelt to salute the emperor as he sat motionless on his throne, it is clear that they must have kissed either his feet or knees. It is only singular that Anna should not have amply supplied the silence or ambiguity of the Latins. The abasement of their princes would have added a fine chapter to the Ceremoniale Aulæ Byzantinæ.

[3] He called himself Φραγγὸς κάθαρος τῶν εὐγένων (Alexias, l. x. p. 301). What a title of *noblesse* of the eleventh century, if any one could now prove his inheritance! Anna relates, with visible pleasure, that the swelling barbarian, Λατινὸς τετυφωμένος, was killed, or wounded, after fighting in the front in the battle of Dorylæum (l. xi. p. 317). This circumstance may justify the suspicion of Ducange (Not. p. 362), that he was no other than Robert of Paris, of the district most peculiarly styled the Duchy or Island of France (*L'Isle de France*).

himself by the side of Alexius. The sage reproof of Baldwin
provoked him to exclaim, in his barbarous idiom, " Who is this
rustic, that keeps his seat while so many valiant captains are
standing round him? " The emperor maintained his silence,
dissembled his indignation, and questioned his interpreter concerning the meaning of the words, which he partly suspected
from the universal language of gesture and countenance. Before
the departure of the pilgrims he endeavoured to learn the name
and condition of the audacious baron. " I am a Frenchman,"
replied Robert, " of the purest and most ancient nobility of my
country. All that I know is, that there is a church in my neighbourhood,[1] the resort of those who are desirous of approving
their valour in single combat. Till an enemy appears, they
address their prayers to God and his saints. That church I have
frequently visited, but never have I found an antagonist who
dared to accept my defiance." Alexius dismissed the challenger
with some prudent advice for his conduct in the Turkish warfare;
and history repeats with pleasure this lively example of the
manners of his age and country.

The conquest of Asia was undertaken and achieved by Alexander, with thirty-five thousand Macedonians and Greeks;[2] and
his best hope was in the strength and discipline of his phalanx
of infantry. The principal force of the crusaders consisted in
their cavalry; and when that force was mustered in the plains
of Bithynia, the knights and their martial attendants on horseback amounted to one hundred thousand fighting men, completely armed with the helmet and coat of mail. The value of
these soldiers deserved a strict and authentic account; and the
flower of European chivalry might furnish, in a first effort, this
formidable body of heavy horse. A part of the infantry might
be enrolled for the service of scouts, pioneers, and archers; but
the promiscuous crowd were lost in their own disorder; and we
depend not on the eyes or knowledge, but on the belief and
fancy, of a chaplain of Count Baldwin,[3] in the estimate of six

[1] With the same penetration, Ducange discovers his church to be that of
St. Drausus, or Drosin, of Soissons, quem duello dimicaturi solent invo-
care: pugiles qui ad memoriam ejus (*his tomb*) pernoctant invictos reddit,
ut et de Burgundiâ et Italiâ tali necessitate confugiatur ad eum. Joan.
Sariberiensis, epist. 139.

[2] There is some diversity on the numbers of his army; but no authority
can be compared with that of Ptolemy, who states it at five thousand horse
and thirty thousand foot (see Usher's Annales, p. 152).

[3] Fulcher. Carnotensis, p. 387. He enumerates nineteen nations of
different names and languages (p. 389); but I do not clearly apprehend
his difference between the *Franci* and *Galli, Itali* and *Apuli*. Elsewhere
(p. 385) he contemptuously brands the deserters.

hundred thousand pilgrims able to bear arms, besides the priests
and monks, the women and children, of the Latin camp.   The
reader starts; and before he is recovered from his surprise I
shall add, on the same testimony, that, if all who took the cross
had accomplished their vow, above SIX MILLIONS would have
migrated from Europe to Asia.   Under this oppression of faith
I derive some relief from a more sagacious and thinking writer,[1]
who, after the same review of the cavalry, accuses the credulity
of the priest of Chartres, and even doubts whether the *Cisalpine*
regions (in the geography of a Frenchman) were sufficient to
produce and pour forth such incredible multitudes.   The coolest
scepticism will remember that of these religious volunteers great
numbers never beheld Constantinople and Nice.   Of enthusiasm
the influence is irregular and transient: many were detained at
home by reason or cowardice, by poverty or weakness; and
many were repulsed by the obstacles of the way, the more
insuperable as they were unforeseen to these ignorant fanatics.
The savage countries of Hungary and Bulgaria were whitened
with their bones: their vanguard was cut in pieces by the
Turkish sultan; and the loss of the first adventure, by the sword,
or climate, or fatigue, has already been stated at three hundred
thousand men.   Yet the myriads that survived, that marched,
that pressed forwards on the holy pilgrimage, were a subject of
astonishment to themselves and to the Greeks.   The copious
energy of her language sinks under the efforts of the princess
Anna: [2] the images of locusts, of leaves and flowers, of the sands
of the sea, or the stars of heaven, imperfectly represent what
she had seen and heard; and the daughter of Alexius exclaims
that Europe was loosened from its foundations, and hurled
against Asia.   The ancient hosts of Darius and Xerxes labour
under the same doubt of a vague and indefinite magnitude;
but I am inclined to believe that a larger number has never been
contained within the lines of a single camp than at the siege of
Nice, the first operation of the Latin princes.   Their motives,
their characters, and their arms, have been already displayed.
Of their troops, the most numerous portion were natives of
France: the Low Countries, the banks of the Rhine, and Apulia

[1] Guibert, p. 556 [l. vii. c. 39].   Yet even his gentle opposition implies an
immense multitude.   By Urban II., in the fervour of his zeal, it is only
rated at 300,000 pilgrims (Epist. xvi. Concil. tom. xii. p. 731).
[2] Alexias, l. x. p. 283, 305.   Her fastidious delicacy complains of their
strange and inarticulate names, and indeed there is scarcely one that she
has not contrived to disfigure with the proud ignorance so dear and familiar
to a polished people.   I shall select only one example, *Sangeles*, for the
count of St. Giles.

sent a powerful reinforcement: some bands of adventurers were drawn from Spain, Lombardy, and England;[1] and from the distant bogs and mountains of Ireland and Scotland[2] issued some naked and savage fanatics, ferocious at home, but unwarlike abroad. Had not superstition condemned the sacrilegious prudence of depriving the poorest or weakest Christian of the merit of the pilgrimage, the useless crowd, with mouths but without hands, might have been stationed in the Greek empire till their companions had opened and secured the way of the Lord. A small remnant of the pilgrims, who passed the Bosphorus, was permitted to visit the holy sepulchre. Their northern constitution was scorched by the rays, and infected by the vapours, of a Syrian sun. They consumed, with heedless prodigality, their stores of water and provision: their numbers exhausted the inland country: the sea was remote, the Greeks were unfriendly, and the Christians of every sect fled before the voracious and cruel rapine of their brethren. In the dire necessity of famine, they sometimes roasted and devoured the flesh of their infant or adult captives. Among the Turks and Saracens, the idolaters of Europe were rendered more odious by the name and reputation of cannibals; the spies, who introduced themselves into the kitchen of Bohemond, were shown several human bodies turning on the spit: and the artful Norman encouraged a report which increased at the same time the abhorrence and the terror of the infidels.[3]

I have expatiated with pleasure on the first steps of the crusaders, as they paint the manners and character of Europe: but I shall abridge the tedious and uniform narrative of their blind achievements, which were performed by strength and are

[1] William of Malmesbury (who wrote about the year 1130) has inserted in his history (l. iv. p. 130-154 [Script. post Bedam]) a narrative of the first crusade: but I wish that, instead of listening to the tenue murmur which had passed the British ocean (p. 143), he had confined himself to the numbers, families, and adventures of his countrymen. I find in Dugdale, that an English Norman, Stephen earl of Albemarle and Holdernesse, led the rear-guard with duke Robert at the battle of Antioch (Baronage, part i. p. 61).

[2] Videres Scotorum apud se ferocium alias imbellium cuneos (Guibert, p. 471): the *crus intectum* and *hispida chlamys* may suit the Highlanders, but the finibus uliginosis may rather apply to the Irish bogs. William of Malmesbury expressly mentions the Welsh and Scots, etc. (l. iv. p. 133), who quitted, the former venationem saltuum, the latter familiaritatem pulicum.

[3] This cannibal hunger, sometimes real, more frequently an artifice or a lie, may be found in Anna Comnena (Alexias, l. x. p. 288), Guibert (p. 546), Radulph. Cadom. (c. 97). The stratagem is related by the author of the Gesta Francorum, the monk Robert Baldric, and Raymond de Agiles, in the siege and famine of Antioch.

described by ignorance. From their first station in the neighbourhood of Nicomedia, they advanced in successive divisions;
passed the contracted limit of the Greek empire; opened a road
through the hills; and commenced, by the siege of his capital,
their pious warfare against the Turkish sultan. His kingdom
of Roum extended from the Hellespont to the confines of Syria,
and barred the pilgrimage of Jerusalem: his name was Kilidge-
Arslan, or Soliman,[1] of the race of Seljuk, and son of the first
conqueror; and in the defence of a land which the Turks considered as their own, he deserved the praise of his enemies, by
whom alone he is known to posterity. Yielding to the first
impulse of the torrent, he deposited his family and treasure in
Nice; retired to the mountains with fifty thousand horse; and
twice descended to assault the camps or quarters of the Christian
besiegers, which formed an imperfect circle of above six miles.
The lofty and solid walls of Nice were covered by a deep ditch,
and flanked by three hundred and seventy towers; and on the
verge of Christendom the Moslems were trained in arms, and
inflamed by religion. Before this city the French princes
occupied their stations, and prosecuted their attacks without
correspondence or subordination: emulation prompted their
valour; but their valour was sullied by cruelty, and their emulation degenerated into envy and civil discord. In the siege of
Nice the arts and engines of antiquity were employed by the
Latins; the mine and the battering-ram, the tortoise, and the
belfry or movable turret, artificial fire, and the *catapult* and
balist, the sling, and the crossbow for the casting of stones and
darts.[2] In the space of seven weeks much labour and blood
were expended, and some progress, especially by Count Raymond,
was made on the side of the besiegers. But the Turks could
protract their resistance and secure their escape, as long as they
were masters of the lake[3] Ascanius, which stretches several

---

[1] His Musulman appellation of Soliman is used by the Latins, and his
character is highly embellished by Tasso. His Turkish name of Kilidge-
Arslan (A.H. 485-500, A.D. 1192-1206: see De Guignes's Tables, tom. i.
p. 245) is employed by the Orientals, and with some corruption by the
Greeks; but little more than his name can be found in the Mohammedan
writers, who are dry and sulky on the subject of the first crusade (De
Guignes, tom. iii. p. ii. p. 10-30).

[2] On the fortifications, engines, and sieges of the middle ages, see Muratori (Antiquitat. Italiæ, tom. ii. dissert. xxvi. p. 452-524). The *belfredus*,
from whence our belfry, was the movable tower of the ancients (Ducange,
tom. i. p. 608).

[3] I cannot forbear remarking the resemblance between the siege and
lake of Nice with the operations of Hernan Cortez before Mexico. See
Dr. Robertson, Hist. of America, l. v.

miles to the westward of the city.   The means of conquest were
supplied by the prudence and industry of Alexius; a great
number of boats was transported on sledges from the sea to the
lake; they were filled with the most dexterous of his archers;
the flight of the sultana was intercepted; Nice was invested by
land and water; and a Greek emissary persuaded the inhabitants
to accept his master's protection, and to save themselves, by a
timely surrender, from the rage of the savages of Europe.   In
the moment of victory, or at least of hope, the crusaders, thirsting
for blood and plunder, were awed by the Imperial banner that
streamed from the citadel; and Alexius guarded with jealous
vigilance this important conquest.   The murmurs of the chiefs
were stifled by honour or interest; and after a halt of nine days
they directed their march towards Phrygia under the guidance of
a Greek general, whom they suspected of a secret connivance
with the sultan.   The consort and the principal servants of
Soliman had been honourably restored without ransom; and the
emperor's generosity to the *miscreants* [1] was interpreted as
treason to the Christian cause.

Soliman was rather provoked than dismayed by the loss of his
capital; he admonished his subjects and allies of this strange
invasion of the Western barbarians; the Turkish emirs obeyed
the call of loyalty or religion, the Turkman hordes encamped
round his standard, and his whole force is loosely stated by the
Christians at two hundred, or even three hundred and sixty
thousand horse.   Yet he patiently waited till they had left
behind them the sea and the Greek frontier, and, hovering on the
flanks, observed their careless and confident progress in two
columns beyond the view of each other.   Some miles before they
could reach Dorylæum in Phrygia, the left, and least numerous,
division was surprised and attacked, and almost oppressed, by
the Turkish cavalry. [2]   The heat of the weather, the clouds of
arrows, and the barbarous onset overwhelmed the crusaders;
they lost their order and confidence, and the fainting fight was
sustained by the personal valour, rather than by the military

---

[1] *Mécréant*, a word invented by the French crusaders, and confined in
that language to its primitive sense.   It should seem that the zeal of our
ancestors boiled higher, and that they branded every unbeliever as a
rascal.   A similar prejudice still lurks in the minds of many who think
themselves Christians.
[2] Baronius has produced a very doubtful letter to his brother Roger
(A.D. 1098, No. 15).   The enemies consisted of Medes, Persians, Chaldæans: be it so.   The first attack was cum nostro incommodo; true and
tender.   But why Godfrey of Bouillon and Hugh *brothers* ?   Tancred is
styled *filius*—of whom?   certainly not of Roger, nor of Bohemond.

conduct, of Bohemond, Tancred, and Robert of Normandy.
They were revived by the welcome banners of duke Godfrey,
who flew to their succour, with the count of Vermandois and
sixty thousand horse, and was followed by Raymond of Toulouse,
the bishop of Puy, and the remainder of the sacred army.   Without a moment's pause they formed in new order, and advanced
to a second battle.   They were received with equal resolution,
and, in their common disdain for the unwarlike people of Greece
and Asia, it was confessed on both sides that the Turks and the
Franks were the only nations entitled to the appellation of
soldiers.[1]   Their encounter was varied, and balanced by the contrast of arms and discipline: of the direct charge and wheeling
evolutions, of the couched lance and the brandished javelin, of a
weighty broadsword and a crooked sabre, of cumbrous armour
and thin flowing robes, and of the long Tartar bow and the
arbalist, or crossbow, a deadly weapon, yet unknown to the
Orientals.[2]   As long as the horses were fresh, and the quivers
full, Soliman maintained the advantage of the day, and four
thousand Christians were pierced by the Turkish arrows.   In
the evening swiftness yielded to strength; on either side the
numbers were equal, or at least as great as any ground could
hold, or any generals could manage; but, in turning the hills,
the last division of Raymond and his *provincials* was led, perhaps
without design, on the rear of an exhausted enemy, and the long
contest was determined.   Besides a nameless and unaccounted
multitude, three thousand *pagan* knights were slain in the battle
and pursuit; the camp of Soliman was pillaged, and in the
variety of precious spoil the curiosity of the Latins was amused
with foreign arms and apparel, and the new aspect of dromedaries
and camels.   The importance of the victory was proved by the
hasty retreat of the sultan: reserving ten thousand guards of the
relics of his army, Soliman evacuated the kingdom of Roum,
and hastened to implore the aid, and kindle the resentment, of
his Eastern brethren.   In a march of five hundred miles the
crusaders traversed the Lesser Asia, through a wasted land and
deserted towns, without finding either a friend or an enemy.

[1] Verumtamen dicunt se esse de Francorum generatione; et quia nullus
homo naturaliter debet esse miles nisi Franci et Turci (Gesta Francorum,
p. 7).   The same community of blood and valour is attested by archbishop Baldric (p. 99).
[2] *Balista, Balestra, Arbalestre.*   See Muratori, Antiq. tom. ii. p. 517-524;
Ducange, Gloss. Latin. tom. i. p. 531, 532.   In the time of Anna Comnena,
this weapon, which she describes under the name of *tzangra*, was unknown
in the East (l. x. p. 291).   By a humane inconsistency, the pope strove to
prohibit it in Christian wars.

The geographer [1] may trace the position of Dorylæum, Antioch
of Pisidia, Iconium, Archelais, and Germanicia, and may compare those classic appellations with the modern names of
Eskishehr the old city, Akshehr the white city, Cogni, Erekli, and
Marash. As the pilgrims passed over a desert, where a draught
of water is exchanged for silver, they were tormented by intolerable thirst, and on the banks of the first rivulet their haste
and intemperance were still more pernicious to the disorderly
throng. They climbed with toil and danger the steep and
slippery sides of Mount Taurus; many of the soldiers cast away
their arms to secure their footsteps; and had not terror preceded
their van, the long and trembling file might have been driven
down the precipice by a handful of resolute enemies. Two of
their most respectable chiefs, the duke of Lorraine and the count
of Toulouse, were carried in litters; Raymond was raised, as it
is said, by miracle, from a hopeless malady; and Godfrey had
been torn by a bear, as he pursued that rough and perilous chase
in the mountains of Pisidia.

To improve the general consternation, the cousin of Bohemond
and the brother of Godfrey were detached from the main army
with their respective squadrons of five and of seven hundred
knights. They overran in a rapid career the hills and sea-coast
of Cilicia, from Cogni to the Syrian gates; the Norman standard
was first planted on the walls of Tarsus and Malmistra; but the
proud injustice of Baldwin at length provoked the patient and
generous Italian, and they turned their consecrated swords
against each other in a private and profane quarrel.[2] Honour
was the motive, and fame the reward, of Tancred, but fortune
smiled on the more selfish enterprise of his rival.[3] He was

---

[1] The curious reader may compare the classic learning of Cellarius and
the geographical science of D'Anville. William of Tyre is the only
historian of the crusades who has any knowledge of antiquity; and
M. Otter trod almost in the footsteps of the Franks from Constantinople
to Antioch (Voyage en Turquie et en Perse, tom. i. p. 35-88).

[2] [The origin of the quarrel was that Tancred, who had arrived first with
his troops before Tarsus, persuaded the citizens to hoist his flag on the
fortifications. Baldwin, on his arrival, induced them, partly by threats,
partly by promises, to haul it down and substitute his. It is singular that
a similar dispute had occurred in the same city between Cassius and Dola-
bella during the civil wars of Rome. Cf. Appian, Bell. Civ. lib. iv. cap. 8;
Chronicle of Matthew of Edessa translated by Dulaurier, p. 218.—O. S.]

[3] This detached conquest of Edessa is best represented by Fulcherius
Carnotensis, or of Chartres (in the collections of Bongarsius, Duchesne, and
Martenne), the valiant chaplain of Count Baldwin (Esprit des Croisades,
tom. i. p. 13, 14). In the disputes of that prince with Tancred, his partiality is encountered by the partiality of Radulphus Cadomensis, the
soldier and historian of the gallant marquis.

called to the assistance of a Greek or Armenian tyrant, who had
been suffered, under the Turkish yoke, to reign over the Christians of Edessa.   Baldwin accepted the character of his son and
champion, but no sooner was he introduced into the city than
he inflamed the people to the massacre of his father, occupied
the throne and treasure, extended his conquests over the hills
of Armenia and the plain of Mesopotamia, and founded the first
principality of the Franks or Latins, which subsisted fifty-four
years beyond the Euphrates.[1]

Before the Franks could enter Syria, the summer, and even
the autumn, were completely wasted; the siege of Antioch, or
the separation and repose of the army during the winter season,
was strongly debated in their council; the love of arms and the
holy sepulchre urged them to advance, and reason perhaps was
on the side of resolution, since every hour of delay abates the
fame and force of the invader, and multiplies the resources of
defensive war.   The capital of Syria was protected by the river
Orontes, and the *iron bridge* of nine arches derives its name
from the massy gates of the two towers which are constructed
at either end.   They were opened by the sword of the duke of
Normandy; his victory gave entrance to three hundred thousand
crusaders, an account which may allow some scope for losses and
desertion, but which clearly detects much exaggeration in the
review of Nice.   In the description of Antioch [2] it is not easy to
define a middle term between her ancient magnificence, under the
successors of Alexander and Augustus, and the modern aspect
of Turkish desolation.   The Tetrapolis, or four cities, if they
retained their name and position, must have left a large vacuity
in a circumference of twelve miles; and that measure, as well as
the number of four hundred towers, are not perfectly consistent
with the five gates so often mentioned in the history of the siege.
Yet Antioch must have still flourished as a great and populous
capital.   At the head of the Turkish emirs, Baghisian, a veteran
chief, commanded in the place; his garrison was composed of
six or seven thousand horse, and fifteen or twenty thousand
foot; one hundred thousand Moslems are said to have fallen by
the sword, and their numbers were probably inferior to the
Greeks, Armenians, and Syrians, who had been no more than

---

[1] See De Guignes, Hist. des Huns, tom. i. p. 456.

[2] For Antioch, see Pococke (Description of the East, vol. ii. p. i. p. 188-
193), Otter (Voyage en Turquie, etc., tom. i. p. 81, etc.), the Turkish
geographer (in Otter's notes), the Index Geographicus of Schultens (ad
calcem Bohadin. Vit. Saladin.), and Abulfeda (Tabula Syriæ, p. 115, 116,
vers. Reiske).

fourteen years the slaves of the house of Seljuk. From the
remains of a solid and stately wall it appears to have arisen to
the height of threescore feet in the valleys; and wherever less
art and labour had been applied, the ground was supposed to be
defended by the river, the morass, and the mountains. Notwithstanding these fortifications, the city had been repeatedly
taken by the Persians, the Arabs, the Greeks, and the Turks; so
large a circuit must have yielded many pervious points of attack,
and in a siege that was formed about the middle of October the
vigour of the execution could alone justify the boldness of the
attempt. Whatever strength and valour could perform in the
field was abundantly discharged by the champions of the cross:
in the frequent occasions of sallies, of forage, of the attack and
defence of convoys, they were often victorious; and we can only
complain that their exploits are sometimes enlarged beyond the
scale of probability and truth. The sword of Godfrey [1] divided
a Turk from the shoulder to the haunch, and one half of the
infidel fell to the ground, while the other was transported by his
horse to the city gate. As Robert of Normandy rode against
his antagonist, " I devote thy head," he piously exclaimed, " to
the demons of hell; " and that head was instantly cloven to the
breast by the resistless stroke of his descending falchion. But
the reality or the report of such gigantic prowess [2] must have
taught the Moslems to keep within their walls, and against those
walls of earth or stone the sword and the lance were unavailing
weapons. In the slow and successive labours of a siege the
crusaders were supine and ignorant, without skill to contrive, or
money to purchase, or industry to use the artificial engines and
implements of assault. In the conquest of Nice they had been
powerfully assisted by the wealth and knowledge of the Greek
emperor; his absence was poorly supplied by some Genoese and
Pisan vessels that were attracted by religion or trade to the
coast of Syria; the stores were scanty, the return precarious,
and the communication difficult and dangerous. Indolence or

---

[1] Ensem elevat, eumque à sinistrâ parte scapularum tantâ virtute in-
torsit, quòd pectus medium disjunxit, spinam et vitalia interrupit, et sic
lubricus ensis super crus dextrum integer exivit; sicque caput integrum
cum dextrâ parte corporis immersit gurgite, partemque quæ equo præside-
bat remisit civitati (Robert. Mon. p. 50). Cujus ense trajectus, Turcus duo
factus est Turci; ut inferior alter in urbem equitaret, alter arcitenens in
flumine nataret (Radulph. Cadom. c. 53, p. 304). Yet he justifies the
deed by the *stupendis* viribus of Godfrey; and William of Tyre covers it
by obstupuit populus facti novitate . . . mirabilis (l. v. c. 6, p. 701). Yet
it must not have appeared incredible to the knights of that age.

[2] See the exploits of Robert, Raymond, and the modest Tancred, who
imposed silence on his squire (Radulph. Cadom. c. 53).

weakness had prevented the Franks from investing the entire circuit, and the perpetual freedom of two gates relieved the wants and recruited the garrison of the city. At the end of seven months, after the ruin of their cavalry and an enormous loss by famine, desertion, and fatigue, the progress of the crusaders was imperceptible, and their success remote, if the Latin Ulysses, the artful and ambitious Bohemond, had not employed the arms of cunning and deceit. The Christians of Antioch were numerous and discontented: Phirouz, a Syrian renegado, had acquired the favour of the emir and the command of three towers, and the merit of his repentance disguised to the Latins, and perhaps to himself, the foul design of perfidy and treason. A secret correspondence, for their mutual interest, was soon established between Phirouz and the prince of Tarento; and Bohemond declared in the council of the chiefs that he could deliver the city into their hands. But he claimed the sovereignty of Antioch as the reward of his service, and the proposal which had been rejected by the envy, was at length extorted from the distress, of his equals. The nocturnal surprise was executed by the French and Norman princes, who ascended in person the scaling-ladders that were thrown from the walls; their new proselyte, after the murder of his too scrupulous brother, embraced and introduced the servants of Christ, the army rushed through the gates, and the Moslems soon found that, although mercy was hopeless, resistance was impotent. But the citadel still refused to surrender, and the victors themselves were speedily encompassed and besieged by the innumerable forces of Kerboga, prince of Mosul, who, with twenty-eight Turkish emirs, advanced to the deliverance of Antioch. Five-and-twenty days the Christians spent on the verge of destruction, and the proud lieutenant of the caliph and the sultan left them only the choice of servitude or death.[1] In this extremity they collected the relics of their strength, sallied from the town, and in a single memorable day annihilated or dispersed the host of Turks and Arabians, which they might safely report to have consisted of six hundred thousand men.[2] Their supernatural

---

[1] After mentioning the distress and humble petition of the Franks, Abul-pharagius adds the haughty reply of Codbuka, or Kerboga: " Non evasuri estis nisi per gladium " (Dynast. p. 242).

[2] In describing the host of Kerboga, most of the Latin historians, the author of the Gesta (p. 17), Robert Monachus (p. 56), Baldric (p. 111), Fulcherius Carnotensis (p. 392), Guibert (p. 512), William of Tyre (l. vi. c. 3, p. 714), Bernard Thesaurarius (c. 39, p. 695), are content with the vague expressions of infinita multitudo, immensum agmen, innumeræ copiæ or gentes, which correspond with the μετὰ ἀναριθμήτων χιλιάδων of Anna

allies I shall proceed to consider: the human causes of the
victory of Antioch were the fearless despair of the Franks, and
the surprise, the discord, perhaps the errors, of their unskilful
and presumptuous adversaries. The battle is described with as
much disorder as it was fought; but we may observe the tent
of Kerboga, a movable and spacious palace, enriched with the
luxury of Asia, and capable of holding above two thousand
persons; we may distinguish his three thousand guards, who
were cased, the horses as well as the men, in complete steel.

In the eventful period of the siege and defence of Antioch,
the crusaders were alternately exalted by victory or sunk in
despair; either swelled with plenty or emaciated with hunger.
A speculative reasoner might suppose that their faith had a
strong and serious influence on their practice; and that the
soldiers of the cross, the deliverers of the holy sepulchre, prepared themselves by a sober and virtuous life for the daily
contemplation of martyrdom. Experience blows away this
charitable illusion; and seldom does the history of profane
war display such scenes of intemperance and prostitution as
were exhibited under the walls of Antioch. The grove of
Daphne no longer flourished; but the Syrian air was still impregnated with the same vices; the Christians were seduced by
every temptation [1] that nature either prompts or reprobates;
the authority of the chiefs was despised; and sermons and edicts
were alike fruitless against those scandalous disorders, not less
pernicious to military discipline than repugnant to evangelic
purity. In the first days of the siege and the possession of
Antioch the Franks consumed with wanton and thoughtless
prodigality the frugal subsistence of weeks and months: the
desolate country no longer yielded a supply; and from that
country they were at length excluded by the arms of the besieging Turks. Disease, the faithful companion of want, was
envenomed by the rains of the winter, the summer heats, unwholesome food, and the close imprisonment of multitudes.
The pictures of famine and pestilence are always the same, and
always disgustful; and our imagination may suggest the nature
of their sufferings and their resources. The remains of treasure
or spoil were eagerly lavished in the purchase of the vilest

Comnena (Alexias, l. xi. p. 318-320). The numbers of the Turks are fixed
by Albert Aquensis at 200,000 (l. iv. c. 10, p. 242), and by Radulphus
Cadomensis at 400,000 horse (c. 72, p. 309).

[1] See the tragic and scandalous fate of an archdeacon of royal birth, who
was slain by the Turks as he reposed in an orchard, playing at dice with a
Syrian concubine.

nourishment: and dreadful must have been the calamities of
the poor, since, after paying three marks of silver for a goat and
fifteen for a lean camel,[1] the count of Flanders was reduced to
beg a dinner, and duke Godfrey to borrow a horse. Sixty thousand horses had been reviewed in the camp; before the end of
the siege they were diminished to two thousand, and scarcely
two hundred fit for service could be mustered on the day of
battle. Weakness of body and terror of mind extinguished the
ardent enthusiasm of the pilgrims; and every motive of honour
and religion was subdued by the desire of life.[2] Among the
chiefs, three heroes may be found without fear or reproach:
Godfrey of Bouillon was supported by his magnanimous piety;
Bohemond by ambition and interest; and Tancred declared, in
the true spirit of chivalry, that, as long as he was at the head
of forty knights, he would never relinquish the enterprise of
Palestine. But the count of Toulouse and Provence was suspected of a voluntary indisposition; the duke of Normandy
was recalled from the sea-shore by the censures of the church;
Hugh the Great, though he led the vanguard of the battle,
embraced an ambiguous opportunity of returning to France; and
Stephen count of Chartres basely deserted the standard which
he bore, and the council in which he presided. The soldiers
were discouraged by the flight of William viscount of Melun,
surnamed the *Carpenter*, from the weighty strokes of his axe;
and the saints were scandalised by the fall of Peter the Hermit,
who, after arming Europe against Asia, attempted to escape
from the penance of a necessary fast. Of the multitude of
recreant warriors, the names (says an historian) are blotted
from the book of life; and the opprobrious epithet of the rope-
dancers was applied to the deserters who dropped in the night
from the walls of Antioch. The emperor Alexius,[3] who seemed
to advance to the succour of the Latins, was dismayed by the

---

[1] The value of an ox rose from five solidi (fifteen shillings) at Christmas
to two marks (four pounds), and afterwards much higher; a kid or lamb,
from one shilling to eighteen of our present money: in the second famine, a
loaf of bread, or the head of an animal, sold for a piece of gold. More
examples might be produced; but it is the ordinary, not the extraordinary,
prices that deserve the notice of the philosopher.

[2] Alii multi, quorum nomina non tenemus; quia, deleta de libro vitæ,
præsenti operi non sunt inserenda (Will. Tyr l. vi. c. 5, p. 715). Guibert
(p. 518, 523 [l. v. c. 25; l. vi. c. 11]) attempts to excuse Hugh the Great,
and even Stephen of Chartres.

[3] See the progress of the crusade, the retreat of Alexius, the victory of
Antioch, and the conquest of Jerusalem, in the Alexiad. l. xi. p. 317-327.
Anna was so prone to exaggeration, that she magnifies the exploits of the
Latins.

assurance of their hopeless condition. They expected their fate
in silent despair; oaths and punishments were tried without
effect; and to rouse the soldiers to the defence of the walls, it
was found necessary to set fire to their quarters.

For their salvation and victory they were indebted to the
same fanaticism which had led them to the brink of ruin. In
such a cause, and in such an army, visions, prophecies, and
miracles were frequent and familiar. In the distress of Antioch,
they were repeated with unusual energy and success: St.
Ambrose had assured a pious ecclesiastic that two years of trial
must precede the season of deliverance and grace; the deserters
were stopped by the presence and reproaches of Christ himself;
the dead had promised to arise and combat with their brethren;
the Virgin had obtained the pardon of their sins; and their confidence was revived by a visible sign, the seasonable and splendid
discovery of the HOLY LANCE. The policy of their chiefs has on
this occasion been admired, and might surely be excused; but
a pious fraud is seldom produced by the cool conspiracy of many
persons; and a voluntary impostor might depend on the support
of the wise and the credulity of the people. Of the diocese of
Marseilles, there was a priest of low cunning and loose manners,
and his name was Peter Bartholemy. He presented himself at
the door of the council-chamber, to disclose an apparition of St.
Andrew, which had been thrice reiterated in his sleep, with a
dreadful menace if he presumed to suppress the commands of
heaven. " At Antioch," said the apostle, " in the church of my
brother St. Peter, near the high altar, is concealed the steel head
of the lance that pierced the side of our Redeemer. In three
days, that instrument of eternal, and now of temporal, salvation,
will be manifested to his disciples. Search, and ye shall find:
bear it aloft in battle; and that mystic weapon shall penetrate
the souls of the miscreants." The pope's legate, the bishop of
Puy, affected to listen with coldness and distrust; but the
revelation was eagerly accepted by Count Raymond, whom his
faithful subject, in the name of the apostle, had chosen for the
guardian of the holy lance. The experiment was resolved; and
on the third day, after a due preparation of prayer and fasting,
the priest of Marseilles introduced twelve trusty spectators,
among whom were the count and his chaplain; and the church
doors were barred against the impetuous multitude. The ground
was opened in the appointed place; but the workmen, who
relieved each other, dug to the depth of twelve feet without discovering the object of their search. In the evening, when Count

Raymond had withdrawn to his post, and the weary assistants began to murmur, Bartholemy, in his shirt, and without his shoes, boldly descended into the pit; the darkness of the hour and of the place enabled him to secrete and deposit the head of a Saracen lance; and the first sound, the first gleam, of the steel was saluted with a devout rapture. The holy lance was drawn from its recess, wrapped in a veil of silk and gold, and exposed to the veneration of the crusaders; their anxious suspense burst forth in a general shout of joy and hope, and the desponding troops were again inflamed with the enthusiasm of valour. Whatever had been the arts, and whatever might be the sentiments of the chiefs, they skilfully improved this fortunate revolution by every aid that discipline and devotion could afford. The soldiers were dismissed to their quarters with an injunction to fortify their minds and bodies for the approaching conflict, freely to bestow their last pittance on themselves and their horses, and to expect with the dawn of day the signal of victory. On the festival of St. Peter and St. Paul the gates of Antioch were thrown open: a martial psalm, "Let the Lord arise, and let his enemies be scattered!" was chanted by a procession of priests and monks; the battle array was marshalled in twelve divisions, in honour of the twelve apostles; and the holy lance, in the absence of Raymond, was intrusted to the hands of his chaplain. The influence of this relic or trophy was felt by the servants, and perhaps by the enemies, of Christ; [1] and its potent energy was heightened by an accident, a stratagem, or a rumour, of a miraculous complexion. Three knights, in white garments and resplendent arms, either issued, or seemed to issue, from the hills: the voice of Adhemar, the pope's legate, proclaimed them as the martyrs St. George, St. Theodore, and St. Maurice: the tumult of battle allowed no time for doubt or scrutiny; and the welcome apparition dazzled the eyes or the imagination of a fanatic army. In the season of danger and triumph the revelation of Bartholemy of Marseilles was unanimously asserted; but as soon as the temporary service was accomplished, the personal dignity and liberal alms which the count of Toulouse derived from the custody of the holy lance provoked the envy, and awakened the reason, of his rivals. A Norman clerk presumed to sift, with a philosophic spirit, the truth of the legend,

[1] The Mohammedan Aboulmahasen (apud De Guignes, tom. ii. p. ii. p. 95) is more correct in his account of the holy lance than the Christians, Anna Comnena and Abulpharagius: the Greek princess confounds it with the nail of the cross (l. xi. p. 326); the Jacobite primate, with St. Peter's staff (p. 242).

the circumstances of the discovery, and the character of the prophet; and the pious Bohemond ascribed their deliverance to the merits and intercession of Christ alone. For a while the Provincials defended their national palladium with clamours and arms; and new visions condemned to death and hell the profane sceptics who presumed to scrutinise the truth and merit of the discovery. The prevalence of incredulity compelled the author to submit his life and veracity to the judgment of God. A pile of dry faggots, four feet high and fourteen long, was erected in the midst of the camp; the flames burnt fiercely to the elevation of thirty cubits; and a narrow path of twelve inches was left for the perilous trial. The unfortunate priest of Marseilles traversed the fire with dexterity and speed; but his thighs and belly were scorched by the intense heat; he expired the next day; and the logic of believing minds will pay some regard to his dying protestations of innocence and truth. Some efforts were made by the Provincials to substitute a cross, a ring, or a tabernacle, in the place of the holy lance, which soon vanished in contempt and oblivion.[1] Yet the revelation of Antioch is gravely asserted by succeeding historians: and such is the progress of credulity, that miracles, most doubtful on the spot and at the moment, will be received with implicit faith at a convenient distance of time and space.

The prudence or fortune of the Franks had delayed their invasion till the decline of the Turkish empire.[2] Under the manly government of the three first sultans, the kingdoms of Asia were united in peace and justice; and the innumerable armies which they led in person were equal in courage, and superior in discipline, to the barbarians of the West. But at the time of the crusade, the inheritance of Malek Shaw was disputed by his four sons; their private ambition was insensible of the public danger; and, in the vicissitudes of their fortune, the royal vassals were ignorant, or regardless, of the true object of their allegiance. The twenty-eight emirs who marched with the standard of Kerboga were his rivals or enemies: their hasty levies were drawn from the towns and tents of Mesopotamia and Syria; and the Turkish veterans were employed or consumed

[1] The two antagonists who express the most intimate knowledge and the strongest conviction of the *miracle* and of the *fraud* are Raymond de Agiles and Radulphus Cadomensis, the one attached to the count of Toulouse, the other to the Norman prince. Fulcherius Carnotensis presumes to say, Audite fraudem et non fraudem! and afterwards, Invenit lanceam, fallaciter occultatam forsitan. The rest of the herd are loud and strenuous.

[2] See M. de Guignes, tom. ii. p. ii. p. 223, etc.; and the articles of *Barkiarok, Mohammed, Sangiar,* in D'Herbelot.

in the civil wars beyond the Tigris. The caliph of Egypt embraced this opportunity of weakness and discord to recover his ancient possessions; and his sultan Aphdal besieged Jerusalem and Tyre, expelled the children of Ortok, and restored in Palestine the civil and ecclesiastical authority of the Fatimites.[1] They heard with astonishment of the vast armies of Christians that had passed from Europe to Asia, and rejoiced in the sieges and battles which broke the power of the Turks, the adversaries of their sect and monarchy. But the same Christians were the enemies of the prophet; and from the overthrow of Nice and Antioch, the motive of their enterprise, which was gradually understood, would urge them forwards to the banks of the Jordan, or perhaps of the Nile. An intercourse of epistles and embassies, which rose and fell with the events of war, was maintained between the throne of Cairo and the camp of the Latins; and their adverse pride was the result of ignorance and enthusiasm. The ministers of Egypt declared in a haughty, or insinuated in a milder, tone, that their sovereign, the true and lawful commander of the faithful, had rescued Jerusalem from the Turkish yoke; and that the pilgrims, if they would divide their numbers, and lay aside their arms, should find a safe and hospitable reception at the sepulchre of Jesus. In the belief of their lost condition, the caliph Mostali despised their arms and imprisoned their deputies: the conquest and victory of Antioch prompted him to solicit those formidable champions with gifts of horses and silk robes, of vases, and purses of gold and silver; and in his estimate of their merit or power the first place was assigned to Bohemond, and the second to Godfrey. In either fortune, the answer of the crusaders was firm and uniform: they disdained to inquire into the private claims or possessions of the followers of Mohammed: whatsoever was his name or nation, the usurper of Jerusalem was their enemy; and instead of prescribing the mode and terms of their pilgrimage, it was only by a timely surrender of the city and province, their sacred right, that he could deserve their alliance, or deprecate their impending and irresistible attack.[2]

Yet this attack, when they were within the view and reach of

[1] The emir, or sultan Aphdal, recovered Jerusalem and Tyre, A.H. 489 (Renaudot, Hist. Patriarch. Alexandrin. p. 478; De Guignes, tom. i. p. 249, from Abulfeda and Ben Schounah). Jerusalem ante adventum vestrum recuperavimus, Turcos ejecimus, say the Fatimite ambassadors.

[2] See the transactions between the caliph of Egypt and the crusaders in William of Tyre (l. iv. c. 24, l. vi. c. 19) and Albert Aquensis (l. iii. c. 59 [p. 234]), who are more sensible of their importance than the contemporary writers.

their glorious prize, was suspended above ten months after the defeat of Kerboga. The zeal and courage of the crusaders were chilled in the moment of victory; and instead of marching to improve the consternation, they hastily dispersed to enjoy the luxury, of Syria. The causes of this strange delay may be found in the want of strength and subordination. In the painful and various service of Antioch the cavalry was annihilated; many thousands of every rank had been lost by famine, sickness, and desertion: the same abuse of plenty had been productive of a third famine; and the alternative of intemperance and distress had generated a pestilence which swept away above fifty thousand of the pilgrims. Few were able to command, and none were willing to obey: the domestic feuds, which had been stifled by common fear, were again renewed in acts, or at least in sentiments, of hostility; the fortune of Baldwin and Bohemond excited the envy of their companions; the bravest knights were enlisted for the defence of their new principalities; and Count Raymond exhausted his troops and treasures in an idle expedition into the heart of Syria. The winter was consumed in discord and disorder; a sense of honour and religion was rekindled in the spring; and the private soldiers, less susceptible of ambition and jealousy, awakened with angry clamours the indolence of their chiefs. In the month of May the relics of this mighty host proceeded from Antioch to Laodicea: about forty thousand Latins, of whom no more than fifteen hundred horse and twenty thousand foot were capable of immediate service. Their easy march was continued between Mount Libanus and the sea-shore: their wants were liberally supplied by the coasting traders of Genoa and Pisa; and they drew large contributions from the emirs of Tripoli, Tyre, Sidon, Acre, and Cæsarea, who granted a free passage and promised to follow the example of Jerusalem. From Cæsarea they advanced into the midland country: their clerks recognised the sacred geography of Lydda, Ramla, Emmaus, and Bethlem, and as soon as they descried the holy city, the crusaders forgot their toils and claimed their reward.[1]

Jerusalem has derived some reputation from the number and importance of her memorable sieges. It was not till after a long and obstinate contest that Babylon and Rome could prevail against the obstinacy of the people, the craggy ground that

---

[1] The greatest part of the march of the Franks is traced, and most accurately traced, in Maundrell's Journey from Aleppo to Jerusalem (p. 11-67); un des meilleurs morçeaux, sans contredit, qu'on ait dans ce genre (D'Anville, Mémoire sur Jérusalem, p. 27).

might supersede the necessity of fortifications, and the walls and towers that would have fortified the most accessible plain.[1] These obstacles were diminished in the age of the crusades. The bulwarks had been completely destroyed and imperfectly restored: the Jews, their nation and worship, were for ever banished: but nature is less changeable than man, and the site of Jerusalem, though somewhat softened and somewhat removed, was still strong against the assaults of an enemy. By the experience of a recent siege, and a three years' possession, the Saracens of Egypt had been taught to discern, and in some degree to remedy, the defects of a place which religion as well as honour forbade them to resign. Aladin, or Iftikhar, the caliph's lieutenant, was intrusted with the defence: his policy strove to restrain the native Christians by the dread of their own ruin and that of the holy sepulchre; to animate the Moslems by the assurance of temporal and eternal rewards. His garrison is said to have consisted of forty thousand Turks and Arabians; and if he could muster twenty thousand of the inhabitants, it must be confessed that the besieged were more numerous than the besieging army.[2] Had the diminished strength and numbers of the Latins allowed them to grasp the whole circumference of four thousand yards (about two English miles and a half [3]), to what useful purpose should they have descended into the valley of Ben Hinnom and torrent of Kedron,[4] or approached the precipices of the south and east, from whence they had nothing either to hope or fear? Their siege was more reasonably

---

[1] See the masterly description of Tacitus (Hist. v. 11, 12, 13), who supposes that the Jewish lawgivers had provided for a perpetual state of hostility against the rest of mankind.

[2] The lively scepticism of Voltaire is balanced with sense and erudition by the French author of the Esprit des Croisades (tom. iv. p. 386-388), who observes, that, according to the Arabians, the inhabitants of Jerusalem must have exceeded 200,000; that, in the siege of Titus, Josephus collects 1,300,000 Jews; that they are stated by Tacitus himself at 600,000; and that the largest defalcation that his *accepimus* can justify will still leave them more numerous than the Roman army.

[3] Maundrell, who diligently perambulated the walls, found a circuit of 4630 paces, or 4167 English yards (p. 109, 110): from an authentic plan D'Anville concludes a measure nearly similar, of 1960 French *toises* (p. 23-29), in his scarce and valuable tract. For the topography of Jerusalem, see Reland (Palestina, tom. ii. p. 832-860).

[4] Jerusalem was possessed only of the torrent of Kedron, dry in summer, and of the little spring or brook of Siloe (Reland, tom. i. p. 294, 300). Both strangers and natives complained of the want of water, which, in time of war, was studiously aggravated. Within the city, Tacitus mentions a perennial fountain, an aqueduct and cisterns for rain-water. The aqueduct was conveyed from the rivulet Tekoe or Etham, which is likewise mentioned by Bohadin (in Vit. Saladin. p. 238).

directed against the northern and western sides of the city. Godfrey of Bouillon erected his standard on the first swell of Mount Calvary: to the left, as far as St. Stephen's gate, the line of attack was continued by Tancred and the two Roberts; and Count Raymond established his quarters from the citadel to the foot of Mount Sion, which was no longer included within the precincts of the city. On the fifth day the crusaders made a general assault, in the fanatic hope of battering down the walls without engines, and of scaling them without ladders. By the dint of brutal force they burst the first barrier, but they were driven back with shame and slaughter to the camp: the influence of vision and prophecy was deadened by the too frequent abuse of those pious stratagems; and time and labour were found to be the only means of victory. The time of the siege was indeed fulfilled in forty days, but they were forty days of calamity and anguish. A repetition of the old complaint of famine may be imputed in some degree to the voracious or disorderly appetite of the Franks; but the stony soil of Jerusalem is almost destitute of water; the scanty springs and hasty torrents were dry in the summer season: nor was the thirst of the besiegers relieved, as in the city, by the artificial supply of cisterns and aqueducts. The circumjacent country is equally destitute of trees for the uses of shade or building; but some large beams were discovered in a cave by the crusaders: a wood near Sichem, the enchanted grove of Tasso,[1] was cut down: the necessary timber was transported to the camp by the vigour and dexterity of Tancred; and the engines were framed by some Genoese artists, who had fortunately landed in the harbour of Jaffa. Two movable turrets were constructed at the expense, and in the stations, of the duke of Lorraine and the count of Toulouse, and rolled forwards with devout labour, not to the most accessible, but to the most neglected, parts of the fortification. Raymond's tower was reduced to ashes by the fire of the besieged, but his colleague was more vigilant and successful; the enemies were driven by his archers from the rampart; the drawbridge was let down; and on a Friday, at three in the afternoon, the day and hour of the Passion, Godfrey of Bouillon stood victorious on the walls of Jerusalem. His example was followed on every side by the emulation of valour; and about four hundred and sixty years after the conquest of Omar, the holy city was rescued from the Mohammedan yoke. In the pillage of public and private

---

[1] Gierusalemme Liberata, canto xiii. It is pleasant enough to observe how Tasso has copied and embellished the minutest details of the siege.

wealth, the adventurers had agreed to respect the exclusive
property of the first occupant; and the spoils of the great mosque,
seventy lamps and massy vases of gold and silver, rewarded the
diligence, and displayed the generosity, of Tancred. A bloody
sacrifice was offered by his mistaken votaries to the God of the
Christians: resistance might provoke, but neither age nor sex
could mollify, their implacable rage: they indulged themselves
three days in a promiscuous massacre; [1] and the infection of the
dead bodies produced an epidemical disease. After seventy
thousand Moslems had been put to the sword, and the harmless
Jews had been burnt in their synagogue, they could still reserve
a multitude of captives whom interest or lassitude persuaded
them to spare. Of these savage heroes of the cross, Tancred
alone betrayed some sentiments of compassion; yet we may
praise the more selfish lenity of Raymond, who granted a
capitulation and safe-conduct to the garrison of the citadel. [2]
The holy sepulchre was now free; and the bloody victors prepared to accomplish their vow. Bareheaded and barefoot, with
contrite hearts and in a humble posture, they ascended the hill
of Calvary, amidst the loud anthems of the clergy; kissed the
stone which had covered the Saviour of the world; and bedewed
with tears of joy and penitence the monument of their redemption.
This union of the fiercest and most tender passions has been
variously considered by two philosophers: by the one, [3] as easy
and natural; by the other, [4] as absurd and incredible.   Perhaps
it is too rigorously applied to the same persons and the same
hour: the example of the virtuous Godfrey awakened the piety
of his companions; while they cleansed their bodies they purified
their minds; nor shall I believe that the most ardent in slaughter
and rapine were the foremost in the procession to the holy
sepulchre.

Eight days after this memorable event, which pope Urban
did not live to hear, the Latin chiefs proceeded to the election
of a king, to guard and govern their conquests in Palestine.
Hugh the Great and Stephen of Chartres had retired with some

---

[1] Besides the Latins, who are not ashamed of the massacre, see Elmacin
(Hist. Saracen. p. 363), Abulpharagius (Dynast. p. 243), and M. de Guignes
(tom. ii. p. ii. p. 99), from Aboulmahasen.

[2] The old tower Psephina, in the middle ages Neblosa, was named
Castellum Pisanum, from the patriarch Daimbert. It is still the citadel,
the residence of the Turkish aga, and commands a prospect of the Dead
Sea, Judea, and Arabia (D'Anville, p. 19-23). It was likewise called the
Tower of David, πυργὸς παμμεγεθέστατος.

[3] Hume, in his History of England, vol. i. p. 311, 312, octavo edition.

[4] Voltaire, in his Essai sur l'Histoire Générale, tom. ii. c. 54, p. 345, 346.

loss of reputation, which they strove to regain by a second
crusade and an honourable death. Baldwin was established at
Edessa, and Bohemond at Antioch; and two Roberts, the duke
of Normandy [1] and the count of Flanders, preferred their fair
inheritance in the West to a doubtful competition or a barren
sceptre. The jealousy and ambition of Raymond were condemned by his own followers, and the free, the just, the unanimous voice of the army proclaimed Godfrey of Bouillon the
first and most worthy of the champions of Christendom. His
magnanimity accepted a trust as full of danger as of glory; but
in a city where his Saviour had been crowned with thorns, the
devout pilgrim rejected the name and ensigns of royalty; and
the founder of the kingdom of Jerusalem contented himself with
the modest title of Defender and Baron of the Holy Sepulchre.
His government of a single year,[2] too short for the public happiness, was interrupted in the first fortnight by a summons to the
field, by the approach of the vizir or sultan of Egypt, who had
been too slow to prevent, but who was impatient to avenge,
the loss of Jerusalem. His total overthrow in the battle of
Ascalon sealed the establishment of the Latins in Syria, and
signalised the valour of the French princes, who in this action
bade a long farewell to the holy wars. Some glory might be
derived from the prodigious inequality of numbers, though I
shall not count the myriads of horse and foot on the side of the
Fatimites; but, except three thousand Ethiopians or Blacks,
who were armed with flails or scourges of iron, the barbarians of
the South fled on the first onset, and afforded a pleasing comparison between the active valour of the Turks and the sloth
and effeminacy of the natives of Egypt. After suspending
before the holy sepulchre the sword and standard of the sultan,
the new king (he deserves the title) embraced his departing companions, and could retain only with the gallant Tancred three
hundred knights, and two thousand foot soldiers, for the defence
of Palestine. His sovereignty was soon attacked by a new
enemy, the only one against whom Godfrey was a coward.
Adhemar, bishop of Puy, who excelled both in council and action,
had been swept away in the last plague of Antioch: the remain-

[1] The English ascribe to Robert of Normandy, and the Provincials to
Raymond of Toulouse, the glory of refusing the crown; but the honest
voice of tradition has preserved the memory of the ambition and revenge
(Villehardouin, No. 136) of the count of St. Giles. He died at the siege of
Tripoli, which was possessed by his descendants.
[2] See the election, the battle of Ascalon, etc., in William of Tyre, l. ix.
c. 1-12, and in the conclusion of the Latin historians of the first crusade.

ing ecclesiastics preserved only the pride and avarice of their character; and their seditious clamours had required that the choice of a bishop should precede that of a king. The revenue and jurisdiction of the lawful patriarch were usurped by the Latin clergy: the exclusion of the Greeks and Syrians was justified by the reproach of heresy or schism;[1] and, under the iron yoke of their deliverers, the Oriental Christians regretted the tolerating government of the Arabian caliphs. Daimbert, archbishop of Pisa, had long been trained in the secret policy of Rome: he brought a fleet of his countrymen to the succour of the Holy Land, and was installed, without a competitor, the spiritual and temporal head of the church. The new patriarch[2] immediately grasped the sceptre which had been acquired by the toil and blood of the victorious pilgrims; and both Godfrey and Bohemond submitted to receive at his hands the investiture of their feudal possessions. Nor was this sufficient; Daimbert claimed the immediate property of Jerusalem and Jaffa; instead of a firm and generous refusal, the hero negotiated with the priest; a quarter of either city was ceded to the church; and the modest bishop was satisfied with an eventual reversion of the rest, on the death of Godfrey without children, or on the future acquisition of a new seat at Cairo or Damascus.

Without this indulgence the conqueror would have almost been stripped of his infant kingdom, which consisted only of Jerusalem and Jaffa, with about twenty villages and towns of the adjacent country.[3] Within this narrow verge the Mohammedans were still lodged in some impregnable castles; and the husbandman, the trader, and the pilgrim were exposed to daily and domestic hostility. By the arms of Godfrey himself, and of the two Baldwins, his brother and cousin, who succeeded to the throne, the Latins breathed with more ease and safety; and at length they equalled, in the extent of their dominions, though not in the millions of their subjects, the ancient princes of Judah and Israel.[4] After the reduction of the maritime cities

[1] Renaudot, Hist. Patriarch. Alex. p. 479.

[2] See the claims of the patriarch Daimbert, in William of Tyre (l. ix. c. 15-18, x. 4, 7, 9), who asserts with marvellous candour the independence of the conquerors and kings of Jerusalem.

[3] Willerm. Tyr. l. x. 19. The Historia Hierosolimitana of Jacobus à Vitriaco (l. i. c. 21-50), and the Secreta Fidelium Crucis of Marinus Sanutus (l. iii. p. 1 [7?]), describe the state and conquests of the Latin kingdom of Jerusalem.

[4] An actual muster, not including the tribes of Levi and Benjamin, gave David an army of 1,300,000 or 1,574,000 fighting men; which, with the addition of women, children, and slaves, may imply a population of thirteen millions, in a country sixty leagues in length and thirty broad. The

of Laodicea, Tripoli, Tyre, and Ascalon,[1] which were powerfully
assisted by the fleets of Venice, Genoa, and Pisa, and even of
Flanders and Norway,[2] the range of sea-coast from Scanderoon
to the borders of Egypt was possessed by the Christian pilgrims.
If the prince of Antioch disclaimed his supremacy, the counts
of Edessa and Tripoli owned themselves the vassals of the king
of Jerusalem: the Latins reigned beyond the Euphrates; and the
four cities of Hems, Hamah, Damascus, and Aleppo were the
only relics of the Mohammedan conquests in Syria.[3]   The laws
and language, the manners and titles, of the French nation and
Latin church, were introduced into these transmarine colonies.
According to the feudal jurisprudence, the principal states and
subordinate baronies descended in the line of male and female
succession:[4] but the children of the first conquerors,[5] a motley
and degenerate race, were dissolved by the luxury of the climate;
the arrival of new crusaders from Europe was a doubtful hope
and a casual event.   The service of the feudal tenures [6] was performed by six hundred and sixty-six knights, who might expect
the aid of two hundred more under the banner of the count of
Tripoli; and each knight was attended to the field by four

honest and rational Le Clerc (Comment. on 2nd Samuel, xxiv. and 1st
Chronicles, xxi.) æstuat augusto in limite, and mutters his suspicion of a
false transcript; a dangerous suspicion!

[1] These sieges are related, each in its proper place, in the great history of
William of Tyre, from the ninth to the eighteenth book, and more briefly
told by Bernardus Thesaurarius (de Acquisitione Terræ Sanctæ, c. 87-98,
p. 732-740).   Some domestic facts are celebrated in the Chronicles of Pisa,
Genoa, and Venice, in the sixth, tenth, and twelfth tomes of Muratori.

[2] Quidam populus de insulis occidentis egressus, et maxime de eâ parte
quæ Norvegia dicitur.   William of Tyre (l. xi. c. 14, p. 804) marks their
course per Britannicum mare et Calpen to the siege of Sidon.

[3] Benelathir, apud De Guignes, Hist. des Huns, tom. ii. part ii. p. 150,
151, A.D. 1127.   He must speak of the inland country.

[4] Sanut very sensibly descants on the mischiefs of female succession in
a land hostibus circumdata, ubi cuncta virilia et virtuosa esse deberent.
Yet, at the summons and with the approbation of her feudal lord, a noble
damsel was obliged to choose a husband and champion (Assises de Jérusalem, c. 242, etc.).   See in M. de Guignes (tom. i. p. 441-471) the accurate
and useful tables of these dynasties, which are chiefly drawn from the
Lignages d'Outremer.

[5] They were called by derision Poullains, Pullani, and their name is
never pronounced without contempt (Ducange. Gloss. Latin. tom. v. p. 535;
and Observations sur Joinville, p. 84, 85; Jacob. à Vitriaco, Hist. Hierosol.
l. i. c. 67, 72; and Sanut, l. iii. p. viii. c. 2, p. 182).   Illustrium virorum
qui ad Terræ Sanctæ . . . liberationem in ipsâ manserunt degeneres
filii . . . in deliciis enutriti, molles et effeminati, etc.

[6] This authentic detail is extracted from the Assises de Jérusalem (c. 324,
326-331).   Sanut (l. iii. p. viii. c. 1, p. 174) reckons only 518 knights and
5775 followers.

squires or archers on horseback.[1] Five thousand and seventy-five *serjeants*, most probably foot-soldiers, were supplied by the churches and cities; and the whole legal militia of the kingdom could not exceed eleven thousand men, a slender defence against the surrounding myriads of Saracens and Turks.[2] But the firmest bulwark of Jerusalem was founded on the knights of the Hospital of St. John,[3] and of the temple of Solomon;[4] on the strange association of a monastic and military life, which fanaticism might suggest, but which policy must approve. The flower of the nobility of Europe aspired to wear the cross, and to profess the vows, of these respectable orders; their spirit and discipline were immortal; and the speedy donation of twenty-eight thousand farms, or manors,[5] enabled them to support a regular force of cavalry and infantry for the defence of Palestine. The austerity of the convent soon evaporated in the exercise of arms: the world was scandalised by the pride, avarice, and corruption of these Christian soldiers; their claims of immunity and jurisdiction disturbed the harmony of the church and state; and the public peace was endangered by their jealous emulation. But in their most dissolute period the knights of the hospital and temple maintained their fearless and fanatic character: they neglected to live, but they were prepared to die, in the service of Christ; and the spirit of chivalry, the parent and offspring of the crusades, has been transplanted by this institution from the holy sepulchre to the isle of Malta.[6]

[1] The sum total, and the division, ascertain the service of the three great baronies at 100 knights each; and the text of the Assises, which extends the number to 500, can only be justified by this supposition.

[2] Yet on great emergencies (says Sanut) the barons brought a voluntary aid; decentem comitivam militum juxta statum suum.

[3] William of Tyre (l. xviii. c. 3, 4, 5) relates the ignoble origin and early insolence of the Hospitalers, who soon deserted their humble patron, St. John the Eleemosynary, for the more august character of St. John the Baptist (see the ineffectual struggles of Pagi, Critica, A.D. 1099, No. 14-18). They assumed the profession of arms about the year 1120; the Hospital was *mater*; the Temple *filia*; the Teutonic order was founded A.D. 1190, at the siege of Acre (Mosheim, Institut. p. 389, 390).

[4] See St. Bernard de Laude Novæ Militiæ Templi, composed A.D. 1132-1136, in Opp. tom. i. p. ii. p. 547-563, edit. Mabillon, Venet. 1750. Such an encomium, which is thrown away on the dead Templars, would be highly valued by the historians of Malta.

[5] Matthew Paris, Hist. Major, p. 544. He assigns to the Hospitalers 19,000, to the Templars 9000 *maneria*, a word of much higher import (as Ducange has rightly observed) in the English than in the French idiom. *Manor* is a lordship, *manoir* a dwelling.

[6] In the three first books of the Histoire des Chevaliers de Malthe, par l'Abbé de Vertot, the reader may amuse himself with a fair, and sometimes flattering, picture of the order, while it was employed for the defence of Palestine. The subsequent books pursue their emigrations to Rhodes and Malta.

The spirit of freedom, which pervades the feudal institutions, was felt in its strongest energy by the volunteers of the cross, who elected for their chief the most deserving of his peers. Amidst the slaves of Asia, unconscious of the lesson or example, a model of political liberty was introduced; and the laws of the French kingdom are derived from the purest source of equality and justice. Of such laws, the first and indispensable condition is the assent of those whose obedience they require, and for whose benefit they are designed. No sooner had Godfrey of Bouillon accepted the office of supreme magistrate than he solicited the public and private advice of the Latin pilgrims who were the best skilled in the statutes and customs of Europe. From these materials, with the counsel and approbation of the patriarch and barons, of the clergy and laity, Godfrey composed the ASSISE OF JERUSALEM,[1] a precious monument of feudal jurisprudence. The new code, attested by the seals of the king, the patriarch, and the viscount of Jerusalem, was deposited in the holy sepulchre, enriched with the improvements of succeeding times, and respectfully consulted as often as any doubtful question arose in the tribunals of Palestine. With the kingdom and city all was lost;[2] the fragments of the written law were preserved by jealous tradition[3] and variable practice till the middle of the thirteenth century: the code was restored by the pen of John d'Ibelin, count of Jaffa, one of the principal feudatories;[4] and the final revision was accomplished in the year thirteen

[1] The Assises de Jérusalem, in old law French, were printed with Beaumanoir's Coûtumes de Beauvoisis (Bourges and Paris, 1690, in folio), and illustrated by Gaspard Thaumas de la Thaumassière with a comment and glossary. An Italian version had been published in 1535, at Venice, for the use of the kingdom of Cyprus.

[2] A la terre perdue, tout fut perdû, is the vigorous expression of the Assise (c. 281). Yet Jerusalem capitulated with Saladin; the queen and the principal Christians departed in peace; and a code so precious and so portable could not provoke the avarice of the conquerors. I have sometimes suspected the existence of this original copy of the Holy Sepulchre, which might be invented to sanctify and authenticate the traditionary customs of the French in Palestine.

[3] A noble lawyer, Raoul de Tabarie, denied the prayer of king Amauri (A.D. 1195-1205), that he would commit his knowledge to writing, and frankly declared, que de ce qu'il savoit ne feroit-il ja nul borjois son pareill, ne nul sage homme lettré (c. 281).

[4] The compiler of this work, Jean d'Ibelin, was count of Jaffa and Ascalon, lord of Baruth (Berytus) and Rames, and died A.D. 1266 (Sanut, l. iii. p. xii. c. 5, 8 [p. 220, 222]). The family of Ibelin, which descended from a younger brother of a count of Chartres in France, long flourished in Palestine and Cyprus (see the Lignages de deça Mer, or d'Outremer, c. 6, at the end of the Assises de Jérusalem, an original book, which records the pedigrees of the French adventurers).

hundred and sixty-nine, for the use of the Latin kingdom of Cyprus.[1]

The justice and freedom of the constitution were maintained by two tribunals of unequal dignity, which were instituted by Godfrey of Bouillon after the conquest of Jerusalem. The king, in person, presided in the upper court, the court of the barons. Of these the four most conspicuous were the prince of Galilee, the lord of Sidon and Cæsarea, and the counts of Jaffa and Tripoli, who, perhaps with the constable and marshal,[2] were in a special manner the compeers and judges of each other. But all the nobles who held their lands immediately of the crown were entitled and bound to attend the king's court; and each baron exercised a similar jurisdiction in the subordinate assemblies of his own feudatories. The connection of lord and vassal was honourable and voluntary: reverence was due to the benefactor, protection to the dependent; but they mutually pledged their faith to each other; and the obligation on either side might be suspended by neglect or dissolved by injury. The cognisance of marriages and testaments was blended with religion, and usurped by the clergy: but the civil and criminal causes of the nobles, the inheritance and tenure of their fiefs, formed the proper occupation of the supreme court. Each member was the judge and guardian both of public and private rights. It was his duty to assert with his tongue and sword the lawful claims of the lord: but if an unjust superior presumed to violate the freedom or property of a vassal, the confederate peers stood forth to maintain his quarrel by word and deed. They boldly affirmed his innocence and his wrongs; demanded the restitution of his liberty or his lands; suspended, after a fruitless demand, their own service; rescued their brother from prison; and employed every weapon in his defence, without offering direct violence to the person of their lord, which was ever sacred in their eyes.[3] In their pleadings, replies, and rejoinders, the

[1] By sixteen commissioners chosen in the states of the island: the work was finished the 3rd of November, 1369, sealed with four seals, and deposited in the cathedral of Nicosia (see the preface to the Assises).

[2] The cautious John d'Ibelin argues, rather than affirms, that Tripoli is the fourth barony, and expresses some doubt concerning the right or pretension of the constable and marshal ([Assises de Jérus.] c. 324).

[3] Entre seignor et homme ne n'a que la foi; . . . mais tant que l'homme doit à son seignor reverence en toutes choses (c. 206). Tous les hommes dudit royaume sont par ladite Assise tenus les uns as autres . . . et en celle maniere que le seignor mette main ou face mettre au cors ou au fié d'aucun d'yaus sans esgard et sans connoissance de court, que tous les autres doivent venir devant le seignor, etc. (212). The form of their remonstrances is conceived with the noble simplicity of freedom.

advocates of the court were subtle and copious; but the use of
argument and evidence was often superseded by judicial combat;
and the Assise of Jerusalem admits in many cases this barbarous
institution, which has been slowly abolished by the laws and
manners of Europe.

The trial by battle was established in all criminal cases which
affected the life, or limb, or honour of any person; and in all
civil transactions of or above the value of one mark of silver.
It appears that in criminal cases the combat was the privilege
of the accuser, who, except in a charge of treason, avenged his
personal injury, or the death of those persons whom he had a
right to represent; but wherever, from the nature of the charge,
testimony could be obtained, it was necessary for him to produce
witnesses of the fact. In civil cases the combat was not allowed
as the means of establishing the claim of the demandant, but
he was obliged to produce witnesses who had, or assumed to
have, knowledge of the fact. The combat was then the privilege
of the defendant, because he charged the witness with an attempt
by perjury to take away his right. He came therefore to be in
the same situation as the appellant in criminal cases. It was
not, then, as a mode of proof that the combat was received, nor
as making negative evidence (according to the supposition of
Montesquieu); [1] but in every case the right to offer battle was
founded on the right to pursue by arms the redress of an injury,
and the judicial combat was fought on the same principle and
with the same spirit as a private duel. Champions were only
allowed to women, and to men maimed or past the age of sixty.
The consequence of a defeat was death to the person accused, or
to the champion or witness, as well as to the accuser himself;
but in civil cases the demandant was punished with infamy and
the loss of his suit, while his witness and champion suffered an
ignominious death. In many cases it was in the option of the
judge to award or to refuse the combat: but two are specified
in which it was the inevitable result of the challenge; if a faithful
vassal gave the lie to his compeer who unjustly claimed any
portion of their lord's demesnes, or if an unsuccessful suitor
presumed to impeach the judgment and veracity of the court.
He might impeach them, but the terms were severe and perilous;
in the same day he successively fought *all* the members of the
tribunal, even those who had been absent; a single defeat was

---

[1] See l'Esprit des Loix, l. xxviii. In the forty years since its publication,
no work has been more read and criticised; and the spirit of inquiry which
it has excited is not the least of our obligations to the author.

followed by death and infamy, and where none could hope for victory it is highly probable that none would adventure the trial. In the Assise of Jerusalem, the legal subtlety of the count of Jaffa is more laudably employed to elude, than to facilitate, the judicial combat, which he derives from a principle of honour rather than of superstition.[1]

Among the causes which enfranchised the plebeians from the yoke of feudal tyranny, the institution of cities and corporations is one of the most powerful; and if those of Palestine are coeval with the first crusade, they may be ranked with the most ancient of the Latin world. Many of the pilgrims had escaped from their lords under the banner of the cross, and it was the policy of the French princes to tempt their stay by the assurance of the rights and privileges of freemen. It is expressly declared in the Assise of Jerusalem, that after instituting, for his knights and barons, the court of peers, in which he presided himself, Godfrey of Bouillon established a second tribunal, in which his person was represented by his viscount. The jurisdiction of this inferior court extended over the burgesses of the kingdom, and it was composed of a select number of the most discreet and worthy citizens, who were sworn to judge, according to the laws, of the actions and fortunes of their equals.[2] In the conquest and settlement of new cities, the example of Jerusalem was imitated by the kings and their great vassals, and above thirty similar corporations were founded before the loss of the Holy Land. Another class of subjects, the Syrians,[3] or Oriental Christians, were oppressed by the zeal of the clergy, and protected by the toleration of the state. Godfrey listened to their reasonable prayer that they might be judged by their own national laws. A third court was instituted for their use, of limited and domestic jurisdiction; the sworn members were Syrians, in blood, language, and religion, but the office of the president (in Arabic, of the

---

[1] For the intelligence of this obscure and obsolete jurisprudence (c. 80-111) I am deeply indebted to the friendship of a learned lord, who, with an accurate and discerning eye, has surveyed the philosophic history of law. By his studies posterity might be enriched: the merit of the orator and the judge can be *felt* only by his contemporaries.

[2] Louis le Gros, who is considered as the father of this institution in France, did not begin his reign till nine years (A.D. 1108) after Godfrey of Bouillon (Assises, c. 2, 324). For its origin and effects see the judicious remarks of Dr. Robertson (History of Charles V. vol. i. p. 30-36, 251-265, quarto edition).

[3] Every reader conversant with the historians of the crusades will understand, by the peuple des Suriens, the Oriental Christians, Melchites, Jacobites, or Nestorians, who had all adopted the use of the Arabic language (vol. iv. p. 593).

rais) was sometimes exercised by the viscount of the city. At an immeasurable distance below the *nobles*, the *burgesses*, and the *strangers*, the Assise of Jerusalem condescends to mention the *villains* and *slaves*, the peasants of the land and the captives of war, who were almost equally considered as the objects of property. The relief or protection of these unhappy men was not esteemed worthy of the care of the legislator: but he diligently provides for the recovery, though not indeed for the punishment, of the fugitives. Like hounds or hawks, who had strayed from the lawful owner, they might be lost and claimed; the slave and falcon were of the same value, but three slaves or twelve oxen were accumulated to equal the price of the war-horse, and a sum of three hundred pieces of gold was fixed, in the age of chivalry, as the equivalent of the more noble animal.[1]

CHAPTER LIX

Preservation of the Greek Empire—Numbers, Passage, and Event of the Second and Third Crusades—St. Bernard—Reign of Saladin in Egypt and Syria—His Conquest of Jerusalem—Naval Crusades—Richard the First of England—Pope Innocent the Third; and the Fourth and Fifth Crusades—The Emperor Frederic the Second—Louis the Ninth of France; and the two last Crusades—Expulsion of the Latins or Franks by the Mamalukes

IN a style less grave than that of history I should perhaps compare the emperor Alexius [2] to the jackal, who is said to follow the steps, and to devour the leavings, of the lion. Whatever had been his fears and toils in the passage of the first crusade, they were amply recompensed by the subsequent benefits which he derived from the exploits of the Franks. His dexterity and vigilance secured their first conquest of Nice, and from this threatening station the Turks were compelled to evacuate the neighbourhood of Constantinople. While the crusaders, with blind valour, advanced into the midland countries of Asia, the crafty Greek improved the favourable occasion when the emirs of the sea-coast were recalled to the standard of the

[1] See the Assises de Jérusalem (c. 310, 311, 312). These laws were enacted as late as the year 1350, in the kingdom of Cyprus. In the same century, in the reign of Edward I., I understand, from a late publication (of his Book of Account), that the price of a war-horse was not less exorbitant in England.

[2] Anna Comnena relates her father's conquests in Asia Minor, Alexiad, l. xi. p. 321-325, l. xiv. p. 419; his Cilician war against Tancred and Bohemond, p. 328-342; the war of Epirus, with tedious prolixity, l. xii. xiii. p. 345-406; the death of Bohemond, l. xiv. p. 419.

sultan. The Turks were driven from the isles of Rhodes and Chios: the cities of Ephesus and Smyrna, of Sardes, Philadelphia, and Laodicea, were restored to the empire, which Alexius enlarged from the Hellespont to the banks of the Mæander and the rocky shores of Pamphylia. The churches resumed their splendour, the towns were rebuilt and fortified, and the desert country was peopled with colonies of Christians, who were gently removed from the more distant and dangerous frontier. In these paternal cares we may forgive Alexius if he forgot the deliverance of the holy sepulchre; but by the Latins he was stigmatised with the foul reproach of treason and desertion. They had sworn fidelity and obedience to his throne, but *he* had promised to assist their enterprise in person, or, at least, with his troops and treasures; his base retreat dissolved their obligations; and the sword, which had been the instrument of their victory, was the pledge and title of their just independence. It does not appear that the emperor attempted to revive his obsolete claims over the kingdom of Jerusalem,[1] but the borders of Cilicia and Syria were more recent in his possession, and more accessible to his arms. The great army of the crusaders was annihilated or dispersed; the principality of Antioch was left without a head by the surprise and captivity of Bohemond; his ransom had oppressed him with a heavy debt, and his Norman followers were insufficient to repel the hostilities of the Greeks and Turks. In this distress Bohemond embraced a magnanimous resolution of leaving the defence of Antioch to his kinsman the faithful Tancred, of arming the West against the Byzantine empire, and of executing the design which he inherited from the lessons and example of his father Guiscard. His embarkation was clandestine, and, if we may credit a tale of the princess Anna, he passed the hostile sea closely secreted in a coffin.[2] But his reception in France was dignified by the public applause and his marriage with the king's daughter; his return was glorious, since the bravest spirits of the age enlisted under his veteran command; and he repassed the Adriatic at the head of five thousand horse and forty thousand foot, assembled from

[1] The kings of Jerusalem submitted however to a nominal dependence, and in the dates of their inscriptions (one is still legible in the church of Bethlem) they respectfully placed before their own the name of the reigning emperor (Ducange, Dissertations sur Joinville, xxvii. p. 319).

[2] Anna Comnena adds [l. xi. p. 341], that, to complete the imitation, he was shut up with a dead cock; and condescends to wonder how the barbarian could endure the confinement and putrefaction. This absurd tale is unknown to the Latins.

the most remote climates of Europe.[1]   The strength of Durazzo and prudence of Alexius, the progress of famine and approach of winter, eluded his ambitious hopes, and the venal confederates were seduced from his standard.   A treaty of peace [2] suspended the fears of the Greeks, and they were finally delivered by the death of an adversary whom neither oaths could bind, nor dangers could appal, nor prosperity could satiate.   His children succeeded to the principality of Antioch, but the boundaries were strictly defined, the homage was clearly stipulated, and the cities of Tarsus and Malmistra were restored to the Byzantine emperors.   Of the coast of Anatolia, they possessed the entire circuit from Trebizond to the Syrian gates.   The Seljukian dynasty of Roum [3] was separated on all sides from the sea and their Musulman brethren; the power of the sultans was shaken by the victories and even the defeats of the Franks; and after the loss of Nice they removed their throne to Cogni or Iconium, an obscure and inland town above three hundred miles from Constantinople.[4]   Instead of trembling for their capital, the Comnenian princes waged an offensive war against the Turks, and the first crusade prevented the fall of the declining empire.

In the twelfth century three great emigrations marched by land from the West to the relief of Palestine.   The soldiers and pilgrims of Lombardy, France, and Germany were excited by the example and success of the first crusade.[5]   Forty-eight years after the deliverance of the holy sepulchre, the emperor and the French king, Conrad the Third and Louis the Seventh, undertook the second crusade to support the falling fortunes of the Latins.[6]   A grand division of the third crusade was led by the

---

[1] Ἀπὸ Θύλης, in the Byzantine geography, must mean England; yet we are more credibly informed that our Henry I. would not suffer him to levy any troops in his kingdom (Ducange, Not. ad Alexiad. p. 41).

[2] The copy of the treaty (Alexiad, l. xiii. p. 406-416) is an original and curious piece, which would require, and might afford, a good map of the principality of Antioch.

[3] See in the learned work of M. de Guignes (tom. ii. part ii.) the history of the Seljukians of Iconium, Aleppo, and Damascus, as far as it may be collected from the Greeks, Latins, and Arabians.   The last are ignorant or regardless of the affairs of *Roum*.

[4] Iconium is mentioned as a station by Xenophon, and by Strabo with the ambiguous title of Κωμόπολις (Cellarius, tom. ii. p. 121.)   Yet St. Paul found in that place a multitude (πλῆθος) of Jews and Gentiles.   Under the corrupt name of *Kunijah*, it is described as a great city, with a river and gardens, three leagues from the mountains, and decorated (I know not why) with Plato's tomb (Abulfeda, tabul. xvii. p. 303, vers. Reiske; and the Index Geographicus of Schultens from Ibn Said).

[5] For this supplement to the first crusade see Anna Comnena (Alexias, l. xi. p. 331, etc., and the eighth book of Albert Aquensis).

[6] For the second crusade, of Conrad III. and Louis VII. see William of

emperor Frederic Barbarossa,[1] who sympathised with his brothers of France and England in the common loss of Jerusalem. These three expeditions may be compared, in their resemblance of the greatness of numbers, their passage through the Greek empire, and the nature and event of their Turkish warfare; and a brief parallel may save the repetition of a tedious narrative. However splendid it may seem, a regular story of the crusades would exhibit the perpetual return of the same causes and effects, and the frequent attempts for the defence or recovery of the Holy Land would appear so many faint and unsuccessful copies of the original.

I. Of the swarms that so closely trod in the footsteps of the first pilgrims, the chiefs were equal in rank, though unequal in fame and merit, to Godfrey of Bouillon and his fellow adventurers. At their head were displayed the banners of the dukes of Burgundy, Bavaria, and Aquitain: the first a descendant of Hugh Capet, the second a father of the Brunswick line; the archbishop of Milan, a temporal prince, transported, for the benefit of the Turks, the treasures and ornaments of his church and palace; and the veteran crusaders, Hugh the Great and Stephen of Chartres, returned to consummate their unfinished vow. The huge and disorderly bodies of their followers moved forwards in two columns; and if the first consisted of two hundred and sixty thousand persons, the second might possibly amount to sixty thousand horse and one hundred thousand foot.[2] The armies of the second crusade might have claimed the conquest of Asia; the nobles of France and Germany were animated by the presence of their sovereigns, and both the rank and personal characters of Conrad and Louis gave a dignity to their cause, and a discipline to their force, which might be vainly expected from the feudatory chiefs. The cavalry of the emperor and that of the king was each composed of seventy thousand knights

Tyre (l. xvi. c. 18-29), Otho of Frisingen (l. i. c. 34-45, 59, 60), Matthew Paris (Hist. Major. p. 68), Struvius (Corpus Hist. Germanicæ, p. 372, 373). Scriptores Rerum Francicarum à Duchesne, tom. iv.; Nicetas, in Vit. Manuel, l. i. c. 4, 5, 6, p. 41-48 [p. 80-96, ed. Bonn]; Cinnamus, l. ii. p. 41-49 [ed. Par.; p. 73-89, ed. Bonn].

[1] For the third crusade of Frederic Barbarossa, see Nicetas in Isaac. Angel. l. ii. c. 3-8, p. 257-266 [p. 524-544, ed. Bonn]; Struv. (Corpus Hist. Germ. p. 414); and two historians, who probably were spectators, Tagino (in Scriptor. Freher. tom. i. p. 406-416, edit. Struv.), and the Anonymus de Expeditione Asiaticâ Fred. I. (in Canisii Antiq. Lection. tom. iii. p. ii. p. 498-526, edit. Basnage).

[2] Anna, who states these later swarms at 40,000 horse and 100,000 foot, calls them Normans, and places at their head two brothers of Flanders. The Greeks were strangely ignorant of the names, families, and possessions of the Latin princes.

and their immediate attendants in the field;[1] and if the light-armed troops, the peasant infantry, the women and children, the priests and monks, be rigorously excluded, the full account will scarcely be satisfied with four hundred thousand souls. The West, from Rome to Britain, was called into action; the kings of Poland and Bohemia obeyed the summons of Conrad; and it is affirmed by the Greeks and Latins, that, in the passage of a strait or river, the Byzantine agents, after a tale of nine hundred thousand, desisted from the endless and formidable computation.[2] In the third crusade, as the French and English preferred the navigation of the Mediterranean, the host of Frederic Barbarossa was less numerous. Fifteen thousand knights and as many squires were the flower of the German chivalry; sixty thousand horse and one hundred thousand foot were mustered by the emperor in the plains of Hungary; and after such repetitions we shall no longer be startled at the six hundred thousand pilgrims which credulity has ascribed to this last emigration.[3] Such extravagant reckonings prove only the astonishment of contemporaries, but their astonishment most strongly bears testimony to the existence of an enormous though indefinite multitude. The Greeks might applaud their superior knowledge of the arts and stratagems of war, but they confessed the strength and courage of the French cavalry and the infantry of the Germans;[4] and the strangers are described as an iron race, of gigantic stature, who darted fire from their eyes, and spilt blood like water on the ground. Under the banners of Conrad a troop of females rode in the attitude and armour of men, and the chief

---

[1] William of Tyre, and Matthew Paris, reckon 70,000 loricati in each of the armies.

[2] The imperfect enumeration is mentioned by Cinnamus (ἐννενήκοντα μυριάδες [p. 69, ed. Bonn]), and confirmed by Odo de Diogilo apud Ducange ad Cinnamum, with the more precise sum of 900,556. Why must therefore the version and comment suppose the modest and insufficient reckoning of 90,000? Does not Godfrey of Viterbo (Pantheon, p. xix. in Muratori, tom. vii. p. 462) exclaim—

> —— Numerum si noscere quæras,
> Millia millena militis agmen erat.

[3] This extravagant account is given by Albert of Stade (apud Struvium, p. 414); my calculation is borrowed from Odo of Viterbo, Arnold of Lubeck, apud eundem, and Bernard Thesaur. (c. 169, p. 804). The original writers are silent. The Mohammedans gave him 200,000 or 260,000 men (Bohadin, in Vit. Saladin. p. 110 [P. ii. c 61]).

[4] I must observe that, in the second and third crusades, the subjects of Conrad and Frederic are styled by the Greeks and Orientals Alamanni. The Lechi and Tzechi of Cinnamus are the Poles and Bohemians; and it is for the French that he reserves the ancient appellation of Germans. He likewise names the Βρίττιοι, or Βριταννοί.

of these Amazons, from her gilt spurs and buskins, obtained the epithet of the Golden-footed Dame.

II. The numbers and character of the strangers was an object of terror to the effeminate Greeks, and the sentiment of fear is nearly allied to that of hatred. This aversion was suspended or softened by the apprehension of the Turkish power; and the invectives of the Latins will not bias our more candid belief that the emperor Alexius dissembled their insolence, eluded their hostilities, counselled their rashness, and opened to their ardour the road of pilgrimage and conquest. But when the Turks had been driven from Nice and the sea-coast, when the Byzantine princes no longer dreaded the distant sultans of Cogni, they felt with purer indignation the free and frequent passage of the Western barbarians, who violated the majesty and endangered the safety of the empire. The second and third crusades were undertaken under the reign of Manuel Comnenus and Isaac Angelus. Of the former, the passions were always impetuous, and often malevolent; and the natural union of a cowardly and a mischievous temper was exemplified in the latter, who, without merit or mercy, could punish a tyrant and occupy his throne. It was secretly, and perhaps tacitly, resolved by the prince and people to destroy, or at least to discourage, the pilgrims by every species of injury and oppression; and their want of prudence and discipline continually afforded the pretence or the opportunity. The Western monarchs had stipulated a safe passage and fair market in the country of their Christian brethren; the treaty had been ratified by oaths and hostages; and the poorest soldier of Frederic's army was furnished with three marks of silver to defray his expenses on the road. But every engagement was violated by treachery and injustice; and the complaints of the Latins are attested by the honest confession of a Greek historian, who has dared to prefer truth to his country.[1] Instead of an hospitable reception, the gates of the cities, both in Europe and Asia, were closely barred against the crusaders; and the scanty pittance of food was let down in baskets from the walls. Experience or foresight might excuse this timid jealousy; but the common duties of humanity prohibited the mixture of chalk, or other poisonous ingredients, in the bread; and should Manuel be acquitted of any foul connivance, he is guilty of coining base money for the purpose of trading with the pilgrims. In every

---

[1] Nicetas was a child at the second crusade, but in the third he commanded against the Franks the important post of Philippopolis. Cinnamus is infected with national prejudice and pride.

step of their march they were stopped or misled: the governors had private orders to fortify the passes and break down the bridges against them: the stragglers were pillaged and murdered: the soldiers and horses were pierced in the woods by arrows from an invisible hand; the sick were burnt in their beds; and the dead bodies were hung on gibbets along the highways. These injuries exasperated the champions of the cross, who were not endowed with evangelical patience; and the Byzantine princes, who had provoked the unequal conflict, promoted the embarkation and march of these formidable guests. On the verge of the Turkish frontier Barbarossa spared the guilty Philadelphia,[1] rewarded the hospitable Laodicea, and deplored the hard necessity that had stained his sword with any drops of Christian blood. In their intercourse with the monarchs of Germany and France, the pride of the Greeks was exposed to an anxious trial. They might boast that on the first interview the seat of Louis was a low stool beside the throne of Manuel; [2] but no sooner had the French king transported his army beyond the Bosphorus than he refused the offer of a second conference unless his brother would meet him on equal terms either on the sea or land. With Conrad and Frederic the ceremonial was still nicer and more difficult: like the successors of Constantine, they styled themselves emperors of the Romans,[3] and firmly maintained the purity of their title and dignity. The first of these representatives of Charlemagne would only converse with Manuel on horseback in the open field; the second, by passing the Hellespont rather than the Bosphorus, declined the view of Constantinople and its sovereign. An emperor who had been crowned at Rome was reduced in the Greek epistles to the humble appellation of *Rex*, or prince, of the Alemanni; and the vain and feeble Angelus affected to be ignorant of the name of one of the greatest men and monarchs of the age. While they viewed

[1] The conduct of the Philadelphians is blamed by Nicetas, while the anonymous German accuses the rudeness of his countrymen (culpâ nostrâ). History would be pleasant if we were embarrassed only by *such* contradictions. It is likewise from Nicetas that we learn the pious and humane sorrow of Frederic.

[2] Χθαμάλη ἕδρα, which Cinnamus translates into Latin by the word Σέλλιον [p. 83, ed. Bonn]. Ducange works very hard to save his king and country from such ignominy (sur Joinville, dissertat. xxvii. p. 317-320). Louis afterwards insisted on a meeting in mari ex æquo, not ex equo, according to the laughable readings of some MSS.

[3] Ego Romanorum imperator sum, ille Romaniorum (Anonym. Canis. p. 512). The public and historical style of the Greeks was Ρὴξ . . . *princeps*. Yet Cinnamus owns that Ἱμπεράτωρ is synonymous to Βασιλεύς [p. 69, ed. Bonn].

with hatred and suspicion the Latin pilgrims, the Greek emperors maintained a strict, though secret, alliance with the Turks and Saracens. Isaac Angelus complained that by his friendship for the great Saladin he had incurred the enmity of the Franks; and a mosque was founded at Constantinople for the public exercise of the religion of Mohammed.[1]

III. The swarms that followed the first crusade were destroyed in Anatolia by famine, pestilence, and the Turkish arrows; and the princes only escaped with some squadrons of horse to accomplish their lamentable pilgrimage. A just opinion may be formed of their knowledge and humanity; of their knowledge, from the design of subduing Persia and Chorasan in their way to Jerusalem; of their humanity, from the massacre of the Christian people, a friendly city, who came out to meet them with palms and crosses in their hands. The arms of Conrad and Louis were less cruel and imprudent; but the event of the second crusade was still more ruinous to Christendom; and the Greek Manuel is accused by his own subjects of giving seasonable intelligence to the sultan, and treacherous guides to the Latin princes. Instead of crushing the common foe by a double attack at the same time, but on different sides, the Germans were urged by emulation, and the French were retarded by jealousy. Louis had scarcely passed the Bosphorus when he was met by the returning emperor, who had lost the greatest part of his army in glorious, but unsuccessful, action on the banks of the Mæander. The contrast of the pomp of his rival hastened the retreat of Conrad: the desertion of his independent vassals reduced him to his hereditary troops: and he borrowed some Greek vessels to execute by sea the pilgrimage of Palestine. Without studying the lessons of experience, or the nature of the war, the king of France advanced through the same country to a similar fate. The vanguard, which bore the royal banner and the oriflamme of St. Denys,[2] had doubled their march with rash and inconsiderate speed; and the rear, which the king commanded in person, no longer found their companions in the evening camp. In darkness and disorder, they were encompassed, assaulted,

---

[1] In the Epistles of Innocent III. (xiii. p. 184); and the History of Bohadin (p. 129, 130), see the views of a pope and a cadhi on this *singular* toleration.

[2] As counts of Vexin, the kings of France were the vassals and advocates of the monastery of St. Denys. The saint's peculiar banner, which they received from the abbot, was of a square form, and a red or *flaming* colour. The *oriflamme* appeared at the head of the French armies from the twelfth to the fifteenth century (Ducange sur Joinville, dissert. xviii. p. 244-253).

and overwhelmed by the innumerable host of Turks, who, in the
art of war, were superior to the Christians of the twelfth century.
Louis, who climbed a tree in the general discomfiture, was saved
by his own valour and the ignorance of his adversaries; and with
the dawn of day he escaped alive, but almost alone, to the camp
of the vanguard. But instead of pursuing his expedition by
land, he was rejoiced to shelter the relics of his army in the
friendly seaport of Satalia. From thence he embarked for
Antioch; but so penurious was the supply of Greek vessels that
they could only afford room for his knights and nobles; and
the plebeian crowd of infantry was left to perish at the foot of
the Pamphylian hills. The emperor and the king embraced and
wept at Jerusalem; their martial trains, the remnant of mighty
armies, were joined to the Christian powers of Syria, and a fruitless siege of Damascus was the final effort of the second crusade.
Conrad and Louis embarked for Europe with the personal fame
of piety and courage; but the Orientals had braved these potent
monarchs of the Franks, with whose names and military forces
they had been so often threatened.[1] Perhaps they had still
more to fear from the veteran genius of Frederic the First, who
in his youth had served in Asia under his uncle Conrad. Forty
campaigns in Germany and Italy had taught Barbarossa to
command; and his soldiers, even the princes of the empire, were
accustomed under his reign to obey. As soon as he lost sight
of Philadelphia and Laodicea, the last cities of the Greek frontier,
he plunged into the salt and barren desert, a land (says the
historian) of horror and tribulation.[2] During twenty days every
step of his fainting and sickly march was besieged by the
innumerable hordes of Turkmans,[3] whose numbers and fury
seemed after each defeat to multiply and inflame. The emperor
continued to struggle and to suffer; and such was the measure of
his calamities, that when he reached the gates of Iconium no
more than one thousand knights were able to serve on horseback.
By a sudden and resolute assault he defeated the guards, and
stormed the capital, of the sultan,[4] who humbly sued for pardon

[1] The original French histories of the second crusade are the Gesta
Ludovici VII., published in the fourth volume of Duchesne's collection.
The same volume contains many original letters of the king, of Suger his
minister, etc., the best documents of authentic history.

[2] Terram horroris et salsuginis, terram siccam, sterilem, inamœnam.
Anonym. Canis. p. 517. The emphatic language of a sufferer.

[3] Gens innumera, sylvestris, indomita, prædones sine ductore. The
sultan of Cogni might sincerely rejoice in their defeat. Anonym. Canis.
p. 517, 518.

[4] See in the anonymous writer in the Collection of Canisius, Tagino, and

and peace. The road was now open, and Frederic advanced in a career of triumph till he was unfortunately drowned in a petty torrent of Cilicia.[1] The remainder of his Germans was consumed by sickness and desertion; and the emperor's son expired with the greatest part of his Swabian vassals at the siege of Acre. Among the Latin heroes Godfrey of Bouillon and Frederic Barbarossa could alone achieve the passage of the Lesser Asia; yet even their success was a warning; and in the last and most experienced age of the crusades every nation preferred the sea to the toils and perils of an island expedition.[2]

The enthusiasm of the first crusade is a natural and simple event, while hope was fresh, danger untried, and enterprise congenial to the spirit of the times. But the obstinate perseverance of Europe may indeed excite our pity and admiration; that no instruction should have been drawn from constant and adverse experience; that the same confidence should have repeatedly grown from the same failures; that six succeeding generations should have rushed headlong down the precipice that was open before them; and that men of every condition should have staked their public and private fortunes on the desperate adventure of possessing or recovering a tombstone two thousand miles from their country. In a period of two centuries after the council of Clermont, each spring and summer produced a new emigration of pilgrim warriors for the defence of the Holy Land; but the seven great armaments or crusades were excited by some impending or recent calamity: the nations were moved by the authority of their pontiffs and the example of their kings: their zeal was kindled, and their reason was silenced, by the voice of their holy orators; and among these, Bernard,[3] the monk, or the

Bohadin (Vit. Saladin. p. 119, 120 [P. ii. c. 69]), the ambiguous conduct of Kilidge Arslan, sultan of Cogni, who hated and feared both Saladin and Frederic.

[1] The desire of comparing two great men has tempted many writers to drown Frederic in the river Cydnus, in which Alexander so imprudently bathed (Q. Curt. l. iii. c. 4, 5). But, from the march of the emperor, I rather judge that his Saleph is the Calycadnus, a stream of less fame, but of a longer course.

[2] Marinus Sanutus, A.D. 1321, lays it down as a precept, Quod stolus ecclesiæ per terram nullatenus est ducenda. He resolves, by the Divine aid, the objection, or rather exception, of the first crusade (Secreta Fidelium Crucis, l. ii. pars. ii. c. i. p. 37).

[3] The most authentic information of St. Bernard must be drawn from his own writings, published in a correct edition by Père Mabillon, and reprinted at Venice, 1750, in six volumes in folio. Whatever friendship could recollect, or superstition could add, is contained in the two lives, by his disciples, in the sixth volume: whatever learning and criticism could ascertain, may be found in the prefaces of the Benedictine editor.

saint, may claim the most honourable place. About eight years before the first conquest of Jerusalem he was born of a noble family in Burgundy; at the age of three-and-twenty he buried himself in the monastery of Citeaux, then in the primitive fervour of the institution; at the end of two years he led forth her third colony, or daughter, to the valley of Clairvaux [1] in Champagne; and was content, till the hour of his death, with the humble station of abbot of his own community. A philosophic age has abolished, with too liberal and indiscriminate disdain, the honours of these spiritual heroes. The meanest among them are distinguished by some energies of the mind; they were at least superior to their votaries and disciples; and, in the race of superstition, they attained the prize for which such numbers contended. In speech, in writing, in action, Bernard stood high above his rivals and contemporaries; his compositions are not devoid of wit and eloquence; and he seems to have preserved as much reason and humanity as may be reconciled with the character of a saint. In a secular life he would have shared the seventh part of a private inheritance; by a vow of poverty and penance, by closing his eyes against the visible world,[2] by the refusal of all ecclesiastical dignities, the abbot of Clairvaux became the oracle of Europe, and the founder of one hundred and sixty convents. Princes and pontiffs trembled at the freedom of his apostolical censures: France, England, and Milan consulted and obeyed his judgment in a schism of the church: the debt was repaid by the gratitude of Innocent the Second: and his successor, Eugenius the Third, was the friend and disciple of the holy Bernard. It was in the proclamation of the second crusade that he shone as the missionary and prophet of God, who called the nations to the defence of his holy sepulchre.[3]   At the parlia-

---

[1] Clairvaux, surnamed the Valley of Absynth, is situate among the woods near Bar sur Aube in Champagne. St. Bernard would blush at the pomp of the church and monastery; he would ask for the library, and I know not whether he would be much edified by a tun of 800 muids (914 1-7th hogsheads), which almost rivals that of Heidelberg (Mélanges tirés d'une Grande Bibliothèque, tom. xlvi. p. 15-20).

[2] The disciples of the saint (Vit. ima. l. iii. c. 2, p. 1232; Vit. iida. c. 16, No. 45, p. 1383) record a marvellous example of his pious apathy. Juxta lacum etiam Lausannensem totius diei itinere pergens, penitus non attendit aut se videre non vidit. Cum enim vespere facto de eodem lacû socii colloquerentur, interrogabat eos ubi lacus ille esset; et mirati sunt universi. To admire or despise St. Bernard as he ought, the reader, like myself, should have before the windows of his library the beauties of that incomparable landscape.

[3] Otho Frising. l. i. c. 4 [34]; Bernard. Epist. 363, ad Francos Orientales; Opp. tom. i. p. 328; Vit. ima. l. iii. c. 4, tom. vi. p. 1235.

[Bernard had a nobler object in view than merely preaching another

ment of Vezelay he spoke before the king; and Louis the Seventh, with his nobles, received their crosses from his hand. The abbot of Clairvaux then marched to the less easy conquest of the emperor Conrad: a phlegmatic people, ignorant of his language, was transported by the pathetic vehemence of his tone and gestures; and his progress, from Constance to Cologne, was the triumph of eloquence and zeal. Bernard applauds his own success in the depopulation of Europe; affirms that cities and castles were emptied of their inhabitants; and computes that only one man was left behind for the consolation of seven widows.[1] The blind fanatics were desirous of electing him for their general; but the example of the hermit Peter was before his eyes; and while he assured the crusaders of the divine favour, he prudently declined a military command, in which failure and victory would have been almost equally disgraceful to his character.[2] Yet, after the calamitous event, the abbot of Clairvaux was loudly accused as a false prophet, the author of the public and private mourning; his enemies exulted, his friends blushed, and his apology was slow and unsatisfactory. He justifies his obedience to the commands of the pope; expatiates on the mysterious ways of Providence; imputes the misfortunes of the pilgrims to their own sins; and modestly insinuates that his mission had been approved by signs and wonders.[3] Had the fact been certain, the argument would be decisive; and his faithful disciples, who enumerate twenty or thirty miracles in a day, appeal to the public assemblies of France and Germany, in which

crusade for the defence of the Holy Sepulchre. His design was to arrest the fierce and merciless persecution of the Jews which was preparing under the monk Radulph, to renew the frightful scenes which had preceded the first crusade, in the flourishing cities on the banks of the Rhine. The Jews have always acknowledged the Christian intervention of St. Bernard. —O. S.]

[1] Mandastis et obedivi . . . multiplicati sunt super numerum; vacuantur urbes et castella; et *pene* jam non inveniunt quem apprehendant septem mulieres unum virum; adeo ubique viduæ vivis remanent viris. Bernard, Epist. 247 [p. 246, ed. Bened.]. We must be careful not to construe *pene* as a substantive.

[2] Quis ego sum ut disponam acies, ut egrediar ante facies armatorum? aut quid tam remo⸱ᵘᵐ a professione meâ, [etiam] si vires, [suppeterent, etiam] si peritia [non deesset], etc. Epist. 256, tom. i. p. 259 [p. 258, ed. Bened.]. He speaks with contempt of the hermit Peter, vir quidam. Epist. 363.

[3] Sic [sed] dicunt forsitan isti, unde scimus quòd a Domino sermo egressus sit? Quæ signa tu facis ut credamus tibi? Non est quod ad ista ipse respondeam; parcendum verecundiæ meæ. Responde tu pro me, et pro te ipso, secundum quæ vidisti et audisti, et [aut certe] secundum quod te [tibi] inspiraverit Deus. Consolat. [De Considerat.] l. ii. c. 1; Opp. tom. ii. p. 421-423 [p. 417, ed. Bened.].

they were performed.[1] At the present hour such prodigies will not obtain credit beyond the precincts of Clairvaux; but in the preternatural cures of the blind, the lame, and the sick, who were presented to the man of God, it is impossible for us to ascertain the separate shares of accident, of fancy, of imposture, and of fiction.

Omnipotence itself cannot escape the murmurs of its discordant votaries; since the same dispensation which was applauded as a deliverance in Europe, was deplored, and perhaps arraigned, as a calamity in Asia. After the loss of Jerusalem the Syrian fugitives diffused their consternation and sorrow: Bagdad mourned in the dust; the cadhi Zeineddin of Damascus tore his beard in the caliph's presence; and the whole divan shed tears at his melancholy tale.[2] But the commanders of the faithful could only weep; they were themselves captives in the hands of the Turks: some temporal power was restored to the last age of the Abbassides; but their humble ambition was confined to Bagdad and the adjacent province. Their tyrants, the Seljukian sultans, had followed the common law of the Asiatic dynasties, the unceasing round of valour, greatness, discord, degeneracy, and decay: their spirit and power were unequal to the defence of religion; and, in his distant realm of Persia, the Christians were strangers to the name and the arms of Sangiar, the last hero of his race.[3] While the sultans were involved in the silken web of the harem, the pious task was undertaken by their slaves, the Atabeks,[4] a Turkish name, which, like the Byzantine patricians, may be translated by Father of the Prince. Ascansar, a valiant Turk, had been the favourite of Malek Shah, from whom he received the privilege of standing on the right hand of the throne; but, in the civil wars that ensued on the monarch's death, he lost his head and the government of Aleppo. His

---

[1] See the testimonies in Vita ima. l. iv. c. 5, 6; Opp. tom. vi. p. 1258-1261, l. vi. c. 1-17, p. 1286-1314.

[2] Abulmahasen apud De Guignes, Hist. des Huns, tom. ii. p. ii. p. 99.

[3] See his *article* in the Bibliothèque Orientale of D'Herbelot, and De Guignes, tom. ii. p. i. p. 230-261. Such was his valour, that he was styled the second Alexander; and such the extravagant love of his subjects, that they prayed for the sultan a year after his decease. Yet Sangiar might have been made prisoner by the Franks, as well as by the Uzes. He reigned near fifty years (A.D. 1103-1152), and was a munificent patron of Persian poetry.

[4] See the Chronology of the Atabeks of Irak and Syria, in De Guignes, tom. i. p. 254; and the reigns of Zenghi and Noureddin in the same writer (tom. ii. p. ii. p. 147-221), who uses the Arabic text of Benelathir, Ben Schounah, and Abulfeda; the Bibliothèque Orientale, under the articles *Atabeks* and *Noureddin*, and the Dynasties of Abulpharagius, p. 250-267, vers. Pocock.

domestic emirs persevered in their attachment to his son Zenghi, who proved his first arms against the Franks in the defeat of Antioch: thirty campaigns in the service of the caliph and sultan established his military fame; and he was invested with the command of Mosul, as the only champion that could avenge the cause of the prophet. The public hope was not disappointed: after a siege of twenty-five days he stormed the city of Edessa, and recovered from the Franks their conquests beyond the Euphrates:[1] the martial tribes of Curdistan were subdued by the independent sovereign of Mosul and Aleppo: his soldiers were taught to behold the camp as their only country; they trusted to his liberality for their rewards; and their absent families were protected by the vigilance of Zenghi. At the head of these veterans his son Noureddin gradually united the Mohammedan powers, added the kingdom of Damascus to that of Aleppo, and waged a long and successful war against the Christians of Syria; he spread his ample reign from the Tigris to the Nile, and the Abbassides rewarded their faithful servant with all the titles and prerogatives of royalty. The Latins themselves were compelled to own the wisdom and courage, and even the justice and piety, of this implacable adversary.[2] In his life and government the holy warrior revived the zeal and simplicity of the first caliphs. Gold and silk were banished from his palace, the use of wine from his dominions; the public revenue was scrupulously applied to the public service; and the frugal household of Noureddin was maintained from his legitimate share of the spoil which he vested in the purchase of a private estate. His favourite sultana sighed for some female object of expense. " Alas," replied the king, " I fear God, and am no more than the treasurer of the Moslems. Their property I cannot alienate; but I still possess three shops in the city of Hems: these you may take; and these alone can I bestow." His chamber of justice was the terror of the great and the refuge of the poor. Some years after the sultan's death an oppressed subject called aloud in the

[1] William of Tyre (l. xvi. c. 4, 5, 7) describes the loss of Edessa, and the death of Zenghi. The corruption of his name into *Sanguin* afforded the Latins a comfortable allusion to his *sanguinary* character and end, fit sanguine sanguinolentus.

[2] Noradinus (says William of Tyre, l. xx. 33 [p. 995]) maximus nominis et fidei Christianæ persecutor; princeps tamen justus, vafer, providus, et secundum gentis suæ traditiones religiosus. To this Catholic witness we may add the primate of the Jacobites (Abulpharag. p. 267), quo non alter erat inter reges vitæ ratione magis laudabili, aut quæ pluribus justitiæ experimentis abundaret. The true praise of kings is after their death, and from the mouth of their enemies.

streets of Damascus, " O Noureddin, Noureddin, where art thou
now? Arise, arise, to pity and protect us!" A tumult was
apprehended, and a living tyrant blushed or trembled at the
name of a departed monarch.

By the arms of the Turks and Franks the Fatimites had been
deprived of Syria. In Egypt the decay of their character and
influence was still more essential. Yet they were still revered as
the descendants and successors of the prophet; they maintained
their invisible state in the palace of Cairo; and their person was
seldom violated by the profane eyes of subjects or strangers.
The Latin ambassadors [1] have described their own introduction
through a series of gloomy passages and glittering porticoes:
the scene was enlivened by the warbling of birds and the murmur
of fountains: it was enriched by a display of rich furniture and
rare animals; of the Imperial treasures, something was shown,
and much was supposed; and the long order of unfolding doors
was guarded by black soldiers and domestic eunuchs. The
sanctuary of the presence chamber was veiled with a curtain;
and the vizir, who conducted the ambassadors, laid aside his
scimitar, and prostrated himself three times on the ground;
the veil was then removed; and they beheld the commander of
the faithful, who signified his pleasure to the first slave of the
throne. But this slave was his master: the vizirs or sultans
had usurped the supreme administration of Egypt; the claims
of the rival candidates were decided by arms; and the name
of the most worthy, of the strongest, was inserted in the royal
patent of command. The factions of Dargham and Shawer
alternately expelled each other from the capital and country;
and the weaker side implored the dangerous protection of the
sultan of Damascus, or the king of Jerusalem, the perpetual
enemies of the sect and monarchy of the Fatimites. By his arms
and religion the Turk was most formidable; but the Frank, in
an easy direct march, could advance from Gaza to the Nile;
while the intermediate situation of his realm compelled the
troops of Noureddin to wheel round the skirts of Arabia, a long
and painful circuit, which exposed them to thirst, fatigue, and
the burning winds of the desert. The secret zeal and ambition
of the Turkish prince aspired to reign in Egypt under the name
of the Abbassides; but the restoration of the suppliant Shawer

---

[1] From the ambassador, William of Tyre (l. xix. c. 17, 18) describes the
palace of Cairo. In the caliph's treasure were found a pearl as large as a
pigeon's egg, a ruby weighing seventeen Egyptian drachms, an emerald a
palm and a half in length, and many vases of crystal and porcelain of
China (Renaudot, p. 536).

was the ostensible motive of the first expedition; and the success was intrusted to the emir Shiracouh, a valiant and veteran commander. Dargham was oppressed and slain; but the ingratitude, the jealousy, the just apprehensions, of his more fortunate rival, soon provoked him to invite the king of Jerusalem to deliver Egypt from his insolent benefactors. To this union the forces of Shiracouh were unequal: he relinquished the premature conquest; and the evacuation of Belbeis or Pelusium was the condition of his safe retreat. As the Turks defiled before the enemy, and their general closed the rear, with a vigilant eye, and a battle-axe in his hand, a Frank presumed to ask him if he were not afraid of an attack? "It is doubtless in your power to begin the attack," replied the intrepid emir; "but rest assured that not one of my soldiers will go to paradise till he has sent an infidel to hell." His report of the riches of the land, the effeminacy of the natives, and the disorders of the government, revived the hopes of Noureddin; the caliph of Bagdad applauded the pious design; and Shiracouh descended into Egypt a second time with twelve thousand Turks and eleven thousand Arabs. Yet his forces were still inferior to the confederate armies of the Franks and Saracens; and I can discern an unusual degree of military art in his passage of the Nile, his retreat into Thebais, his masterly evolutions in the battle of Babain, the surprise of Alexandria, and his marches and countermarches in the flats and valley of Egypt, from the tropic to the sea. His conduct was seconded by the courage of his troops, and on the eve of action a Mamaluke [1] exclaimed, "If we cannot wrest Egypt from the Christian dogs, why do we not renounce the honours and rewards of the sultan, and retire to labour with the peasants, or to spin with the females of the harem?" Yet, after all his efforts in the field,[2] after the obstinate defence of Alexandria [3] by his nephew Saladin, an honourable capitulation and retreat concluded the second enterprise of Siracouh; and Noureddin reserved his abilities for a third and more propitious

[1] *Mamluc*, plur. *Mamalic*, is defined by Pocock (Prolegom. ad Abulpharag. p. 7) and D'Herbelot (p. 545), servum emptitium, seu qui pretio numerato in domini possessionem cedit. They frequently occur in the wars of Saladin (Bohadin, p. 236, etc.); and it was only the *Bahartie* Mamalukes that were first introduced into Egypt by his descendants.
[2] Jacobus à Vitriaco (p. 1116) gives the king of Jerusalem no more than 370 knights. Both the Franks and the Moslems report the superior numbers of the enemy—a difference which may be solved by counting or omitting the unwarlike Egyptians.
[3] It was the Alexandria of the Arabs, a middle term in extent and riches between the period of the Greeks and Romans and that of the Turks (Savary, Lettres sur l'Egypte, tom. i. p. 25, 26).

occasion. It was soon offered by the ambition and avarice of Amalric or Amaury, king of Jerusalem, who had imbibed the pernicious maxim that no faith should be kept with the enemies of God. A religious warrior, the great master of the hospital, encouraged him to proceed; the emperor of Constantinople either gave, or promised, a fleet to act with the armies of Syria; and the perfidious Christian, unsatisfied with spoil and subsidy, aspired to the conquest of Egypt. In this emergency the Moslems turned their eyes towards the sultan of Damascus; the vizir, whom danger encompassed on all sides, yielded to their unanimous wishes; and Noureddin seemed to be tempted by the fair offer of one third of the revenue of the kingdom. The Franks were already at the gates of Cairo; but the suburbs, the old city, were burnt on their approach; they were deceived by an insidious negotiation, and their vessels were unable to surmount the barriers of the Nile. They prudently declined a contest with the Turks in the midst of a hostile country; and Amaury retired into Palestine with the shame and reproach that always adhere to unsuccessful injustice. After this deliverance, Shiracouh was invested with a robe of honour, which he soon stained with the blood of the unfortunate Shawer. For a while the Turkish emirs condescended to hold the office of vizir; but this foreign conquest precipitated the fall of the Fatimites themselves; and the bloodless change was accomplished by a message and a word. The caliphs had been degraded by their own weakness and the tyranny of the vizirs: their subjects blushed when the descendant and successor of the prophet presented his naked hand to the rude gripe of a Latin ambassador; they wept when he sent the hair of his women, a sad emblem of their grief and terror, to excite the pity of the sultan of Damascus. By the command of Noureddin, and the sentence of the doctors, the holy names of Abubeker, Omar, and Othman were solemnly restored: the caliph Mosthadi, of Bagdad, was acknowledged in the public prayers as the true commander of the faithful; and the green livery of the sons of Ali was exchanged for the black colour of the Abbassides. The last of his race, the caliph Adhed, who survived only ten days, expired in happy ignorance of his fate: his treasures secured the loyalty of the soldiers, and silenced the murmurs of the sectaries; and in all subsequent revolutions Egypt has never departed from the orthodox tradition of the Moslems.[1]

[1] For this great revolution of Egypt, see William of Tyre (l. xix. 5, 6, 7, 12-31; xx. 5-12), Bohadin (in Vit. Saladin. p. 30-39), Abulfeda (in

The hilly country beyond the Tigris is occupied by the pastoral tribes of the Curds; [1] a people hardy, strong, savage, impatient of the yoke, addicted to rapine, and tenacious of the government of their national chiefs. The resemblance of name, situation, and manners, seems to identify them with the Carduchians of the Greeks; [2] and they still defend against the Ottoman Porte the antique freedom which they asserted against the successors of Cyrus. Poverty and ambition prompted them to embrace the profession of mercenary soldiers: the service of his father and uncle prepared the reign of the great Saladin; [3] and the son of Job or Ayub, a simple Curd, magnanimously smiled at his pedigree, which flattery deduced from the Arabian caliphs. [4] So unconscious was Noureddin of the impending ruin of his house, that he constrained the reluctant youth to follow his uncle Shiracouh into Egypt: his military character was established by the defence of Alexandria; and if we may believe the Latins, he solicited and obtained from the Christian general the *profane* honours of knighthood. [5] On the death of Shiracouh, the office of grand vizir was bestowed on Saladin, as the youngest and least powerful of the emirs; but with the advice of his father, whom he invited to Cairo, his genius obtained the ascendant over his equals, and attached the army to his person and interest. While Noureddin lived, these ambitious Curds were the most humble of his slaves; and the indiscreet murmurs of the divan

Excerpt. Schultens, p. 1-12), D'Herbelot (Biblioth. Orient. *Adhed, Fathemah*, but very incorrect), Renaudot (Hist. Patriarch. Alex. p. 522-525, 532-537), Vertot (Hist. des Chevaliers de Malthe, tom. i. p. 141-163, in 4to), and M. de Guignes (tom. ii. p. ii. p. 185-215).

[1] For the Curds, see De Guignes, tom. i. p. 416, 417; the Index Geographicus of Schultens; and Tavernier, Voyages, p. i. p. 308, 309. The Ayoubites descended from the tribe of the Rawadiæi, one of the noblest; but as *they* were infected with the heresy of the Metempsychosis, the orthodox sultans insinuated that their descent was only on the mother's side, and that their ancestor was a stranger who settled among the Curds.

[2] See the fourth book of the Anabasis of Xenophon. The ten thousand suffered more from the arrows of the free Carduchians than from the splendid weakness of the Great King.

[3] We are indebted to the Professor Schultens (Lugd. Bat. 1755, in folio) for the richest and most authentic materials, a Life of Saladin by his friend and minister the Cadhi Bohadin, and copious extracts from the history of his kinsman the prince Abulfeda of Hamah. To these we may add the article of *Salaheddin* in the Bibliothèque Orientale, and all that may be gleaned from the Dynasties of Abulpharagius.

[4] Since Abulfeda was himself an Ayoubite, he may share the praise for imitating, at least tacitly, the modesty of the founder.

[5] Hist. Hierosol. in the Gesta Dei per Francos, p. 1152. A similar example may be found in Joinville (p. 42, édition du Louvre); but the pious St. Louis refused to dignify infidels with the order of Christian knighthood (Ducange, Observations, p. 70).

were silenced by the prudent Ayub, who loudly protested that at the command of the sultan he himself would lead his son in chains to the foot of the throne. "Such language," he added in private, "was prudent and proper in an assembly of your rivals; but we are now above fear and obedience; and the threats of Noureddin shall not extort the tribute of a sugar-cane." His seasonable death relieved them from the odious and doubtful conflict: his son, a minor of eleven years of age, was left for a while to the emirs of Damascus; and the new lord of Egypt was decorated by the caliph with every title [1] that could sanctify his usurpation in the eyes of the people. Nor was Saladin long content with the possession of Egypt: he despoiled the Christians of Jerusalem, and the Atabeks of Damascus, Aleppo, and Diarbekir: Mecca and Medina acknowledged him for their temporal protector: his brother subdued the distant regions of Yemen, or the happy Arabia; and at the hour of his death his empire was spread from the African Tripoli to the Tigris, and from the Indian Ocean to the mountains of Armenia. In the judgment of his character, the reproaches of treason and ingratitude strike forcibly on *our* minds, impressed, as they are, with the principle and experience of law and loyalty. But his ambition may in some measure be excused by the revolutions of Asia,[2] which had erased every notion of legitimate succession; by the recent example of the Atabeks themselves; by his reverence to the son of his benefactor; his humane and generous behaviour to the collateral branches; by *their* incapacity and *his* merit; by the approbation of the caliph, the sole source of all legitimate power; and, above all, by the wishes and interest of the people, whose happiness is the first object of government. In *his* virtues, and in those of his patron, they admired the singular union of the hero and the saint; for both Noureddin and Saladin are ranked among the Mohammedan saints; and the constant meditation of the holy war appears to have shed a serious and sober colour over their lives and actions. The youth of the latter [3] was addicted to wine and women; but his aspiring spirit soon renounced the temptations of pleasure for the graver follies of fame and dominion: the garment of Saladin was a

---

[1] In these Arabic titles *religionis* must always be understood; *Noureddin*, lumen r.; *Ezzodin*, decus; *Amadoddin*, columen: our hero's proper name was Joseph, and he was styled *Salahoddin*, salus; *Al Malichus*, *Al Nasirus*, rex defensor; *Abu Modaffir*, pater victoriæ. Schultens, Præfat.

[2] Abulfeda, who descended from a brother of Saladin, observes, from many examples, that the founders of dynasties took the guilt for themselves, and left the reward to their innocent collaterals (Excerpt. p. 10).

[3] See his life and character in Renaudot, p. 537-548.

coarse woollen; water was his only drink; and, while he emulated the temperance, he surpassed the chastity, of his Arabian prophet. Both in faith and practice he was a rigid Musulman; he ever deplored that the defence of religion had not allowed him to accomplish the pilgrimage of Mecca; but at the stated hours, five times each day, the sultan devoutly prayed with his brethren: the involuntary omission of fasting was scrupulously repaid; and his perusal of the Koran, on horseback between the approaching armies, may be quoted as a proof, however ostentatious, of piety and courage.[1] The superstitious doctrine of the sect of Shafei was the only study that he deigned to encourage: the poets were safe in his contempt; but all profane science was the object of his aversion; and a philosopher who had vented some speculative novelties was seized and strangled by the command of the royal saint. The justice of his divan was accessible to the meanest suppliant against himself and his ministers; and it was only for a kingdom that Saladin would deviate from the rule of equity. While the descendants of Seljuk and Zenghi held his stirrup and smoothed his garments, he was affable and patient with the meanest of his servants. So boundless was his liberality that he distributed twelve thousand horses at the siege of Acre; and at the time of his death no more than forty-seven drachms of silver and one piece of gold coin were found in the treasury; yet, in a martial reign, the tributes were diminished, and the wealthy citizens enjoyed, without fear or danger, the fruits of their industry. Egypt, Syria, and Arabia were adorned by the royal foundations of hospitals, colleges, and mosques; and Cairo was fortified with a wall and citadel; but his works were consecrated to public use;[2] nor did the sultan indulge himself in a garden or palace of private luxury. In a fanatic age, himself a fanatic, the genuine virtues of Saladin commanded the esteem of the Christians: the emperor of Germany gloried in his friendship;[3] the Greek emperor solicited his alliance;[4] and the conquest of Jerusalem diffused, and perhaps magnified, his fame both in the East and West.

During its short existence the kingdom of Jerusalem[5] was

[1] His civil and religious virtues are celebrated in the first chapter of Bohadin (p. 4-30), himself an eye-witness and an honest bigot.

[2] In many works, particularly Joseph's well in the castle of Cairo, the sultan and the patriarch have been confounded by the ignorance of natives and travellers.

[3] Anonym. Canisii, tom. iii. p. ii. p. 504.   [4] Bohadin, p. 129, 130.

[5] For the Latin kingdom of Jerusalem, see William of Tyre, from the ninth to the twenty-second book; Jacob. à Vitriaco, Hist. Hierosolym. l. i.; and Sanutus, Secreta Fidelium Crucis, l. iii. p. vi. vii. viii. ix.

supported by the discord of the Turks and Saracens; and both the Fatimite caliphs and the sultans of Damascus were tempted to sacrifice the cause of their religion to the meaner considerations of private and present advantage. But the powers of Egypt, Syria, and Arabia were now united by a hero whom nature and fortune had armed against the Christians. All without now bore the most threatening aspect; and all was feeble and hollow in the internal state of Jerusalem. After the two first Baldwins, the brother and cousin of Godfrey of Bouillon, the sceptre devolved by female succession to Melisenda, daughter of the second Baldwin, and her husband Fulk, count of Anjou, the father, by a former marriage, of our English Plantagenets. Their two sons, Baldwin the Third and Amaury, waged a strenuous, and not unsuccessful, war against the infidels; but the son of Amaury, Baldwin the Fourth, was deprived, by the leprosy, a gift of the crusades, of the faculties both of mind and body. His sister Sybilla, the mother of Baldwin the Fifth, was his natural heiress: after the suspicious death of her child, she crowned her second husband, Guy of Lusignan, a prince of a handsome person, but of such base renown that his own brother Jeffrey was heard to exclaim, " Since they have made *him* a king, surely they would have made *me* a god!" The choice was generally blamed; and the most powerful vassal, Raymond count of Tripoli, who had been excluded from the succession and regency, entertained an implacable hatred against the king, and exposed his honour and conscience to the temptations of the sultan. Such were the guardians of the holy city; a leper, a child, a woman, a coward, and a traitor: yet its fate was delayed twelve years by some supplies from Europe, by the valour of the military orders, and by the distant or domestic avocations of their great enemy. At length, on every side, the sinking state was encircled and pressed by a hostile line; and the truce was violated by the Franks, whose existence it protected. A soldier of fortune, Reginald of Châtillon, had seized a fortress on the edge of the desert, from whence he pillaged the caravans, insulted Mohammed, and threatened the cities of Mecca and Medina. Saladin condescended to complain; rejoiced in the denial of justice; and at the head of fourscore thousand horse and foot invaded the Holy Land. The choice of Tiberias for his first siege was suggested by the count of Tripoli, to whom it belonged; and the king of Jerusalem was persuaded to drain his garrison,[1] and to arm his people, for the relief of that important place.

---

[1] Templarii ut apes bombatant et Hospitalarii ut venti stridebant, et

By the advice of the perfidious Raymond the Christians were
betrayed into a camp destitute of water: he fled on the first
onset, with the curses of both nations:[1] Lusignan was overthrown, with the loss of thirty thousand men; and the wood of
the true cross, a dire misfortune! was left in the power of the
infidels. The royal captive was conducted to the tent of
Saladin; and as he fainted with thirst and terror, the generous
victor presented him with a cup of sherbet, cooled in snow,
without suffering his companion, Reginald of Châtillon, to
partake of this pledge of hospitality and pardon. "The person
and dignity of a king," said the sultan, "are sacred; but this
impious robber must instantly acknowledge the prophet, whom
he has blasphemed, or meet the death which he has so often
deserved." On the proud or conscientious refusal of the
Christian warrior, Saladin struck him on the head with his
scimitar, and Reginald was despatched by the guards.[2] The
trembling Lusignan was sent to Damascus to an honourable
prison and speedy ransom; but the victory was stained by the
execution of two hundred and thirty knights of the hospital, the
intrepid champions and martyrs of their faith. The kingdom
was left without a head; and of the two grand masters of the
military orders, the one was slain and the other was a prisoner.
From all the cities, both of the sea-coast and the inland country,
the garrisons had been drawn away for this fatal field: Tyre and
Tripoli alone could escape the rapid inroad of Saladin; and three
months after the battle of Tiberias he appeared in arms before
the gates of Jerusalem.[3]

barones se exitio offerebant, et Turcopuli (the Christian light troops) semet
ipsi in ignem injiciebant (Ispahani de Expugnatione Kudsiticâ, p. 18, apud
Schultens)—a specimen of Arabian eloquence somewhat different from
the style of Xenophon!

[The number of Saladin's army has been greatly exaggerated. Some
authorities make it 80,000, others, such as Oman in *The Art of War*, at
70,000. But if he had 25,000 men he had as many as he could find a
commissariat able to support. That was always the chief difficulty in
Syrian campaigns in the Middle Ages. Cf. Col. Moncrieff's tractate, *Commissariat in the Middle Ages*.—O. S.]

[1] The Latins affirm, the Arabians insinuate, the treason of Raymond;
but, had he really embraced their religion, he would have been a saint and
a hero in the eyes of the latter.

[2] Renaud, Reginald, or Arnold de Châtillon, is celebrated by the Latins
in his life and death; but the circumstances of the latter are more distinctly related by Bohadin and Abulfeda; and Joinville (Hist. de St.
Louis, p. 70) alludes to the practice of Saladin, of never putting to death a
prisoner who had tasted his bread and salt. Some of the companions of
Arnold had been slaughtered, and almost sacrificed, in a valley of Mecca,
ubi sacrificia mactantur (Abulfeda, p. 32).

[3] Vertot, who well describes the loss of the kingdom and city (Hist. des
Chevaliers de Malthe, tom. i. l. ii. p. 226-278), inserts two original epistles
of a knight templar.

He might expect that the siege of a city so venerable on earth and in heaven, so interesting to Europe and Asia, would rekindle the last sparks of enthusiasm; and that, of sixty thousand Christians, every man would be a soldier, and every soldier a candidate for martyrdom. But queen Sybilla trembled for herself and her captive husband; and the barons and knights, who had escaped from the sword and chains of the Turks, displayed the same factious and selfish spirit in the public ruin. The most numerous portion of the inhabitants was composed of the Greek and Oriental Christians, whom experience had taught to prefer the Mohammedan before the Latin yoke;[1] and the holy sepulchre attracted a base and needy crowd, without arms or courage, who subsisted only on the charity of the pilgrims. Some feeble and hasty efforts were made for the defence of Jerusalem: but in the space of fourteen days a victorious army drove back the sallies of the besieged, planted their engines, opened the wall to the breadth of fifteen cubits, applied their scaling-ladders, and erected on the breach twelve banners of the prophet and the sultan. It was in vain that a barefoot procession of the queen, the women, and the monks, implored the Son of God to save his tomb and his inheritance from impious violation. Their sole hope was in the mercy of the conqueror, and to the first suppliant deputation that mercy was sternly denied. " He had sworn to avenge the patience and long-suffering of the Moslems; the hour of forgiveness was elapsed, and the moment was now arrived to expiate, in blood, the innocent blood which had been spilt by Godfrey and the first crusaders." But a desperate and successful struggle of the Franks admonished the sultan that his triumph was not yet secure; he listened with reverence to a solemn adjuration in the name of the common Father of mankind; and a sentiment of human sympathy mollified the rigour of fanaticism and conquest. He consented to accept the city and to spare the inhabitants. The Greek and Oriental Christians were permitted to live under his dominion; but it was stipulated that in forty days all the Franks and Latins should evacuate Jerusalem and be safely conducted to the sea-ports of Syria and Egypt; that ten pieces of gold should be paid for each man, five for each woman, and one for every child; and that those who were unable to purchase their freedom should be detained in perpetual slavery. Of some writers it is a favourite and invidious theme to compare the humanity of Saladin with the massacre of the first crusade. The difference would be

---

[1] Renaudot, Hist. Patriarch. Alex. p. 545.

merely personal; but we should not forget that the Christians
had offered to capitulate, and that the Mohammedans of Jerusalem
sustained the last extremities of an assault and storm. Justice
is indeed due to the fidelity with which the Turkish conqueror
fulfilled the conditions of the treaty; and he may be deservedly
praised for the glance of pity which he cast on the misery of the
vanquished. Instead of a rigorous exaction of his debt, he
accepted a sum of thirty thousand byzants for the ransom of
seven thousand poor; two or three thousand more were dismissed by his gratuitous clemency; and the number of slaves
was reduced to eleven or fourteen thousand persons. In his
interview with the queen, his words, and even his tears, suggested the kindest consolations: his liberal alms were distributed
among those who had been made orphans or widows by the
fortune of war; and while the knights of the hospital were in
arms against him, he allowed their more pious brethren to continue, during the term of a year, the care and service of the sick.
In these acts of mercy the virtue of Saladin deserves our admiration and love: he was above the necessity of dissimulation, and
his stern fanaticism would have prompted him to dissemble,
rather than to affect, this profane compassion for the enemies
of the Koran. After Jerusalem had been delivered from the
presence of the strangers, the sultan made his triumphant entry,
his banners waving in the wind, and to the harmony of martial
music. The great mosque of Omar, which had been converted
into a church, was again consecrated to one God and his prophet
Mohammed: the walls and pavement were purified with rose-
water; and a pulpit, the labour of Noureddin, was erected in the
sanctuary. But when the golden cross that glittered on the
dome was cast down and dragged through the streets, the Christians of every sect uttered a lamentable groan, which was
answered by the joyful shouts of the Moslems. In four ivory
chests the patriarch had collected the crosses, the images, the
vases, and the relics of the holy place; they were seized by the
conqueror, who was desirous of presenting the caliph with the
trophies of Christian idolatry. He was persuaded, however, to
intrust them to the patriarch and prince of Antioch; and the
pious pledge was redeemed by Richard of England, at the
expense of fifty-two thousand byzants of gold.[1]

[1] For the conquest of Jerusalem, Bohadin (p. 67-75 [P. ii. c. 35, 36]) and
Abulfeda (p. 40-43) are our Moslem witnesses. Of the Christian, Bernard
Thesaurarius (c. 151-167) is the most copious and authentic; see likewise
Matthew Paris (p. 120-124).

The nations might fear and hope the immediate and final
expulsion of the Latins from Syria, which was yet delayed above
a century after the death of Saladin.[1]   In the career of victory
he was first checked by the resistance of Tyre; the troops and
garrisons, which had capitulated, were imprudently conducted
to the same port: their numbers were adequate to the defence
of the place; and the arrival of Conrad of Montferrat inspired
the disorderly crowd with confidence and union.   His father,
a venerable pilgrim, had been made prisoner in the battle of
Tiberias; but that disaster was unknown in Italy and Greece,
when the son was urged by ambition and piety to visit the inheritance of his royal nephew, the infant Baldwin.   The view of the
Turkish banners warned him from the hostile coast of Jaffa;
and Conrad was unanimously hailed as the prince and champion
of Tyre, which was already besieged by the conqueror of Jerusalem.   The firmness of his zeal, and perhaps his knowledge of
a generous foe, enabled him to brave the threats of the sultan,
and to declare that, should his aged parent be exposed before
the walls, he himself would discharge the first arrow, and glory
in his descent from a Christian martyr.[2]   The Egyptian fleet
was allowed to enter the harbour of Tyre; but the chain was
suddenly drawn, and five galleys were either sunk or taken: a
thousand Turks were slain in a sally; and Saladin, after burning
his engines, concluded a glorious campaign by a disgraceful
retreat to Damascus.   He was soon assailed by a more formidable tempest.   The pathetic narratives, and even the
pictures, that represented in lively colours the servitude and
profanation of Jerusalem, awakened the torpid sensibility of
Europe: the emperor Frederic Barbarossa, and the kings of
France and England, assumed the cross; and the tardy magnitude of their armaments was anticipated by the maritime states
of the Mediterranean and the Ocean.   The skilful and provident
Italians first embarked in the ships of Genoa, Pisa, and Venice.
They were speedily followed by the most eager pilgrims of
France, Normandy, and the Western Isles.   The powerful
succour of Flanders, Frise, and Denmark filled near a hundred
vessels; and the Northern warriors were distinguished in the

[1] The sieges of Tyre and Acre are most copiously described by Bernard
Thesaurarius (de Acquisitione Terræ Sanctæ, c. 167-179), the author of the
Historia Hierosolymitana (p. 1150-1172, in Bongarsius), Abulfeda (p. 43-
50), and Bohadin (p. 75-179).
[2] I have followed a moderate and probable representation of the fact:
by Vertot, who adopts without reluctance a romantic tale, the old marquis
is actually exposed to the darts of the besieged.

field by a lofty stature and a ponderous battle-axe.[1] Their increasing multitudes could no longer be confined within the walls of Tyre, or remain obedient to the voice of Conrad. They pitied the misfortunes and revered the dignity of Lusignan, who was released from prison, perhaps to divide the army of the Franks. He proposed the recovery of Ptolemais, or Acre, thirty miles to the south of Tyre; and the place was first invested by two thousand horse and thirty thousand foot under his nominal command. I shall not expatiate on the story of this memorable siege, which lasted near two years, and consumed, in a narrow space, the forces of Europe and Asia. Never did the flame of enthusiasm burn with fiercer and more destructive rage; nor could the true believers, a common appellation, who consecrated their own martyrs, refuse some applause to the mistaken zeal and courage of their adversaries. At the sound of the holy trumpet the Moslems of Egypt, Syria, Arabia, and the Oriental provinces assembled under the servant of the prophet:[2] his camp was pitched and removed within a few miles of Acre; and he laboured night and day for the relief of his brethren and the annoyance of the Franks. Nine battles, not unworthy of the name, were fought in the neighbourhood of Mount Carmel, with such vicissitude of fortune, that in one attack the sultan forced his way into the city; that in one sally the Christians penetrated to the royal tent. By the means of divers and pigeons a regular correspondence was maintained with the besieged; and, as often as the sea was left open, the exhausted garrison was withdrawn, and a fresh supply was poured into the place. The Latin camp was thinned by famine, the sword, and the climate; but the tents of the dead were replenished with new pilgrims, who exaggerated the strength and speed of their approaching countrymen. The vulgar was astonished by the report that the pope himself, with an innumerable crusade, was advanced as far as Constantinople. The march of the emperor filled the East with more serious alarms: the obstacles which he encountered in Asia, and perhaps in Greece, were raised by the policy of Saladin: his joy on the death of Barbarossa was measured by his esteem; and the

---

[1] Northmanni et Gothi, et cæteri populi insularum quæ inter occidentem et septemtrionem sitæ sunt, gentes bellicosæ, corporis proceri, mortis intrepidæ, bipennibus armatæ, navibus rotundis, quæ Ysnachiæ dicuntur, advectæ.

[2] The historian of Jerusalem (p. 1168) adds the nations of the East from the Tigris to India, and the swarthy tribes of Moors and Getulians, so that Asia and Africa fought against Europe.

Christians were rather dismayed than encouraged at the sight of the duke of Swabia and his way-worn remnant of five thousand Germans. At length, in the spring of the second year, the royal fleets of France and England cast anchor in the bay of Acre, and the siege was more vigorously prosecuted by the youthful emulation of the two kings, Philip Augustus and Richard Plantagenet. After every resource had been tried, and every hope was exhausted, the defenders of Acre submitted to their fate; a capitulation was granted, but their lives and liberties were taxed at the hard conditions of a ransom of two hundred thousand pieces of gold, the deliverance of one hundred nobles and fifteen hundred inferior captives, and the restoration of the wood of the holy cross. Some doubts in the agreement, and some delay in the execution, rekindled the fury of the Franks, and three thousand Moslems, almost in the sultan's view, were beheaded by the command of the sanguinary Richard.[1] By the conquest of Acre the Latin powers acquired a strong town and a convenient harbour; but the advantage was most dearly purchased. The minister and historian of Saladin computes, from the report of the enemy, that their numbers, at different periods, amounted to five or six hundred thousand; that more than one hundred thousand Christians were slain; that a far greater number was lost by disease or shipwreck; and that a small portion of this mighty host could return in safety to their native countries.[2]

Philip Augustus and Richard the First are the only kings of France and England who have fought under the same banners; but the holy service in which they were enlisted was incessantly disturbed by their national jealousy; and the two factions which they protected in Palestine were more averse to each other than to the common enemy. In the eyes of the Orientals the French monarch was superior in dignity and power; and, in the emperor's absence, the Latins revered him as their temporal chief.[3] His exploits were not adequate to his fame. Philip was

---

[1] Bohadin, p. 183 [P. ii. c. 115]; and this massacre is neither denied nor blamed by the Christian historians. Alacriter jussa complentes (the English soldiers), says Galfridus à Vinesauf (l. iv. c. 4, p. 346), who fixes at 2700 the number of victims, who are multiplied to 5000 by Roger Hoveden (p. 697, 698). The humanity or avarice of Philip Augustus was persuaded to ransom his prisoners (Jacob à Vitriaco, l. i. c. 99, p. 1122).

[2] Bohadin, p. 14. He quotes the judgment of Balianus and the prince of Sidon, and adds, ex illo mundo quasi hominum paucissimi redierunt. Among the Christians who died before St. John d'Acre, I find the English names of De Ferrers earl of Derby (Dugdale, Baronage, part i. p. 260), Mowbray (idem. p. 124), De Mandevil, De Fiennes, St. John, Scrope, Pigot, Talbot, etc.

[3] Magnus hic apud eos, interque reges eorum tum virtute, tum majestate

brave, but the statesman predominated in his character; he was soon weary of sacrificing his health and interest on a barren coast: the surrender of Acre became the signal of his departure; nor could he justify this unpopular desertion by leaving the duke of Burgundy, with five hundred knights and ten thousand foot, for the service of the Holy Land. The king of England, though inferior in dignity, surpassed his rival in wealth and military renown;[1] and if heroism be confined to brutal and ferocious valour, Richard Plantagenet will stand high among the heroes of the age. The memory of *Cœur de Lion*, of the lion-hearted prince, was long dear and glorious to his English subjects; and at the distance of sixty years it was celebrated in proverbial sayings by the grandsons of the Turks and Saracens against whom he had fought: his tremendous name was employed by the Syrian mothers to silence their infants; and if a horse suddenly started from the way, his rider was wont to exclaim, " Dost thou think king Richard is in that bush?"[2] His cruelty to the Mohammedans was the effect of temper and zeal; but I cannot believe that a soldier, so free and fearless in the use of his lance, would have descended to whet a dagger against his valiant brother Conrad of Montferrat, who was slain at Tyre by some secret assassins.[3] After the surrender of Acre, and the departure of Philip, the king of England led the crusaders to the recovery of the sea-coast; and the cities of Cæsarea and Jaffa were added to the fragments of the kingdom of Lusignan. A march of one hundred miles from Acre to Ascalon was a great and perpetual battle of eleven days. In the disorder of his troops, Saladin remained on the field with seventeen guards, without lowering his standard, or suspending the sound of his brazen kettle-drum: he again rallied and renewed the charge; and his preachers or heralds called aloud on the *Unitarians* manfully to stand up against the Christian idolaters. But the

eminens . . . summus rerum arbiter (Bohadin, p. 159 [P. ii. c. 95]). He does not seem to have known the names either of Philip or Richard.

[1] Rex Angliæ, præstrenuus . . . rege Gallorum minor apud eos censebatur ratione regni atque dignitatis; sed tum divitiis florentior, tum bellicâ virtute multo erat celebrior (Bohadin, p. 161 [P. ii. c. 97]). A stranger might admire those riches; the national historians will tell with what lawless and wasteful oppression they were collected.

[2] Joinville, p. 17. Cuides-tu que ce soit le roi Richart?

[3] Yet he was guilty in the opinion of the Moslems, who attest the confession of the assassins that they were sent by the king of England (Bohadin, p. 225 [P. ii. c. 144]); and his only defence is an absurd and palpable forgery (Hist. de l'Académie des Inscriptions, tom. xvi. p. 155-163), a pretended letter from the prince of the assassins, the Sheich, or old man of the mountain, who justified Richard, by assuming to himself the guilt or merit of the murder.

progress of these idolaters was irresistible; and it was only by demolishing the walls and buildings of Ascalon that the sultan could prevent them from occupying an important fortress on the confines of Egypt. During a severe winter the armies slept; but in the spring the Franks advanced within a day's march of Jerusalem, under the leading standard of the English king; and his active spirit intercepted a convoy, or caravan, of seven thousand camels. Saladin [1] had fixed his station in the holy city; but the city was struck with consternation and discord: he fasted; he prayed; he preached; he offered to share the dangers of the siege; but his Mamalukes, who remembered the fate of their companions at Acre, pressed the sultan, with loyal or seditious clamours, to reserve *his* person and *their* courage for the future defence of the religion and empire.[2] The Moslems were delivered by the sudden, or, as they deemed, the miraculous, retreat of the Christians;[3] and the laurels of Richard were blasted by the prudence, or envy, of his companions. The hero, ascending a hill, and veiling his face, exclaimed with an indignant voice, " Those who are unwilling to rescue, are unworthy to view, the sepulchre of Christ! " After his return to Acre, on the news that Jaffa was surprised by the sultan, he sailed with some merchant vessels, and leaped foremost on the beach: the castle was relieved by his presence; and sixty thousand Turks and Saracens fled before his arms. The discovery of his weakness provoked them to return in the morning; and they found him carelessly encamped before the gates with only seventeen knights and three hundred archers. Without counting their numbers, he sustained their charge; and we learn from the evidence of his enemies that the king of England, grasping his lance, rode furiously along their front, from the right to the left wing, without meeting an adversary who dared to encounter his career.[4] Am I writing the history of Orlando or Amadis?

[1] See the distress and pious firmness of Saladin, as they are described by Bohadin (p. 7-9, 235-237), who himself harangued the defenders of Jerusalem; their fears were not unknown to the enemy (Jacob. à Vitriaco, l. i. c. 100, p. 1123; Vinisauf, l. v. c. 50, p. 399).

[2] Yet, unless the sultan, or an Ayoubite prince, remained in Jerusalem, nec Curdi Turcis, nec Turci essent obtemperaturi Curdis (Bohadin, p. 236 [P. ii. c. 156]). He draws aside a corner of the political curtain.

[3] Bohadin (p. 237), and even Jeffrey de Vinisauf (l. vi. c. 1-8, p. 403-409), ascribe the retreat to Richard himself; and Jacobus à Vitriaco observes that, in his impatience to depart, in alterum virum mutatus est (p. 1123). Yet Joinville, a French knight, accuses the envy of Hugh duke of Burgundy (p. 116), without supposing, like Matthew Paris, that he was bribed by Saladin.

[4] The expeditions to Ascalon, Jerusalem, and Jaffa, are related by Bohadin (p. 184-249) and Abulfeda (p. 51, 52). The author of the Itine-

During these hostilities a languid and tedious negotiation [1] between the Franks and Moslems was started, and continued, and broken, and again resumed, and again broken. Some acts of royal courtesy, the gift of snow and fruit, the exchange of Norway hawks and Arabian horses, softened the asperity of religious war; from the vicissitude of success the monarchs might learn to suspect that Heaven was neuter in the quarrel: nor, after the trial of each other, could either hope for a decisive victory.[2] The health both of Richard and Saladin appeared to be in a declining state; and they respectively suffered the evils of distant and domestic warfare: Plantagenet was impatient to punish a perfidious rival who had invaded Normandy in his absence; and the indefatigable sultan was subdued by the cries of the people, who was the victim, and of the soldiers, who were the instruments, of his martial zeal. The first demands of the king of England were the restitution of Jerusalem, Palestine, and the true cross; and he firmly declared that himself and his brother pilgrims would end their lives in the pious labour, rather than return to Europe with ignomiry and remorse. But the conscience of Saladin refused, without some weighty compensation, to restore the idols, or promote the idolatry, of the Christians: he asserted, with equal firmness, his religious and civil claim to the sovereignty of Palestine; descanted on the importance and sanctity of Jerusalem; and rejected all terms of the establishment, or partition, of the Latins. The marriage which Richard proposed, of his sister with the sultan's brother, was defeated by the difference of faith: the princess abhorred the embraces of a Turk; and Adel, or Saphadin, would not easily renounce a plurality of wives. A personal interview was declined by Saladin, who alleged their mutual ignorance of each other's language; and the negotiation was managed with much art and delay by their interpreters and envoys. The final agreement

rary, or the monk of St. Alban's, cannot exaggerate the cadhi's account of the prowess of Richard (Vinisauf, l. vi. c. 14-24, p. 412-421; Hist. Major, p. 137-143); and on the whole of this war there is a marvellous agreement between the Christian and Mohammedan writers, who mutually praise the virtues of their enemies.

[1] See the progress of negotiation and hostility in Bohadin (p. 207-260), who was himself an actor in the treaty. Richard declared his intention of returning with new armies to the conquest of the Holy Land; and Saladin answered the menace with a civil compliment (Vinisauf, l. vi. c. 28, p. 423).

[2] The most copious and original account of this holy war is Galfridi à Vinisauf, Itinerarium Regis Anglorum Richardi et aliorum in Terram Hierosolymorum, in six books, published in the second volume of Gale's Scriptores Hist. Anglicanæ (p. 247-429). Roger Hoveden and Matthew Paris afford likewise many valuable materials; and the former describes with accuracy the discipline and navigation of the English fleet.

was equally disapproved by the zealots of both parties, by the Roman pontiff and the caliph of Bagdad. It was stipulated that Jerusalem and the holy sepulchre should be open, without tribute or vexation, to the pilgrimage of the Latin Christians; that, after the demolition of Ascalon, they should inclusively possess the sea-coast from Jaffa to Tyre; that the count of Tripoli and the prince of Antioch should be comprised in the truce; and that, during three years and three months, all hostilities should cease. The principal chiefs of the two armies swore to the observance of the treaty; but the monarchs were satisfied with giving their word and their right hand; and the royal majesty was excused from an oath, which always implies some suspicion of falsehood and dishonour. Richard embarked for Europe, to seek a long captivity and a premature grave; and the space of a few months concluded the life and glories of Saladin. The Orientals described his edifying death, which happened at Damascus; but they seem ignorant of the equal distribution of his alms among the three religions,[1] or of the display of a shroud, instead of a standard, to admonish the East of the instability of human greatness. The unity of empire was dissolved by his death; his sons were oppressed by the stronger arm of their uncle Saphadin; the hostile interests of the sultans of Egypt, Damascus, and Aleppo [2] were again revived; and the Franks or Latins stood, and breathed, and hoped, in their fortresses along the Syrian coast.

The noblest monument of a conqueror's fame, and of the terror which he inspired, is the Saladine tenth, a general tax, which was imposed on the laity and even the clergy of the Latin church for the service of the holy war. The practice was too lucrative to expire with the occasion; and this tribute became the foundation of all the tithes and tenths on ecclesiastical benefices which have been granted by the Roman pontiffs to Catholic sovereigns, or reserved for the immediate use of the apostolic see.[3] This pecuniary emolument must have tended to increase the interest of the popes in the recovery of Palestine:

---

[1] Even Vertot (tom. i. p. 251) adopts the foolish notion of the indifference of Saladin, who professed the Koran with his last breath.

[2] See the succession of the Ayoubites, in Abulpharagius (Dynast. p. 277, etc.), and the tables of M. de Guignes, l'Art de Vérifier les Dates, and the Bibliothèque Orientale.

[3] Thomassin (Discipline de l'Eglise, tom. iii. p. 311-374) has copiously treated of the origin, abuses, and restrictions of these *tenths*. A theory was started, but not pursued, that they were rightfully due to the pope, a tenth of the Levite's tenth to the high priest (Selden on Tithes; see his Works, vol. iii. p. ii. p. 1083).

after the death of Saladin they preached the crusade by their epistles, their legates, and their missionaries; and the accomplishment of the pious work might have been expected from the zeal and talents of Innocent the Third.[1] Under that young and ambitious priest the successors of St. Peter attained the full meridian of their greatness: and in a reign of eighteen years he exercised a despotic command over the emperors and kings, whom he raised and deposed; over the nations, whom an interdict of months or years deprived, for the offence of their rulers, of the exercise of Christian worship. In the council of the Lateran he acted as the ecclesiastical, almost as the temporal, sovereign of the East and West. It was at the feet of his legate that John of England surrendered his crown; and Innocent may boast of the two most signal triumphs over sense and humanity, the establishment of transubstantiation and the origin of the inquisition. At his voice two crusades, the fourth and the fifth, were undertaken; but, except a king of Hungary, the princes of the second order were at the head of the pilgrims; the forces were inadequate to the design, nor did the effects correspond with the hopes and wishes of the pope and the people. The fourth crusade was diverted from Syria to Constantinople; and the conquest of the Greek or Roman empire by the Latins will form the proper and important subject of the next chapter. In the fifth,[2] two hundred thousand Franks were landed at the eastern mouth of the Nile. They reasonably hoped that Palestine must be subdued in Egypt, the seat and storehouse of the sultan; and after a siege of sixteen months the Moslems deplored the loss of Damietta. But the Christian army was ruined by the pride and insolence of the legate Pelagius, who, in the pope's name, assumed the character of general; the sickly Franks were encompassed by the waters of the Nile and the Oriental forces; and it was by the evacuation of Damietta that they obtained a safe retreat, some concessions for the pilgrims, and the tardy restitution of the doubtful relic of the true cross. The failure may in some measure be ascribed to the abuse and multiplication of the crusades, which were preached at the same time against the pagans of Livonia, the Moors of Spain, the

---

[1] See the Gesta Innocentii III. in Muratori, Script. Rer. Ital. (tom. iii. p. i. p. 486-568).

[2] See the fifth crusade, and the siege of Damietta, in Jacobus à Vitriaco (l. iii. p. 1125-1149, in the Gesta Dei of Bongarsius), an eye-witness; Bernard Thesaurarius (in Script. Muratori, tom. vii. p. 825-846, c. 194-207), a contemporary; and Sanutus (Secreta Fidel. Crucis, l. iii. p. xi. c. 4-9), a diligent compiler; and of the Arabians, Abulpharagius (Dynast. p. 294), and the Extracts at the end of Joinville (p. 533, 537, 540, 547, etc.).

Albigeois of France, and the kings of Sicily of the Imperial family.[1] In these meritorious services the volunteers might acquire at home the same spiritual indulgence and a larger measure of temporal rewards; and even the popes, in their zeal against a domestic enemy, were sometimes tempted to forget the distress of their Syrian brethren. From the last age of the crusades they derived the occasional command of an army and revenue, and some deep reasoners have suspected that the whole enterprise, from the first synod of Placentia, was contrived and executed by the policy of Rome. The suspicion is not founded either in nature or in fact. The successors of St. Peter appear to have followed, rather than guided, the impulse of manners and prejudice; without much foresight of the seasons or cultivation of the soil, they gathered the ripe and spontaneous fruits of the superstition of the times. They gathered these fruits without toil or personal danger: in the council of the Lateran, Innocent the Third declared an ambiguous resolution of animating the crusaders by his example; but the pilot of the sacred vessel could not abandon the helm, nor was Palestine ever blessed with the presence of a Roman pontiff.[2]

The persons, the families, and estates of the pilgrims were under the immediate protection of the popes; and these spiritual patrons soon claimed the prerogative of directing their operations, and enforcing, by commands and censures, the accomplishment of their vow. Frederic the Second,[3] the grandson of Barbarossa, was successively the pupil, the enemy, and the victim of the church. At the age of twenty-one years, and in obedience to his guardian Innocent the Third, he assumed the cross; the same promise was repeated at his royal and imperial coronations, and his marriage with the heiress of Jerusalem for ever bound him to defend the kingdom of his son Conrad. But as Frederic advanced in age and authority, he

[1] To those who took the cross against Mainfroy, the pope (A.D. 1255) granted plenissimam peccatorum remissionem. Fideles mirabantur quòd tantum eis promitteret pro sanguine Christianorum effundendo quantum pro cruore infidelium aliquando (Matthew Paris, p. 785). A high flight for the reason of the thirteenth century.

[2] This simple idea is agreeable to the good sense of Mosheim (Institut. Hist. Eccles. p. 332) and the fine philosophy of Hume (Hist. of England, vol. i. p. 330).

[3] The original materials for the crusade of Frederic II. may be drawn from Richard de St. Germano (in Muratori, Script. Rerum Ital. tom. vii. p. 1002-1013) and Matthew Paris (p. 286, 291, 300, 302, 304). The most rational moderns are Fleury (Hist. Eccles. tom. xvi.), Vertot (Chevaliers de Malthe, tom. i. l. iii.), Giannone (Istoria Civile di Napoli, tom. ii. l. xvi.), and Muratori (Annali d'Italia, tom. x.).

repented of the rash engagements of his youth: his liberal sense and knowledge taught him to despise the phantoms of super-stition and the crowns of Asia; he no longer entertained the same reverence for the successors of Innocent; and his ambition was occupied by the restoration of the Italian monarchy from Sicily to the Alps. But the success of this project would have reduced the popes to their primitive simplicity, and, after the delays and excuses of twelve years, they urged the emperor, with entreaties and threats, to fix the time and place of his departure for Palestine. In the harbours of Sicily and Apulia he prepared a fleet of one hundred galleys, and of one hundred vessels, that were framed to transport and land two thousand five hundred knights, with their horses and attendants; his vassals of Naples and Germany formed a powerful army, and the number of English crusaders was magnified to sixty thousand by the report of fame. But the inevitable or affected slowness of these mighty preparations consumed the strength and provisions of the more indigent pilgrims; the multitude was thinned by sickness and desertion, and the sultry summer of Calabria anticipated the mischiefs of a Syrian campaign. At length the emperor hoisted sail at Brundusium, with a fleet and army of forty thousand men; but he kept the sea no more than three days, and his hasty retreat, which was ascribed by his friends to a grievous indisposition, was accused by his enemies as a volun-tary and obstinate disobedience. For suspending his vow was Frederic excommunicated by Gregory the Ninth; for presuming, the next year, to accomplish his vow, he was again excommuni-cated by the same pope.[1] While he served under the banner of the cross a crusade was preached against him in Italy; and after his return he was compelled to ask pardon for the injuries which he had suffered. The clergy and military orders of Palestine were previously instructed to renounce his communion and dispute his commands, and in his own kingdom the emperor was forced to consent that the orders of the camp should be issued in the name of God and of the Christian republic. Frederic entered Jerusalem in triumph, and with his own hands (for no priest would perform the office) he took the crown from the altar of the holy sepulchre. But the patriarch cast an interdict on the church which his presence had profaned; and the knights of the hospital and temple informed the sultan how easily he might be surprised and slain in his unguarded visit to the river Jordan.

---

[1] Poor Muratori knows what to think, but knows not what to say: " Chinò qui il capo," etc., p. 322.

In such a state of fanaticism and faction, victory was hopeless and defence was difficult; but the conclusion of an advantageous peace may be imputed to the discord of the Mohammedans, and their personal esteem for the character of Frederic. The enemy of the church is accused of maintaining with the miscreants an intercourse of hospitality and friendship unworthy of a Christian; of despising the barrenness of the land; and of indulging a profane thought that if Jehovah had seen the kingdom of Naples, he never would have selected Palestine for the inheritance of his chosen people. Yet Frederic obtained from the sultan the restitution of Jerusalem, of Bethlem and Nazareth, of Tyre and Sidon; the Latins were allowed to inhabit and fortify the city; an equal code of civil and religious freedom was ratified for the sectaries of Jesus and those of Mohammed; and, while the former worshipped at the holy sepulchre, the latter might pray and preach in the mosque of the temple [1] from whence the prophet undertook his nocturnal journey to heaven. The clergy deplored this scandalous toleration, and the weaker Moslems were gradually expelled; but every rational object of the crusades was accomplished without bloodshed; the churches were restored, the monasteries were replenished, and, in the space of fifteen years, the Latins of Jerusalem exceeded the number of six thousand. This peace and prosperity, for which they were ungrateful to their benefactor, was terminated by the irruption of the strange and savage hordes of Carizmians.[2] Flying from the arms of the Moguls, those shepherds of the Caspian rolled headlong on Syria; and the union of the Franks with the sultans of Aleppo, Hems, and Damascus was insufficient to stem the violence of the torrent. Whatever stood against them was cut off by the sword or dragged into captivity; the military orders were almost exterminated in a single battle; and in the pillage of the city, in the profanation of the holy sepulchre, the Latins confess and regret the modesty and discipline of the Turks and Saracens.

Of the seven crusades, the two last were undertaken by Louis the Ninth, king of France, who lost his liberty in Egypt, and his life on the coast of Africa. Twenty-eight years after his death he was canonised at Rome, and sixty-five miracles were readily found and solemnly attested to justify the claim of the royal

[1] The clergy artfully confounded the mosque or church of the temple with the holy sepulchre, and their wilful error has deceived both Vertot and Muratori.

[2] The irruption of the Carizmians, or Corasmins, is related by Matthew Paris (p. 546, 547), and by Joinville, Nangis, and the Arabians (p. 111, 112, 191, 192, 528, 530).

saint.[1] The voice of history renders a more honourable testimony, that he united the virtues of a king, a hero, and a man; that his martial spirit was tempered by the love of private and public justice; and that Louis was the father of his people, the friend of his neighbours, and the terror of the infidels. Superstition alone, in all the extent of her baleful influence,[2] corrupted his understanding and his heart; his devotion stooped to admire and imitate the begging friars of Francis and Dominic; he pursued with blind and cruel zeal the enemies of the faith; and the best of kings twice descended from his throne to seek the adventures of a spiritual knight-errant. A monkish historian would have been content to applaud the most despicable part of his character; but the noble and gallant Joinville,[3] who shared the friendship and captivity of Louis, has traced with the pencil of nature the free portrait of his virtues as well as of his failings. From this intimate knowledge we may learn to suspect the political views of depressing their great vassals, which are so often imputed to the royal authors of the crusades. Above all the princes of the middle ages Louis the Ninth successfully laboured to restore the prerogatives of the crown; but it was at home, and not in the East, that he acquired for himself and his posterity; his vow was the result of enthusiasm and sickness; and if he were the promoter, he was likewise the victim, of this holy madness. For the invasion of Egypt, France was exhausted of her troops and treasures; he covered the sea of Cyprus with eighteen hundred sails; the most modest enumeration amounts to fifty thousand men; and, if we might trust his own confession, as it is reported by Oriental vanity, he disembarked nine thousand five hundred horse, and one hundred and thirty thousand foot, who performed their pilgrimage under the shadow of his power.[4]

In complete armour, the oriflamme waving before him, Louis

[1] Read, if you can, the Life and Miracles of St. Louis, by the confessor of Queen Margaret (p. 291-523, Joinville, du Louvre).

[2] He believed all that mother church taught (Joinville, p. 10), but he cautioned Joinville against disputing with infidels. " L'omme lay (said he in his old language), quand il ot medire de la loy Crestienne, ne doit pas deffendre la loy Crestienne ne mais que de l'espée, dequoi il doit donner parmi le ventre dedens, tant comme elle y peut entrer (p. 12).

[3] I have two editions of Joinville: the one (Paris, 1668) most valuable for the observations of Ducange; the other (Paris au Louvre, 1761) most precious for the pure and authentic text, a MS. of which has been recently discovered. The last editor proves that the history of St. Louis was finished A.D. 1309, without explaining, or even admiring, the age of the author, which must have exceeded ninety years (Preface, p. xi.; Observations de Ducange, p. 17).

[4] Joinville, p. 32; Arabic Extracts. p. 549.

leaped foremost on the beach; and the strong city of Damietta, which had cost his predecessors a siege of sixteen months, was abandoned on the first assault by the trembling Moslems. But Damietta was the first and the last of his conquests; and in the fifth and sixth crusades the same causes, almost on the same ground, were productive of similar calamities.[1] After a ruinous delay, which introduced into the camp the seeds of an epidemical disease, the Franks advanced from the sea-coast towards the capital of Egypt, and strove to surmount the unseasonable inundation of the Nile which opposed their progress. Under the eye of their intrepid monarch, the barons and knights of France displayed their invincible contempt of danger and discipline; his brother, the count of Artois, stormed with inconsiderate valour the town of Massoura; and the carrier pigeons announced to the inhabitants of Cairo that all was lost. But a soldier, who afterwards usurped the sceptre, rallied the flying troops: the main body of the Christians was far behind their vanguard, and Artois was overpowered and slain. A shower of Greek fire was incessantly poured on the invaders; the Nile was commanded by the Egyptian galleys, the open country by the Arabs; all provisions were intercepted; each day aggravated the sickness and famine; and about the same time a retreat was found to be necessary and impracticable. The Oriental writers confess that Louis might have escaped if he would have deserted his subjects: he was made prisoner, with the greatest part of his nobles; all who could not redeem their lives by service or ransom were inhumanly massacred, and the walls of Cairo were decorated with a circle of Christian heads.[2] The king of France was loaded with chains, but the generous victor, a great-grandson of the brother of Saladin, sent a robe of honour to his royal captive, and his deliverance, with that of his soldiers, was obtained by the restitution of Damietta[3] and the payment of four hundred thousand pieces of gold. In a soft and luxurious climate the

---

[1] The last editors have enriched their Joinville with large and curious extracts from the Arabic historians, Macrizi, Abulfeda, etc. See likewise Abulpharagius (Dynast. p. 322-325), who calls him by the corrupt name of *Redefrans*. Matthew Paris (p. 683, 684) has described the rival folly of the French and English who fought and fell at Massoura.

[2] Savary, in his agreeable Lettres sur l'Egypte, has given a description of Damietta (tom. i. lettre xxiii. p. 274-290), and a narrative of the expedition of St. Louis (xxv. p. 306-350).

[3] For the ransom of St. Louis a million of byzants was asked and granted; but the sultan's generosity reduced that sum to 800,000 byzants, which are valued by Joinville at 400,000 French livres of his own time, and expressed by Matthew Paris by 100,000 marks of silver (Ducange, Dissertation xx. sur Joinville).

degenerate children of the companions of Noureddin and Saladin were incapable of resisting the flower of European chivalry; they triumphed by the arms of their slaves or Mamalukes, the hardy natives of Tartary, who at a tender age had been purchased of the Syrian merchants, and were educated in the camp and palace of the sultan. But Egypt soon afforded a new example of the danger of prætorian bands; and the rage of these ferocious animals, who had been let loose on the strangers, was provoked to devour their benefactor. In the pride of conquest, Touran Shaw, the last of his race, was murdered by his Mamalukes; and the most daring of the assassins entered the chamber of the captive king, with drawn scimitars, and their hands imbrued in the blood of their sultan. The firmness of Louis commanded their respect;[1] their avarice prevailed over cruelty and zeal, the treaty was accomplished, and the king of France, with the relics of his army, was permitted to embark for Palestine. He wasted four years within the walls of Acre, unable to visit Jerusalem, and unwilling to return without glory to his native country.

The memory of his defeat excited Louis, after sixteen years of wisdom and repose, to undertake the seventh and last of the crusades. His finances were restored, his kingdom was enlarged; a new generation of warriors had arisen, and he embarked with fresh confidence at the head of six thousand horse and thirty thousand foot. The loss of Antioch had provoked the enterprise; a wild hope of baptising the king of Tunis tempted him to steer for the African coast; and the report of an immense treasure reconciled his troops to the delay of their voyage to the Holy Land. Instead of a proselyte, he found a siege; the French panted and died on the burning sands; St. Louis expired in his tent; and no sooner had he closed his eyes than his son and successor gave the signal of the retreat.[2] " It is thus," says a lively writer, " that a Christian king died near the ruins of Carthage, waging war against the sectaries of Mohammed, in a land to which Dido had introduced the deities of Syria." [3]

A more unjust and absurd constitution cannot be devised

---

[1] The idea of the emirs to choose Louis for their sultan is seriously attested by Joinville (p. 77, 78), and does not appear to me so absurd as to M. de Voltaire (Hist. Générale, tom. ii. p. 386, 387). The Mamalukes themselves were strangers, rebels, and equals: they had felt his valour, they hoped his conversion; and such a motion, which was not seconded, might be made perhaps by a secret Christian in their tumultuous assembly.

[2] See the expedition in the Annals of St. Louis, by William de Nangis, p. 270-287; and the Arabic Extracts, p. 545, 555, of the Louvre edition of Joinville.

[3] Voltaire, Hist. Générale, tom. ii. p. 391.

than that which condemns the natives of a country to perpetual
servitude under the arbitrary dominion of strangers and slaves.
Yet such has been the state of Egypt above five hundred years.
The most illustrious sultans of the Baharite and Borgite dynasties[1]
were themselves promoted from the Tartar and Circassian bands;
and the four-and-twenty beys, or military chiefs, have ever been
succeeded, not by their sons, but by their servants. They
produce the great charter of their liberties, the treaty of Selim
the First with the republic;[2] and the Othman emperor still
accepts from Egypt a slight acknowledgment of tribute and
subjection. With some breathing intervals of peace and order,
the two dynasties are marked as a period of rapine and bloodshed;[3] but their throne, however shaken, reposed on the two
pillars of discipline and valour; their sway extended over Egypt,
Nubia, Arabia, and Syria; their Mamalukes were multiplied
from eight hundred to twenty-five thousand horse; and their
numbers were increased by a provincial militia of one hundred
and seven thousand foot, and the occasional aid of sixty-six
thousand Arabs.[4] Princes of such power and spirit could not
long endure on their coast a hostile and independent nation;
and if the ruin of the Franks was postponed about forty years,
they were indebted to the cares of an unsettled reign, to the
invasion of the Mogols, and to the occasional aid of some warlike
pilgrims. Among these the English reader will observe the name
of our first Edward, who assumed the cross in the lifetime of his
father Henry. At the head of a thousand soldiers the future
conqueror of Wales and Scotland delivered Acre from a siege;
marched as far as Nazareth with an army of nine thousand men;
emulated the fame of his uncle Richard; extorted, by his

---

[1] The chronology of the two dynasties of Mamalukes, the Baharites,
Turks or Tartars of Kipzak, and the Borgites, Circassians, is given by
Pocock (Prolegom. ad Abulpharag. p. 6-31) and De Guignes (tom. i. p. 264-
270); their history from Abulfeda, Macrizi, etc., to the beginning of the
fifteenth century, by the same M. de Guignes (tom. iv. p. 110-328).

[2] Savary, Lettres sur l'Egypte, tom. ii. lettre xv. p. 189-208. I much
question the authenticity of this copy; yet it is true that sultan Selim concluded a treaty with the Circassians or Mamalukes of Egypt, and left them
in possession of arms, riches, and power. See a new Abrégé de l'Histoire
Ottomane, composed in Egypt, and translated by M. Digeon (tom. i. p. 55-
58; Paris, 1781), a curious, authentic, and national history.

[3] Si totum quo regnum occupârunt tempus respicias, præsertim quod
fini propius, reperies illud bellis, pugnis, injuriis, ac rapinis refertum (Al
Jannabi, apud Pocock, p. 31). The reign of Mohammed (A.D. 1311-1341)
affords an happy exception (De Guignes, tom. iv. p. 208-210).

[4] They are now reduced to 8500: but the expense of each Mamaluke
may be rated at 100 louis: and Egypt groans under the avarice and insolence of these strangers (Voyages de Volney, tom. i. p. 89-187).

valour, a ten years' truce; and escaped, with a dangerous
wound, from the dagger of a fanatic *assassin*.[1]   Antioch,[2] whose
situation had been less exposed to the calamities of the holy war,
was finally occupied and ruined by Bondocdar, or Bibars, sultan
of Egypt and Syria; the Latin principality was extinguished;
and the first seat of the Christian name was dispeopled by the
slaughter of seventeen, and the captivity of one hundred, thousand of her inhabitants.   The maritime towns of Laodicea,
Gabala, Tripoli, Berytus, Sidon, Tyre, and Jaffa, and the stronger
castles of the Hospitalers and Templars, successively fell; and
the whole existence of the Franks was confined to the city and
colony of St. John of Acre, which is sometimes described by the
more classic title of Ptolemais.

After the loss of Jerusalem, Acre,[3] which is distant about
seventy miles, became the metropolis of the Latin Christians,
and was adorned with strong and stately buildings, with
aqueducts, an artificial port, and a double wall.   The population
was increased by the incessant streams of pilgrims and fugitives;
in the pauses of hostility the trade of the East and West was
attracted to this convenient station, and the market could offer
the produce of every clime and the interpreters of every tongue.
But in this conflux of nations every vice was propagated and
practised: of all the disciples of Jesus and Mohammed, the male
and female inhabitants of Acre were esteemed the most corrupt,
nor could the abuse of religion be corrected by the discipline of
law.   The city had many sovereigns and no government.   The
kings of Jerusalem and Cyprus, of the house of Lusignan, the
princes of Antioch, the counts of Tripoli and Sidon, the great
masters of the hospital, the temple, and the Teutonic order, the
republics of Venice, Genoa, and Pisa, the pope's legate, the kings
of France and England, assumed an independent command;
seventeen tribunals exercised the power of life and death; every
criminal was protected in the adjacent quarter; and the perpetual jealousy of the nations often burst forth in acts of violence
and blood.   Some adventurers, who disgraced the ensign of the

---

[1] See Carte's History of England, vol. ii. p. 165-175, and his original
authors, Thomas Wikes and Walter Hemingford (l. iii. c. 34, 35), in Gale's
Collection (tom. ii. p. 97, 589-592).   They are both ignorant of the princess
Eleanor's piety in sucking the poisoned wound, and saving her husband
at the risk of her own life.

[2] Sanutus, Secret. Fidelium Crucis, l. iii. p. xii. c. 9, and De Guignes,
Hist. des Huns, tom. iv. p. 143, from the Arabic historians.

[3] The state of Acre is represented in all the chronicles of the times, and
most accurately in John Villani, l. vii. c. 144, in Muratori, Scriptores Rerum
Italicarum, tom. xiii. p. 337, 338.

cross, compensated their want of pay by the plunder of the
Mohammedan villages; nineteen Syrian merchants, who traded
under the public faith, were despoiled and hanged by the Christians, and the denial of satisfaction justified the arms of the
sultan Khalil.   He marched against Acre at the head of sixty
thousand horse and one hundred and forty thousand foot; his
train of artillery (if I may use the word) was numerous and
weighty;   the separate timbers of a single engine were transported in one hundred waggons;   and the royal historian
Abulfeda, who served with the troops of Hamah, was himself a
spectator of the holy war.   Whatever might be the vices of the
Franks, their courage was rekindled by enthusiasm and despair;
but they were torn by the discord of seventeen chiefs, and overwhelmed on all sides by the powers of the sultan.   After a siege
of thirty-three days the double wall was forced by the Moslems;
the principal tower yielded to their engines;   the Mamalukes
made a general assault;   the city was stormed, and death or
slavery was the lot of sixty thousand Christians.   The convent,
or rather fortress, of the Templars resisted three days longer;
but the great master was pierced with an arrow, and, of five
hundred knights, only ten were left alive, less happy than the
victims of the sword, if they lived to suffer on a scaffold in the
unjust and cruel proscription of the whole order.   The king of
Jerusalem, the patriarch, and the great master of the hospital
effected their retreat to the shore; but the sea was rough, the
vessels were insufficient, and great numbers of the fugitives were
drowned before they could reach the isle of Cyprus, which might
comfort Lusignan for the loss of Palestine.   By the command
of the sultan the churches and fortifications of the Latin cities
were demolished: a motive of avarice or fear still opened the
holy sepulchre to some devout and defenceless pilgrims: and a
mournful and solitary silence prevailed along the coast which had
so long resounded with the WORLD'S DEBATE.[1]

[1] See the final expulsion of the Franks in Sanutus, l. iii. p. xii. c. 11-22;
Abulfeda, Macrizi, etc., in De Guignes, tom. iv. p. 162, 164; and Vertot,
tom. i. l. iii. p. 407-428.

CHAPTER LX

Schism of the Greeks and Latins—State of Constantinople—Revolt of the
Bulgarians—Isaac Angelus dethroned by his Brother Alexius—
Origin of the Fourth Crusade—Alliance of the French and Venetians
with the Son of Isaac—Their Naval Expedition to Constantinople—
The two Sieges and Final Conquest of the City by the Latins

THE restoration of the Western empire by Charlemagne was
speedily followed by the separation of the Greek and Latin
churches.[1] A religious and national animosity still divides the
two largest communions of the Christian world; and the schism
of Constantinople, by alienating her most useful allies, and provoking her most dangerous enemies, has precipitated the decline
and fall of the Roman empire in the East.

In the course of the present history the aversion of the Greeks
for the Latins has been often visible and conspicuous. It was
originally derived from the disdain of servitude, inflamed, after
the time of Constantine, by the pride of equality or dominion,
and finally exasperated by the preference which their rebellious
subjects had given to the alliance of the Franks. In every age
the Greeks were proud of their superiority in profane and
religious knowledge: they had first received the light of Christianity; they had pronounced the decrees of the seven general
councils; they alone possessed the language of Scripture and
philosophy: nor should the barbarians, immersed in the darkness of the West,[2] presume to argue on the high and mysterious
questions of theological science. Those barbarians despised in
their turn the restless and subtle levity of the Orientals, the
authors of every heresy, and blessed their own simplicity, which
was content to hold the tradition of the apostolic church. Yet
in the seventh century the synods of Spain, and afterwards
of France, improved or corrupted the Nicene creed, on the
mysterious subject of the third person of the Trinity.[3] In the

[1] In the successive centuries, from the ninth to the eighteenth, Mosheim
traces the schism of the Greeks with learning, clearness, and impartiality:
the *filioque* (Institut. Hist. Eccles. p. 277), Leo III. p. 303; Photius, p. 307,
308; Michael Cerularius, p. 370, 371, etc.

[2] Ἄνδρες δυσσεβεῖς καὶ ἀποτρόπαιοι, ἄνδρες ἐκ σκότους ἀνάδυντες, τῆς γὰρ
Ἑσπερίου μοίρας ὑπῆρχον γεννήματα (Phot. Epist. p. 47, edit. Montacut.).
The Oriental patriarch continues to apply the images of thunder, earth-
quake, hail, wild boar, precursors of Antichrist, etc. etc.

[3] The mysterious subject of the procession of the Holy Ghost is discussed in the historical, theological, and controversial sense, or nonsense,
by the Jesuit Petavius. (Dogmata Theologica, tom. ii. l. vii. p. 362-440.)

long controversies of the East the nature and generation of the Christ had been scrupulously defined; and the well-known relation of father and son seemed to convey a faint image to the human mind. The idea of birth was less analogous to the Holy Spirit, who, instead of a divine gift or attribute, was considered by the Catholics as a substance, a person, a god; he was not begotten, but in the orthodox style he *proceeded*. Did he proceed from the Father alone, perhaps *by* the Son? or from the Father *and* the Son? The first of these opinions was asserted by the Greeks, the second by the Latins; and the addition to the Nicene creed of the word *filioque* kindled the flame of discord between the Oriental and the Gallic churches. In the origin of the dispute the Roman pontiffs affected a character of neutrality and moderation: they condemned the innovation, but they acquiesced in the sentiment, of their Transalpine brethren: they seemed desirous of casting a veil of silence and charity over the superfluous research; and in the correspondence of Charlemange and Leo the Third, the pope assumes the liberality of a statesman,[1] and the prince descends to the passions and prejudices of a priest.[2] But the orthodoxy of Rome spontaneously obeyed the impulse of her temporal policy; and the *filioque*, which Leo wished to erase, was transcribed in the symbol and chanted in the liturgy of the Vatican. The Nicene and Athanasian creeds are held as the Catholic faith, without which none can be saved; and both Papists and Protestants must now sustain and return the anathemas of the Greeks, who deny the procession of the Holy Ghost from the Son as well as from the Father. Such articles of faith are not susceptible of treaty; but the rules of discipline will vary in remote and independent churches; and the reason, even of divines, might allow that the difference is inevitable and harmless. The craft or superstition of Rome has imposed on her priests and deacons the rigid obligation of celibacy; among the Greeks it is confined to the bishops; the loss is compensated by dignity or annihilated

[1] Before the shrine of St. Peter he placed two shields of the weight of 94½ pounds of pure silver; on which he inscribed the text of both creeds (utroque symbolo) pro amore et *cautelá* orthodoxæ fidei (Anastas. in Leon. III. in Muratori, tom. iii. pars i. p. 208). His language most clearly proves that neither the *filioque* nor the Athanasian creed were received at Rome about the year 830.

[2] The Missi of Charlemagne pressed him to declare that all who rejected the *filioque*, at least the doctrine, must be damned. All, replies the pope, are not capable of reaching the altiora mysteria; qui potuerit, et non voluerit, salvus esse non potest (Collect. Concil. tom. ix. p. 277-286). The *potuerit* would leave a large loophole of salvation!

by age; and the parochial clergy, the papas, enjoy the conjugal society of the wives whom they have married before their entrance into holy orders. A question concerning the *Azyms* was fiercely debated in the eleventh century, and the essence of the Eucharist was supposed in the East and West to depend on the use of leavened or unleavened bread. Shall I mention in a serious history the furious reproaches that were urged against the Latins, who for a long while remained on the defensive? They neglected to abstain, according to the apostolical decree, from things strangled, and from blood: they fasted, a Jewish observance! on the Saturday of each week: during the first week of Lent they permitted the use of milk and cheese; [1] their infirm monks were indulged in the taste of flesh; and animal grease was substituted for the want of vegetable oil: the holy chrism or unction in baptism was reserved to the episcopal order; the bishops, as the bridegrooms of their churches, were decorated with rings; their priests shaved their faces, and baptised by a single immersion. Such were the crimes which provoked the zeal of the patriarchs of Constantinople, and which were justified with equal zeal by the doctors of the Latin church. [2]

Bigotry and national aversion are powerful magnifiers of every object of dispute; but the immediate cause of the schism of the Greeks may be traced in the emulation of the leading prelates, who maintained the supremacy of the old metropolis, superior to all, and of the reigning capital, inferior to none, in the Christian world. About the middle of the ninth century, Photius, [3] an ambitious layman, the captain of the guards and principal secretary, was promoted by merit and favour to the more desirable office of patriarch of Constantinople. In science, even ecclesiastical science, he surpassed the clergy of the age; and the purity of his morals has never been impeached: but his ordination was hasty, his rise was irregular; and Ignatius, his abdicated predecessor, was yet supported by the public compassion and the obstinacy of his adherents. They appealed to

---

[1] In France, after some harsher laws, the ecclesiastical discipline is now relaxed: milk, cheese, and butter are become a perpetual, and eggs an annual, indulgence in Lent (Vie privée des François, tom. ii. p. 27-38).

[2] The original monuments of the schism, of the charges of the Greeks against the Latins, are deposited in the epistles of Photius (Epist. Encyclica, ii. p. 47-61) and of Michael Cerularius (Canisii Antiq. Lectiones, tom. iii. p. i. p. 281-324, edit. Basnage, with the prolix answer of Cardinal Humbert).

[3] The tenth volume of the Venice edition of the Councils contains all the acts of the synods, and history of Photius: they are abridged, with a faint tinge of prejudice or prudence, by Dupin and Fleury.

the tribunal of Nicholas the First, one of the proudest and most aspiring of the Roman pontiffs, who embraced the welcome opportunity of judging and condemning his rival of the East. Their quarrel was embittered by a conflict of jurisdiction over the king and nation of the Bulgarians; nor was their recent conversion to Christianity of much avail to either prelate, unless he could number the proselytes among the subjects of his power. With the aid of his court the Greek patriarch was victorious; but in the furious contest he deposed in his turn the successor of St. Peter, and involved the Latin church in the reproach of heresy and schism. Photius sacrificed the peace of the world to a short and precarious reign: he fell with his patron, the Cæsar Bardas; and Basil the Macedonian performed an act of justice in the restoration of Ignatius, whose age and dignity had not been sufficiently respected. From his monastery, or prison, Photius solicited the favour of the emperor by pathetic complaints and artful flattery; and the eyes of his rival were scarcely closed when he was again restored to the throne of Constantinople. After the death of Basil he experienced the vicissitudes of courts and the ingratitude of a royal pupil: the patriarch was again deposed, and in his last solitary hours he might regret the freedom of a secular and studious life. In each revolution the breath, the nod, of the sovereign had been accepted by a submissive clergy; and a synod of three hundred bishops was always prepared to hail the triumph, or to stigmatise the fall, of the holy, or the execrable, Photius.[1] By a delusive promise of succour or reward, the popes were tempted to countenance these various proceedings; and the synods of Constantinople were ratified by their epistles or legates. But the court and the people, Ignatius and Photius, were equally adverse to their claims; their ministers were insulted or imprisoned; the procession of the Holy Ghost was forgotten; Bulgaria was for ever annexed to the Byzantine throne; and the schism was prolonged by their rigid censure of all the multiplied ordinations of an irregular patriarch. The darkness and corruption of the tenth century suspended the intercourse, without reconciling the minds, of the two nations. But when the Norman sword restored the churches of Apulia to the jurisdiction of Rome, the departing flock was warned, by a petulant epistle of the Greek patriarch,

[1] The synod of Constantinople, held in the year 869, is the eighth of the general councils, the last assembly of the East which is recognised by the Roman church. She rejects the synods of Constantinople of the years 867 and 879, which were, however, equally numerous and noisy; but they were favourable to Photius.

to avoid and abhor the errors of the Latins. The rising majesty
of Rome could no longer brook the insolence of a rebel; and
Michael Cerularius was excommunicated in the heart of Constantinople by the pope's legates. Shaking the dust from their
feet, they deposited on the altar of St. Sophia a direful anathema,[1]
which enumerates the seven mortal heresies of the Greeks, and
devotes the guilty teachers, and their unhappy sectaries, to the
eternal society of the devil and his angels. According to the
emergencies of the church and state, a friendly correspondence
was sometimes resumed; the language of charity and concord
was sometimes affected; but the Greeks have never recanted
their errors, the popes have never repealed their sentence; and
from this thunderbolt we may date the consummation of the
schism. It was enlarged by each ambitious step of the Roman
pontiffs: the emperors blushed and trembled at the ignominious
fate of their royal brethren of Germany; and the people was
scandalised by the temporal power and military life of the Latin
clergy.[2]

The aversion of the Greeks and Latins was nourished and
manifested in the three first expeditions to the Holy Land.
Alexius Comnenus contrived the absence at least of the formidable pilgrims: his successors, Manuel and Isaac Angelus, conspired with the Moslems for the ruin of the greatest princes of the
Franks; and their crooked and malignant policy was seconded
by the active and voluntary obedience of every order of their
subjects. Of this hostile temper a large portion may doubtless
be ascribed to the difference of language, dress, and manners,
which severs and alienates the nations of the globe. The pride
as well as the prudence of the sovereign was deeply wounded by
the intrusion of foreign armies that claimed a right of traversing
his dominions, and passing under the walls of his capital: his
subjects were insulted and plundered by the rude strangers of
the West: and the hatred of the pusillanimous Greeks was
sharpened by secret envy of the bold and pious enterprises of
the Franks. But these profane causes of national enmity were
fortified and inflamed by the venom of religious zeal. Instead of
a kind embrace, an hospitable reception from their Christian
brethren of the East, every tongue was taught to repeat the

[1] See this anathema in the Councils, tom. xi. p. 1457-1460.
[2] Anna Comnena (Alexiad, l. i. p. 31-33 [tom. i. p. 63-68, ed. Bonn]) represents the abhorrence, not only of the church, but of the palace, for
Gregory VII., the popes, and the Latin communion. The style of Cinnamus
and Nicetas is still more vehement. Yet how calm is the voice of history
compared with that of polemics!

names of schismatic and heretic, more odious to an orthodox
ear than those of pagan and infidel: instead of being loved for
the general conformity of faith and worship, they were abhorred
for some rules of discipline, some questions of theology, in which
themselves or their teachers might differ from the Oriental church.
In the crusade of Louis the Seventh the Greek clergy washed and
purified the altars which had been defiled by the sacrifice of a
French priest. The companions of Frederic Barbarossa deplore
the injuries which they endured, both in word and deed, from
the peculiar rancour of the bishops and monks. Their prayers
and sermons excited the people against the impious barbarians;
and the patriarch is accused of declaring that the faithful might
obtain the redemption of all their sins by the extirpation of the
schismatics.[1] An enthusiast named Dorotheus alarmed the
fears and restored the confidence of the emperor by a prophetic
assurance that the German heretic, after assaulting the gate
of Blachernes, would be made a signal example of the divine
vengeance. The passage of these mighty armies were rare and
perilous events; but the crusades introduced a frequent and
familiar intercourse between the two nations, which enlarged
their knowledge without abating their prejudices. The wealth
and luxury of Constantinople demanded the productions of every
climate: these imports were balanced by the art and labour of
her numerous inhabitants; her situation invites the commerce of
the world; and, in every period of her existence, that commerce
has been in the hands of foreigners. After the decline of
Amalphi, the Venetians, Pisans, and Genoese introduced their
factories and settlements into the capital of the empire: their
services were rewarded with honours and immunities; they
acquired the possession of lands and houses, their families were
multiplied by marriages with the natives, and, after the toleration of a Mohammedan mosque, it was impossible to interdict the
churches of the Roman rite.[2] The two wives of Manuel Com-

---

[1] His anonymous historian (de Expedit. Asiat. Fred. I. in Canisii Lection.
Antiq. tom. iii. pars ii. p. 511, edit. Basnage) mentions the sermons of the
Greek patriarch, quomodo Græcis injunxerat in remissionem peccatorum
peregrinos occidere et delere de terrâ. Tagino observes (in Scriptores Freher.
tom. i. p. 409, edit. Struv.), Græci hæreticos nos appellant: clerici et monachi
dictis et factis persequuntur. We may add the declaration of the emperor
Baldwin fifteen years afterwards: Hæc est (gens) quæ Latinos omnes non
hominum nomine, sed canum dignabatur; quorum sanguinem effundere
penè inter merita reputabant (Gesta Innocent. III. c. 92, in Muratori,
Script. Rerum Italicarum, tom. iii. pars i. p. 536). There may be some
exaggeration, but it was as effectual for the action and re-action of hatred.
[2] See Anna Comnena (Alexiad. l. vi. p. 161, 162 [tom. i. p. 286, sq., ed.
Bonn]) and a remarkable passage of Nicetas (in Manuel. l. v. c. 9 [p. 223,

nenus [1] were of the race of the Franks: the first, a sister-in-law of
the emperor Conrad; the second, a daughter of the prince of
Antioch: he obtained for his son Alexius a daughter of Philip
Augustus king of France; and he bestowed his own daughter on
a marquis of Montferrat, who was educated and dignified in the
palace of Constantinople. The Greek encountered the arms,
and aspired to the empire, of the West: he esteemed the valour,
and trusted the fidelity, of the Franks; [2] their military talents
were unfitly recompensed by the lucrative offices of judges and
treasurers; the policy of Manuel had solicited the alliance of the
pope; and the popular voice accused him of a partial bias to
the nation and religion of the Latins.[3] During his reign and
that of his successor Alexius, they were exposed at Constantinople
to the reproach of foreigners, heretics, and favourites; and this
triple guilt was severely expiated in the tumult which announced
the return and elevation of Andronicus.[4] The people rose in
arms: from the Asiatic shore the tyrant despatched his troops
and galleys to assist the national revenge; and the hopeless
resistance of the strangers served only to justify the rage and
sharpen the daggers of the assassins. Neither age, nor sex, nor
the ties of friendship or kindred, could save the victims of
national hatred, and avarice, and religious zeal: the Latins were
slaughtered in their houses and in the streets; their quarter was
reduced to ashes; the clergy were burnt in their churches, and
the sick in their hospitals; and some estimate may be formed
of the slain from the clemency which sold above four thousand
Christians in perpetual slavery to the Turks. The priests and
monks were the loudest and most active in the destruction of
the schismatics; and they chanted a thanksgiving to the Lord
when the head of a Roman cardinal, the pope's legate, was

ed. Bonn]), who observes of the Venetians, κατὰ σμήνη καὶ φρατρίας τὴν
Κωνσταντίνου πόλιν τῆς οἰκείας ἠλλάξαντο, etc.

[1] Ducange, Fam. Byzant. p. 186, 187.

[2] Nicetas in Manuel. l. vii. c. 2 [p. 267, ed. Bonn]. Regnante enim
(Manuele) . . . apud eum tantam Latinus populus repererat gratiam ut
neglectis Græculis suis tanquam viris mollibus et effeminatis, . . . solis
Latinis grandia committeret negotia . . . erga eos profusâ liberalitate
abundabat, ex omni orbe ad eum tanquam ad benefactorem nobiles et
ignobiles concurrebant. Willelm. Tyr. xxii. c. 10.

[3] The suspicions of the Greeks would have been confirmed, if they had
seen the political epistles of Manuel to pope Alexander III., the enemy of
his enemy Frederic I., in which the emperor declares his wish of uniting
the Greeks and Latins as one flock under one shepherd, etc. (See Fleury,
Hist. Ecclés. tom. xv. p. 187, 213, 243.)

[4] See the Greek and Latin narratives in Nicetas (in Alexio Comneno, c. 10
[p. 320, ed. Bonn]) and William of Tyre (l. xxii. c. 10, 11, 12, 13); the first
soft and concise, the second loud, copious, and tragical.

severed from his body, fastened to the tail of a dog, and dragged,
with savage mockery, through the city. The more diligent of
the strangers had retreated, on the first alarm, to their vessels,
and escaped through the Hellespont from the scene of blood. In
their flight they burnt and ravaged two hundred miles of the sea-
coast, inflicted a severe revenge on the guiltless subjects of the
empire, marked the priests and monks as their peculiar enemies,
and compensated, by the accumulation of plunder, the loss of
their property and friends. On their return they exposed to
Italy and Europe the wealth and weakness, the perfidy and
malice of the Greeks, whose vices were painted as the genuine
characters of heresy and schism. The scruples of the first
crusaders had neglected the fairest opportunities of securing, by
the possession of Constantinople, the way to the Holy Land:
a domestic revolution invited, and almost compelled, the French
and Venetians to achieve the conquest of the Roman empire of
the East.

In the series of the Byzantine princes I have exhibited the
hypocrisy and ambition, the tyranny and fall, of Andronicus,
the last male of the Comnenian family who reigned at Constantinople. The revolution which cast him headlong from the
throne saved and exalted Isaac Angelus,[1] who descended by the
females from the same Imperial dynasty. The successor of a
second Nero might have found it an easy task to deserve the
esteem and affection of his subjects: they sometimes had reason
to regret the administration of Andronicus. The sound and
vigorous mind of the tyrant was capable of discerning the connection between his own and the public interest; and while he
was feared by all who could inspire him with fear, the unsus-
pected people, and the remote provinces, might bless the inexorable justice of their master. But his successor was vain
and jealous of the supreme power, which he wanted courage and
abilities to exercise: his vices were pernicious, his virtues (if he
possessed any virtues) were useless, to mankind; and the Greeks,
who imputed their calamities to his negligence, denied him the
merit of any transient or accidental benefits of the times.
Isaac slept on the throne, and was awakened only by the sound
of pleasure: his vacant hours were amused by comedians and
buffoons, and even to these buffoons the emperor was an object

---

[1] The history of the reign of Isaac Angelus is composed in three books,
by the senator Nicetas (p. 228-290); and his offices of logothete, or principal secretary, and judge of the veil or palace, could not bribe the impartiality of the historian. He wrote, it is true, after the fall and death of his
benefactor.

of contempt: his feasts and buildings exceeded the examples of
royal luxury: the number of his eunuchs and domestics amounted
to twenty thousand; and a daily sum of four thousand pounds
of silver would swell to four millions sterling the annual expense
of his household and table.   His poverty was relieved by oppression; and the public discontent was inflamed by equal abuses in
the collection and the application of the revenue.   While the
Greeks numbered the days of their servitude, a flattering prophet,
whom he rewarded with the dignity of patriarch, assured him of
a long and victorious reign of thirty-two years, during which he
should extend his sway to Mount Libanus, and his conquests
beyond the Euphrates.   But his only step towards the accomplishment of the prediction was a splendid and scandalous
embassy to Saladin,[1] to demand the restitution of the holy
sepulchre, and to propose an offensive and defensive league with
the enemy of the Christian name.   In these unworthy hands, of
Isaac and his brother, the remains of the Greek empire crumbled
into dust.   The island of Cyprus, whose name excites the ideas of
elegance and pleasure, was usurped by his namesake, a Comnenian prince; and by a strange concatenation of events, the
sword of our English Richard bestowed that kingdom on the
house of Lusignan, a rich compensation for the loss of Jerusalem.

The honour of the monarchy and the safety of the capital
were deeply wounded by the revolt of the Bulgarians and
Wallachians.   Since the victory of the second Basil, they had
supported, above a hundred and seventy years, the loose
dominion of the Byzantine princes; but no effectual measures
had been adopted to impose the yoke of laws and manners on
these savage tribes.   By the command of Isaac, their sole means
of subsistence, their flocks and herds, were driven away to contribute towards the pomp of the royal nuptials; and their fierce
warriors were exasperated by the denial of equal rank and pay in
the military service.   Peter and Asan, two powerful chiefs, of the
race of the ancient kings,[2] asserted their own rights and the
national freedom: their demoniac impostors proclaimed to the
crowd that their glorious patron St. Demetrius had for ever
deserted the cause of the Greeks: and the conflagration spread

[1] See Bohadin, Vit. Saladin. p. 129-131, 226, vers. Schultens.   The
ambassador of Isaac was equally versed in the Greek, French, and Arabic
languages; a rare instance in those times.   His embassies were received
with honour, dismissed without effect, and reported with scandal in the
West.

[2] Ducange, Familiæ Dalmaticæ, p. 318, 319, 320.   The original correspondence of the Bulgarian king and the Roman pontiff is inscribed in the
Gesta Innocent. III. c. 66-82, p. 513-525.

from the banks of the Danube to the hills of Macedonia and
Thrace. After some faint efforts, Isaac Angelus and his brother
acquiesced in their independence; and the Imperial troops were
soon discouraged by the bones of their fellow-soldiers that were
scattered along the passes of Mount Hæmus. By the arms and
policy of John, or Joannices, the second kingdom of Bulgaria
was firmly established. The subtle barbarian sent an embassy
to Innocent the Third to acknowledge himself a genuine son of
Rome in descent and religion,[1] and humbly received from the
pope the licence of coining money, the royal title, and a Latin
archbishop or patriarch. The Vatican exulted in the spiritual
conquest of Bulgaria, the first object of the schism; and if the
Greeks could have preserved the prerogatives of the church, they
would gladly have resigned the rights of the monarchy.

The Bulgarians were malicious enough to pray for the long
life of Isaac Angelus, the surest pledge of their freedom and
prosperity. Yet their chiefs could involve in the same indiscriminate contempt the family and nation of the emperor. " In
all the Greeks," said Asan to his troops, " the same climate, and
character, and education, will be productive of the same fruits.
Behold my lance," continued the warrior, " and the long
streamers that float in the wind. They differ only in colour;
they are formed of the same silk, and fashioned by the same
workman; nor has the stripe that is stained in purple any
superior price or value above its fellows." [2] Several of these
candidates for the purple successively rose and fell under the
empire of Isaac: a general who had repelled the fleets of Sicily
was driven to revolt and ruin by the ingratitude of the prince;
and his luxurious repose was disturbed by secret conspiracies
and popular insurrections. The emperor was saved by accident,
or the merit of his servants: he was at length oppressed by an
ambitious brother, who, for the hope of a precarious diadem,
forgot the obligations of nature, of loyalty, and of friendship.[3]

---

[1] The pope acknowledges his pedigree, a nobili urbis Romæ prosapiâ
genitores tui originem traxerunt. This tradition, and the strong resem-
blance of the Latin and Wallachian idioms, are explained by M. D'Anville
(Etats de l'Europe, p. 258-262). The Italian colonies of the Dacia of
Trajan were swept away by the tide of emigration from the Danube to the
Volga, and brought back by another wave from the Volga to the Danube.
Possible, but strange!

[2] This parable is in the best savage style; but I wish the Wallach had
not introduced the classic name of Mysians, the experiment of the magnet
or loadstone, and the passage of an old comic poet (Nicetas, in Alex.
Comneno, l. i. p. 299, 300 [ed. Par.; p. 613, ed. Bonn]).

[3] The Latins aggravate the ingratitude of Alexius, by supposing that he
had been released by his brother Isaac from Turkish captivity. This

While Isaac in the Thracian valleys pursued the idle and solitary pleasures of the chase, his brother, Alexius Angelus, was invested with the purple by the unanimous suffrage of the camp: the capital and the clergy subscribed to their choice; and the vanity of the new sovereign rejected the name of his fathers for the lofty and royal appellation of the Comnenian race. On the despicable character of Isaac I have exhausted the language of contempt, and can only add that in a reign of eight years the baser Alexius [1] was supported by the masculine vices of his wife Euphrosyne. The first intelligence of his fall was conveyed to the late emperor by the hostile aspect and pursuit of the guards, no longer his own: he fled before them above fifty miles as far as Stagyra in Macedonia; but the fugitive, without an object or a follower, was arrested, brought back to Constantinople, deprived of his eyes, and confined in a lonesome tower, on a scanty allowance of bread and water. At the moment of the revolution, his son Alexius, whom he educated in the hope of empire, was twelve years of age. He was spared by the usurper, and reduced to attend his triumph both in peace and war; but as the army was encamped on the sea-shore, an Italian vessel facilitated the escape of the royal youth; and, in the disguise of a common sailor, he eluded the search of his enemies, passed the Hellespont, and found a secure refuge in the isle of Sicily. After saluting the threshold of the apostles, and imploring the protection of pope Innocent the Third, Alexius accepted the kind invitation of his sister Irene, the wife of Philip of Swabia, king of the Romans. But in his passage through Italy he heard that the flower of Western chivalry was assembled at Venice for the deliverance of the Holy Land; and a ray of hope was kindled in his bosom that their invincible swords might be employed in his father's restoration.

About ten or twelve years after the loss of Jerusalem, the nobles of France were again summoned to the holy war by the voice of a third prophet, less extravagant, perhaps, than Peter the Hermit, but far below St. Bernard in the merit of an orator and a statesman. An illiterate priest of the neighbourhood of Paris, Fulk of Neuilly,[2] forsook his parochial duty, to assume

---

pathetic tale had doubtless been repeated at Venice and Zara; but I do not readily discover its grounds in the Greek historians.

[1] See the reign of Alexius Angelus, or Comnenus, in the three books of Nicetas, p. 291-352.

[2] See Fleury, Hist. Ecclés. tom. xvi. p. 26, etc., and Villehardouin, No. 1, with the observations of Ducange, which I always mean to quote with the original text.

the more flattering character of a popular and itinerant
missionary. The fame of his sanctity and miracles was spread
over the land: he declaimed, with severity and vehemence,
against the vices of the age; and his sermons, which he preached
in the streets of Paris, converted the robbers, the usurers, the
prostitutes, and even the doctors and scholars of the university.
No sooner did Innocent the Third ascend the chair of St. Peter
than he proclaimed in Italy, Germany, and France, the obligation of a new crusade.[1] The eloquent pontiff described the ruin
of Jerusalem, the triumph of the Pagans, and the shame of
Christendom: his liberality proposed the redemption of sins, a
plenary indulgence to all who should serve in Palestine, either
a year in person, or two years by a substitute:[2] and among his
legates and orators who blew the sacred trumpet, Fulk of Neuilly
was the loudest and most successful. The situation of the
principal monarchs was averse to the pious summons. The
emperor Frederic the Second was a child; and his kingdom of
Germany was disputed by the rival houses of Brunswick and
Swabia, the memorable factions of the Guelphs and Ghibelines.
Philip Augustus of France had performed, and could not be
persuaded to renew, the perilous vow; but as he was not less
ambitious of praise than of power, he cheerfully instituted a
perpetual fund for the defence of the Holy Land. Richard of
England was satiated with the glory and misfortunes of his first
adventure, and he presumed to deride the exhortations of Fulk
of Neuilly, who was not abashed in the presence of kings. " You
advise me," said Plantagenet, " to dismiss my three daughters,
pride, avarice, and incontinence: I bequeath them to the most
deserving; my pride to the knights-templars, my avarice to the
monks of Cisteaux, and my incontinence to the prelates." But
the preacher was heard and obeyed by the great vassals, the
princes of the second order; and Theobald, or Thibaut, count of
Champagne, was the foremost in the holy race. The valiant
youth, at the age of twenty-two years, was encouraged by the
domestic examples of his father, who marched in the second
crusade, and of his elder brother, who had ended his days in
Palestine with the title of King of Jerusalem: two thousand

---

[1] The contemporary life of Pope Innocent III., published by Baluze and
Muratori (Scriptores Rerum Italicarum, tom. iii. pars i. p. 486-568), is most
valuable for the important and original documents which are inserted in
the text. The bull of the crusade may be read, c. 84, 85 [p. 526].

[2] Por-ce que cil pardon fut issi gran, si s'en esmeurent mult li cuers des
genz, et mult s'en croisierent, porce que li pardons ere si gran. Villehardouin, No. 1. Our philosophers may refine on the causes of the crusades,
but such were the genuine feelings of a French knight.

two hundred knights owed service and homage to his peerage: [1]
the nobles of Champagne excelled in all the exercises of war; [2]
and, by his marriage with the heiress of Navarre, Thibaut could
draw a band of hardy Gascons from either side of the Pyrenæan
mountains.   His companion in arms was Louis count of Blois
and Chartres; like himself of regal lineage, for both the princes
were nephews, at the same time, of the kings of France and
England.   In a crowd of prelates and barons, who imitated their
zeal, I distinguish the birth and merit of Matthew of Montmorency; the famous Simon of Montfort, the scourge of the
Albigeois; and a valiant noble, Jeffrey of Villehardouin, [3]
marshal of Champagne, [4] who has condescended, in the rude
idiom of his age and country, [5] to write or dictate [6] an original
narrative of the councils and actions in which he bore a
memorable part.   At the same time, Baldwin count of Flanders,
who had married the sister of Thibaut, assumed the cross at
Bruges, with his brother Henry and the principal knights and
citizens of that rich and industrious province. [7]   The vow which
the chiefs had pronounced in churches, they ratified in tournaments: the operations of the war were debated in full and
frequent assemblies: and it was resolved to seek the deliverance

---

[1] This number of fiefs (of which 1800 owed liege homage) was enrolled in
the church of St. Stephen at Troyes, and attested, A.D. 1213, by the marshal
and butler of Champagne (Ducange, Observ. p. 254).

[2] Campania . . . militiæ privilegio singularius excellit . . . in tyro-
ciniis . . . prolusione armorum, etc. Ducange, p. 249, from the old
Chronicle of Jerusalem, A.D. 1177-1199.

[3] The name of Villehardouin was taken from a village and castle in the
diocese of Troyes, near the river Aube, between Bar and Arcis.   The family
was ancient and noble: the elder branch of our historian existed after the
year 1400; the younger, which acquired the principality of Achaia, merged
in the house of Savoy (Ducange, p. 235-245).

[4] This office was held by his father and his descendants; but Ducange
has not hunted it with his usual sagacity.   I find that, in the year 1356, it
was in the family of Conflans: but these provincial have been long since
eclipsed by the national marshals of France.

[5] This language, of which I shall produce some specimens, is explained
by Vigenere and Ducange, in a version and glossary.   The President Des
Brosses (Méchanisme des Langues, tom. ii. p. 83) gives it as the example of
a language which has ceased to be French, and is understood only by
grammarians.

[6] His age, and his own expression, moi qui ceste œuvre *dicta* (No. 62,
etc.), may justify the suspicion (more probable than Mr. Wood's on Homer)
that he could neither read nor write.   Yet Champagne may boast of the
two first historians, the noble authors of French prose, Villehardouin and
Joinville.

[7] The crusade and reigns of the counts of Flanders, Baldwin and his
brother Henry, are the subject of a particular history by the Jesuit Doutre-
mens (Constantinopolis Belgica; Turnaci, 1638, in 4to), which I have only
seen with the eyes of Ducange.

of Palestine in Egypt, a country, since Saladin's death, which was almost ruined by famine and civil war. But the fate of so many royal armies displayed the toils and perils of a land expedition; and if the Flemings dwelt along the ocean, the French barons were destitute of ships and ignorant of navigation. They embraced the wise resolution of choosing six deputies or representatives, of whom Villehardouin was one, with a discretionary trust to direct the motions, and to pledge the faith, of the whole confederacy. The maritime states of Italy were alone possessed of the means of transporting the holy warriors with their arms and horses; and the six deputies proceeded to Venice to solicit, on motives of piety or interest, the aid of that powerful republic.

In the invasion of Italy by Attila, I have mentioned [1] the flight of the Venetians from the fallen cities of the continent, and their obscure shelter in the chain of islands that line the extremity of the Adriatic Gulf. In the midst of the waters, free, indigent, laborious, and inaccessible, they gradually coalesced into a republic: the first foundations of Venice were laid in the island of Rialto; and the annual election of the twelve tribunes was superseded by the permanent office of a duke or doge. On the verge of the two empires, the Venetians exult in the belief of primitive and perpetual independence.[2] Against the Latins their antique freedom has been asserted by the sword, and may be justified by the pen. Charlemagne himself resigned all claims of sovereignty to the islands of the Adriatic Gulf: his son Pepin was repulsed in the attacks of the *lagunas* or canals, too deep for the cavalry, and too shallow for the vessels; and in every age, under the German Cæsars, the lands of the republic have been clearly distinguished from the kingdom of Italy. But the inhabitants of Venice were considered by themselves, by strangers, and by their sovereigns, as an inalienable portion of the Greek empire:[3] in the ninth and tenth centuries the

---

[1] History, etc., vol. iii. p. 396.

[2] The foundation and independence of Venice, and Pepin's invasion, are discussed by Pagi (Critica, tom. iii. A.D. 810, No. 4, etc.) and Beretti (Dissert. Chorograph. Italiæ medii Ævi, in Muratori, Script. tom. x. p. 153). The two critics have a slight bias, the Frenchman adverse, the Italian favourable, to the republic.

[3] When the son of Charlemagne asserted his right of sovereignty, he was answered by the loyal Venetians, ὅτι ἡμεῖς δοῦλοι θέλομεν εἶναι τοῦ Ῥωμαίων βασιλέως (Constantin. Porphyrogenit. de Administrat. Imperii, pars ii. c. 28, p. 85); and the report of the ninth establishes the fact of the tenth century, which is confirmed by the embassy of Liutprand of Cremona. The annual tribute, which the emperor allows them to pay to the king of Italy, alleviates, by doubling, their servitude; but the hateful word δοῦλοι must

proofs of their subjection are numerous and unquestionable;
and the vain titles, the servile honours, of the Byzantine court,
so ambitiously solicited by their dukes, would have degraded
the magistrates of a free people. But the bands of this
dependence, which was never absolute or rigid, were imperceptibly relaxed by the ambition of Venice and the weakness of
Constantinople. Obedience was softened into respect, privilege
ripened into prerogative, and the freedom of domestic government was fortified by the independence of foreign dominion.
The maritime cities of Istria and Dalmatia bowed to the
sovereigns of the Adriatic; and when they armed against the
Normans in the cause of Alexius, the emperor applied, not to
the duty of his subjects, but to the gratitude and generosity of
his faithful allies. The sea was their patrimony: [1] the western
parts of the Mediterranean, from Tuscany to Gibraltar, were
indeed abandoned to their rivals of Pisa and Genoa; but the
Venetians acquired an early and lucrative share of the commerce of Greece and Egypt. Their riches increased with the
increasing demand of Europe: their manufactures of silk and
glass, perhaps the institution of their bank, are of high antiquity;
and they enjoyed the fruits of their industry in the magnificence
of public and private life. To assert her flag, to avenge her
injuries, to protect the freedom of navigation, the republic could
launch and man a fleet of a hundred galleys; and the Greeks,
the Saracens, and the Normans were encountered by her naval
arms. The Franks of Syria were assisted by the Venetians in
the reduction of the sea-coast; but their zeal was neither blind
nor disinterested; and in the conquest of Tyre they shared the

be translated, as in the charter of 827 (Laugier, Hist. de Venise, tom. i.
p. 67, etc.), by the softer appellation of *subditi*, or *fideles*.

[Venice was dependent upon Constantinople until about 836, about
which time the weakness of the Eastern empire permitted her to throw off
the yoke. Under the Doge Peter Tradonicus, by military expeditions
against the Slavonic pirates that invested the Adriatic, and the Saracens
who carried their depredations to Dalmatia and the northern section of
the Eastern Riviera, and by entering into independent compacts with the
neighbouring cities of Italy, Venice changed her condition from that of a
province to that of a responsible power, and when the Eastern empire
regained strength under Basil it was impossible to recall her to her former
subordinate position. From the eleventh century onward, Venice slowly
but surely grew in influence and power. Cf. *The Venetian Republic*, by
Horatio Brown (Dent's Cyclopædic Primers, 1903).—O. S.]

[1] See the twenty-fifth and thirtieth dissertations of the Antiquitates
medii Ævi of Muratori. From Anderson's History of Commerce, I understand that the Venetians did not trade to England before the year 1323.
The most flourishing state of their wealth and commerce in the beginning
of the fifteenth century is agreeably described by the Abbé Dubos (Hist.
de la Ligue de Cambray, tom. ii. p. 443-480).

sovereignty of a city, the first seat of the commerce of the world. The policy of Venice was marked by the avarice of a trading, and the insolence of a maritime power; yet her ambition was prudent: nor did she often forget that, if armed galleys were the effect and safeguard, merchant vessels were the cause and supply, of her greatness. In her religion she avoided the schism of the Greeks, without yielding a servile obedience to the Roman pontiff; and a free intercourse with the infidels of every clime appears to have allayed betimes the fever of superstition. Her primitive government was a loose mixture of democracy and monarchy: the doge was elected by the votes of the general assembly; as long as he was popular and successful, he reigned with the pomp and authority of a prince; but in the frequent revolutions of the state, he was deposed, or banished, or slain, by the justice or injustice of the multitude. The twelfth century produced the first rudiments of the wise and jealous aristocracy, which has reduced the doge to a pageant, and the people to a cipher.[1]

When the six ambassadors of the French pilgrims arrived at Venice, they were hospitably entertained in the palace of St. Mark, by the reigning duke: his name was Henry Dandolo;[2] and he shone in the last period of human life as one of the most illustrious characters of the times. Under the weight of years, and after the loss of his eyes,[3] Dandolo retained a sound understanding and a manly courage; the spirit of a hero, ambitious to signalise his reign by some memorable exploits; and the wisdom of a patriot, anxious to build his fame on the glory and advantage of his country. He praised the bold enthusiasm and

---

[1] The Venetians have been slow in writing and publishing their history. Their most ancient monuments are, 1. The rude Chronicle (perhaps) of John Sagorninus (Venezia, 1765, in octavo), which represents the state and manners of Venice in the year 1008. 2. The larger history of the doge (1342-1354) Andrew Dandolo, published for the first time in the twelfth tom. of Muratori, A.D. 1728. The History of Venice by the Abbé Laugier (Paris, 1728) is a work of some merit, which I have chiefly used for the constitutional part.

[2] Henry Dandolo was eighty-four at his election (A.D. 1192), and ninety-seven at his death (A.D. 1205). See the Observations of Ducange sur Ville-hardouin, No. 204. But this *extraordinary* longevity is not observed by the original writers, nor does there exist another example of a hero near a hundred years of age. Theophrastus might afford an instance of a writer of ninety-nine; but instead of ἐννενήκοντα (Procem. ad Character.), I am much inclined to read ἑβδομήκοντα, with his last editor Fischer, and the first thoughts of Casaubon. It is scarcely possible that the powers of the mind and body should support themselves till such a period of life.

[3] The modern Venetians (Laugier, tom. ii. p. 119) accuse the emperor Manuel; but the calumny is refuted by Villehardouin and the older writers, who suppose that Dandolo lost his eyes by a wound (No. 34, and Ducange).

liberal confidence of the barons and their deputies: in such a cause, and with such associates, he should aspire, were he a private man, to terminate his life; but he was the servant of the republic, and some delay was requisite to consult, on this arduous business, the judgment of his colleagues. The proposal of the French was first debated by the six *sages* who had been recently appointed to control the administration of the doge: it was next disclosed to the forty members of the council of state; and finally communicated to the legislative assembly of four hundred and fifty representatives, who were annually chosen in the six quarters of the city. In peace and war the doge was still the chief of the republic; his legal authority was supported by the personal reputation of Dandolo; his arguments of public interest were balanced and approved; and he was authorised to inform the ambassadors of the following conditions of the treaty.[1] It was proposed that the crusaders should assemble at Venice on the feast of St. John of the ensuing year; that flat-bottomed vessels should be prepared for four thousand five hundred horses and nine thousand squires, with a number of ships sufficient for the embarkation of four thousand five hundred knights and twenty thousand foot: that during a term of nine months they should be supplied with provisions, and transported to what-soever coast the service of God and Christendom should require; and that the republic should join the armament with a squadron of fifty galleys. It was required that the pilgrims should pay, before their departure, a sum of eighty-five thousand marks of silver; and that all conquests, by sea and land, should be equally divided between the confederates. The terms were hard; but the emergency was pressing, and the French barons were not less profuse of money than of blood. A general assembly was convened to ratify the treaty: the stately chapel and place of St. Mark were filled with ten thousand citizens; and the noble deputies were taught a new lesson of humbling themselves before the majesty of the people. "Illustrious Venetians," said the marshal of Champagne, "we are sent by the greatest and most powerful barons of France to implore the aid of the masters of the sea for the deliverance of Jerusalem. They have enjoined us to fall prostrate at your feet; nor will we rise from the ground till you have promised to avenge with us the injuries of Christ." The eloquence of their words and tears,[2] their martial aspect

---

[1] See the original treaty in the Chronicle of Andrew Dandolo, p. 323-326 [Murat. Script. Ital. t. xii.].

[2] A reader of Villehardouin must observe the frequent tears of the

its allegiance to Venice, and implored the protection of the king
of Hungary.[1] The crusaders burst the chain or boom of the
harbour; landed their horses, troops, and military engines; and
compelled the inhabitants, after a defence of five days, to
surrender at discretion: their lives were spared, but the revolt
was punished by the pillage of their houses and the demolition
of their walls. The season was far advanced; the French and
Venetians resolved to pass the winter in a secure harbour and
plentiful country; but their repose was disturbed by national
and tumultuous quarrels of the soldiers and mariners. The
conquest of Zara had scattered the seeds of discord and scandal:
the arms of the allies had been stained in their outset with the
blood, not of infidels, but of Christians: the king of Hungary and
his new subjects were themselves enlisted under the banner
of the cross; and the scruples of the devout were magnified by
the fear or lassitude of the reluctant pilgrims. The pope had
excommunicated the false crusaders who had pillaged and
massacred their brethren,[2] and only the marquis Boniface and
Simon of Montfort escaped these spiritual thunders; the one
by his absence from the siege, the other by his final departure
from the camp. Innocent might absolve the simple and submissive penitents of France; but he was provoked by the
stubborn reason of the Venetians, who refused to confess their
guilt, to accept their pardon, or to allow, in their temporal
concerns, the interposition of a priest.

The assembly of such formidable powers by sea and land had
revived the hopes of young [3] Alexius, and both at Venice and
Zara he solicited the arms of the crusaders for his own restoration
and his father's [4] deliverance. The royal youth was recommended by Philip king of Germany; his prayers and presence
excited the compassion of the camp, and his cause was embraced

[1] Katona (Hist. Critica Reg. Hungariæ, Stirpis Arpad. tom. iv. p. 536-
558) collects all the facts and testimonies most adverse to the conquerors
of Zara.

[2] See the whole transaction, and the sentiments of the pope, in the
Epistles of Innocent III. Gesta, c. 86, 87, 88.

[3] A modern reader is surprised to hear of the valet de Constantinople,
as applied to young Alexius, on account of his youth, like the *infants* of
Spain, and the *nobilissimus puer* of the Romans. The pages and *valets* of
the knights were as noble as themselves (Villehardouin and Ducange,
No. 36).

[4] The emperor Isaac is styled by Villehardouin *Sursac* (No. 35, etc.),
which may be derived from the French *Sire*, or the Greek Κυρ (κίριος)
melted into his proper name; the farther corruptions of Tursac and Con-
serac will instruct us what licence may have been used in the old dynasties
of Assyria and Egypt.

and pleaded by the marquis of Montferrat and the doge of Venice.
A double alliance, and the dignity of Cæsar, had connected with
the Imperial family the two elder brothers of Boniface;[1] he
expected to derive a kingdom from the important service; and
the more generous ambition of Dandolo was eager to secure the
inestimable benefits of trade and dominion that might accrue
to his country.[2] Their influence procured a favourable audience
for the ambassadors of Alexius; and if the magnitude of his
offers excited some suspicion, the motives and rewards which he
displayed might justify the delay and diversion of those forces
which had been consecrated to the deliverance of Jerusalem.
He promised, in his own and his father's name, that, as soon as
they should be seated on the throne of Constantinople, they
would terminate the long schism of the Greeks, and submit
themselves and their people to the lawful supremacy of the
Roman church. He engaged to recompense the labours and
merits of the crusaders by the immediate payment of two
hundred thousand marks of silver; to accompany them in
person to Egypt; or, if it should be judged more advantageous,
to maintain, during a year, ten thousand men, and, during his
life, five hundred knights, for the service of the Holy Land.
These tempting conditions were accepted by the republic of
Venice, and the eloquence of the doge and marquis persuaded
the counts of Flanders, Blois, and St. Pol, with eight barons of
France, to join in the glorious enterprise. A treaty of offensive
and defensive alliance was confirmed by their oaths and seals;
and each individual, according to his situation and character,
was swayed by the hope of public or private advantage; by
the honour of restoring an exiled monarch; or by the sincere
and probable opinion that their efforts in Palestine would be
fruitless and unavailing, and that the acquisition of Constantinople must precede and prepare the recovery of Jerusalem.
But they were the chiefs or equals of a valiant band of freemen
and volunteers, who thought and acted for themselves: the
soldiers and clergy were divided; and, if a large majority
subscribed to the alliance, the numbers and arguments of the

---

[1] Reinier and Conrad: the former married Maria, daughter of the
emperor Manuel Comnenus; the latter was the husband of Theodora
Angela, sister of the emperors Isaac and Alexius. Conrad abandoned the
Greek court and princess for the glory of defending Tyre against Saladin
(Ducange, Fam. Byzant. p. 187, 203).

[2] Nicetas (in Alexio Comneno, l. iii. c. 9 [p. 715, ed. Bonn]) accuses the
doge and Venetians as the first authors of the war against Constantinople,
and considers only as a κῦμα ἐπὶ κύματι the arrival and shameful offers of
the royal exile.

dissidents were strong and respectable.[1] The boldest hearts
were appalled by the report of the naval power and impregnable strength of Constantinople, and their apprehensions were
disguised to the world, and perhaps to themselves, by the more
decent objections of religion and duty. They alleged the
sanctity of a vow which had drawn them from their families
and homes to the rescue of the holy sepulchre; nor should the
dark and crooked counsels of human policy divert them from
a pursuit, the event of which was in the hands of the Almighty.
Their first offence, the attack of Zara, had been severely
punished by the reproach of their conscience and the censures
of the pope, nor would they again imbrue their hands in the
blood of their fellow Christians. The apostle of Rome had
pronounced; nor would they usurp the right of avenging with
the sword the schism of the Greeks and the doubtful usurpation
of the Byzantine monarch. On these principles or pretences
many pilgrims, the most distinguished for their valour and piety,
withdrew from the camp; and their retreat was less pernicious
than the open or secret opposition of a discontented party that
laboured, on every occasion, to separate the army and disappoint
the enterprise.

Notwithstanding this defection, the departure of the fleet and
army was vigorously pressed by the Venetians, whose zeal for
the service of the royal youth concealed a just resentment to his
nation and family. They were mortified by the recent preference
which had been given to Pisa, the rival of their trade; they had
a long arrear of debt and injury to liquidate with the Byzantine
court; and Dandolo might not discourage the popular tale that
he had been deprived of his eyes by the emperor Manuel, who
perfidiously violated the sanctity of an ambassador. A similar
armament, for ages, had not rode the Adriatic: it was composed
of one hundred and twenty flat-bottomed vessels or *palanders*
for the horses, two hundred and forty transports filled with men
and arms, seventy store-ships laden with provisions, and fifty
stout galleys well prepared for the encounter of an enemy.[2]
While the wind was favourable, the sky serene, and the water

---

[1] Villehardouin and Gunther represent the sentiments of the two parties.
The abbot Martin left the army at Zara, proceeded to Palestine, was sent
ambassador to Constantinople, and became a reluctant witness of the
second siege.

[2] The birth and dignity of Andrew Dandolo gave him the motive and
the means of searching in the archives of Venice the memorable story of
his ancestor. His brevity seems to accuse the copious and more recent
narratives of Sanudo (in Muratori, Script. Rerum Italicarum, tom. xxii.),
Blondus, Sabellicus, and Rhamnusius.

smooth, every eye was fixed with wonder and delight on the
scene of military and naval pomp which overspread the sea.
The shields of the knights and squires, at once an ornament and
a defence, were arranged on either side of the ships; the banners
of the nations and families were displayed from the stern; our
modern artillery was supplied by three hundred engines for
casting stones and darts; the fatigues of the way were cheered
with the sound of music; and the spirits of the adventurers
were raised by the mutual assurance that forty thousand
Christian heroes were equal to the conquest of the world.[1]   In
the navigation [2] from Venice and Zara the fleet was successfully
steered by the skill and experience of the Venetian pilots: at
Durazzo the confederates first landed on the territories of the
Greek empire; the isle of Corfu afforded a station and repose;
they doubled, without accident, the perilous cape of Malea, the
southern point of Peloponnesus or the Morea; made a descent
in the islands of Negropont and Andros; and cast anchor at
Abydus on the Asiatic side of the Hellespont.   These preludes
of conquest were easy and bloodless; the Greeks of the provinces,
without patriotism or courage, were crushed by an irresistible
force; the presence of the lawful heir might justify their
obedience, and it was rewarded by the modesty and discipline
of the Latins.   As they penetrated through the Hellespont, the
magnitude of their navy was compressed in a narrow channel,
and the face of the waters was darkened with innumerable sails.
They again expanded in the basin of the Propontis, and traversed
that placid sea, till they approached the European shore at the
abbey of St. Stephen, three leagues to the west of Constantinople.
The prudent doge dissuaded them from dispersing themselves
in a populous and hostile land; and, as their stock of provisions
was reduced, it was resolved, in the season of harvest, to replenish
their storeships in the fertile islands of the Propontis.   With this
resolution they directed their course; but a strong gale and their
own impatience drove them to the eastward, and so near did
they run to the shore and the city, that some volleys of stones
and darts were exchanged between the ships and the rampart.
As they passed along, they gazed with admiration on the capital

---

[1] Villehardouin, No. 62.   His feelings and expressions are original: he
often weeps, but he rejoices in the glories and perils of war with a spirit
unknown to a sedentary writer.

[2] In this voyage almost all the geographical names are corrupted by
the Latins.   The modern appellation of Chalcis, and all Euboea, is derived
from its *Euripus, Evripo, Negri-po, Negropont,* which dishonours our maps
(D'Anville, Géographie Ancienne, tom. i. p. 263).

of the East, or, as it should seem, of the earth, rising from her seven hills, and towering over the continents of Europe and Asia. The swelling domes and lofty spires of five hundred palaces and churches were gilded by the sun and reflected in the waters; the walls were crowded with soldiers and spectators, whose numbers they beheld, of whose temper they were ignorant; and each heart was chilled by the reflection that, since the beginning of the world, such an enterprise had never been undertaken by such a handful of warriors. But the momentary apprehension was dispelled by hope and valour; and every man, says the marshal of Champagne, glanced his eye on the sword or lance which he must speedily use in the glorious conflict.[1] The Latins cast anchor before Chalcedon; the mariners only were left in the vessels; the soldiers, horses, and arms were safely landed; and, in the luxury of an Imperial palace, the barons tasted the first fruits of their success. On the third day the fleet and army moved towards Scutari, the Asiatic suburb of Constantinople: a detachment of five hundred Greek horse was surprised and defeated by fourscore French knights; and in a halt of nine days the camp was plentifully supplied with forage and provisions.

In relating the invasion of a great empire, it may seem strange that I have not described the obstacles which should have checked the progress of the strangers. The Greeks, in truth, were an unwarlike people; but they were rich, industrious, and subject to the will of a single man; had that man been capable of fear when his enemies were at a distance, or of courage when they approached his person. The first rumour of his nephew's alliance with the French and Venetians was despised by the usurper Alexius: his flatterers persuaded him that in this contempt he was bold and sincere; and each evening, in the close of the banquet, he thrice discomfited the barbarians of the West. These barbarians had been justly terrified by the report of his naval power; and the sixteen hundred fishing-boats of Constantinople[2] could have manned a fleet to sink them in the Adriatic, or stop their entrance in the mouth of the Hellespont. But all force may be annihilated by the negligence of the prince and the venality of his ministers. The great duke or admiral

---

[1] Et sachiez que il ni ot si hardi cui le cuer ne fremist (c. 66). . . . Chascuns regardoit ses armes . . . que par tems en arons mestier (c. 67). Such is the honesty of courage.

[2] Eandem urbem plus in solis navibus piscatorum abundare, quam illos in toto navigio. Habebat enim mille et sexcentas piscatorias naves. . . . Bellicas autem sive mercatorias habebant infinitæ multitudinis et portum tutissimum. Gunther, Hist. C. P. c. 8, p. 10 [in Canisius. Ant. Lect. t. iv.].

made a scandalous, almost a public, auction of the sails, the
masts, and the rigging; the royal forests were reserved for the
more important purpose of the chase; and the trees, says
Nicetas, were guarded by the eunuchs like the groves of religious
worship.[1] From his dream of pride Alexius was awakened by
the siege of Zara and the rapid advances of the Latins; as soon
as he saw the danger was real, he thought it inevitable, and his
vain presumption was lost in abject despondency and despair.
He suffered these contemptible barbarians to pitch their camp
in the sight of the palace, and his apprehensions were thinly disguised by the pomp and menace of a suppliant embassy. The
sovereign of the Romans was astonished (his ambassadors were
instructed to say) at the hostile appearance of the strangers.
If these pilgrims were sincere in their vow for the deliverance of
Jerusalem, his voice must applaud, and his treasures should
assist, their pious design; but should they dare to invade the
sanctuary of empire, their numbers, were they ten times more
considerable, should not protect them from his just resentment.
The answer of the doge and barons was simple and magnanimous.
" In the cause of honour and justice," they said, " we despise
the usurper of Greece, his threats, and his offers. *Our* friendship
and *his* allegiance are due to the lawful heir, to the young prince
who is seated among us, and to his father the emperor Isaac, who
has been deprived of his sceptre, his freedom, and his eyes by
the crime of an ungrateful brother. Let that brother confess his
guilt and implore forgiveness, and we ourselves will intercede
that he may be permitted to live in affluence and security. But
let him not insult us by a second message: our reply will be
made in arms, in the palace of Constantinople."

On the tenth day of their encampment at Scutari the
crusaders prepared themselves, as soldiers and as Catholics, for
the passage of the Bosphorus. Perilous indeed was the adventure: the stream was broad and rapid; in a calm the current of
the Euxine might drive down the liquid and unextinguishable
fires of the Greeks, and the opposite shores of Europe were
defended by seventy thousand horse and foot in formidable
array. On this memorable day, which happened to be bright
and pleasant, the Latins were distributed in six battles or
divisions; the first, or vanguard, was led by the count of Flanders,
one of the most powerful of the Christian princes in the skill and
number of his cross-bows. The four successive battles of the

---

[1] Καθάπερ ἱερῶν ἀλσέων, εἰπεῖν δὲ καὶ θεοφυτεύτων παραδείσων ἐφείδοντο
τουτωνί. Nicetas in Alex. Comneno, l. iii. c. 9, p. 348 [p. 716, ed. Bonn].

French were commanded by his brother Henry, the counts of St. Pol and Blois, and Matthew of Montmorency, the last of whom was honoured by the voluntary service of the marshal and nobles of Champagne. The sixth division, the rear-guard and reserve of the army, was conducted by the marquis of Montferrat, at the head of the Germans and Lombards. The chargers, saddled, with their long caparisons dragging on the ground, were embarked in the flat *palanders*,[1] and the knights stood by the side of their horses, in complete armour, their helmets laced, and their lances in their hands. Their numerous train of *serjeants* [2] and archers occupied the transports, and each transport was towed by the strength and swiftness of a galley. The six divisions traversed the Bosphorus without encountering an enemy or an obstacle; to land the foremost was the wish, to conquer or die was the resolution, of every division and of every soldier. Jealous of the pre-eminence of danger, the knights in their heavy armour leaped into the sea when it rose as high as their girdle; the serjeants and archers were animated by their valour; and the squires, letting down the drawbridges of the palanders, led the horses to the shore. Before the squadrons could mount, and form, and couch their lances, the seventy thousand Greeks had vanished from their sight; the timid Alexius gave the example to his troops, and it was only by the plunder of his rich pavilions that the Latins were informed that they had fought against an emperor. In the first consternation of the flying enemy, they resolved, by a double attack, to open the entrance of the harbour. The tower of Galata,[3] in the suburb of Pera, was attacked and stormed by the French, while the Venetians assumed the more difficult task of forcing the boom or chain that was stretched from that tower to the Byzantine shore. After some fruitless attempts their intrepid perseverance

---

[1] From the version of Vigenere I adopt the well-sounding word *palander*, which is still used, I believe, in the Mediterranean. But had I written in French, I should have preferred the original and expressive denomination of *vessiers* or *huissiers*, from the *huis*, or door, which was let down as a drawbridge; but which, at sea, was closed into the side of the ship. (See Ducange au Villehardouin, No. 14, and Joinville, p. 27, 28, édit. du Louvre.)

[2] To avoid the vague expressions of followers, etc., I use, after Villehardouin, the word *serjeants* for all horsemen who were not knights. There were serjeants at arms and serjeants at law; and if we visit the parade and Westminster Hall, we may observe the strange result of the distinction (Ducange, Glossar. Latin. *Servientes*, etc., tom. vi. p. 226-231).

[3] It is needless to observe that on the subject of Galata, the chain, etc., Ducange is accurate and full. Consult likewise the proper chapters of the C. P. Christiana of the same author. The inhabitants of Galata were so vain and ignorant, that they applied to themselves St. Paul's Epistle to the Galatians.

prevailed; twenty ships of war, the relics of the Grecian navy, were either sunk or taken; the enormous and massy links of iron were cut asunder by the shears or broken by the weight of the galleys; [1] and the Venetian fleet, safe and triumphant, rode at anchor in the port of Constantinople. By these daring achievements a remnant of twenty thousand Latins solicited the licence of besieging a capital which contained above four hundred thousand inhabitants, [2] able, though not willing, to bear arms in the defence of their country. Such an account would indeed suppose a population of near two millions: but whatever abatement may be required in the numbers of the Greeks, the *belief* of those numbers will equally exalt the fearless spirit of their assailants.

In the choice of the attack the French and Venetians were divided by their habits of life and warfare. The latter affirmed with truth that Constantinople was most accessible on the side of the sea and the harbour. The former might assert with honour that they had long enough trusted their lives and fortunes to a frail bark and a precarious element, and loudly demanded a trial of knighthood, a firm ground, and a close onset, either on foot or horseback. After a prudent compromise of employing the two nations by sea and land in the service best suited to their character, the fleet covering the army, they both proceeded from the entrance to the extremity of the harbour: the stone bridge of the river was hastily repaired; and the six battles of the French formed their encampment against the front of the capital, the basis of the triangle which runs about four miles from the port to the Propontis. [3] On the edge of a broad ditch, at the foot of a lofty rampart, they had leisure to contemplate the difficulties of their enterprise. The gates to

---

[1] The vessel that broke the chain was named the Eagle, *Aquila* (Dandol. Chronicon, p. 322), which Blondus (de Gestis Venet.) has changed into *Aquilo*, the north-wind. Ducange, Observations, No. 83, maintains the latter reading; but he had not seen the respectable text of Dandolo, nor did he enough consider the topography of the harbour. The south-east would have been a more effectual wind. [Note to Wilken, vol. v. p. 215.]

[2] Quatre cens mil homes ou plus (Villehardouin, No. 133) must be understood of *men* of a military age. Le Beau (Hist. du Bas Empire, tom. xx. p. 417) allows Constantinople a million of inhabitants, of whom 60,000 horse, and an infinite number of foot soldiers. In its present decay, the capital of the Ottoman empire may contain 400,000 souls (Bell's Travels, vol. ii. p. 401, 402); but as the Turks keep no registers, and as circumstances are fallacious, it is impossible to ascertain (Niebuhr, Voyage en Arabie, tom. i. p. 18, 19) the real populousness of their cities.

[3] On the most correct plans of Constantinople, I know not how to measure more than 4000 paces. Yet Villehardouin computes the space at three leagues (No. 86). If his eye were not deceived, he must reckon by the old Gallic league of 1500 paces, which might still be used in Champagne.

the right and left of their narrow camp poured forth frequent sallies of cavalry and light infantry, which cut off their stragglers, swept the country of provisions, sounded the alarm five or six times in the course of each day, and compelled them to plant a palisade and sink an entrenchment for their immediate safety In the supplies and convoys the Venetians had been too sparing, or the Franks too voracious: the usual complaints of hunger and scarcity were heard, and perhaps felt: their stock of flour would be exhausted in three weeks; and their disgust of salt meat tempted them to taste the flesh of their horses. The trembling usurper was supported by Theodore Lascaris, his son-in-law, a valiant youth, who aspired to save and to rule his country; the Greeks, regardless of that country, were awakened to the defence of their religion; but their firmest hope was in the strength and spirit of the Varangian guards, of the Danes and English, as they are named in the writers of the times.[1] After ten days' incessant labour the ground was levelled, the ditch filled, the approaches of the besiegers were regularly made, and two hundred and fifty engines of assault exercised their various powers to clear the rampart, to batter the walls, and to sap the foundations. On the first appearance of a breach the scaling-ladders were applied: the numbers that defended the vantage-ground repulsed and oppressed the adventurous Latins: but they admired the resolution of fifteen knights and serjeants, who had gained the ascent, and maintained their perilous station till they were precipitated or made prisoners by the Imperial guards. On the side of the harbour the naval attack was more successfully conducted by the Venetians; and that industrious people employed every resource that was known and practised before the invention of gunpowder. A double line, three bow-shots in front, was formed by the galleys and ships; and the swift motion of the former was supported by the weight and loftiness of the latter, whose decks, and poops, and turret, were the platforms of military engines, that discharged their shot over the heads of the first line. The soldiers, who leaped from the galleys on shore, immediately planted and ascended their scaling-ladders, while the large ships, advancing more slowly into the intervals, and lowering a drawbridge, opened a way through the air from their masts to the rampart. In the midst of the conflict the doge, a venerable and

---

[1] The guards, the Varangi, are styled by Villehardouin (No. 89, 95, etc.) Englois et Danois avec leurs haches. Whatever had been their origin, a French pilgrim could not be mistaken in the nations of which they were at that time composed.

conspicuous form, stood aloft in complete armour on the prow
of his galley. The great standard of St. Mark was displayed
before him; his threats, promises, and exhortations urged the
diligence of the rowers; his vessel was the first that struck;
and Dandolo was the first warrior on the shore. The nations
admired the magnanimity of the blind old man, without reflect-
ing that his age and infirmities diminished the price of life and
enhanced the value of immortal glory. On a sudden, by an
invisible hand (for the standard-bearer was probably slain), the
banner of the republic was fixed on the rampart: twenty-five
towers were rapidly occupied; and, by the cruel expedient of
fire, the Greeks were driven from the adjacent quarter. The
doge had despatched the intelligence of his success, when he was
checked by the danger of his confederates. Nobly declaring
that he would rather die with the pilgrims than gain a victory by
their destruction, Dandolo relinquished his advantage, recalled
his troops, and hastened to the scene of action. He found the
six weary diminutive *battles* of the French encompassed by sixty
squadrons of the Greek cavalry, the least of which was more
numerous than the largest of their divisions. Shame and despair
had provoked Alexius to the last effort of a general sally; but
he was awed by the firm order and manly aspect of the Latins;
and, after skirmishing at a distance, withdrew his troops in the
close of the evening. The silence or tumult of the night exasperated his fears; and the timid usurper, collecting a treasure of
ten thousand pounds of gold, basely deserted his wife, his people,
and his fortune; threw himself into a bark; stole through the
Bosphorus; and landed in shameful safety in an obscure harbour
of Thrace. As soon as they were apprised of his flight, the Greek
nobles sought pardon and peace in the dungeon where the blind
Isaac expected each hour the visit of the executioner. Again
saved and exalted by the vicissitudes of fortune, the captive in
his Imperial robes was replaced on the throne, and surrounded
with prostrate slaves, whose real terror and affected joy he was
incapable of discerning. At the dawn of day hostilities were
suspended, and the Latin chiefs were surprised by a message
from the lawful and reigning emperor, who was impatient to
embrace his son and to reward his generous deliverers.[1]

[1] For the first siege and conquest of Constantinople, we may read the
original letter of the crusaders to Innocent III., Gesta, c. 91, p. 533, 534;
Villehardouin, No. 75-99; Nicetas, in Alexio Comnen. l. iii. c. 10, p. 349-
352 [p. 718-725, ed. Bonn]; Dandolo, in Chron. p. 322. Gunther and his
abbot Martin were not yet returned from their obstinate pilgrimage to
Jerusalem, or St. John d'Acre, where the greatest part of the company had
died of the plague.

But these generous deliverers were unwilling to release their hostage till they had obtained from his father the payment, or at least the promise, of their recompense.   They chose four ambassadors, Matthew of Montmorency, our historian the marshal of Champagne, and two Venetians, to congratulate the emperor. The gates were thrown open on their approach, the streets on both sides were lined with the battle-axes of the Danish and English guard: the presence-chamber glittered with gold and jewels, the false substitutes of virtue and power: by the side of the blind Isaac his wife was seated, the sister of the king of Hungary: and by her appearance, the noble matrons of Greece were drawn from their domestic retirement and mingled with the circle of senators and soldiers.   The Latins, by the mouth of the marshal, spoke like men conscious of their merits, but who respected the work of their own hands; and the emperor clearly understood that his son's engagements with Venice and the pilgrims must be ratified without hesitation or delay.   Withdrawing into a private chamber with the empress, a chamberlain, an interpreter, and the four ambassadors, the father of young Alexius inquired with some anxiety into the nature of his stipulations.   The submission of the Eastern empire to the pope, the succour of the Holy Land, and a present contribution of two hundred thousand marks of silver.—" These conditions are weighty," was his prudent reply: " they are hard to accept, and difficult to perform.   But no conditions can exceed the measure of your services and deserts."   After this satisfactory assurance, the barons mounted on horseback and introduced the heir of Constantinople to the city and palace: his youth and marvellous adventures engaged every heart in his favour, and Alexius was solemnly crowned with his father in the dome of St. Sophia.   In the first days of his reign, the people, already blessed with the restoration of plenty and peace, was delighted by the joyful catastrophe of the tragedy; and the discontent of the nobles, their regret, and their fears, were covered by the polished surface of pleasure and loyalty.   The mixture of two discordant nations in the same capital might have been pregnant with mischief and danger; and the suburb of Galata, or Pera, was assigned for the quarters of the French and Venetians.   But the liberty of trade and familiar intercourse was allowed between the friendly nations; and each day the pilgrims were tempted by devotion or curiosity to visit the churches and palaces of Constantinople.   Their rude minds, insensible perhaps of the finer arts, were astonished by the magnificent scenery: and the poverty of their native towns enhanced the populousness and riches of the first metropolis of Christendom.[1] Descending from his state, young Alexius was prompted by interest and gratitude to repeat his frequent and familiar visits to his Latin allies; and in the freedom of the table the gay petulance of the French sometimes forgot the emperor of the East.[2] In their more serious conferences it was agreed that the re-union of the two churches must be the result of patience and time; but avarice was less tractable than zeal; and a large sum was instantly disbursed to appease the wants, and silence the importunity, of the crusaders.[3] Alexius was alarmed by the approaching hour of their departure: their absence might have relieved him from the engagement which he was yet incapable of performing; but his friends would have left him, naked and alone, to the caprice and prejudice of a perfidious nation. He wished to bribe their stay, the delay of a year, by undertaking to defray their expense, and to satisfy, in their name, the freight of the Venetian vessels. The offer was agitated in the council of the barons; and, after a repetition of their debates and scruples, a majority of votes again acquiesced in the advice of the doge and the prayer of the young emperor. At the price of sixteen hundred pounds of gold, he prevailed on the marquis of Montferrat to lead him with an army round the provinces of Europe; to establish his authority, and pursue his uncle, while Constantinople was awed by the presence of Baldwin and his confederates of France and Flanders. The expedition was successful: the blind emperor exulted in the success of his arms, and listened to the predictions of his flatterers, that the same Providence which had raised him from the dungeon to the throne would heal his gout, restore his sight, and watch over the long prosperity of his reign. Yet the mind of the suspicious old man was tormented by the rising glories of his son; nor could his

---

[1] Compare, in the rude energy of Villehardouin (No. 66, 100), the inside and outside views of Constantinople, and their impression on the minds of the pilgrims: cette ville (says he) que de totes les autres ére souveraine. See the parallel passages of Fulcherius Carnotensis, Hist. Hierosol. l. i. c. 4 [p. 386], and Will. Tyr. ii. 3, xx. 26.

[2] As they played at dice, the Latins took off his diadem, and clapped on his head a woollen or hairy cap, τὸ μεγαλοπρεπὲς καὶ παγκλέϊστον κατερρύπαινεν ὄνομα (Nicetas, p. 358 [p. 736, ed. Bonn])'. If these merry companions were Venetians, it was the insolence of trade and a commonwealth.

[3] Villehardouin, No. 101; Dandolo, p. 322. The doge affirms that the Venetians were paid more slowly than the French; but he owns that the histories of the two nations differed on that subject. Had he read Villehardouin? The Greeks complained, however, quòd totius Græciæ opes transtulisset (Gunther, Hist. C. P. c. 13). See the lamentations and invectives of Nicetas (p. 355 [p. 729, ed. Bonn]).

pride conceal from his envy, that, while his own name was pronounced in faint and reluctant acclamations, the royal youth
was the theme of spontaneous and universal praise.[1]

By the recent invasion the Greeks were awakened from a
dream of nine centuries; from the vain presumption that the
capital of the Roman empire was impregnable to foreign arms.
The strangers of the West had violated the city, and bestowed
the sceptre, of Constantine: their Imperial clients soon became
as unpopular as themselves: the well-known vices of Isaac were
rendered still more contemptible by his infirmities, and the young
Alexius was hated as an apostate who had renounced the manners
and religion of his country. His secret covenant with the Latins
was divulged or suspected; the people, and especially the clergy,
were devoutly attached to their faith and superstition; and
every convent, and every shop, resounded with the danger of
the church and the tyranny of the pope.[2] An empty treasury
could ill supply the demands of regal luxury and foreign extor-
tion: the Greeks refused to avert, by a general tax, the impending evils of servitude and pillage; the oppression of the rich
excited a more dangerous and personal resentment; and if the
emperor melted the plate and despoiled the images of the
sanctuary, he seemed to justify the complaints of heresy and
sacrilege. During the absence of marquis Boniface and his
Imperial pupil, Constantinople was visited with a calamity
which might be justly imputed to the zeal and indiscretion of the
Flemish pilgrims.[3] In one of their visits to the city they were
scandalised by the aspect of a mosque or synagogue, in which
one God was worshipped, without a partner or a son. Their
effectual mode of controversy was to attack the infidels with the
sword, and their habitation with fire: but the infidels, and some
Christian neighbours, presumed to defend their lives and properties; and the flames which bigotry had kindled consumed the
most orthodox and innocent structures. During eight days and

---

[1] The reign of Alexius Comnenus occupies three books in Nicetas, p. 291-
352. The short restoration of Isaac and his son is despatched in five
chapters, p. 352-362.

[2] When Nicetas reproaches Alexius for his impious league, he bestows
the harshest names on the pope's new religion, μεῖζον καὶ ἀτοπώτατον
. . . παρεκτροπὴν πίστεως . . . τῶν τοῦ Πάπα προνομίων καινισμὸν,
μετάθεσίν τε καὶ μεταποίησιν τῶν παλαιῶν Ῥωμαίοις ἐθῶν (p. 348 [p. 715,
ed. Bonn]). Such was the sincere language of every Greek to the last gasp
of the empire.

[3] Nicetas (p. 355 [p. 731, ed. Bonn]) is positive in the charge, and speci-
fies the Flemings (Φλαμίονες), though he is wrong in supposing it an
ancient name. Villehardouin (No. 107) exculpates the barons, and is
ignorant (perhaps affectedly ignorant) of the names of the guilty.

nights the conflagration spread above a league in front, from the harbour to the Propontis, over the thickest and most populous regions of the city. It is not easy to count the stately churches and palaces that were reduced to a smoking ruin, to value the merchandise that perished in the trading streets, or to number the families that were involved in the common destruction. By this outrage, which the doge and the barons in vain affected to disclaim, the name of the Latins became still more unpopular; and the colony of that nation, above fifteen thousand persons, consulted their saftey in a hasty retreat from the city to the protection of their standard in the suburb of Pera. The emperor returned in triumph; but the firmest and most dexterous policy would have been insufficient to steer him through the tempest which overwhelmed the person and government of that unhappy youth. His own inclination, and his father's advice, attached him to his benefactors; but Alexius hesitated between gratitude and patriotism, between the fear of his subjects and of his allies.[1] By his feeble and fluctuating conduct he lost the esteem and confidence of both; and, while he invited the marquis of Montferrat to occupy the palace, he suffered the nobles to conspire, and the people to arm, for the deliverance of their country. Regardless of his painful situation, the Latin chiefs repeated their demands, resented his delays, suspected his intentions, and exacted a decisive answer of peace or war. The haughty summons was delivered by three French knights and three Venetian deputies, who girded their swords, mounted their horses, pierced through the angry multitude, and entered, with a fearless countenance, the palace and presence of the Greek emperor. In a peremptory tone they recapitulated their services and his engagements; and boldly declared that, unless their just claims were fully and immediately satisfied, they should no longer hold him either as a sovereign or a friend. After this defiance, the first that had ever wounded an Imperial ear, they departed without betraying any symptoms of fear; but their escape from a servile palace and a furious city astonished the ambassadors themselves: and their return to the camp was the signal of mutual hostility.

Among the Greeks all authority and wisdom were overborne by the impetuous multitude, who mistook their rage for valour, their numbers for strength, and their fanaticism for the support and inspiration of Heaven. In the eyes of both nations Alexius

[1] Compare the suspicions and complaints of Nicetas (p. 359-362 [p. 740-747, ed. Bonn]) with the blunt charges of Baldwin of Flanders (Gesta Innocent. III. c. 92, p. 534), cum patriarcha et mole nobilium, nobis promissis perjurus et mendax.

was false and contemptible: the base and spurious race of the
Angeli was rejected with clamorous disdain; and the people of
Constantinople encompassed the senate to demand at their
hands a more worthy emperor. To every senator, conspicuous
by his birth or dignity, they successively presented the purple:
by each senator the deadly garment was repulsed: the contest
lasted three days; and we may learn from the historian Nicetas,
one of the members of the assembly, that fear and weakness
were the guardians of their loyalty. A phantom, who vanished
in oblivion, was forcibly proclaimed by the crowd: [1] but the
author of the tumult, and the leader of the war, was a prince of
the house of Ducas; and his common appellation of Alexius
must be discriminated by the epithet of Mourzoufle, [2] which in
the vulgar idiom expressed the close junction of his black and
shaggy eyebrows. At once a patriot and a courtier, the perfidious Mourzoufle, who was not destitute of cunning and courage,
opposed the Latins both in speech and action, inflamed the
passions and prejudices of the Greeks, and insinuated himself
into the favour and confidence of Alexius, who trusted him with
the office of great chamberlain, and tinged his buskins with the
colours of royalty. At the dead of night he rushed into the bed-
chamber with an affrighted aspect, exclaiming that the palace
was attacked by the people and betrayed by the guards. Starting from his couch, the unsuspecting prince threw himself into
the arms of his enemy, who had contrived his escape by a private
staircase. But that staircase terminated in a prison: Alexius
was seized, stripped, and loaded with chains; and, after tasting
some days the bitterness of death, he was poisoned, or strangled,
or beaten with clubs, at the command, and in the presence, of the
tyrant. The emperor Isaac Angelus soon followed his son to
the grave; and Mourzoufle, perhaps, might spare the superfluous crime of hastening the extinction of impotence and
blindness.

The death of the emperors, and the usurpation of Mourzoufle,
had changed the nature of the quarrel. It was no longer the dis-
agreement of allies who overvalued their services, or neglected
their obligations: the French and Venetians forgot their complaints against Alexius, dropped a tear on the untimely fate of

---

[1] His name was Nicholas Canabus: he deserved the praise of Nicetas and
the vengeance of Mourzoufle (p. 362 [p. 744, ed. Bonn]).

[2] Villehardouin (No. 116) speaks of him as a favourite, without knowing
that he was a prince of the blood, *Angelus* and *Ducas*. Ducange, who
pries into every corner, believes him to be the son of Isaac Ducas Sebastocrator, and second cousin of young Alexius.

their companion, and swore revenge against the perfidious nation who had crowned his assassin. Yet the prudent doge was still inclined to negotiate: he asked as a debt, a subsidy, or a fine, fifty thousand pounds of gold, about two millions sterling; nor would the conference have been abruptly broken if the zeal, or policy, of Mourzoufle had not refused to sacrifice the Greek church to the safety of the state.[1] Amidst the invectives of his foreign and domestic enemies, we may discern that he was not unworthy of the character which he had assumed, of the public champion: the second siege of Constantinople was far more laborious than the first; the treasury was replenished, and discipline was restored, by a severe inquisition into the abuses of the former reign; and Mourzoufle, an iron mace in his hand, visiting the posts, and affecting the port and aspect of a warrior, was an object of terror to his soldiers, at least, and to his kinsmen. Before and after the death of Alexius, the Greeks made two vigorous and well-conducted attempts to burn the navy in the harbour; but the skill and courage of the Venetians repulsed the fire-ships; and the vagrant flames wasted themselves without injury in the sea.[2] In a nocturnal sally the Greek emperor was vanquished by Henry, brother of the count of Flanders: the advantages of number and surprise aggravated the shame of his defeat: his buckler was found on the field of battle; and the Imperial standard,[3] a divine image of the Virgin, was presented, as a trophy and a relic, to the Cistercian monks, the disciples of St. Bernard. Near three months, without excepting the holy season of Lent, were consumed in skirmishes and preparations, before the Latins were ready or resolved for a general assault. The land fortifications had been found impregnable; and the Venetian pilots represented, that, on the shore of the Propontis, the anchorage was unsafe, and the ships must be driven by the current far away to the straits of the Hellespont; a prospect not unpleasing to the reluctant pilgrims, who sought every opportunity of breaking the army. From the harbour, therefore, the

---

[1] This negotiation, probable in itself, and attested by Nicetas (p. 365 [p. 751, ed. Bonn]), is omitted as scandalous by the delicacy of Dandolo and Villehardouin.

[2] Baldwin mentions both attempts to fire the fleet (Gest. c. 92, p. 534, 535); Villehardouin (No. 113-115) only describes the first. It is remarkable that neither of these warriors observe any peculiar properties in the Greek fire.

[3] Ducange (No. 119) pours forth a torrent of learning on the *Gonfanon Imperial.* This banner of the Virgin is shown at Venice as a trophy and relic: if it be genuine, the pious doge must have cheated the monks of ~eaux.

assault was determined by the assailants and expected by the besieged; and the emperor had placed his scarlet pavilions on a neighbouring height, to direct and animate the efforts of his troops. A fearless spectator, whose mind could entertain the ideas of pomp and pleasure, might have admired the long array of two embattled armies, which extended above half a league, the one on the ships and galleys, the other on the walls and towers raised above the ordinary level by several stages of wooden turrets. Their first fury was spent in the discharge of darts, stones, and fire, from the engines; but the water was deep; the French were bold; the Venetians were skilful; they approached the walls; and a desperate conflict of swords, spears, and battle-axes, was fought on the trembling bridges that grappled the floating to the stable batteries. In more than a hundred places the assault was urged and the defence was sustained; till the superiority of ground and numbers finally prevailed, and the Latin trumpets sounded a retreat. On the ensuing days the attack was renewed with equal vigour and a similar event; and, in the night, the doge and the barons held a council, apprehensive only for the public danger: not a voice pronounced the words of escape or treaty; and each warrior, according to his temper, embraced the hope of victory or the assurance of a glorious death.[1] By the experience of the former siege the Greeks were instructed, but the Latins were animated; and the knowledge that Constantinople *might* be taken was of more avail than the local precautions which that knowledge had inspired for its defence. In the third assault two ships were linked together to double their strength; a strong north wind drove them on the shore; the bishops of Troyes and Soissons led the van; and the auspicious names of the *Pilgrim* and the *Paradise* resounded along the line.[2] The episcopal banners were displayed on the walls; a hundred marks of silver had been promised to the first adventurers; and if their reward was intercepted by death, their names have been immortalised by fame. Four towers were scaled; three gates were burst open; and the French knights, who might tremble on the waves, felt themselves invincible on horseback on the solid ground. Shall I relate that the thousands who guarded the emperor's person fled on the

---

[1] Villehardouin (No. 126) confesses that mult ere grant peril; and Guntherus (Hist. C. P. c. 13 [c. 14, p. xiv.]) affirms that nulla spes victoriæ arridere poterat. Yet the knight despises those who thought of flight, and the monk praises his countrymen who were resolved on death.

[2] Baldwin and all the writers honour the names of these two galleys, felici auspicio.

approach, and before the lance, of a single warrior? Their
ignominious flight is attested by their countryman Nicetas: an
army of phantoms marched with the French hero, and he was
magnified to a giant in the eyes of the Greeks.[1] While the fugitives deserted their posts and cast away their arms, the Latins
entered the city under the banners of their leaders: the streets
and gates opened for their passage; and either design or accident
kindled a third conflagration, which consumed in a few hours the
measure of three of the largest cities of France.[2] In the close
of evening the barons checked their troops and fortified their
stations: they were awed by the extent and populousness of the
capital, which might yet require the labour of a month, if the
churches and palaces were conscious of their internal strength.
But in the morning a suppliant procession, with crosses and
images, announced the submission of the Greeks and deprecated
the wrath of the conquerors: the usurper escaped through the
golden gate: the palaces of Blachernæ and Boucoleon were
occupied by the count of Flanders and the marquis of Montferrat;
and the empire, which still bore the name of Constantine and
the title of Roman, was subverted by the arms of the Latin
pilgrims.[3]

Constantinople had been taken by storm; and no restraints
except those of religion and humanity were imposed on the conquerors by the laws of war. Boniface, marquis of Montferrat,
still acted as their general; and the Greeks, who revered his
name as that of their future sovereign, were heard to exclaim in
a lamentable tone, " Holy marquis-king, have mercy upon us! "
His prudence or compassion opened the gates of the city to the
fugitives, and he exhorted the soldiers of the cross to spare the
lives of their fellow-Christians. The streams of blood that flow

[1] With an allusion to Homer, Nicetas calls him ἐννεόργυιος, nine orgyæ, or
eighteen yards, high—a stature which would, indeed, have excused the
terror of the Greek. On this occasion the historian seems fonder of the
marvellous than of his country, or perhaps of truth. Baldwin exclaims,
in the words of the psalmist, persequitur unus ex nobis centum alienos.

[2] Villehardouin (No. 130) is again ignorant of the authors of *this* more
legitimate fire, which is ascribed by Gunther to a quidam comes Teutonicus
(c. 14 [c. 17, p. xv.]). They seem ashamed, the incendiaries!

[3] For the second siege and conquest of Constantinople, see Villehardouin
(No. 113-132), Baldwin's second Epistle to Innocent III. (Gesta, c. 92,
p. 534-537), with the whole reign of Mourzoufle, in Nicetas (p. 363-375
[p. 748-770, ed. Bonn]), and borrow some hints from Dandolo (Chron.
Venet. p. 323-330) and Gunther (Hist. C. P. c. 14-18), who add the decorations of prophecy and vision. The former produces an oracle of the Ery-
thræan sibyl, of a great armament on the Adriatic, under a blind chief,
against Byzantium, etc. Curious enough, were the prediction anterior to
the fact.

down the pages of Nicetas may be reduced to the slaughter of
two thousand of his unresisting countrymen; [1] and the greater
part was massacred, not by the strangers, but by the Latins who
had been driven from the city, and who exercised the revenge
of a triumphant faction. Yet of these exiles, some were less
mindful of injuries than of benefits; and Nicetas himself was
indebted for his safety to the generosity of a Venetian merchant.
Pope Innocent the Third accuses the pilgrims of respecting, in
their lust, neither age, nor sex, nor religious profession; and
bitterly laments that the deeds of darkness, fornication, adultery,
and incest, were perpetrated in open day; and that noble
matrons and holy nuns were polluted by the grooms and peasants
of the Catholic camp. [2] It is indeed probable that the licence of
victory prompted and covered a multitude of sins: but it is
certain that the capital of the East contained a stock of venal or
willing beauty sufficient to satiate the desires of twenty thousand
pilgrims, and female prisoners were no longer subject to the right
or abuse of domestic slavery. The marquis of Montferrat was
the patron of discipline and decency: the count of Flanders was
the mirror of chastity: they had forbidden, under pain of death,
the rape of married women, or virgins, or nuns; and the proclamation was sometimes invoked by the vanquished [3] and
respected by the victors. Their cruelty and lust were moderated
by the authority of the chiefs and feelings of the soldiers; for
we are no longer describing an irruption of the northern savages;
and however ferocious they might still appear, time, policy, and
religion had civilised the manners of the French, and still more
of the Italians. But a free scope was allowed to their avarice,
which was glutted, even in the holy week, by the pillage of
Constantinople. The right of victory, unshackled by any
promise or treaty, had confiscated the public and private wealth
of the Greeks; and every hand, according to its size and strength,
might lawfully execute the sentence and seize the forfeiture. A
portable and universal standard of exchange was found in the

---

[1] Ceciderunt tamen eâ die civium quasi duo millia, etc. (Gunther, c. 18.)
Arithmetic is an excellent touchstone to try the amplifications of passion
and rhetoric.

[2] Quidam (says Innocent III., Gesta, c. 94, p. 538) nec religioni, nec
ætati, nec sexui pepercerunt: sed fornicationes, adulteria, et incestus in
oculis omnium exercentes, non solùm maritatas et viduas, sed et matronas
et virgines Deoque dicatas, exposuerunt spurcitiis garcionum. Villehardouin takes no notice of these common incidents.

[3] Nicetas saved, and afterwards married, a noble virgin (p. 380 [p. 781,
ed. Bonn]), whom a soldier, ἐπὶ μάρτυσι πολλοῖς ὀνηδὸν ἐπιβρωμώμενος,
had almost violated, in spite of the ἐντολαί, ἐντάλματα εὖ γεγονότων.

coined and uncoined metals of gold and silver, which each captor, at home or abroad, might convert into the possessions most suitable to his temper and situation. Of the treasures which trade and luxury had accumulated, the silks, velvets, furs, the gems, spices, and rich movables, were the most precious, as they could not be procured for money in the ruder countries of Europe. An order of rapine was instituted; nor was the share of each individual abandoned to industry or chance. Under the tremendous penalties of perjury—excommunication and death—the Latins were bound to deliver their plunder into the common stock; three churches were selected for the deposit and distribution of the spoil: a single share was allotted to a foot soldier, two for a serjeant on horseback, four to a knight, and larger proportions according to the rank and merit of the barons and princes. For violating this sacred engagement, a knight belonging to the count of St. Paul was hanged with his shield and coat of arms round his neck: his example might render similar offenders more artful and discreet, but avarice was more powerful than fear, and it is generally believed that the secret far exceeded the acknowledged plunder. Yet the magnitude of the prize surpassed the largest scale of experience or expectation.[1] After the whole had been equally divided between the French and Venetians, fifty thousand marks were deducted to satisfy the debts of the former and the demands of the latter. The residue of the French amounted to four hundred thousand marks of silver,[2] about eight hundred thousand pounds sterling; nor can I better appreciate the value of that sum in the public and private transactions of the age than by defining it as seven times the annual revenue of the kingdom of England.[3]

In this great revolution we enjoy the singular felicity of comparing the narratives of Villehardouin and Nicetas, the opposite feelings of the marshal of Champagne and the Byzantine senator.[4]

[1] Of the general mass of wealth, Gunther observes, ut de pauperibus et advenis cives ditissimi redderentur (Hist. C. P. c. 18); Villehardouin (No. 132), that since the creation, ne fu tant gaaignié en une ville; Baldwin (Gesta, c. 92), ut tantum tota non videatur possidere Latinitas [p. 535].

[2] Villehardouin, No. 133-135. Instead of 400,000, there is a various reading of 500,000. The Venetians had offered to take the whole booty, and to give 400 marks to each knight, 200 to each priest and horseman, and 100 to each foot soldier: they would have been great losers (Le Beau, Hist. du Bas-Empire, tom. xx. p. 506: I know not from whence).

[3] At the council of Lyons (A.D. 1245) the English ambassadors stated the revenue of the crown as below that of the foreign clergy, which amounted to 60,000 marks a-year (Matthew Paris, p. 451; Hume's History of England, vol. ii. p. 170).

[4] The disorders of the sack of Constantinople, and his own adventures, are feelingly described by Nicetas, p. 367-369 [p. 757-761, ed. Bonn], and

At the first view it should seem that the wealth of Constantinople was only transferred from one nation to another, and that the loss and sorrow of the Greeks is exactly balanced by the joy and advantage of the Latins. But in the miserable account of war the gain is never equivalent to the loss, the pleasure to the pain; the smiles of the Latins were transient and fallacious; the Greeks for ever wept over the ruins of their country, and their real calamities were aggravated by sacrilege and mockery. What benefits accrued to the conquerors from the three fires which annihilated so vast a portion of the buildings and riches of the city? What a stock of such things as could neither be used nor transported was maliciously or wantonly destroyed! How much treasure was idly wasted in gaming, debauchery, and riot! And what precious objects were bartered for a vile price by the impatience or ignorance of the soldiers, whose reward was stolen by the base industry of the last of the Greeks! These alone who had nothing to lose might derive some profit from the revolution; but the misery of the upper ranks of society is strongly painted in the personal adventures of Nicetas himself. His stately palace had been reduced to ashes in the second conflagration; and the senator, with his family and friends, found an obscure shelter in another house which he possessed near the church of St. Sophia. It was the door of this mean habitation that his friend the Venetian merchant guarded, in the disguise of a soldier, till Nicetas could save by a precipitate flight the relics of his fortune and the chastity of his daughter. In a cold wintry season these fugitives, nursed in the lap of prosperity, departed on foot; his wife was with child; the desertion of their slaves compelled them to carry their baggage on their own shoulders; and their women, whom they placed in the centre, were exhorted to conceal their beauty with dirt, instead of adorning it with paint and jewels. Every step was exposed to insult and danger: the threats of the strangers were less painful than the taunts of the plebeians, with whom they were now levelled; nor did the exiles breathe in safety till their mournful pilgrimage was concluded at Selymbria, above forty miles from the capital. On the way they overtook the patriarch, without attendance and almost without apparel, riding on an ass, and reduced to a state of apostolical poverty, which, had it been voluntary, might perhaps have been meritorious. In the meanwhile his desolate

in the Status Urb. C. P. p. 375-384 [p. 771-790, ed. Bonn]. His complaints, even of sacrilege, are justified by Innocent III. (Gesta, c. 92); but Villehardouin does not betray a symptom of pity or remorse.

churches were profaned by the licentiousness and party zeal of
the Latins. After stripping the gems and pearls, they converted
the chalices into drinking-cups; their tables, on which they
gamed and feasted, were covered with the pictures of Christ and
the saints; and they trampled under foot the most venerable
objects of the Christian worship. In the cathedral of St. Sophia
the ample veil of the sanctuary was rent asunder for the sake of
the golden fringe; and the altar, a monument of art and riches,
was broken in pieces and shared among the captors. Their
mules and horses were laden with the wrought silver and gilt
carvings which they tore down from the doors and pulpit; and if
the beasts stumbled under the burden, they were stabbed by
their impatient drivers, and the holy pavement streamed with
their impure blood. A prostitute was seated on the throne of the
patriarch; and that daughter of Belial, as she is styled, sung and
danced in the church to ridicule the hymns and processions of
the Orientals. Nor were the repositories of the royal dead secure
from violation: in the church of the Apostles the tombs of the
emperors were rifled; and it is said that after six centuries the
corpse of Justinian was found without any signs of decay or putrefaction. In the streets the French and Flemings clothed themselves and their horses in painted robes and flowing head-dresses
of linen; and the coarse intemperance of their feasts [1] insulted
the splendid sobriety of the East. To expose the arms of a
people of scribes and scholars, they affected to display a pen, an
inkhorn, and a sheet of paper, without discerning that the instruments of science and valour were *alike* feeble and useless in the
hands of the modern Greeks.

Their reputation and their language encouraged them, however, to despise the ignorance and to overlook the progress of
the Latins.[2] In the love of the arts the national difference was
still more obvious and real; the Greeks preserved with reverence
the works of their ancestors, which they could not imitate; and,
in the destruction of the statues of Constantinople, we are provoked to join in the complaints and invectives of the Byzantine

[1] If I rightly apprehend the Greek of Nicetas's receipts, their favourite
dishes were boiled buttocks of beef, salt pork and peas, and soup made of
garlic and sharp or sour herbs (p. 382 [p. 786, ed. Bonn]).
[2] Nicetas uses very harsh expressions, παρ' ἀγραμμάτοις Βαρβάροις, καὶ
τέλεον ἀναλφαβήτοις (Fragment. apud Fabric. Biblioth. Græc. tom. vi. p.
414). This reproach, it is true, applies most strongly to their ignorance of
Greek and of Homer. In their own language, the Latins of the twelfth and
thirteenth centuries were not destitute of literature. See Harris's Philological Inquiries, p. iii. c. 9, 10, 11.

historian.[1] We have seen how the rising city was adorned by
the vanity and despotism of the Imperial founder: in the ruins
of paganism some gods and heroes were saved from the axe of
superstition; and the forum and hippodrome were dignified
with the relics of a better age. Several of these are described
by Nicetas [2] in a florid and affected style; and from his descriptions I shall select some interesting particulars. 1. The
victorious charioteers were cast in bronze, at their own, or the
public, charge, and fitly placed in the hippodrome: they stood
aloft in their chariots wheeling round the goal: the spectators
could admire their attitude and judge of the resemblance; and of
these figures, the most perfect might have been transported from
the Olympic stadium. 2. The sphinx, river-horse, and crocodile,
denote the climate and manufacture of Egypt and the spoils of
that ancient province. 3. The she-wolf suckling Romulus and
Remus, a subject alike pleasing to the *old* and the *new* Romans,
but which could rarely be treated before the decline of the Greek
sculpture. 4. An eagle holding and tearing a serpent in his
talons—a domestic monument of the Byzantines, which they
ascribed, not to a human artist, but to the magic power of the
philosopher Apollonius, who, by this talisman, delivered the
city from such venomous reptiles. 5. An ass and his driver,
which were erected by Augustus in his colony of Nicopolis, to
commemorate a verbal omen of the victory of Actium. 6. An
equestrian statue, which passed in the vulgar opinion for Joshua,
the Jewish conqueror, stretching out his hand to stop the course
of the descending sun. A more classical tradition recognised
the figures of Bellerophon and Pegasus; and the free attitude of
the steed seemed to mark that he trod on air rather than on the
earth. 7. A square and lofty obelisk of brass; the sides were
embossed with a variety of picturesque and rural scenes: birds
singing, rustics labouring or playing on their pipes, sheep bleating, lambs skipping, the sea, and a scene of fish and fishing, little
naked Cupids laughing, playing, and pelting each other with

[1] Nicetas was of Chonæ in Phrygia (the old Colossæ of St. Paul): he
raised himself to the honours of senator, judge of the veil, and great logothete; beheld the fall of the empire, retired to Nice, and composed an
elaborate history from the death of Alexius Commenus to the reign of
Henry.

[2] A manuscript of Nicetas in the Bodleian library contains this curious
fragment on the statues of Constantinople, which fraud, or shame, or
rather carelessness, has dropped in the common editions. It is published
by Fabricius (Biblioth. Græc. tom. vi. p. 405-416), and immoderately
praised by the late ingenious Mr. Harris of Salisbury (Philological Inquiries,
p. iii. c. 5, p. 301-312).

apples, and on the summit a female figure turning with the slightest breath, and thence denominated *the wind's attendant.* 8. The Phrygian shepherd presenting to Venus the prize of beauty, the apple of discord. 9. The incomparable statue of Helen, which is delineated by Nicetas in the words of admiration and love: her well-turned feet, snowy arms, rosy lips, bewitching smiles, swimming eyes, arched eyebrows, the harmony of her shape, the lightness of her drapery, and her flowing locks that waved in the wind—a beauty that might have moved her barbarian destroyers to pity and remorse. 10. The manly, or divine, form of Hercules,[1] as he was restored to life by the master-hand of Lysippus, of such magnitude that his thumb was equal to the waist, his leg to the stature, of a common man:[2] his chest ample, his shoulders broad, his limbs strong and muscular, his hair curled, his aspect commanding. Without his bow, or quiver, or club, his lion's skin carelessly thrown over him, he was seated on an osier basket, his right leg and arm stretched to the utmost, his left knee bent and supporting his elbow, his head reclining on his left hand, his countenance indignant and pensive. 11. A colossal statue of Juno, which had once adorned her temple of Samos; the enormous head by four yoke of oxen was laboriously drawn to the palace. 12. Another colossus, of Pallas or Minerva, thirty feet in height, and representing with admirable spirit the attributes and character of the martial maid. Before we accuse the Latins, it is just to remark that this Pallas was destroyed after the first siege by the fear and superstition of the Greeks themselves.[3] The other statues of brass which I have enumerated were broken and melted by the unfeeling avarice of the crusaders: the cost and labour were consumed in a moment; the soul of genius evaporated in smoke, and the remnant of base metal was coined into money for the payment of the troops. Bronze is not the most durable of monuments: from the marble forms of Phidias and Praxiteles the Latins might turn aside with stupid contempt;[4] but unless

[1] To illustrate the statue of Hercules, Mr. Harris quotes a Greek epigram, and engraves a beautiful gem, which does not, however, copy the attitude of the statue: in the latter, Hercules had not his club, and his right leg and arm were extended.

[2] I transcribe these proportions, which appear to me inconsistent with each other, and may possibly show that the boasted taste of Nicetas was no more than affectation and vanity.

[3] Nicetas in Isaaco Angelo et Alexio, c. 3, p. 359 [p. 738, ed Bonn]. The Latin editor very properly observes that the historian, in his bombast style, produces ex pulice elephantem.

[4] In two passages of Nicetas (edit. Paris, p. 360; Fabric. p. 408) the Latins are branded with the lively reproach of οἱ τοῦ καλοῦ ἀνέραστοι βάρ-

they were crushed by some accidental injury, those useless stones stood secure on their pedestals.[1] The most enlightened of the strangers, above the gross and sensual pursuits of their country-men, more piously exercised the right of conquest in the search and seizure of the relics of the saints.[2] Immense was the supply of heads and bones, crosses and images, that were scattered by this revolution over the churches of Europe; and such was the increase of pilgrimage and oblation, that no branch, perhaps, of more lucrative plunder was imported from the East.[3] Of the writings of antiquity many that still existed in the twelfth century are now lost. But the pilgrims were not solicitous to save or transport the volumes of an unknown tongue: the perishable substance of paper or parchment can only be preserved by the multiplicity of copies; the literature of the Greeks had almost centered in the metropolis; and, without computing the extent of our loss, we may drop a tear over the libraries that have perished in the triple fire of Constantinople.[4]

βαροι, and their avarice of brass is clearly expressed. Yet the Venetians had the merit of removing four bronze horses from Constantinople to the place of St. Mark (Sanuto, Vite de' Dogi, in Muratori, Script. Rerum Italicarum, tom. xxii. p. 534).

[1] Winckelman, Hist. de l'Art, tom. iii. p. 269, 270.

[2] See the pious robbery of the abbot Martin, who transferred a rich cargo to his monastery of Paris, diocese of Basil (Gunther, Hist. C. P. c. 19, 23, 24). Yet, in secreting this booty, the saint incurred an excommunication, and perhaps broke his oath. [Compare Wilken, vol. v. p. 308.—M.]

[3] Fleury, Hist. Ecclés. tom. xvi. p. 139-145.

[4] I shall conclude this chapter with the notice of a modern history, which illustrates the taking of Constantinople by the Latins, but which has fallen somewhat late into my hands. Paolo Ramusio, the son of the compiler of Voyages, was directed by the senate of Venice to write the history of the conquest; and this order, which he received in his youth, he executed in a mature age, by an elegant Latin work, de Bello Constantino-politano et Imperatoribus Comnenis per Gallos et Venetos restitutis (Venet. 1635, in folio). Ramusio, or Rhamnusus, transcribes and translates, sequitur ad unguem, a MS. of Villehardouin, which he possessed; but he enriches his narrative with Greek and Latin materials, and we are in-debted to him for a correct state of the fleet, the names of the fifty Venetian nobles who commanded the galleys of the republic, and the patriot opposi-tion of Pantaleon Barbus to the choice of the doge for emperor.

CHAPTER LXI

Partition of the Empire by the French and Venetians—Five Latin
    Emperors of the Houses of Flanders and Courtenay—Their Wars
    against the Bulgarians and Greeks—Weakness and Poverty of the
    Latin Empire—Recovery of Constantinople by the Greeks—General
    Consequences of the Crusades

AFTER the death of the lawful princes, the French and Venetians,
confident of justice and victory, agreed to divide and regulate
their future possessions.[1] It was stipulated by treaty that
twelve electors, six of either nation, should be nominated; that
a majority should choose the emperor of the East; and that, if
the votes were equal, the decision of chance should ascertain the
successful candidate. To him, with all the titles and prerogatives of the Byzantine throne, they assigned the two palaces of
Boucoleon and Blachernæ, with a fourth part of the Greek
monarchy. It was defined that the three remaining portions
should be equally shared between the republic of Venice and the
barons of France; that each feudatory, with an honourable
exception for the doge, should acknowledge and perform the
duties of homage and military service to the supreme head of the
empire; that the nation which gave an emperor should resign
to their brethren the choice of a patriarch; and that the pilgrims,
whatever might be their impatience to visit the Holy Land, should
devote another year to the conquest and defence of the Greek
provinces. After the conquest of Constantinople by the Latins,
the treaty was confirmed and executed; and the first and most
important step was the creation of an emperor. The six electors
of the French nation were all ecclesiastics, the abbot of Loces,
the archbishop elect of Acre in Palestine, and the bishops of
Troyes, Soissons, Halberstadt, and Bethlehem, the last of whom
exercised in the camp the office of pope's legate: their profession
and knowledge were respectable; and as *they* could not be the
objects, they were best qualified to be the authors, of the choice.
The six Venetians were the principal servants of the state, and
in this list the noble families of Querini and Contarini are still
proud to discover their ancestors. The twelve assembled in the
chapel of the palace; and after the solemn invocation of the
Holy Ghost, they proceeded to deliberate and vote. A just

---

[1] See the original treaty of partition in the Venetian Chronicle of Andrew
Dandolo, p. 326-330, and the subsequent election in Villehardouin, No.
136-140, with Ducange in his Observations, and the 1st book of his Histoire
de Constantinople sous l'Empire des Francois.

impulse of respect and gratitude prompted them to crown the virtues of the doge: his wisdom had inspired their enterprise; and the most youthful knights might envy and applaud the exploits of blindness and age. But the patriot Dandolo was devoid of all personal ambition, and fully satisfied that he had been judged worthy to reign. His nomination was overruled by the Venetians themselves: his countrymen, and perhaps his friends,[1] represented, with the eloquence of truth, the mischiefs that might arise to national freedom and the common cause from the union of two incompatible characters, of the first magistrate of a republic and the emperor of the East. The exclusion of the doge left room for the more equal merits of Boniface and Baldwin; and at their names all meaner candidates respectfully withdrew. The marquis of Montferrat was recommended by his mature age and fair reputation, by the choice of the adventurers, and the wishes of the Greeks; nor can I believe that Venice, the mistress of the sea, could be seriously apprehensive of a petty lord at the foot of the Alps.[2] But the count of Flanders was the chief of a wealthy and warlike people; he was valiant, pious, and chaste; in the prime of life, since he was only thirty-two years of age; a descendant of Charlemagne, a cousin of the king of France, and a compeer of the prelates and barons who had yielded with reluctance to the command of a foreigner. Without the chapel, these barons, with the doge and marquis at their head, expected the decision of the twelve electors. It was announced by the bishop of Soissons, in the name of his colleagues: " Ye have sworn to obey the prince whom we should choose: by our unanimous suffrage, Baldwin count of Flanders and Hainault is now your sovereign, and the emperor of the East." He was saluted with loud applause, and the proclamation was re-echoed through the city by the joy of the Latins and the trembling adulation of the Greeks. Boniface was the first to kiss the hand of his rival, and to raise him on the buckler; and Baldwin was transported to the cathedral, and solemnly invested with the purple buskins. At the end of three weeks he was crowned by the legate, in the vacancy of a patriarch; but the Venetian clergy soon filled the

---

[1] After mentioning the nomination of the doge by a French elector, his kinsman Andrew Dandolo approves his exclusion, quidam Venetorum fidelis et nobilis senex, usus oratione satis probabili, etc. [p. 330], which has been embroidered by modern writers from Blondus to Le Beau.

[2] Nicetas (p. 384 [p. 789, ed. Bonn]), with the vain ignorance of a Greek, describes the marquis of Montferrat as a *maritime* power. Λαμπαρδίαν δὲ οἰκεῖσθαι παράλιον. Was he deceived by the Byzantine theme of Lombardy, which extended along the coast of Calabria?

chapter of St. Sophia, seated Thomas Morosini on the ecclesiastical throne, and employed every art to perpetuate in their own nation the honours and benefices of the Greek church.[1] Without delay the successor of Constantine instructed Palestine, France, and Rome, of this memorable revolution.   To Palestine he sent, as a trophy, the gates of Constantinople, and the chain of the harbour;[2] and adopted, from the Assise of Jerusalem, the laws or customs best adapted to a French colony and conquest in the East.   In his epistles the natives of France are encouraged to swell that colony, and to secure that conquest, to people a magnificent city and a fertile land, which will reward the labours both of the priest and the soldier.   He congratulates the Roman pontiff on the restoration of his authority in the East; invites him to extinguish the Greek schism by his presence in a general council; and implores his blessing and forgiveness for the disobedient pilgrims.   Prudence and dignity are blended in the answer of Innocent.[3]   In the subversion of the Byzantine empire, he arraigns the vices of man, and adores the providence of God: the conquerors will be absolved or condemned by their future conduct; the validity of their treaty depends on the judgment of St. Peter; but he inculcates their most sacred duty of establishing a just subordination of obedience and tribute, from the Greeks to the Latins, from the magistrate to the clergy, and from the clergy to the pope.

In the division of the Greek provinces [4] the share of the Venetians was more ample than that of the Latin emperor.   No more than one fourth was appropriated to his domain; a clear moiety of the remainder was reserved for Venice; and the other moiety was distributed among the adventurers of France and Lombardy.   The venerable Dandolo was proclaimed despot of Romania, and invested after the Greek fashion with the purple buskins.   He ended at Constantinople his long and glorious life;

[1] They exacted an oath from Thomas Morosini to appoint no canons of St. Sophia the lawful electors, except Venetians who had lived ten years at Venice, etc.   But the foreign clergy was envious, the pope disapproved this national monopoly, and of the six Latin patriarchs of Constantinople only the first and the last were Venetians.

[2] Nicetas, p. 383 [p. 788, ed. Bonn].

[3] The Epistles of Innocent III. are a rich fund for the ecclesiastical and civil institution of the Latin empire of Constantinople; and the most important of these epistles (of which the collection in 2 vols. in folio is published by Stephen Baluze) are inserted in his Gesta, in Muratori, Script. Rerum Italicarum, tom. iii. p. 1, c. 94-105.

[4] In the treaty of partition most of the names are corrupted by the scribes: they might be restored, and a good map, suited to the last age of the Byzantine empire, would be an improvement of geography.   But, alas! D'Anville is no more!

and if the prerogative was personal, the title was used by his successors till the middle of the fourteenth century, with the singular, though true, addition of lords of one fourth and a half of the Roman empire.[1]   The doge, a slave of state, was seldom permitted to depart from the helm of the republic; but his place was supplied by the *bail*, or regent, who exercised a supreme jurisdiction over the colony of Venetians: they possessed three of the eight quarters of the city; and his independent tribunal was composed of six judges, four counsellors, two chamberlains, two fiscal advocates, and a constable.   Their long experience of the Eastern trade enabled them to select their portion with discernment: they had rashly accepted the dominion and defence of Adrianople; but it was the more reasonable aim of their policy to form a chain of factories, and cities, and islands, along the maritime coast, from the neighbourhood of Ragusa to the Hellespont and the Bosphorus.   The labour and cost of such extensive conquests exhausted their treasury: they abandoned their maxims of government, adopted a feudal system, and contented themselves with the homage of their nobles [2] for the possessions which these private vassals undertook to reduce and maintain.   And thus it was that the family of Sanut acquired the duchy of Naxos, which involved the greatest part of the archipelago.   For the price of ten thousand marks the republic purchased of the marquis of Montferrat the fertile island of Crete or Candia with the ruins of a hundred cities; [3] but its improvement was stinted by the proud and narrow spirit of an aristocracy; [4] and the wisest senators would confess that the sea, not the land, was the treasury of St. Mark.   In the moiety of the adventurers the marquis Boniface might claim the most liberal reward; and, besides the isle of Crete, his exclusion from the throne was compensated by the royal title and the provinces

[1] Their style was dominus quartæ partis et dimidiæ [cum dimidio totius] imperii Romani, till Giovanni Dolfino, who was elected doge in the year 1356 (Sanuto, p. 530, 641).   For the government of Constantinople see Ducange, Historie de C. P. i. 37.

[2] Ducange (Hist. de C. P. ii. 6) has marked the conquests made by the state or nobles of Venice of the islands of Candia, Corfu, Cephalonia, Zante, Naxos, Paros, Melos, Andros, Mycone, Scyro, Cea, and Lemnos.

[3] Boniface sold the isle of Candia, August 12, A.D. 1204.   See the act in Sanuto, p. 533: but I cannot understand how it could be his mother's portion, or how she could be the daughter of an emperor Alexius.

[4] In the year 1212 the doge Peter Zani sent a colony to Candia, drawn from every quarter of Venice.   But in their savage manners and frequent rebellions the Candiots may be compared to the Corsicans under the yoke of Genoa; and when I compare the accounts of Belon and Tournefort, I cannot discern much difference between the Venetian and the Turkish island.

beyond the Hellespont. But he prudently exchanged that distant and difficult conquest for the kingdom of Thessalonica or Macedonia, twelve days' journey from the capital, where he might be supported by the neighbouring powers of his brother-in-law the king of Hungary. His progress was hailed by the voluntary or reluctant acclamations of the natives; and Greece, the proper and ancient Greece, again received a Latin conqueror,[1] who trod with indifference that classic ground. He viewed with a careless eye the beauties of the valley of Tempe; traversed with a cautious step the straits of Thermopylæ; occupied the unknown cities of Thebes, Athens, and Argos; and assaulted the fortifications of Corinth and Napoli,[2] which resisted his arms. The lots of the Latin pilgrims were regulated by chance, or choice, or subsequent exchange; and they abused, with intemperate joy, their triumph over the lives and fortunes of a great people. After a minute survey of the provinces, they weighed in the scales of avarice the revenue of each district, the advantage of the situation, and the ample or scanty supplies for the maintenance of soldiers and horses. Their presumption claimed and divided the long-lost dependencies of the Roman sceptre: the Nile and Euphrates rolled through their imaginary realms; and happy was the warrior who drew for his prize the palace of the Turkish sultan of Iconium.[3] I shall not descend to the pedigree of families and the rent-roll of estates, but I wish to specify that the counts of Blois and St. Pol were invested with the duchy of Nice and the lordship of Demotica:[4] the principal fiefs were held by the service of constable, chamberlain, cap-bearer, butler, and chief cook; and our historian, Jeffrey of Villehardouin, obtained a fair establishment on the banks of the Hebrus, and united the double office of marshal of Champagne

---

[1] Villehardouin (No. 159, 160, 173-177) and Nicetas (p. 387-394) describe the expedition into Greece of the marquis Boniface. The Choniate might derive his information from his brother Michael, archbishop of Athens, whom he paints as an orator, a statesman, and a saint. His encomium of Athens, and the description of Tempe, should be published from the Bodleian MS. of Nicetas (Fabric. Biblioth. Græc. tom. vi. p. 405), and would have deserved Mr. Harris's inquiries.

[2] Napoli di Romania, or Nauplia, the ancient seaport of Argos, is still a place of strength and consideration, situate on a rocky peninsula, with a good harbour (Chandler's Travels into Greece, p. 227).

[3] I have softened the expression of Nicetas, who strives to expose the presumption of the Franks. See de Rebus C. P. expugnatam, p. 375-384.

[4] A city surrounded by the river Hebrus, and six leagues to the south of Adrianople, received from its double wall the Greek name of Didymotei-chos, insensibly corrupted into Demotica and Dimot. I have preferred the more convenient and modern appellation of Demotica. This place was the last Turkish residence of Charles XII.

and Romania. At the head of his knights and archers each
baron mounted on horseback to secure the possession of his
share, and their first efforts were generally successful. But the
public force was weakened by their dispersion; and a thousand
quarrels must arise under a law, and among men, whose sole
umpire was the sword. Within three months after the conquest
of Constantinople, the emperor and the king of Thessalonica
drew their hostile followers into the field: they were reconciled
by the authority of the doge, the advice of the marshal, and the
firm freedom of their peers.[1]

Two fugitives, who had reigned at Constantinople, still
asserted the title of emperor; and the subjects of their fallen
throne might be moved to pity by the misfortunes of the elder
Alexius, or excited to revenge by the spirit of Mourzoufle. A
domestic alliance, a common interest, a similar guilt, and the
merit of extinguishing his enemies, a brother and a nephew,
induced the more recent usurper to unite with the former the
relics of his power. Mourzoufle was received with smiles and
honours in the camp of his father Alexius; but the wicked can
never love, and should rarely trust, their fellow criminals: he
was seized in the bath, deprived of his eyes, stripped of his
troops and treasures, and turned out to wander an object of
horror and contempt to those who with more propriety could
hate, and with more justice could punish, the assassin of the
emperor Isaac and his son. As the tyrant, pursued by fear or
remorse, was stealing over to Asia, he was seized by the Latins
of Constantinople, and condemned, after an open trial, to
an ignominious death. His judges debated the mode of his
execution, the axe, the wheel, or the stake; and it was resolved
that Mourzoufle [2] should ascend the Theodosian column, a pillar

---

[1] Their quarrel is told by Villehardouin (No. 146-158) with the spirit of
freedom. The merit and reputation of the marshal are acknowledged by
the Greek historian (p. 387 [p. 794, ed. Bonn]), μέγα παρὰ τοῖς τῶν Λατίνων
δυναμένου στρατεύμασι; unlike some modern heroes, whose exploits are only
visible in their own memoirs.

[William de Champlite, brother of the Count of Dijon, assumed the title
of Prince of Achaia: on the death of his brother he returned with regret to
France, to assume his paternal inheritance, and left Villehardouin his
"bailli," on condition that, if he did not return within a year, Villehardouin
was to retain the investiture. By an unknightly trick (as Milman says),
Villehardouin disembarrassed himself from the troublesome claim of
Robert, the cousin of the count of Dijon, to the succession. He contrived that Robert should arrive just fifteen days too late; and with the
general concurrence of the assembled knights was himself invested with
the principality.—O. S.]

[2] See the fate of Mourzoufle, in Nicetas (p. 392 [p. 804, ed. Bonn]),
Villehardouin (No. 141-145, 163), and Guntherus (c. 20, 21). Neither the

of white marble of one hundred and forty-seven feet in height.[1]
From the summit he was cast down headlong and dashed in
pieces on the pavement, in the presence of innumerable
spectators, who filled the forum of Taurus, and admired the
accomplishment of an old prediction, which was explained by
this singular event.[2]   The fate of Alexius is less tragical: he
was sent by the marquis a captive to Italy, and a gift to the
king of the Romans; but he had not much to applaud his fortune
if the sentence of imprisonment and exile were changed from a
fortress in the Alps to a monastery in Asia.   But his daughter,
before the national calamity, had been given in marriage to a
young hero, who continued the succession, and restored the
throne, of the Greek princes.[3]   The valour of Theodore Lascaris
was signalised in the two sieges of Constantinople.   After the
flight of Mourzoufle, when the Latins were already in the city,
he offered himself as their emperor to the soldiers and people;
and his ambition, which might be virtuous, was undoubtedly
brave.   Could he have infused a soul into the multitude, they
might have crushed the strangers under their feet: their abject
despair refused his aid; and Theodore retired to breathe the air
of freedom in Anatolia, beyond the immediate view and pursuit
of the conquerors.   Under the title, at first of despot, and afterwards of emperor, he drew to his standard the bolder spirits, who
were fortified against slavery by the contempt of life; and as
every means was lawful for the public safety, implored without
scruple the alliance of the Turkish sultan.   Nice, where Theodore
established his residence, Prusa and Philadelphia, Smyrna and
Ephesus, opened their gates to their deliverer: he derived
strength and reputation from his victories, and even from his
defeats; and the successor of Constantine preserved a fragment
of the empire from the banks of the Mæander to the suburbs of

marshal nor the monk afford a grain of pity for a tyrant or rebel, whose
punishment, however, was more unexampled than his crime.
[1] The column of Arcadius, which represents in basso relievo his victories,
or those of his father Theodosius, is still extant at Constantinople.   It is
described and measured, Gyllius (Topograph. iv. 7), Banduri (ad l. i.
Antiquit. C. P. p. 507, etc.), and Tournefort (Voyage du Levant, tom. ii.
lettre xii. p. 231).   [Compare Wilken, note, vol. v. p. 388.—M.]
[2] The nonsense of Gunther and the modern Greeks concerning this
columna fatidica is unworthy of notice; but it is singular enough, that,
fifty years before the Latin conquest, the poet Tzetzes (Chiliad, ix. 277)
relates the dream of a matron, who saw an army in the forum, and a man
sitting on the column, clapping his hands and uttering a loud exclamation.
[3] The dynasties of Nice, Trebizond, and Epirus (of which Nicetas saw
the origin without much pleasure or hope), are learnedly explored, and
clearly represented, in the Familiæ Byzantinæ of Ducange.

Nicomedia, and at length of Constantinople. Another portion, distant and obscure, was possessed by the lineal heir of the Comneni, a son of the virtuous Manuel, a grandson of the tyrant Andronicus. His name was Alexius; and the epithet of great was applied perhaps to his stature, rather than to his exploits. By the indulgence of the Angeli, he was appointed governor or duke of Trebizond: [1] his birth gave him ambition, the revolution independence; and without changing his title, he reigned in peace from Sinope to the Phasis, along the coast of the Black Sea. His nameless son and successor is described as the vassal of the sultan, whom he served with two hundred lances: that Comnenian prince was no more than duke of Trebizond, and the title of emperor was first assumed by the pride and envy of the grandson of Alexius. In the West a third fragment was saved from the common shipwreck by Michael, a bastard of the house of Angeli, who, before the revolution, had been known as an hostage, a soldier, and a rebel. His flight from the camp of the marquis Boniface secured his freedom; by his marriage with the governor's daughter he commanded the important place of Durazzo, assumed the title of despot, and founded a strong and conspicuous principality in Epirus, Ætolia, and Thessaly, which have ever been peopled by a warlike race. The Greeks, who had offered their service to their new sovereigns, were excluded by the haughty Latins [2] from all civil and military honours, as a nation born to tremble and obey. Their resentment prompted

[1] Except some facts in Pachymer and Nicephorus Gregoras, which will hereafter be used, the Byzantine writers disdain to speak of the empire of Trebizond, or principality of the *Lazi ;* and among the Latins it is conspicuous only in the romances of the fourteenth or fifteenth centuries. Yet the indefatigable Ducange has dug out (Fam. Byz. p. 192) two authentic passages in Vincent of Beauvais (l. xxxi. c. 144), and the protonotary Ogerius (apud Wading, A.D. 1279, No. 4).

[Alexius was not appointed governor of Trebizond by the indulgence of the Angeli; it was rather through the help of his aunt, queen Thamar of Iberia. When Andronicus died in 1185, his two grandsons, Alexius and David, succeeded in escaping to Iberia. Thamar helped Alexius to found, in 1204, the independent principality of Trapezus, where he assumed the title of Grand Komnenos. At the same time his brother seized Paphlagonia, Theodore Lascaris went against David, defeated him (1212), and took his kingdom from him, all but a little bit round Sinope, which they left him. But in 1214 the Turks attacked him, and he fell in battle. Alexius, on the other hand, maintained himself at Trebizond, and the empire of Trebizond survived the Turkish conquest of Constantinople by eight years.—O. S.]

[2] The portrait of the French Latins is drawn in Nicetas by the hand of prejudice and resentment: οὐδὲν τῶν ἄλλων ἐθνῶν εἰς Ἄρεος ἔργα παρασυμβεβλῆσθαί σφισιν ἠνείχοντο· ἀλλ' οὐδέ τις τῶν Χαρίτων ἢ τῶν Μουσῶν παρὰ τοῖς βαρβάροις τούτοις ἐπεξενίζετο, καὶ παρὰ τοῦτο οἶμαι τὴν φύσιν ἦσαν ἀνήμεροι, καὶ τὸν χόλον εἶχον τοῦ λόγου προτρέχοντα [P. 791, ed. Bonn.]

them to show that they might have been useful friends, since they could be dangerous enemies: their nerves were braced by adversity: whatever was learned or holy, whatever was noble or valiant, rolled away into the independent states of Trebizond, Epirus, and Nice; and a single patrician is marked by the ambiguous praise of attachment and loyalty to the Franks. The vulgar herd of the cities and the country would have gladly submitted to a mild and regular servitude; and the transient disorders of war would have been obliterated by some years of industry and peace. But peace was banished, and industry was crushed, in the disorders of the feudal system. The *Roman* emperors of Constantinople, if they were endowed with abilities, were armed with power for the protection of their subjects: their laws were wise, and their administration was simple. The Latin throne was filled by a titular prince, the chief, and often the servant, of his licentious confederates: the fiefs of the empire, from a kingdom to a castle, were held and ruled by the sword of the barons; and their discord, poverty, and ignorance extended the ramifications of tyranny to the most sequestered villages. The Greeks were oppressed by the double weight of the priest, who was invested with temporal power, and of the soldier, who was inflamed by fanatic hatred; and the insuperable bar of religion and language for ever separated the stranger and the native. As long as the crusaders were united at Constantinople, the memory of their conquest, and the terror of their arms, imposed silence on the captive land: their dispersion betrayed the smallness of their numbers and the defects of their discipline; and some failures and mischances revealed the secret that they were not invincible. As the fear of the Greeks abated, their hatred increased. They murmured; they conspired; and before a year of slavery had elapsed, they implored, or accepted, the succour of a barbarian, whose power they had felt, and whose gratitude they trusted.[1]

The Latin conquerors had been saluted with a solemn and early embassy from John, or Joannice, or Calo-John, the revolted chief of the Bulgarians and Wallachians. He deemed himself their brother, as the votary of the Roman pontiff, from whom he had received the regal title and a holy banner; and in the subversion of the Greek monarchy he might aspire to the name of their friend and accomplice. But Calo-John was astonished

[1] I here begin to use, with freedom and confidence, the eight books of the Histoire de C. P. sous l'Empire des François, which Ducange has given as a supplement to Villehardouin; and which, in a barbarous style, deserves the praise of an original and classic work.

to find that the count of Flanders had assumed the pomp and
pride of the successors of Constantine; and his ambassadors were
dismissed with a haughty message, that the rebel must deserve
a pardon by touching with his forehead the footstool of the
Imperial throne.   His resentment [1] would have exhaled in acts
of violence and blood: his cooler policy watched the rising
discontent of the Greeks, affected a tender concern for their
sufferings, and promised that their first struggles for freedom
should be supported by his person and kingdom.   The conspiracy was propagated by national hatred, the firmest band of
association and secrecy; the Greeks were impatient to sheathe
their daggers in the breasts of the victorious strangers; but the
execution was prudently delayed till Henry, the emperor's
brother, had transported the flower of his troops beyond the
Hellespont.   Most of the towns and villages of Thrace were true
to the moment and the signal; and the Latins, without arms or
suspicion, were slaughtered by the vile and merciless revenge of
their slaves.   From Demotica, the first scene of the massacre,
the surviving vassals of the count of St. Pol escaped to Adrianople, but the French and Venetians, who occupied that city,
were slain or expelled by the furious multitude; the garrisons
that could effect their retreat fell back on each other towards the
metropolis; and the fortresses, that separately stood against
the rebels, were ignorant of each other's and of their sovereign's
fate.   The voice of fame and fear announced the revolt of the
Greeks and the rapid approach of their Bulgarian ally; and
Calo-John, not depending on the forces of his own kingdom, had
drawn from the Scythian wilderness a body of fourteen thousand
Comans, who drank, as it was said, the blood of their captives,
and sacrificed the Christians on the altars of their gods.[2]

Alarmed by this sudden and growing danger, the emperor
despatched a swift messenger to recall Count Henry and his
troops; and had Baldwin expected the return of his gallant
brother, with a supply of twenty thousand Armenians, he might
have encountered the invader with equal numbers and a decisive
superiority of arms and discipline.   But the spirit of chivalry
could seldom discriminate caution from cowardice, and the

---

[1] In Calo-John's answer to the pope we may find his claims and complaints (Gesta Innocent. III. c. 108, 109): he was cherished at Rome as the
prodigal son.

[2] The Comans were a Tartar or Turkman horde, which encamped in the
twelfth and thirteenth centuries on the verge of Moldavia.   The greater
part were pagans, but some were Mohammedans, and the whole horde was
converted to Christianity (A.D. 1370) by Lewis, king of Hungary.

emperor took the field with a hundred and forty knights, and
their train of archers and serjeants. The marshal, who dissuaded and obeyed, led the vanguard in their march to Adrianople; the main body was commanded by the count of Blois;
the aged doge of Venice followed with the rear; and their scanty
numbers were increased from all sides by the fugitive Latins.
They undertook to besiege the rebels of Adrianople; and such
was the pious tendency of the crusades, that they employed the
holy week in pillaging the country for their subsistence, and in
framing engines for the destruction of their fellow-Christians.
But the Latins were soon interrupted and alarmed by the light
cavalry of the Comans, who boldly skirmished to the edge of
their imperfect lines; and a proclamation was issued by the
marshal of Romania, that, on the trumpet's sound, the cavalry
should mount and form; but that none, under pain of death,
should abandon themselves to a desultory and dangerous pursuit.
This wise injunction was first disobeyed by the count of Blois,
who involved the emperor in his rashness and ruin. The
Comans, of the Parthian or Tartar school, fled before their first
charge; but after a career of two leagues, when the knights and
their horses were almost breathless, they suddenly turned,
rallied, and encompassed the heavy squadrons of the Franks.
The count was slain on the field, the emperor was made prisoner;
and if the one disdained to fly, if the other refused to yield, their
personal bravery made a poor atonement for their ignorance or
neglect of the duties of a general.[1]

Proud of his victory and his royal prize, the Bulgarian
advanced to relieve Adrianople and achieve the destruction of
the Latins. They must inevitably have been destroyed if the
marshal of Romania had not displayed a cool courage and
consummate skill, uncommon in all ages, but most uncommon
in those times, when war was a passion rather than a science.
His grief and fears were poured into the firm and faithful bosom
of the doge; but in the camp he diffused an assurance of safety,
which could only be realised by the general belief. All day he
maintained his perilous station between the city and the barbarians; Villehardouin decamped in silence at the dead of night,
and his masterly retreat of three days would have deserved the
praise of Xenophon and the ten thousand. In the rear, the
marshal supported the weight of the pursuit; in the front, he

---

[1] Nicetas, from ignorance or malice, imputes the defeat to the cowardice
of Dandolo (p. 383 [p. 397, ed. Par.; p. 814, ed. Bonn]): but Villehardouin
shares his own glory with his venerable friend, qui viels home ére et gote
ne veoit, mais mult ére sages et preus et vigueros (No. 193).

moderated the impatience of the fugitives, and wherever the
Comans approached they were repelled by a line of impenetrable
spears. On the third day the weary troops beheld the sea, the
solitary town of Rodosto,[1] and their friends, who had landed
from the Asiatic shore. They embraced, they wept; but they
united their arms and counsels; and, in his brother's absence,
Count Henry assumed the regency of the empire, at once in a
state of childhood and caducity.[2] If the Comans withdrew
from the summer heats, seven thousand Latins, in the hour of
danger, deserted Constantinople, their brethren, and their vows.
Some partial success was overbalanced by the loss of one
hundred and twenty knights in the field of Rusium; and of the
Imperial domain no more was left than the capital, with two or
three adjacent fortresses on the shores of Europe and Asia. The
king of Bulgaria was resistless and inexorable; and Calo-John
respectfully eluded the demands of the pope, who conjured his
new proselyte to restore peace and the emperor to the afflicted
Latins. The deliverance of Baldwin was no longer, he said, in
the power of man: that prince had died in prison, and the manner
of his death is variously related by ignorance and credulity.
The lovers of a tragic legend will be pleased to hear that the
royal captive was tempted by the amorous queen of the Bulgarians; that his chaste refusal exposed him to the falsehood
of a woman and the jealousy of a savage; that his hands and
feet were severed from his body; that his bleeding trunk was
cast among the carcases of dogs and horses; and that he breathed
three days before he was devoured by the birds of prey.[3] About
twenty years afterwards, in a wood of the Netherlands, a
hermit announced himself as the true Baldwin, the emperor of
Constantinople, and lawful sovereign of Flanders. He related
the wonders of his escape, his adventures, and his penance,
among a people prone to believe and to rebel; and, in the first
transport, Flanders acknowledged her long-lost sovereign. A

[1] The truth of geography, and the original text of Villehardouin (No.
194), place Rodosto three days' journey (trois jornées) from Adrianople:
but Vigenere, in his version, has most absurdly substituted *trois heures*
[lieuẽs]; and this error, which is not corrected by Ducange, has entrapped
several moderns, whose names I shall spare.

[2] The reign and end of Baldwin are related by Villehardouin and Nicetas
(p. 386-416 [p. 791-853, ed. Bonn]); and their omissions are supplied by
Ducange in his Observations, and to the end of his first book.

[3] After brushing away all doubtful and improbable circumstances, we
may prove the death of Baldwin—1. By the firm belief of the French barons
(Villehardouin, No. 230); 2. By the declaration of Calo-John himself, who
excuses his not releasing the captive emperor, quia debitum carnis exsol-
verat cum carcere teneretur (Gesta Innocent III. c. 109 [p. 550]).

short examination before the French court detected the impostor, who was punished with an ignominious death; but the Flemings still adhered to the pleasing error, and the countess Jane is accused by the gravest historians of sacrificing to her ambition the life of an unfortunate father. [1]

In all civilised hostility a treaty is established for the exchange or ransom of prisoners; and if their captivity be prolonged, their condition is known, and they are treated according to their rank with humanity or honour. But the savage Bulgarian was a stranger to the laws of war; his prisons were involved in darkness and silence; and above a year elapsed before the Latins could be assured of the death of Baldwin, before his brother, the regent Henry, would consent to assume the title of emperor. His moderation was applauded by the Greeks as an act of rare and inimitable virtue. Their light and perfidious ambition was eager to seize or anticipate the moment of a vacancy, while a law of succession, the guardian both of the prince and people, was gradually defined and confirmed in the hereditary monarchies of Europe. In the support of the Eastern empire Henry was gradually left without an associate, as the heroes of the crusade retired from the world or from the war. The doge of Venice, the venerable Dandolo, in the fulness of years and glory, sunk into the grave. The marquis of Montferrat was slowly recalled from the Peloponnesian war to the revenge of Baldwin and the defence of Thessalonica. Some nice disputes of feudal homage and service were reconciled in a personal interview between the emperor and the king; they were firmly united by mutual esteem and the common danger; and their alliance was sealed by the nuptials of Henry with the daughter of the Italian prince. He soon deplored the loss of his friend and father. At the persuasion of some faithful Greeks, Boniface made a bold and successful inroad among the hills of Rhodope; the Bulgarians fled on his approach; they assembled to harass his retreat. On the intelligence that his rear was attacked, without waiting for any defensive armour, he leaped on horseback, couched his lance, and drove the enemies before him; but in the rash pursuit he was pierced with a mortal wound, and the head of the king of Thessalonica was presented to Calo-John, who enjoyed the honours, without the merit, of victory. It is here, at this melancholy event, that the pen or the voice of Jeffrey of Ville-

---

[1] See the story of this impostor from the French and Flemish writers, in Ducange, Hist. de C. P. iii. 9; and the ridiculous fables that were believed by the monks of St. Alban's, in Matthew Paris, Hist. Major, p. 271, 272.

hardouin seems to drop or to expire;[1] and if he still exercised
his military office of marshal of Romania, his subsequent
exploits are buried in oblivion.[2]   The character of Henry was
not unequal to his arduous situation: in the siege of Constantinople, and beyond the Hellespont, he had deserved the fame of
a valiant knight and a skilful commander, and his courage was
tempered with a degree of prudence and mildness unknown to his
impetuous brother.   In the double war against the Greeks of
Asia and the Bulgarians of Europe he was ever the foremost on
shipboard or on horseback; and though he cautiously provided
for the success of his arms, the drooping Latins were often roused
by his example to save and to second their fearless emperor.
But such efforts, and some supplies of men and money from
France, were of less avail than the errors, the cruelty, and death
of their most formidable adversary.   When the despair of the
Greek subjects invited Calo-John as their deliverer, they hoped
that he would protect their liberty and adopt their laws; they
were soon taught to compare the degrees of national ferocity,
and to execrate the savage conqueror, who no longer dissembled
his intention of dispeopling Thrace, of demolishing the cities,
and of transplanting the inhabitants beyond the Danube.
Many towns and villages of Thrace were already evacuated; a
heap of ruins marked the place of Philippopolis, and a similar
calamity was expected at Demotica and Adrianople by the first
authors of the revolt.   They raised a cry of grief and repentance
to the throne of Henry; the emperor alone had the magnanimity
to forgive and trust them.   No more than four hundred knights,
with their serjeants and archers, could be assembled under his
banner; and with this slender force he fought and repulsed the
Bulgarian, who, besides his infantry, was at the head of forty
thousand horse.[3]   In this expedition Henry felt the difference
between a hostile and a friendly country: the remaining cities

[1] Villehardouin, No. 257.   I quote, with regret, this lamentable conclusion, where we lose at once the original history, and the rich illustra-
tions of Ducange.   The last pages may derive some light from Henry's
two epistles to Innocent III. (Gesta, c. 106, 107).

[2] The marshal was alive in 1212, but he probably died soon afterwards,
without returning to France (Ducange, Observations sur Villehardouin,
p. 238).   His fief of Messinople, the gift of Boniface, was the ancient
Maximianopolis, which flourished in the time of Ammianus Marcellinus,
among the cities of Thrace.   (No. 141.)

[3] [There was no battle.   On the advance of the Latins, Kalo-John
suddenly broke up his camp and retreated.   The Latins considered this
unexpected deliverance almost in the light of a miracle.   It has been suggested by Le Beau that the defection of the Comans, who usually quitted
the camp during the heat of summer, may have occasioned the defection
of the Bulgarians.—O. S.]

were preserved by his arms, and the savage, with shame and loss, was compelled to relinquish his prey. The siege of Thessalonica was the last of the evils which Calo-John inflicted or suffered; he was stabbed in the night in his tent, and the general, perhaps the assassin, who found him weltering in his blood, ascribed the blow with general applause to the lance of St. Demetrius.[1] After several victories the prudence of Henry concluded an honourable peace with the successor of the tyrant, and with the Greek princes of Nice and Epirus. If he ceded some doubtful limits, an ample kingdom was reserved for himself and his feudatories; and his reign, which lasted only ten years, afforded a short interval of prosperity and peace. Far above the narrow policy of Baldwin and Boniface, he freely intrusted to the Greeks the most important offices of the state and army; and this liberality of sentiment and practice was the more seasonable, as the princes of Nice and Epirus had already learned to seduce and employ the mercenary valour of the Latins. It was the aim of Henry to unite and reward his deserving subjects of every nation and language; but he appeared less solicitous to accomplish the impracticable union of the two churches. Pelagius, the pope's legate, who acted as the sovereign of Constantinople, had interdicted the worship of the Greeks, and sternly imposed the payment of tithes, the double procession of the Holy Ghost, and a blind obedience to the Roman pontiff. As the weaker party, they pleaded the duties of conscience, and implored the rights of toleration: " Our bodies," they said, " are Cæsar's, but our souls belong only to God." The persecution was checked by the firmness of the emperor;[2] and if we can believe that the same prince was poisoned by the Greeks themselves, we must entertain a contemptible idea of the sense and gratitude of mankind. His valour was a vulgar attribute, which he shared with ten thousand knights: but Henry possessed the superior courage to oppose, in a superstitious age, the pride and avarice of the clergy. In the cathedral of St. Sophia he presumed to place his throne on the right hand of the patriarch; and this presumption excited the sharpest censure of pope Innocent the Third. By a salutary edict, one of the first examples of the laws of mortmain, he prohibited the alienation of fiefs; many of the Latins, desirous of returning to Europe, resigned their estates to

---

[1] The church of this patron of Thessalonica was served by the canons of the holy sepulchre, and contained a divine ointment which distilled daily and stupendous miracles (Ducange, Hist. de C. P. ii. 4).

[2] Acropolita (c. 17) observes the persecution of the legate, and the toleration of Henry (Ερη, as he calls him), κλύδωνα κατεστόρεσε.

the church for a spiritual or temporal reward; these holy lands
were immediately discharged from military service, and a colony
of soldiers would have been gradually transformed into a college
of priests.[1]

The virtuous Henry died at Thessalonica in the defence of that
kingdom, and of an infant, the son of his friend Boniface. In
the two first emperors of Constantinople the male line of the
counts of Flanders was extinct. But their sister Yolande was
the wife of a French prince, the mother of a numerous progeny;
and one of her daughters had married Andrew king of Hungary,
a brave and pious champion of the cross. By seating him on the
Byzantine throne, the barons of Romania would have acquired
the forces of a neighbouring and warlike kingdom; but the
prudent Andrew revered the laws of succession; and the princess
Yolande, with her husband Peter of Courtenay, count of Auxerre,
was invited by the Latins to assume the empire of the East. The
royal birth of his father, the noble origin of his mother, recommended to the barons of France the first-cousin of their king.
His reputation was fair, his possessions were ample, and, in the
bloody crusade against the Albigeois, the soldiers and the priests
had been abundantly satisfied of his zeal and valour. Vanity
might applaud the elevation of a French emperor of Constantinople; but prudence must pity, rather than envy, his treacherous
and imaginary greatness. To assert and adorn his title, he was
reduced to sell or mortgage the best of his patrimony. By these
expedients, the liberality of his royal kinsman Philip Augustus,
and the national spirit of chivalry, he was enabled to pass the
Alps at the head of one hundred and forty knights, and five
thousand five hundred serjeants and archers. After some
hesitation, pope Honorius the Third was persuaded to crown
the successor of Constantine: but he performed the ceremony
in a church without the walls, lest he should seem to imply or to
bestow any right of sovereignty over the ancient capital of the
empire. The Venetians had engaged to transport Peter and
his forces beyond the Adriatic, and the empress, with her four
children, to the Byzantine palace; but they required, as the
price of their service, that he should recover Durazzo from the
despot of Epirus. Michael Angelus, or Comnenus, the first of
his dynasty, had bequeathed the succession of his power and

---

[1] See the reign of HENRY, in Ducange (Hist. de C. P. l. i. c. 35-41, l. ii.
c. 1-22), who is much indebted to the Epistles of the Popes. Le Beau
(Hist. du Bas Empire, tom. xxi. p. 120-122) has found, perhaps in Doutre-
man, some laws of Henry which determined the service of fiefs and the
prerogatives of the emperor.

ambition to Theodore, his legitimate brother, who already threatened and invaded the establishments of the Latins. After discharging his debt by a fruitless assault, the emperor raised the siege to prosecute a long and perilous journey over land from Durazzo to Thessalonica. He was soon lost in the mountains of Epirus: the passes were fortified; his provisions exhausted; he was delayed and deceived by a treacherous negotiation; and, after Peter of Courtenay and the Roman legate had been arrested in a banquet, the French troops, without leaders or hopes, were eager to exchange their arms for the delusive promise of mercy and bread. The Vatican thundered; and the impious Theodore was threatened with the vengeance of earth and heaven; but the captive emperor and his soldiers were forgotten, and the reproaches of the pope are confined to the imprisonment of his legate. No sooner was he satisfied by the deliverance of the priest and a promise of spiritual obedience, than he pardoned and protected the despot of Epirus. His peremptory commands suspended the ardour of the Venetians and the king of Hungary; and it was only by a natural or untimely death [1] that Peter of Courtenay was released from his hopeless captivity.[2]

The long ignorance of his fate, and the presence of the lawful sovereign, of Yolande, his wife or widow, delayed the proclamation of a new emperor. Before her death, and in the midst of her grief, she was delivered of a son, who was named Baldwin, the last and most unfortunate of the Latin princes of Constantinople. His birth endeared him to the barons of Romania; but his childhood would have prolonged the troubles of a minority, and his claims were superseded by the elder claims of his brethren. The first of these, Philip of Courtenay, who derived from his mother the inheritance of Namur, had the wisdom to prefer the substance of a marquisate to the shadow of an empire; and on his refusal, Robert, the second of the sons of Peter and Yolande, was called to the throne of Constantinople. Warned by his father's mischance, he pursued his slow and secure journey through Germany and along the Danube: a passage was opened by his sister's marriage with the king of Hungary; and the

---

[1] Acropolita (c. 14) affirms that Peter of Courtenay died by the sword (ἔργον μαχαίρας γενέσθαι); but from his dark expressions I should conclude a previous captivity, ὡς πάντας ἄρδην δεσμώτας ποιῆσαι σὺν πᾶσι σκεύεσι. The Chronicle of Auxerre delays the emperor's death till the year 1219; and Auxerre is in the neighbourhood of Courtenay.

[2] See the reign and death of Peter of Courtenay, in Ducange (Hist. de C. P. l. ii. c. 22-28), who feebly strives to excuse the neglect of the emperor by Honorius III.

emperor Robert was crowned by the patriarch in the cathedral of St. Sophia. But his reign was an era of calamity and disgrace; and the colony, as it was styled, of NEW FRANCE yielded on all sides to the Greeks of Nice and Epirus. After a victory, which he owed to his perfidy rather than his courage, Theodore Angelus entered the kingdom of Thessalonica; expelled the feeble Demetrius, the son of the marquis Boniface; erected his standard on the walls of Adrianople; and added, by his vanity, a third or a fourth name to the list of rival emperors. The relics of the Asiatic province were swept away by John Vataces, the son-in-law and successor of Theodore Lascaris, and who, in a triumphant reign of thirty-three years, displayed the virtues both of peace and war. Under his discipline, the swords of the French mercenaries were the most effectual instrument of his conquests, and their desertion from the service of their country was at once a symptom and a cause of the rising ascendant of the Greeks. By the construction of a fleet he obtained the command of the Hellespont, reduced the islands of Lesbos and Rhodes,[1] attacked the Venetians of Candia, and intercepted the rare and parsimonious succours of the West. Once, and once only, the Latin emperor sent an army against Vataces; and in the defeat of that army, the veteran knights, the last of the original con querors, were left on the field of battle. But the success of a foreign enemy was less painful to the pusillanimous Robert than the insolence of his Latin subjects, who confounded the weakness of the emperor and of the empire. His personal misfortunes will prove the anarchy of the government and the ferociousness of the times. The amorous youth had neglected his Greek bride, the daughter of Vataces, to introduce into the palace a beautiful maid, of a private, though noble, family of Artois; and her mother had been tempted by the lustre of the purple to forfeit her engagements with a gentleman of Burgundy. His love was converted into rage; he assembled his friends, forced the palace gates, threw the mother into the sea, and inhumanly cut off the nose and lips of the wife or concubine of the emperor. Instead of punishing the offender, the barons avowed and applauded the savage deed,[2] which, as a prince and as a man, it was impossible

---

[1] [On the empire being overwhelmed by the crusaders, Leo Gabalas seized the chief power and made himself master of Rhodes. In 1233 John Vatatzes defeated Gabalas, and obliged him to own his suzerainty, but left him in possession. The island was finally conquered by the knights of St. John in 1310.—O. S.]

[2] Marinus Sanutus (Secreta Fidelium Crucis, l. ii. p. 4, c. 18, p. 73) is so much delighted with this bloody deed, that he has transcribed it in his margin as a bonum exemplum. Yet he acknowledges the damsel for the lawful wife of Robert.

that Robert should forgive. He escaped from the guilty city
to implore the justice or compassion of the pope: the emperor
was coolly exhorted to return to his station; before he could
obey, he sunk under the weight of grief, shame, and impotent
resentment.[1]

It was only in the age of chivalry that valour could ascend
from a private station to the thrones of Jerusalem and Constantinople. The titular kingdom of Jerusalem had devolved to
Mary, the daughter of Isabella and Conrad of Montferrat, and
the grand-daughter of Almeric or Amaury. She was given to
John of Brienne, of a noble family in Champagne, by the public
voice, and the judgment of Philip Augustus, who named him as
the most worthy champion of the Holy Land.[2] In the fifth
crusade he led a hundred thousand Latins to the conquest of
Egypt: by him the siege of Damietta was achieved; and the
subsequent failure was justly ascribed to the pride and avarice
of the legate. After the marriage of his daughter with Frederic
the Second[3] he was provoked by the emperor's ingratitude to
accept the command of the army of the church; and though
advanced in life, and despoiled of royalty, the sword and spirit
of John of Brienne were still ready for the service of Christendom.
In the seven years of his brother's reign, Baldwin of Courtenay
had not emerged from a state of childhood, and the barons of
Romania felt the strong necessity of placing the sceptre in the
hands of a man and a hero. The veteran king of Jerusalem
might have disdained the name and office of regent; they
agreed to invest him for his life with the title and prerogatives
of emperor, on the sole condition that Baldwin should marry his
second daughter, and succeed at a mature age to the throne
of Constantinople. The expectation, both of the Greeks and
Latins, was kindled by the renown, the choice, and the presence
of John of Brienne; and they admired his martial aspect, his
green and vigorous age of more than fourscore years, and his
size and stature, which surpassed the common measure of mankind.[4] But avarice, and the love of ease, appear to have chilled

---

[1] See the reign of Robert, in Ducange (Hist. de C. P. l. iii. c. 1-12).

[2] Rex igitur Franciæ, deliberatione habitâ, respondit nuntiis, se daturum
hominem Syriæ partibus aptum; in armis probum (*preux*), in bellis
securum, in agendis providum, Johannem comitem Brennensem. Sanut.
Secret. Fidelium, l. iii. p. xi. c. 4, p. 205; Matthew Paris, p. 159.

[3] Giannone (Istoria Civile, tom. ii. l. xvi. p. 380-385) discusses the
marriage of Frederic II. with the daughter of John of Brienne, and the
double union of the crowns of Naples and Jerusalem.

[4] Acropolita, c. 27. The historian was at that time a boy, and educated
at Constantinople. In 1233, when he was eleven years old, his father

the ardour of enterprise: his troops were disbanded, and two
years rolled away without action or honour, till he was awakened
by the dangerous alliance of Vataces emperor of Nice, and of
Azan king of Bulgaria.[1] They besieged Constantinople by sea
and land, with an army of one hundred thousand men, and a
fleet of three hundred ships of war; while the entire force of the
Latin emperor was reduced to one hundred and sixty knights,
and a small addition of serjeants and archers. I tremble to
relate, that, instead of defending the city, the hero made a sally
at the head of his cavalry; and that, of forty-eight squadrons
of the enemy, no more than three escaped from the edge of his
invincible sword. Fired by his example, the infantry and the
citizens boarded the vessels that anchored close to the walls;
and twenty-five were dragged in triumph into the harbour of
Constantinople. At the summons of the emperor, the vassals
and allies armed in her defence; broke through every obstacle
that opposed their passage; and, in the succeeding year, obtained
a second victory over the same enemies. By the rude poets of
the age John of Brienne is compared to Hector, Roland, and
Judas Maccabæus:[2] but their credit, and his glory, receives some
abatement from the silence of the Greeks. The empire was soon
deprived of the last of her champions; and the dying monarch
was ambitious to enter paradise in the habit of a Franciscan
friar.[3]

In the double victory of John of Brienne I cannot discover
the name or exploits of his pupil Baldwin, who had attained the

broke the Latin chain, left a splendid fortune, and escaped to the Greek
court of Nice, where his son was raised to the highest honours.

[1] [Azan, king of Bulgaria, was one of the most enlightened and religious
princes of his time. In the battle of Klokotnitza, not far from the banks
of the river Strymon, in the year 1230 he defeated the armies of Epirus
and Thessalonica, and subsequently brought under his sway Albania, Macedonia, and the greater part of Thrace. He built the cathedral of Tirnovo in
commemoration of his successful campaign. With regard to his antagonist,
John de Brienne, he was elected emperor in 1229, but did not arrive at
Constantinople until 1231. The siege did not begin until 1234.—O. S.]

[2] Philip Mouskes, bishop of Tournay (A.D. 1274-1282), has composed a
poem, or rather a string of verses, in bad old Flemish French, on the Latin
emperors of Constantinople, which Ducange has published at the end of
Villehardouin; see p. 224, for the prowess of John of Brienne.

> N'Aie, Ector, Roll' ne Ogiers
> Ne Judas Machabeus li fiers
> Tant ne fit d'armes en estors
> Com fist li Rois Jehans cel jors
> Et il defors et il dedans
> La paru sa force et ses sens
> Et li hardiment qu'il avoit.

[3] See the reign of John de Brienne, in Ducange, Hist. de C. P. l. iii. c. 13-26.

age of military service, and who succeeded to the imperial dignity
on the decease of his adoptive father.[1] The royal youth was
employed on a commission more suitable to his temper; he was
sent to visit the Western courts, of the pope more especially, and
of the king of France; to excite their pity by the view of his
innocence and distress; and to obtain some supplies of men or
money for the relief of the sinking empire. He thrice repeated
these mendicant visits, in which he seemed to prolong his stay,
and postpone his return; of the five-and-twenty years of his
reign, a greater number were spent abroad than at home; and in
no place did the emperor deem himself less free and secure than
in his native country and his capital. On some public occasions,
his vanity might be soothed by the title of Augustus, and by
the honours of the purple; and at the general council of Lyons,
when Frederic the Second was excommunicated and deposed,
his Oriental colleague was enthroned on the right hand of the
pope. But how often was the exile, the vagrant, the Imperial
beggar, humbled with scorn, insulted with pity, and degraded
in his own eyes and those of the nations! In his first visit to
England he was stopped at Dover by a severe reprimand, that
he should presume, without leave, to enter an independent
kingdom. After some delay, Baldwin, however, was permitted
to pursue his journey, was entertained with cold civility, and
thankfully departed with a present of seven hundred marks.[2]
From the avarice of Rome he could only obtain the proclamation
of a crusade, and a treasure of indulgences: a coin whose currency
was depreciated by too frequent and indiscriminate abuse. His
birth and misfortunes recommended him to the generosity of his
cousin Louis the Ninth; but the martial zeal of the saint was
diverted from Constantinople to Egypt and Palestine; and the
public and private poverty of Baldwin was alleviated, for a
moment, by the alienation of the marquisate of Namur and the
lordship of Courtenay, the last remains of his inheritance.[3] By
such shameful or ruinous expedients he once more returned to

---

[1] See the reign of Baldwin II. till his expulsion from Constantinople, in
Ducange, Hist. de C. P. l. iv. c. 1-34; the end, l. v. c. 1-33.

[2] Matthew Paris relates the two visits of Baldwin II. to the English
court, p. 396, 637; his return to Greece armatâ manû, p. 407; his letters of
his nomen formidabile, etc., p. 481 (a passage which had escaped Ducange);
his expulsion, p. 850.

[3] Louis IX. disapproved and stopped the alienation of Courtenay
(Ducange, l. iv. c. 23). It is now annexed to the royal demesne, but
granted for a term (engagé) to the family of Boulainvilliers. Courtenay, in
the election of Nemours in the Isle de France, is a town of 900 inhabitants,
with the remains of a castle (Mélanges tirés d'une Grande Bibliothèque,
tom. xlv. p. 74-77).

Romania, with an army of thirty thousand soldiers, whose
numbers were doubled in the apprehension of the Greeks. His
first despatches to France and England announced his victories
and his hopes: he had reduced the country round the capital
to the distance of three days' journey; and if he succeeded
against an important, though nameless, city (most probably
Chiorli), the frontier would be safe and the passage accessible.
But these expectations (if Baldwin was sincere) quickly vanished
like a dream: the troops and treasures of France melted away in
his unskilful hands: and the throne of the Latin emperor was
protected by a dishonourable alliance with the Turks and Comans.
To secure the former, he consented to bestow his niece on the
unbelieving sultan of Cogni; to please the latter, he complied
with their pagan rites; a dog was sacrificed between the two
armies; and the contracting parties tasted each other's blood,
as a pledge of their fidelity.[1] In the palace, or prison, of Constantinople, the successor of Augustus demolished the vacant
houses for winter-fuel, and stripped the lead from the churches
for the daily expense of his family. Some usurious loans were
dealt with a scanty hand by the merchants of Italy; and Philip,
his son and heir, was pawned at Venice as the security for a
debt.[2] Thirst, hunger, and nakedness are positive evils: but
wealth is relative; and a prince, who would be rich in a private
station, may be exposed by the increase of his wants to all the
anxiety and bitterness of poverty.

But in this abject distress the emperor and empire were still
possessed of an ideal treasure, which drew its fantastic value
from the superstition of the Christian world. The merit of the
true cross was somewhat impaired by its frequent division; and
a long captivity among the infidels might shed some suspicion
on the fragments that were produced in the East and West.
But another relic of the Passion was preserved in the Imperial
chapel of Constantinople; and the crown of thorns which had
been placed on the head of Christ was equally precious and
authentic. It had formerly been the practice of the Egyptian
debtors to deposit, as a security, the mummies of their parents;
and both their honour and religion were bound for the redemption of the pledge. In the same manner, and in the absence of
the emperor, the barons of Romania borrowed the sum of thirteen

---

[1] Joinville, p. 104, édit. du Louvre. A Coman prince, who died without
baptism, was buried at the gates of Constantinople with a live retinue of
slaves and horses.

[2] Sanut. Secret. Fidel. Crucis, l. ii. p. iv. c. 18, p. 73.

thousand one hundred and thirty-four pieces of gold [1] on the credit of the holy crown: they failed in the performance of their contract; and a rich Venetian, Nicholas Querini, undertook to satisfy their impatient creditors, on condition that the relic should be lodged at Venice, to become his absolute property if it were not redeemed within a short and definite term. The barons apprised their sovereign of the hard treaty and impending loss; and as the empire could not afford a ransom of seven thousand pounds sterling, Baldwin was anxious to snatch the prize from the Venetians, and to vest it with more honour and emolument in the hands of the most Christian king.[2] Yet the negotiation was attended with some delicacy. In the purchase of relics the saint would have started at the guilt of simony; but if the mode of expression were changed, he might lawfully repay the debt, accept the gift, and acknowledge the obligation. His ambassadors, two Dominicans, were despatched to Venice to redeem and receive the holy crown, which had escaped the dangers of the sea and the galleys of Vataces. On opening a wooden box they recognised the seals of the doge and barons, which were applied on a shrine of silver; and within this shrine the monument of the Passion was enclosed in a golden vase. The reluctant Venetians yielded to justice and power; the emperor Frederic granted a free and honourable passage; the court of France advanced as far as Troyes in Champagne to meet with devotion this inestimable relic: it was borne in triumph through Paris by the king himself, barefoot, and in his shirt; and a free gift of ten thousand marks of silver reconciled Baldwin to his loss. The success of this transaction tempted the Latin emperor to offer with the same generosity the remaining furniture of his chapel;[3] a large and authentic portion of the true cross; the baby-linen of the Son of God; the lance, the sponge, and the chain of his Passion; the rod of Moses; and part of the skull of St. John the Baptist. For the reception of these spiritual treasures twenty thousand marks were expended by St. Louis on

[1] Under the words *Perparus, Perpera, Hyperperum,* Ducange is short and vague: Monetæ genus. From a corrupt passage of Guntherus (Hist. C. P. c. 8, p. 10) I guess that the Perpera was the nummus aureus, the fourth part of a mark of silver, or about ten shillings sterling in value. In lead it would be too contemptible.

[2] For the translation of the holy crown, etc., from Constantinople to Paris, see Ducange (Hist. de C. P. l. iv. c. 11-14, 24, 35) and Fleury (Hist. Ecclés. tom. xvii. p. 201-204).

[3] Mélanges tirés d'une Grande Bibliothèque, tom. xliii. p. 201-205. The Lutrin of Boileau exhibits the inside, the soul and manners of the *Sainte Chapelle*; and many facts relative to the institution are collected and explained by his commentators, Brosset and De St. Marc.

a stately foundation, the holy chapel of Paris, on which the muse
of Boileau has bestowed a comic immortality. The truth of such
remote and ancient relics, which cannot be proved by any
human testimony, must be admitted by those who believe in the
miracles which they have performed. About the middle of the
last age, an inveterate ulcer was touched and cured by a holy
prickle of the holy crown: [1] the prodigy is attested by the most
pious and enlightened Christians of France; nor will the fact be
easily disproved, except by those who are armed with a general
antidote against religious credulity. [2]

The Latins of Constantinople [3] were on all sides encompassed
and pressed: their sole hope, the last delay of their ruin, was in
the division of their Greek and Bulgarian enemies; and of this
hope they were deprived by the superior arms and policy of
Vataces emperor of Nice. From the Propontis to the rocky
coast of Pamphylia, Asia was peaceful and prosperous under his
reign; and the events of every campaign extended his influence
in Europe. The strong cities of the hills of Macedonia and
Thrace were rescued from the Bulgarians, and their kingdom
was circumscribed by its present and proper limits along the
southern banks of the Danube. The sole emperor of the
Romans could no longer brook that a lord of Epirus, a Comnenian prince of the West, should presume to dispute or share
the honours of the purple; and the humble Demetrius changed
the colour of his buskins, and accepted with gratitude the
appellation of despot. His own subjects were exasperated by
his baseness and incapacity; they implored the protection of
their supreme lord. After some resistance, the kingdom of
Thessalonica was united to the empire of Nice; and Vataces
reigned without a competitor from the Turkish borders to the
Adriatic gulf. The princes of Europe revered his merit and

---

[1] It was performed A.D. 1656, March 24, on the niece of Pascal; and that
superior genius, with Arnauld, Nicole, etc., were on the spot, to believe
and attest a miracle which confounded the Jesuits and saved Port Royal
(Œuvres de Racine, tom. vi. p. 176-187, in his eloquent History of Port
Royal).

[2] Voltaire (Siècle de Louis XIV. c. 37; Œuvres, tom. ix. p. 178, 179)
strives to invalidate the fact: but Hume (Essays, vol. ii. p. 483, 484), with
more skill and success, seizes the battery, and turns the cannon against
his enemies.

[3] The gradual losses of the Latins may be traced in the third, fourth, and
fifth books of the compilation of Ducange: but of the Greek conquests he
has dropped many circumstances which may be recovered from the larger
history of George Acropolita and the three first books of Nicephorus
Gregoras, two writers of the Byzantine series who have had the good
fortune to meet with learned editors, Leo Allatius at Rome, and John
Boivin in the Academy of Inscriptions of Paris.

power; and had he subscribed an orthodox creed, it should seem that the pope would have abandoned without reluctance the Latin throne of Constantinople. But the death of Vataces, the short and busy reign of Theodore his son, and the helpless infancy of his grandson John, suspended the restoration of the Greeks. In the next chapter I shall explain their domestic revolutions; in this place it will be sufficient to observe that the young prince was oppressed by the ambition of his guardian and colleague Michael Palæologus, who displayed the virtues and vices that belong to the founder of a new dynasty. The emperor Baldwin had flattered himself that he might recover some provinces or cities by an impotent negotiation. His ambassadors were dismissed from Nice with mockery and contempt. At every place which they named Palæologus alleged some special reason which rendered it dear and valuable in his eyes: in the one he was born; in another he had been first promoted to military command; and in a third he had enjoyed, and hoped long to enjoy, the pleasures of the chase. " And what then do you propose to give us? " said the astonished deputies. " Nothing," replied the Greek; " not a foot of land. If your master be desirous of peace, let him pay me, as an annual tribute, the sum which he receives from the trade and customs of Constantinople. On these terms I may allow him to reign. If he refuses, it is war. I am not ignorant of the art of war, and I trust the event to God and my sword." [1] An expedition against the despot of Epirus was the first prelude of his arms. If a victory was followed by a defeat, if the race of the Comneni or Angeli survived in those mountains his efforts and his reign, the captivity of Villehardouin prince of Achaia deprived the Latins of the most active and powerful vassal of their expiring monarchy. The republics of Venice and Genoa disputed, in the first of their naval wars, the command of the sea and the commerce of the East. Pride and interest attached the Venetians to the defence of Constantinople; their rivals were tempted to promote the designs of her enemies, and the alliance of the Genoese with the schismatic conqueror provoked the indignation of the Latin church. [2]

Intent on his great object, the emperor Michael visited in

---

[1] George Acropolita, c. 78, p. 89, 90, edit. Paris [p. 171 sq. ed. Bonn].

[2] The Greeks, ashamed of any foreign aid, disguise the alliance and succour of the Genoese; but the fact is proved by the testimony of J. Villani (Chron. l. vi. c. 71, in Muratori, Script. Rerum Italicarum, tom. xiii. p. 202, 203) and William de Nangis (Annales de St. Louis, p. 248, in the Louvre Joinville), two impartial foreigners; and Urban IV. threatened to deprive Genoa of her archbishop.

person and strengthened the troops and fortifications of Thrace.
The remains of the Latins were driven from their last possessions:
he assaulted without success the suburb of Galata, and corresponded with a perfidious baron, who proved unwilling, or unable,
to open the gates of the metropolis.   The next spring his favourite
general, Alexius Strategopulus, whom he had decorated with the
title of Cæsar, passed the Hellespont with eight hundred horse
and some infantry [1] on a secret expedition.   His instructions
enjoined him to approach, to listen, to watch, but not to risk any
doubtful or dangerous enterprise against the city.   The adjacent
territory between the Propontis and the Black Sea was cultivated
by a hardy race of peasants and outlaws, exercised in arms,
uncertain in their allegiance, but inclined by language, religion,
and present advantage, to the party of the Greeks.   They were
styled the *volunteers*,[2] and by their free service the army of
Alexius, with the regulars of Thrace and the Coman auxiliaries,[3]
was augmented to the number of five-and-twenty thousand men.
By the ardour of the volunteers, and by his own ambition, the
Cæsar was stimulated to disobey the precise orders of his master,
in the just confidence that success would plead his pardon and
reward.   The weakness of Constantinople and the distress and
terror of the Latins were familiar to the observation of the
volunteers; and they represented the present moment as the
most propitious to surprise and conquest.   A rash youth, the
new governor of the Venetian colony, had sailed away with
thirty galleys and the best of the French knights on a wild
expedition to Daphnusia, a town on the Black Sea, at the distance
of forty leagues, and the remaining Latins were without strength
or suspicion.   They were informed that Alexius had passed the
Hellespont; but their apprehensions were lulled by the smallness of his original numbers, and their imprudence had not
watched the subsequent increase of his army.   If he left his
main body to second and support his operations, he might
advance unperceived in the night with a chosen detachment.
While some applied scaling-ladders to the lowest part of the
walls, they were secure of an old Greek who would introduce their

---

[1] Some precautions must be used in reconciling the discordant numbers;
the 800 soldiers of Nicetas, the 25,000 of Spandugino (apud Ducange, l. v.
c. 24); the Greeks and Scythians of Acropolita; and the numerous army
of Michael, in the Epistles of pope Urban IV. (i. 129.)

[2] Θεληματάριοι.   They are described and named by Pachymer (l. ii. c. 14).

[3] It is needless to seek these Comans in the deserts of Tartary, or even of
Moldavia.   A part of the horde had submitted to John Vataces, and was
probably settled as a nursery of soldiers on some waste lands of Thrace
Cantacuzen (l. i. c. 2).

companions through a subterraneous passage into his house;
they could soon on the inside break an entrance through the
golden gate, which had been long obstructed; and the conqueror
would be in the heart of the city before the Latins were conscious
of their danger. After some debate, the Cæsar resigned himself
to the faith of the volunteers; they were trusty, bold, and
successful; and, in describing the plan, I have already related
the execution and success.[1] But no sooner had Alexius passed
the threshold of the golden gate than he trembled at his own
rashness; he paused, he deliberated, till the desperate volunteers
urged him forwards by the assurance that in retreat lay the
greatest and most inevitable danger. Whilst the Cæsar kept
his regulars in firm array, the Comans dispersed themselves on
all sides; an alarm was sounded, and the threats of fire and
pillage compelled the citizens to a decisive resolution. The
Greeks of Constantinople remembered their native sovereigns;
the Genoese merchants their recent alliance and Venetian foes;
every quarter was in arms; and the air resounded with a general
acclamation of " Long life and victory to Michael and John, the
august emperors of the Romans!" Their rival, Baldwin, was
awakened by the sound; but the most pressing danger could
not prompt him to draw his sword in the defence of a city which
he deserted perhaps with more pleasure than regret: he fled
from the palace to the sea-shore, where he descried the welcome
sails of the fleet returning from the vain and fruitless attempt
on Daphnusia. Constantinople was irrecoverably lost; but the
Latin emperor and the principal families embarked on board the
Venetian galleys, and steered for the isle of Eubœa, and afterwards for Italy, where the royal fugitive was entertained by the
pope and Sicilian king with a mixture of contempt and pity.
From the loss of Constantinople to his death he consumed
thirteen years soliciting the Catholic powers to join in his restoration: the lesson had been familiar to his youth; nor was his last
exile more indigent or shameful than his three former pilgrimages
to the courts of Europe. His son Philip was the heir of an ideal
empire; and the pretensions of *his* daughter Catherine were
transported by her marriage, to Charles of Valois, the brother of
Philip the Fair, king of France. The house of Courtenay was
represented in the female line by successive alliances, till the

---

[1] The loss of Constantinople is briefly told by the Latins: the conquest
is described with more satisfaction by the Greeks; by Acropolita (c. 85),
Pachymer (l. ii. c. 26, 27), Nicephorus Gregoras (l. iv. c. 1, 2). See Ducange,
Hist. de C. P. l. v. c. 19-27.

title of emperor of Constantinople, too bulky and sonorous for
a private name, modestly expired in silence and oblivion.[1]

After this narrative of the expeditions of the Latins to Palestine
and Constantinople, I cannot dismiss the subject without re-
volving the general consequences on the countries that were the
scene, and on the nations that were the actors, of these memorable
crusades.[2]   As soon as the arms of the Franks were withdrawn,
the impression, though not the memory, was erased in the
Mohammedan realms of Egypt and Syria.   The faithful disciples
of the prophet were never tempted by a profane desire to study
the laws or language of the idolaters; nor did the simplicity of
their primitive manners receive the slightest alteration from
their intercourse in peace and war with the unknown strangers
of the West.   The Greeks, who thought themselves proud, but
who were only vain, showed a disposition somewhat less inflexible.
In the efforts for the recovery of their empire they emulated the
valour, discipline, and tactics of their antagonists.   The modern
literature of the West they might justly despise; but its free
spirit would instruct them in the rights of man; and some
institutions of public and private life were adopted from the
French.   The correspondence of Constantinople and Italy
diffused the knowledge of the Latin tongue; and several of the
fathers and classics were at length honoured with a Greek
version.[3]   But the national and religious prejudices of the
Orientals were inflamed by persecution; and the reign of the
Latins confirmed the separation of the two churches.

If we compare the era of the crusades, the Latins of Europe
with the Greeks and Arabians, their respective degrees of knowledge, industry, and art, our rude ancestors must be content
with the third rank in the scale of nations.   Their successive
improvement and present superiority may be ascribed to a
peculiar energy of character, to an active and imitative spirit,

[1] See the three last books (l. v.-viii.) and the genealogical tables of
Ducange. In the year 1382 the titular emperor of Constantinople was
James de Baux, duke of Andria in the kingdom of Naples, the son of
Margaret, daughter of Catherine de Valois, daughter of Catherine, daughter
of Philip, son of Baldwin II. (Ducange, l. viii. c. 37, 38). It is uncertain
whether he left any posterity.

[2] Abulfeda, who saw the conclusion of the crusades, speaks of the kingdoms of the Franks and those of the Negroes as equally unknown (Prolegom.
ad Geograph.). Had he not disdained the Latin language, how easily
might the Syrian prince have found books and interpreters!

[3] A short and superficial account of these versions from Latin into Greek
is given by Huet (de Interpretatione et de claris Interpretibus, p. 131-135).
Maximus Planudes, a monk of Constantinople (A.D. 1327-1353), has translated Cæsar's Commentaries, the Somnium Scipionis, the Metamorphoses
and Heroides of Ovid, etc. (Fabric. Bib. Græc. tom. x. p. 533).

unknown to their more polished rivals, who at that time were in a stationary or retrograde state. With such a disposition the Latins should have derived the most early and essential benefits from a series of events which opened to their eyes the prospect of the world, and introduced them to a long and frequent intercourse with the more cultivated regions of the East. The first and most obvious progress was in trade and manufactures, in the arts which are strongly prompted by the thirst of wealth, the calls of necessity, and the gratification of the sense or vanity. Among the crowd of unthinking fanatics a captive or a pilgrim might sometimes observe the superior refinements of Cairo and Constantinople: the first importer of windmills [1] was the benefactor of nations; and if such blessings are enjoyed without any grateful remembrance, history has condescended to notice the more apparent luxuries of silk and sugar, which were transported into Italy from Greece and Egypt. But the intellectual wants of the Latins were more slowly felt and supplied; the ardour of studious curiosity was awakened in Europe by different causes and more recent events; and, in the age of the crusades, they viewed with careless indifference the literature of the Greeks and Arabians. Some rudiments of mathematical and medicinal knowledge might be imparted in practice and in figures; necessity might produce some interpreters for the grosser business of merchants and soldiers; but the commerce of the Orientals had not diffused the study and knowledge of their languages in the schools of Europe.[2] If a similar principle of religion repulsed the idiom of the Koran, it should have excited their patience and curiosity to understand the original text of the Gospel; and the same grammar would have unfolded the sense of Plato and the beauties of Homer. Yet, in a reign of sixty years, the Latins of Constantinople disdained the speech and learning of their subjects; and the manuscripts were the only treasures which the natives might enjoy without rapine or envy. Aristotle was indeed the oracle of the Western universities, but it was a barbarous Aristotle; and, instead of ascending to the fountain head, his Latin votaries humbly accepted a corrupt and remote version from the Jews and Moors of Andalusia. The principle of the crusades was a savage fanaticism; and the most important

[1] Windmills, first invented in the dry country of Asia Minor, were used in Normandy as early as the year 1105 (Vie privée des François, tom. i. p. 42, 43; Ducange, Gloss. Latin. tom. iv. p. 474).
[2] See the complaints of Roger Bacon (Biographia Britannica, vol. i. p. 418, Kippis's edition). If Bacon himself, or Gerbert, understood some Greek, they were prodigies, and owed nothing to the commerce of the East.

effects were analogous to the cause. Each pilgrim was ambitious
to return with his sacred spoils, the relics of Greece and Palestine;[1]
and each relic was preceded and followed by a train of miracles
and visions. The belief of the Catholics was corrupted by new
legends, their practice by new superstitions; and the establishment of the inquisition, the mendicant orders of monks and
friars, the last abuse of indulgences, and the final progress of
idolatry, flowed from the baleful fountain of the holy war. The
active spirit of the Latins preyed on the vitals of their reason
and religion; and if the ninth and tenth centuries were the times
of darkness, the thirteenth and fourteenth were the age of
absurdity and fable.

In the profession of Christianity, in the cultivation of a fertile
land, the northern conquerors of the Roman empire insensibly
mingled with the provincials and rekindled the embers of the
arts of antiquity. Their settlements about the age of Charlemagne had acquired some degree of order and stability, when
they were overwhelmed by new swarms of invaders, the Normans,
Saracens,[2] and Hungarians, who replunged the western countries
of Europe into their former state of anarchy and barbarism.
About the eleventh century the second tempest had subsided by
the expulsion or conversion of the enemies of Christendom: the
tide of civilisation, which had so long ebbed, began to flow with
a steady and accelerated course; and a fairer prospect was opened
to the hopes and efforts of the rising generations. Great was
the increase, and rapid the progress, during the two hundred
years of the crusades; and some philosophers have applauded
the propitious influence of these holy wars, which appear to me
to have checked rather than forwarded the maturity of Europe.[3]
The lives and labours of millions which were buried in the East
would have been more profitably employed in the improvement
of their native country: the accumulated stock of industry and
wealth would have overflowed in navigation and trade; and the
Latins would have been enriched and enlightened by a pure and

---

[1] Such was the opinion of the great Leibnitz (Œuvres de Fontenelle,
tom. v. p. 458), a master of the history of the middle ages. I shall only
instance the pedigree of the Carmelites and the flight of the house of
Loretto, which were both derived from Palestine.

[2] If I rank the Saracens with the barbarians, it is only relative to their
wars, or rather inroads, in Italy and France, where their sole purpose was
to plunder and destroy.

[3] On this interesting subject, the progress of society in Europe, a strong
ray of philosophic light has broke from Scotland in our own times; and
it is with private, as well as public regard, that I repeat the names of
Hume, Robertson, and Adam Smith.

friendly correspondence with the climates of the East. In one respect I can indeed perceive the accidental operation of the crusades, not so much in producing a benefit as in removing an evil. The larger portion of the inhabitants of Europe was chained to the soil, without freedom, or property, or knowledge; and the two orders of ecclesiastics and nobles, whose numbers were comparatively small, alone deserved the name of citizens and men. This oppressive system was supported by the arts of the clergy and the swords of the barons. The authority of the priests operated in the darker ages as a salutary antidote: they prevented the total extinction of letters, mitigated the fierceness of the times, sheltered the poor and defenceless, and preserved or revived the peace and order of civil society. But the independence, rapine, and discord of the feudal lords were unmixed with any semblance of good; and every hope of industry and improvement was crushed by the iron weight of the martial aristocracy. Among the causes that undermined that Gothic edifice, a conspicuous place must be allowed to the crusades. The estates of the barons were dissipated, and their race was often extinguished in these costly and perilous expeditions. Their poverty extorted from their pride those charters of freedom which unlocked the fetters of the slave, secured the farm of the peasant and the shop of the artificer, and gradually restored a substance and a soul to the most numerous and useful part of the community. The conflagration which destroyed the tall and barren trees of the forest gave air and scope to the vegetation of the smaller and nutritive plants of the soil.

Digression on the Family of Courtenay

THE purple of three emperors who have reigned at Constantinople will authorise or excuse a digression on the origin and singular fortunes of the house of COURTENAY,[1] in the three principal branches, I. Of Edessa; II. Of France; and III. Of England; of which the last only has survived the revolutions of eight hundred years.

I. Before the introduction of trade, which scatters riches, and

---

[1] I have applied but not confined myself to *A Genealogical History of the noble and illustrious Family of Courtenay, by Ezra Cleaveland, Tutor to Sir William Courtenay, and Rector of Honiton: Exon.* 1735, *in folio.* The first part is extracted from William of Tyre; the second from Bouchet's French history; and the third from various memorials, public, provincial, and private, of the Courtenays of Devonshire. The rector of Honiton has more gratitude than industry, and more industry than criticism.

of knowledge, which dispels prejudice, the prerogative of birth is most strongly felt and most humbly acknowledged. In every age the laws and manners of the Germans have discriminated the ranks of society: the dukes and counts who shared the empire of Charlemagne converted their office to an inheritance; and to his children each feudal lord bequeathed his honour and his sword. The proudest families are content to lose, in the darkness of the middle ages, the tree of their pedigree, which, however deep and lofty, must ultimately rise from a plebeian róot; and their historians must descend ten centuries below the Christian era, before they can ascertain any lineal succession by the evidence of surnames, of arms, and of authentic records. With the first rays of light [1] we discern the nobility and opulence of Atho, a French knight: his nobility, in the rank and title of a nameless father; his opulence, in the foundation of the castle of Courtenay in the district of Gatinois, about fifty-six miles to the south of Paris. From the reign of Robert, the son of Hugh Capet, the barons of Courtenay are conspicuous among the immediate vassals of the crown; and Joscelin, the grandson of Atho and a noble dame, is enrolled among the heroes of the first crusade. A domestic alliance (their mothers were sisters) attached him to the standard of Baldwin of Bruges, the second count of Edessa; a princely fief, which he was worthy to receive and able to maintain, announces the number of his martial followers; and after the departure of his cousin, Joscelin himself was invested with the county of Edessa on both sides of the Euphrates. By economy in peace his territories were replenished with Latin and Syrian subjects; his magazines with corn, wine, and oil; his castles with gold and silver, with arms and horses. In a holy warfare of thirty years he was alternately a conqueror and a captive: but he died like a soldier, in a horse litter at the head of his troops; and his last glance beheld the flight of the Turkish invaders who had presumed on his age and infirmities. His son and successor, of the same name, was less deficient in valour than in vigilance; but he sometimes forgot that dominion is acquired and maintained by the same arts. He challenged the hostility of the Turks without securing the friendship of the prince of Antioch; and, amidst the peaceful luxury of Turbessel, in Syria,[2] Joscelin neglected the defence of the Christian frontier

---

[1] The primitive record of the family is a passage of the continuator of Aimoin, a monk of Fleury, who wrote in the twelfth century. See his Chronicle, in the Historians of France (tom. xi. p. 276).

[2] Turbessel, or, as it is now styled, Telbesher, is fixed by D'Anville four-and-twenty miles from the great passage over the Euphrates at Zeugma.

beyond the Euphrates. In his absence, Zenghi, the first of the
Atabeks, besieged and stormed his capital, Edessa, which was
feebly defended by a timorous and disloyal crowd of Orientals:
the Franks were oppressed in a bold attempt for its recovery,
and Courtenay ended his days in the prison of Aleppo. He still
left a fair and ample patrimony. But the victorious Turks
oppressed on all sides the weakness of a widow and orphan; and,
for the equivalent of an annual pension, they resigned to the
Greek emperor the charge of defending, and the shame of losing,
the last relics of the Latin conquest. The countess-dowager of
Edessa retired to Jerusalem with her two children: the daughter,
Agnes, became the wife and mother of a king; the son, Joscelin
the Third, accepted the office of seneschal, the first of the
kingdom, and held his new estates in Palestine by the service of
fifty knights. His name appears with honour in all the trans-
actions of peace and war; but he finally vanishes in the fall of
Jerusalem; and the name of Courtenay, in this branch of
Edessa, was lost by the marriage of his two daughters with a
French and a German baron.[1]

II. While Joscelin reigned beyond the Euphrates, his elder
brother Milo, the son of Joscelin, the son of Atho, continued,
near the Seine, to possess the castle of their fathers, which was at
length inherited by Rainaud, or Reginald, the youngest of his
three sons. Examples of genius or virtue must be rare in the
annals of the oldest families; and, in a remote age, their pride
will embrace a deed of rapine and violence; such, however, as
could not be perpetrated without some superiority of courage,
or, at least, of power. A descendant of Reginald of Courtenay
may blush for the public robber who stripped and imprisoned
several merchants after they had satisfied the king's duties at
Sens and Orleans. He will glory in the offence, since the bold
offender could not be compelled to obedience and restitution till
the regent and the count of Champagne prepared to march
against him at the head of an army.[2] Reginald bestowed his
estates on his eldest daughter, and his daughter on the seventh
son of king Louis the Fat; and their marriage was crowned with
a numerous offspring. We might expect that a private should

[1] His possessions are distinguished in the Assises of Jerusalem (c. 326)
among the feudal tenures of the kingdom, which must therefore have been
collected between the years 1153 and 1187. His pedigree may be found
in the Lignages d'Outremer, c. 16.

[2] The rapine and satisfaction of Reginald de Courtenay are preposter-
ously arranged in the Epistles of the abbot and regent Suger (cxiv. cxvi.),
the best memorials of the age (Duchesne, Scriptores Hist. Franc. tom. iv.
p. 530).

have merged in a royal name; and that the descendants of Peter of France and Elizabeth of Courtenay would have enjoyed the title and honours of princes of the blood. But this legitimate claim was long neglected, and finally denied; and the causes of their disgrace will represent the story of this second branch. 1. Of all the families now extant, the most ancient, doubtless, and the most illustrious, is the house of France, which has occupied the same throne above eight hundred years, and descends, in a clear and lineal series of males, from the middle of the ninth century.[1] In the age of the crusades it was already revered both in the East and West. But from Hugh Capet to the marriage of Peter no more than five reigns or generations had elapsed; and so precarious was their title, that the eldest sons, as a necessary precaution, were previously crowned during the lifetime of their fathers. The peers of France have long maintained their precedency before the younger branches of the royal line, nor had the princes of the blood, in the twelfth century, acquired that hereditary lustre which is now diffused over the most remote candidates for the succession. 2. The barons of Courtenay must have stood high in their own estimation, and in that of the world, since they could impose on the son of a king the obligation of adopting for himself and all his descendants the name and arms of their daughter and his wife. In the marriage of an heiress with her inferior or her equal, such exchange was often required and allowed: but as they continued to diverge from the regal stem, the sons of Louis the Fat were insensibly confounded with their maternal ancestors; and the new Courtenays might deserve to forfeit the honours of their birth, which a motive of interest had tempted them to renounce. 3. The shame was far more permanent than the reward, and a momentary blaze was followed by a long darkness. The eldest son of these nuptials, Peter of Courtenay, had married, as I have

[1] In the beginning of the eleventh century, after naming the father and grandfather of Hugh Capet, the monk Glaber is obliged to add, cujus genus valde in-ante reperitur obscurum. Yet we are assured that the great-grandfather of Hugh Capet was Robert the Strong, count of Anjou (A.D. 863-873), a noble Frank of Neustria, Neustricus . . . generosæ stirpis, who was slain in the defence of his country against the Normans, dum patriæ fines tuebatur. Beyond Robert all is conjecture or fable. It is a probable conjecture that the third race descended from the second by Childebrand, the brother of Charles Martel. It is an absurd fable that the second was allied to the first by the marriage of Ansbert, a Roman senator and the ancestor of St. Arnoul, with Blitilde, a daughter of Clotaire I. The Saxon origin of the house of France is an ancient but incredible opinion. See a judicious memoir of M. de Foncemagne (Mémoires de l'Académie des Inscriptions, tom. xx. p. 548-579). He had promised to declare his own opinion in a second memoir, which has never appeared.

already mentioned, the sister of the counts of Flanders, the two first emperors of Constantinople: he rashly accepted the invitation of the barons of Romania; his two sons, Robert and Baldwin, successively held and lost the remains of the Latin empire in the East, and the grand-daughter of Baldwin the Second again mingled her blood with the blood of France and of Valois. To support the expenses of a troubled and transitory reign, their patrimonial estates were mortgaged or sold; and the last emperors of Constantinople depended on the annual charity of Rome and Naples.

While the elder brothers dissipated their wealth in romantic adventures, and the castle of Courtenay was profaned by a plebeian owner, the younger branches of that adopted name were propagated and multiplied. But their splendour was clouded by poverty and time: after the decease of Robert, great butler of France, they descended from princes to barons; the next generations were confounded with the simple gentry; the descendants of Hugh Capet could no longer be visible in the rural lords of Tanlay and of Champignelles. The more adventurous embraced without dishonour the profession of a soldier: the least active and opulent might sink, like their cousins of the branch of Dreux, into the condition of peasants. Their royal descent in a dark period of four hundred years became each day more obsolete and ambiguous; and their pedigree, instead of being enrolled in the annals of the kingdom, must be painfully searched by the minute diligence of heralds and genealogists. It was not till the end of the sixteenth century, on the accession of a family almost as remote as their own, that the princely spirit of the Courtenays again revived; and the question of the nobility provoked them to assert the royalty of their blood. They appealed to the justice and compassion of Henry the Fourth; obtained a favourable opinion from twenty lawyers of Italy and Germany, and modestly compared themselves to the descendants of king David, whose prerogatives were not impaired by the lapse of ages or the trade of a carpenter.[1] But every ear was deaf,

---

[1] Of the various petitions, apologies, etc., published by the *princes* of Courtenay, I have seen the three following, all in octavo:—1. De Stirpe et Origine Domus de Courtenay: addita sunt Responsa celeberrimorum Europæ Jurisconsultorum: Paris, 1607. 2. Representation du Procedé tenû a l'instance faicte devant le Roi, par Messieurs de Courtenay, pour la conservation de l'Honneur et Dignité de leur Maison, branche de la royalle Maison de France: à Paris, 1613. 3. Representation du subject qui a porté Messieurs de Salles et de Fraville, de la Maison de Courtenay, à se retirer hors du Royaume, 1614. It was a homicide, for which the Courtenays expected to be pardoned, or tried, as princes of the blood.

and every circumstance was adverse, to their lawful claims.
The Bourbon kings were justified by the neglect of the Valois;
the princes of the blood, more recent and lofty, disdained the
alliance of this humble kindred: the parliament, without deny-
ing their proofs, eluded a dangerous precedent by an arbitrary
distinction, and established St. Louis as the first father of the
royal line.[1] A repetition of complaints and protests was
repeatedly disregarded; and the hopeless pursuit was terminated
in the present century by the death of the last male of the family.[2]
Their painful and anxious situation was alleviated by the pride
of conscious virtue: they sternly rejected the temptations of
fortune and favour; and a dying Courtenay would have sacrificed
his son if the youth could have renounced, for any temporal
interest, the right and title of a legitimate prince of the blood of
France.[3]

III. According to the old register of Ford Abbey, the
Courtenays of Devonshire are descended from prince *Florus*, the
second son of Peter, and the grandson of Louis the Fat.[4] This
fable of the grateful or venal monks was too respectfully entertained by our antiquaries, Camden [5] and Dugdale: [6] but it is so
clearly repugnant to truth and time, that the rational pride of
the family now refuses to accept this imaginary founder. Their
most faithful historians believe that, after giving his daughter to

[1] The sense of the parliaments is thus expressed by Thuanus: Principis
nomen nusquam in Galliâ tributum, nisi iis qui per mares e regibus nostris
originem repetunt; qui nunc tantum a Ludovico Nono beatæ memoriæ
numerantur; nam *Cortinæi* et Drocenses, a Ludovico crasso genus
ducentes, hodie inter eos minime recensentur—a distinction of expediency
rather than justice. The sanctity of Louis IX. could not invest him with
any special prerogative, and all the descendants of Hugh Capet must be
included in his original compact with the French nation.

[2] The last male of the Courtenays was Charles Roger, who died in the
year 1730, without leaving any sons. The last female was Hélène de
Courtenay, who married Louis de Beaufremont. Her title of Princesse du
Sang Royal de France was suppressed (February 7th, 1737) by an *arrêt* of
the parliament of Paris.

[3] The singular anecdote to which I allude is related in the Recueil des
Pièces interessantes et peu connues (Maestricht, 1786, in 4 vols. 12mo);
and the unknown editor quotes his author, who had received it from
Hélène de Courtenay, marquise de Beaufremont.

[4] Dugdale, Monasticon Anglicanum, vol. i. p. 786. Yet this fable must
have been invented before the reign of Edward III. The profuse devotion
of the three first generations to Ford Abbey was followed by oppression on
one side and ingratitude on the other; and in the sixth generation the
monks ceased to register the births, actions, and deaths of their patrons.

[5] In his Britannia, in the list of the earls of Devonshire. His expression,
e regio sanguine ortos credunt, betrays, however, some doubt or suspicion.

[6] In his Baronage, P. i. p. 634, he refers to his own Monasticon. Should
he not have corrected the register of Ford Abbey, and annihilated the
phantom Florus, by the unquestionable evidence of the French historians?

the king's son, Reginald of Courtenay abandoned his possessions
in France, and obtained from the English monarch a second wife
and a new inheritance. It is certain, at least, that Henry the
Second distinguished in his camps and councils a Reginald, of
the name and arms, and, as it may be fairly presumed, of the
genuine race, of the Courtenays of France. The right of ward-
ship enabled a feudal lord to reward his vassal with the marriage
and estate of a noble heiress; and Reginald of Courtenay
acquired a fair establishment in Devonshire, where his posterity
has been seated above six hundred years.[1] From a Norman
baron, Baldwin de Brioniis, who had been invested by the
Conqueror, Hawise, the wife of Reginald, derived the honour of
Okehampton, which was held by the service of ninety-three
knights; and a female might claim the manly offices of hereditary
viscount or sheriff, and of captain of the royal castle of Exeter.
Their son Robert married the sister of the earl of Devon: at the
end of a century, on the failure of the family of Rivers,[2] his
great-grandson, Hugh the Second, succeeded to a title which was
still considered as a territorial dignity; and twelve earls of
Devonshire, of the name of Courtenay, have flourished in a
period of two hundred and twenty years. They were ranked
among the chief of the barons of the realm; nor was it till after
a strenuous dispute that they yielded to the fief of Arundel the
first place in the parliament of England: their alliances were
contracted with the noblest families, the Veres, Despensers,
St. Johns, Talbots, Bohuns, and even the Plantagenets themselves; and in a contest with John of Lancaster, a Courtenay,
bishop of London, and afterwards archbishop of Canterbury,
might be accused of profane confidence in the strength and
number of his kindred. In peace the earls of Devon resided in
their numerous castles and manors of the west: their ample
revenue was appropriated to devotion and hospitality: and the
epitaph of Edward, surnamed, from his misfortune, the *blind*,
from his virtues, the *good*, earl, inculcates with much ingenuity
a moral sentence, which may however be abused by thoughtless
generosity. After a grateful commemoration of the fifty-five

---

[1] Besides the third and most valuable book of Cleaveland's History, I
have consulted Dugdale, the father of our genealogical science (Baronage,
P. i. p. 634-643).

[2] This great family, de Ripuariis, de Redvers, de Rivers, ended, in Edward
the First's time, in Isabella de Fortibus, a famous and potent dowager,
who long survived her brother and husband (Dugdale, Baronage, P. i.
p. 254-257).

years of union and happiness which he enjoyed with Mabel his
wife, the good earl thus speaks from the tomb:—

> What we gave, we have;
> What we spent, we had;
> What we left, we lost.[1]

But their *losses*, in this sense, were far superior to their gifts and
expenses; and their heirs, not less than the poor, were the
objects of their paternal care. The sums which they paid for
livery and seisin attest the greatness of their possessions; and
several estates have remained in their family since the thirteenth
and fourteenth centuries. In war the Courtenays of England
fulfilled the duties, and deserved the honours of chivalry. They
were often intrusted to levy and command the militia of Devonshire and Cornwall; they often attended their supreme lord to
the borders of Scotland; and in foreign service, for a stipulated
price, they sometimes maintained fourscore men-at-arms and as
many archers. By sea and land they fought under the standard
of the Edwards and Henries: their names are conspicuous in
battles, in tournaments, and in the original list of the Order of
the Garter; three brothers shared the Spanish victory of the
Black Prince; and in the lapse of six generations the English
Courtenays had learned to despise the nation and country from
which they derived their origin. In the quarrel of the two Roses
the earls of Devon adhered to the house of Lancaster, and three
brothers successively died either in the field or on the scaffold.
Their honours and estates were restored by Henry the Seventh:
a daughter of Edward the Fourth was not disgraced by the
nuptials of a Courtenay; their son, who was created marquis of
Exeter, enjoyed the favour of his cousin Henry the Eighth; and
in the camp of Cloth of Gold he broke a lance against the French
monarch. But the favour of Henry was the prelude of disgrace;
his disgrace was the signal of death; and of the victims of the
jealous tyrant the marquis of Exeter is one of the most noble and
guiltless. His son Edward lived a prisoner in the Tower, and
died an exile at Padua; and the secret love of queen Mary,
whom he slighted, perhaps for the princess Elizabeth, has shed
a romantic colour on the story of this beautiful youth. The
relics of his patrimony were conveyed into strange families by
the marriages of his four aunts; and his personal honours, as if
they had been legally extinct, were revived by the patents of

---

[1] Cleaveland, p. 142. By some it is assigned to a Rivers earl of Devon;
but the English denotes the fifteenth rather than the thirteenth century.

succeeding princes. But there still survived a lineal descendant of Hugh the first earl of Devon, a younger branch of the Courtenays, who have been seated at Powderham Castle above four hundred years, from the reign of Edward the Third to the present hour. Their estates have been increased by the grant and improvement of lands in Ireland, and they have been recently restored to the honours of the peerage. Yet the Courtenays still retain the plaintive motto which asserts the innocence and deplores the fall of their ancient house.[1] While they sigh for past greatness, they are doubtless sensible of present blessings: in the long series of the Courtenay annals the most splendid era is likewise the most unfortunate; nor can an opulent peer of Britain be inclined to envy the emperors of Constantinople who wandered over Europe to solicit alms for the support of their dignity and the defence of their capital.

CHAPTER LXII

The Greek Emperors of Nice and Constantinople—Elevation and Reign of Michael Palæologus—His false Union with the Pope and the Latin Church—Hostile Designs of Charles of Anjou—Revolt of Sicily—War of the Catalans in Asia and Greece—Revolutions and present State of Athens

THE loss of Constantinople restored a momentary vigour to the Greeks. From their palaces the princes and nobles were driven into the field; and the fragments of the falling monarchy were grasped by the hands of the most vigorous or the most skilful candidates. In the long and barren pages of the Byzantine annals [2] it would not be an easy task to equal the two characters of Theodore Lascaris and John Ducas Vataces,[3] who replanted and upheld the Roman standard at Nice in Bithynia. The differ-

---

[1] *Ubi lapsus ! Quid feci ?* a motto which was probably adopted by the Powderham branch after the loss of the earldom of Devonshire, etc. The primitive arms of the Courtenays were *Or, three torteaux, Gules*, which seem to denote their affinity with Godfrey of Bouillon and the ancient counts of Boulogne.

[2] For the reigns of the Nicene emperors, more especially of John Vataces and his son, their minister, George Acropolita, is the only genuine contemporary; but George Pachymer returned to Constantinople with the Greeks at the age of nineteen (Hanckius de Script. Byzant. c. 33, 34, p. 564-578; Fabric. Biblioth. Græc. tom. vi. p. 448-460). Yet the history of Nicephorus Gregoras, though of the fourteenth century, is a valuable narrative from the taking of Constantinople by the Latins.

[3] Nicephorus Gregoras (l. ii. c. 1) distinguishes between the ὀξεῖα ὁρμή of Lascaris and the εὐστάθεια of Vataces. The two portraits are in a very good style.

ence of their virtues was happily suited to the diversity of their situation. In his first efforts the fugitive Lascaris commanded only three cities and two thousand soldiers: his reign was the season of generous and active despair; in every military operation he staked his life and crown; and his enemies of the Hellespont and the Mæander were surprised by his celerity and subdued by his boldness. A victorious reign of eighteen years expanded the principality of Nice to the magnitude of an empire. The throne of his successor and son-in-law Vataces was founded on a more solid basis, a larger scope, and more plentiful resources; and it was the temper, as well as the interest, of Vataces to calculate the risk, to expect the moment, and to insure the success, of his ambitious designs. In the decline of the Latins I have briefly exposed the progress of the Greeks; the prudent and gradual advances of a conqueror who, in a reign of thirty-three years, rescued the provinces from national and foreign usurpers, till he pressed on all sides the Imperial city, a leafless and sapless trunk, which must fall at the first stroke of the axe. But his interior and peaceful administration is still more deserving of notice and praise.[1] The calamities of the times had wasted the numbers and the substance of the Greeks: the motives and the means of agriculture were extirpated; and the most fertile lands were left without cultivation or inhabitants. A portion of this vacant property was occupied and improved by the command, and for the benefit, of the emperor: a powerful hand and a vigilant eye supplied and surpassed, by a skilful management, the minute diligence of a private farmer: the royal domain became the garden and granary of Asia; and, without impoverishing the people, the sovereign acquired a fund of innocent and productive wealth. According to the nature of the soil, his lands were sown with corn or planted with vines; the pastures were filled with horses and oxen, with sheep and hogs; and when Vataces presented to the empress a crown of diamonds and pearls, he informed her, with a smile, that this precious ornament arose from the sale of the eggs of his innumerable poultry. The produce of his domain was applied to the maintenance of his palace and hospitals, the calls of dignity and benevolence: the lesson was still more useful than the revenue: the plough was restored to its ancient security and honour; and the nobles were taught to seek a sure and independent revenue from their estates,

---

[1] Pachymer, l. i. c. 23, 24; Nic. Greg. l. ii. c. 6 [tom. i. p. 42, ed. Bonn]. The reader of the Byzantines must observe how rarely we are indulged with such precious details.

instead of adorning their splendid beggary by the oppression of the people, or (what is almost the same) by the favours of the court. The superfluous stock of corn and cattle was eagerly purchased by the Turks, with whom Vataces preserved a strict and sincere alliance; but he discouraged the importation of foreign manufactures, the costly silks of the East and the curious labours of the Italian looms. "The demands of nature and necessity," was he accustomed to say, "are indispensable; but the influence of fashion may rise and sink at the breath of a monarch:" and both his precept and example recommended simplicity of manners and the use of domestic industry. The education of youth and the revival of learning were the most serious objects of his care; and, without deciding the precedency, he pronounced with truth that a prince and a philosopher [1] are the two most eminent characters of human society. His first wife was Irene, the daughter of Theodore Lascaris, a woman more illustrious by her personal merit, the milder virtues of her sex, than by the blood of the Angeli and Comneni that flowed in her veins, and transmitted the inheritance of the empire. After her death he was contracted to Anne or Constance, a natural daughter of the emperor Frederic the Second; but as the bride had not attained the years of puberty, Vataces placed in his solitary bed an Italian damsel of her train; [2] and his amorous weakness bestowed on the concubine the honours, though not the title, of lawful empress. His frailty was censured as a flagitious and damnable sin by the monks; and their rude invectives exercised and displayed the patience of the royal lover. A philosophic age may excuse a single vice, which was redeemed by a crowd of virtues; and in the review of his faults, and the more intemperate passions of Lascaris, the judgment of their contemporaries was softened by gratitude to the second founders of the empire. [3] The slaves of the Latins, without law or peace, applauded the happiness of their brethren who had resumed their national freedom; and Vataces employed the laudable

[1] Μόνοι γὰρ ἁπάντων ἀνθρώπων ὀνομαστότατοι βασιλεὺς καὶ φιλόσοφος (Greg. Acropol. c. 32). The emperor, in a familiar conversation, examined and encouraged the studies of his future logothete.

[2] [Frederick ultimately married the lady and legitimised her children. She passed by the name of the "Marchioness," and the question as to whether she was or was not to be allowed to be present at Holy Communion was the cause of the rupture between the emperor and Nicephorus Blemmydes.—O. S.]

[3] Compare Acropolita (c. 18, 52), and the two first books of Nicephorus Gregoras.

policy of convincing the Greeks of every dominion that it was their interest to be enrolled in the number of his subjects.

A strong shade of degeneracy is visible between John Vataces and his son Theodore; between the founder who sustained the weight, and the heir who enjoyed the splendour, of the Imperial crown.[1] Yet the character of Theodore was not devoid of energy; he had been educated in the school of his father, in the exercise of war and hunting: Constantinople was yet spared; but in the three years of a short reign he thrice led his armies into the heart of Bulgaria. His virtues were sullied by a choleric and suspicious temper: the first of these may be ascribed to the ignorance of control; and the second might naturally arise from a dark and imperfect view of the corruption of mankind. On a march in Bulgaria he consulted on a question of policy his principal ministers; and the Greek logothete, George Acropolita, presumed to offend him by the declaration of a free and honest opinion. The emperor half unsheathed his scimitar; but his more deliberate rage reserved Acropolita for a baser punishment. One of the first officers of the empire was ordered to dismount, stripped of his robes, and extended on the ground in the presence of the prince and army. In this posture he was chastised with so many and such heavy blows from the clubs of two guards or executioners, that, when Theodore commanded them to cease, the great logothete was scarcely able to arise and crawl away to his tent. After a seclusion of some days he was recalled by a peremptory mandate to his seat in council; and so dead were the Greeks to the sense of honour and shame, that it is from the narrative of the sufferer himself that we acquire the knowledge of his disgrace.[2] The cruelty of the emperor was exasperated by the pangs of sickness, the approach of a premature end, and the suspicion of poison and magic. The lives and fortunes, the eyes and limbs, of his kinsmen and nobles, were sacrificed to each sally of passion; and before he died, the son of Vataces might deserve from the people, or at least from the court, the appellation of tyrant. A matron of the family of the Palæologi had

---

[1] A Persian saying, that Cyrus was the *father*, and Darius the *master*, of his subjects, was applied to Vacates and his son. But Pachymer (l. i. c. 23) has mistaken the mild Darius for the cruel Cambyses, despot or tyrant of his people. By the institution of taxes, Darius had incurred the less odious, but more contemptible, name of Κάπηλος, merchant or broker (Herodotus, iii. 89).

[2] Acropolita (c. 63) seems to admire his own firmness in sustaining a beating, and not returning to council till he was called. He relates the exploits of Theodore, and his own services, from c. 53 to c. 74 of his history. See the third book of Nicephorus Gregoras.

provoked his anger by refusing to bestow her beauteous daughter
on the vile plebeian who was recommended by his caprice.
Without regard to her birth or age, her body, as high as the
neck, was enclosed in a sack with several cats, who were pricked
with pins to irritate their fury against their unfortunate fellow-
captive.   In his last hours the emperor testified a wish to forgive
and be forgiven, a just anxiety for the fate of John his son and
successor, who, at the age of eight years, was condemned to the
dangers of a long minority.   His last choice intrusted the office
of guardian to the sanctity of the patriarch Arsenius, and to the
courage of George Muzalon, the great domestic, who was equally
distinguished by the royal favour and the public hatred.   Since
their connection with the Latins, the names and privileges of
hereditary rank had insinuated themselves into the Greek
monarchy;   and the noble families [1] were provoked by the
elevation of a worthless favourite, to whose influence they
imputed the errors and calamities of the late reign.   In the first
council after the emperor's death, Muzalon, from a lofty throne,
pronounced a laboured apology of his conduct and intentions:
his modesty was subdued by a unanimous assurance of esteem
and fidelity; and his most inveterate enemies were the loudest
to salute him as the guardian and saviour of the Romans.
Eight days were sufficient to prepare the execution of the conspiracy.   On the ninth, the obsequies of the deceased monarch
were solemnised in the cathedral of Magnesia, [2] an Asiatic city,
where he expired, on the banks of the Hermus and at the foot
of Mount Sipylus.   The holy rites were interrupted by a sedition
of the guards; Muzalon, his brothers, and his adherents, were
massacred at the foot of the altar; and the absent patriarch
was associated with a new colleague, with Michael Palæologus,
the most illustrious, in birth and merit, of the Greek nobles. [3]

Of those who are proud of their ancestors the far greater part
must be content with local or domestic renown, and few there
are who dare trust the memorials of their family to the public

[1] Pachymer (l. i. c. 21 [tom. i. p. 65, ed. Bonn]) names and discriminates
fifteen or twenty Greek families, καὶ ὅσοι ἄλλοι, οἷς ἡ μεγαλογενὴς σειρὰ καὶ
χρυσῆ συγκεκρότητο.   Does he mean, by this decoration, a figurative or a
real golden chain?   Perhaps both.

[2] The old geographers, with Cellarius and D'Anville, and our travellers,
particularly Pocock and Chandler, will teach us to distinguish the two
Magnesias of Asia Minor, of the Mæander and of Sipylus.   The latter, our
present object, is still flourishing for a Turkish city, and lies eight hours, or
leagues, to the north-east of Smyrna (Tournefort, Voyage du Levant, tom.
iii. lettre xxii. p. 365-370; Chandler's Travels into Asia Minor, p. 267).

[3] See Acropolita (c. 75, 76, etc.), who lived too near the times; Pachymer
(l. i. c. 13-25); Gregoras (l. iii. c. 3, 4, 5).

annals of their country. As early as the middle of the eleventh century, the noble race of the Palæologi [1] stands high and conspicuous in the Byzantine history: it was the valiant George Palæologus who placed the father of the Comneni on the throne; and his kinsmen or descendants continued, in each generation, to lead the armies and councils of the state. The purple was not dishonoured by their alliance; and had the law of succession, and female succession, been strictly observed, the wife of Theodore Lascaris must have yielded to her elder sister, the mother of Michael Palæologus, who afterwards raised his family to the throne. In his person the splendour of birth was dignified by the merit of the soldier and statesman; in his early youth he was promoted to the office of *constable* or commander of the French mercenaries: the private expense of a day never exceeded three pieces of gold; but his ambition was rapacious and profuse, and his gifts were doubled by the graces of his conversation and manners. The love of the soldiers and people excited the jealousy of the court; and Michael thrice escaped from the dangers in which he was involved by his own imprudence or that of his friends. I. Under the reign of Justice and Vataces, a dispute arose [2] between two officers, one of whom accused the other of maintaining the hereditary right of the Palæologi. The cause was decided, according to the new jurisprudence of the Latins, by single combat; the defendant was overthrown; but he persisted in declaring that himself alone was guilty, and that he had uttered these rash or treasonable speeches without the approbation or knowledge of his patron. Yet a cloud of suspicion hung over the innocence of the constable: he was still pursued by the whispers of malevolence, and a subtle courtier, the archbishop of Philadelphia, urged him to accept the judgment of God in the fiery proof of the ordeal. [3] Three days before the trial the patient's arm was enclosed in a bag, and secured by the royal signet; and it was incumbent on him to bear a red-hot ball of iron three times from the altar to the rails of the

[1] The pedigree of Palæologus is explained by Ducange (Famil. Byzant. p. 230, etc.): the events of his private life are related by Pachymer (l. i. c. 7-12) and Gregoras (l. ii. 8; l. iii. 2, 4; l. iv. 1) with visible favour to the father of the reigning dynasty.

[2] Acropolita (c. 50) relates the circumstances of this curious adventure, which seem to have escaped the more recent writers.

[3] Pachymer (l. i. c. 12 [tom. i. p. 33, ed. Bonn]), who speaks with proper contempt of this barbarous trial, affirms that he had seen in his youth many persons who had sustained, without injury, the fiery ordeal. As a Greek, he is credulous; but the ingenuity of the Greeks might furnish some remedies of art or fraud against their own superstition or that of their tyrant.

sanctuary, without artifice and without injury. Palæologus
eluded the dangerous experiment with sense and pleasantry.
" I am a soldier," said he, " and will boldly enter the lists with
my accusers; but a layman, a sinner like myself, is not endowed
with the gift of miracles. *Your* piety, most holy prelate, may
deserve the interposition of Heaven, and from your hands I will
receive the fiery globe, the pledge of my innocence." The archbishop started; the emperor smiled; and the absolution or
pardon of Michael was approved by new rewards and new
services. II. In the succeeding reign, as he held the government of Nice, he was secretly informed that the mind of the
absent prince was poisoned with jealousy, and that death or
blindness would be his final reward. Instead of awaiting the
return and sentence of Theodore, the constable, with some
followers, escaped from the city and the empire, and, though he
was plundered by the Turkmans of the desert, he found an
hospitable refuge in the court of the sultan. In the ambiguous
state of an exile, Michael reconciled the duties of gratitude and
loyalty: drawing his sword against the Tartars; admonishing
the garrisons of the Roman limit; and promoting, by his
influence, the restoration of peace, in which his pardon and recall
were honourably included. III. While he guarded the West
against the despot of Epirus, Michael was again suspected and
condemned in the palace; and such was his loyalty or weakness,
that he submitted to be led in chains above six hundred miles
from Durazzo to Nice. The civility of the messenger alleviated
his disgrace, the emperor's sickness dispelled his danger; and
the last breath of Theodore, which recommended his infant
son, at once acknowledged the innocence and the power of
Palæologus.

But his innocence had been too unworthily treated, and his
power was too strongly felt, to curb an aspiring subject in the
fair field that was opened to his ambition.[1] In the council after
the death of Theodore, he was the first to pronounce, and the
first to violate, the oath of allegiance to Muzalon; and so dexterous was his conduct that he reaped the benefit, without
incurring the guilt, or at least the reproach, of the subsequent
massacre. In the choice of a regent he balanced the interests
and passions of the candidates, turned their envy and hatred
from himself against each other, and forced every competitor to

[1] Without comparing Pachymer to Thucydides or Tacitus, I will praise
his narrative (l. i. c. 13-32, l. ii. c. 1-9), which pursues the ascent of Palæologus with eloquence, perspicuity, and tolerable freedom. Acropolita is
more cautious, and Gregoras more concise.

own that, after his own claims, those of Palæologus were best
entitled to the preference. Under the title of great duke, he
accepted or assumed, during a long minority, the active powers
of government; the patriarch was a venerable name, and the
factious nobles were seduced or oppressed by the ascendant of his
genius. The fruits of the economy of Vataces were deposited in
a strong castle on the banks of the Hermus, in the custody of the
faithful Varangians; the constable retained his command or
influence over the foreign troops; he employed the guards to
possess the treasure, and the treasure to corrupt the guards;
and whatsoever might be the abuse of the public money, his
character was above the suspicion of private avarice. By himself, or by his emissaries, he strove to persuade every rank of
subjects that their own prosperity would rise in just proportion
to the establishment of his authority. The weight of taxes was
suspended, the perpetual theme of popular complaint; and he
prohibited the trials by the ordeal and judicial combat. These
barbaric institutions were already abolished or undermined in
France [1] and England; [2] and the appeal to the sword offended
the sense of a civilised,[3] and the temper of an unwarlike, people.
For the future maintenance of their wives and children the
veterans were grateful; the priest and the philosopher applauded
his ardent zeal for the advancement of religion and learning; and
his vague promise of rewarding merit was applied by every
candidate to his own hopes. Conscious of the influence of the
clergy, Michael successfully laboured to secure the suffrage of
that powerful order. Their expensive journey from Nice to
Magnesia afforded a decent and ample pretence: the leading
prelates were tempted by the liberality of his nocturnal visits;
and the incorruptible patriarch was flattered by the homage of

[1] The judicial combat was abolished by St. Louis in his own territories;
and his example and authority were at length prevalent in France (Esprit
des Loix, l. xxviii. c. 29).

[2] In civil cases Henry II. gave an option to the defendant: Glanvile
prefers the proof by evidence; and that by judicial combat is reprobated
in the Fleta. Yet the trial by battle has never been abrogated in the
English law. [It was abolished by statute in 1817.]

[3] Yet an ingenious friend has urged to me in mitigation of this practice,
1. That in nations emerging from barbarism it moderates the licence of
private war and arbitrary revenge. 2. That it is less absurd than the
trials by the ordeal, or boiling water, or the cross, which it has contributed
to abolish. 3. That it served at least as a test of personal courage; a
quality so seldom united with a base disposition, that the danger of a trial
might be some check to a malicious prosecutor, and a useful barrier against
injustice supported by power. The gallant and unfortunate earl of Surrey
might probably have escaped his unmerited fate, had not his demand of
the combat against his accuser been overruled.

his new colleague, who led his mule by the bridle into the town,
and removed to a respectful distance the importunity of the
crowd. Without renouncing his title by royal descent, Palæologus encouraged a free discussion into the advantages of elective
monarchy; and his adherents asked, with the insolence of
triumph, what patient would trust his health, or what merchant
would abandon his vessel, to the *hereditary* skill of a physician
or a pilot? The youth of the emperor, and the impending
dangers of a minority, required the support of a mature and
experienced guardian; of an associate raised above the envy of
his equals, and invested with the name and prerogatives of royalty.
For the interest of the prince and people, without any selfish
views for himself or his family, the great duke consented to
guard and instruct the son of Theodore: but he sighed for the
happy moment when he might restore to his firmer hands the
administration of his patrimony, and enjoy the blessings of a
private station. He was first invested with the title and prerogatives of *despot*, which bestowed the purple ornaments and
the second place in the Roman monarchy. It was afterwards
agreed that John and Michael should be proclaimed as joint
emperors, and raised on the buckler, but that the pre-eminence
should be reserved for the birthright of the former. A mutual
league of amity was pledged between the royal partners; and
in case of a rupture, the subjects were bound, by their oath of
allegiance, to declare themselves against the aggressor: an
ambiguous name, the seed of discord and civil war. Palæologus
was content; but on the day of the coronation, and in the
cathedral of Nice, his zealous adherents most vehemently urged
the just priority of his age and merit. The unseasonable dispute
was eluded by postponing to a more convenient opportunity the
coronation of John Lascaris; and he walked with a slight diadem
in the train of his guardian, who alone received the Imperial
crown from the hands of the patriarch. It was not without
extreme reluctance that Arsenius abandoned the cause of his
pupil; but the Varangians brandished their battle-axes; a sign
of assent was extorted from the trembling youth; and some
voices were heard, that the life of a child should no longer impede
the settlement of the nation. A full harvest of honours and
employments was distributed among his friends by the grateful
Palæologus. In his own family he created a despot and two
sebastocrators; Alexius Strategopulus was decorated with the
title of Cæsar ; and that veteran commander soon repaid the
obligation by restoring Constantinople to the Greek emperor.

It was in the second year of his reign, while he resided in the palace and gardens of Nymphæum,[1] near Smyrna, that the first messenger arrived at the dead of night; and the stupendous intelligence was imparted to Michael, after he had been gently waked by the tender precaution of his sister Eulogia. The man was unknown or obscure; he produced no letters from the victorious Cæsar; nor could it easily be credited, after the defeat of Vataces and the recent failure of Palæologus himself, that the capital had been surprised by a detachment of eight hundred soldiers. As a hostage, the doubtful author was confined, with the assurance of death or an ample recompense; and the court was left some hours in the anxiety of hope and fear, till the messengers of Alexius arrived with the authentic intelligence, and displayed the trophies of the conquest, the sword and sceptre,[2] the buskins and bonnet,[3] of the usurper Baldwin, which he had dropped in his precipitate flight. A general assembly of the bishops, senators, and nobles was immediately convened, and never perhaps was an event received with more heartfelt and universal joy. In a studied oration the new sovereign of Constantinople congratulated his own and the public fortune. " There was a time," said he, " a far distant time, when the Roman empire extended to the Adriatic, the Tigris, and the confines of Æthiopia. After the loss of the provinces, our capital itself, in these last and calamitous days, has been wrested from our hands by the barbarians of the West. From the lowest ebb the tide of prosperity has again returned in our favour; but our prosperity was that of fugitives and exiles; and when we were asked which was the country of the Romans, we indicated with a blush the climate of the globe, and the quarter of the heavens. The divine Providence has now restored to our arms the city of Constantine, the sacred seat of religion and empire; and it will depend on our valour and conduct to render this important acquisition the pledge and omen of future victories."

---

[1] The site of Nymphæum is not clearly defined in ancient or modern geography. But from the last hours of Vataces (Acropolita, c. 52), it is evident the palace and gardens of his favourite residence were in the neighbourhood of Smyrna. Nymphæum might be loosely placed in Lydia (Gregoras, l. vi. 6 [tom. i. p. 190, ed. Bonn]).

[2] This sceptre, the emblem of justice and power, was a long staff, such as was used by the heroes in Homer. By the latter Greeks it was named Dicanice, and the Imperial sceptre was distinguished as usual by the red or purple colour.

[3] Acropolita affirms (c. 87) that this bonnet was after the French fashion; but from the ruby at the point or summit, Ducange (Hist. de C. P. l. v. c. 28, 29) believes that it was the high-crowned hat of the Greeks. Could Acropolita mistake the dress of his own court?

So eager was the impatience of the prince and people, that
Michael made his triumphal entry into Constantinople only
twenty days after the expulsion of the Latins.   The golden gate
was thrown open at his approach; the devout conqueror dismounted from his horse; and a miraculous image of Mary the
Conductress was borne before him, that the divine Virgin in person
might appear to conduct him to the temple of her Son, the
cathedral of St. Sophia.   But after the first transport of devotion
and pride, he sighed at the dreary prospect of solitude and ruin.
The palace was defiled with smoke and dirt, and the gross intemperance of the Franks; whole streets had been consumed by
fire, or were decayed by the injuries of time; the sacred and
profane edifices were stripped of their ornaments; and, as if they
were conscious of their approaching exile, the industry of the
Latins had been confined to the work of pillage and destruction.
Trade had expired under the pressure of anarchy and distress,
and the numbers of inhabitants had decreased with the opulence
of the city.   It was the first care of the Greek monarch to rein-
state the nobles in the palaces of their fathers, and the houses, or
the ground which they occupied, were restored to the families
that could exhibit a legal right of inheritance.   But the far
greater part was extinct or lost; the vacant property had devolved to the lord; he repeopled Constantinople by a liberal
invitation to the provinces, and the brave *volunteers* were seated
in the capital which had been recovered by their arms.   The
French barons and the principal families had retired with their
emperor, but the patient and humble crowd of Latins was
attached to the country, and indifferent to the change of masters.
Instead of banishing the factories of the Pisans, Venetians, and
Genoese, the prudent conqueror accepted their oaths of allegiance,
encouraged their industry, confirmed their privileges, and
allowed them to live under the jurisdiction of their proper magistrates.   Of these nations the Pisans and Venetians preserved
their respective quarters in the city; but the services and power
of the Genoese deserved at the same time the gratitude and
the jealousy of the Greeks.   Their independent colony was first
planted at the seaport town of Heraclea in Thrace.   They were
speedily recalled, and settled in the exclusive possession of the
suburb of Galata, an advantageous post, in which they revived
the commerce and insulted the majesty of the Byzantine empire.[1]

---

[1] See Pachymer (l. ii. c. 28-33), Acropolita (c. 88), Nicephorus Gregoras
(l. iv. 7); and for the treatment of the subject Latins, Ducange (l. v.
c. 30, 31).

The recovery of Constantinople was celebrated as the era of a new empire; the conqueror, alone, and by the right of the sword, renewed his coronation in the church of St. Sophia; and the name and honours of John Lascaris, his pupil and lawful sovereign, were insensibly abolished. But his claims still lived in the minds of the people, and the royal youth must speedily attain the years of manhood and ambition. By fear or conscience Palæologus was restrained from dipping his hands in innocent and royal blood; but the anxiety of a usurper and a parent urged him to secure his throne by one of those imperfect crimes so familiar to the modern Greeks. The loss of sight incapacitated the young prince for the active business of the world: instead of the brutal violence of tearing out his eyes, the visual nerve was destroyed by the intense glare of a red-hot basin,[1] and John Lascaris was removed to a distant castle, where he spent many years in privacy and oblivion. Such cool and deliberate guilt may seem incompatible with remorse; but if Michael could trust the mercy of Heaven, he was not inaccessible to the reproaches and vengeance of mankind, which he had provoked by cruelty and treason. His cruelty imposed on a servile court the duties of applause or silence; but the clergy had a right to speak in the name of their invisible Master, and their holy legions were led by a prelate whose character was above the temptations of hope or fear. After a short abdication of his dignity, Arsenius[2] had consented to ascend the ecclesiastical throne of Constantinople, and to preside in the restoration of the church. His pious simplicity was long deceived by the arts of Palæologus, and his patience and submission might soothe the usurper, and protect the safety of the young prince. On the news of his inhuman treatment the patriarch unsheathed the spiritual sword, and superstition, on this occasion, was enlisted in the cause of humanity and justice. In a synod of bishops, who were stimulated by the example of his zeal, the patriarch pronounced a sentence of excommunication, though his prudence

---

[1] This milder invention for extinguishing the sight was tried by the philosopher Democritus on himself, when he sought to withdraw his mind from the visible world: a foolish story! The word *abacinare*, in Latin and Italian, has furnished Ducange (Gloss. Latin.) with an opportunity to review the various modes of blinding: the more violent were scooping, burning with an iron or hot vinegar, and binding the head with a strong cord till the eyes burst from their sockets. Ingenious tyrants!

[2] See the first retreat and restoration of Arsenius, in Pachymer (l. ii. c. 15, l. iii. c. 1, 2) and Nicephorus Gregoras (l. iii. c. 1, l. iv. c. 1). Posterity justly accused the ἀφέλεια and ῥαθυμία of Arsenius, the virtues of a hermit, the vices of a minister (l. xii. c. 2).

still repeated the name of Michael in the public prayers. The
Eastern prelates had not adopted the dangerous maxims of
ancient Rome; nor did they presume to enforce their censures
by deposing princes or absolving nations from their oaths of
allegiance. But the Christian who had been separated from God
and the church became an object of horror, and, in a turbulent and
fanatic capital, that horror might arm the hand of an assassin,
or inflame a sedition of the people. Palæologus felt his danger,
confessed his guilt, and deprecated his judge: the act was
irretrievable, the prize was obtained; and the most rigorous
penance, which he solicited, would have raised the sinner to the
reputation of a saint. The unrelenting patriarch refused to
announce any means of atonement or any hopes of mercy, and
condescended only to pronounce that, for so great a crime, great
indeed must be the satisfaction. " Do you require," said
Michael, " that I should abdicate the empire? " And at these
words he offered, or seemed to offer, the sword of state. Arsenius
eagerly grasped this pledge of sovereignty; but when he perceived that the emperor was unwilling to purchase absolution
at so dear a rate, he indignantly escaped to his cell, and left the
royal sinner kneeling and weeping before the door.[1]

The danger and scandal of this excommunication subsisted
above three years, till the popular clamour was assuaged by
time and repentance; till the brethren of Arsenius condemned
his inflexible spirit, so repugnant to the unbounded forgiveness
of the Gospel. The emperor had artfully insinuated, that, if he
were still rejected at home, he might seek, in the Roman pontiff,
a more indulgent judge; but it was far more easy and effectual
to find or to place that judge at the head of the Byzantine
church.

Arsenius was involved in a vague rumour of conspiracy and
disaffection; some irregular steps in his ordination and government were liable to censure; a synod deposed him from the
episcopal office; and he was transported under a guard of soldiers
to a small island of the Propontis. Before his exile he sullenly
requested that a strict account might be taken of the treasures
of the church; boasted that his sole riches, three pieces of gold,
had been earned by transcribing the psalms; continued to assert
the freedom of his mind; and denied, with his last breath, the
pardon which was implored by the royal sinner.[2] After some

---

[1] The crime and excommunication of Michael are fairly told by
Pachymer (l. iii. c. 10, 14, 19, etc.) and Gregoras (l. iv. c. 4). His confession and penance restored their freedom.

[2] Pachymer relates the exile of Arsenius (l. iv. c. 1-16): he was one of

delay, Gregory, bishop of Adrianople, was translated to the
Byzantine throne; but his authority was found insufficient to
support the absolution of the emperor; and Joseph, a reverend
monk, was substituted to that important function. This edifying scene was represented in the presence of the senate and
people; at the end of six years the humble penitent was restored
to the communion of the faithful; and humanity will rejoice
that a milder treatment of the captive Lascaris was stipulated
as a proof of his remorse. But the spirit of Arsenius still survived in a powerful faction of the monks and clergy, who
persevered above forty-eight years in an obstinate schism.
Their scruples were treated with tenderness and respect by
Michael and his son, and the reconciliation of the Arsenites was
the serious labour of the church and state. In the confidence of
fanaticism, they had proposed to try their cause by a miracle;
and when the two papers, that contained their own and the
adverse cause, were cast into a fiery brazier, they expected that
the Catholic verity would be respected by the flames. Alas!
the two papers were indiscriminately consumed, and this unforeseen accident produced the union of a day, and renewed the
quarrel of an age.[1] The final treaty displayed the victory of the
Arsenites; the clergy abstained during forty days from all
ecclesiastical functions; a slight penance was imposed on the
laity, the body of Arsenius was deposited in the sanctuary, and
in the name of the departed saint the prince and people were
released from the sins of their fathers.[2]

The establishment of his family was the motive, or at least

the commissaries who visited him in the desert island. The last testament
of the unforgiving patriarch is still extant (Dupin, Bibliothèque Ecclésiastique, tom. x. p. 95).

[The charges of Arsenius were of a wholly different nature from what is
stated here. He was charged with omitting the name of the emperor
from his prayers, with allowing the sultan of Iconium to bathe in vessels
signed with the cross, and to have admitted him to the church, though un-
baptised, during the service. It was pleaded in favour of Arsenius, among
other proofs of the sultan's Christianity, that he had offered to eat ham. It
was after his exile that Arsenius was involved in the charge of conspiracy.
—O. S.]

[1] Pachymer (l. vii. c. 22 [tom. ii. p. 60, ed. Bonn]) relates this miraculous
trial like a philosopher, and treats with similar contempt a plot of the
Arsenites, to hide a revelation in the coffin of some old saint (l. vii. c. 13
[tom. ii. p. 40, ed. Bonn]). He compensates this incredulity by an image
that weeps, another that bleeds (l. vii. c. 30 [tom. ii. p. 82, ed. Bonn]), and
the miraculous cures of a deaf and a mute patient (l. xi. c. 32 [tom. ii.
p. 453, ed. Bonn]).

[2] The story of the Arsenites is spread through the thirteen books of
Pachymer. Their union and triumph are reserved for Nicephorus Gregoras
(l. vii. c. 9 [tom. i. p. 262, ed. Bonn]), who neither loves nor esteems
these sectaries.

the pretence, of the crime of Palæologus; and he was impatient
to confirm the succession, by sharing with his eldest son the
honours of the purple. Andronicus, afterwards surnamed the
Elder, was proclaimed and crowned emperor of the Romans in
the fifteenth year of his age; and, from the first era of a prolix
and inglorious reign, he held that august title nine years as the
colleague, and fifty as the successor, of his father. Michael
himself, had he died in a private station, would have been
thought more worthy of the empire; and the assaults of his
temporal and spiritual enemies left him few moments to labour
for his own fame or the happiness of his subjects. He wrested
from the Franks several of the noblest islands of the Archipelago
—Lesbos, Chios, and Rhodes: his brother Constantine was sent
to command in Malvasia and Sparta; and the eastern side of the
Morea, from Argos and Napoli to Cape Tænarus, was repossessed
by the Greeks. This effusion of Christian blood was loudly condemned by the patriarch; and the insolent priest presumed to
interpose his fears and scruples between the arms of princes.
But in the prosecution of these western conquests the countries
beyond the Hellespont were left naked to the Turks; and their
depredations verified the prophecy of a dying senator, that the
recovery of Constantinople would be the ruin of Asia. The
victories of Michael were achieved by his lieutenants; his sword
rusted in the palace; and, in the transactions of the emperor
with the popes and the king of Naples, his political arts were
stained with cruelty and fraud.[1]

I. The Vatican was the most natural refuge of a Latin emperor
who had been driven from his throne; and pope Urban the
Fourth appeared to pity the misfortunes, and vindicate the
cause, of the fugitive Baldwin. A crusade, with plenary indulgence, was preached by his command against the schismatic
Greeks: he excommunicated their allies and adherents; solicited
Louis the Ninth in favour of his kinsman; and demanded a
tenth of the ecclesiastic revenues of France and England for the
service of the holy war.[2] The subtle Greek, who watched the
rising tempest of the West, attempted to suspend or soothe the
hostility of the pope by suppliant embassies and respectful
letters; but he insinuated that the establishment of peace must

---

[1] Of the thirteen books of Pachymer, the first six (as the fourth and fifth
of Nicephorus Gregoras) contain the reign of Michael, at the time of whose
death he was forty years of age. Instead of breaking, like his editor the
Père Poussin, his history into two parts, I follow Ducange and Cousin, who
number the thirteen books in one series.

[2] Ducange, Hist. de C. P. l. v. c. 33, etc., from the Epistles of Urban IV.

prepare the reconciliation and obedience of the Eastern church.
The Roman court could not be deceived by so gross an artifice;
and Michael was admonished that the repentance of the son
should precede the forgiveness of the father; and that *faith* (an
ambiguous word) was the only basis of friendship and alliance.
After a long and affected delay, the approach of danger, and the
importunity of Gregory the Tenth, compelled him to enter on a
more serious negotiation: he alleged the example of the great
Vataces; and the Greek clergy, who understood the intentions
of their prince, were not alarmed by the first steps of reconciliation and respect. But when he pressed the conclusion of the
treaty, they strenuously declared that the Latins, though not
in name, were heretics in fact, and that they despised those
strangers as the vilest and most despicable portion of the human
race.[1] It was the task of the emperor to persuade, to corrupt,
to intimidate the most popular ecclesiastics, to gain the vote
of each individual, and alternately to urge the arguments of
Christian charity and the public welfare. The texts of the
fathers and the arms of the Franks were balanced in the theological and political scale; and without approving the addition
to the Nicene creed, the most moderate were taught to confess
that the two hostile propositions of proceeding from the Father
BY the Son, and of proceeding from the Father AND the Son,
might be reduced to a safe and Catholic sense.[2] The supremacy
of the pope was a doctrine more easy to conceive, but more
painful to acknowledge; yet Michael represented to his monks
and prelates that they might submit to name the Roman bishop
as the first of the patriarchs; and that their distance and discretion would guard the liberties of the Eastern church from the
mischievous consequences of the right of appeal. He protested
that he would sacrifice his life and empire rather than yield the
smallest point of orthodox faith or national independence; and
this declaration was sealed and ratified by a golden bull. The
patriarch Joseph withdrew to a monastery, to resign or resume
his throne, according to the event of the treaty: the letters of
union and obedience were subscribed by the emperor, his son

---

[1] From their mercantile intercourse with the Venetians and Genoese,
they branded the Latins as κάπηλοι and βάναυσοι (Pachymer, l. v. c. 10).
" Some are heretics in name; others, like the Latins, in fact," said the
learned Veccus (l. v. c. 12), who soon afterwards became a convert (c. 15,
16) and a patriarch (c. 24).

[2] In this class we may place Pachymer himself, whose copious and
candid narrative occupies the fifth and sixth books of his history. Yet the
Greek is silent on the council of Lyons, and seems to believe that the
popes always resided in Rome and Italy (l. v. c. 17, 21).

Andronicus, and thirty-five archbishops and metropolitans,
with their respective synods; and the episcopal list was multiplied by many dioceses which were annihilated under the yoke
of the infidels. An embassy was composed of some trusty
ministers and prelates: they embarked for Italy, with rich
ornaments and rare perfumes, for the altar of St. Peter; and
their secret orders authorised and recommended a boundless
compliance. They were received in the general council of Lyons,
by pope Gregory the Tenth, at the head of five hundred bishops.[1]
He embraced with tears his long-lost and repentant children;
accepted the oath of the ambassadors, who abjured the schism
in the name of the two emperors; adorned the prelates with the
ring and mitre; chanted in Greek and Latin the Nicene creed
with the addition of *filioque;* and rejoiced in the union of the
East and West, which had been reserved for his reign. To consummate this pious work, the Byzantine deputies were speedily
followed by the pope's nuncios; and their instruction discloses
the policy of the Vatican, which could not be satisfied with the
vain title of supremacy. After viewing the temper of the prince
and people, they were enjoined to absolve the schismatic clergy
who should subscribe and swear their adjuration and obedience;
to establish in all the churches the use of the perfect creed; to
prepare the entrance of a cardinal legate, with the full powers
and dignity of his office; and to instruct the emperor in the
advantages which he might derive from the temporal protection
of the Roman pontiff.[2]

But they found a country without a friend, a nation in which
the names of Rome and Union were pronounced with abhorrence.
The patriarch Joseph was indeed removed: his place was filled
by Veccus, an ecclesiastic of learning and moderation; and the
emperor was still urged by the same motives to persevere in the
same professions.[3] But in his private language Palæologus
affected to deplore the pride, and to blame the innovations, of
the Latins; and while he debased his character by this double

[1] See the acts of the council of Lyons in the year 1274; Fleury, Hist.
Ecclésiastique, tom. xviii. p. 181-199; Dupin, Biblioth. Ecclés. tom. x.
p. 135.
[2] This curious instruction, which has been drawn with more or less
honesty by Wading and Leo Allatius from the archives of the Vatican, is
given in an abstract or version by Fleury (tom. xviii. p. 252-258).
[3] [Joannes Veccus, who became patriarch of Constantinople in 1275, was
the leading theologian who threw the weight of his name in favour of the
union. His treatise " On the Union and Peace of the Churches of Old and
New Rome," together with others on the same subject, were issued in the
Græcia Orthodoxa of Leo Allatius. His chief antagonist in theological discussion was Gregory of Cyprus, who became patriarch in 1283.—O. S.]

hypocrisy, he justified and punished the opposition of his subjects. By the joint suffrage of the new and the ancient Rome,
a sentence of excommunication was pronounced against the
obstinate schismatics: the censures of the church were executed
by the sword of Michael; on the failure of persuasion, he tried
the arguments of prison and exile, of whipping and mutilation
—those touchstones, says an historian, of cowards and the brave.
Two Greeks still reigned in Ætolia, Epirus, and Thessaly, with
the appellation of despots: they had yielded to the sovereign
of Constantinople, but they rejected the chains of the Roman
pontiff, and supported their refusal by successful arms. Under
their protection, the fugitive monks and bishops assembled in
hostile synods, and retorted the name of heretic with the galling
addition of apostate: the prince of Trebizond was tempted to
assume the forfeit title of emperor; and even the Latins of
Negropont, Thebes, Athens, and the Morea forgot the merits of
the convert, to join, with open or clandestine aid, the enemies
of Palæologus. His favourite generals, of his own blood and
family, successively deserted, or betrayed, the sacrilegious trust.
His sister Eulogia, a niece, and two female cousins conspired
against him; another niece, Mary queen of Bulgaria, negotiated
his ruin with the sultan of Egypt; and, in the public eye, their
treason was consecrated as the most sublime virtue.[1] To the
pope's nuncios, who urged the consummation of the work,
Palæologus exposed a naked recital of all that he had done and
suffered for their sake. They were assured that the guilty
sectaries, of both sexes and every rank, had been deprived of their
honours, their fortunes, and their liberty; a spreading list of
confiscation and punishment, which involved many persons the
dearest to the emperor, or the best deserving of his favour.
They were conducted to the prison, to behold four princes of the
royal blood chained in the four corners, and shaking their fetters
in an agony of grief and rage. Two of these captives were afterwards released; the one by submission, the other by death: but
the obstinacy of their two companions was chastised by the loss
of their eyes; and the Greeks, the least adverse to the union,
deplore that cruel and inauspicious tragedy.[2] Persecutors must

---

[1] This frank and authentic confession of Michael's distress is exhibited
in barbarous Latin by Ogerius, who signs himself Protonotarius Inter-
pretum, and transcribed by Wading from the MSS. of the Vatican (A.D.
1278, No. 3). His annals of the Franciscan order, the Fratres Minores,
in seventeen volumes in folio (Rome, 1741), I have now accidentally seen
among the waste paper of a bookseller.

[2] See the sixth book of Pachymer, particularly the chapters 1, 11, 16, 18,

expect the hatred of those whom they oppress; but they
commonly find some consolation in the testimony of their conscience, the applause of their party, and, perhaps, the success of
their undertaking. But the hypocrisy of Michael, which was
prompted only by political motives, must have forced him to
hate himself, to despise his followers, and to esteem and envy
the rebel champions by whom he was detested and despised.
While his violence was abhorred at Constantinople, at Rome his
slowness was arraigned, and his sincerity suspected; till at
length pope Martin the Fourth excluded the Greek emperor from
the pale of a church into which he was striving to reduce a
schismatic people. No sooner had the tyrant expired than the
union was dissolved and abjured by unanimous consent; the
churches were purified; the penitents were reconciled; and his
son Andronicus, after weeping the sins and errors of his youth,
most piously denied his father the burial of a prince and a
Christian.[1]

II. In the distress of the Latins the walls and towers of Constantinople had fallen to decay; they were restored and fortified
by the policy of Michael, who deposited a plenteous store of corn
and salt provisions, to sustain the siege which he might hourly
expect from the resentment of the Western powers. Of these,
the sovereign of the Two Sicilies was the most formidable neighbour; but as long as they were possessed by Mainfroy, the
bastard of Frederic the Second, his monarchy was the bulwark,
rather than the annoyance, of the Eastern empire. The usurper,
though a brave and active prince, was sufficiently employed in
the defence of his throne: his proscription by successive popes
had separated Mainfroy from the common cause of the Latins;
and the forces that might have besieged Constantinople were
detained in a crusade against the domestic enemy of Rome.
The prize of her avenger, the crown of the Two Sicilies, was won

24-27. He is the more credible, as he speaks of this persecution with less
anger than sorrow.

[The following is the summing up of Michael's character by Finlay in
his *Byzantine Empire* (vol. iii. p. 372): " He was a type of the empire he re-
established and transmitted to his descendants. He was selfish, hypo-
critical, able, and accomplished, an inborn liar, vain, meddling, ambitious,
cruel, and rapacious. He has gained renown in history as the restorer of
the Eastern empire; he ought to be execrated as the corrupter of the Greek
race, for his reign affords a signal example of the extent to which a nation
may be degraded by the misconduct of its sovereign when he is entrusted
with despotic power."—O. S.]

[1] Pachymer, l. vii. c. 1, 11, 17 [tom. ii. p. 11, 36, 50, ed. Bonn]. The
speech of Andronicus the Elder (lib. xii. c. 2) is a curious record which
proves that, if the Greeks were the slaves of the emperor, the emperor was
not less the slave of superstition and the clergy.

and worn by the brother of St. Louis, by Charles count of Anjou
and Provence, who led the chivalry of France on this holy expedition.[1] The disaffection of his Christian subjects compelled
Mainfroy to enlist a colony of Saracens whom his father had
planted in Apulia; and this odious succour will explain the
defiance of the Catholic hero, who rejected all terms of accommodation. " Bear this message," said Charles, " to the sultan
of Nocera, that God and the sword are umpire between us; and
that he shall either send me to paradise, or I will send him to the
pit of hell." The armies met; and though I am ignorant of
Mainfroy's doom in the other world, in this he lost his friends,
his kingdom, and his life, in the bloody battle of Benevento.
Naples and Sicily were immediately peopled with a warlike race
of French nobles; and their aspiring leader embraced the future
conquest of Africa, Greece, and Palestine. The most specious
reasons might point his first arms against the Byzantine empire;
and Palæologus, diffident of his own strength, repeatedly
appealed from the ambition of Charles to the humanity of St.
Louis, who still preserved a just ascendant over the mind of his
ferocious brother. For a while the attention of that brother was
confined at home by the invasion of Conradin, the last heir of the
Imperial house of Swabia: but the hapless boy sunk in the
unequal conflict; and his execution on a public scaffold taught
the rivals of Charles to tremble for their heads as well as their
dominions. A second respite was obtained by the last crusade
of St. Louis to the African coast; and the double motive of
interest and duty urged the king of Naples to assist, with his
powers and his presence, the holy enterprise. The death of
St. Louis released him from the importunity of a virtuous censor:
the king of Tunis confessed himself the tributary and vassal of
the crown of Sicily; and the boldest of the French knights were
free to enlist under his banner against the Greek empire. A
treaty and a marriage united his interest with the house of
Courtenay; his daughter Beatrice was promised to Philip, son
and heir of the emperor Baldwin; a pension of six hundred
ounces of gold was allowed for his maintenance; and his generous
father distributed among his allies the kingdoms and provinces

---

[1] The best accounts, the nearest the time, the most full and entertaining,
of the conquest of Naples by Charles of Anjou, may be found in the Florentine Chronicles of Ricordano Malespina (c. 175-193) and Giovanni Villani
(l. vii. c. 1-10, 25-30), which are published by Muratori in the eighth and
thirteenth volumes of the Historians of Italy. In his Annals (tom. xi.
p. 56-72), he has abridged these great events, which are likewise described
in the Istoria Civile of Giannone, tom. ii. l. xix., tom. iii. l. xx.

of the East, reserving only Constantinople, and one day's journey round the city, for the Imperial domain.[1] In this perilous moment Palæologus was the most eager to subscribe the creed, and implore the protection, of the Roman pontiff, who assumed, with propriety and weight, the character of an angel of peace, the common father of the Christians. By his voice the sword of Charles was chained in the scabbard; and the Greek ambassadors beheld him, in the pope's antechamber, biting his ivory sceptre in a transport of fury, and deeply resenting the refusal to enfranchise and consecrate his arms. He appears to have respected the disinterested mediation of Gregory the Tenth; but Charles was insensibly disgusted by the pride and partiality of Nicholas the Third; and his attachment to his kindred, the Ursini family, alienated the most strenuous champion from the service of the church. The hostile league against the Greeks, of Philip the Latin emperor, the king of the Two Sicilies, and the republic of Venice, was ripened into execution; and the election of Martin the Fourth, a French pope, gave a sanction to the cause. Of the allies, Philip supplied his name; Martin, a bull of excommunication; the Venetians, a squadron of forty galleys; and the formidable powers of Charles consisted of forty counts, ten thousand men-at-arms, a numerous body of infantry, and a fleet of more than three hundred ships and transports. A distant day was appointed for assembling this mighty force in the harbour of Brindisi; and a previous attempt was risked with a detachment of three hundred knights, who invaded Albania and besieged the fortress of Belgrade. Their defeat might amuse with a triumph the vanity of Constantinople; but the more sagacious Michael, despairing of his arms, depended on the effects of a conspiracy; on the secret workings of a rat who gnawed the bow-string[2] of the Sicilian tyrant.

Among the proscribed adherents of the house of Swabia, John of Procida forfeited a small island of that name in the bay of Naples. His birth was noble, but his education was learned; and in the poverty of exile he was relieved by the practice of physic, which he had studied in the school of Salerno. Fortune had left him nothing to lose, except life; and to despise life is the first qualification of a rebel. Procida was endowed with the art of negotiation to enforce his reasons and disguise his motives;

[1] Ducange, Hist. de C. P. l. v. c. 49-56, l. vi. c. 1-13. See Pachymer, l. iv. c. 29, l. v. c. 7-10, 25, l. vi. c. 30, 32, 33; and Nicephorus Gregoras, l. iv. 5, l. v. 1, 6.

[2] The reader of Herodotus will recollect how miraculously the Assyrian host of Sennacherib was disarmed and destroyed (l. ii. c. 141).

and in his various transactions with nations and men, he could
persuade each party that he laboured solely for *their* interest.
The new kingdoms of Charles were afflicted by every species of
fiscal and military oppression;[1] and the lives and fortunes of
his Italian subjects were sacrificed to the greatness of their
master and the licentiousness of his followers. The hatred of
Naples was repressed by his presence; but the looser government of his vicegerents excited the contempt, as well as the
aversion, of the Sicilians: the island was roused to a sense of
freedom by the eloquence of Procida; and he displayed to every
baron his private interest in the common cause. In the confidence of foreign aid, he successively visited the courts of the
Greek emperor, and of Peter king of Arragon,[2] who possessed
the maritime countries of Valentia and Catalonia. To the
ambitious Peter a crown was presented, which he might justly
claim by his marriage with the sister of Mainfroy, and by the
dying voice of Conradin, who from the scaffold had cast a ring
to his heir and avenger. Palæologus was easily persuaded to
divert his enemy from a foreign war by a rebellion at home; and
a Greek subsidy of twenty-five thousand ounces of gold was
most profitably applied to arm a Catalan fleet, which sailed under
a holy banner to the specious attack of the Saracens of Africa.
In the disguise of a monk or beggar, the indefatigable missionary
of revolt flew from Constantinople to Rome, and from Sicily to
Saragossa: the treaty was sealed with the signet of pope Nicholas
himself, the enemy of Charles; and his deed of gift transferred
the fiefs of St. Peter from the house of Anjou to that of Arragon
So widely diffused and so freely circulated, the secret was preserved above two years with impenetrable discretion; and each
of the conspirators imbibed the maxim of Peter, who declared
that he would cut off his left hand if it were conscious of the
intentions of his right. The mine was prepared with deep and
dangerous artifice; but it may be questioned whether the
instant explosion of Palermo were the effect of accident or
design.

On the vigil of Easter a procession of the disarmed citizens

[1] According to Sabas Malaspina (Hist. Sicula, l. iii. c. 16, in Muratori
tom. viii. p. 832), a zealous Guelph, the subjects of Charles, who had reviled
Mainfroy as a wolf, began to regret him as a lamb; and he justifies their
discontent by the oppressions of the French government (l. vi. c. 2, 7)
See the Sicilian manifesto in Nicholas Specialis (l. i. c. 11, in Muratori
tom. x. p. 930).
[2] See the character and counsels of Peter king of Arragon, in Mariana
(Hist. Hispan. l. xiv. c. 6, tom. ii. p. 133). The reader forgives the Jesuit's
defects, in favour, always of his style, and often of his sense.

visited a church without the walls, and a noble damsel was rudely insulted by a French soldier.[1] The ravisher was instantly punished with death; and if the people was at first scattered by a military force, their numbers and fury prevailed: the conspirators seized the opportunity; the flame spread over the island, and eight thousand French were exterminated in a promiscuous massacre, which has obtained the name of the SICILIAN VESPERS.[2] From every city the banners of freedom and the church were displayed: the revolt was inspired by the presence or the soul of Procida; and Peter of Arragon, who sailed from the African coast to Palermo, was saluted as the king and saviour of the isle. By the rebellion of a people on whom he had so long trampled with impunity, Charles was astonished and confounded; and in the first agony of grief and devotion he was heard to exclaim, " O God! if thou hast decreed to humble me, grant me at least a gentle and gradual descent from the pinnacle of greatness!" His fleet and army, which already filled the seaports of Italy, were hastily recalled from the service of the Grecian war; and the situation of Messina exposed that town to the first storm of his revenge. Feeble in themselves, and yet hopeless of foreign succour, the citizens would have repented and submitted on the assurance of full pardon and their ancient privileges. But the pride of the monarch was already rekindled; and the most fervent entreaties of the legate could extort no more than a promise that he would forgive the remainder after a chosen list of eight hundred rebels had been yielded to his discretion. The despair of the Messinese renewed their courage: Peter of Arragon approached to their relief,[3] and his rival was driven back by the failure of provision and the terrors of the equinox to the Calabrian shore. At the same moment the Catalan admiral, the famous Roger de Loria, swept the channel with an invincible squadron: the French fleet,

[1] After enumerating the sufferings of his country, Nicholas Specialis adds, in the true spirit of Italian jealousy, Quæ omnia et graviora quidem, ut arbitror, patienti animo Siculi tolerassent, nisi (quod primum cunctis dominantibus cavendum est) alienas feminas invasissent (l. i. c. 2, p. 924).

[2] The French were long taught to remember this bloody lesson: " If I am provoked (said Henry the Fourth), I will breakfast at Milan, and dine at Naples." " Your majesty (replied the Spanish ambassador) may perhaps arrive in Sicily for vespers."

[3] This revolt, with the subsequent victory, are related by two national writers, Bartholemy à Neocastro (in Muratori, tom. xiii.) and Nicholas Specialis (in Muratori, tom. x.), the one a contemporary, the other of the next century. The patriot Specialis disclaims the name of rebellion, and all previous correspondence with Peter of Arragon (nullo communicato consilio), who *happened* to be with a fleet and army on the African coast (l. i. c. 4, 9).

more numerous in transports than in galleys, was either burnt
or destroyed; and the same blow assured the independence of
Sicily and the safety of the Greek empire. A few days before
his death the emperor Michael rejoiced in the fall of an enemy
whom he hated and esteemed; and perhaps he might be content
with the popular judgment, that, had they not been matched
with each other, Constantinople and Italy must speedily have
obeyed the same master.[1] From this disastrous moment the
life of Charles was a series of misfortunes: his capital was
insulted, his son was made prisoner, and he sunk into the grave
without recovering the isle of Sicily, which, after a war of
twenty years, was finally severed from the throne of Naples, and
transferred, as an independent kingdom, to a younger branch of
the house of Arragon.[2]

I shall not, I trust, be accused of superstition; but I must
remark that, even in this world, the natural order of events will
sometimes afford the strong appearances of moral retribution.
The first Palæologus had saved his empire by involving the
kingdoms of the West in rebellion and blood; and from these
seeds of discord uprose a generation of iron men, who assaulted
and endangered the empire of his son. In modern times our
debts and taxes are the secret poison which still corrodes the
bosom of peace; but in the weak and disorderly government
of the middle ages it was agitated by the present evil of the
disbanded armies. Too idle to work, too proud to beg, the
mercenaries were accustomed to a life of rapine: they could rob
with more dignity and effect under a banner and a chief; and the
sovereign, to whom their service was useless and their presence
importunate, endeavoured to discharge the torrent on some
neighbouring countries. After the peace of Sicily, many
thousands of Genoese, *Catalans*,[3] etc., who had fought by sea
and land under the standard of Anjou or Arragon, were blended
into one nation by the resemblance of their manners and interest.
They heard that the Greek provinces of Asia were invaded by

[1] Nicephorus Gregoras (l. v. c. 6) admires the wisdom of Providence in
this equal balance of states and princes. For the honour of Palæologus I
had rather this balance had been observed by an Italian writer.

[2] See the Chronicle of Villani, the eleventh volume of the Annali d'Italia
of Muratori, and the twentieth and twenty-first books of the Istoria Civile
of Giannone.

[3] In this motley multitude the Catalans and Spaniards, the bravest of
the soldiery, were styled by themselves and the Greeks *Amogavares*.
Moncada derives their origin from the Goths, and Pachymer (l. xi. c. 22
[tom. ii. p. 416, ed. Bonn]) from the Arabs, and, in spite of national and
religious pride, I am afraid the latter is in the right.

the Turks: they resolved to share the harvest of pay and plunder; and Frederic king of Sicily most liberally contributed the means of their departure. In a warfare of twenty years a ship or a camp was become their country; arms were their sole profession and property; valour was the only virtue which they knew; their women had imbibed the fearless temper of their lovers and husbands: it was reported that with a stroke of their broad-sword the Catalans could cleave a horseman and a horse; and the report itself was a powerful weapon. Roger de Flor [1] was the most popular of their chiefs; and his personal merit overshadowed the dignity of his prouder rivals of Arragon. The offspring of a marriage between a German gentleman of the court of Frederic the Second and a damsel of Brindisi, Roger was successively a templar, an apostate, a pirate, and at length the richest and most powerful admiral of the Mediterranean. He sailed from Messina to Constantinople with eighteen galleys, four great ships, and eight thousand adventurers; and his previous treaty was faithfully accomplished by Andronicus the Elder, who accepted with joy and terror this formidable succour. A palace was allotted for his reception, and a niece of the emperor was given in marriage to the valiant stranger, who was immediately created great duke or admiral of Romania. After a decent repose he transported his troops over the Propontis, and boldly led them against the Turks: in two bloody battles thirty thousand of the Moslems were slain: he raised the siege of Philadelphia, and deserved the name of the deliverer of Asia. But after a short season of prosperity the cloud of slavery and ruin again burst on that unhappy province. The inhabitants escaped (says a Greek historian) from the smoke into the flames; and the hostility of the Turks was less pernicious than the friend-ship of the Catalans. The lives and fortunes which they had rescued they considered as their own: the willing or reluctant maid was saved from the race of circumcision for the embraces of a Christian soldier: the exaction of fines and supplies was enforced by licentious rapine and arbitrary executions; and, on the resistance of Magnesia, the great duke besieged a city of the Roman empire. [2] These disorders he excused by the wrongs and

[1] [The name of Roger de Flor is one of note in the Middle Ages. He was said to have been the son of a falconer, his true name being Richard Blum, the statement that he was the son of a gentleman of the court of Frederic II. being denied. His career was romantic in the extreme. As to the numbers that constituted his expedition, Ramon de Montaner informs us that they were 36 sail, 1500 horsemen, 4000 Amogavares, 1000 foot soldiers, as well as the oarsmen and sailors.—O. S.]

[2] Some idea may be formed of the population of these cities from the

passions of a victorious army; nor would his own authority or
person have been safe had he dared to punish his faithful followers,
who were defrauded of the just and covenanted price of their
services. The threats and complaints of Andronicus disclosed
the nakedness of the empire. His golden bull had invited no
more than five hundred horse and a thousand foot soldiers; yet
the crowds of volunteers who migrated to the East had been
enlisted and fed by his spontaneous bounty. While his bravest
allies were content with three byzants or pieces of gold for their
monthly pay, an ounce or even two ounces of gold were assigned
to the Catalans, whose annual pension would thus amount to
near a hundred pounds sterling: one of their chiefs had
modestly rated at three hundred thousand crowns the value of
his *future* merits; and above a million had been issued from the
treasury for the maintenance of these costly mercenaries. A
cruel tax had been imposed on the corn of the husbandman:
one-third was retrenched from the salaries of the public officers;
and the standard of the coin was so shamefully debased, that of
the four-and-twenty parts only five were of pure gold.[1] At the
summons of the emperor, Roger evacuated a province which no
longer supplied the materials of rapine; but he refused to
disperse his troops; and while his style was respectful, his
conduct was independent and hostile. He protested that, if the
emperor should march against him, he would advance forty
paces to kiss the ground before him; but in rising from this
prostrate attitude Roger had a life and sword at the service of his
friends. The great duke of Romania condescended to accept
the title and ornaments of Cæsar; but he rejected the new
proposal of the government of Asia with a subsidy of corn and
money, on condition that he should reduce his troops to the
harmless number of three thousand men. Assassination is the
last resource of cowards. The Cæsar was tempted to visit the
royal residence of Adrianople; in the apartment, and before the

36,000 inhabitants of Tralles, which, in the preceding reign, was rebuilt by
the emperor, and ruined by the Turks. (Pachymer, l. vi. c. 20, 21.)

[1] I have collected these pecuniary circumstances from Pachymer (l. xi.
c. 21, l. xii. c. 4, 5, 8, 14, 19 [tom. ii. p. 493, 494, ed. Bonn]), who describes
the progressive degradation of the gold coin. Even in the prosperous
times of John Ducas Vataces, the byzants were composed in equal proportions of the pure and the baser metal. The poverty of Michael Palæologus compelled him to strike a new coin, with nine parts, or carats, of gold,
and fifteen of copper alloy. After his death the standard rose to ten carats,
till in the public distress it was reduced to the moiety. The prince was
relieved for a moment, while credit and commerce were for ever blasted.
In France the gold coin is of twenty-two carats (one twelfth alloy), and the
standard of England and Holland is still higher.

eyes, of the empress he was stabbed by the Alani guards; and, though the deed was imputed to their private revenge, his countrymen, who dwelt at Constantinople in the security of peace, were involved in the same proscription by the prince or people. The loss of their leader intimidated the crowd of adventurers, who hoisted the sails of flight, and were soon scattered round the coasts of the Mediterranean. But a veteran band of fifteen hundred Catalans or French stood firm in the strong fortress of Gallipoli on the Hellespont, displayed the banners of Arragon, and offered to revenge and justify their chief by an equal combat of ten or a hundred warriors. Instead of accepting this bold defiance, the emperor Michael, the son and colleague of Andronicus, resolved to oppress them with the weight of multitudes: every nerve was strained to form an army of thirteen thousand horse and thirty thousand foot, and the Propontis was covered with the ships of the Greeks and Genoese. In two battles by sea and land these mighty forces were encountered and overthrown by the despair and discipline of the Catalans: the young emperor fled to the palace, and an insufficient guard of light-horse was left for the protection of the open country. Victory renewed the hopes and numbers of the adventurers; every nation was blended under the name and standard of the *great company ;* and three thousand Turkish proselytes deserted from the Imperial service to join this military association. In the possession of Gallipoli the Catalans intercepted the trade of Constantinople and the Black Sea, while they spread their devastations on either side of the Hellespont over the confines of Europe and Asia. To prevent their approach the greatest part of the Byzantine territory was laid waste by the Greeks themselves: the peasants and their cattle retired into the city; and myriads of sheep and oxen, for which neither place nor food could be procured, were unprofitably slaughtered on the same day. Four times the emperor Andronicus sued for peace, and four times he was inflexibly repulsed, till the want of provisions and the discord of the chiefs compelled the Catalans to evacuate the banks of the Hellespont and the neighbourhood of the capital. After their separation from the Turks, the remains of the great company pursued their march through Macedonia and Thessaly, to seek a new establishment in the heart of Greece.[1]

---

[1] The Catalan war is most copiously related by Pachymer, in the eleventh, twelfth, and thirteenth books, till he breaks off in the year 1308. Nicephorus Gregoras (l. vii. 3-6) is more concise and complete. Ducange, who adopts these adventurers as French, has hunted their footsteps with his usual diligence (Hist. de C. P. l. vi. c. 22-46). He quotes an Arragonese

After some ages of oblivion Greece was awakened to new
misfortunes by the arms of the Latins.   In the two hundred and
fifty years between the first and the last conquest of Constantinople that venerable land was disputed by a multitude of petty
tyrants; without the comforts of freedom and genius, her
ancient cities were again plunged in foreign and intestine war;
and, if servitude be preferable to anarchy, they might repose
with joy under the Turkish yoke.   I shall not pursue the obscure
and various dynasties that rose and fell on the continent or in the
isles; but our silence on the fate of ATHENS [1] would argue a
strange ingratitude to the first and purest school of liberal
science and amusement.   In the partition of the empire the
principality of Athens and Thebes was assigned to Otho de la
Roche, a noble warrior of Burgundy,[2] with the title of great
duke,[3] which the Latins understood in their own sense, and the

history, which I have read with pleasure, and which the Spaniards extol
as a model of style and composition (Expedicion de los Catalanes y Arra-
goneses contra Turcos y Griegos: Barcelona, 1623, in quarto: Madrid,
1777, in octavo). Don Francisco de Moncada, Conde de Osona, may
imitate Cæsar or Sallust; he may transcribe the Greek or Italian contemporaries: but he never quotes his authorities, and I cannot discern any
national records of the exploits of his countrymen.
    [Ramon de Montaner, one of the Catalans who accompanied Roger de
Flor and who was governor of Gallipoli, records that Roger de Flor, other-
wise the Great Duke, was recalled from Natolia on account of the war that
had arisen on the death of Azan, king of Bulgaria. Andronicus claimed
the kingdom for his nephews, the sons of Azan by his sister. Roger
turned the tide of success in favour of the emperor and made peace. But
Andronicus alienated the troops by paying them in debased coin. According to Ramon, Roger was murdered by order of Kyr Michael, son of the
emperor. Ramon was left the governor and chancellor; all the scribes of
the army remained with him, and with their aid he kept the books in
which were registered the number of foot and horse employed on each
expedition.—O. S.]
    [1] See the laborious history of Ducange, whose accurate table of the
French dynasties recapitulates the thirty-five passages in which he mentions the dukes of Athens.
    [2] He is twice mentioned by Villehardouin with honour (No. 151, 235);
and under the first passage Ducange observes all that can be known of
his person and family.
    [3] From these Latin princes of the fourteenth century, Boccace, Chaucer,
and Shakspeare have borrowed their Theseus *duke* of Athens. An
ignorant age transfers its own language and manners to the most distant
times.
    [Otto de la Roche did not take any ducal title.   The designation he did
take was that of Sire, Μέγας Κυριός, or Grand Lord.   In the year 1254 a
question having arisen between Guy de la Roche and the prince of Achaia
respecting personal homage due to the former, it was referred to Louis
XI., and Guy undertook a journey to the court of France.   Louis deemed
the case of so frivolous a nature that, in order to indemnify Guy for his
trouble and expense, he authorised him to assume the title of Duke of
Athens, instead of " Grand Sire."   Otto de la Roche had resigned the
government of Athens and of Thebes to his nephew Guy, son of his

Greeks more foolishly derived from the age of Constantine.[1]
Otho followed the standard of the marquis of Montferrat: the
ample state which he acquired by a miracle of conduct or
fortune,[2] was peaceably inherited by his son and two grandsons,
till the family, though not the nation, was changed by the
marriage of an heiress into the elder branch of the house of
Briennne. The son of that marriage, Walter de Brienne,
succeeded to the duchy of Athens; and, with the aid of some
Catalan mercenaries, whom he invested with fiefs, reduced above
thirty castles of the vassal or neighbouring lords. But when he
was informed of the approach and ambition of the great company, he collected a force of seven hundred knights, six thousand
four hundred horse, and eight thousand foot, and boldly met
them on the banks of the river Cephisus in Bœotia. The Catalans
amounted to no more than three thousand five hundred horse
and four thousand foot; but the deficiency of numbers was
compensated by stratagem and order. They formed round
their camp an artificial inundation; the duke and his knights
advanced without fear or precaution on the verdant meadow;
their horses plunged into the bog; and he was cut in pieces,
with the greatest part of the French cavalry. His family and
nation were expelled; and his son Walter de Brienne, the titular
duke of Athens, the tyrant of Florence, and the constable of
France, lost his life in the field of Poitiers. Attica and Bœotia
were the rewards of the victorious Catalans; they married the
widows and daughters of the slain; and during fourteen years
the great company was the terror of the Grecian states. Their
factions drove them to acknowledge the sovereignty of the house
of Arragon; and during the remainder of the fourteenth century

brother, Pons de Ray, and returned to end his days on his own moderate
fief in France. Guy was succeeded by his eldest son John and, on the
death of the latter without issue, by his second son William. The last
named died in 1290, and was succeeded by his son Guy II. (great grand-
nephew of Otto de la Roche), after whose death it was that Walter de
Brienne succeeded to the duchy. Thus Gibbon's sentence should read,
instead of " inherited by his son and two grandsons," " inherited by his
nephew, two grand-nephews, and a great grand-nephew."—O. S.]
[1] The same Constantine gave to Sicily a king, to Russia the *magnus
dapifer* of the empire, to Thebes the *primicerius ;* and these absurd fables
are properly lashed by Ducange (ad Nicephor. Greg. l. vii. c. 5). By the
Latins the lord of Thebes was styled, by corruption, the Megas Kurios, or
Grand Sire!
[2] *Quodam miraculo,* says Alberic. He was probably received by Michael
Choniates, the archbishop who had defended Athens against the tyrant
Leo Sgurus (Nicetas urbs capta, p. 805, ed. Bek.). Michael was the
brother of the historian Nicetas; and his encomium of Athens is still
extant in MS. in the Bodleian library (Fabric. Biblioth. Græc. tom. vi.
p. 405).

Athens, as a government or an appanage, was successively bestowed by the kings of Sicily. After the French and Catalans, the third dynasty was that of the Accaioli,[1] a family, plebeian at Florence, potent at Naples, and sovereign in Greece. Athens, which they embellished with new buildings, became the capital of a state that extended over Thebes, Argos, Corinth, Delphi, and a part of Thessaly; and their reign was finally determined by Mohammed the Second, who strangled the last duke, and educated his sons in the discipline and religion of the seraglio.

Athens,[2] though no more than the shadow of her former self, still contains about eight or ten thousand inhabitants: of these, three-fourths are Greeks in religion and language; and the Turks, who compose the remainder, have relaxed, in their intercourse with the citizens, somewhat of the pride and gravity of their national character. The olive-tree, the gift of Minerva, flourishes in Attica; nor has the honey of Mount Hymettus lost any part of its exquisite flavour:[3] but the languid trade is monopolised by strangers, and the agriculture of a barren land is abandoned to the vagrant Wallachians. The Athenians are still distin-

---

[1] [Of the Acciajoli, and their influence in Greece, Finlay states the following facts:—

"Several members of the family of the Acciajoli had formed a distinguished commercial company at Florence in the thirteenth century, settled in the Peloponnesus about the middle of the fourteenth, under the protection of Robert, king of Naples. Nicolas Acciajoli was invested in the year 1334 with the administration of the lands which the company had acquired in payment or in security of the loans it had made to the royal house of Anjou, and he acquired additional possessions in the principality of Achaia, both by purchase and grant, from Catherine of Valois, titular empress of Romania and regent of Achaia for her son prince Robert. He was the founder of the fortunes of the family. Nicolas was invested by Catherine with the power of mortgaging, exchanging, and selling his fiefs without any previous authorisation from his suzerain. Nicolas acted as principal minister of Catherine, during a residence of three years in the Morea; and he made use of his position, like a prudent banker, to obtain considerable grants of territory. He returned to Italy in 1341, and never again visited Greece; but his estates in Achaia were administered by his relatives and other members of the banking house in Florence, many of whom obtained considerable fiefs for themselves through his influence." —O. S.]

[2] The modern account of Athens and the Athenians is extracted from Spon (Voyage en Grèce, tom. ii. p. 79-199) and Wheeler (Travels into Greece, p. 337-414), Stuart (Antiquities of Athens, passim) and Chandler (Travels into Greece, p. 23-172). The first of these travellers visited Greece in the year 1676; the last 1765; and ninety years had not produced much difference in the tranquil scene.

[3] The ancients, or at least the Athenians, believed that all the bees in the world had been propagated from Mount Hymettus. They taught that health might be preserved, and life prolonged, by the external use of oil and the internal use of honey (Geoponica, l. xv. c. 7, p. 1089-1094, edit. Niclas.).

guished by the subtlety and acuteness of their understandings;
but these qualities, unless ennobled by freedom and enlightened
by study, will degenerate into a low and selfish cunning: and it
is a proverbial saying of the country, " From the Jews of Thessalonica, the Turks of Negropont, and the Greeks of Athens,
good Lord deliver us ! " This artful people has eluded the
tyranny of the Turkish bashaws by an expedient which alleviates
their servitude and aggravates their shame. About the middle of
the last century the Athenians chose for their protector the Kislar
Aga, or chief black eunuch of the seraglio. This Æthiopian
slave, who possesses the sultan's ear, condescends to accept the
tribute of thirty thousand crowns: his lieutenant, the Waywode,
whom he annually confirms, may reserve for his own about five
or six thousand more; and such is the policy of the citizens,
that they seldom fail to remove and punish an oppressive
governor. Their private differences are decided by the archbishop, one of the richest prelates of the Greek church, since he
possesses a revenue of one thousand pounds sterling; and by a
tribunal of the eight *geronti* or elders, chosen in the eight quarters
of the city: the noble families cannot trace their pedigree above
three hundred years; but their principal members are distinguished by a grave demeanour, a fur cap, and the lofty
appellation of *archon*. By some, who delight in the contrast,
the modern language of Athens is represented as the most corrupt
and barbarous of the seventy dialects of the vulgar Greek: [1]
this picture is too darkly coloured; but it would not be easy,
in the country of Plato and Demosthenes, to find a reader or
a copy of their works. The Athenians walk with supine indifference among the glorious ruins of antiquity; and such is the
debasement of their character, that they are incapable of
admiring the genius of their predecessors.[2]

[1] Ducange, Glossar. Græc. Præfat. p. 8, who quotes for his author Theodosius Zygomalas, a modern grammarian. Yet Spon (tom. ii. p. 194) and
Wheeler (p. 355), no incompetent judges, entertain a more favourable
opinion of the Attic dialect.

[2] Yet we must not accuse them of corrupting the name of Athens, which
they still call Athini. From the εἰς τὴν Ἀθήνην we have formed our own
barbarism of *Setines.*

CHAPTER LXIII

Civil Wars, and Ruin of the Greek Empire—Reigns of Andronicus the Elder and Younger, and John Palæologus—Regency, Revolt, Reign, and Abdication of John Cantacuzene—Establishment of a Genoese Colony at Pera or Galata—Their Wars with the Empire and City of Constantinople

THE long reign of Andronicus [1] the elder is chiefly memorable by the disputes of the Greek church, the invasion of the Catalans, and the rise of the Ottoman power. He is celebrated as the most learned and virtuous prince of the age; but such virtue, and such learning, contributed neither to the perfection of the individual nor to the happiness of society. A slave of the most abject superstition, he was surrounded on all sides by visible and invisible enemies; nor were the flames of hell less dreadful to his fancy than those of a Catalan or Turkish war. Under the reign of the Palæologi the choice of the patriarch was the most important business of the state; the heads of the Greek church were ambitious and fanatic monks; and their vices or virtues, their learning or ignorance, were equally mischievous or contemptible. By his intemperate discipline the patriarch Athanasius [2] excited the hatred of the clergy and people: he was heard to declare that the sinner should swallow the last dregs of the cup of penance; and the foolish tale was propagated of his punishing a sacrilegious ass that had tasted the lettuce of a convent garden. Driven from the throne by the universal clamour, Athanasius composed before his retreat two papers of a very opposite cast. His public testament was in the tone of charity and resignation; the private codicil breathed the direst anathemas against the authors of his disgrace, whom he excluded for ever from the communion of the Holy Trinity, the angels, and the saints. This last paper he enclosed in an earthen pot, which was placed, by his order, on the top of one of the pillars in the dome of St. Sophia, in the distant hope of discovery and revenge. At the end of four years some youths, climbing by a ladder in search of pigeons' nests, detected the fatal secret; and, as Andronicus felt himself touched and bound by the

---

[1] Andronicus himself will justify our freedom in the invective (Nicephorus Gregoras, l. i. c. 1) which he pronounced against historic falsehood. It is true that his censure is more pointedly urged against calumny than against adulation.

[2] For the anathema in the pigeon's nest, see Pachymer (l. ix. c. 24 [tom. ii. p. 249, ed. Bonn]), who relates the general history of Athanasius (l. viii. c. 13-16, 20-24, l. x. c. 27-29, 31-36, l. xi. c. 1-3, 5, 6, l. xiii. c. 8, 10, 23, 35), and is followed by Nicephorus Gregoras (l. vi. c. 5, 7, l. vii. c. 1, 9), who includes the second retreat of this second Chrysostom.

excommunication, he trembled on the brink of the abyss which had been so treacherously dug under his feet. A synod of bishops was instantly convened to debate this important question: the rashness of these clandestine anathemas was generally condemned; but as the knot could be untied only by the same hand, as that hand was now deprived of the crosier, it appeared that this posthumous decree was irrevocable by any earthly power. Some faint testimonies of repentance and pardon were extorted from the author of the mischief; but the conscience of the emperor was still wounded, and he desired, with no less ardour than Athanasius himself, the restoration of a patriarch by whom alone he could be healed. At the dead of night a monk rudely knocked at the door of the royal bed-chamber, announcing a revelation of plague and famine, of inundations and earthquakes. Andronicus started from his bed and spent the night in prayer, till he felt, or thought that he felt, a slight motion of the earth. The emperor on foot led the bishops and monks to the cell of Athanasius; and, after a proper resistance, the saint, from whom this message had been sent, consented to absolve the prince and govern the church of Constantinople. Untamed by disgrace, and hardened by solitude, the shepherd was again odious to the flock, and his enemies contrived a singular, and, as it proved, a successful, mode of revenge. In the night they stole away the foot-stool or foot-cloth of his throne, which they secretly replaced with the decoration of a satirical picture. The emperor was painted with a bridle in his mouth, and Athanasius leading the tractable beast to the feet of Christ. The authors of the libel were detected and punished; but as their lives had been spared, the Christian priest in sullen indignation retired to his cell; and the eyes of Andronicus, which had been opened for a moment, were again closed by his successor.

If this transaction be one of the most curious and important of a reign of fifty years, I cannot at least accuse the brevity of my materials, since I reduce into some few pages the enormous folios of Pachymer,[1] Cantacuzene,[2] and Nicephorus Gregoras,[3]

[1] Pachymer, in seven books, 377 folio pages, describes the first twenty-six years of Andronicus the Elder; and marks the date of his composition by the current news or lie of the day (A.D. 1308). Either death or disgust prevented him from resuming the pen.

[2] After an interval of twelve years from the conclusion of Pachymer, Cantacuzenus takes up the pen; and his first book (c. 1-59, p. 9-150 [ed. Ven.]) relates the civil war and the eight last years of the elder Andronicus. The ingenious comparison with Moses and Cæsar is fancied by his French translator, the president Cousin.

[3] Nicephorus Gregoras more briefly includes the entire life and reign of

who have composed the prolix and languid story of the times.
The name and situation of the emperor John Cantacuzene might
inspire the most lively curiosity. His memorials of forty years
extend from the revolt of the younger Andronicus to his own
abdication of the empire; and it is observed that, like Moses and
Cæsar, he was the principal actor in the scenes which he describes.
But in this eloquent work we should vainly seek the sincerity of
a hero or a penitent. Retired in a cloister from the vices and
passions of the world, he presents not a confession, but an
apology, of the life of an ambitious statesman. Instead of unfolding the true counsels and characters of men, he displays the
smooth and specious surface of events, highly varnished with his
own praises and those of his friends. Their motives are always
pure; their ends always legitimate: they conspire and rebel
without any views of interest; and the violence which they
inflict or suffer is celebrated as the spontaneous effect of reason
and virtue.

After the example of the first of the Palæologi, the elder
Andronicus associated his son Michael to the honours of the
purple; and from the age of eighteen to his premature death,
that prince was acknowledged, above twenty-five years, as the
second emperor of the Greeks.[1] At the head of an army he
excited neither the fears of the enemy nor the jealousy of the
court: his modesty and patience were never tempted to compute
the years of his father; nor was that father compelled to repent
of his liberality either by the virtues or vices of his son. The
son of Michael was named Andronicus from his grandfather,
to whose early favour he was introduced by that nominal
resemblance. The blossoms of wit and beauty increased the
fondness of the elder Andronicus; and, with the common vanity
of age, he expected to realise in the second, the hope which
had been disappointed in the first, generation. The boy was
educated in the palace as an heir and a favourite; and in the
oaths and acclamations of the people, the *august triad* was
formed by the names of the father, the son, and the grandson.

Andronicus the Elder (l. vi. c. 1—l. x. c. 1, p. 96-291). This is the part of
which Cantacuzene complains as a false and malicious representation of his
conduct.

[1] He was crowned May 21st, 1295, and died October 12th, 1320 (Ducange,
Fam. Byz. p. 239). His brother Theodore, by a second marriage, inherited
the marquisate of Montferrat, apostatised to the religion and manners of
the Latins (ὅτι καὶ γνώμῃ καὶ πίστει καὶ σχήματι, καὶ γενείων κουρᾷ καὶ πᾶσιν
ἔθεσιν Λατῖνος ἦν ἀκραιφνής. Nic. Greg. l. ix. c. 1), and founded a
dynasty of Italian princes, which was extinguished A.D. 1533 (Ducange,
Fam. Byz. p. 249-253).

But the younger Andronicus was speedily corrupted by his infant greatness, while he beheld with puerile impatience the double obstacle that hung, and might long hang, over his rising ambition. It was not to acquire fame, or to diffuse happiness, that he so eagerly aspired: wealth and impunity were in his eyes the most precious attributes of a monarch; and his first indiscreet demand was the sovereignty of some rich and fertile island, where he might lead a life of independence and pleasure. The emperor was offended by the loud and frequent intemperance which disturbed his capital; the sums which his parsimony denied were supplied by the Genoese usurers of Pera; and the oppressive debt, which consolidated the interest of a faction, could be discharged only by a revolution. A beautiful female, a matron in rank, a prostitute in manners, had instructed the younger Andronicus in the rudiments of love; but he had reason to suspect the nocturnal visits of a rival; and a stranger passing through the street was pierced by the arrows of his guards, who were placed in ambush at her door. That stranger was his brother, prince Manuel, who languished and died of his wound; and the emperor Michael, their common father, whose health was in a declining state, expired on the eighth day, lamenting the loss of both his children.[1] However guiltless in his intention, the younger Andronicus might impute a brother's and a father's death to the consequence of his own vices; and deep was the sigh of thinking and feeling men when they perceived, instead of sorrow and repentance, his ill-dissembled joy on the removal of two odious competitors. By these melancholy events, and the increase of his disorders, the mind of the elder emperor was gradually alienated; and, after many fruitless reproofs, he transferred on another grandson[2] his hopes and affection. The change was announced by the new oath of allegiance to the reigning sovereign, and the *person* whom he should appoint for his successor; and the acknowledged heir, after a repetition of insults and complaints, was exposed to the indignity of a public trial. Before the sentence, which would probably have condemned him to a dungeon or a cell, the emperor was informed that the palace courts were filled with the armed followers of his

---

[1] We are indebted to Nicephorus Gregoras (l. viii. c. 1) for the knowledge of this tragic adventure; while Cantacuzene more discreetly conceals the vices of Andronicus the Younger, of which he was the witness, and perhaps the associate (l. i. c. 1, etc.).

[2] His destined heir was Michael Catharus, the bastard of Constantine his second son. In this project of excluding his grandson Andronicus, Nicephorus Gregoras (l. viii. c. 3 [6?]) agrees with Cantacuzene (l. i. c. 1, 2).

grandson; the judgment was softened to a treaty of reconcila-
tion; and the triumphant escape of the prince encouraged the
ardour of the younger faction.

Yet the capital, the clergy, and the senate adhered to the
person, or at least to the government, of the old emperor; and
it was only in the provinces, by flight, and revolt, and foreign
succour, that the malcontents could hope to vindicate their
cause and subvert his throne. The soul of the enterprise was
the great domestic John Cantacuzene: the sally from Constantinople is the first date of his actions and memorials; and if his
own pen be most descriptive of his patriotism, an unfriendly
historian has not refused to celebrate the zeal and ability which
he displayed in the service of the young emperor.[1] That prince
escaped from the capital under the pretence of hunting; erected
his standard at Adrianople; and, in a few days, assembled fifty
thousand horse and foot, whom neither honour nor duty could
have armed against the barbarians. Such a force might have
saved or commanded the empire; but their counsels were discordant, their motions were slow and doubtful, and their progress
was checked by intrigue and negotiation. The quarrel of the
two Andronici was protracted, and suspended, and renewed,
during a ruinous period of seven years. In the first treaty the
relics of the Greek empire were divided: Constantinople, Thessalonica, and the islands were left to the elder, while the younger
acquired the sovereignty of the greatest part of Thrace, from
Philippi to the Byzantine limit. By the second treaty he
stipulated the payment of his troops, his immediate coronation,
and an adequate share of the power and revenue of the state.
The third civil war was terminated by the surprise of Constantinople, the final retreat of the old emperor, and the sole reign
of his victorious grandson. The reasons of this delay may be
found in the characters of the men and of the times. When the
heir of the monarchy first pleaded his wrongs and his apprehensions, he was heard with pity and applause; and his adherents
repeated on all sides the inconsistent promise that he would
increase the pay of the soldiers and alleviate the burdens of the
people. The grievances of forty years were mingled in his
revolt; and the rising generation was fatigued by the endless
prospect of a reign whose favourites and maxims were of other

---

[1] [The conduct of Cantacuzene was inexplicable even on his own showing.
He was unwilling to dethrone the old emperor, and dissuaded the troops
from the immediate march on Constantinople. The young Andronicus,
he says, entered into his views, and wrote to warn the emperor of his
danger when the march was determined.—O. S.]

times. The youth of Andronicus had been without spirit, his age was without reverence: his taxes produced an annual revenue of five hundred thousand pounds; yet the richest of the sovereigns of Christendom was incapable of maintaining three thousand horse and twenty galleys, to resist the destructive progress of the Turks.[1] "How different," said the younger Andronicus, "is my situation from that of the son of Philip! Alexander might complain that his father would leave him nothing to conquer: alas! my grandsire will leave me nothing to lose." But the Greeks were soon admonished that the public disorders could not be healed by a civil war; and that their young favourite was not destined to be the saviour of a falling empire. On the first repulse his party was broken by his own levity, their intestine discord, and the intrigues of the ancient court, which tempted each malcontent to desert or betray the cause of rebellion. Andronicus the younger was touched with remorse, or fatigued with business, or deceived by negotiation: pleasure rather than power was his aim; and the licence of maintaining a thousand hounds, a thousand hawks, and a thousand huntsmen, was sufficient to sully his fame and disarm his ambition.

Let us now survey the catastrophe of this busy plot and the final situation of the principal actors.[2] The age of Andronicus was consumed in civil discord; and, amidst the events of war and treaty, his power and reputation continually decayed, till the fatal night in which the gates of the city and palace were opened without resistance to his grandson. His principal commander scorned the repeated warnings of danger; and, retiring to rest in the vain security of ignorance, abandoned the feeble monarch, with some priests and pages, to the terrors of a sleepless night. These terrors were quickly realised by the hostile shouts which proclaimed the titles and victory of Andronicus the younger; and the aged emperor, falling prostrate before an image of the Virgin, despatched a suppliant message to resign the sceptre and to obtain his life at the hands of the conqueror. The answer of his grandson was decent and pious; at the prayer of his friends

[1] See Nicephorus Gregoras, l. viii. c. 6 [tom. i. p. 317, ed. Bonn]. The younger Andronicus complained that in four years and four months a sum of 350,000 byzants of gold was due to him for the expenses of his household (Cantacuzen. l. i. c. 48 [tom. i. p. 237, ed. Bonn]). Yet he would have remitted the debt, if he might have been allowed to squeeze the farmers of the revenue.

[2] I follow the chronology of Nicephorus Gregoras, who is remarkably exact. It is proved that Cantacuzene has mistaken the dates of his own actions, or rather that his text has been corrupted by ignorant transcribers.

the younger Andronicus assumed the sole administration; but
the elder still enjoyed the name and pre-eminence of the first
emperor, the use of the great palace, and a pension of twenty-
four thousand pieces of gold, one half of which was assigned on
the royal treasure and the other on the fishery of Constantinople.
But his impotence was soon exposed to contempt and oblivion;
the vast silence of the palace was disturbed only by the cattle
and poultry of the neighbourhood, which roved with impunity
through the solitary courts; and a reduced allowance of ten
thousand pieces of gold [1] was all that he could ask and more
than he could hope. His calamities were embittered by the
gradual extinction of sight; his confinement was rendered each
day more rigorous; and during the absence and sickness of his
grandson, his inhuman keepers, by the threats of instant death,
compelled him to exchange the purple for the monastic habit
and profession. The monk *Antony* had renounced the pomp
of the world: yet he had occasion for a coarse fur in the winter
season; and as wine was forbidden by his confessor, and water
by his physician, the sherbet of Egypt was his common drink.
It was not without difficulty that the late emperor could procure
three or four pieces to satisfy these simple wants; and if he
bestowed the gold to relieve the more painful distress of a friend,
the sacrifice is of some weight in the scale of humanity and
religion. Four years after his abdication Andronicus, or Antony,
expired in a cell, in the seventy-fourth year of his age: and the
last strain of adulation could only promise a more splendid
crown of glory in heaven than he had enjoyed upon earth.[2]

Nor was the reign of the younger, more glorious or fortunate
than that of the elder, Andronicus.[3] He gathered the fruits of
ambition; but the taste was transient and bitter: in the
supreme station he lost the remains of his early popularity; and
the defects of his character became still more conspicuous to the
world. The public reproach urged him to march in person
against the Turks; nor did his courage fail in the hour of trial;
but a defeat and a wound were the only trophies of his expedition

---

[1] I have endeavoured to reconcile the 24,000 pieces of Cantacuzene (l. ii.
c. 1) with the 10,000 of Nicephorus Gregoras (l. ix. c. 2); the one of whom
wished to soften, the other to magnify, the hardships of the old emperor.

[2] See Nicephorus Gregoras (l. ix. 6, 7, 8, 10, 14, l. x. c. 1). The historian
had tasted of the prosperity, and shared the retreat, of his benefactor; and
that friendship which " waits or to the scaffold or the cell " should not
lightly be accused as " a hireling, a prostitute to praise."

[3] The sole reign of Andronicus the younger is described by Cantacuzene
(l. ii. c. 1-40, p. 191-339 [ed. Par.]), and Nicephorus Gregoras (l. ix. c. 7—
l. xi. c. 11, p. 262-351).

in Asia, which confirmed the establishment of the Ottoman
monarchy.   The abuses of the civil government attained their
full maturity and perfection: his neglect of forms and the confusion of national dresses are deplored by the Greeks as the fatal
symptoms of the decay of the empire.   Andronicus was old
before his time; the intemperance of youth had accelerated the
infirmities of age; and after being rescued from a dangerous
malady by nature, or physic, or the Virgin, he was snatched
away before he had accomplished his forty-fifth year.   He was
twice married; and as the progress of the Latins in arms and
arts had softened the prejudices of the Byzantine court, his two
wives were chosen in the princely houses of Germany and Italy.
The first, Agnes at home, Irene in Greece, was daughter of the
duke of Brunswick.   Her father[1] was a petty lord[2] in the poor
and savage regions of the north of Germany;[3] yet he derived
some revenue from his silver-mines;[4] and his family is celebrated by the Greeks as the most ancient and noble of the
Teutonic name.[5]   After the death of this childless princess,

[1] Agnes, or Irene, was the daughter of duke Henry the Wonderful, the
chief of the house of Brunswick, and the fourth in descent from the famous
Henry the Lion, duke of Saxony and Bavaria, and conqueror of the Slavi
on the Baltic coast.   Her brother Henry was surnamed the *Greek*, from
his two journeys into the East: but these journeys were subsequent to his
sister's marriage; and I am ignorant *how* Agnes was discovered in the
heart of Germany, and recommended to the Byzantine court.   (Rimius,
Memoirs of the House of Brunswick, p. 126-137.)

[2] Henry the Wonderful was the founder of the branch of Grubenhagen,
extinct in the year 1596.   (Rimius, p. 287.)   He resided in the castle of
Wolfenbüttel, and possessed no more than a sixth part of the allodial
estates of Brunswick and Luneburg, which the Guelph family had saved
from the confiscation of their great fiefs.   The frequent partitions among
brothers had almost ruined the princely houses of Germany, till that just,
but pernicious, law was slowly superseded by the right of primogeniture.
The principality of Grubenhagen, one of the last remains of the Hercynian
forest, is a woody, mountainous, and barren tract.   (Busching's Geography, vol. vi. p. 270-286, English translation.)

[3] The royal author of the Memoirs of Brandenburg will teach us how
justly, in a much later period, the north of Germany deserved the epithets
of poor and barbarous.   (Essai sur les Mœurs, etc.)   In the year 1306, in
the woods of Luneburg, some wild people of the Vened race were allowed
to bury alive their infirm and useless parents.   (Rimius, p. 136.)

[4] The assertion of Tacitus, that Germany was destitute of the precious
metals, must be taken, even in his own time, with some limitation.   (Germania, c. 5; Annal. xi. 20.)   According to Spener (Hist. Germaniæ Prag-
matica, tom. i. p. 351), *Argentifodinæ* in Hercyniis montibus, imperante
Othone magno (A.D. 968) primum apertæ, largam etiam opes augendi
dederunt copiam: but Rimius (p. 258, 259) defers till the year 1016 the
discovery of the silver-mines of Grubenhagen, or the Upper Hartz, which
were productive in the beginning of the fourteenth century, and which still
yield a considerable revenue to the house of Brunswick.

[5] Cantacuzene has given a most honourable testimony, ἦν δ᾽ ἐκ Γερμανῶν
αὔτη θυγάτηρ δουκὸς ντὶ Μπρουζουὴκ (the modern Greeks employ the ντ for the

Andronicus sought in marriage Jane, the sister of the count of Savoy; [1] and his suit was preferred to that of the French king. [2] The count respected in his sister the superior majesty of a Roman empress: her retinue was composed of knights and ladies; she was regenerated and crowned in St. Sophia under the more orthodox appellation of Anne; and, at the nuptial feast, the Greeks and Italians vied with each other in the martial exercises of tilts and tournaments.

The empress Anne of Savoy survived her husband: their son, John Palæologus, was left an orphan and an emperor in the ninth year of his age; and his weakness was protected by the first and most deserving of the Greeks. The long and cordial friendship of his father for John Cantacuzene is alike honourable to the prince and the subject. It had been formed amidst the pleasures of their youth: their families were almost equally noble; [3] and the recent lustre of the purple was amply compensated by the energy of a private education. We have seen that the young emperor was saved by Cantacuzene from the power of his grandfather; and, after six years of civil war, the same favourite brought him back in triumph to the palace of Constantinople. Under the reign of Andronicus the younger, the great domestic ruled the emperor and the empire; and it was by his valour and conduct that the isle of Lesbos and the principality of Ætolia were restored to their ancient allegiance. His enemies confess that among the public robbers Cantacuzene alone was moderate and abstemious; and the free and voluntary account which he produces of his own wealth [4] may sustain the presumption that it was devolved by inheritance, and not accumulated by rapine. He does not indeed specify the value of his money, plate, and jewels, yet, after a voluntary gift of two hundred vases of silver, after much had been secreted by his friends and plundered by

δ, and the μπ for the β, and the whole will read in the Italian idiom di Brunzuic), τοῦ παρ' αὐτοῖς ἐπιφανεστάτου, καὶ λαμπρότητι πάντας τοὺς ὁμοφύλους ὑπερβάλλοντος τοῦ γένους [l. i. c. 10, tom. i. p. 52, ed. Bonn]. The praise is just in itself, and pleasing to an English ear.

[1] Anne, or Jane, was one of the four daughters of Amedée the Great, by a second marriage, and half sister of his successor Edward count of Savoy (Anderson's Tables, p. 650). See Cantacuzene (l. i. c. 40-42).

[2] That king, if the fact be true, must have been Charles the Fair, who in five years (1321-1326) was married to three wives (Anderson, p. 628). Anne of Savoy arrived at Constantinople in February 1326.

[3] The noble race of the Cantacuzeni (illustrious from the eleventh century in the Byzantine annals) was drawn from the Paladins of France, the heroes of those romances which, in the thirteenth century, were translated and read by the Greeks (Ducange, Fam. Byzant. p. 258).

[4] See Cantacuzene (l. iii. c. 24, 30, 36).

his foes, his forfeit treasures were sufficient for the equipment
of a fleet of seventy galleys. He does not measure the size and
number of his estates; but his granaries were heaped with an
incredible store of wheat and barley; and the labour of a thousand yoke of oxen might cultivate, according to the practice of
antiquity, about sixty-two thousand five hundred acres of arable
land.[1]   His patures were stocked with two thousand five hundred
brood mares, two hundred camels, three hundred mules, five
hundred asses, five thousand horned cattle, fifty thousand hogs,
and seventy thousand sheep: [2] a precious record of rural opulence
in the last period of the empire, and in a land, most probably in
Thrace, so repeatedly wasted by foreign and domestic hostility.
The favour of Cantacuzene was above his fortune.   In the
moments of familiarity, in the hour of sickness, the emperor was
desirous to level the distance between them, and pressed his
friend to accept the diadem and purple.   The virtue of the great
domestic, which is attested by his own pen, resisted the dangerous
proposal; but the last testament of Andronicus the younger
named him the guardian of his son, and the regent of the empire.

Had the regent found a suitable return of obedience and gratitude, perhaps he would have acted with pure and zealous fidelity
in the service of his pupil.[3]   A guard of five hundred soldiers
watched over his person and the palace; the funeral of the late
emperor was decently performed, the capital was silent and
submissive, and five hundred letters, which Cantacuzene
despatched in the first month, informed the provinces of their
loss and their duty.   The prospect of a tranquil minority was
blasted by the great duke or admiral Apocaucus; and to
exaggerate *his* perfidy, the Imperial historian is pleased to
magnify his own imprudence in raising him to that office against
the advice of his more sagacious sovereign.   Bold and subtle,
rapacious and profuse, the avarice and ambition of Apocaucus

---

[1] Saserna in Gaul, and Columella in Italy or Spain, allow two yoke of
oxen, two drivers, and six labourers, for two hundred jugera (125 English
acres) of arable land, and three more men must be added if there be much
underwood (Columella de Re Rusticâ, l. ii. c. 13, p. 441, edit. Gesner).

[2] In this enumeration (l. iii. c. 30) the French translation of the president
Cousin is blotted with three palpable and essential errors.   1. He omits
the 1000 yoke of working oxen.   2. He interprets the πεντακόσιαι πρὸς
δισχιλίαις by the number of fifteen hundred.   3. He confounds myriads
with chiliads, and gives Cantacuzene no more than 5000 hogs.   Put not
your trust in translations!

[3] See the regency and reign of John Cantacuzenus, and the whole pro
gress of the civil war, in his own history (l. iii. c. 1-100, p. 348-700 [ed.
Par.]), and in that of Nicephorus Gregoras (l. xii. c. 1—l. xv. c. 9, p. 353
492).

were by turns subservient to each other, and his talents were
applied to the ruin of his country. His arrogance was heightened
by the command of a naval force and an impregnable castle, and
under the mask of oaths and flattery he secretly conspired
against his benefactor. The female court of the empress was
bribed and directed; he encouraged Anne of Savoy to assert, by
the law of nature, the tutelage of her son; the love of power
was disguised by the anxiety of maternal tenderness; and the
founder of the Palæologi had instructed his posterity to dread
the example of a perfidious guardian. The patriarch John of
Apri was a proud and feeble old man, encompassed by a
numerous and hungry kindred. He produced an obsolete
epistle of Andronicus, which bequeathed the prince and people
to his pious care: the fate of his predecessor Arsenius prompted
him to prevent, rather than punish, the crimes of a usurper;
and Apocaucus smiled at the success of his own flattery when he
beheld the Byzantine priest assuming the state and temporal
claims of the Roman pontiff.[1] Between three persons so
different in their station and character a private league was concluded: a shadow of authority was restored to the senate, and
the people was tempted by the name of freedom. By this
powerful confederacy the great domestic was assaulted at first
with clandestine, at length with open arms. His prerogatives
were disputed, his opinions slighted, his friends persecuted, and
his safety was threatened both in the camp and city. In his
absence on the public service he was accused of treason, proscribed as an enemy of the church and state, and delivered, with
all his adherents, to the sword of justice, the vengeance of the
people, and the power of the devil; his fortunes were confiscated,
his aged mother was cast into prison, all his past services were
buried in oblivion, and he was driven by injustice to perpetrate
the crime of which he was accused.[2] From the review of his preceding conduct, Cantacuzene appears to have been guiltless of
any treasonable designs; and the only suspicion of his innocence
must arise from the vehemence of his protestations, and the
sublime purity which he ascribes to his own virtue. While the

---

[1] He assumed the royal privilege of red shoes or buskins; placed on his
head a mitre of silk and gold; subscribed his epistles with hyacinth or
green ink; and claimed for the new whatever Constantine had given to
the ancient Rome (Cantacuzen. l. iii. c. 26 [tom. ii. p. 162, ed. Bonn];
Nic. Gregoras, l. xiv. c. 3).

[2] Nic. Gregoras (l. xii. c. 5) confesses the innocence and virtues of Cantacuzenus, the guilt and flagitious vices of Apocaucus; nor does he dissemble
the motive of his personal and religious enmity to the former; νῦν δὲ διὰ
κακίαν ἄλλων, αἴτιος ὁ πραότατος τῆς τῶν ὅλων ἔδοξεν εἶναι φθορᾶς [tom. ii.
p. 590, ed. Bonn].

*I 476

empress and the patriarch still affected the appearances of harmony, he repeatedly solicited the permission of retiring to a private, and even a monastic life. After he had been declared a public enemy it was his fervent wish to throw himself at the feet of the young emperor, and to receive without a murmur the stroke of the executioner: it was not without reluctance that he listened to the voice of reason, which inculcated the sacred duty of saving his family and friends, and proved that he could only save them by drawing the sword and assuming the Imperial title.

In the strong city of Demotica, his peculiar domain, the emperor John Cantacuzenus was invested with the purple buskins: his right leg was clothed by his noble kinsmen, the left by the Latin chiefs, on whom he conferred the order of knighthood. But even in this act of revolt he was still studious of loyalty; and the titles of John Palæologus and Anne of Savoy were proclaimed before his own name and that of his wife Irene. Such vain ceremony is a thin disguise of rebellion; nor are there perhaps any *personal* wrongs that can authorise a subject to take arms against his sovereign: but the want of preparation and success may confirm the assurance of the usurper that this decisive step was the effect of necessity rather than of choice. Constantinople adhered to the young emperor; the king of Bulgaria was invited to the relief of Adrianople; the principal cities of Thrace and Macedonia, after some hesitation, renounced their obedience to the great domestic; and the leaders of the troops and provinces were induced by their private interest to prefer the loose dominion of a woman and a priest. The army of Cantacuzene, in sixteen divisions, was stationed on the banks of the Melas to tempt or intimidate the capital: it was dispersed by treachery or fear, and the officers, more especially the mercenary Latins, accepted the bribes and embraced the service of the Byzantine court. After this loss, the rebel emperor (he fluctuated between the two characters) took the road of Thessalonica with a chosen remnant; but he failed in his enterprise on that important place; and he was closely pursued by the great duke, his enemy Apocaucus, at the head of a superior power by sea and land. Driven from the coast, in his march, or rather flight, into the mountains of Servia, Cantacuzene assembled his troops to scrutinise those who were worthy and willing to accompany his broken fortunes. A base majority bowed and retired; and his trusty band was diminished to two thousand, and at last to five hundred, volunteers. The *cral*,[1] or despot of the Servians,

[1] The princes of Servia (Ducange, Famil. Dalmaticæ, etc., c. 2, 3, 4, 9)

received him with generous hospitality; but the ally was insensibly degraded to a suppliant, a hostage, a captive; and, in this
miserable dependence, he waited at the door of the barbarian,
who could dispose of the life and liberty of a Roman emperor.
The most tempting offers could not persuade the cral to violate
his trust; but he soon inclined to the stronger side, and his
friend was dismissed without injury to a new vicissitude of hopes
and perils. Near six years the flame of discord burnt with
various success and unabated rage; the cities were distracted
by the faction of the nobles and the plebeians—the Cantacuzeni
and Palæologi: and the Bulgarians, the Servians, and the Turks
were invoked on both sides as the instruments of private ambition
and the common ruin. The regent deplored the calamities of
which he was the author and victim: and his own experience
might dictate a just and lively remark on the different nature of
foreign and civil war. "The former," said he, "is the external
warmth of summer, always tolerable, and often beneficial; the
latter is the deadly heat of a fever, which consumes without a
remedy the vitals of the constitution." [1]

were styled Despots in Greek, and Cral in their native idiom. (Ducange,
Gloss. Græc. p. 751.) That title, the equivalent of king, appears to be of
Sclavonic origin, from whence it has been borrowed by the Hungarians,
the modern Greeks, and even by the Turks (Leunclavius, Pandect. Turc.
p. 422), who reserve the name of Padishah for the emperor. To obtain
the latter instead of the former is the ambition of the French at Constantinople (Avertissement à l'Histoire de Timur Bec, p. 39).

[The word *Kral* (king) was derived from Karl the Great, as Kaiser is
derived from Cæsar.—O. S.]

[1] Nic. Gregoras, l. xii. c. 14 [tom. ii. p. 622, ed. Bonn]. It is surprising
that Cantacuzene has not inserted this just and lively image in his own
writings.

[Under Stephan Dushan (1331-1355) Servia became at this time the
strongest power in the peninsula. Finlay says of him that his empire extended from the Danube to the Gulf of Arta. "He was a man of great
ambition, and was celebrated for his gigantic stature and personal courage.
His subjects boasted of his liberality and success in war; his enemies reproached him with faithlessness and cruelty. He had driven his father,
Stephen VII., from the throne, and the old man had been murdered in
prison by the rebellious nobles of Servia, who feared lest a reconciliation
should take place with his son. He then began to extend his conquests
on all sides. To the east he rendered himself master of the whole valley
of the Strymon, took the large and flourishing city of Serres, and garrisoned
all the fortresses as far as the wall that defended the pass of Christopolis.
He then extended his dominions along the shores of the Adriatic, and to
the south he carried his arms as far as the Gulf of Ambracia. He subdued
the Wallachians of Thessaly, and placed strong garrisons in Achrida,
Kastoria, and Joannina." Flushed with victory, he at last formed the
ambitious scheme of depriving the Greeks of their political and ecclesiastical supremacy in the Eastern empire and transferring it to the Servian.
He was crowned at Skopia in 1346 "Tzar of the Serbs and Greeks," and
gave his son the title of "kral"—king. In a word, Stephen did for Servia
what Yaroslav did for Russia.—O. S.]

The introduction of barbarians and savages into the contests of civilised nations is a measure pregnant with shame and mischief, which the interest of the moment may compel, but which is reprobated by the best principles of humanity and reason. It is the practice of both sides to accuse their enemies of the guilt of the first alliances; and those who fail in their negotiations are loudest in their censure of the example which they envy and would gladly imitate. The Turks of Asia were less barbarous perhaps than the shepherds of Bulgaria and Servia, but their religion rendered them the implacable foes of Rome and Christianity. To acquire the friendship of their emirs, the two factions vied with each other in baseness and profusion: the dexterity of Cantacuzene obtained the preference: but the succour and victory were dearly purchased by the marriage of his daughter with an infidel, the captivity of many thousand Christians, and the passage of the Ottomans into Europe, the last and fatal stroke in the fall of the Roman empire. The inclining scale was decided in his favour by the death of Apocaucus, the just though singular retribution of his crimes. A crowd of nobles or plebeians whom he feared or hated had been seized by his orders in the capital and the provinces, and the old palace of Constantine was assigned for the place of their confinement. Some alterations in raising the walls and narrowing the cells had been ingeniously contrived to prevent their escape and aggravate their misery, and the work was incessantly pressed by the daily visits of the tyrant. His guards watched at the gate; and as he stood in the inner court to overlook the architects, without fear or suspicion, he was assaulted and laid breathless on the ground by two resolute prisoners of the Palæologian race,[1] who were armed with sticks and animated by despair. On the rumour of revenge and liberty, the captive multitude broke their fetters, fortified their prison, and exposed from the battlements the tyrant's head, presuming on the favour of the people and the clemency of the empress. Anne of Savoy might rejoice in the fall of a haughty and ambitious minister; but while she delayed to resolve or to act, the populace, more especially the mariners, were excited by the widow of the great duke to a sedition, an assault, and a massacre. The prisoners (of whom the far greater part were guiltless or inglorious of the deed) escaped to a neighbouring church: they were slaughtered at the

[1] The two avengers were both Palæologi, who might resent, with royal indignation, the shame of their chains. The tragedy of Apocaucus may deserve a peculiar reference to Cantacuzene (l. iii. c. 88) and Nic. Gregoras (l. xiv. c. 10).

foot of the altar; and in his death the monster was not less bloody and venomous than in his life. Yet his talents alone upheld the cause of the young emperor; and his surviving associates, suspicious of each other, abandoned the conduct of the war, and rejected the fairest terms of accommodation. In the beginning of the dispute the empress felt and complained that she was deceived by the enemies of Cantacuzene: the patriarch was employed to preach against the forgiveness of injuries; and her promise of immortal hatred was sealed by an oath under the penalty of excommunication.[1] But Anne soon learned to hate without a teacher: she beheld the misfortunes of the empire with the indifference of a stranger; her jealousy was exasperated by the competition of a rival empress; and on the first symptoms of a more yielding temper, she threatened the patriarch to convene a synod and degrade him from his office. Their incapacity and discord would have afforded the most decisive advantage; but the civil war was protracted by the weakness of both parties; and the moderation of Cantacuzene has not escaped the reproach of timidity and indolence. He successively recovered the provinces and cities; and the realm of his pupil was measured by the walls of Constantinople; but

[1] Cantacuzene accuses the patriarch, and spares the empress, the mother of his sovereign (l. iii. 33, 34), against whom Nic. Gregoras expresses a particular animosity (l. xiv. 10, 11; xv. 5). It is true that they do not speak exactly of the same time.

[It is well that the reader should know what exactly is meant by the term "The Greek Empire." Finlay gives us the following excellent *résumé*: "The Greek empire consisted of several detached provinces when Cantacuzenos seated himself on the throne, and the inhabitants of these different parts could only communicate freely by sea. The nucleus of the imperial power consisted of the city of Constantinople and the greater part of Thrace. On the Asiatic side of the Bosphorus the Greek possessions consisted of the suburb Skutari, a few forts, and a narrow strip of coast running from Chalcedon to the Black Sea. In Thrace the frontier extended from Sozopolis along the mountains to the south-west, passing about a day's journey to the north of Adrianople, and descending to the Ægean Sea at the pass and fortress of Christopolis. It included the districts of Morrah and the Thracian Chalkidike. The second portion of the empire in importance consisted of the rich and populous city of Thessalonica, with the western part of the Macedonian Chalkidike and its three peninsulas of Cassandra, Longos, and Agionoros. The third detached portion of the empire consisted of a part of Wallachian Thessaly and of Albanian Epirus, which formed a small province interposed between the Servian empire and the Catalan Duchy of Athens and Neopatras. The fourth detached part consisted of the Greek province in the Peloponnesus, which obtained the name of the Despotat of Misithra, and embraced about one-third of the peninsula. The remaining fragments of the empire consisted of a few islands in the Ægean Sea, which had escaped the domination of the Venetians, the Genoese, and the Knights of St. John, and of the cities of Philadelphia and Phocæa, which still recognised the suzerainty of Constantinople."—O. S.]

the metropolis alone counterbalanced the rest of the empire;
nor could he attempt that important conquest till he had
secured in his favour the public voice and a private correspondence.   An Italian, of the name of Facciolati,[1] had succeeded to
the office of great duke: the ships, the guards, and the golden
gate were subject to his command; but his humble ambition
was bribed to become the instrument of treachery; and the
revolution was accomplished without danger or bloodshed.
Destitute of the powers of resistance or the hope of relief, the
inflexible Anne would have still defended the palace, and have
smiled to behold the capital in flames rather than in the possession of a rival.   She yielded to the prayers of her friends and
enemies, and the treaty was dictated by the conqueror, who
professed a loyal and zealous attachment to the son of his benefactor.   The marriage of his daughter with John Palæologus was
at length consummated; the hereditary right of the pupil was
acknowledged, but the sole administration during ten years
was vested in the guardian.   Two emperors and three empresses
were seated on the Byzantine throne; and a general amnesty
quieted the apprehensions and confirmed the property of the
most guilty subjects.   The festival of the coronation and
nuptials was celebrated with the appearances of concord and
magnificence, and both were equally fallacious.   During the
late troubles the treasures of the state, and even the furniture
of the palace, had been alienated or embezzled; the royal banquet
was served in pewter or earthenware; and such was the proud
poverty of the times, that the absence of gold and jewels was
supplied by the paltry artifices of glass and gilt leather.[2]

I hasten to conclude the personal history of John Cantacuzene.[3]
He triumphed and reigned; but his reign and triumph were
clouded by the discontent of his own and the adverse faction.
His followers might style the general amnesty an act of pardon
for his enemies, and of oblivion for his friends: in his cause their

---

[1] The traitor and treason are revealed by Nic. Gregoras (l. xv. c. 8); but
the name is more discreetly suppressed by his great accomplice (Cantacuzen. l. iii. c. 99).

[2] Nic. Greg. l. xv. 11 [tom. ii. p. 788, ed. Bonn].   There were, however,
some true pearls, but very thinly sprinkled.   The rest of the stones had
only παντοδαπὴν χροιὰν πρὸς τὸ διαυγές.

[3] From his return to Constantinople, Cantacuzene continues his history
and that of the empire one year beyond the abdication of his son Matthew,
A.D. 1357 (l. iv. c. 1-50, p. 705-911).   Nicephorus Gregoras ends with the
synod of Constantinople, in the year 1351 (l. xxii. c. 3, p. 660; the rest, to
the conclusion of the twenty-fourth book, p. 717, is all controversy); and
his fourteen last books are still MSS. in the king of France's library.

estates had been forfeited or plundered; and as they wandered naked and hungry through the streets, they cursed the selfish generosity of a leader who, on the throne of the empire, might relinquish without merit his private inheritance.[1] The adherents of the empress blushed to hold their lives and fortunes by the precarious favour of a usurper, and the thirst of revenge was concealed by a tender concern for the succession, and even the safety, of her son. They were justly alarmed by a petition of the friends of Cantacuzene, that they might be released from their oath of allegiance to the Palæologi, and intrusted with the defence of some cautionary towns; a measure supported with argument and eloquence, and which was rejected (says the Imperial historian) "by *my* sublime and almost incredible virtue." His repose was disturbed by the sound of plots and seditions, and he trembled lest the lawful prince should be stolen away by some foreign or domestic enemy, who would inscribe his name and his wrongs in the banners of rebellion. As the son of Andronicus advanced in the years of manhood he began to feel and to act for himself, and his rising ambition was rather stimulated than checked by the imitation of his father's vices. If we may trust his own professions, Cantacuzene laboured with honest industry to correct these sordid and sensual appetites, and to raise the mind of the young prince to a level with his fortune. In the Servian expedition the two emperors showed themselves in cordial harmony to the troops and provinces, and the younger colleague was initiated by the elder in the mysteries of war and government. After the conclusion of the peace, Palæologus was left at Thessalonica, a royal residence and a frontier station, to secure by his absence the peace of Constantinople, and to withdraw his youth from the temptations of a luxurious capital. But the distance weakened the powers of control, and the son of Andronicus was surrounded with artful or unthinking companions, who taught him to hate his guardian, to deplore his exile, and to vindicate his rights. A private treaty with the cral or despot of Servia was soon followed by an open revolt; and Cantacuzene, on the throne of the elder Andronicus, defended the cause of age and prerogative, which in his youth he had so vigorously attacked. At his request the empress-mother undertook the voyage of Thessalonica and the office of mediation: she returned without success; and unless Anne of Savoy was

---

[1] The emperor (Cantacuzen. l. iv. c. 1) represents his own virtues, and Nic. Gregoras (l. xv. c. 11) the complaints of his friends, who suffered by its effects. I have lent them the words of our poor cavaliers after the Restoration.

instructed by adversity, we may doubt the sincerity, or at least
the fervour, of her zeal. While the regent grasped the sceptre
with a firm and vigorous hand, she had been instructed to declare
that the ten years of his legal administration would soon elapse;
and that, after a full trial of the vanity of the world, the emperor
Cantacuzene sighed for the repose of a cloister, and was ambitious
only of a heavenly crown. Had these sentiments been genuine,
his voluntary abdication would have restored the peace of the
empire, and his conscience would have been relieved by an act
of justice. Palæologus alone was responsible for his future
government; and whatever might be his vices, they were surely
less formidable than the calamities of a civil war, in which the
barbarians and infidels were again invited to assist the Greeks
in their mutual destruction. By the arms of the Turks, who
now struck a deep and everlasting root in Europe, Cantacuzene
prevailed in the third contest in which he had been involved, and
the young emperor, driven from the sea and land, was compelled
to take shelter among the Latins of the isle of Tenedos. His
insolence and obstinacy provoked the victor to a step which
must render the quarrel irreconcilable; and the association of
his son Matthew, whom he invested with the purple, established
the succession in the family of the Cantacuzeni. But Constantinople was still attached to the blood of her ancient princes, and
this last injury accelerated the restoration of the rightful heir.
A noble Genoese espoused the cause of Palæologus, obtained a
promise of his sister, and achieved the revolution with two
galleys and two thousand five hundred auxiliaries. Under the
pretence of distress they were admitted into the lesser port; a
gate was opened, and the Latin shout of " Long life and victory
to the emperor John Palæologus! " was answered by a general
rising in his favour. A numerous and loyal party yet adhered
to the standard of Cantacuzene; but he asserts in his history
(does he hope for belief?) that his tender conscience rejected
the assurance of conquest; that, in free obedience to the voice
of religion and philosophy, he descended from the throne, and
embraced with pleasure the monastic habit and profession.[1]
So soon as he ceased to be a prince, his successor was not unwilling that he should be a saint; the remainder of his life was
devoted to piety and learning; in the cells of Constantinople
and Mount Athos the monk Joasaph was respected as the

[1] The awkward apology of Cantacuzene (l. iv. c. 39-42), who relates, with
visible confusion, his own downfall, may be supplied by the less accurate,
but more honest, narratives of Matthew Villani (l. iv. c. 46, in the Script.
Rerum Ital. tom. xiv. p. 268) and Ducas (c. 10, 11).

temporal and spiritual father of the emperor; and if he issued
from his retreat, it was as the minister of peace, to subdue the
obstinacy and solicit the pardon of his rebellious son.[1]

Yet in the cloister the mind of Cantacuzene was still exercised
by theological war. He sharpened a controversial pen against
the Jews and Mohammedans;[2] and in every state he defended
with equal zeal the divine light of Mount Thabor, a memorable
question which consummates the religious follies of the Greeks.
The fakirs of India[3] and the monks of the Oriental church were
alike persuaded that, in total abstraction of the faculties of the
mind and body, the purer spirit may ascend to the enjoyment
and vision of the Deity. The opinion and practice of the
monasteries of Mount Athos[4] will be best represented in the
words of an abbot who flourished in the eleventh century.
"When thou art alone in thy cell," says the ascetic teacher, "shut
thy door, and seat thyself in a corner: raise thy mind above all
things vain and transitory; recline thy beard and chin on thy
breast; turn thy eyes and thy thought towards the middle of thy
belly, the region of the navel; and search the place of the heart,
the seat of the soul. At first all will be dark and comfortless;
but if you persevere day and night, you will feel an ineffable joy;
and no sooner has the soul discovered the place of the heart, than
it is involved in a mystic and etherial light." This light, the
production of a distempered fancy, the creature of an empty
stomach and an empty brain, was adored by the Quietists as the
pure and perfect essence of God himself; and as long as the folly
was confined to Mount Athos, the simple solitaries were not
inquisitive how the divine essence could be a *material* substance,
or how an *immaterial* substance could be perceived by the eyes
of the body. But in the reign of the younger Andronicus these

[1] Cantacuzene, in the year 1375, was honoured with a letter from the
pope (Fleury, Hist. Ecclés. tom. xx. p. 250). His death is placed by a
respectable authority on the 20th of November, 1411 (Ducange, Fam.
Byzant. p. 260). But if he were of the age of his companion Andronicus
the Younger, he must have lived 116 years—a rare instance of longevity,
which in so illustrious a person would have attracted universal notice.

[2] His four discourses, or books, were printed at Basil 1543 (Fabric.
Biblioth. Græc. tom. vi. p. 473). He composed them to satisfy a proselyte
who was assaulted with letters from his friends of Ispahan. Cantacuzene
had read the Koran; but I understand from Maracci that he adopts the
vulgar prejudices and fables against Mohammed and his religion.

[3] See the Voyages de Bernier, tom. i. p. 127.

[4] Mosheim, Institut. Hist. Eccles. p. 522, 523; Fleury, Hist. Ecclés.
tom. xx. p. 22, 24, 107-114, etc. The former unfolds the causes with the
judgment of a philosopher, the latter transcribes and translates with the
prejudices of a Catholic priest.

monasteries were visited by Barlaam,[1] a Calabrian monk, who was
equally skilled in philosophy and theology, who possessed the
languages of the Greeks and Latins, and whose versatile genius
could maintain their opposite creeds, according to the interest
of the moment. The indiscretion of an ascetic revealed to the
curious traveller the secrets of mental prayer; and Barlaam
embraced the opportunity of ridiculing the Quietists, who placed
the soul in the navel; of accusing the monks of Mount Athos of
heresy and blasphemy. His attack compelled the more learned
to renounce or dissemble the simple devotion of their brethren,
and Gregory Palamas introduced a scholastic distinction between
the essence and operation of God. His inaccessible essence
dwells in the midst of an uncreated and eternal light; and this
beatific vision of the saints had been manifested to the disciples
on Mount Thabor in the transfiguration of Christ. Yet this
distinction could not escape the reproach of polytheism; the
eternity of the light of Thabor was fiercely denied, and Barlaam
still charged the Palamites with holding two eternal substances,
a visible and an invisible God. From the rage of the monks of
Mount Athos, who threatened his life, the Calabrian retired to
Constantinople, where his smooth and specious manners introduced him to the favour of the great domestic and the emperor.
The court and the city were involved in this theological dispute,
which flamed amidst the civil war; but the doctrine of Barlaam was disgraced by his flight and apostacy; the Palamites
triumphed; and their adversary, the patriarch John of Apri,
was deposed by the consent of the adverse factions of the state.
In the character of emperor and theologian, Cantacuzene
presided in the synod of the Greek church, which established, as
an article of faith, the uncreated light of Mount Thabor: and,
after so many insults, the reason of mankind was slightly
wounded by the addition of a single absurdity. Many rolls of
paper or parchment have been blotted; and the impenitent
sectaries, who refused to subscribe the orthodox creed, were
deprived of the honours of Christian burial; but in the next age
the question was forgotten, nor can I learn that the axe or the
faggot were employed for the extirpation of the Barlaamite
heresy.[2]

[1] Basnage (in Canisii Antiq. Lectiones, tom. iv. p. 363-368) has investigated the character and story of Barlaam. The duplicity of his opinions
had inspired some doubts of the identity of his person. See likewise
Fabricius (Biblioth. Græc. tom. x. p. 427-432).

[2] See Cantacuzene (l. ii. c. 39, 40; l. iv. c. 3, 23, 24, 25) and Nic. Gregoras
(l. xi. c. 10; l. xv. 3, 7, etc.), whose last books, from the nineteenth to the

For the conclusion of this chapter I have reserved the Genoese
war, which shook the throne of Cantacuzene and betrayed the
debility of the Greek empire. The Genoese, who, after the
recovery of Constantinople, were seated in the suburb of Pera
or Galata, received that honourable fief from the bounty of the
emperor. They were indulged in the use of their laws and
magistrates, but they submitted to the duties of vassals and subjects; the forcible word of *liegemen* [1] was borrowed from the
Latin jurisprudence, and their *podestà*, or chief, before he entered
on his office, saluted the emperor with loyal acclamations and
vows of fidelity. Genoa sealed a firm alliance with the Greeks;
and, in the case of a defensive war, a supply of fifty empty galleys,
and a succour of fifty galleys completely armed and manned, was
promised by the republic to the empire. In the revival of a
naval force it was the aim of Michael Palæologus to deliver
himself from a foreign aid; and his vigorous government contained the Genoese of Galata within those limits which the
insolence of wealth and freedom provoked them to exceed. A
sailor threatened that they should soon be masters of Constantinople, and slew the Greek who resented this national affront;
and an armed vessel, after refusing to salute the palace, was
guilty of some acts of piracy in the Black Sea. Their countrymen threatened to support their cause: but the long and open
village of Galata was instantly surrounded by the Imperial
troops; till, in the moment of the assault, the prostrate Genoese
implored the clemency of their sovereign. The defenceless
situation which secured their obedience exposed them to the
attack of their Venetian rivals, who, in the reign of the elder
Andronicus, presumed to violate the majesty of the throne. On
the approach of their fleets, the Genoese, with their families and
effects, retired into the city; their empty habitations were
reduced to ashes; and the feeble prince, who had viewed the
destruction of his suburb, expressed his resentment, not by arms,
but by ambassadors. This misfortune, however, was advantageous to the Genoese, who obtained, and imperceptibly abused,
the dangerous licence of surrounding Galata with a strong wall,
of introducing into the ditch the waters of the sea, of erecting

twenty-fourth, are almost confined to a subject so interesting to the authors.
Boivin (in Vit. Nic. Gregoræ), from the unpublished books, and Fabricius
(Biblioth. Græc. tom. x. p. 462-473), or rather Montfaucon, from the MSS.
of the Coislin library, have added some facts and documents.

[1] Pachymer (l. v. c. 10 [tom. i. p. 366, ed. Bonn]) very properly explains
λυζίους (*ligios*) by ιδίους. The use of these words in the Greek and Latin
of the feudal times may be amply understood from the Glossaries of
Ducange (Græc. p. 811, 812; Latin. tom. iv. p. 109-111).

lofty turrets, and of mounting a train of military engines on the
rampart. The narrow bounds in which they had been circumscribed were insufficient for the growing colony; each day they
acquired some addition of landed property, and the adjacent
hills were covered with their villas and castles, which they joined
and protected by new fortifications.[1]   The navigation and trade
of the Euxine was the patrimony of the Greek emperors, who
commanded the narrow entrance, the gates, as it were, of that
inland sea. In the reign of Michael Palæologus their prerogative
was acknowledged by the sultan of Egypt, who solicited and
obtained the liberty of sending an annual ship for the purchase
of slaves in Circassia and the Lesser Tartary: a liberty pregnant
with mischief to the Christian cause, since these youths were
transformed by education and discipline into the formidable
Mamalukes.[2]   From the colony of Pera the Genoese engaged
with superior advantage in the lucrative trade of the Black Sea,
and their industry supplied the Greeks with fish and corn, two
articles of food almost equally important to a superstitious people.
The spontaneous bounty of nature appears to have bestowed the
harvests of the Ukraine, the produce of a rude and savage
husbandry; and the endless exportation of salt-fish and caviar is
annually renewed by the enormous sturgeons that are caught at
the mouth of the Don or Tanais, in their last station of the rich
mud and shallow water of the Mæotis.[3]   The waters of the Oxus,
the Caspian, the Volga, and the Don opened a rare and laborious
passage for the gems and spices of India; and after three months'
march the caravans of Carizme met the Italian vessels in the
harbours of Crimea.[4]   These various branches of trade were
monopolised by the diligence and power of the Genoese.   Their

[1] The establishment and progress of the Genoese at Pera, or Galata, is
described by Ducange (C. P. Christiana, l. i. p. 68, 69) from the Byzantine
historians, Pachymer (l. ii. c. 35; l. v. 10, 30; l. ix. 15; l. xii. 6, 9), Nicephorus Gregoras (l. v. c. 4; l. vi. c. 11; l. ix. c. 5; l. xi. c. 1; l. xv. c. 1, 6),
and Cantacuzene (l. i. c. 12; l. ii. c. 29, etc.).

[2] Both Pachymer (l. iii. c. 3, ., 5) and Nic. Greg. (l. iv. c. 7) understand
and deplore the effects of this dangerous indulgence.   Bibars, sultan of
Egypt, himself a Tartar, but a devout Musulman, obtained from the
children of Zingis the permission to build a stately mosque in the capital
of Crimea (De Guignes, Hist. des Huns, tom. iii. p. 343).

[3] Chardin (Voyages en Perse, tom. i. p. 48) was assured at Caffa that
these fishes were sometimes twenty-four or twenty-six feet long, weighed
eight or nine hundred pounds, and yielded three or four quintals of caviar.
The corn of the Bosphorus had supplied the Athenians in the time of
Demosthenes.

[4] De Guignes, Hist. des Huns, tom. iii. p. 343, 344; Viaggi di Ramusiol
tom. i. fol. 400.   But this land or water carriage could only be practicable
when Tartary was united under a wise and powerful monarch.

rivals of Venice and Pisa were forcibly expelled; the natives were awed by the castles and cities which arose on the foundations of their humble factories; and their principal establishment of Caffa [1] was besieged without effect by the Tartar powers. Destitute of a navy, the Greeks were oppressed by these haughty merchants, who fed or famished Constantinople according to their interest. They proceeded to usurp the customs, the fishery, and even the toll, of the Bosphorus; and while they derived from these objects a revenue of two hundred thousand pieces of gold, a remnant of thirty thousand was reluctantly allowed to the emperor.[2] The colony of Pera or Galata acted, in peace and war, as an independent state; and, as it will happen in distant settlements, the Genoese podestà too often forgot that he was the servant of his own masters.

These usurpations were encouraged by the weakness of the elder Andronicus, and by the civil wars that afflicted his age and the minority of his grandson. The talents of Cantacuzene were employed to the ruin, rather than the restoration, of the empire; and after his domestic victory he was condemned to an ignominious trial, whether the Greeks or the Genoese should reign in Constantinople. The merchants of Pera were offended by his refusal of some contiguous lands, some commanding heights, which they proposed to cover with new fortifications; and in the absence of the emperor, who was detained at Demotica by sickness, they ventured to brave the debility of a female reign. A Byzantine vessel, which had presumed to fish at the mouth of the harbour, was sunk by these audacious strangers; the fishermen were murdered. Instead of suing for pardon, the Genoese demanded satisfaction; required, in a haughty strain, that the Greeks should renounce the exercise of navigation; and encountered with regular arms the first sallies of the popular indignation. They instantly occupied the debatable land; and by the labour of a whole people, of either sex and of every age, the wall was raised, and the ditch was sunk, with incredible speed. At the same time they attacked and burnt two Byzantine galleys; while the three others, the remainder of the Imperial navy, escaped from their hands: the habitations without the gates, or along the shore, were pillaged and destroyed; and the care of the regent, of the empress Irene, was confined to

---

[1] Nic. Gregoras (l. xiii. c. 12) is judicious and well-informed on the trade and colonies of the Black Sea. Chardin describes the present ruins of Caffa, where, in forty days, he saw above 400 sail employed in the corn and fish trade (Voyages en Perse, tom. i p. 46-48).

[2] See Nic. Gregoras, l. xvii. c. 1.

the preservation of the city. The return of Cantacuzene dispelled the public consternation: the emperor inclined to peaceful counsels; but he yielded to the obstinacy of his enemies, who rejected all reasonable terms, and to the ardour of his subjects, who threatened, in the style of Scripture, to break them in pieces like a potter's vessel. Yet they reluctantly paid the taxes that he imposed for the construction of ships, and the expenses of the war; and as the two nations were masters, the one of the land, the other of the sea, Constantinople and Pera were pressed by the evils of a mutual siege. The merchants of the colony, who had believed that a few days would terminate the war, already murmured at their losses: the succours from their mother-country were delayed by the factions of Genoa; and the most cautious embraced the opportunity of a Rhodian vessel to remove their families and effects from the scene of hostility. In the spring, the Byzantine fleet, seven galleys and a train of smaller vessels, issued from the mouth of the harbour, and steered in a single line along the shore of Pera; unskilfully presenting their sides to the beaks of the adverse squadron. The crews were composed of peasants and mechanics; nor was their ignorance compensated by the native courage of barbarians: the wind was strong, the waves were rough; and no sooner did the Greeks perceive a distant and inactive enemy, than they leaped headlong into the sea, from a doubtful, to an inevitable, peril. The troops that marched to the attack of the lines of Pera were struck at the same moment with a similar panic; and the Genoese were astonished, and almost ashamed, at their double victory. Their triumphant vessels, crowned with flowers, and dragging after them the captive galleys, repeatedly passed and repassed before the palace: the only virtue of the emperor was patience; and the hope of revenge his sole consolation. Yet the distress of both parties interposed a temporary agreement; and the shame of the empire was disguised by a thin veil of dignity and power. Summoning the chiefs of the colony, Cantacuzene affected to despise the trivial object of the debate; and, after a mild reproof, most liberally granted the lands, which had been previously resigned to the seeming custody of his officers.[1]

But the emperor was soon solicited to violate the treaty, and to join his arms with the Venetians, the perpetual enemies of

[1] The events of this war are related by Cantacuzene (l. iv. c. 11) with obscurity and confusion, and by Nic. Gregoras (l. xvii. c. 1-7) in a clear and honest narrative. The priest was less responsible than the prince for the defeat of the fleet.

Genoa and her colonies. While he compared the reasons of peace and war, his moderation was provoked by a wanton insult of the inhabitants of Pera, who discharged from their rampart a large stone that fell in the midst of Constantinople. On his just complaint, they coldly blamed the imprudence of their engineer; but the next day the insult was repeated; and they exulted in a second proof that the royal city was not beyond the reach of their artillery. Cantacuzene instantly signed his treaty with the Venetians; but the weight of the Roman empire was scarcely felt in the balance of these opulent and powerful republics.[1] From the straits of Gibraltar to the mouth of the Tanais, their fleets encountered each other with various success; and a memorable battle was fought in the narrow sea, under the walls of Constantinople. It would not be an easy task to reconcile the accounts of the Greeks, the Venetians, and the Genoese;[2] and while I depend on the narrative of an impartial historian,[3] I shall borrow from each nation the facts that redound to their own disgrace and the honour of their foes. The Venetians, with their allies the Catalans, had the advantage of number; and their fleet, with the poor addition of eight Byzantine galleys, amounted to seventy-five sail: the Genoese did not exceed sixty-four; but in those times their ships of war were distinguished by the superiority of their size and strength. The names and families of their naval commanders, Pisani and Doria, are illustrious in the annals of their country; but the personal merit of the former was eclipsed by the fame and abilities of his rival. They engaged in tempestuous weather; and the tumultuary conflict was continued from the dawn to the extinction of light. The enemies of the Genoese applaud their prowess; the friends of the Venetians are dissatisfied with their behaviour; but all parties agree in praising the skill and boldness of the Catalans, who, with many wounds, sustained the brunt of the action. On the separation of the fleets, the event might appear doubtful; but the thirteen Genoese galleys that had been sunk or taken were compensated by a double loss of the allies; of fourteen

[1] This second war is darkly told by Cantacuzene (l. iv. c. 18, 24, 25, 28-32), who wishes to disguise what he dares not deny. I regret this part of Nic. Gregoras, which is still in MS. at Paris.

[2] Muratori (Annali d'Italia, tom. xii. p. 144) refers to the most ancient Chronicles of Venice (Caresinus, the continuator of Andrew Dandulus, tom. xii. p. 421, 422) and Genoa (George Stella, Annales Genuenses, tom. xvii. p. 1091, 1092), both which I have diligently consulted in his great Collection of the Historians of Italy.

[3] See the Chronicle of Matteo Villani of Florence, l. ii. c. 59, 60, p. 145-147; c. 74, 75, p. 156, 157, in Muratori's Collection, tom. xiv.

Venetians, ten Catalans, and two Greeks; and even the grief of
the conquerors expressed the assurance and habit of more
decisive victories. Pisani confessed his defeat by retiring into a
fortified harbour, from whence, under the pretext of the orders
of the senate, he steered with a broken and flying squadron for
the isle of Candia, and abandoned to his rivals the sovereignty
of the sea. In a public epistle,[1] addressed to the doge and senate,
Petrarch employs his eloquence to reconcile the maritime powers,
the two luminaries of Italy. The orator celebrates the valour
and victory of the Genoese, the first of men in the exercise of
naval war: he drops a tear on the misfortunes of their Venetian
brethren; but he exhorts them to pursue with fire and sword the
base and perfidious Greeks; to purge the metropolis of the East
from the heresy with which it was infected. Deserted by their
friends, the Greeks were incapable of resistance; and three
months after the battle the emperor Cantacuzene solicited and
subscribed a treaty, which for ever banished the Venetians and
Catalans, and granted to the Genoese a monopoly of trade, and
almost a right of dominion. The Roman empire (I smile in
transcribing the name) might soon have sunk into a province of
Genoa, if the ambition of the republic had not been checked by
the ruin of her freedom and naval power. A long contest of
one hundred and thirty years was determined by the triumph
of Venice; and the factions of the Genoese compelled them to
seek for domestic peace under the protection of a foreign lord,
the duke of Milan, or the French king. Yet the spirit of commerce survived that of conquest; and the colony of Pera still
awed the capital and navigated the Euxine, till it was involved
by the Turks in the final servitude of Constantinople itself.

[1] The Abbé de Sade (Mémoires sur la Vie de Pétrarque, tom. iii. p. 257-
263) translates this letter, which he had copied from a MS. in the king of
France's library. Though a servant of the duke of Milan, Petrarch pours
forth his astonishment and grief at the defeat and despair of the Genoese
in the following year (p. 323-332).

CHAPTER LXIV

Conquests of Zingis Khan and the Moguls from China to Poland—Escape
of Constantinople and the Greeks—Origin of the Ottoman Turks in
Bithynia—Reigns and Victories of Othman, Orchan, Amurath the
First, and Bajazet the First—Foundation and Progress of the Turkish
Monarchy in Asia and Europe—Danger of Constantinople and the
Greek Empire

FROM the petty quarrels of a city and her suburbs, from the
cowardice and discord of the falling Greeks, I shall now ascend to
the victorious Turks; whose domestic slavery was ennobled by
martial discipline, religious enthusiasm, and the energy of the
national character. The rise and progress of the Ottomans, the
present sovereigns of Constantinople, are connected with the
most important scenes of modern history; but they are founded
on a previous knowledge of the great eruption of the Moguls and
Tartars, whose rapid conquests may be compared with the
primitive convulsions of nature, which have agitated and altered
the surface of the globe. I have long since asserted my claim
to introduce the nations, the immediate or remote authors of the
fall of the Roman empire; nor can I refuse myself to those events
which, from their uncommon magnitude, will interest a philosophic mind in the history of blood.[1]

From the spacious highlands between China, Siberia, and the
Caspian Sea the tide of emigration and war has repeatedly been
poured. These ancient seats of the Huns and Turks were
occupied in the twelfth century by many pastoral tribes, of the
same descent and similar manners, which were united and led
to conquest by the formidable Zingis. In his ascent to greatness
that barbarian (whose private appellation was Temugin) had
trampled on the necks of his equals. His birth was noble; but

---

[1] The reader is invited to review chapters xxii. to xxvi., and xxxiii. to
xxxviii., the manners of pastoral nations, the conquests of Attila and the
Huns, which were composed at a time when I entertained the wish, rather
than the hope, of concluding my history.
[In these volumes the names Moguls (or Mongols), Tartars, and Turks
are frequently used indiscriminately, but it may be well to affirm again
what has been stated again and again, that the Tartars (or Tatars) were
probably a Mongolian tribe which occupied so conspicuous a place in the
army of Zenghis Khan that their name was given to the whole race. The
Turks are one of the most numerous of the families of the world, and almost
all the nomad Asiatic tribes that devastated Europe from the fourth to the
twelfth centuries belonged to this race—the Huns, Chazars, Avars, Bulgarians, Petcheneges, and Comanians, were all Turks. The only Asiatic
invaders who were not so were the Hungarians, or the Magyars, and they
were a Finnish or Tschudish people.—O. S.]

it was in the pride of victory that the prince or people deduced his seventh ancestor from the immaculate conception of a virgin. His father had reigned over thirteen hordes, which composed about thirty or forty thousand families: above two-thirds refused to pay tithes or obedience to his infant son; and at the age of thirteen Temugin fought a battle against his rebellious subjects. The future conqueror of Asia was reduced to fly and to obey; but he rose superior to his fortune, and in his fortieth year he had established his fame and dominion over the circumjacent tribes. In a state of society in which policy is rude and valour is universal, the ascendant of one man must be founded on his power and resolution to punish his enemies and recompense his friends. His first military league was ratified by the simple rites of sacrificing a horse and tasting of a running stream: Temugin pledged himself to divide with his followers the sweets and the bitters of life; and when he had shared among them his horses and apparel, he was rich in their gratitude and his own hopes. After his first victory he placed seventy caldrons on the fire, and seventy of the most guilty rebels were cast headlong into the boiling water. The sphere of his attraction was continually enlarged by the ruin of the proud and the submission of the prudent; and the boldest chieftains might tremble when they beheld, enchased in silver, the skull of the khan of the Keraites;[1] who, under the name of Prester John, had corresponded with the Roman pontiff and the princes of Europe. The ambition of Temugin condescended to employ the arts of superstition; and it was from a naked prophet, who could ascend to heaven on a white horse, that he accepted the title of Zingis,[2] the *most great;* and a divine right to the conquest and dominion of the earth. In a general *couroultai*, or diet, he was seated on a felt, which was long afterwards revered as a relic, and solemnly

[1] The khans of the Keraites were most probably incapable of reading the pompous epistles composed in their name by the Nestorian missionaries, who endowed them with the fabulous wonders of an Indian kingdom. Perhaps these Tartars (the Presbyter or Priest John) had submitted to the rites of baptism and ordination (Asseman. Biblioth. Orient. tom. iii. p. ii. p. 487-503).
[The fact is now pretty definitely established that the Keraites were not a Mongol but a Turkish race, whose territory lay near the Upper Orchon, between the rivers Selinga and Kernlen. They were a Christian race, having been converted early in the eleventh century.—O. S.]
[2] Since the history and tragedy of Voltaire, *Gengis*, at least in French, seems to be the more fashionable spelling; but Abulghazi Khan must have known the true name of his ancestor. His etymology appears just: *Zin*, in the Mogul tongue, signifies *great*, and *gis* is the superlative termination (Hist. Généalogique des Tatars, part iii. p. 194, 195). From the same idea of magnitude the appellation of *Zingis* is bestowed on the ocean.

proclaimed great khan or emperor of the Moguls [1] and Tartars.[2] Of these kindred, though rival, names, the former had given birth to the imperial race, and the latter has been extended by accident or error over the spacious wilderness of the north.

The code of laws which Zingis dictated to his subjects was adapted to the preservation of domestic peace and the exercise of foreign hostility. The punishment of death was inflicted on the crimes of adultery, murder, perjury, and the capital thefts of a horse or ox; and the fiercest of men were mild and just in their intercourse with each other. The future election of the great khan was vested in the princes of his family and the heads of the tribes; and the regulations of the chase were essential to the pleasures and plenty of a Tartar camp. The victorious nation was held sacred from all servile labours, which were abandoned to slaves and strangers; and every labour was servile except the profession of arms. The service and discipline of the troops, who were armed with bows, scimitars, and iron maces, and divided by hundreds, thousands, and ten thousands, were the institutions of a veteran commander. Each officer and soldier was made responsible, under pain of death, for the safety and honour of his companions; and the spirit of conquest breathed in the law that peace should never be granted unless to a vanquished and suppliant enemy. But it is the religion of Zingis that best deserves our wonder and applause. The Catholic inquisitors of Europe, who defended nonsense by cruelty, might have been confounded by the example of a barbarian, who anticipated the lessons of philosophy,[3] and established by his laws a system of pure theism and perfect toleration. His first and only article of faith was the existence of one God, the

[1] The name of Moguls has prevailed among the Orientals, and still adheres to the titular sovereign, the Great Mogul of Hindostan.

[2] The Tartars (more properly Tatars) were descended from Tatar Khan, the brother of Mogul Khan (see Abulghazi, parts i. and ii.), and once formed a horde of 70,000 families on the borders of Kitay (p. 103-112). In the great invasion of Europe (A.D. 1238) they seem to have led the vanguard; and the similitude of the name of *Tartarei* recommended that of Tartars to the Latins (Matt. Paris, p. 398 [p. 546, ed. Lond. 1640], etc.).

[3] A singular conformity may be found between the religious laws of Zingis Khan and of Mr. Locke (Constitutions of Carolina, in his works, vol. iv. p. 535, 4to edition, 1777).
[Before his armies entered Tibet, Zenghis Khan sent an embassy to Bogdosott-nam-Dsimmo, a Lama high priest, with a letter to this effect: " I have chosen thee as high priest for myself and my empire. Repair then to me, and promote the present and future happiness of man. I will be thy supporter and protector. Let us establish a system of religion, and unite it with the monarchy." The high priest accepted the invitation, and Mongol historians term this epoch " The Period of the First Respect for Religion."—O. S.]

Author of all good, who fills by his presence the heavens and
earth, which he has created by his power. The Tartars and
Moguls were addicted to the idols of their peculiar tribes; and
many of them had been converted by the foreign missionaries to
the religions of Moses, of Mohammed, and of Christ. These
various systems in freedom and concord were taught and practised
within the precincts of the same camp; and the Bonze, the Imam,
the Rabbi, the Nestorian, and the Latin priest, enjoyed the same
honourable exemption from service and tribute: in the mosque
of Bochara the insolent victor might trample the Koran under
his horse's feet, but the calm legislator respected the prophets
and pontiffs of the most hostile sects. The reason of Zingis was
not informed by books: the khan could neither read nor write;
and, except the tribe of the Igours, the greatest part of the
Moguls and Tartars were as illiterate as their sovereign. The
memory of their exploits was preserved by tradition: sixty-
eight years after the death of Zingis these traditions were
collected and transcribed;[1] the brevity of their domestic annals
may be supplied by the Chinese,[2] Persians,[3] Armenians,[4]

[1] In the year 1294, by the command of Cazan, khan of Persia, the fourth
in descent from Zingis. From these traditions his vizir Fadlallah composed a Mogul history in the Persian language, which has been used by
Petit de la Croix (Hist. de Genghizcan, p. 537-539). The Histoire Généalogique des Tatars (à Leyde, 1726, in 12mo, 2 tomes) was translated by
the Swedish prisoners in Siberia from the Mogul MS. of Abulgasi Bahadur
Khan, a descendant of Zingis, who reigned over the Usbeks of Charasm, or
Carizme (A.D. 1644-1663). He is of most value and credit for the names,
pedigrees, and manners of his nation. Of his nine parts, the first descends
from Adam to Mogul Khan; the second, from Mogul to Zingis; the third
is the life of Zingis; the fourth, fifth, sixth, and seventh, the general
history of his four sons and their posterity; the eighth and ninth, the
particular history of the descendants of Sheibani Khan, who reigned in
Maurenahar and Charasm.

[The Igours (or more correctly Ouigours) were Turks, not Mongols. The
Ouigour minister of Zenghis, Tha-tha-toung-o, was said to be the instructor
of the Mongols in writing, of which they were ignorant previously. The
Ouigour alphabet or characters, therefore, cannot be placed earlier than
1204-1205, nor later than Khubilai.—O. S.]

[2] Histoire de Gentchiscan, et de toute la Dinastie des Mongous ses Suc-
cesseurs, Conquérans de la Chine; tirée de l'Histoire de la Chine par le
R. P. Gaubil, de la Société de Jésus, Missionaire à Peking; à Paris, 1739,
in 4to. This translation is stamped with the Chinese character of domestic
accuracy and foreign ignorance.

[3] See the Histoire du Grand Genghizcan, premier Empereur des Moguls et
Tartares, par M. Petit de la Croix, à Paris, 1710, in 12mo: a work of ten
years' labour, chiefly drawn from the Persian writers, among whom Nisavi,
the secretary of sultan Gelaleddin, has the merit and prejudices of a contemporary. A slight air of romance is the fault of the originals, or the
compiler. See likewise the articles of Genghizcan, Mohammed, Gelaleddin,
etc., in the Bibliothèque Orientale of D'Herbelot.

[4] Haithonus, or Aithonus, an Armenian prince, and afterwards a monk

Syrians,[1] Arabians,[2] Greeks,[3] Russians,[4] Poles,[5] Hungarians,[6] and Latins;[7] and each nation will deserve credit in the relation of their own disasters and defeats.[8]

The arms of Zingis and his lieutenants successively reduced the hordes of the desert, who pitched their tents between the wall of China and the Volga; and the Mogul emperor became the monarch of the pastoral world, the lord of many millions of shepherds and soldiers, who felt their united strength, and were impatient to rush on the mild and wealthy climates of the south. His ancestors had been the tributaries of the Chinese emperors;

of Premontré (Fabric. Biblioth. Lat. medii Ævi, tom. i. p. 34), dictated in the French language his book *de Tartaris*, his old fellow-soldiers. It was immediately translated into Latin, and is inserted in the Novus Orbis of Simon Grynæus (Basil, 1555, in folio).

[1] Zingis Khan, and his first successors, occupy the conclusion of the ninth Dynasty of Abulpharagius (vers. Pocock, Oxon. 1663, in 4to); and his tenth Dynasty is that of the Moguls of Persia. Assemannus (Biblioth. Orient. tom. ii.) has extracted some facts from his Syriac writings, and the lives of the Jacobite maphrians, or primates of the East.

[2] Among the Arabians, in language and religion, we may distinguish Abulfeda, sultan of Hamah in Syria, who fought in person, under the Mameluke standard, against the Moguls.

[3] Nicephorus Gregoras (l. ii. c. 5, 6) has felt the necessity of connecting the Scythian and Byzantine histories. He describes with truth and elegance the settlement and manners of the Moguls of Persia, but he is ignorant of their origin, and corrupts the names of Zingis and his sons.

[4] M. Levesque (Histoire de Russie, tom. ii.) has described the conquest of Russia by the Tartars, from the patriarch Nicon and the old chronicles.

[5] For Poland I am content with the Sarmatia Asiatica et Europæa of Matthew à Michou, or De Michoviâ, a canon and physician of Cracow (A.D. 1506), inserted in the Novus Orbis of Grynæus. Fabric. Biblioth. Latin. mediæ et infimæ Ætatis, tom. v. p. 56.

[6] I should quote Thuroczius, the oldest general historian (pars ii. c. 74, p. 150), in the first volume of the Scriptores Rerum Hungaricarum, did not the same volume contain the original narrative of a contemporary, an eye-witness, and a sufferer (M. Rogerii, Hungari, Varadiensis Capituli Canonici, Carmen miserabile, seu Historia super Destructione Regni Hungariæ Temporibus Belæ IV. Regis per Tartaros facta, p. 292-321); the best picture that I have ever seen of all the circumstances of a barbaric invasion.

[7] Matthew Paris has represented, from authentic documents, the danger and distress of Europe (consult the word *Tartari* in his copious Index). From motives of zeal and curiosity, the court of the great khan in the thirteenth century was visited by two friars, John de Plano Carpini, and William Rubruquis, and by Marco Polo, a Venetian gentleman. The Latin relations of the two former are inserted in the first volume of Hakluyt; the Italian original or version of the third (Fabric. Biblioth. Latin. medii Ævi, tom. ii. p. 198, tom. v. p. 25) may be found in the second tome of Ramusio.

[8] In his great History of the Huns M. de Guignes has most amply treated of Zingis Khan and his successors. See tom. iii. l. xv.-xix. and in the collateral articles of the Seljukians of Roum, tom. ii. l. xi.; the Carizmians, l. xiv.; and the Mamelukes, tom. iv. l. xxi.: consult likewise the tables of the first volume. He is ever learned and accurate; yet I am only indebted to him for a general view, and some passages of Abulfeda, which are still latent in the Arabic text.

and Temugin himself had been disgraced by a title of honour and servitude. The court of Pekin was astonished by an embassy from its former vassal, who, in the tone of the king of nations, exacted the tribute and obedience which he had paid, and who affected to treat the *son of heaven* as the most contemptible of mankind. A haughty answer disguised their secret apprehensions; and their fears were soon justified by the march of innumerable squadrons, who pierced on all sides the feeble rampart of the great wall. Ninety cities were stormed, or starved, by the Moguls; ten only escaped; and Zingis, from a knowledge of the filial piety of the Chinese, covered his vanguard with their captive parents; an unworthy, and by degrees a fruitless, abuse of the virtue of his enemies. His invasion was supported by the revolt of a hundred thousand Khitans, who guarded the frontier: yet he listened to a treaty; and a princess of China, three thousand horses, five hundred youths and as many virgins, and a tribute of gold and silk, were the price of his retreat. In his second expedition he compelled the Chinese emperor to retire beyond the Yellow River to a more southern residence. The siege of Pekin [1] was long and laborious: the inhabitants were reduced by famine to decimate and devour their fellow-citizens; when their ammunition was spent, they discharged ingots of gold and silver from their engines; but the Moguls introduced a mine to the centre of the capital; and the conflagration of the palace burnt above thirty days. China was desolated by Tartar war and domestic faction; and the five northern provinces were added to the empire of Zingis.

In the West he touched the dominions of Mohammed sultan of Carizme, who reigned from the Persian Gulf to the borders of India and Turkestan; and who, in the proud imitation of Alexander the Great, forgot the servitude and ingratitude of his fathers to the house of Seljuk. It was the wish of Zingis to establish a friendly and commercial intercourse with the most powerful of the Moslem princes; nor could he be tempted by the secret solicitations of the caliph of Bagdad, who sacrificed to his personal wrongs the safety of the church and state. A rash and inhuman deed provoked and justified the Tartar arms in the invasion of the southern Asia. A caravan of three ambassadors and one hundred and fifty merchants was arrested and murdered

[1] More properly *Yen-king*, an ancient city, whose ruins still appear some furlongs to the south-east of the modern *Pekin*, which was built by Cublai Khan (Gaubil, p. 146). Pe-king and Nan-king are vague titles, the courts of the north and of the south. The identity and change of names perplex the most skilful readers of the Chinese geography (p. 177).

at Otrar, by the command of Mohammed; nor was it till after a demand and denial of justice, till he had prayed and fasted three nights on a mountain, that the Mogul emperor appealed to the judgment of God and his sword. Our European battles, says a philosophic writer,[1] are petty skirmishes, if compared to the numbers that have fought and fallen in the fields of Asia. Seven hundred thousand Moguls and Tartars are said to have marched under the standard of Zingis and his four sons. In the vast plains that extend to the north of the Sihon or Jaxartes they were encountered by four hundred thousand soldiers of the sultan; and in the first battle, which was suspended by the night, one hundred and sixty thousand Carizmians were slain. Mohammed was astonished by the multitude and valour of his enemies; he withdrew from the scene of danger, and distributed his troops in the frontier towns; trusting that the barbarians, invincible in the field, would be repulsed by the length and difficulty of so many regular sieges. But the prudence of Zingis had formed a body of Chinese engineers, skilled in the mechanic arts; informed perhaps of the secret of gunpowder, and capable, under his discipline, of attacking a foreign country with more vigour and success than they had defended their own. The Persian historians will relate the sieges and reduction of Otrar, Cogende, Bochara, Samarcand, Carizme, Herat, Merou, Nisabour, Balch, and Candahar; and the conquest of the rich and populous countries of Transoxiana, Carizme, and Chorazan. The destructive hostilities of Attila and the Huns have long since been elucidated by the example of Zingis and the Moguls; and in this more proper place I shall be content to observe, that, from the Caspian to the Indus, they ruined a tract of many hundred miles, which was adorned with the habitations and labours of mankind, and that five centuries have not been sufficient to repair the ravages of four years. The Mogul emperor encouraged or indulged the fury of his troops: the hope of future possession was lost in the ardour of rapine and slaughter; and the cause of the war exasperated their native fierceness by the pretence of justice and revenge. The downfall and death of the sultan Mohammed, who expired, unpitied and alone, in a desert island of the Caspian Sea, is a poor atonement for the calamities of which he was the author. Could the Carizmian empire have been saved by a single hero, it would have been saved by his son Gelaleddin,

---

[1] M. de Voltaire, Essai sur l'Histoire Générale, tom. iii. c. 60, p. 8. His account of Zingis and the Moguls contains, as usual, much general sense and truth, with some particular errors.

whose active valour repeatedly checked the Moguls in the career of victory. Retreating, as he fought, to the banks of the Indus, he was oppressed by their innumerable host, till, in the last moment of despair, Gelaleddin spurred his horse into the waves, swam one of the broadest and most rapid rivers of Asia, and extorted the admiration and applause of Zingis himself. It was in this camp that the Mogul conqueror yielded with reluctance to the murmurs of his weary and wealthy troops, who sighed for the enjoyment of their native land. Incumbered with the spoils of Asia, he slowly measured back his footsteps, betrayed some pity for the misery of the vanquished, and declared his intention of rebuilding the cities which had been swept away by the tempest of his arms. After he had repassed the Oxus and Jaxartes he was joined by two generals whom he had detached with thirty thousand horse to subdue the western provinces of Persia. They had trampled on the nations which opposed their passage, penetrated through the gates of Derbend, traversed the Volga and the desert, and accomplished the circuit of the Caspian Sea, by an expedition which had never been attempted, and has never been repeated. The return of Zingis was signalised by the overthrow of the rebellious or independent kingdoms of Tartary; and he died in the fulness of years and glory, with his last breath exhorting and instructing his sons to achieve the conquest of the Chinese empire.

The harem of Zingis was composed of five hundred wives and concubines; and of his numerous progeny, four sons, illustrious by their birth and merit, exercised under their father the principal offices of peace and war. Toushi was his great huntsman, Zagatai [1] his judge, Octai his minister, and Tuli his general; and their names and actions are often conspicuous in the history of his conquests. Firmly united for their own and the public interest, the three brothers and their families were content with dependent sceptres; and Octai, by general consent, was proclaimed great khan, or emperor of the Moguls and Tartars. He was succeeded by his son Gayuk, after whose death the empire devolved to his cousins Mangou and Cublai, the sons of Tuli, and the grandsons of Zingis. In the sixty-eight years of his four first successors, the Mogul subdued almost all Asia and a large portion of Europe. Without confining myself to the order of

---

[1] Zagatai gave his name to his dominions of Maurenahar, or Transoxiana; and the Moguls of Hindostan, who emigrated from that country, are styled Zagatais by the Persians. This certain etymology, and the similar example of Uzbek, Nogai, etc., may warn us not absolutely to reject the derivations of a national, from a personal, name.

time, without expatiating on the detail of events, I shall present
a general picture of the progress of their arms; I. In the East;
II. In the South; III. In the West; and IV. In the North.

I. Before the invasion of Zingis, China was divided into two
empires or dynasties of the North and South; [1] and the difference
of origin and interest was smoothed by a general conformity of
laws, language, and national manners. The Northern empire,
which had been dismembered by Zingis, was finally subdued
seven years after his death. After the loss of Pekin, the
emperor had fixed his residence at Kaifong, a city many leagues
in circumference, and which contained, according to the Chinese
annals, fourteen hundred thousand families of inhabitants and
fugitives. He escaped from thence with only seven horsemen,
and made his last stand in a third capital, till at length the hopeless monarch, protesting his innocence and accusing his fortune,
ascended a funeral pile, and gave orders that, as soon as he had
stabbed himself, the fire should be kindled by his attendants.
The dynasty of the *Song*, the native and ancient sovereigns of
the whole empire, survived about forty-five years the fall of the
Northern usurpers; and the perfect conquest was reserved for
the arms of Cublai. During this interval the Moguls were often
diverted by foreign wars; and, if the Chinese seldom dared to
meet their victors in the field, their passive courage presented
an endless succession of cities to storm and of millions to slaughter.
In the attack and defence of places the engines of antiquity and
the Greek fire were alternately employed: the use of gunpowder
in cannon and bombs appears as a familiar practice; [2] and the
sieges were conducted by the Mohammedans and Franks, who had
been liberally invited into the service of Cublai. After passing

[1] In Marco Polo, and the Oriental geographers, the names of Cathay and
Mangi distinguish the northern and southern empires, which, from A.D.
1234 to 1279, were those of the great khan and of the Chinese. The search
of Cathay, after China had been found, excited and misled our navigators
of the sixteenth century in their attempts to discover the north-east
passage.

[2] I depend on the knowledge and fidelity of the Père Gaubil, who translates the Chinese text of the annals of the Moguls or Yuen (p. 71, 93, 153);
but I am ignorant at what time these annals were composed and published.
The two uncles of Marco Polo, who served as engineers at the siege of
Siengyangfou (l. ii. c. 61, in Ramusio, tom. ii.; see Gaubil, p. 155, 157),
must have felt and related the effects of this destructive powder; and
their silence is a weighty, and almost decisive, objection. I entertain a
suspicion that the recent discovery was carried from Europe to China by
the caravans of the fifteenth century, and falsely adopted as an old national
discovery before the arrival of the Portuguese and Jesuits in the sixteenth.
Yet the Père Gaubil affirms that the use of gunpowder has been known to
the Chinese above 1600 years.

the great river the troops and artillery were conveyed along a
series of canals, till they invested the royal residence of Hamcheu,
or Quinsay, in the country of silk, the most delicious climate
of China. The emperor, a defenceless youth, surrendered his
person and sceptre; and before he was sent in exile into Tartary
he struck nine times the ground with his forehead, to adore in
prayer or thanksgiving the mercy of the great khan. Yet the
war (it was now styled a rebellion) was still maintained in the
southern provinces from Hamcheu to Canton; and the obstinate
remnant of independence and hostility was transported from the
land to the sea. But when the fleet of the *Song* was surrounded
and oppressed by a superior armament, their last champion
leaped into the waves with his infant emperor in his arms. " It
is more glorious," he cried, " to die a prince than to live a slave."
A hundred thousand Chinese imitated his example; and the
whole empire, from Tonkin to the great wall, submitted to the
dominion of Cublai. His boundless ambition aspired to the
conquest of Japan: his fleet was twice shipwrecked; and the
lives of a hundred thousand Moguls and Chinese were sacrificed
in the fruitless expedition. But the circumjacent kingdoms,
Corea, Tonkin, Cochin-china, Pegu, Bengal, and Thibet, were
reduced in different degrees of tribute and obedience by the
effort or terror of his arms. He explored the Indian Ocean with a
fleet of a thousand ships: they sailed in sixty-eight days, most
probably to the isle of Borneo, under the equinoctial line; and
though they returned not without spoil or glory, the emperor
was dissatisfied that the savage king had escaped from their
hands.

II. The conquest of Hindostan by the Moguls was reserved in
a later period for the house of Timour; but that of Iran, or
Persia, was achieved by Holagou Khan, the grandson of Zingis,
the brother and lieutenant of the two successive emperors,
Mangou and Cublai. I shall not enumerate the crowd of sultans,
emirs, and atabeks whom he trampled into dust; but the extirpation of the *Assassins,* or Ismaelians [1] of Persia, may be considered as a service to mankind. Among the hills to the south of
the Caspian these odious sectaries had reigned with impunity
above a hundred and sixty years; and their prince, or imam,
established his lieutenant to lead and govern the colony of
Mount Libanus, so famous and formidable in the history of the

[1] All that can be known of the Assassins of Persia and Syria is poured
from the copious, and even profuse, erudition of M. Falconet, in two
Mémoires read before the Academy of Inscriptions (tom. xvii. p. 127-170).

crusades.[1] With the fanaticism of the Koran the Ismaelians had blended the Indian transmigration and the visions of their own prophets; and it was their first duty to devote their souls and bodies in blind obedience to the vicar of God. The daggers of his missionaries were felt both in the East and West: the Christians and the Moslems enumerate, and perhaps multiply, the illustrious victims that were sacrificed to the zeal, avarice, or resentment of *the old man* (as he was corruptly styled) *of the mountain*. But these daggers, his only arms, were broken by the sword of Holagou, and not a vestige is left of the enemies of mankind, except the word *assassin*, which, in the most odious sense, has been adopted in the languages of Europe. The extinction of the Abbassides cannot be indifferent to the spectators of their greatness and decline. Since the fall of their Seljukian tyrants the caliphs had recovered their lawful dominion of Bagdad and the Arabian Irak; but the city was distracted by theological factions, and the commander of the faithful was lost in a harem of seven hundred concubines. The invasion of the Moguls he encountered with feeble arms and haughty embassies. "On the divine decree," said the caliph Mostasem, " is founded the throne of the sons of Abbas: and their foes shall surely be destroyed in this world and in the next. Who is this Holagou that dares to rise against them? If he be desirous of peace, let him instantly depart from the sacred territory; and perhaps he may obtain from our clemency the pardon of his fault." This presumption was cherished by a perfidious vizir, who assured his master that, even if the barbarians had entered the city, the women and children from the terraces would be sufficient to overwhelm them with stones. But when Holagou touched the phantom, it instantly vanished into smoke. After a siege of two months Bagdad was stormed and sacked by the Moguls; and their savage commander pronounced the death of the caliph Mostasem, the last of the temporal successors of Mohammed; whose noble kinsmen, of the race of Abbas, had reigned in Asia above five hundred years. Whatever might be the designs of the conqueror, the holy cities of Mecca and Medina[2]

[1] The Ismaelians of Syria, 40,000 Assassins, had acquired or founded ten castles in the hills above Tortosa. About the year 1280 they were extirpated by the Mamalukes.

[2] As a proof of the ignorance of the Chinese in foreign transactions, I must observe that some of their historians extend the conquests of Zingis himself to Medina, the country of Mohammed (Gaubil, p. 42).

[Zenghis Khan did not carry on the military operations of his armies. He only approved of the suggestions made by his illustrious commanders, Sabutai and Samuka, who deserve to rank among the great generals of the world. He never interfered with them.—O. S.]

were protected by the Arabian desert; but the Moguls spread beyond the Tigris and Euphrates, pillaged Aleppo and Damascus, and threatened to join the Franks in the deliverance of Jerusalem. Egypt was lost had she been defended only by her feeble offspring; but the Mamalukes had breathed in their infancy the keenness of a Scythian air: equal in valour, superior in discipline, they met the Moguls in many a well-fought field; and drove back the stream of hostility to the eastward of the Euphrates. But it overflowed with resistless violence the kingdoms of Armenia and Anatolia, of which the former was possessed by the Christians and the latter by the Turks. The sultans of Iconium opposed some resistance to the Mogul arms till Azzadin sought a refuge among the Greeks of Constantinople, and his feeble successors, the last of the Seljukian dynasty, were finally extirpated by the khans of Persia.

III. No sooner had Octai subverted the northern empire of China than he resolved to visit with his arms the most remote countries of the West. Fifteen hundred thousand Moguls and Tartars were inscribed on the military roll: of these the great khan selected a third, which he intrusted to the command of his nephew Batou, the son of Tuli; who reigned over his father's conquests to the north of the Caspian Sea. After a festival of forty days Batou set forwards on this great expedition; and such was the speed and ardour of his innumerable squadrons, that in less than six years they had measured a line of ninety degrees of longitude, a fourth part of the circumference of the globe. The great rivers of Asia and Europe, the Volga and Kama, the Don and Borysthenes, the Vistula and Danube, they either swam with their horses or passed on the ice, or traversed in leathern boats, which followed the camp and transported their waggons and artillery. By the first victories of Batou the remains of national freedom were eradicated in the immense plains of Turkestan and Kipzak.[1] In his rapid progress he overran the kingdoms, as they are now styled, of Astracan and Cazan; and the troops which he detached towards Mount Caucasus explored the most secret recesses of Georgia and Circassia. The civil discord of the great dukes, or princes, of Russia betrayed their country to the Tartars. They spread from Livonia to the Black Sea, and both Moscow and Kiow, the modern and the ancient capitals, were reduced to ashes; a

[1] The *Dashté Kipzak*, or plain of Kipzak, extends on either side of the Volga, in a boundless space towards the Jaik and Borysthenes, and is supposed to contain the primitive name and nation of the Cosacks.

temporary ruin, less fatal than the deep, and perhaps indelible, mark which a servitude of two hundred years has imprinted on the character of the Russians. The Tartars ravaged with equal fury the countries which they hoped to possess and those which they were hastening to leave. From the permanent conquest of Russia they made a deadly, though transient, inroad into the heart of Poland, and as far as the borders of Germany. The cities of Lublin and Cracow were obliterated: they approached the shores of the Baltic; and in the battle of Lignitz they defeated the dukes of Silesia, the Polish palatines, and the great master of the Teutonic order, and filled nine sacks with the right ears of the slain. From Lignitz, the extreme point of their western march, they turned aside to the invasion of Hungary; and the presence or spirit of Batou inspired the host of five hundred thousand men: the Carpathian hills could not be long impervious to their divided columns; and their approach had been fondly disbelieved till it was irresistibly felt. The king, Bela the Fourth, assembled the military force of his counts and bishops; but he had alienated the nation by adopting a vagrant horde of forty thousand families of Comans, and these savage guests were provoked to revolt by the suspicion of treachery and the murder of their prince. The whole country north of the Danube was lost in a day and depopulated in a summer; and the ruins of cities and churches were overspread with the bones of the natives who expiated the sins of their Turkish ancestors. An ecclesiastic who fled from the sack of Waradin describes the calamities which he had seen or suffered; and the sanguinary rage of sieges and battles is far less atrocious than the treatment of the fugitives, who had been allured from the woods under a promise of peace and pardon, and who were coolly slaughtered as soon as they had performed the labours of the harvest and vintage. In the winter the Tartars passed the Danube on the ice and advanced to Gran or Strigonium, a German colony, and the metropolis of the kingdom. Thirty engines were planted against the walls; the ditches were filled with sacks of earth and dead bodies; and after a promiscuous massacre, three hundred noble matrons were slain in the presence of the khan. Of all the cities and fortresses of Hungary three alone survived the Tartar invasion, and the unfortunate Bela hid his head among the islands of the Adriatic.

The Latin world was darkened by this cloud of savage hostility: a Russian fugitive carried the alarm to Sweden; and the remote nations of the Baltic and the ocean trembled at the approach of the Tartars,[1] whom their fear and ignorance were inclined to separate from the human species. Since the invasion of the Arabs in the eighth century Europe had never been exposed to a similar calamity; and if the disciples of Mohammed would have oppressed her religion and liberty, it might be apprehended that the shepherds of Scythia would extinguish her cities, her arts, and all the institutions of civil society. The Roman pontiff attempted to appease and convert these invincible pagans by a mission of Franciscan and Dominican friars; but he was astonished by the reply of the khan, that the sons of God and of Zingis were invested with a divine power to subdue or extirpate the nations; and that the pope would be involved in the universal destruction, unless he visited in person and as a suppliant the royal horde. The emperor Frederic the Second embraced a more generous mode of defence; and his letters to the kings of France and England and the princes of Germany represented the common danger, and urged them to arm their vassals in this just and rational crusade.[2] The Tartars themselves were awed by the fame and valour of the Franks: the town of Neustadt in Austria was bravely defended against them by fifty knights and twenty cross-bows; and they raised the siege on the appearance of a German army. After wasting the adjacent kingdoms of Servia, Bosnia, and Bulgaria, Batou slowly retreated from the Danube to the Volga to enjoy the rewards of victory in the city and palace of Serai, which started at his command from the midst of the desert.

IV. Even the poor and frozen regions of the north attracted the arms of the Moguls: Sheibani khan, the brother of the great Batou, led a horde of fifteen thousand families into the wilds of Siberia; and his descendants reigned at Tobolskoi above three

[1] In the year 1238 the inhabitants of Gothia (*Sweden*) and Frise were prevented, by their fear of the Tartars, from sending, as usual, their ships to the herring-fishery on the coast of England; and, as there was no exportation, forty or fifty of these fish were sold for a shilling (Matthew Paris, p. 396). It is whimsical enough that the orders of a Mogul khan, who reigned on the borders of China, should have lowered the price of herrings in the English market.

[2] I shall copy his characteristic or flattering epithets of the different countries of Europe: Furens ac fervens ad arma Germania, strenuæ militiæ genitrix et alumna Francia, bellicosa et audax Hispania, virtuosa viris et classe munita fertilis Anglia, impetuosis bellatoribus referta Alemannia, navalis Dacia, indomita Italia, pacis ignara Burgundia, inquieta Apulia, cum maris Græci, Adriatici et Tyrrheni insulis pyraticis et invictis, Cretâ, Cypro, Siciliâ, cum Oceano conterminis insulis, et regionibus, cruenta Hybernia, cum agili Wallia, palustris Scotia, glacialis Norwegia, suam electam militiam sub vexillo Crucis destinabunt, etc. Matthew Paris, p. 498.)

centuries till the Russian conquest. The spirit of enterprise which pursued the course of the Oby and Yenisei must have led to the discovery of the Icy Sea. After brushing away the monstrous fables of men with dogs' heads and cloven feet, we shall find that, fifteen years after the death of Zingis, the Moguls were informed of the name and manners of the Samoyedes in the neighbourhood of the polar circle, who dwelt in subterraneous huts and derived their furs and their food from the sole occupation of hunting.[1]

While China, Syria, and Poland were invaded at the same time by the Moguls and Tartars, the authors of the mighty mischief were content with the knowledge and declaration that their word was the sword of death. Like the first caliphs, the first successors of Zingis seldom appeared in person at the head of their victorious armies. On the banks of the Onon and Selinga the royal or *golden horde* exhibited the contrast of simplicity and greatness; of the roasted sheep and mare's milk which composed their banquets; and of a distribution in one day of five hundred waggons of gold and silver. The ambassadors and princes of Europe and Asia were compelled to undertake this distant and laborious pilgrimage; and the life and reign of the great dukes of Russia, the kings of Georgia and Armenia, the sultans of Iconium, and the emirs of Persia, were decided by the frown or smile of the great khan. The sons and grandsons of Zingis had been accustomed to the pastoral life; but the village of Caracorum [2] was gradually ennobled by their election and residence. A change of manners is implied in the removal of Octai and Mangou from a tent to a house; and their example was imitated by the princes of their family and the great officers of the empire. Instead of the boundless forest, the enclosure of a park afforded the more indolent pleasures of the chase; their new habitations were decorated with painting and sculpture; their superfluous treasures were cast in fountains, and basins, and statues of massy silver; and the artists of China and Paris vied with each other in the service of the great khan.[3] Caracorum contained two streets, the one of Chinese mechanics, the other of

[1] See Carpin's relation in Hakluyt, vol. i. p. 30. The pedigree of the khans of Siberia is given by Abulghazi (part viii. p. 485-495). Have the Russians found no Tartar chronicles at Tobolskoi?

[2] The Map of D'Anville and the Chinese Itineraries (De Guignes, tom. i. part ii. p. 57) seem to mark the position of Holin, or Caracorum, about six hundred miles to the north-west of Pekin. The distance between Selinginsky and Pekin is near 2000 Russian versts, between 1300 and 1400 English miles (Bell's Travels, vol. ii. p. 67).

[3] Rubruquis found at Caracorum his countryman *Guillaume Boucher*,

Mohammedan traders; and the places of religious worship, one
Nestorian church, two mosques, and twelve temples of various
idols, may represent in some degree the number and division of
inhabitants. Yet a French missionary declares that the town of
St. Denys, near Paris, was more considerable than the Tartar
capital; and that the whole palace of Mangou was scarcely equal
to a tenth part of that Benedictine abbey. The conquests of
Russia and Syria might amuse the vanity of the great khans;
but they were seated on the borders of China; the acquisition
of that empire was the nearest and most interesting object; and
they might learn from their pastoral economy that it is for the
advantage of the shepherd to protect and propagate his flock.
I have already celebrated the wisdom and virtue of a mandarin
who prevented the desolation of five populous and cultivated
provinces. In a spotless administration of thirty years this
friend of his country and of mankind continually laboured to
mitigate, or suspend, the havoc of war; to save the monuments,
and to rekindle the flame, of science; to restrain the military
commander by the restoration of civil magistrates; and to
instil the love of peace and justice into the minds of the Moguls.
He struggled with the barbarism of the first conquerors; but his
salutary lessons produced a rich harvest in the second generation.
The northern, and by degrees the southern, empire acquiesced in
the government of Cublai, the lieutenant, and afterwards the
successor, of Mangou; and the nation was loyal to a prince who
had been educated in the manners of China. He restored the
forms of her venerable constitution; and the victors submitted
to the laws, the fashions, and even the prejudices, of the vanquished people. This peaceful triumph, which has been more
than once repeated, may be ascribed, in a great measure, to the
numbers and servitude of the Chinese. The Mogul army was
dissolved in a vast and populous country; and their emperors
adopted with pleasure a political system which gives to the
prince the solid substance of despotism, and leaves to the subject the empty names of philosophy, freedom, and filial obedience.
Under the reign of Cublai, letters and commerce, peace and
justice, were restored; the great canal of five hundred miles was
opened from Nankin to the capital; he fixed his residence at
Pekin; and displayed in his court the magnificence of the greatest
monarch of Asia. Yet this learned prince declined from the

orfèvre de Paris, who had executed for the khan a silver tree, supported
by four lions, and ejecting four different liquors. Abulghazi (part iv.
p. 366) mentions the painters of Kitay or China.

pure and simple religion of his great ancestor: he sacrificed to
the idol Fo; and his blind attachment to the lamas of Thibet and
the bonzes of China [1] provoked the censure of the disciples of
Confucius. His successors polluted the palace with a crowd of
eunuchs, physicians, and astrologers, while thirteen millions of
their subjects were consumed in the provinces by famine. One
hundred and forty years after the death of Zingis, his degenerate
race, the dynasty of the Yuen, was expelled by a revolt of the
native Chinese; and the Mogul emperors were lost in the oblivion
of the desert. Before this revolution they had forfeited their
supremacy over the dependent branches of their house, the
khans of Kipzak and Russia, the khans of Zagatai or Transoxiana, and the khans of Iran or Persia. By their distance and
power these royal lieutenants had soon been released from the
duties of obedience; and after the death of Cublai they scorned
to accept a sceptre or a title from his unworthy successors.
According to their respective situation, they maintained the
simplicity of the pastoral life, or assumed the luxury of the cities
of Asia; but the princes and their hordes were alike disposed
for the reception of a foreign worship. After some hesitation
between the Gospel and the Koran, they conformed to the
religion of Mohammed; and while they adopted for their brethren
the Arabs and Persians, they renounced all intercourse with the
ancient Moguls, the idolaters of China.

In this shipwreck of nations some surprise may be excited by
the escape of the Roman empire, whose relics, at the time of the
Mogul invasion, were dismembered by the Greeks and Latins.
Less potent than Alexander, they were pressed, like the Macedonian, both in Europe and Asia, by the shepherds of Scythia;
and had the Tartars undertaken the siege, Constantinople must
have yielded to the fate of Pekin, Samarcand, and Bagdad. The
glorious and voluntary retreat of Batou from the Danube was
insulted by the vain triumph of the Franks and Greeks; [2] and in
a second expedition death surprised him in full march to attack
the capital of the Cæsars. His brother Borga carried the Tartar

---

[1] The attachment of the khans, and the hatred of the mandarins, to the
bonzes and lamas (Duhalde, Hist. de la Chine, tom. i. p. 502, 503) seems
to represent them as the priests of the same god, of the Indian *Fo*, whose
worship prevails among the sects of Hindostan, Siam, Thibet, China, and
Japan. But this mysterious subject is still lost in a cloud, which the re-
searches of our Asiatic Society may gradually dispel.

[2] Some repulse of the Moguls in Hungary (Matthew Paris, p. 545, 546)
might propagate and colour the report of the union and victory of the
kings of the Franks on the confines of Bulgaria. Abulpharagius (Dynast.
p. 310), after forty years beyond the Tigris, might be easily deceived.

arms into Bulgaria and Thrace; but he was diverted from the
Byzantine war by a visit to Novogorod, in the fifty-seventh
degree of latitude, where he numbered the inhabitants, and
regulated the tributes, of Russia.   The Mogul khan formed an
alliance with the Mamalukes against his brethren of Persia:
three hundred thousand horse penetrated through the gates of
Derbend, and the Greeks might rejoice in the first example of
domestic war.   After the recovery of Constantinople, Michael
Palæologus,[1] at a distance from his court and army, was surprised and surrounded in a Thracian castle by twenty thousand
Tartars.   But the object of their march was a private interest:
they came to the deliverance of Azzadin the Turkish sultan,
and were content with his person and the treasure of the emperor.
Their general Noga, whose name is perpetuated in the hordes of
Astracan, raised a formidable rebellion against Mengo Timour,
the third of the khans of Kipzak, obtained in marriage Maria the
natural daughter of Palæologus, and guarded the dominions of
his friend and father.   The subsequent invasions of a Scythian
cast were those of outlaws and fugitives; and some thousands
of Alani and Comans, who had been driven from their native
seats, were reclaimed from a vagrant life and enlisted in the
service of the empire.   Such was the influence in Europe of the
invasion of the Moguls.   The first terror of their arms secured
rather than disturbed the peace of the Roman Asia.   The sultan
of Iconium solicited a personal interview with John Vataces;
and his artful policy encouraged the Turks to defend their barrier
against the common enemy.[2]   That barrier indeed was soon
overthrown, and the servitude and ruin of the Seljukians exposed the nakedness of the Greeks.   The formidable Holagou
threatened to march to Constantinople at the head of four
hundred thousand men; and the groundless panic of the citizens
of Nice will present an image of the terror which he had inspired.
The accident of a procession, and the sound of a doleful litany,
" From the fury of the Tartars, good Lord, deliver us," had
scattered the hasty report of an assault and massacre.   In the
blind credulity of fear the streets of Nice were crowded with
thousands of both sexes, who knew not from what or to whom
they fled; and some hours elapsed before the firmness of the
military officers could relieve the city from this imaginary foe.
But the ambition of Holagou and his successors was fortunately

[1] See Pachymer, l. iii. c. 25, and l. ix. c. 26, 27; and the false alarm at
Nice, l. iii. c. 27 [c. 28, tom. i. p. 244, ed. Bonn]; Nicephorus Gregoras,
l. iv. c. 6.
[2] G. Acropolita, p. 36, 37; Nic. Greg. l. ii. c. 6, l. iv. c. 5.

diverted by the conquest of Bagdad and a long vicissitude of
Syrian wars; their hostility to the Moslems inclined them to
unite with the Greeks and Franks;[1] and their generosity or contempt had offered the kingdom of Anatolia as the reward of an
Armenian vassal. The fragments of the Seljukian monarchy
were disputed by the emirs who had occupied the cities or the
mountains; but they all confessed the supremacy of the khans
of Persia; and he often interposed his authority, and sometimes
his arms, to check their depredations, and to preserve the peace
and balance of his Turkish frontier. The death of Cazan,[2] one
of the greatest and most accomplished princes of the house of
Zingis, removed this salutary control; and the decline of the
Moguls gave a free scope to the rise and progress of the OTTO-
MAN EMPIRE.[3]

After the retreat of Zingis the sultan Gelaleddin of Carizme
had returned from India to the possession and defence of his
Persian kingdoms. In the peace of eleven years that hero
fought in person fourteen battles; and such was his activity
that he led his cavalry in seventeen days from Teflis to Kerman,
a march of a thousand miles. Yet he was oppressed by the
jealousy of the Moslem princes and the innumerable armies
of the Moguls; and after his last defeat Gelaleddin perished
ignobly in the mountains of Curdistan. His death dissolved a
veteran and adventurous army, which included under the name
of Carizmians or Corasmins many Turkman hordes that had
attached themselves to the sultan's fortune. The bolder and
more powerful chiefs invaded Syria, and violated the holy
sepulchre of Jerusalem: the more humble engaged in the service
of Aladin sultan of Iconium, and among these were the obscure
fathers of the Ottoman line. They had formerly pitched their
tents near the southern banks of the Oxus, in the plains of
Mahan and Nesa; and it is somewhat remarkable that the same
spot should have produced the first authors of the Parthian and

---

[1] Abulpharagius, who wrote in the year 1284, declares that the Moguls,
since the fabulous defeat of Batou, had not attacked either the Franks or
Greeks; and of this he is a competent witness. Hayton likewise, the
Armeniac prince, celebrates their friendship for himself and his nation.

[2] Pachymer gives a splendid character of Cazan Khan, the rival of Cyrus
and Alexander (l. xii. c. 1). In the conclusion of his history (l. xiii. c. 36
[tom. ii. p. 651, ed. Bonn]), he *hopes* much from the arrival of 30,000
Tochars, or Tartars, who were ordered by the successor of Cazan to restrain
the Turks of Bithynia, A.D. 1308.

[3] The origin of the Ottoman dynasty is illustrated by the critical learning of MM. de Guignes (Hist. des Huns, tom. iv. p. 329-337) and D'Anville
(Empire Turc, p. 14-22), two inhabitants of Paris, from whom the Orientals
may learn the history and geography of their own country.

Turkish empires. At the head, or in the rear, of a Carizmian
army, Soliman Shah was drowned in the passage of the Euphrates:
his son Orthogrul became the soldier and subject of Aladin, and
established at Surgut, on the banks of the Sangar, a camp of
four hundred families or tents, whom he governed fifty-two
years both in peace and war. He was the father of Thaman, or
Athman, whose Turkish name has been melted into the appellation of the caliph Othman:[1] and if we describe that pastoral
chief as a shepherd and a robber, we must separate from those
characters all idea of ignominy and baseness. Othman possessed, and perhaps surpassed, the ordinary virtues of a soldier;
and the circumstances of time and place were propitious to his
independence and success. The Seljukian dynasty was no more,
and the distance and decline of the Mogul khans soon enfranchised him from the control of a superior. He was situate on
the verge of the Greek empire: the Koran sanctified his *gazi*,
or holy war, against the infidels; and their political errors
unlocked the passes of Mount Olympus, and invited him to
descend into the plains of Bithynia. Till the reign of Palæologus these passes had been vigilantly guarded by the militia of
the country, who were repaid by their own safety and an exemption from taxes. The emperor abolished their privilege and
assumed their office; but the tribute was rigorously collected,
the custody of the passes was neglected, and the hardy moun-
taineers degenerated into a trembling crowd of peasants without
spirit or discipline. It was on the twenty-seventh of July, in
the year twelve hundred and ninety-nine of the Christian era,
that Othman first invaded the territory of Nicomedia;[2] and the
singular accuracy of the date seems to disclose some foresight of
the rapid and destructive growth of the monster. The annals
of the twenty-seven years of his reign would exhibit a repetition
of the same inroads; and his hereditary troops were multiplied in
each campaign by the accession of captives and volunteers.
Instead of retreating to the hills, he maintained the most useful
and defensible posts, fortified the towns and castles which he had
first pillaged, and renounced the pastoral life for the baths and
palaces of his infant capitals. But it was not till Othman was
oppressed by age and infirmities that he received the welcome

---

[1] [Osman is the real Turkish name, which has been corrupted into
Othman. The descendants of his subjects style themselves *Osmanlis*,
which has been corrupted into Ottoman.—O. S.]

[2] See Pachymer, l. x. c. 25, 26, l. xiii. c. 33, 34, 36, and concerning the
guard of the mountains, l. i. c. 3-6; Nicephorus Gregoras, l. vii. c. 1; and
the first book of Laonicus Chalcocondyles, the Athenian.

news of the conquest of Prusa, which had been surrendered by
famine or treachery to the arms of his son Orchan. The glory
of Othman is chiefly founded on that of his descendants; but the
Turks have transcribed or composed a royal testament of his
last counsels of justice and moderation.[1]

From the conquest of Prusa we may date the true era of the
Ottoman empire. The lives and possessions of the Christian
subjects were redeemed by a tribute or ransom of thirty thousand crowns of gold; and the city, by the labours of Orchan,
assumed the aspect of a Mohammedan capital; Prusa was
decorated with a mosque, a college, and an hospital, of royal
foundation; the Seljukian coin was changed for the name and
impression of the new dynasty; and the most skilful professors
of human and divine knowledge attracted the Persian and
Arabian students from the ancient schools of Oriental learning.
The office of vizir was instituted for Aladin, the brother of
Orchan; and a different habit distinguished the citizens from
the peasants, the Moslems from the infidels. All the troops of
Othman had consisted of loose squadrons of Turkman cavalry,
who served without pay and fought without discipline; but a
regular body of infantry was first established and trained by the
prudence of his son. A great number of volunteers was enrolled
with a small stipend, but with the permission of living at home,
unless they were summoned to the field: their rude manners and
seditious temper disposed Orchan to educate his young captives as
his soldiers and those of the prophet; but the Turkish peasants
were still allowed to mount on horseback and follow his standard,
with the appellation and the hopes of *freebooters*. By these arts
he formed an army of twenty-five thousand Moslems: a train of

[1] I am ignorant whether the Turks have any writers older than
Mohammed II., nor can I reach beyond a meagre chronicle (Annales
Turcici ad Annum 1550), translated by John Gaudier, and published by
Leunclavius (ad calcem Laonic. Chalcocond. p. 311-350), with copious
pandects, or commentaries. The History of the Growth and Decay (A.D.
1300-1683) of the Othman Empire was translated into English from the
Latin MS. of Demetrius Cantemir, prince of Moldavia (London, 1734, in
folio). The author is guilty of strange blunders in Oriental history; but
he was conversant with the language, the annals, and institutions of the
Turks. Cantemir partly draws his materials from the Synopsis of Saadi
Effendi of Larissa, dedicated in the year 1696 to sultan Mustapha, and a
valuable abridgment of the original historians. In one of the Ramblers
Dr. Johnson praises Knolles (A General History of the Turks to the
present Year: London, 1603) as the first of historians, unhappy only in
the choice of his subject. Yet I much doubt whether a partial and verbose
compilation from Latin writers, thirteen hundred folio pages of speeches
and battles, can either instruct or amuse an enlightened age, which requires
from the historian some tincture of philosophy and criticism.

battering engines was framed for the use of sieges; and the first successful experiment was made on the cities of Nice and Nicomedia. Orchan granted a safe-conduct to all who were desirous of departing with their families and effects; but the widows of the slain were given in marriage to the conquerors; and the sacrilegious plunder, the books, the vases, and the images, were sold or ransomed at Constantinople. The emperor Andronicus the Younger was vanquished and wounded by the son of Othman:[1] he subdued the whole province or kingdom of Bithynia as far as the shores of the Bosphorus and Hellespont; and the Christians confessed the justice and clemency of a reign which claimed the voluntary attachment of the Turks of Asia. Yet Orchan was content with the modest title of emir; and in the list of his compeers, the princes of Roum or Anatolia,[2] his military forces were surpassed by the emirs of Ghermian and Caramania, each of whom could bring into the field an army of forty thousand men. Their dominions were situate in the heart of the Seljukian kingdom: but the holy warriors, though of inferior note, who formed new principalities on the Greek empire, are more conspicuous in the light of history. The maritime country from the Propontis to the Mæander and the isle of Rhodes, so long threatened and so often pillaged, was finally lost about the thirtieth year of Andronicus the Elder.[3] Two Turkish chieftains, Sarukhan and Aidin, left their names to their conquests, and their conquests to their posterity. The captivity or ruin of the *seven* churches of Asia was consummated; and the barbarous lords of Ionia and Lydia still trample on the monuments of classic and Christian antiquity. In the loss of Ephesus the Christians deplored the fall of the first angel, the extinction of the first candlestick, of the Revelations;[4] the desolation is

---

[1] Cantacuzene, though he relates the battle and heroic flight of the younger Andronicus (l. ii. c. 6, 7, 8), dissembles by his silence the loss of Prusa, Nice, and Nicomedia, which are fairly confessed by Nicephorus Gregoras (l. viii. 15; ix. 9, 13; xi. 6). It appears that Nice was taken by Orchan in 1330, and Nicomedia in 1339, which are somewhat different from the Turkish dates.

[2] The partition of the Turkish emirs is extracted from two contemporaries, the Greek Nicephorus Gregoras (l. vii. 1) and the Arabian Marakeschi (De Guignes, tom. ii. P. ii. p. 76, 77). See likewise the first book of Laonicus Chalcocondyles.

[3] Pachymer, l. xiii. c. 13.

[4] See the Travels of Wheeler and Spon, of Pococke and Chandler, and more particularly Smith's Survey of the Seven Churches of Asia, p. 205-276. The more pious antiquaries labour to reconcile the promises and threats of the author of the Revelations with the *present* state of the seven cities. Perhaps it would be more prudent to confine his predictions to the characters and events of his own times.

complete; and the temple of Diana or the church of Mary will equally elude the search of the curious traveller. The circus and three stately theatres of Laodicea are now peopled with wolves and foxes; Sardes is reduced to a miserable village; the God of Mohammed, without a rival or a son, is invoked in the mosques of Thyatira and Pergamus; and the populousness of Smyrna is supported by the foreign trade of the Franks and Armenians. Philadelphia alone has been saved by prophecy, or courage. At a distance from the sea, forgotten by the emperors, encompassed on all sides by the Turks, her valiant citizens defended their religion and freedom above fourscore years, and at length capitulated with the proudest of the Ottomans. Among the Greek colonies and churches of Asia, Philadelphia is still erect—a column in a scene of ruins—a pleasing example that the paths of honour and safety may sometimes be the same. The servitude of Rhodes was delayed above two centuries by the establishment of the knights of St. John of Jerusalem:[1] under the discipline of the order that island emerged into fame and opulence; the noble and warlike monks were renowned by land and sea; and the bulwark of Christendom provoked and repelled the arms of the Turks and Saracens.

The Greeks, by their intestine divisions, were the authors of their final ruin. During the civil wars of the elder and younger Andronicus, the son of Othman achieved, almost without resistance, the conquest of Bithynia; and the same disorders encouraged the Turkish emirs of Lydia and Ionia to build a fleet, and to pillage the adjacent islands and the sea-coast of Europe. In the defence of his life and honour, Cantacuzene was tempted to prevent, or imitate, his adversaries, by calling to his aid the public enemies of his religion and country. Amir, the son of Aidin, concealed under a Turkish garb the humanity and politeness of a Greek; he was united with the great domestic by mutual esteem and reciprocal services; and their friendship is compared, in the vain rhetoric of the times, to the perfect union of Orestes and Pylades.[2] On the report of the danger of his

[1] Consult the fourth book of the Histoire de l'Ordre de Malthe, par l'Abbé de Vertot. That pleasing writer betrays his ignorance in supposing that Othman, a freebooter of the Bithynian hills, could besiege Rhodes by sea and land.

[2] Nicephorus Gregoras has expatiated with pleasure on this amiable character (l. xii. 7; xiii. 4, 10; xiv. 1, 9; xvi. 6). Cantacuzene speaks with honour and esteem of his ally (l. iii. c. 56, 57, 63, 64, 66, 67, 68, 86, 89, 95, 96), but he seems ignorant of his own sentimental passion for the Turk, and indirectly denies the possibility of such unnatural friendship (l. iv. c. 40 [tom. iii. p. 297, ed. Bonn]).

friend, who was persecuted by an ungrateful court, the prince of Ionia assembled at Smyrna a fleet of three hundred vessels, with an army of twenty-nine thousand men; sailed in the depth of winter, and cast anchor at the mouth of the Hebrus. From thence, with a chosen band of two thousand Turks, he marched along the banks of the river, and rescued the empress, who was besieged in Demotica by the wild Bulgarians. At that disastrous moment the life or death of his beloved Cantacuzene was concealed by his flight into Servia; but the grateful Irene, impatient to behold her deliverer, invited him to enter the city, and accompanied her message with a present of rich apparel and a hundred horses. By a peculiar strain of delicacy, the gentle barbarian refused, in the absence of an unfortunate friend, to visit his wife, or to taste the luxuries of the palace; sustained in his tent the rigour of the winter; and rejected the hospitable gift, that he might share the hardships of two thousand companions, all as deserving as himself of that honour and distinction. Necessity and revenge might justify his predatory excursions by sea and land; he left nine thousand five hundred men for the guard of his fleet; and persevered in the fruitless search of Cantacuzene, till his embarkation was hastened by a fictitious letter, the severity of the season, the clamours of his independent troops, and the weight of his spoil and captives. In the prosecution of the civil war, the prince of Ionia twice returned to Europe, joined his arms with those of the emperor, besieged Thessalonica, and threatened Constantinople. Calumny might affix some reproach on his imperfect aid, his hasty departure, and a bribe of ten thousand crowns which he accepted from the Byzantine court; but his friend was satisfied; and the conduct of Amir is excused by the more sacred duty of defending against the Latins his hereditary dominions. The maritime power of the Turks had united the pope, the king of Cyprus, the republic of Venice, and the order of St. John, in a laudable crusade; their galleys invaded the coast of Ionia; and Amir was slain with an arrow, in the attempt to wrest from the Rhodian knights the citadel of Smyrna.[1] Before his death he generously recommended another ally of his own nation, not more sincere or zealous than himself, but more able to afford a prompt and powerful succour, by his situation along the Propontis and in the front of Constantinople. By the prospect of a more advantageous treaty, the Turkish

---

[1] After the conquest of Smyrna by the Latins, the defence of this fortress was imposed by Pope Gregory XI. on the knights of Rhodes (see Vertot, l. v.).

prince of Bithynia was detached from his engagements with Anne of Savoy; and the pride of Orchan dictated the most solemn protestations, that, if he could obtain the daughter of Cantacuzene, he would invariably fulfil the duties of a subject and a son. Parental tenderness was silenced by the voice of ambition: the Greek clergy connived at the marriage of a Christian princess with a sectary of Mohammed; and the father of Theodora describes, with shameful satisfaction, the dishonour of the purple.[1] A body of Turkish cavalry attended the ambassadors, who disembarked from thirty vessels, before his camp of Selymbria. A stately pavilion was erected, in which the empress Irene passed the night with her daughters. In the morning Theodora ascended a throne, which was surrounded with curtains of silk and gold: the troops were under arms; but the emperor alone was on horseback. At a signal the curtains were suddenly withdrawn, to disclose the bride, or the victim, encircled by kneeling eunuchs and hymeneal torches: the sound of flutes and trumpets proclaimed the joyful event; and her pretended happiness was the theme of the nuptial song, which was chanted by such poets as the age could produce. Without the rites of the church, Theodora was delivered to her barbarous lord: but it had been stipulated that she should preserve her religion in the harem of Bursa; and her father celebrates her charity and devotion in this ambiguous situation. After his peaceful establishment on the throne of Constantinople, the Greek emperor visited his Turkish ally, who, with four sons, by various wives, expected him at Scutari, on the Asiatic shore. The two princes partook, with seeming cordiality, of the pleasures of the banquet and the chase; and Theodora was permitted to repass the Bosphorus, and to enjoy some days in the society of her mother. But the friendship of Orchan was subservient to his religion and interest; and in the Genoese war he joined without a blush the enemies of Cantacuzene.

In the treaty with the empress Anne the Ottoman prince had inserted a singular condition, that it should be lawful for him to sell his prisoners at Constantinople, or transport them into Asia. A naked crowd of Christians of both sexes and every age,

---

[1] See Cantacuzenus, l. iii. c. 95 [tom. ii. p. 586, ed. Bonn]. Nicephorus Gregoras, who, for the light of Mount Thabor, brands the emperor with the names of tyrant and Herod, excuses, rather than blames, this Turkish marriage, and alleges the passion and power of Orchan. ἐγγύτατος, καὶ τῇ δυνάμει τοὺς κατ᾽ αὐτὸν ἤδη Περσικοὺς (*Turkish*) ὑπεραίρων Σατράπας (l. xv. 5). He afterwards celebrates his kingdom and armies. See his reign in Cantemir, p. 24-30.

of priests and monks, of matrons and virgins, was exposed in the
public market; the whip was frequently used to quicken the
charity of redemption; and the indigent Greeks deplored the
fate of their brethren, who were led away to the worst evils of
temporal and spiritual bondage.[1] Cantacuzene was reduced to
subscribe the same terms; and their execution must have been
still more pernicious to the empire: a body of ten thousand
Turks had been detached to the assistance of the empress Anne;
but the entire forces of Orchan were exerted in the service of his
father. Yet these calamities were of a transient nature; as soon
as the storm had passed away, the fugitives might return to their
habitations; and at the conclusion of the civil and foreign wars
Europe was completely evacuated by the Moslems of Asia. It
was in his last quarrel with his pupil that Cantacuzene inflicted
the deep and deadly wound which could never be healed by
his successors, and which is poorly expiated by his theological
dialogues against the prophet Mohammed. Ignorant of their
own history, the modern Turks confound their first and their
final passage of the Hellespont,[2] and describe the son of Orchan
as a nocturnal robber, who, with eighty companions, explores
by stratagem a hostile and unknown shore. Soliman, at the
head of ten thousand horse, was transported in the vessels, and
entertained as the friend, of the Greek emperor. In the civil
wars of Romania he performed some service and perpetrated
more mischief; but the Chersonesus was insensibly filled with a
Turkish colony; and the Byzantine court solicited in vain the
restitution of the fortresses of Thrace. After some artful delays
between the Ottoman prince and his son, their ransom was valued
at sixty thousand crowns, and the first payment had been made
when an earthquake shook the walls and cities of the provinces;
the dismantled places were occupied by the Turks; and Gallipoli,
the key of the Hellespont, was rebuilt and repeopled by the policy
of Soliman. The abdication of Cantacuzene dissolved the
feeble bands of domestic alliance; and his last advice admonished
his countrymen to decline a rash contest, and to compare their
own weakness with the numbers and valour, the discipline and

---

[1] The most lively and concise picture of this captivity may be found in
the history of Ducas (c. 8 [p. 32, ed. Bonn]), who fairly describes what
Cantacuzene confesses with a guilty blush!

[2] In this passage, and the first conquests in Europe, Cantemir (p. 27,
etc.) gives a miserable idea of his Turkish guides; nor am I much better
satisfied with Chalcocondyles (l. i. p. 12, etc. [ed. Par.; p. 25, ed.
Bonn]). They forget to consult the most authentic record, the fourth
book of Cantacuzene. I likewise regret the last books, which are still
manuscript, of Nicephorus Gregoras.

enthusiasm, of the Moslems. His prudent counsels were despised by the headstrong vanity of youth, and soon justified by the victories of the Ottomans. But as he practised in the field the exercise of the *jerid*, Soliman was killed by a fall from his horse; and the aged Orchan wept and expired on the tomb of his valiant son.

But the Greeks had not time to rejoice in the death of their enemies; and the Turkish scimitar was wielded with the same spirit by Amurath the First, the son of Orchan, and the brother of Soliman. By the pale and fainting light of the Byzantine annals [1] we can discern that he subdued without resistance the whole province of Romania or Thrace, from the Hellespont to Mount Hæmus and the verge of the capital; and that Adrianople was chosen for the royal seat of his government and religion in Europe. Constantinople, whose decline is almost coeval with her foundation, had often, in the lapse of a thousand years, been assaulted by the barbarians of the East and West; but never till this fatal hour had the Greeks been surrounded, both in Asia and Europe, by the arms of the same hostile monarchy. Yet the prudence or generosity of Amurath postponed for a while this easy conquest; and his pride was satisfied with the frequent and humble attendance of the emperor John Palæologus and his four sons, who followed at his summons the court and camp of the Ottoman prince. He marched against the Sclavonian nations between the Danube and the Adriatic, the Bulgarians, Servians, Bosnians, and Albanians; and these warlike tribes, who had so often insulted the majesty of the empire, were repeatedly broken by the destructive inroads. Their countries did not abound either in gold or silver; nor were their rustic hamlets and townships enriched by commerce or decorated by the arts of luxury. But the natives of the soil have been distinguished in every age by their hardiness of mind and body; and they were converted by a prudent institution into the firmest and most faithful supporters of the Ottoman greatness.[2] The vizir of Amurath reminded his sovereign that, according to the Mohammedan law, he was entitled to a fifth part of the spoil and captives; and that the duty might easily be levied, if vigilant officers were stationed at Gallipoli, to watch the passage, and to select for his use the stoutest and most beautiful of the Christian youth. The advice was followed: the edict was proclaimed;

After the conclusion of Cantacuzene and Gregoras there follows a dark interval of a hundred years. George Phranza, Michael Ducas, and Laonicus Chalcocondyles, all three wrote after the taking of Constantinople.

[2] See Cantemir, p. 37-41, with his own large and curious annotations.

many thousands of the European captives were educated in
religion and arms; and the new militia was consecrated and
named by a celebrated dervish. Standing in the front of their
ranks, he stretched the sleeve of his gown over the head of the
foremost soldier, and his blessing was delivered in these words:
" Let them be called Janizaries (*Yengi cheri*, or new soldiers);
may their countenance be ever bright! their hand victorious!
their sword keen! may their spear always hang over the heads
of their enemies; and wheresoever they go, may they return
with a *white face !* " [1] Such was the origin of these haughty
troops, the terror of the nations, and sometimes of the sultans
themselves. Their valour has declined, their discipline is relaxed,
and their tumultary array is incapable of contending with the
order and weapons of modern tactics; but at the time of their
institution they possessed a decisive superiority in war; since a
regular body of infantry, in constant exercise and pay, was not
maintained by any of the princes of Christendom. The Janizaries fought with the zeal of proselytes against their *idolatrous*
countrymen; and in the battle of Cossova the league and independence of the Sclavonian tribes was finally crushed. As the
conqueror walked over the field, he observed that the greatest
part of the slain consisted of beardless youths; and listened to
the flattering reply of his vizir, that age and wisdom would have
taught them not to oppose his irresistible arms. But the sword
of his Janizaries could not defend him from the dagger of despair;
a Servian soldier started from the crowd of dead bodies, and
Amurath was pierced to the belly with a mortal wound. The
grandson of Othman was mild in his temper, modest in his
apparel, and a lover of learning and virtue; but the Moslems
were scandalised at his absence from public worship; and he was
corrected by the firmness of the mufti, who dared to reject his
testimony in a civil cause; a mixture of servitude and freedom
not unfrequent in Oriental history.[2]

The character of Bajazet, the son and successor of Amurath,
is strongly expressed in his surname of *Ilderim*, or the lightning;
and he might glory in an epithet which was drawn from the fiery

---

[1] *White* and *black* face are common and proverbial expressions of praise
and reproach in the Turkish language. Hic *niger* est, hunc tu Romane
caveto, was likewise a Latin sentence.

[2] See the life and death of Morad, or Amurath I., in Cantemir (p. 33-45),
the first book of Chalcocondyles, and the Annales Turcici of Leunclavius.
According to another story, the sultan was stabbed by a Croat in his tent;
and this accident was alleged to Busbequius (Epist. i. p. 98) as an excuse
for the unworthy precaution of pinioning, as it were, between two attendants, an ambassador's arms, when he is introduced to the royal presence.

energy of his soul and the rapidity of his destructive march. In
the fourteen years of his reign [1] he incessantly moved at the head
of his armies, from Boursa to Adrianople, from the Danube to
the Euphrates; and, though he strenuously laboured for the
propagation of the law, he invaded, with impartial ambition, the
Christian and Mohammedan princes of Europe and Asia. From
Angora to Amasia and Erzeroum, the northern regions of
Anatolia were reduced to his obedience: he stripped of their
hereditary possessions his brother emirs of Ghermian and Caramania, of Aidin and Sarukhan; and after the conquest of Iconium
the ancient kingdom of the Seljukians again revived in the
Ottoman dynasty. Nor were the conquests of Bajazet less
rapid or important in Europe. No sooner had he imposed a
regular form of servitude on the Servians and Bulgarians than
he passed the Danube to seek new enemies and new subjects in
the heart of Moldavia. [2] Whatever yet adhered to the Greek
empire in Thrace, Macedonia, and Thessaly, acknowledged a
Turkish master: an obsequious bishop led him through the
gates of Thermopylæ into Greece; and we may observe, as a
singular fact, that the widow of a Spanish chief, who possessed
the ancient seat of the oracle of Delphi, deserved his favour by
the sacrifice of a beauteous daughter. The Turkish communication between Europe and Asia had been dangerous and doubtful,
till he stationed at Gallipoli a fleet of galleys, to command the
Hellespont and intercept the Latin succours of Constantinople.
While the monarch indulged his passions in a boundless range
of injustice and cruelty, he imposed on his soldiers the most rigid
laws of modesty and abstinence; and the harvest was peaceably
reaped and sold within the precincts of his camp. Provoked by
the loose and corrupt administration of justice, he collected in a
house the judges and lawyers of his dominions, who expected
that in a few moments the fire would be kindled to reduce them
to ashes. His ministers trembled in silence: but an Æthiopian
buffoon presumed to insinuate the true cause of the evil; and
future venality was left without excuse by annexing an adequate
salary to the office of cadhi. [3] The humble title of emir was no

[1] The reign of Bajazet I., or Ilderim Bayazid, is contained in Cantemir
(p. 46), the second book of Chalcocondyles, and the Annales Turcici. The
surname of Ilderim, or lightning, is an example that the conquerors and
poets of every age have *felt* the truth of a system which derives the sublime
from the principle of terror.

[2] Cantemir, who celebrates the victories of the great Stephen over the
Turks (p. 47), had composed the ancient and modern state of his principality of Moldavia, which has been long promised, and is still unpublished.

[3] Leunclav. Annal. Turcici, p. 318, 319. The venality of the cadhis has

longer suitable to the Ottoman greatness; and Bajazet condescended to accept a patent of sultan from the caliphs who served
in Egypt under the yoke of the Mamalukes:[1] a last and frivolous
homage that was yielded by force to opinion; by the Turkish conquerors to the house of Abbas and the successors of the Arabian
prophet.   The ambition of the sultan was inflamed by the
obligation of deserving this august title; and he turned his arms
against the kingdom of Hungary, the perpetual theatre of the
Turkish victories and defeats.   Sigismond, the Hungarian king,
was the son and brother of the emperors of the West: his cause
was that of Europe and the church; and, on the report of his
danger, the bravest knights of France and Germany were eager
to march under his standard and that of the cross.   In the battle
of Nicopolis Bajazet defeated a confederate army of a hundred
thousand Christians, who had proudly boasted that if the sky
should fall they could uphold it on their lances.   The far greater
part were slain or driven into the Danube; and Sigismond,
escaping to Constantinople by the river and the Black Sea,
returned after a long circuit to his exhausted kingdom.[2]   In the
pride of victory Bajazet threatened that he would besiege Buda;
that he would subdue the adjacent countries of Germany and
Italy; and that he would feed his horse with a bushel of oats on
the altar of St. Peter at Rome.   His progress was checked, not
by the miraculous interposition of the apostle, not by a crusade
of the Christian powers, but by a long and painful fit of the gout.
The disorders of the moral are sometimes corrected by those of
the physical world; and an acrimonious humour falling on a
single fibre of one man may prevent or suspend the misery of
nations.

Such is the general idea of the Hungarian war; but the
disastrous adventure of the French has procured us some
memorials which illustrate the victory and character of Bajazet.[3]

long been an object of scandal and satire; and, if we distrust the observations of our travellers, we may consult the feeling of the Turks themselves
(D'Herbelot, Biblioth. Orientale, p. 216, 217, 229, 230).
    [1] The fact, which is attested by the Arabic history of Ben Schounah,
a contemporary Syrian (De Guignes, Hist. des Huns, tom. iv. p. 336),
destroys the testimony of Saad Effendi and Cantemir (p. 14, 15), of the
election of Othman to the dignity of sultan.
    [2] See the Decades Rerum Hungaricarum (Dec. iii. l. ii. p. 379) of Bon-
finius, an Italian, who, in the fifteenth century, was invited into Hungary
to compose an eloquent history of that kingdom.   Yet, if it be extant and
accessible, I should give the preference to some homely chronicle of the
time and country.
    [3] I should not complain of the labour of this work, if my materials were
always derived from such books as the Chronicle of honest Froissard (vol.

The duke of Burgundy, sovereign of Flanders and uncle of
Charles the Sixth, yielded to the ardour of his son, John count
of Nevers; and the fearless youth was accompanied by four
princes, *his* cousins, and those of the French monarch. Their
inexperience was guided by the Sire de Coucy, one of the best
and oldest captains of Christendom; [1] but the constable, admiral,
and marshal of France [2] commanded an army which did not
exceed the number of a thousand knights and squires. These
splendid names were the source of presumption and the bane of
discipline. So many might aspire to command, that none were
willing to obey; their national spirit despised both their enemies
and their allies; and in the persuasion that Bajazet *would* fly,
or *must* fall, they began to compute how soon they should visit
Constantinople and deliver the holy sepulchre. When their
scouts announced the approach of the Turks, the gay and
thoughtless youths were at table, already heated with wine:
they instantly clasped their armour, mounted their horses, rode
full speed to the vanguard, and resented as an affront the advice
of Sigismond, which would have deprived them of the right and
honour of the foremost attack. The battle of Nicopolis would not
have been lost if the French would have obeyed the prudence
of the Hungarians: but it might have been gloriously won had
the Hungarians imitated the valour of the French. They dispersed the first line, consisting of the troops of Asia; forced a
rampart of stakes which had been planted against the cavalry;
broke, after a bloody conflict, the Janizaries themselves; and
were at length overwhelmed by the numerous squadrons that
issued from the woods and charged on all sides this handful of
intrepid warriors. In the speed and secrecy of his march, in the
order and evolutions of the battle, his enemies felt and admired
the military talents of Bajazet. They accuse his cruelty in the

iv. c. 67, 69, 72, 74, 79-83, 85, 87, 89), who read little, inquired much, and
believed all. The original Mémoires of the Maréchal de Boucicault (partie
i. c. 22-28) add some facts, but they are dry and deficient, if compared
with the pleasant garrulity of Froissard.

[1] An accurate Memoir on the Life of Enguerrand VII., Sire de Coucy,
has been given by the Baron de Zurlauben (Hist. de l'Académie des Inscriptions, tom. xxv.). His rank and possessions were equally considerable in France and England; and, in 1375, he led an army of adventurers
into Switzerland, to recover a large patrimony which he claimed in right
of his grandmother, the daughter of the emperor Albert I. of Austria
(Sinner, Voyage dans la Suisse Occidentale, tom. i. p. 118-124).

[2] That military office, so respectable at present, was still more conspicuous when it was divided between two persons (Daniel, Hist. de la
Milice Françoise, tom. ii. p. 5). One of these, the marshal of the crusade,
was the famous Boucicault, who afterwards defended Constantinople,
governed Genoa, invaded the coast of Asia, and died in the field of Azincour.

use of victory. After reserving the count of Nevers and four-and-twenty lords, whose birth and riches were attested by his Latin interpreters, the remainder of the French captives, who had survived the slaughter of the day, were led before his throne; and, as they refused to abjure their faith, were successively beheaded in his presence. The sultan was exasperated by the loss of his bravest Janizaries; and if it be true that, on the eve of the engagement, the French had massacred their Turkish prisoners,[1] they might impute to themselves the consequences of a just retaliation. A knight, whose life had been spared, was permitted to return to Paris, that he might relate the deplorable tale, and solicit the ransom of the noble captives. In the meanwhile the count of Nevers, with the princes and barons of France, were dragged along in the marches of the Turkish camp, exposed as a grateful trophy to the Moslems of Europe and Asia, and strictly confined at Boursa as often as Bajazet resided in his capital. The sultan was pressed each day to expiate with their blood the blood of his martyrs; but he had pronounced that they should live, and either for mercy or destruction his word was irrevocable. He was assured of their value and importance by the return of the messenger, and the gifts and intercessions of the kings of France and of Cyprus. Lusignan presented him with a gold saltcellar of curious workmanship, and of the price of ten thousand ducats; and Charles the Sixth despatched by the way of Hungary a cast of Norwegian hawks, and six horse-loads of scarlet cloth, of fine linen of Rheims, and of Arras tapestry, representing the battles of the great Alexander. After much delay, the effect of distance rather than of art, Bajazet agreed to accept a ransom of two hundred thousand ducats for the count of Nevers and the surviving princes and barons: the marshal Boucicault, a famous warrior, was of the number of the fortunate; but the admiral of France had been slain in the battle; and the constable, with the Sire de Coucy, died in the prison of Boursa. This heavy demand, which was doubled by incidental costs, fell chiefly on the duke of Burgundy, or rather on his Flemish subjects, who were bound by the feudal laws to contribute for the knighthood and captivity of the eldest son of their lord. For the faithful discharge of the debt some merchants of Genoa gave security to the amount of five times the sum; a lesson to those warlike times, that commerce and credit are the links of the society of nations. It had been stipulated in the treaty

[1] For this odious fact, the Abbé de Vertot quotes the Hist. Anonyme de St. Denys, l. xvi. c. 10, 11. (Ordre de Malthe, tom. ii. p. 310.)

that the French captives should swear never to bear arms against
the person of their conqueror; but the ungenerous restraint was
abolished by Bajazet himself. " I despise," said he to the heir
of Burgundy, " thy oaths and thy arms. Thou art young, and
mayest be ambitious of effacing the disgrace or misfortune of
thy first chivalry. Assemble thy powers, proclaim thy design,
and be assured that Bajazet will rejoice to meet thee a second
time in a field of battle." Before their departure they were
indulged in the freedom and hospitality of the court of Boursa.
The French princes admired the magnificence of the Ottoman,
whose hunting and hawking equipage was composed of seven
thousand huntsmen and seven thousand falconers.[1] In their
presence, and at his command, the belly of one of his chamberlains was cut open, on a complaint against him for drinking the
goat's milk of a poor woman. The strangers were astonished
by this act of justice; but it was the justice of a sultan who dis-
dains to balance the weight of evidence or to measure the degrees
of guilt.

After his enfranchisement from an oppressive guardian, John
Palæologus remained thirty-six years the helpless, and, as it
should seem, the careless, spectator of the public ruin.[2] Love,
or rather lust, was his only vigorous passion; and in the embraces
of the wives and virgins of the city the Turkish slave forgot
the dishonour of the emperor of the *Romans*. Andronicus, his
eldest son, had formed, at Adrianople, an intimate and guilty
friendship with Sauzes, the son of Amurath; and the two youths
conspired against the authority and lives of their parents.
The presence of Amurath in Europe soon discovered and dissipated their rash counsels; and, after depriving Sauzes of his
sight, the Ottoman threatened his vassal with the treatment of
an accomplice and an enemy unless he inflicted a similar punishment on his own son. Palæologus trembled and obeyed, and a
cruel precaution involved in the same sentence the childhood and
innocence of John the son of the criminal. But the operation

---

[1] Sherefeddin Ali (Hist. de Timour Bec, l. v. c. 13) allows Bajazet a
round number of 12,000 officers and servants of the chase. A part of his
spoils was afterwards displayed in a hunting-match of Timour:—1, hounds
with satin housings; 2, leopards with collars set with jewels; 3, Grecian
greyhounds; and 4, dogs from Europe, as strong as African lions (idem,
l. vi. c. 15). Bajazet was particularly fond of flying his hawks at cranes
(Chalcocondyles, l. ii. p. 35 [p. 67, ed. Bonn]).

[2] For the reigns of John Palæologus and his son Manuel, from 1354 to
1402, see Ducas, c. 9-15; Phranza, l. i. c. 16-21; and the first and second
books of Chalcocondyles, whose proper subject is drowned in a sea of
episode.

was so mildly or so unskilfully performed that the one retained the sight of an eye, and the other was afflicted only with the infirmity of squinting. Thus excluded from the succession, the two princes were confined in the tower of Anema; and the piety of Manuel, the second son of the reigning monarch, was rewarded with the gift of the Imperial crown. But at the end of two years the turbulence of the Latins and the levity of the Greeks produced a revolution, and the two emperors were buried in the tower from whence the two prisoners were exalted to the throne. Another period of two years afforded Palæologus and Manuel the means of escape; it was contrived by the magic or subtlety of a monk, who was alternately named the angel or the devil; they fled to Scutari; their adherents armed in their cause, and the two Byzantine factions displayed the ambition and animosity with which Cæsar and Pompey had disputed the empire of the world. The Roman world was now contracted to a corner of Thrace, between the Propontis and the Black Sea, about fifty miles in length and thirty in breadth: a space of ground not more extensive than the lesser principalities of Germany or Italy, if the remains of Constantinople had not still represented the wealth and populousness of a kingdom. To restore the public peace it was found necessary to divide this fragment of the empire; and while Palæologus and Manuel were left in possession of the capital, almost all that lay without the walls was ceded to the blind princes, who fixed their residence at Rhodosto and Selymbria. In the tranquil slumber of royalty the passions of John Palæologus survived his reason and his strength: he deprived his favourite and heir of a blooming princess of Trebizond; and while the feeble emperor laboured to consummate his nuptials, Manuel, with a hundred of the noblest Greeks, was sent on a peremptory summons to the Ottoman *Porte*. They served with honour in the wars of Bajazet; but a plan of fortifying Constantinople excited his jealousy; he threatened their lives; the new works were instantly demolished; and we shall bestow a praise, perhaps above the merit of Palæologus, if we impute this last humiliation as the cause of his death.

The earliest intelligence of that event was communicated to Manuel, who escaped with speed and secrecy from the palace of Boursa to the Byzantine throne. Bajazet affected a proud indifference at the loss of this valuable pledge; and while he pursued his conquests in Europe and Asia, he left the emperor to struggle with his blind cousin John of Selymbria, who, in eight years of civil war, asserted his right of primogeniture. At

307

length the ambition of the victorious sultan pointed to the conquest of Constantinople: but he listened to the advice of his vizir, who represented that such an enterprise might unite the powers of Christendom in a second and more formidable crusade. His epistle to the emperor was conceived in these words:—" By the divine clemency, our invincible scimitar has reduced to our obedience almost all Asia, with many and large countries in Europe, excepting only the city of Constantinople; for beyond the walls thou hast nothing left. Resign that city; stipulate thy reward; or tremble, for thyself and thy unhappy people, at the consequences of a rash refusal." But his ambassadors were instructed to soften their tone, and to propose a treaty, which was subscribed with submission and gratitude. A truce of ten years was purchased by an annual tribute of thirty thousand crowns of gold; the Greeks deplored the public toleration of the law of Mohammed; and Bajazet enjoyed the glory of establishing a Turkish cadhi, and founding a royal mosque, in the metropolis of the Eastern church.[1] Yet this truce was soon violated by the restless sultan; in the cause of the prince of Selymbria, the lawful emperor, an army of Ottomans again threatened Constantinople, and the distress of Manuel implored the protection of the king of France. His plaintive embassy obtained much pity and some relief, and the conduct of the succour was intrusted to the marshal Boucicault,[2] whose religious chivalry was inflamed by the desire of revenging his captivity on the infidels. He sailed, with four ships of war, from Aiguesmortes to the Hellespont; forced the passage, which was guarded by seventeen Turkish galleys; landed at Constantinople a supply of six hundred men-at-arms and sixteen hundred archers, and reviewed them in the adjacent plain without condescending to number or array the multitude of Greeks. By his presence the blockade was raised both by sea and land; the flying squadrons of Bajazet were driven to a more respectful distance; and several castles in Europe and Asia were stormed by the emperor and the marshal, who fought with equal valour by each other's side. But the Ottomans soon returned with an increase of numbers; and the intrepid Boucicault, after a year's struggle, resolved to evacuate a country which could no longer afford either pay or provisions for his soldiers. The marshal offered to conduct

[1] Cantemir, p. 50-53. Of the Greeks, Ducas alone (c. 13, 15) acknowledges the Turkish cadhi at Constantinople. Yet even Ducas dissembles the mosque.

[2] Mémoires du bon Messire Jean le Maingre, dit *Boucicault*, Maréchal de France, partie ire., c. 30-35.

Manuel to the French court, where he might solicit in person a supply of men and money; and advised, in the meanwhile, that, to extinguish all domestic discord, he should leave his blind competitor on the throne. The proposal was embraced: the prince of Selymbria was introduced to the capital; and such was the public misery that the lot of the exile seemed more fortunate than that of the sovereign. Instead of applauding the success of his vassal, the Turkish sultan claimed the city as his own; and, on the refusal of the emperor John, Constantinople was more closely pressed by the calamities of war and famine. Against such an enemy prayers and resistance were alike unavailing; and the savage would have devoured his prey if, in the fatal moment, he had not been overthrown by another savage stronger than himself. By the victory of Timour or Tamerlane the fall of Constantinople was delayed about fifty years; and this important though accidental service may justly introduce the life and character of the Mogul conqueror.

CHAPTER LXV

Elevation of Timour or Tamerlane to the Throne of Samarcand—His Conquests in Persia, Georgia, Tartary, Russia, India, Syria, and Anatolia—His Turkish War—Defeat and Captivity of Bajazet—Death of Timour—Civil War of the Sons of Bajazet—Restoration of the Turkish Monarchy by Mohammed the First—Siege of Constantinople by Amurath the Second

THE conquest and monarchy of the world was the first object of the ambition of TIMOUR. To live in the memory and esteem of future ages was the second wish of his magnanimous spirit. All the civil and military transactions of his reign were diligently recorded in the journals of his secretaries:[1] the authentic narrative was revised by the persons best informed of each particular transaction; and it is believed in the empire and family of Timour that the monarch himself composed the *com-*

---

[1] These journals were communicated to Sherefeddin, or Cherefeddin, Ali, a native of Yezd, who composed in the Persian language a history of Timour Beg, which has been translated into French by M. Petit de la Croix (Paris, 1722, in 4 vols. 12mo), and has always been my faithful guide. His geography and chronology are wonderfully accurate; and he may be trusted for public facts, though he servilely praises the virtue and fortune of the hero. Timour's attention to procure intelligence from his own and foreign countries may be seen in the Institutions, p. 215, 217, 349, 351.

mentaries [1] of his life and the *institutions* [2] of his government.[3] But these cares were ineffectual for the preservation of his fame, and these precious memorials in the Mogul or Persian language were concealed from the world, or, at least, from the knowledge of Europe. The nations which he vanquished exercised a base and impotent revenge; and ignorance has long repeated the tale of calumny [4] which had disfigured the birth and character, the person, and even the name, of *Tamerlane*.[5] Yet his real merit would be enhanced rather than debased by the elevation of a peasant to the throne of Asia; nor can his lameness be a theme of reproach, unless he had the weakness to blush at a natural, or perhaps an honourable, infirmity.

In the eyes of the Moguls, who held the indefeasible succession

[1] These Commentaries are yet unknown in Europe: but Mr. White gives some hope that they may be imported and translated by his friend Major Davy, who had read in the East this " minute and faithful narrative of an interesting and eventful period."

[2] I am ignorant whether the original institution, in the Turki or Mogul language, be still extant. The Persic version, with an English translation, and most valuable index, was published (Oxford, 1783, in 4to) by the joint labours of Major Davy and Mr. White the Arabic professor. This work has been since translated from the Persic into French (Paris, 1787) by M. Langlès, a learned Orientalist, who has added the Life of Timour and many curious notes.

[3] Shaw Allum, the present Mogul, reads, values, but cannot imitate, the institutions of his great ancestor. The English translator relies on their internal evidence; but if any suspicion should arise of fraud and fiction, they will not be dispelled by Major Davy's letter. The Orientals have never cultivated the art of criticism; the patronage of a prince, less honourable perhaps, is not less lucrative than that of a bookseller; nor can it be deemed incredible that a Persian, the *real* author, should renounce the credit, to raise the value and price, of the work.

[4] The original of the tale is found in the following work, which is much esteemed for its florid elegance of style: *Ahmedis Arabsiadæ* (Ahmed Ebn Arabshah) *Vitæ et Rerum Gestarum Timuri. Arabice et Latine. Edidit Samuel Henricus Manger. Franequeræ*, 1767, 2 tom. *in* 4to. This Syrian author is ever a malicious, and often an ignorant, enemy: the very titles of his chapters are injurious; as how the wicked, as how the impious, as how the viper, etc. The copious article of TIMUR, in Bibliothèque Orientale, is of a mixed nature, as D'Herbelot indifferently draws his materials (p. 877-888) from Khondemir, Ebn Schounah, and the Lebtarikh.

[5] *Demir* or *Timour* signifies, in the Turkish language, Iron; and *Beg* is the appellation of a lord or prince. By the change of a letter or accent it is changed into *Lenc* or Lame; and a European corruption confounds the two words in the name of Tamerlane.

[The extraordinary stories that were told about Timour did not even omit his birth. According to his Memoirs he was so called by a sheikh who, when visited by his mother on the day after the future conqueror's birth, was reading the verse of the Koran, " Are you sure that He who dwelleth in heaven will not cause the earth to swallow you up? and, behold, it shall shake, Tamarū." The sheikh then stopped and said, " We have named your son Timour." His lameness has been cited as matter for reproach. He was lamed by an arrow wound at the siege of the capital of Sistan when he was over-running the countries south of the Oxus.—O. S.]

of the house of Zingis, he was doubtless a rebel subject; yet he sprang from the noble tribe of Berlass: his fifth ancestor, Carashar Nevian, had been the vizir of Zagatai, in his new realm of Transoxiana; and in the ascent of some generations, the branch of Timour is confounded, at least by the females,[1] with the Imperial stem.[2] He was born forty miles to the south of Samarcand, in the village of Sebzar, in the fruitful territory of Cash, of which his fathers were the hereditary chiefs, as well as of a toman of ten thousand horse.[3] His birth[4] was cast on one of those periods of anarchy which announce the fall of the Asiatic dynasties, and open a new field to adventurous ambition. The khans of Zagatai were extinct; the emirs aspired to independence, and their domestic feuds could only be suspended by the conquest and tyranny of the khans of Kashgar, who, with an army of Getes or Calmucks,[5] invaded the Transoxian kingdom. From the twelfth year of his age Timour had entered the field of action; in the twenty-fifth he stood forth as the deliverer of his country, and the eyes and wishes of the people were turned towards a hero who suffered in their cause.[6] The chiefs of the law and of the

---

[1] After relating some false and foolish tales of Timour *Lenc*, Arabshah is compelled to speak truth, and to own him for a kinsman of Zingis, per mulieres (as he peevishly adds) laqueos Satanæ (pars i. c. i. p. 25). The testimony of Abulghazi Khan (P. ii. c. 5, P. v. c. 4) is clear, unquestionable, and decisive.

[2] According to one of the pedigrees, the fourth ancestor of Zingis, and the ninth of Timour, were brothers; and they agreed that the posterity of the elder should succeed to the dignity of khan, and that the descendants of the younger should fill the office of their minister and general. This tradition was at least convenient to justify the *first* steps of Timour's ambition (Institutions, p. 24, 25, from the MS. fragments of Timour's History).

[3] See the preface of Sherefeddin, and Abulfeda's Geography (Chorasmiæ, etc., Descriptio, p. 60, 61), in the third volume of Hudson's Minor Greek Geographers.

[4] See his nativity in Dr. Hyde (Syntagma Dissertat. tom. ii. p. 466) as it was cast by the astrologers of his grandson Ulugh Beg. He was born A.D. 1336, April 9, 11° 57′ P.M. lat. 36. I know not whether they can prove the great conjunction of the planets from whence, like other conquerors and prophets, Timour derived the surname of Saheb Keran, or master of the conjunctions (Biblioth. Orient. p. 878).

[5] In the Institutions of Timour, these subjects of the khan of Kashgar are most improperly styled Ouzbegs or Uzbeks, a name which belongs to another branch and country of Tartars (Abulghazi, P. v. c. 5; P. vii. c. 5). Could I be sure that this word is in the Turkish original, I would boldly pronounce that the Institutions were framed a century after the death of Timour, since the establishment of the Uzbeks in Transoxiana.

[6] [Timour was said to have been twenty-seven when he served in his first campaign under the emir Houssein, who ruled over Khorasan and Mawerainnehr. In the Memoirs written by himself, he says of himself, "At twelve, when but a boy, I fancied that I perceived in myself all the signs of greatness and of wisdom, and whoever came to visit me I used to

army had pledged their salvation to support him with their lives
and fortunes, but in the hour of danger they were silent and
afraid; and, after waiting seven days on the hills of Samarcand,
he retreated to the desert with only sixty horsemen. The fugitives were overtaken by a thousand Getes, whom he repulsed
with incredible slaughter; and his enemies were forced to
exclaim, "Timour is a wonderful man: fortune and the divine
favour are with him." But in this bloody action his own
followers were reduced to ten, a number which was soon
diminished by the desertion of three Carizmians. He wandered
in the desert with his wife, seven companions, and four horses;
and sixty-two days was he plunged in a loathsome dungeon, from
whence he escaped by his own courage and the remorse of the
oppressor.[1] After swimming the broad and rapid stream of the
Jihoon or Oxus, he led, during some months, the life of a vagrant
and outlaw on the borders of the adjacent states. But his fame
shone brighter in adversity; he learned to distinguish the friends
of his person, the associates of his fortune, and to apply the
various characters of men for their advantage, and, above all,
for his own. On his return to his native country Timour was
successively joined by the parties of his confederates, who
anxiously sought him in the desert; nor can I refuse to describe,
in his pathetic simplicity, one of their fortunate encounters. He
presented himself as a guide to three chiefs, who were at the
head of seventy horse. " When their eyes fell upon me," says
Timour, " they were overwhelmed with joy, and they alighted
from their horses, and they came and kneeled, and they kissed
my stirrup. I also came down from my horse, and took each
of them in my arms. And I put my turban on the head of the
first chief; and my girdle, rich in jewels and wrought with gold,
I bound on the loins of the second; and the third I clothed in
my own coat. And they wept, and I wept also; and the hour

receive with great hauteur and dignity." At seventeen he undertook the
management of the flocks and herds of the family. At nineteen he
became religious and left off playing chess, made a kind of Buddhist vow
never to injure living thing, and felt his foot paralysed from having accidentally trod upon an ant. At twenty thoughts of rebellion and of greatness rose in his mind; at twenty-one he appears to have performed his
first feat of arms, and he was a practised warrior when he served in his
twenty-seventh year under emir Houssein. He belonged to the Barlas
family, which in turn belonged to the famous Turkish sept, the Kurikan
Clan. He was therefore not a Mongol but a Turk.—O. S.]

[1] [After this imprisonment of sixty-two days in a loathsome dungeon,
he made a vow to God that though he might be obliged to kill some people
as a punishment or in self-defence, yet he would never keep any human
being in prison or in chains.—O. S.]

of prayer was arrived, and we prayed. And we mounted our horses, and came to my dwelling; and I collected my people, and made a feast." His trusty bands were soon increased by the bravest of the tribes; he led them against a superior foe, and, after some vicissitudes of war, the Getes were finally driven from the kingdom of Transoxiana. He had done much for his own glory; but much remained to be done, much art to be exerted, and some blood to be spilt, before he could teach his equals to obey him as their master. The birth and power of emir Houssein compelled him to accept a vicious and unworthy colleague, whose sister was the best beloved of his wives. Their union was short and jealous; but the policy of Timour, in their frequent quarrels, exposed his rival to the reproach of injustice and perfidy, and, after a final defeat, Houssein was slain by some sagacious friends, who presumed, for the last time, to disobey the commands of their lord. At the age of thirty-four,[1] and in a general diet or *couroultai*, he was invested with *Imperial* command; but he affected to revere the house of Zingis; and while the emir Timour reigned over Zagatai and the East, a nominal khan served as a private officer in the armies of his servant. A fertile kingdom, five hundred miles in length and in breadth, might have satisfied the ambition of a subject; but Timour aspired to the dominion of the world, and before his death the crown of Zagatai was one of the twenty-seven crowns which he had placed on his head. Without expatiating on the victories of thirty-five compaigns; without describing the lines of march which he repeatedly traced over the continent of Asia; I shall briefly represent his conquests in, I. Persia, II. Tartary, and III. India,[2] and from thence proceed to the more interesting narrative of his Ottoman war.

I. For every war a motive of safety or revenge, of honour or zeal, of right or convenience, may be readily found in the jurisprudence of conquerors. No sooner had Timour re-united to the patrimony of Zagatai the dependent countries of Carizme and Candahar, than he turned his eyes towards the kingdoms of Iran or Persia. From the Oxus to the Tigris that extensive country was left without a lawful sovereign since the death of

---

[1] The first book of Sherefeddin is employed on the private life of the hero; and he himself, or his secretary (Institutions, p. 3-77), enlarges with pleasure on the thirteen designs and enterprises which most truly constitute his *personal* merit. It even shines through the dark colouring of Arabshah (P. i. c. 1-12).

[2] The conquests of Persia, Tartary, and India are represented in the second and third books of Sherefeddin, and by Arabshah (c. 13-55). Consult the excellent Indexes to the Institutions.

Abousaid, the last of the descendants of the great Holacou. Peace and justice had been banished from the land above forty years, and the Mogul invader might seem to listen to the cries of an oppressed people. Their petty tyrants might have opposed him with confederate arms: they separately stood, and successively fell; and the difference of their fate was only marked by the promptitude of submission or the obstinacy of resistance. Ibrahim, prince of Shirwan or Albania, kissed the footstool of the Imperial throne. His peace-offerings of silks, horses, and jewels, were composed, according to the Tartar fashion, each article of nine pieces; but a critical spectator observed that there were only eight slaves. " I myself am the ninth," replied Ibrahim, who was prepared for the remark, and his flattery was rewarded by the smile of Timour.[1] Shah Mansour, prince of Fars, or the proper Persia, was one of the least powerful, but most dangerous, of his enemies. In a battle, under the walls of Shiraz, he broke, with three or four thousand soldiers, the *coul* or main-body of thirty thousand horse, where the emperor fought in person. No more than fourteen or fifteen guards remained near the standard of Timour; he stood firm as a rock, and received on his helmet two weighty strokes of a scimitar;[2] the Moguls rallied; the head of Mansour was thrown at his feet; and he declared his esteem of the valour of a foe by extirpating all the males of so intrepid a race. From Shiraz his troops advanced to the Persian Gulf, and the richness and weakness of Ormuz[3] were displayed in an annual tribute of six hundred thousand dinars of gold. Bagdad was no longer the city of peace, the seat of the caliphs; but the noblest conquest of Holacou could not be overlooked by his ambitious successor.

[1] The reverence of the Tartars for the mysterious number of *nine* is declared by Abulghazi Khan, who, for that reason, divides his Genealogical History into nine parts.

[2] According to Arabshah (P. i. c. 28, p. 183), the coward Timour ran away to his tent, and hid himself from the pursuit of Shah Mansour under the women's garments. Perhaps Sherefeddin (l. iii. c. 25) has magnified his courage.

[3] The history of Ormuz is not unlike that of Tyre. The old city, on the continent, was destroyed by the Tartars, and renewed in a neighbouring island without fresh water or vegetation. The kings of Ormuz, rich in the Indian trade and the pearl fishery, possessed large territories both in Persia and Arabia; but they were at first the tributaries of the sultans of Kerman, and at last were delivered (A.D. 1505) by the Portuguese tyrants from the tyranny of their own vizirs (Marco Polo, l. i. c. 15, 16, fol. 7, 8; Abulfeda, Geograph. tabul. xi. p. 261, 262; an original Chronicle of Ormuz, in Texeira, or Stevens' History of Persia, p. 376-416; and the Itineraries inserted in the first volume of Ramusio; of Ludovico Barthema, 1503, fol. 167; of Andrea Corsali, 1517, fol. 202, 203; and of Odoardo Barbessa, in 1516, fol. 315-318).

The whole course of the Tigris and Euphrates, from the mouth
to the sources of those rivers, was reduced to his obedience;
he entered Edessa; and the Turkmans of the black sheep
were chastised for the sacrilegious pillage of a caravan of Mecca.
In the mountains of Georgia the native Christians still braved
the law and the sword of Mohammed; by three expeditions he
obtained the merit of the *gazie*, or holy war; and the prince of
Teflis became his proselyte and friend.

II. A just retaliation might be urged for the invasion of
Turkestan, or the Eastern Tartary. The dignity of Timour
could not endure the impunity of the Getes: he passed the
Sihoon, subdued the kingdom of Kashgar, and marched seven
times into the heart of their country. His most distant camp
was two months' journey, or four hundred and eighty leagues,
to the north-east of Samarcand; and his emirs, who traversed
the river Irtish, engraved in the forests of Siberia a rude
memorial of their exploits. The conquest of Kipzak, or the
western Tartary,[1] was founded on the double motive of aiding
the distressed, and chastising the ungrateful. Toctamish, a
fugitive prince, was entertained and protected in his court: the
ambassadors of Auruss Khan were dismissed with a haughty
denial, and followed on the same day by the armies of Zagatai;
and their success established Toctamish in the Mogul empire of
the North. But, after a reign of ten years, the new khan forgot
the merits and the strength of his benefactor; the base usurper,
as he deemed him, of the sacred rights of the house of Zingis.
Through the gates of Derbend he entered Persia at the head of
ninety thousand horse: with the innumerable forces of Kipzak,
Bulgaria, Circassia, and Russia, he passed the Sihoon, burnt the
palaces of Timour, and compelled him, amidst the winter snows,
to contend for Samarcand and his life. After a mild expostula-
tion, and a glorious victory, the emperor resolved on revenge:
and by the east, and the west, of the Caspian, and the Volga, he
twice invaded Kipzak with such mighty powers, that thirteen
miles were measured from his right to his left wing. In a march
of five months they rarely beheld the footsteps of man: and their
daily subsistence was often trusted to the fortune of the chase.
At length the armies encountered each other; but the treachery
of the standard-bearer, who, in the heat of action, reversed the
Imperial standard of Kipzak determined the victory of the

---

[1] Arabshah had travelled into Kipzak, and acquired a singular knowledge of the geography, cities, and revolutions of that northern region
(P. i. c. 45-49).

Zagatais; and Toctamish (I speak the language of the Institutions) gave the tribe of Toushi to the wind of desolation.[1] He
fled to the Christian duke of Lithuania; again returned to the
banks of the Volga; and, after fifteen battles with a domestic
rival, at last perished in the wilds of Siberia. The pursuit of a
flying enemy carried Timour into the tributary provinces of
Russia: a duke of the reigning family was made prisoner amidst
the ruins of his capital; and Yeletz, by the pride and ignorance
of the Orientals, might easily be confounded with the genuine
metropolis of the nation. Moscow trembled at the approach of
the Tartar, and the resistance would have been feeble, since the
hopes of the Russians were placed in a miraculous image of the
Virgin, to whose protection they ascribed the casual and voluntary
retreat of the conqueror. Ambition and prudence recalled him
to the South, the desolate country was exhausted, and the Mogul
soldiers were enriched with an immense spoil of precious furs, of
linen of Antioch,[2] and of ingots of gold and silver.[3] On the
banks of the Don, or Tanais, he received a humble deputation
from the consuls and merchants of Egypt,[4] Venice, Genoa,
Catalonia, and Biscay, who occupied the commerce and city of
Tana, or Azoph, at the mouth of the river. They offered their
gifts, admired his magnificence, and trusted his royal word.
But the peaceful visit of an emir, who explored the state of the
magazines and harbour, was speedily followed by the destructive
presence of the Tartars. The city was reduced to ashes; the
Moslems were pillaged and dismissed; but all the Christians who
had not fled to their ships were condemned either to death or
slavery.[5] Revenge prompted him to burn the cities of Serai

[1] Institutions of Timour, p. 123, 125. Mr. White, the editor, bestows
some animadversion on the superficial account of Sherefeddin (l. iii. c. 12,
13, 14), who was ignorant of the designs of Timour and the true springs of
action.

[2] The furs of Russia are more credible than the ingots. But the linen of
Antioch has never been famous; and Antioch was in ruins. I suspect
that it was some manufacture of Europe, which the Hanse merchants had
imported by the way of Novogorod.

[3] M. Levesque (Hist. de Russie, tom. ii. p. 247; Vie de Timour, p. 64-67,
before the French version of the Institutes) has corrected the error of
Sherefeddin, and marked the true limit of Timour's conquests. His arguments are superfluous; and a simple appeal to the Russian annals is sufficient to prove that Moscow, which six years before had been taken by
Toctamish, escaped the arms of a more formidable invader.

[4] An Egyptian consul from Grand Cairo is mentioned in Barbaro's
Voyage to Tana in 1436, after the city had been rebuilt (Ramusio, tom. ii.
fol. 92).

[5] The sack of Azoph is described by Sherefeddin (l. iii. c. 55), and much
more particularly by the author of an Italian chronicle (Andreas de
Redusiis de Quero, in Chron. Tarvisiano, in Muratori, Script. Rerum

and Astrachan, the monuments of rising civilisation; and his
vanity proclaimed that he had penetrated to the region of
perpetual daylight, a strange phenomenon, which authorised
his Mohammedan doctors to dispense with the obligation of
evening prayer.[1]

III. When Timour first proposed to his princes and emirs the
invasion of India or Hindostan,[2] he was answered by a murmur
of discontent: " The rivers! and the mountains and deserts!
and the soldiers clad in armour! and the elephants, destroyers
of men!" But the displeasure of the emperor was more dreadful than all these terrors; and his superior reason was convinced
that an enterprise of such tremendous aspect was safe and easy
in the execution. He was informed by his spies of the weakness
and anarchy of Hindostan: the soubahs of the provinces had
erected the standard of rebellion; and the perpetual infancy of
sultan Mahmoud was despised even in the harem of Delhi. The
Mogul army moved in three great divisions; and Timour
observes with pleasure that the ninety-two squadrons of a thousand horse most fortunately corresponded with the ninety-two
names or epithets of the prophet Mohammed. Between the
Jihoon and the Indus they crossed one of the ridges of mountains
which are styled by the Arabian geographers The stony Girdles
of the Earth. The highland robbers were subdued or extirpated;
but great numbers of men and horses perished in the snow; the
emperor himself was let down a precipice on a portable scaffold
—the ropes were one hundred and fifty cubits in length; and
before he could reach the bottom, this dangerous operation was
five times repeated. Timour crossed the Indus at the ordinary
passage of Attok; and successively traversed, in the footsteps
of Alexander, the *Punjab*, or five rivers,[3] that fall into the master
stream. From Attok to Delhi the high road measures no more

Italicarum, tom. xix. p. 802-805). He had conversed with the Mianis, two
Venetian brothers, one of whom had been sent a deputy to the camp of
Timour, and the other had lost at Azoph three sons and 12,000 ducats.

[1] Sherefeddin only says (l. iii. c. 13) that the rays of the setting, and those
of the rising sun, were scarcely separated by any interval; a problem
which may be solved, in the latitude of Moscow (the 56th degree), with the
aid of the Aurora Borealis and a long summer twilight. But a *day* of forty
days (Khondemir apud D'Herbelot, p. 880) would rigorously confine us
within the polar circle.

[2] For the Indian war, see the Institutions (p. 129-139), the fourth book
of Sherefeddin, and the history of Ferishta (in Dow, vol. ii. p. 1-20), which
throws a general light on the affairs of Hindostan.

[3] The rivers of the Punjab, the five eastern branches of the Indus, have
been laid down for the first time with truth and accuracy in Major Rennell's
incomparable map of Hindostan. In his Critical Memoir he illustrates
with judgment and learning the marches of Alexander and Timour.

than six hundred miles; but the two conquerors deviated to the
south-east; and the motive of Timour was to join his grandson,
who had achieved by his command the conquest of Moultan.
On the eastern bank of the Hyphasis, on the edge of the desert,
the Macedonian hero halted and wept: the Mogul entered the
desert, reduced the fortress of Batnir, and stood in arms before
the gates of Delhi, a great and flourishing city, which had subsisted three centuries under the dominion of the Mohammedan
kings. The siege, more especially of the castle, might have been
a work of time; but he tempted, by the appearance of weakness,
the sultan Mahmoud and his vizir to descend into the plain, with
ten thousand cuirassiers, forty thousand of his foot-guards, and
one hundred and twenty elephants, whose tusks are said to have
been armed with sharp and poisoned daggers. Against these
monsters, or rather against the imagination of his troops, he
condescended to use some extraordinary precautions of fire and
a ditch, of iron spikes and a rampart of bucklers; but the event
taught the Moguls to smile at their own fears; and as soon as
these unwieldy animals were routed, the inferior species (the
men of India) disappeared from the field. Timour made his
triumphal entry into the capital of Hindostan; and admired,
with a view to imitate, the architecture of the stately mosque;
but the order or licence of a general pillage and massacre polluted
the festival of his victory. He resolved to purify his soldiers in
the blood of the idolators, or Gentoos, who still surpass, in the
proportion of ten to one, the numbers of the Moslems. In this
pious design he advanced one hundred miles to the north-east
of Delhi, passed the Ganges, fought several battles by land and
water, and penetrated to the famous rock of Coupele, the statue
of the cow, that *seems* to discharge the mighty river, whose source
is far distant among the mountains of Thibet.[1] His return was
along the skirts of the northern hills; nor could this rapid campaign of one year justify the strange foresight of his emirs, that
their children in a warm climate would degenerate into a race of
Hindoos.

It was on the banks of the Ganges that Timour was informed,
by his speedy messengers, of the disturbances which had arisen

[1] The two great rivers, the Ganges and Burrampooter, rise in Thibet,
from the opposite ridges of the same hills, separate from each other to the
distance of 1200 miles, and, after a winding course of 2000 miles, again
meet in one point near the gulf of Bengal. Yet so capricious is Fame, that
the Burrampooter is a late discovery, while his brother Ganges has been
the theme of ancient and modern story. Coupele, the scene of Timour's
last victory, must be situate near Loldong, 1100 miles from Calcutta; and,
in 1774, a British camp! (Rennell's Memoir, p. 7, 59, 90, 91, 99.)

on the confines of Georgia and Anatolia, of the revolt of the
Christians, and the ambitious designs of the sultan Bajazet.
His vigour of mind and body was not impaired by sixty-three
years and innumerable fatigues; and, after enjoying some
tranquil months in the palace of Samarcand, he proclaimed a
new expedition of seven years into the western countries of Asia.[1]
To the soldiers who had served in the Indian war he granted the
choice of remaining at home, or following their prince; but the
troops of all the provinces and kingdoms of Persia were commanded to assemble at Ispahan, and wait the arrival of the
Imperial standard. It was first directed against the Christians
of Georgia, who were strong only in their rocks, their castles,
and the winter season; but these obstacles were overcome by
the zeal and perseverance of Timour: the rebels submitted to
the tribute or the Koran; and if both religions boasted of their
martyrs, that name is more justly due to the Christian prisoners,
who were offered the choice of abjuration or death. On his
descent from the hills, the emperor gave audience to the first
ambassadors of Bajazet, and opened the hostile correspondence
of complaints and menaces which fermented two years before the
final explosion. Between two jealous and haughty neighbours,
the motives of quarrel will seldom be wanting. The Mogul and
Ottoman conquests now touched each other in the neighbourhood of Erzeroum and the Euphrates; nor had the doubtful limit
been ascertained by time and treaty. Each of these ambitious
monarchs might accuse his rival of violating his territory, of
threatening his vassals, and protecting his rebels; and by the
name of rebels each understood the fugitive princes whose
kingdoms he had usurped, and whose life or liberty he implac-
ably pursued. The resemblance of character was still more
dangerous than the opposition of interest; and in their victorious
career, Timour was impatient of an equal, and Bajazet was
ignorant of a superior. The first epistle [2] of the Mogul emperor
must have provoked, instead of reconciling, the Turkish sultan,
whose family and nation he affected to despise.[3] " Dost thou

---

[1] See the Institutions, p. 141, to the end of the first book, and Sherefeddin (l. v. c. 1-16) to the entrance of Timour into Syria.

[2] We have three copies of these hostile epistles in the Institutions (p. 147),
in Sherefeddin (l. v. c. 14), and in Arabshah (tom. ii. c. 19, p. 183-201);
which agree with each other in the spirit and substance rather than in the
style. It is probable that they have been translated, with various latitude,
from the Turkish original into the Arabic and Persian tongues.

[3] The Mogul emir distinguishes himself and his countrymen by the name
of *Turks*, and stigmatises the race and nation of Bajazet with the less
honourable epithet of *Turkmans*. Yet I do not understand how the Otto-

not know that the greatest part of Asia is subject to our arms and our laws? that our invincible forces extend from one sea to the other? that the potentates of the earth form a line before our gate? and that we have compelled Fortune herself to watch over the prosperity of our empire? What is the foundation of thy insolence and folly? Thou hast fought some battles in the woods of Anatolia; contemptible trophies! Thou hast obtained some victories over the Christians of Europe; thy sword was blessed by the apostle of God; and thy obedience to the precept of the Koran, in waging war against the infidels, is the sole consideration that prevents us from destroying thy country, the frontier and bulwark of the Moslem world. Be wise in time; reflect; repent; and avert the thunder of our vengeance, which is yet suspended over thy head. Thou art no more than a pismire; why wilt thou seek to provoke the elephants? Alas! they will trample thee under their feet." In his replies Bajazet poured forth the indignation of a soul which was deeply stung by such unusual contempt. After retorting the basest reproaches on the thief and rebel of the desert, the Ottoman recapitulates his boasted victories in Iran, Touran, and the Indies; and labours to prove that Timour had never triumphed unless by his own perfidy and the vices of his foes. "Thy armies are innumerable: be they so; but what are the arrows of the flying Tartar against the scimitars and battle-axes of my firm and invincible Janizaries? I will guard the princes who have implored my protection: seek them in my tents. The cities of Arzingan and Erzeroum are mine; and unless the tribute be duly paid, I will demand the arrears under the walls of Tauris and Sultania." The ungovernable rage of the sultan at length betrayed him to an insult of a more domestic kind. "If I fly from thy arms," said he, "may *my* wives be thrice divorced from my bed: but if thou hast not courage to meet me in the field, mayest thou again receive *thy* wives after they have thrice endured the embraces of a stranger." [1] Any violation by word or deed of the secrecy of the harem is an unpardonable offence among the Turkish

mans could be descended from a Turkman sailor; those inland shepherds were so remote from the sea and all maritime affairs.

[1] According to the Koran (c. ii. p. 27, and Sale's Discourses, p. 134), a Musulman who had thrice divorced his wife (who had thrice repeated the words of a divorce) could not take her again till after she had been married *to*, and repudiated *by*, another husband; an ignominious transaction, which it is needless to aggravate by supposing that the first husband must see her enjoyed by a second before his face (Rycaut's State of the Ottoman Empire, l. ii. c. 21).

nations;[1] and the political quarrel of the two monarchs was
embittered by private and personal resentment. Yet in his first
expedition Timour was satisfied with the siege and destruction
of Suvas or Sebaste, a strong city on the borders of Anatolia;
and he revenged the indiscretion of the Ottoman on a garrison
of four thousand Armenians, who were buried alive for the brave
and faithful discharge of their duty. As a Musulman he seemed
to respect the pious occupation of Bajazet, who was still engaged
in the blockade of Constantinople; and after this salutary lesson
the Mogul conqueror checked his pursuit, and turned aside to
the invasion of Syria and Egypt. In these transactions, the
Ottoman prince, by the Orientals, and even by Timour, is styled
the *Kaissar of Roum*, the Cæsar of the Romans; a title which, by
a small anticipation, might be given to a monarch who possessed
the provinces, and threatened the city, of the successors of
Constantine.[2]

The military republic of the Mamalukes still reigned in Egypt
and Syria: but the dynasty of the Turks was overthrown by that
of the Circassians;[3] and their favourite Barkok, from a slave and
a prisoner, was raised and restored to the throne. In the midst
of rebellion and discord, he braved the menaces, corresponded
with the enemies, and detained the ambassadors, of the Mogul,
who patiently expected his decease, to revenge the crimes of the
father on the feeble reign of his son Farage. The Syrian emirs[4]
were assembled at Aleppo to repel the invasion: they confided in
the fame and discipline of the Mamalukes, in the temper of their
swords and lances of the purest steel of Damascus, in the strength
of their walled cities, and in the populousness of sixty thousand
villages; and instead of sustaining a siege, they threw open their
gates, and arrayed their forces in the plain. But these forces
were not cemented by virtue and union; and some powerful emirs

---

[1] The common delicacy of the Orientals, in never speaking of their
women, is ascribed in a much higher degree by Arabshah to the Turkish
nations; and it is remarkable enough that Chalcocondyles (l. ii. p. 55
[p. 105, ed. Bonn]) had some knowledge of the prejudice and the insult.

[2] For the style of the Moguls see the Institutions (p. 131, 147), and for
the Persians the Bibliothèque Orientale (p. 882); but I do not find that the
title of Cæsar has been applied by the Arabians, or assumed by the Ottomans themselves.

[3] See the reigns of Barkok and Faradge, in M. de Guignes (tom. iv. l.
xxii.), who, from the Arabic texts of Aboulmahasen, Ebn Schounah, and
Aintabi, has added some facts to our common stock of materials.

[4] For these recent and domestic transactions, Arabshah, though a partial,
is a credible, witness (tom. i. c. 64-68, tom. ii. c. 1-14). Timour must have
been odious to a Syrian; but the notoriety of facts would have obliged
him, in some measure, to respect his enemy and himself. His bitters may
correct the luscious sweets of Sherefeddin (l. v. c. 17-29).

had been seduced to desert or betray their more loyal companions.
Timour's front was covered with a line of Indian elephants,
whose turrets were filled with archers and Greek fire: the rapid
evolutions of his cavalry completed the dismay and disorder;
the Syrian crowds fell back on each other; many thousands were
stifled or slaughtered in the entrance of the great street; the
Moguls entered with the fugitives; and after a short defence,
the citadel, the impregnable citadel of Aleppo, was surrendered
by cowardice or treachery. Among the suppliants and captives
Timour distinguished the doctors of the law, whom he invited
to the dangerous honour of a personal conference.[1] The Mogul
prince was a zealous Musulman; but his Persian schools had
taught him to revere the memory of Ali and Hosein; and he had
imbibed a deep prejudice against the Syrians, as the enemies of
the son of the daughter of the apostle of God. To these doctors
he proposed a captious question, which the casuists of Bochara,
Samarcand, and Herat were incapable of resolving. "Who
are the true martyrs, of those who are slain on my side, or on that
of my enemies?" But he was silenced, or satisfied, by the
dexterity of one of the cadhis of Aleppo, who replied, in the
words of Mohammed himself, that the motive, not the ensign,
constitutes the martyr; and that the Moslems of either party,
who fight only for the glory of God, may deserve that sacred
appellation. The true succession of the caliphs was a controversy of a still more delicate nature; and the frankness of a
doctor, too honest for his situation, provoked the emperor to
exclaim, "Ye are as false as those of Damascus: Moawiyah was
a usurper, Yezid a tyrant, and Ali alone is the lawful successor
of the prophet." A prudent explanation restored his tranquillity; and he passed to a more familiar topic of conversation.
"What is your age?" said he to the cadhi. "Fifty years."—
"It would be the age of my eldest son: you see me here (continued Timour) a poor, lame, decrepit mortal. Yet by my arm
has the Almighty been pleased to subdue the kingdoms of Iran,
Touran, and the Indies. I am not a man of blood; and God is
my witness that in all my wars I have never been the aggressor,
and that my enemies have always been the authors of their own
calamity." During this peaceful conversation the streets of
Aleppo streamed with blood, and re-echoed with the cries of

[1] These interesting conversations appear to have been copied by Arabshah (tom. i. c. 68, p. 625-645) from the cadhi and historian Ebn Schounah,
a principal actor. Yet how could he be alive seventy-five years afterwards (D'Herbelot, p. 792)?

*L 476

mothers and children, with the shrieks of violated virgins.   The
rich plunder that was abandoned to his soldiers might stimulate
their avarice; but their cruelty was enforced by the peremptory
command of producing an adequate number of heads, which,
according to his custom, were curiously piled in columns and
pyramids: the Moguls celebrated the feast of victory, while the
surviving Moslems passed the night in tears and in chains.   I
shall not dwell on the march of the destroyer from Aleppo to
Damascus, where he was rudely encountered, and almost overthrown, by the armies of Egypt.   A retrograde motion was
imputed to his distress and despair: one of his nephews deserted
to the enemy; and Syria rejoiced in the tale of his defeat, when
the sultan was driven by the revolt of the Mamalukes to escape
with precipitation and shame to his palace of Cairo.   Abandoned
by their prince, the inhabitants of Damascus still defended their
walls; and Timour consented to raise the siege, if they would
adorn his retreat with a gift or ransom; each article of nine
pieces.   But no sooner had he introduced himself into the city,
under colour of a truce, than he perfidiously violated the treaty,
imposed a contribution of ten millions of gold; and animated
his troops to chastise the posterity of those Syrians who had
executed, or approved, the murder of the grandson of Mohammed.
A family which had given honourable burial to the head of
Hosein, and a colony of artificers whom he sent to labour at
Samarcand, were alone reserved in the general massacre; and
after a period of seven centuries Damascus was reduced to ashes,
because a Tartar was moved by religious zeal to avenge the blood
of an Arab.   The losses and fatigues of the campaign obliged
Timour to renounce the conquest of Palestine and Egypt; but
in his return to the Euphrates he delivered Aleppo to the flames;
and justified his pious motive by the pardon and reward of two
thousand sectaries of Ali, who were desirous to visit the tomb of
his son.   I have expatiated on the personal anecdotes which
mark the character of the Mogul hero; but I shall briefly mention[1]
that he erected on the ruins of Bagdad a pyramid of ninety
thousand heads; again visited Georgia; encamped on the banks
of the Araxes; and proclaimed his resolution of marching against
the Ottoman emperor.   Conscious of the importance of the war,
he collected his forces from every province: eight hundred thousand men were enrolled on his military list;[2] but the splendid

[1] The marches and occupations of Timour between the Syrian and Ottoman wars are represented by Sherefeddin (l. v. c. 29-43) and Arabshah
(tom. ii. c. 15-18).
[2] This number of 800,000 was extracted by Arabshah, or rather by Ebn

commands of five and ten thousand horse may be rather expressive of the rank and pension of the chiefs than of the genuine number of effective soldiers.[1] In the pillage of Syria the Moguls had acquired immense riches; but the delivery of their pay and arrears for seven years more firmly attached them to the Imperial standard.

During this diversion of the Mogul arms, Bajazet had two years to collect his forces for a more serious encounter. They consisted of four hundred thousand horse and foot,[2] whose merit and fidelity were of an unequal complexion. We may discriminate the Janizaries, who have been gradually raised to an establishment of forty thousand men; a national cavalry, the Spahis of modern times; twenty thousand cuirassiers of Europe, clad in black and impenetrable armour; the troops of Anatolia, whose princes had taken refuge in the camp of Timour; and a colony of Tartars, whom he had driven from Kipzak, and to whom Bajazet had assigned a settlement in the plains of Adrianople. The fearless confidence of the sultan urged him to meet his antagonist; and, as if he had chosen that spot for revenge, he displayed his banners near the ruins of the unfortunate Suvas. In the meanwhile, Timour moved from the Araxes through the countries of Armenia and Anatolia: his boldness was secured by the wisest precautions; his speed was guided by order and discipline; and the woods, the mountains, and the rivers were diligently explored by the flying squadrons who marked his road and preceded his standard. Firm in his plan of fighting in the heart of the Ottoman kingdom, he avoided their camp, dexterously inclined to the left, occupied Cæsarea, traversed the salt desert and the river Halys, and invested Angora; while the sultan, immovable and ignorant in his post, compared the Tartar

---

Schounah, ex rationario Timuri, on the faith of a Carizmian officer (tom. i. c. 68, p. 617); and it is remarkable enough that a Greek historian (Phranza, l. i. c. 29) adds no more than 20,000 men. Poggius reckons 1,000,000; another Latin contemporary (Chron. Tarvisianum, apud Muratori, tom. xix. p. 800) 1,100,000; and the enormous sum of 1,600,000 is attested by a German soldier who was present at the battle of Angora (Leunclav. ad Chalcocondyl. l. iii. p. 82). Timour, in his Institutions, has not deigned to calculate his troops, his subjects, or his revenues.

[1] A wide latitude of non-effectives was allowed by the Great Mogul for his own pride and the benefit of his officers. Bernier's patron was Penge-Hazari, commander of 5000 horse; of which he maintained no more than 500 (Voyages, tom. i. p. 288, 289).

[2] Timour himself fixes at 400,000 men the Ottoman army (Institutions, p. 153), which is reduced to 150,000 by Phranza (l. i. c. 29), and swelled by the German soldier to 1,400,000. It is evident that the Moguls were the more numerous.

swiftness to the crawling of a snail; [1] he returned on the wings of
indignation to the relief of Angora; and as both generals were
alike impatient for action, the plains round that city were the
scene of a memorable battle, which has immortalised the glory of
Timour and the shame of Bajazet. For this signal victory the
Mogul emperor was indebted to himself, to the genius of the
moment, and the discipline of thirty years. He had improved
the tactics, without violating the manners, of his nation,[2] whose
force still consisted in the missile weapons and rapid evolutions
of a numerous cavalry. From a single troop to a great army the
mode of attack was the same: a foremost line first advanced to
the charge, and was supported in a just order by the squadrons
of the great vanguard. The general's eye watched over the field,
and at his command the front and rear of the right and left wings
successively moved forwards in their several divisions, and in a
direct or oblique line; the enemy was pressed by eighteen or
twenty attacks, and each attack afforded a chance of victory.
If they all proved fruitless or unsuccessful, the occasion was
worthy of the emperor himself, who gave the signal of advancing
to the standard and main body, which he led in person.[3] But
in the battle of Angora the main body itself was supported, on
the flanks and in the rear, by the bravest squadrons of the
reserve, commanded by the sons and grandsons of Timour. The
conqueror of Hindostan ostentatiously showed a line of elephants,
the trophies rather than the instruments of victory: the use of
the Greek fire was familiar to the Moguls and Ottomans; but had
they borrowed from Europe the recent invention of gunpowder
and cannon, the artificial thunder, in the hands of either nation,
must have turned the fortune of the day.[4] In that day Bajazet
displayed the qualities of a soldier and a chief; but his genius
sunk under a stronger ascendant, and, from various motives, the
greatest part of his troops failed him in the decisive moment.

[1] It may not be useless to mark the distances between Angora and the
neighbouring cities by the journeys of the caravans, each of twenty or
twenty-five miles; to Smyrna twenty, to Kiotahia ten, to Boursa ten, to
Cæsarea eight, to Sinope ten, to Nicomedia nine, to Constantinople twelve
or thirteen (see Tournefort, Voyage au Levant, tom. ii. lettre xxi.).

[2] See the Systems of Tactics in the Institutions, which the English
editors have illustrated with elaborate plans (p. 373-407).

[3] The sultan himself (says Timour) must then put the foot of courage
into the stirrup of patience. A Tartar metaphor, which is lost in the
English, but preserved in the French, version of the Institutes (p. 156, 157).

[4] The Greek fire, on Timour's side, is attested by Sherefeddin (l. v. c. 47);
but Voltaire's strange suspicion that some cannon, inscribed with strange
characters, must have been sent by that monarch to Delhi, is refuted by
the universal silence of contemporaries.

His rigour and avarice had provoked a mutiny among the Turks, and even his son Soliman too hastily withdrew from the field. The forces of Anatolia, loyal in their revolt, were drawn away to the banners of their lawful princes. His Tartar allies had been tempted by the letters and emissaries of Timour,[1] who reproached their ignoble servitude under the slaves of their fathers, and offered to their hopes the dominion of their new or the liberty of their ancient country. In the right wing of Bajazet the cuirassiers of Europe charged, with faithful hearts and irresistible arms; but these men of iron were soon broken by an artful flight and headlong pursuit; and the Janizaries alone, without cavalry or missile weapons, were encompassed by the circle of the Mogul hunters. Their valour was at length oppressed by heat, thirst, and the weight of numbers; and the unfortunate sultan, afflicted with the gout in his hands and feet, was transported from the field on the fleetest of his horses. He was pursued and taken by the titular khan of Zagatai; and, after his capture and the defeat of the Ottoman powers, the kingdom of Anatolia submitted to the conqueror, who planted his standard at Kiotahia, and dispersed on all sides the ministers of rapine and destruction. Mirza Mehemmed Sultan, the eldest and best beloved of his grandsons, was despatched to Boursa with thirty thousand horse; and such was his youthful ardour, that he arrived with only four thousand at the gates of the capital, after performing in five days a march of two hundred and thirty miles. Yet fear is still more rapid in its course; and Soliman, the son of Bajazet, had already passed over to Europe with the royal treasure. The spoil, however, of the palace and city was immense: the inhabitants had escaped; but the buildings, for the most part of wood, were reduced to ashes. From Boursa the grandson of Timour advanced to Nice, even yet a fair and flourishing city; and the Mogul squadrons were only stopped by the waves of the Propontis. The same success attended the other mirzas and emirs in their excursions; and Smyrna, defended by the zeal and courage of the Rhodian knights, alone deserved the presence of the emperor himself. After an obstinate defence the place was taken by storm: all that breathed was put to the sword; and the heads of the Christian heroes were launched from the engines, on board of two carracks or great ships of Europe that rode at anchor in the harbour. The Moslems of Asia rejoiced in their

[1] Timour has dissembled this secret and important negotiation with the Tartars, which is indisputably proved by the joint evidence of the Arabian (tom. i. c. 47, p. 391), Turkish (Annal. Leunclav. p. 321), and Persian historians (Khondemir apud D'Herbelot, p. 882).

deliverance from a dangerous and domestic foe; and a parallel was drawn between the two rivals by observing that Timour, in fourteen days, had reduced a fortress which had sustained seven years the siege, or at least the blockade, of Bajazet.[1]

The *iron cage* in which Bajazet was imprisoned by Tamerlane, so long and so often repeated as a moral lesson, is now rejected as a fable by the modern writers, who smile at the vulgar credulity.[2] They appeal with confidence to the Persian history of Sherefeddin Ali, which has been given to our curiosity in a French version, and from which I shall collect and abridge a more specious narrative of this memorable transaction. No sooner was Timour informed that the captive Ottoman was at the door of his tent than he graciously stepped forward to receive him, seated him by his side, and mingled with just reproaches a soothing pity for his rank and misfortune. " Alas ! " said the emperor, " the decree of fate is now accomplished by your own fault; it is the web which you have woven, the thorns of the tree which yourself have planted. I wished to spare, and even to assist, the champion of the Moslems: you braved our threats; you despised our friendship; you forced us to enter your kingdom with our invincible armies. Behold the event. Had you vanquished, I am not ignorant of the fate which you reserved for myself and my troops. But I disdain to retaliate: your life and honour are secure; and I shall express my gratitude to God by my clemency to man." The royal captive showed some signs of repentance, accepted the humiliation of a robe of honour, and embraced with tears his son Mousa, who, at his request, was sought and found among the captives of the field. The Ottoman princes were lodged in a splendid pavilion, and the respect of the guards could be surpassed only by their vigilance. On the arrival of the harem from Boursa, Timour restored the queen Despina and her daughter to their father and husband; but he piously required that the Servian princess, who had hitherto been indulged in the profession of Christianity, should embrace without delay the religion of the prophet. In the feast of victory, to which Bajazet was invited, the Mogul emperor

[1] For the war of Anatolia or Roum, I add some hints in the Institutions to the copious narratives of Sherefeddin (l. v. c. 44-65) and Arabshah (tom. ii. c. 20-35). On this part only of Timour's history it is lawful to quote the Turks (Cantemir, p. 53-55; Annal. Leunclav. p. 320-322) and the Greeks (Phranza, l. i. c. 29; Ducas, c. 15-17; Chalcocondyles, l. iii.).

[2] The scepticism of Voltaire (Essai sur l'Histoire Générale, c. 88) is ready on this, as on every occasion, to reject a popular tale, and to diminish the magnitude of vice and virtue; and on most occasions his incredulity is reasonable.

placed a crown on his head and a sceptre in his hand, with a solemn assurance of restoring him with an increase of glory to the throne of his ancestors. But the effect of this promise was disappointed by the sultan's untimely death; amidst the care of the most skilful physicians he expired of an apoplexy at Akshehr, the Antioch of Pisidia, about nine months after his defeat. The victor dropped a tear over his grave: his body, with royal pomp, was conveyed to the mausoleum which he had erected at Boursa; and his son Mousa, after receiving a rich present of gold and jewels, of horses and arms, was invested by a patent in red ink with the kingdom of Anatolia.

Such is the portrait of a generous conqueror, which has been extracted from his own memorials, and dedicated to his son and grandson, nineteen years after his decease; [1] and, at a time when the truth was remembered by thousands, a manifest falsehood would have implied a satire on his real conduct. Weighty indeed is this evidence, adopted by all the Persian histories; [2] yet flattery, more especially in the East, is base and audacious; and the harsh and ignominious treatment of Bajazet is attested by a chain of witnesses, some of whom shall be produced in the order of their time and country. I. The reader has not forgot the garrison of French whom the marshal Boucicault left behind him for the defence of Constantinople. They were on the spot to receive the earliest and most faithful intelligence of the overthrow of their great adversary, and it is more than probable that some of them accompanied the Greek embassy to the camp of Tamerlane. From their account, the *hardships* of the prison and death of Bajazet are affirmed by the marshal's servant and historian, within the distance of seven years.[3] 2. The name of Poggius the Italian [4] is deservedly famous among the revivers

[1] See the History of Sherefeddin (l. v. c. 49, 52, 53, 59, 60). This work was finished at Shiraz, in the year 1424, and dedicated to sultan Ibrahim, the son of Sharokh, the son of Timour, who reigned in Farsistan in his father's lifetime.

[2] After the perusal of Khondemir, Ebn Schounah, etc., the learned D'Herbelot (Biblioth. Orientale, p. 882) may affirm that this fable is not mentioned in the most authentic histories; but his denial of the visible testimony of Arabshah leaves some room to suspect his accuracy.

[3] Et fut lui-même (*Bajazet*) pris, et mené en prison, en laquelle mourut de *dure mort!* Mémoires de Boucicault, P. i. c. 37. These memoirs were composed while the marshal was still governor of Genoa, from whence he was expelled, in the year 1409, by a popular insurrection (Muratori, Annali d'Italia, tom. xii. p. 473, 474).

[4] The reader will find a satisfactory account of the life and writings of Poggius in the Poggiana, an entertaining work of M. Lenfant, and in the Bibliotheca Latina mediæ et infimæ Ætatis of Fabricius (tom. v. p. 305-308). Poggius was born in the year 1380, and died in 1459.

of learning in the fifteenth century. His elegant dialogue on the vicissitudes of fortune [1] was composed in his fiftieth year, twenty-eight years after the Turkish victory of Tamerlane,[2] whom he celebrates as not inferior to the illustrious barbarians of antiquity. Of his exploits and discipline Poggius was informed by several ocular witnesses: nor does he forget an example so apposite to his theme as the Ottoman monarch, whom the Scythian confined like a wild beast in an iron cage, and exhibited a spectacle to Asia. I might add the authority of two Italian chronicles, perhaps of an earlier date, which would prove at least that the same story, whether false or true, was imported into Europe with the first tidings of the revolution.[3] 3. At the time when Poggius flourished at Rome, Ahmed Ebn Arabshah composed at Damascus the florid and malevolent history of Timour, for which he had collected materials in his journeys over Turkey and Tartary.[4] Without any possible correspondence between the Latin and the Arabian writer, they agree in the fact of the iron cage; and their agreement is a striking proof of their common veracity. Ahmed Arabshah likewise relates another outrage which Bajazet endured, of a more domestic and tender nature. His indiscreet mention of women and divorces was deeply resented by the jealous Tartar: in the feast of victory the wine was served by female cupbearers, and the sultan beheld his own concubines and wives confounded among the slaves, and exposed without a veil to the eyes of intemperance. To escape a similar indignity, it is said that his successors, except in a single instance, have abstained from legitimate nuptials; and the Ottoman practice and belief, at least in the sixteenth century, is attested by the observing Busbequius,[5] ambassador from the court of

[1] The dialogue de Varietate Fortunæ (of which a complete and elegant edition has been published at Paris in 1723, in 4to) was composed a short time before the death of pope Martin V. (p. 5), and consequently about the end of the year 1430.

[2] See a splendid and eloquent encomium of Tamerlane, p. 36-39, ipse enim novi (says Poggius) qui uere in ejus castris. . . . Regem vivum cepit, caveâque in modum feræ inclusum per omnem Asiam circumtulit egregium admirandumque spectaculum fortunæ.

[3] The Chronicon Tarvisianum (in Muratori, Script. Rerum Italicarum, tom. xix. p. 800), and the Annales Estenses (tom. xviii. p. 974). The two authors, Andrea de Redusiis de Quero, and James de Delayto, were both contemporaries, and both chancellors, the one of Trevigi, the other of Ferrara. The evidence of the former is the most positive.

[4] See Arabshah, tom. ii. c. 28, 34. He travelled in regiones Rumæas, A.H. 839 (A.D. 1435, July 27), tom. ii. c. 2, p. 13.

[5] Busbequius in Legatione Turcicâ, epist. i. p. 52. Yet his respectable authority is somewhat shaken by the subsequent marriages of Amurath II. with a Servian, and of Mohammed II. with an Asiatic princess Cantemir, p. 83, 93).

Vienna to the great Soliman. 4. Such is the separation of language, that the testimony of a Greek is not less independent than that of a Latin or an Arab. I suppress the names of Chalcocondyles and Ducas, who flourished in a later period, and who speak in a less positive tone; but more attention is due to George Phranza,[1] protovestiare of the last emperors, and who was born a year before the battle of Angora. Twenty-two years after that event he was sent ambassador to Amurath the Second; and the historian might converse with some veteran Janizaries, who had been made prisoners with the sultan, and had themselves seen him in his iron cage. 5. The last evidence, in every sense, is that of the Turkish annals, which have been consulted or transcribed by Leunclavius, Pocock, and Cantemir.[2] They unanimously deplore the captivity of the iron cage; and some credit may be allowed to national historians, who cannot stigmatise the Tartar without uncovering the shame of their king and country.

From these opposite premises a fair and moderate conclusion may be deduced. I am satisfied that Sherefeddin Ali has faithfully described the first ostentatious interview, in which the conqueror, whose spirits were harmonised by success, affected the character of generosity. But his mind was insensibly alienated by the unseasonable arrogance of Bajazet; the complaints of his enemies, the Anatolian princes, were just and vehement; and Timour betrayed a design of leading his royal captive in triumph to Samarcand. An attempt to facilitate his escape, by digging a mine under the tent, provoked the Mogul emperor to impose a harsher restraint; and in his perpetual marches an iron cage on a waggon might be invented, not as a wanton insult, but as a rigorous precaution. Timour had read in some fabulous history a similar treatment of one of his predecessors, a king of Persia; and Bajazet was condemned to represent the person and expiate the guilt of the Roman Cæsar.[3] But the strength of his mind and body fainted under the trial, and his premature death might, without injustice, be ascribed

---

[1] See the testimony of George Phranza (l. i. c. 26 [p. 85, ed. Bonn]), and his life in Hanckius (de Script. Byzant. P. i. c. 40). Chalcocondyles and Ducas speak in general terms of Bajazet's *chains*.

[2] Annales Leunclav. p. 321; Pocock, Prolegomen. ad Abulpharag. Dynast. Cantemir, p. 55.

[3] A Sapor, king of Persia, had been made prisoner, and enclosed in the figure of a cow's hide, by Maximian or Galerius Cæsar. Such is the fable related by Eutychius (Annal. tom. i. p. 421, vers. Pocock). The recollection of the true history (Decline and Fall, etc., vol. i. p. 359-361) will teach us to appreciate the knowledge of the Orientals of the ages which precede the Hegira.

to the severity of Timour. He warred not with the dead: a
tear and a sepulchre were all that he could bestow on a captive
who was delivered from his power; and if Mousa, the son of
Bajazet, was permitted to reign over the ruins of Boursa, the
greatest part of the province of Anatolia had been restored by
the conqueror to their lawful sovereigns.

From the Irtish and Volga to the Persian Gulf, and from the
Ganges to Damascus and the Archipelago, Asia was in the hand
of Timour: his armies were invincible, his ambition was boundless, and his zeal might aspire to conquer and convert the Christian kingdoms of the West, which already trembled at his name.
He touched the utmost verge of the land; but an insuperable,
though narrow sea, rolled between the two continents of Europe
and Asia,[1] and the lord of so many *tomans* or myriads of horse
was not master of a single galley. The two passages of the
Bosphorus and Hellespont, of Constantinople and Gallipoli,
were possessed, the one by the Christians, the other by the Turks.
On this great occasion they forgot the difference of religion, to act
with union and firmness in the common cause: the double straits
were guarded with ships and fortifications, and they separately
withheld the transports which Timour demanded of either nation,
under the pretence of attacking their enemy. At the same time
they soothed his pride with tributary gifts and suppliant
embassies, and prudently tempted him to retreat with the
honours of victory. Soliman, the son of Bajazet, implored his
clemency for his father and himself; accepted, by a red patent,
the investiture of the kingdom of Romania, which he already held
by the sword, and reiterated his ardent wish of casting himself
in person at the feet of the king of the world. The Greek
emperor [2] (either John or Manuel) submitted to pay the same
tribute which he had stipulated with the Turkish sultan, and
ratified the treaty by an oath of allegiance, from which he could
absolve his conscience so soon as the Mogul arms had retired from
Anatolia. But the fears and fancy of nations ascribed to the
ambitious Tamerlane a new design of vast and romantic compass;

---

[1] Arabshah (tom. ii. c. 25) describes, like a curious traveller, the straits
of Gallipoli and Constantinople. To acquire a just idea of these events
I have compared the narratives and prejudices of the Moguls, Turks,
Greeks, and Arabians. The Spanish ambassador mentions this hostile
union of the Christians and Ottomans (Vie de Timour, p. 96).

[2] Since the name of Cæsar had been transferred to the sultans of Roum,
the Greek princes of Constantinople (Sherefeddin, l. v. c. 54) were confounded with the Christian *lords* of Gallipoli, Thessalonica, etc., under the
title of *Tekkur*, which is derived by corruption from the genitive τοῦ κυρίου
(Cantemir, p. 51).

a design of subduing Egypt and Africa, marching from the Nile to the Atlantic Ocean, entering Europe by the Straits of Gibraltar, and, after imposing his yoke on the kingdoms of Christendom, of returning home by the deserts of Russia and Tartary. This remote, and perhaps imaginary danger, was averted by the submission of the sultan of Egypt: the honours of the prayer and the coin attested at Cairo the supremacy of Timour; and a rare gift of a *giraffe* or camelopard, and nine ostriches, represented at Samarcand the tribute of the African world. Our imagination is not less astonished by the portrait of a Mogul, who, in his camp before Smyrna, meditates and almost accomplishes the invasion of the Chinese empire.[1] Timour was urged to this enterprise by national honour and religious zeal. The torrents which he had shed of Musulman blood could be expiated only by an equal destruction of the infidels; and as he now stood at the gates of paradise, he might best secure his glorious entrance by demolishing the idols of China, founding mosques in every city, and establishing the profession of faith in one God and his prophet Mohammed. The recent expulsion of the house of Zingis was an insult on the Mogul name, and the disorders of the empire afforded the fairest opportunity for revenge. The illustrious Hongvou, founder of the dynasty of *Ming*, died four years before the battle of Angora, and his grandson, a weak and unfortunate youth, was burnt in his palace, after a million of Chinese had perished in the civil war.[2] Before he evacuated Anatolia, Timour despatched beyond the Sihoon a numerous army, or rather colony, of his old and new subjects, to open the road, to subdue the pagan Calmucks and Mungals, and to found cities and magazines in the desert; and, by the diligence of his lieutenant, he soon received a perfect map and description of the unknown regions, from the source of the Irtish to the wall of China. During these preparations the emperor achieved the final conquest of Georgia, passed the winter on the banks of the Araxes, appeased the troubles of Persia, and slowly returned to his capital after a campaign of four years and nine months.

On the throne of Samarcand [3] he displayed, in a short repose,

[1] See Sherefeddin, l. v. c. 4, who marks, in a just itinerary, the road to China, which Arabshah (tom. ii. c. 33) paints in vague and rhetorical colours.

[2] Synopsis Hist. Sinicæ, p. 74-76 (in the fourth part of the Relations de Thevenot); Duhalde, Hist. de la Chine (tom. i. p. 507, 508, folio edition); and for the chronology of the Chinese emperors, De Guignes, Hist. des Huns, tom. i. p. 71, 72.

[3] For the return, triumph, and death of Timour, see Sherefeddin (l. vi. c. 1-30) and Arabshah (tom. ii. c. 35-47).

his magnificence and power; listened to the complaints of the
people; distributed a just measure of rewards and punishments;
employed his riches in the architecture of palaces and temples;
and gave audience to the ambassadors of Egypt, Arabia, India,
Tartary, Russia, and Spain, the last of whom presented a suit of
tapestry which eclipsed the pencil of the Oriental artists. The
marriage of six of the emperor's grandsons was esteemed an act
of religion as well as of paternal tenderness; and the pomp of
the ancient caliphs was revived in their nuptials. They were
celebrated in the gardens of Canighul, decorated with innumerable
tents and pavilions, which displayed the luxury of a great city
and the spoils of a victorious camp. Whole forests were cut
down to supply fuel for the kitchens; the plain was spread with
pyramids of meat and vases of every liquor, to which thousands
of guests were courteously invited: the orders of the state and
the nations of the earth were marshalled at the royal banquet;
nor were the ambassadors of Europe (says the haughty Persian)
excluded from the feast; since even the *casses*, the smallest of
fish, find their place in the ocean.[1] The public joy was testified
by illuminations and masquerades; the trades of Samarcand
passed in review; and every trade was emulous to execute some
quaint device, some marvellous pageant, with the materials of
their peculiar art. After the marriage-contracts had been
ratified by the cadhis, the bridegrooms and their brides retired
to the nuptial chambers: nine times, according to the Asiatic
fashion, they were dressed and undressed; and at each change of
apparel pearls and rubies were showered on their heads, and
contemptuously abandoned to their attendants. A general indulgence was proclaimed: every law was relaxed, every pleasure
was allowed; the people was free, the sovereign was idle; and
the historian of Timour may remark, that, after devoting fifty
years to the attainment of empire, the only happy period of his
life were the two months in which he ceased to exercise his power.
But he was soon awakened to the cares of government and war.
The standard was unfurled for the invasion of China: the emirs
made their report of two hundred thousand, the select and
veteran soldiers of Iran and Touran: their baggage and pro-

---

[1] Sherefeddin (l. vi. c. 24) mentions the ambassadors of one of the most
potent sovereigns of Europe. We know that it was Henry III. king of
Castile; and the curious relation of his two embassies is still extant
(Mariana, Hist. Hispan. l. xix. c. 11, tom. ii. p. 329, 330; Avertissement à
l'Hist. de Timur Bec, p. 28-33). There appears likewise to have been some
correspondence between the Mogul emperor and the court of Charles VII.
king of France (Histoire de France, par Velly et Villaret, tom. xii. p. 336).

visions were transported by five hundred great waggons and an immense train of horses and camels; and the troops might prepare for a long absence, since more than six months were employed in the tranquil journey of a caravan from Samarcand to Pekin. Neither age nor the severity of the winter could retard the impatience of Timour; he mounted on horseback, passed the Sihoon on the ice, marched seventy-six parasangs, three hundred miles, from his capital, and pitched his last camp in the neighbourhood of Otrar, where he was expected by the angel of death. Fatigue, and the indiscreet use of iced water, accelerated the progress of his fever; and the conqueror of Asia expired in the seventieth year of his age, thirty-five years after he had ascended the throne of Zagatai. His designs were lost; his armies were disbanded; China was saved; and fourteen years after his decease, the most powerful of his children sent an embassy of friendship and commerce to the court of Pekin.[1]

The fame of Timour has pervaded the East and West: his posterity is still invested with the Imperial *title;* and the admiration of his subjects, who revered him almost as a deity, may be justified in some degree by the praise or confession of his bitterest enemies.[2] Although he was lame of a hand and foot, his form and stature were not unworthy of his rank; and his vigorous health, so essential to himself and to the world, was corroborated by temperance and exercise. In his familiar discourse he was grave and modest; and if he was ignorant of the Arabic language, he spoke with fluency and elegance the Persian and Turkish idioms. It was his delight to converse with the learned on topics of history and science; and the amusement of his leisure hours was the game of chess, which he improved or corrupted with new refinements.[3] In his religion he was a zealous, though not perhaps an orthodox, Musulman;[4] but his

[1] See the translation of the Persian account of their embassy, a curious and original piece (in the fourth part of the Relations de Thevenot). They presented the emperor of China with an old horse which Timour had formerly rode. It was in the year 1419 that they departed from the court of Herat, to which place they returned in 1422 from Pekin.

[2] From Arabshah, tom. ii. c. 96. The bright or softer colours are borrowed from Sherefeddin, D'Herbelot, and the Institutions.

[3] His new system was multiplied from 32 pieces and 64 squares to 56 pieces and 110 or 130 squares: but, except in his court, the old game has been thought sufficiently elaborate. The Mogul emperor was rather pleased than hurt with the victory of a subject: a chess-player will feel the value of this encomium!

[4] See Sherefeddin, l. v. c. 15, 25. Arabshah (tom. ii. c. 96, p. 801, 803) reproves the impiety of Timour and the Moguls, who almost preferred to the Koran the *Yacsa*, or Law of Zingis (cui Deus maledicat); nor will he believe that Sharokh had abolished the use and authority of that pagan code.

sound understanding may tempt us to believe that a superstitious reverence for omens and prophecies, for saints and
astrologers, was only affected as an instrument of policy. In
the government of a vast empire he stood alone and absolute,
without a rebel to oppose his power, a favourite to seduce his
affections, or a minister to mislead his judgment. It was his
firmest maxim, that, whatever might be the consequence, the
word of the prince should never be disputed or recalled; but his
foes have maliciously observed that the commands of anger and
destruction were more strictly executed than those of beneficence
and favour. His sons and grandsons, of whom Timour left six-
and-thirty at his decease, were his first and most submissive
subjects; and whenever they deviated from their duty, they
were corrected, according to the laws of Zingis, with the
bastonade, and afterwards restored to honour and command.
Perhaps his heart was not devoid of the social virtues; perhaps
he was not incapable of loving his friends and pardoning his
enemies; but the rules of morality are founded on the public
interest; and it may be sufficient to applaud the *wisdom* of a
monarch, for the liberality by which he is not impoverished, and
for the justice by which he is strengthened and enriched. To
maintain the harmony of authority and obedience, to chastise
the proud, to protect the weak, to reward the deserving, to
banish vice and idleness from his dominions, to secure the
traveller and merchant, to restrain the depredations of the
soldier, to cherish the labours of the husbandman, to encourage
industry and learning, and, by an equal and moderate assessment,
to increase the revenue without increasing the taxes, are indeed
the duties of a prince; but, in the discharge of these duties, he
finds an ample and immediate recompense. Timour might boast
that, at his accession to the throne, Asia was the prey to anarchy
and rapine, whilst under his prosperous monarchy a child, fearless and unhurt, might carry a purse of gold from the East to the
West. Such was his confidence of merit, that from this reformation he derived an excuse for his victories and a title to universal
dominion. The four following observations will serve to appreciate his claim to the public gratitude; and perhaps we shall
conclude that the Mogul emperor was rather the scourge than
the benefactor of mankind. 1. If some partial disorders, some
local oppressions, were healed by the sword of Timour, the
remedy was far more pernicious than the disease. By their rapine,
cruelty, and discord, the petty tyrants of Persia might afflict their
subjects; but whole nations were crushed under the footsteps

of the reformer. The ground which had been occupied by flourishing cites was often marked by his abominable trophies, by columns, or pyramids, of human heads. Astracan, Carizme, Delhi, Ispahan, Bagdad, Aleppo, Damascus, Boursa, Smyrna, and a thousand others, were sacked, or burnt, or utterly destroyed, in his presence and by his troops: and perhaps his conscience would have been startled if a priest or philosopher had dared to number the millions of victims whom he had sacrificed to the establishment of peace and order.[1] 2. His most destructive wars were rather inroads than conquests. He invaded Turkestan, Kipzak, Russia, Hindostan, Syria, Anatolia, Armenia, and Georgia, without a hope or a desire of preserving those distant provinces. From thence he departed laden with spoil; but he left behind him neither troops to awe the contumacious, nor magistrates to protect the obedient, natives. When he had broken the fabric of their ancient government he abandoned them to the evils which his invasion had aggravated or caused; nor were these evils compensated by any present or possible benefits. 3. The kingdoms of Transoxiana and Persia were the proper field which he laboured to cultivate and adorn as the perpetual inheritance of his family. But his peaceful labours were often interrupted, and sometimes blasted, by the absence of the conqueror. While he triumphed on the Volga or the Ganges, his servants, and even his sons, forgot their master and their duty. The public and private injuries were poorly redressed by the tardy rigour of inquiry and punishment; and we must be content to praise the *Institutions* of Timour as the specious idea of a perfect monarchy. 4. Whatsoever might be the blessings of his administration, they evaporated with his life. To reign, rather than to govern, was the ambition of his children and grandchildren,[2] the enemies of each other and of the people. A fragment of the empire was upheld with some glory by Sharokh, his youngest son; but after *his* decease the scene was again involved in darkness and blood; and before the

---

[1] Besides the bloody passages of this narrative, I must refer to an anticipation in the third volume of the Decline and Fall, which in a single note (p. 355, note [3]) accumulates near 300,000 heads of the monuments of his cruelty. Except in Rowe's play on the fifth of November, I did not expect to hear of Timour's amiable moderation (White's preface, p. 7). Yet I can excuse a generous enthusiasm in the reader, and still more in the editor, of the *Institutions*.

[2] Consult the last chapters of Sherefeddin and Arabshah, and M. de Guignes (Hist. des Huns, tom. iv. l. xx.). Fraser's History of Nadir Shah (p. 1-62). The story of Timour's descendants is imperfectly told; and the second and third parts of Sherefeddin are unknown.

end of a century Transoxiana and Persia were trampled by the
Uzbeks from the north, and the Turkmans of the black and white
sheep. The race of Timour would have been extinct if a hero,
his descendant in the fifth degree, had not fled before the Uzbek
arms to the conquest of Hindostan. His successors (the great
Moguls [1]) extended their sway from the mountains of Cashmir
to Cape Comorin, and from Candahar to the gulf of Bengal.
Since the reign of Aurungzebe their empire has been dissolved;
their treasures of Delhi have been rifled by a Persian robber;
and the richest of their kingdoms is now possessed by a company
of Christian merchants of a remote island in the Northern Ocean.

Far different was the fate of the Ottoman monarchy. The
massy trunk was bent to the ground, but no sooner did the
hurricane pass away than it again rose with fresh vigour and
more lively vegetation. When Timour in every sense had
evacuated Anatolia, he left the cities without a palace, a treasure,
or a king. The open country was overspread with hordes of
shepherds and robbers of Tartar or Turkman origin; the recent
conquests of Bajazet were restored to the emirs, one of whom,
in base revenge, demolished his sepulchre; and his five sons
were eager, by civil discord, to consume the remnant of their
patrimony. I shall enumerate their names in the order of their
age and actions. [2] 1. It is doubtful whether I relate the story
of the true *Mustapha*, or of an impostor who personated that
lost prince. He fought by his father's side in the battle of
Angora: but when the captive sultan was permitted to inquire
for his children, Mousa alone could be found; and the Turkish
historians, the slaves of the triumphant faction, are persuaded
that his brother was confounded among the slain. If Mustapha
escaped from that disastrous field, he was concealed twelve years
from his friends and enemies, till he emerged in Thessaly, and
was hailed by a numerous party as the son and successor of
Bajazet. His first defeat would have been his last, had not the
true or false Mustapha been saved by the Greeks, and restored,
after the decease of his brother Mohammed, to liberty and
empire. A degenerate mind seemed to argue his spurious birth;
and if, on the throne of Adrianople, he was adored as the Ottoman

---

[1] Shah Allum, the present Mogul, is in the fourteenth degree from
Timour, by Miran Shah, his third son. See the second volume of Dow's
History of Hindostan.

[2] The civil wars, from the death of Bajazet to that of Mustapha, are
related, according to the Turks, by Demetrius Cantemir (p. 58-82). Of
the Greeks, Chalcocondyles (l. iv. and v.), Phranza (l. i. c. 30-32), and
Ducas (c. 18-27), the last is the most copious and best informed.

sultan, his flight, his fetters, and an ignominious gibbet delivered the impostor to popular contempt. A similar character and claim was asserted by several rival pretenders: thirty persons are said to have suffered under the name of Mustapha; and these frequent executions may perhaps insinuate that the Turkish court was not perfectly secure of the death of the lawful prince. 2. After his father's captivity Isa [1] reigned for some time in the neighbourhood of Angora, Sinope, and the Black Sea; and his ambassadors were dismissed from the presence of Timour with fair promises and honourable gifts. But their master was soon deprived of his province and life by a jealous brother, the sovereign of Amasia; and the final event suggested a pious allusion that the law of Moses and Jesus, of *Isa* and *Mousa*, had been abrogated by the greater *Mohammed*. 3. *Soliman* is not numbered in the list of the Turkish emperors: yet he checked the victorious progress of the Moguls, and, after their departure, united for a while the thrones of Adrianople and Boursa. In war he was brave, active, and fortunate: his courage was softened by clemency; but it was likewise inflamed by presumption, and corrupted by intemperance and idleness. He relaxed the nerves of discipline in a government where either the subject or the sovereign must continually tremble: his vices alienated the chiefs of the army and the law; and his daily drunkenness, so contemptible in a prince and a man, was doubly odious in a disciple of the prophet. In the slumber of intoxication he was surprised by his brother Mousa; and as he fled from Adrianople towards the Byzantine capital, Soliman was overtaken and slain in a bath, after a reign of seven years and ten months. 4. The investiture of Mousa degraded him as the slave of the Moguls: his tributary kingdom of Anatolia was confined within a narrow limit, nor could his broken militia and empty treasury contend with the hardy and veteran bands of the sovereign of Romania. Mousa fled in disguise from the palace of Boursa; traversed the Propontis in an open boat; wandered over the Wallachian and Servian hills; and after some vain attempts, ascended the throne of Adrianople, so recently stained with the blood of Soliman. In a reign of three years and a half his troops were victorious against the Christians of Hungary and the Morea; but Mousa was ruined by his timorous disposition and unseasonable clemency. After resigning the sovereignty of Anatolia he

---

[1] Arabshah, tom. ii. c. 26, whose testimony on this occasion is weighty and valuable. The existence of Isa (unknown to the Turks) is likewise confirmed by Sherefeddin (l. v. c. 57).

fell a victim to the perfidy of his ministers and the superior ascendant of his brother Mohammed. 5. The final victory of Mohammed was the just recompense of his prudence and moderation. Before his father's captivity the royal youth had been intrusted with the government of Amasia, thirty days' journey from Constantinople, and the Turkish frontier against the Christians of Trebizond and Georgia. The castle in Asiatic warfare was esteemed impregnable; and the city of Amasia,[1] which is equally divided by the river Iris, rises on either side in the form of an amphitheatre, and represents on a smaller scale the image of Bagdad. In his rapid career Timour appears to have overlooked this obscure and contumacious angle of Anatolia; and Mohammed, without provoking the conqueror, maintained his silent independence, and chased from the province the last stragglers of the Tartar host. He relieved himself from the dangerous neighbourhood of Isa; but in the contests of their more powerful brethren his firm neutrality was respected, till, after the triumph of Mousa, he stood forth the heir and avenger of the unfortunate Soliman. Mohammed obtained Anatolia by treaty and Romania by arms; and the soldier who presented him with the head of Mousa was rewarded as the benefactor of his king and country. The eight years of his sole and peaceful reign were usefully employed in banishing the vices of civil discord, and restoring on a firmer basis the fabric of the Ottoman monarchy. His last care was the choice of two vizirs, Bajazet and Ibrahim,[2] who might guide the youth of his son Amurath; and such was their union and prudence, that they concealed above forty days the emperor's death till the arrival of his successor in the palace of Boursa. A new war was kindled in Europe by the prince, or impostor, Mustapha; the first vizir lost his army and his head; but the more fortunate Ibrahim, whose name and family are still revered, extinguished the last pretender to the throne of Bajazet, and closed the scene of domestic hostility.

In these conflicts the wisest Turks, and indeed the body of the nation, were strongly attached to the unity of the empire; and Romania and Anatolia, so often torn asunder by private

---

[1] Arabshah, loc. citat. Abulfeda, Geograph. tab. xvii. p. 302; Busbequius, epist. i. p. 96, 97, in Itinere C. P. et Amasiano.

[2] The virtues of Ibrahim are praised by a contemporary Greek (Ducas, c. 25). His descendants are the sole nobles in Turkey: they content themselves with the administration of his pious foundations, are excused from public offices, and receive two annual visits from the sultan (Cantemir, p. 76).

ambition, were animated by a strong and invincible tendency
of cohesion. Their efforts might have instructed the Christian
powers; and had they occupied, with a confederate fleet, the
straits of Gallipoli, the Ottomans, at least in Europe, must have
been speedily annihilated. But the schism of the West, and the
factions and wars of France and England, diverted the Latins
from this generous enterprise: they enjoyed the present respite,
without a thought of futurity; and were often tempted by a
momentary interest to serve the common enemy of their religion.
A colony of Genoese,[1] which had been planted at Phocæa [2] on
the Ionian coast, was enriched by the lucrative monopoly of
alum; [3] and their tranquillity, under the Turkish empire, was
secured by the annual payment of tribute. In the last civil war
of the Ottomans, the Genoese governor, Adorno, a bold and
ambitous youth, embraced the party of Amurath; and undertook, with seven stout galleys, to transport him from Asia to
Europe. The sultan and five hundred guards embarked on
board the admiral's ship; which was manned by eight hundred
of the bravest Franks. His life and liberty were in their hands;
nor can we, without reluctance, applaud the fidelity of Adorno,
who, in the midst of the passage, knelt before him, and gratefully
accepted a discharge of his arrears of tribute. They landed in
sight of Mustapha and Gallipoli; two thousand Italians, armed
with lances and battle-axes, attended Amurath to the conquest
of Adrianople; and this venal service was soon repaid by the ruin
of the commerce and colony of Phocæa.

If Timour had generously marched at the request, and to the
relief, of the Greek emperor, he might be entitled to the praise
and gratitude of the Christians.[4] But a Musulman who carried

[1] See Pachymer (l. v. c. 29 [c. 30, tom. i. p. 420, ed. Bonn]), Nicephorus
Gregoras (l. ii. c. 1 [xv. 7? vol. ii. p. 766, ed. Bonn]), Sherefeddin (l. v.
c. 57), and Ducas (c. 25). The last of these, a curious and careful observer,
is entitled, from his birth and station, to particular credit in all that
concerns Ionia and the islands. Among the nations that resorted to New
Phocæa, he mentions the English ('Ιγγλῆνοι [p. 161, ed. Bonn]); an early
evidence of Mediterranean trade.

[2] For the spirit of navigation and freedom of ancient Phocæa, or rather
of the Phocæans, consult the first book of Herodotus, and the Geographical
Index of his last and learned French translator, M. Larcher (tom. vii.
p. 299).

[3] Phocæa is not enumerated by Pliny (Hist. Nat. xxxv. 52) among the
places productive of alum: he reckons Egypt as the first, and for the
second the isle of Melos, whose alum-mines are described by Tournefort
(tom. i. lettre iv.), a traveller and a naturalist. After the loss of Phocæa,
the Genoese, in 1459, found that useful mineral in the isle of Ischia (Ismael.
Bouillaud, ad Ducam, c. 25).

[4] The writer who has the most abused this fabulous generosity is our
ingenious Sir William Temple (his Works, vol. iii. p. 349, 350, octavo

into Georgia the sword of persecution, and respected the holy
warfare of Bajazet, was not disposed to pity or succour the
idolaters of Europe. The Tartar followed the impulse of ambition;
and the deliverance of Constantinople was the accidental consequence. When Manuel abdicated the government, it was his
prayer, rather than his hope, that the ruin of the church and
state might be delayed beyond his unhappy days; and after his
return from a western pilgrimage, he expected every hour the
news of the sad catastrophe. On a sudden he was astonished
and rejoiced by the intelligence of the retreat, the overthrow,
and the captivity of the Ottoman. Manuel [1] immediately sailed
from Modon in the Morea; ascended the throne of Constantinople, and dismissed his blind competitor to an easy exile in
the isle of Lesbos. The ambassadors of the son of Bajazet were
soon introduced to his presence; but their pride was fallen, their
tone was modest: they were awed by the just apprehension lest
the Greeks should open to the Moguls the gates of Europe.
Soliman saluted the emperor by the name of father; solicited
at his hands the government or gift of Romania; and promised
to deserve his favour by inviolable friendship, and the restitution of Thessalonica, with the most important places along the
Strymon, the Propontis, and the Black Sea. The alliance of
Soliman exposed the emperor to the enmity and revenge of
Mousa: the Turks appeared in arms before the gates of Constantinople; but they were repulsed by sea and land; and unless
the city was guarded by some foreign mercenaries, the Greeks
must have wondered at their own triumph. But, instead of
prolonging the division of the Ottoman powers, the policy or
passion of Manuel was tempted to assist the most formidable
of the sons of Bajazet. He concluded a treaty with Mohammed,
whose progress was checked by the insuperable barrier of Gallipoli: the sultan and his troops were transported over the
Bosphorus; he was hospitably entertained in the capital; and
his successful sally was the first step to the conquest of Romania.
The ruin was suspended by the prudence and moderation of the
conqueror: he faithfully discharged his own obligations and

edition), that lover of exotic virtue. After the conquest of Russia, etc.,
and the passage of the Danube, his Tartar hero relieves, visits, admires,
and refuses the city of Constantine. His flattering pencil deviates in
every line from the truth of history; yet his pleasing fictions are more
excusable than the gross errors of Cantemir.

[1] For the reigns of Manuel and John, of Mohammed I. and Amurath II.,
see the Othman history of Cantemir (p. 70-95), and the three Greeks,
Chalcocondyles, Phranza, and Ducas, who is still superior to his rivals.

those of Soliman; respected the laws of gratitude and peace;
and left the emperor guardian of his two younger sons, in the
vain hope of saving them from the jealous cruelty of their
brother Amurath. But the execution of his last testament
would have offended the national honour and religion; and the
divan unanimously pronounced that the royal youths should
never be abandoned to the custody and education of a Christian
dog. On this refusal the Byzantine councils were divided: but
the age and caution of Manuel yielded to the presumption of his
son John; and they unsheathed a dangerous weapon of revenge,
by dismissing the true or false Mustapha, who had long been
detained as a captive and hostage, and for whose maintenance
they received an annual pension of three hundred thousand
aspers.[1] At the door of his prison, Mustapha subscribed to
every proposal; and the keys of Gallipoli, or rather of Europe,
were stipulated as the price of his deliverance. But no sooner
was he seated on the throne of Romania than he dismissed the
Greek ambassadors with a smile of contempt, declaring, in a
pious tone, that, at the day of judgment, he would rather answer
for the violation of an oath, than for the surrender of a Musulman city into the hands of the infidels. The emperor was at
once the enemy of the two rivals, from whom he had sustained,
and to whom he had offered, an injury; and the victory of
Amurath was followed, in the ensuing spring, by the siege of
Constantinople.[2]

The religious merit of subduing the city of the Cæsars attracted
from Asia a crowd of volunteers, who aspired to the crown of
martyrdom; their military ardour was inflamed by the promise
of rich spoils and beautiful females; and the sultan's ambition
was consecrated by the presence and prediction of Seid Bechar,
a descendant of the prophet,[3] who arrived in the camp, on a mule,
with a venerable train of five hundred disciples. But he might
blush, if a fanatic could blush, at the failure of his assurances.
The strength of the walls resisted an army of two hundred

---

[1] The Turkish asper (from the Greek ἀσπρός) is, or was, a piece of *white*
or silver money, at present much debased, but which was formerly equivalent to the fifty-fourth part, at least, of a Venetian ducat or sequin; and the
300,000 aspers, a princely allowance or royal tribute, may be computed at
£2500 sterling (Leunclav. Pandect. Turc. p. 406-408).

[2] For the siege of Constantinople in 1422, see the particular and contemporary narrative of John Cananus, published by Leo Allatius, at the
end of his edition of Acropolita (p. 188-199).

[3] Cantemir, p. 80. Cananus, who describes Seid Bechar without naming
him, supposes that the friend of Mohammed assumed in his amours the
privilege of a prophet, and that the fairest of the Greek nuns were promised
to the saint and his disciples.

thousand Turks: their assaults were repelled by the sallies of
the Greeks and their foreign mercenaries; the old resources
of defence were opposed to the new engines of attack; and the
enthusiasm of the dervish, who was snatched to heaven in
visionary converse with Mohammed, was answered by the
credulity of the Christians, who *beheld* the Virgin Mary, in a violet
garment, walking on the rampart and animating their courage.[1]
After a siege of two months Amurath was recalled to Boursa by
a domestic revolt, which had been kindled by Greek treachery,
and was soon extinguished by the death of a guiltless brother.
While he led his Janizaries to new conquests in Europe and Asia,
the Byzantine empire was indulged in a servile and precarious
respite of thirty years. Manuel sank into the grave; and John
Palæologus was permitted to reign, for an annual tribute of three
hundred thousand aspers, and the dereliction of almost all that
he held beyond the suburbs of Constantinople.

In the establishment and restoration of the Turkish empire the
first merit must doubtless be assigned to the personal qualities
of the sultans; since, in human life, the most important scenes
will depend on the character of a single actor. By some shades
of wisdom and virtue they may be discriminated from each other;
but, except in a single instance, a period of nine reigns, and two
hundred and sixty-five years, is occupied, from the elevation of
Othman to the death of Soliman, by a rare series of warlike and
active princes, who impressed their subjects with obedience and
their enemies with terror. Instead of the slothful luxury of the
seraglio, the heirs of royalty were educated in the council and
the field: from early youth they were entrusted by their fathers
with the command of provinces and armies; and this manly
institution, which was often productive of civil war must
have essentially contributed to the discipline and vigour, of the
monarchy. The Ottomans cannot style themselves, like the
Arabian caliphs, the descendants or successors of the apostle of
God; and the kindred which they claim with the Tartar khans
of the house of Zingis appears to be founded in flattery rather than
in truth.[2] Their origin is obscure; but their sacred and indefeasible right, which no time can erase, and no violence can in-
fringe, was soon and unalterably implanted in the minds of their
subjects. A weak or vicious sultan may be deposed and strangled;
but his inheritance devolves to an infant or an idiot: nor has

[1] For this miraculous apparition Cananus appeals to the Musulman
saint; but who will bear testimony for Seid Bechar?
[2] See Rycaut (l. i. c. 13). The Turkish sultans assume the title of khan.
Yet Abulghazi is ignorant of his Ottoman cousins.

the most daring rebel presumed to ascend the throne of his lawful sovereign.[1]

While the transient dynasties of Asia have been continually subverted by a crafty vizir in the palace or a victorious general in the camp, the Ottoman succession has been confirmed by the practice of five centuries, and is now incorporated with the vital principle of the Turkish nation.

To the spirit and constitution of that nation a strong and singular influence may however be ascribed. The primitive subjects of Othman were the four hundred families of wandering Turkmans who had followed his ancestors from the Oxus to the Sangar; and the plains of Anatolia are still covered with the white and black tents of their rustic brethren. But this original drop was dissolved in the mass of voluntary and vanquished subjects, who, under the name of Turks, are united by the common ties of religion, language, and manners. In the cities from Erzeroum to Belgrade, that national appellation is common to all the Moslems, the first and most honourable inhabitants; but they have abandoned, at least in Romania, the villages and the cultivation of the land to the Christian peasants. In the vigorous age of the Ottoman government the Turks were themselves excluded from all civil and military honours; and a servile class, an artificial people, was raised by the discipline of education to obey, to conquer, and to command.[2] From the time of Orchan and the first Amurath the sultans were persuaded that a government of the sword must be renewed in each generation with new soldiers; and that such soldiers must be sought, not in effeminate Asia, but among the hardy and warlike natives of Europe. The provinces of Thrace, Macedonia, Albania, Bulgaria, and Servia became the perpetual seminary of the Turkish army; and when the royal fifth of the captives was diminished by conquest, an inhuman tax of the fifth child, or of every fifth year, was rigorously levied on the Christian families. At the age of twelve or fourteen years the most robust

---

[1] The third grand vizir of the name of Kiuperli, who was slain at the battle of Salankanen in 1691 (Cantemir, p. 382), presumed to say that all the successors of Soliman had been fools or tyrants, and that it was time to abolish the race (Marsigli, Stato Militare, etc., p. 28). This political heretic was a good Whig, and justified against the French ambassador the revolution of England (Mignot, Hist. des Ottomans, tom. iii. p. 434). His presumption condemns the singular exception of continuing offices in the same family.

[2] Chalcocondyles (l. v.) and Ducas (c. 23) exhibit the rude lineaments of the Ottoman policy, and the transmutation of Christian children into Turkish soldiers.

youths were torn from their parents; their names were enrolled
in a book; and from that moment they were clothed, taught, and
maintained for the public service. According to the promise
of their appearance, they were selected for the royal schools of
Boursa, Pera, and Adrianople, intrusted to the care of the
bashaws, or dispersed in the houses of the Anatolian peasantry.
It was the first care of their masters to instruct them in the
Turkish language: their bodies were exercised by every labour
that could fortify their strength; they learned to wrestle, to
leap, to run, to shoot with the bow, and afterwards with the
musket; till they were drafted into the chambers and companies
of the Janizaries, and severely trained in the military or monastic
discipline of the order. The youths most conspicuous for birth,
talents, and beauty, were admitted into the inferior class of
Agiamoglans, or the more liberal rank of *Ichoglans*, of whom the
former were attached to the palace, and the latter to the person
of the prince. In four successive schools, under the rod of the
white eunuchs, the arts of horsemanship and of darting the
javelin were their daily exercise, while those of a more studious
cast applied themselves to the study of the Koran, and the
knowledge of the Arabic and Persian tongues. As they advanced in seniority and merit, they were gradually dismissed to
military, civil, and even ecclesiastical employments: the longer
their stay, the higher was their expectation; till, at a mature
period, they were admitted into the number of the forty agas,
who stood before the sultan, and were promoted by his choice to
the government of provinces and the first honours of the empire.[1]
Such a mode of institution was admirably adapted to the form
and spirit of a despotic monarchy. The ministers and generals
were, in the strictest sense, the slaves of the emperor, to whose
bounty they were indebted for their instruction and support.
When they left the seraglio, and suffered their beards to grow as
the symbol of enfranchisement, they found themselves in an
important office, without faction or friendship, without parents
and without heirs, dependent on the hand which had raised
them from the dust, and which, on the slightest displeasure,
could break in pieces these statues of glass, as they are aptly
termed by the Turkish proverb.[2] In the slow and painful steps

[1] This sketch of the Turkish education and discipline is chiefly borrowed
from Rycaut's State of the Ottoman Empire, the Stato Militare del'
Imperio Ottomanno of Count Marsigli (in Haya, 1732, in folio), and a
Description of the Seraglio, approved by Mr. Greaves himself, a curious
traveller, and inserted in the second volume of his works.

[2] From the series of 115 vizirs, till the siege of Vienna (Marsigli, p. 13),
their place may be valued at three years and a half purchase.

of education, their characters and talents were unfolded to a discerning eye: the *man*, naked and alone, was reduced to the standard of his personal merit; and, if the sovereign had wisdom to choose, he possessed a pure and boundless liberty of choice. The Ottoman candidates were trained by the virtues of abstinence to those of action; by the habits of submission to those of command. A similar spirit was diffused among the troops; and their silence and sobriety, their patience and modesty, have extorted the reluctant praise of their Christian enemies.[1] Nor can the victory appear doubtful, if we compare the discipline and exercise of the Janizaries with the pride of birth, the independence of chivalry, the ignorance of the new levies, the mutinous temper of the veterans, and the vices of intemperance and disorder which so long contaminated the armies of Europe.

The only hope of salvation for the Greek empire and the adjacent kingdoms would have been some more powerful weapon, some discovery in the art of war, that should give them a decisive superiority over their Turkish foes. Such a weapon was in their hands; such a discovery had been made in the critical moment of their fate. The chemists of China or Europe had found, by casual or elaborate experiments, that a mixture of saltpetre, sulphur, and charcoal produces, with a spark of fire, a tremendous explosion. It was soon observed that, if the expansive force were compressed in a strong tube, a ball of stone or iron might be expelled with irresistible and destructive velocity. The precise era of the invention and application of gunpowder [2] is involved in doubtful traditions and equivocal language; yet we may clearly discern that it was known before the middle of the fourteenth century, and that before the end of the same the use of artillery in battles and sieges by sea and land was familiar to the states of Germany, Italy, Spain, France, and England.[3] The priority of nations is of small account; none could derive any exclusive benefit from their previous or

---

[1] See the entertaining and judicious letters of Busbequius.

[2] The first and second volumes of Dr. Watson's Chemical Essays contain two valuable discourses on the discovery and composition of gunpowder.

[3] On this subject modern testimonies cannot be trusted. The original passages are collected by Ducange (Gloss. Latin. tom. i. p. 675, *Bombarda*). But in the early doubtful twilight, the name, sound, fire, and effect, that seem to express *our* artillery, may be fairly interpreted of the old engines and the Greek fire. For the English cannon at Crecy, the authority of John Villani (Chron. l. xii. c. 65) must be weighed against the silence of Froissard. Yet Muratori (Antiquit. Italiæ medii Ævi, tom. ii. Dissert. xxvi. p. 514, 515) has produced a decisive passage from Petrarch (De Remediis utriusque Fortunæ Dialog.), who, before the year 1344, execrates this terrestrial thunder, *nuper* rara, *nunc* communis.

superior knowledge; and in the common improvement they stood on the same level of relative power and military science. Nor was it possible to circumscribe the secret within the pale of the church; it was disclosed to the Turks by the treachery of apostates and the selfish policy of rivals; and the sultans had sense to adopt, and wealth to reward, the talents of a Christian engineer. The Genoese, who transported Amurath into Europe, must be accused as his preceptors; and it was probably by their hands that his cannon was cast and directed at the siege of Constantinople.[1] The first attempt was indeed unsuccessful; but in the general warfare of the age the advantage was on *their* side who were most commonly the assailants; for a while the proportion of the attack and defence was suspended, and this thundering artillery was pointed against the walls and towers which had been erected only to resist the less potent engines of antiquity. By the Venetians the use of gunpowder was communicated without reproach to the sultans of Egypt and Persia, their allies against the Ottoman power; the secret was soon propagated to the extremities of Asia; and the advantage of the European was confined to his easy victories over the savages of the new world. If we contrast the rapid progress of this mischievous discovery with the slow and laborious advances of reason, science, and the arts of peace, a philosopher, according to his temper, will laugh or weep at the folly of mankind.

CHAPTER LXVI

Applications of the Eastern Emperors to the Popes—Visits to the West of John the First, Manuel, and John the Second, Palæologus—Union of the Greek and Latin Churches promoted by the Council of Basil, and concluded at Ferrara and Florence—State of Literature at Constantinople—Its Revival in Italy by the Greek Fugitives—Curiosity and Emulation of the Latins

IN the four last centuries of the Greek emperors their friendly or hostile aspect towards the pope and the Latins may be observed as the thermometer of their prosperity or distress—as the scale of the rise and fall of the barbarian dynasties. When the Turks of the house of Seljuk pervaded Asia, and threatened Constantinople, we have seen at the council of Placentia the suppliant

---

[1] The Turkish cannon, which Ducas (c. 30 [p. 211, ed. Bonn]) first introduces before Belgrade (A.D. 1436), is mentioned by Chalcocondyles (l. v. p. 123 [p. 231, ed. Bonn]) in 1422, at the siege of Constantinople.

ambassadors of Alexius imploring the protection of the common father of the Christians. No sooner had the arms of the French pilgrims removed the sultan from Nice to Iconium than the Greek princes resumed, or avowed, their genuine hatred and contempt for the schismatics of the West, which precipitated the first downfall of their empire. The date of the Mogul invasion is marked in the soft and charitable language of John Vataces. After the recovery of Constantinople the throne of the first Palæologus was encompassed by foreign and domestic enemies: as long as the sword of Charles was suspended over his head he basely courted the favour of the Roman pontiff, and sacrificed to the present danger his faith, his virtue, and the affection of his subjects. On the decease of Michael the prince and people asserted the independence of their church and the purity of their creed: the elder Andronicus neither feared nor loved the Latins; in his last distress pride was the safeguard of superstition; nor could he decently retract in his age the firm and orthodox declarations of his youth. His grandson, the younger Andronicus, was less a slave in his temper and situation; and the conquest of Bithynia by the Turks admonished him to seek a temporal and spiritual alliance with the Western princes. After a separation and silence of fifty years a secret agent, the monk Barlaam, was despatched to Pope Benedict the Twelfth; and his artful instructions appear to have been drawn by the master-hand of the great domestic.[1] "Most holy father," was he commissioned to say, "the emperor is not less desirous than yourself of a union between the two churches; but in this delicate transaction he is obliged to respect his own dignity and the prejudices of his subjects. The ways of union are twofold, force and persuasion. Of force, the inefficacy has been already tried, since the Latins have subdued the empire without subduing the minds of the Greeks. The method of persuasion, though slow, is sure and permanent. A deputation of thirty or forty of our doctors would probably agree with those of the Vatican in the love of truth and the unity of belief; but on their return, what would be the use, the recompense, of such agreement? the scorn of their brethren, and the reproaches of a blind and obstinate nation. Yet that nation is accustomed to reverence the general councils which have fixed the articles of

---

[1] This curious instruction was transcribed (I believe) from the Vatican archives by Odoricus Raynaldus, in his Continuation of the Annals of Baronius (Romæ, 1646-1677, in ten volumes in folio). I have contented myself with the abbé Fleury (Hist. Ecclésiastique, tom. xx. p. 1-8), whose abstracts I have always found to be clear, accurate, and impartial.

our faith; and if they reprobate the decrees of Lyons, it is because
the Eastern churches were neither heard nor represented in that
arbitrary meeting. For this salutary end it will be expedient,
and even necessary, that a well-chosen legate should be sent
into Greece to convene the patriarchs of Constantinople, Alexandria, Antioch, and Jerusalem, and with their aid to prepare
a free and universal synod. But at this moment," continued
the subtle agent, " the empire is assaulted and endangered by
the Turks, who have occupied four of the greatest cities of
Anatolia. The Christian inhabitants have expressed a wish of
returning to their allegiance and religion; but the forces and
revenues of the emperor are insufficient for their deliverance:
and the Roman legate must be accompanied or preceded by an
army of Franks to expel the infidels, and open a way to the holy
sepulchre." If the suspicious Latins should require some pledge,
some previous effect of the sincerity of the Greeks, the answers of
Barlaam were perspicuous and rational. " 1. A general synod
can alone consummate the union of the churches; nor can such
a synod be held till the three Oriental patriarchs and a great
number of bishops are enfranchised from the Mohammedan yoke.
2. The Greeks are alienated by a long series of oppression and
injury: they must be reconciled by some act of brotherly love,
some effectual succour, which may fortify the authority and
arguments of the emperor and the friends of the union. 3. If
some difference of faith or ceremonies should be found incurable,
the Greeks however are the disciples of Christ, and the Turks are
the common enemies of the Christian name. The Armenians,
Cyprians, and Rhodians are equally attacked; and it will become
the piety of the French princes to draw their swords in the
general defence of religion. 4. Should the subjects of Andronicus be treated as the worst of schismatics, of heretics, of pagans,
a judicious policy may yet instruct the powers of the West to
embrace a useful ally, to uphold a sinking empire, to guard the
confines of Europe, and rather to join the Greeks against the
Turks than to expect the union of the Turkish arms with the
troops and treasures of captive Greece." The reasons, the
offers, and the demands of Andronicus were eluded with cold
and stately indifference. The kings of France and Naples
declined the dangers and glory of a crusade: the pope refused to
call a new synod to determine old articles of faith; and his regard
for the obsolete claims of the Latin emperor and clergy engaged
him to use an offensive superscription—" To the *moderator* [1]

[1] The ambiguity of this title is happy or ingenious; and *moderator*, as

of the Greeks, and the persons who style themselves the patriarchs of the Eastern churches." For such an embassy a time and character less propitious could not easily have been found. Benedict the Twelfth [1] was a dull peasant, perplexed with scruples, and immersed in sloth and wine: his pride might enrich with a third crown the papal tiara, but he was alike unfit for the regal and the pastoral office.

After the decease of Andronicus, while the Greeks were distracted by intestine war, they could not presume to agitate a general union of the Christians. But as soon as Cantacuzene had subdued and pardoned his enemies, he was anxious to justify, or at least to extenuate, the introduction of the Turks into Europe and the nuptials of his daughter with a Musulman prince. Two officers of state, with a Latin interpreter, were sent in his name to the Roman court, which was transplanted to Avignon, on the banks of the Rhône, during a period of seventy years: they represented the hard necessity which had urged him to embrace the alliance of the miscreants, and pronounced by his command the specious and edifying sounds of union and crusade. Pope Clement the Sixth,[2] the successor of Benedict, received them with hospitality and honour, acknowledged the innocence of their sovereign, excused his distress, applauded his magnanimity, and displayed a clear knowledge of the state and revolutions of the Greek empire, which he had imbibed from the honest accounts of a Savoyard lady, an attendant of the empress Anne.[3] If Clement was ill endowed with the virtues of

synonymous to *rector*, *gubernator*, is a word of classical, and even Ciceronian, Latinity, which may be found, not in the Glossary of Ducange, but in the Thesaurus of Robert Stephens.

[1] The first epistle (sine titulo) of Petrarch exposes the danger of the *bark* and the incapacity of the *pilot*. Hæc inter, vino madidus, ævo gravis, ac soporifero rore perfusus, jamjam nutitat, dormitat, jam somno præceps, atque (utinam solus) ruit. . . . Heu quanto felicius patrio terram sulcasset aratro, quam scalmum piscatorium ascendisset! This satire engages his biographer to weigh the virtues and vices of Benedict XII., which have been exaggerated by Guelphs and Ghibelines, by Papists and Protestants (see Mémoires sur la Vie de Pétrarque, tom. i. p. 259; ii. not. xv. p. 13-16). He gave occasion to the saying, Bibamus papaliter.

[2] See the original Lives of Clement VI. in Muratori (Script. Rerum Italicarum, tom. iii. P. ii. p. 550-589); Matteo Villani (Chron. l. iii. c. 43, in Muratori, tom. xiv. p. 186), who styles him molto cavallaresco, poco religioso; Fleury (Hist. Ecclés. tom. xx. p. 126); and the Vie de Pétrarque (tom. ii. p. 42-45). The abbé de Sade treats him with the most indulgence; but *he* is a gentleman as well as a priest.

[3] Her name (most probably corrupted) was Zampea. She had accompanied and alone remained with her mistress at Constantinople, where her prudence, erudition, and politeness deserved the praises of the Greeks themselves (Cantacuzen. l. i. c. 42 [tom. i. p. 205, ed. Bonn]).

a priest, he possessed however the spirit and magnificence of a prince whose liberal hand distributed benefices and kingdoms with equal facility. Under his reign Avignon was the seat of pomp and pleasure: in his youth he had surpassed the licentious- ness of a baron; and the palace, nay the bedchamber of the pope, was adorned, or polluted, by the visits of his female favourites. The wars of France and England were adverse to the holy enter- prise; but his vanity was amused by the splendid idea; and the Greek ambassadors returned with two Latin bishops, the ministers of the pontiff. On their arrival at Constantinople the emperor and the nuncios admired each other's piety and elo- quence; and their frequent conferences were filled with mutual praises and promises, by which both parties were amused, and neither could be deceived. " I am delighted," said the devout Cantacuzene, " with the project of our holy war, which must redound to my personal glory as well as to the public benefit of Christendom. My dominions will give a free passage to the armies of France: my troops, my galleys, my treasures, shall be consecrated to the common cause; and happy would be my fate could I deserve and obtain the crown of martyrdom. Words are insufficient to express the ardour with which I sigh for the reunion of the scattered members of Christ. If my death could avail, I would gladly present my sword and my neck: if the spiritual phœnix could arise from my ashes, I would erect the pile and kindle the flame with my own hands." Yet the Greek emperor presumed to observe that the articles of faith which divided the two churches had been introduced by the pride and precipitation of the Latins: he disclaimed the servile and arbitrary steps of the first Palæologus, and firmly declared that he would never submit his conscience unless to the decrees of a free and universal synod. " The situation of the times," continued he, " will not allow the pope and myself to meet either at Rome or Constantinople; but some maritime city may be chosen on the verge of the two empires, to unite the bishops, and to instruct the faithful of the East and West." The nuncios seemed content with the proposition; and Cantacuzene affects to deplore the failure of his hopes, which were soon overthrown by the death of Clement, and the different temper of his suc- cessor. His own life was prolonged, but it was prolonged in a cloister; and, except by his prayers, the humble monk was incapable of directing the counsels of his pupil or the state.[1]

[1] See this whole negotiation in Cantacuzene (l. iv. c. 9), who, amidst the praises and virtues which he bestows on himself, reveals the uneasiness of a guilty conscience.

Yet of all the Byzantine princes, that pupil, John Palæologus, was the best disposed to embrace, to believe, and to obey the shepherd of the West. His mother, Anne of Savoy, was baptised in the bosom of the Latin church: her marriage with Andronicus imposed a change of name, of apparel, and of worship, but her heart was still faithful to her country and religion: she had formed the infancy of her son, and she governed the emperor after his mind, or at least his stature, was enlarged to the size of man. In the first year of his deliverance and restoration the Turks were still masters of the Hellespont; the son of Cantacuzene was in arms at Adrianople, and Palæologus could depend neither on himself nor on his people. By his mother's advice, and in the hope of foreign aid, he abjured the rights both of the church and state; and the act of slavery,[1] subscribed in purple ink, and sealed with the *golden* bull, was privately intrusted to an Italian agent. The first article of the treaty is an oath of fidelity and obedience to Innocent the Sixth and his successors, the supreme pontiffs of the Roman and Catholic church. The emperor promises to entertain with due reverence their legates and nuncios, to assign a palace for their residence and a temple for their worship, and to deliver his second son Manuel as the hostage of his faith. For these condescensions he requires a prompt succour of fifteen galleys, with five hundred men-at-arms and a thousand archers, to serve against his Christian and Musulman enemies. Palæologus engages to impose on his clergy and people the same spiritual yoke; but as the resistance of the Greeks might be justly foreseen, he adopts the two effectual methods of corruption and education. The legate was empowered to distribute the vacant benefices among the ecclesiastics who should subscribe the creed of the Vatican: three schools were instituted to instruct the youth of Constantinople in the language and doctrine of the Latins; and the name of Andronicus, the heir of the empire, was enrolled as the first student. Should he fail in the measures of persuasion or force, Palæologus declares himself unworthy to reign, transfers to the pope all regal and paternal authority, and invests Innocent with full power to regulate the family, the government, and the marriage of his son and successor. But this treaty was neither executed nor published: the Roman galleys were as vain and imaginery as the submission of the Greeks;

---

[1] See this ignominious treaty in Fleury (Hist. Ecclés. p. 151-154), from Raynaldus, who drew it from the Vatican archives. It was not worth the trouble of a pious forgery.

and it was only by the secrecy that their sovereign escaped the dishonour of this fruitless humiliation.

The tempest of the Turkish arms soon burst on his head; and after the loss of Adrianople and Romania he was enclosed in his capital, the vassal of the haughty Amurath, with the miserable hope of being the last devoured by the savage. In this abject state Palæologus embraced the resolution of embarking for Venice, and casting himself at the feet of the pope: he was the first of the Byzantine princes who had ever visited the unknown regions of the West, yet in them alone he could seek consolation or relief; and with less violation of his dignity he might appear in the sacred college than at the Ottoman *Porte*. After a long absence the Roman pontiffs were returning from Avignon to the banks of the Tiber: Urban the Fifth,[1] of a mild and virtuous character, encouraged or allowed the pilgrimage of the Greek prince, and, within the same year, enjoyed the glory of receiving in the Vatican the two Imperial shadows who represented the majesty of Constantine and Charlemagne. In this suppliant visit the emperor of Constantinople, whose vanity was lost in his distress, gave more than could be expected of empty sounds and formal submissions. A previous trial was imposed; and in the presence of four cardinals he acknowledged, as a true Catholic, the supremacy of the pope, and the double procession of the Holy Ghost. After this purification he was introduced to a public audience in the church of St. Peter: Urban, in the midst of the cardinals, was seated on his throne; the Greek monarch, after three genuflexions, devoutly kissed the feet, the hands, and at length the mouth of the holy father, who celebrated high mass in his presence, allowed him to lead the bridle of his mule, and treated him with a sumptuous banquet in the Vatican. The entertainment of Palæologus was friendly and honourable, yet some difference was observed between the emperors of the East and West;[2] nor could the former be entitled to the rare privilege of chanting the Gospel in the rank of a deacon.[3] In favour of his

---

[1] See the two first original Lives of Urban V. (in Muratori, Script. Rerum Italicarum, tom. iii. P. ii. p. 623, 635), and the Ecclesiastical Annals of Spondanus (tom. i. p. 573, A.D. 1369, No. 7), and Raynaldus (Fleury, Hist. Ecclés. tom. xx. p. 223, 224). Yet, from some variations, I suspect the papal writers of slightly magnifying the genuflexions of Palæologus.

[2] Paullo minus quam si fuisset Imperator Romanorum. Yet his title of Imperator Græcorum was no longer disputed (Vit. Urban V., p. 623).

[3] It was confined to the successors of Charlemagne, and to them only on Christmas Day. On all other festivals these Imperial deacons were content to serve the pope, as he said mass, with the book and the *corporal*. Yet the abbé de Sade generously thinks that the merits of Charles IV.

proselyte, Urban strove to rekindle the zeal of the French king
and the other powers of the West; but he found them cold in
the general cause, and active only in their domestic quarrels.
The last hope of the emperor was in an English mercenary, John
Hawkwood,[1] or Acuto, who, with a band of adventurers, the
White Brotherhood, had ravaged Italy from the alps to Calabria,
sold his services to the hostile states, and incurred a just excommunication by shooting his arrows against the papal residence.
A special licence was granted to negotiate with the outlaw, but
the forces, or the spirit, of Hawkwood were unequal to the enterprise: and it was for the advantage perhaps of Palæologus to
be disappointed of a succour that must have been costly, that
could not be effectual, and which might have been dangerous.[2]
The disconsolate Greek[3] prepared for his return, but even his
return was impeded by a most ignominious obstacle. On his
arrival at Venice he had borrowed large sums at exorbitant
usury; but his coffers were empty, his creditors were impatient,
and his person was detained as the best security for the payment.
His eldest son Andronicus, the regent of Constantinople, was
repeatedly urged to exhaust every resource, and even by stripping the churches, to extricate his father from captivity and
disgrace. But the unnatural youth was insensible of the disgrace, and secretly pleased with the captivity of the emperor:
the state was poor, the clergy was obstinate; nor could some
religious scruple be wanting to excuse the guilt of his indifference
and delay. Such undutiful neglect was severely reproved by

might have entitled him, though not on the proper day (A.D. 1368,
November 1), to the whole privilege. He seems to affix a just value on
the privilege and the man (Vie de Pétrarque, tom. iii. p. 735).

[1] Through some Italian corruptions, the etymology of *Falcone in bosco*
(Matteo [Filippo] Villani, l. xi. c. 79, in Muratori, tom. xiv. p. 746) suggests
the English word *Hawkwood*, the true name of our adventurous countryman (Thomas Walsingham, Hist. Anglican. inter Scriptores Camdeni,
p. 184). After two-and-twenty victories and one defeat, he died, in 1394,
general of the Florentines, and was buried with such honours as the republic has not paid to Dante or Petrarch (Muratori, Annali d'Italia, tom.
xii. p. 212-371).

[2] This torrent of English (by birth or service) overflowed from France
into Italy after the peace of Bretigny in 1360. Yet the exclamation of
Muratori (Annali, tom. xii. p. 197) is rather true than civil. " Ci mancava
ancor questo, che dopo essere calpestrata l'Italia da tanti masnadieri
Tedeschi ed Ungheri, venissero fin dall' Inghliterra nuovi *cani* a finire di
divorarla."

[3] Chalcocondyles, l. i. p. 25, 26 [p. 50, *sq.*, ed. Bonn]. The Greek
supposes his journey to the king of France, which is sufficiently refuted by
the silence of the national historians. Nor am I much more inclined to
believe that Palæologus departed from Italy, valde bene consolatus et
contentus (Vit. Urban V. p. 623).

the piety of his brother Manuel, who instantly sold or mortgaged all that he possessed, embarked for Venice, relieved his father, and pledged his own freedom to be responsible for the debt. On his return to Constantinople the parent and king distinguished his two sons with suitable rewards; but the faith and manners of the slothful Palæologus had not been improved by his Roman pilgrimage; and his apostacy or conversion, devoid of any spiritual or temporal effects, was speedily forgotten by the Greeks and Latins.[1]

Thirty years after the return of Palæologus, his son and successor Manuel, from a similar motive, but on a larger scale, again visited the countries of the West. In a preceding chapter I have related his treaty with Bajazet, the violation of that treaty, the siege or blockade of Constantinople, and the French succour under the command of the gallant Boucicault.[2] By his ambassadors Manuel had solicited the Latin powers; but it was thought that the presence of a distressed monarch would draw tears and supplies from the hardest barbarians,[3] and the marshal who advised the journey prepared the reception of the Byzantine prince. The land was occupied by the Turks; but the navigation of Venice was safe and open: Italy received him as the first, or at least as the second, of the Christian princes; Manuel was pitied as the champion and confessor of the faith, and the dignity of his behaviour prevented that pity from sinking into contempt. From Venice he proceeded to Padua and Pavia; and even the Duke of Milan, a secret ally of Bajazet, gave him safe and honourable conduct to the verge of his dominions.[4] On the confines of France[5] the royal officers undertook the care of his person, journey, and expenses; and two thousand of the richest citizens, in arms and on horseback, came forth to meet him as far as Charenton, in the neighbourhood of the capital. At the gates

[1] His return in 1370, and the coronation of Manuel, Sept. 25, 1373 (Ducange, Fam. Byzant. p. 241), leaves some intermediate era for the conspiracy and punishment of Andronicus.

[2] Mémoires de Boucicault, P. i. c. 35, 36.

[3] His journey into the west of Europe is slightly, and I believe reluctantly, noticed by Chalcocondyles (l. ii. p. 44-50 [p. 84-97, ed. Bonn]) and Ducas (c. 14).

[4] Muratori, Annali d'Italia, tom. xii. p. 406. John Galeazzo was the first and most powerful duke of Milan. His connection with Bajazet is attested by Froissard, and he contributed to save and deliver the French captives of Nicopolis.

[5] For the reception of Manuel at Paris, see Spondanus (Annal. Eccles. tom. i. p. 676, 677, A.D. 1400, No. 5), who quotes Juvenal des Ursins, and the monk of St. Denys; and Villaret (Hist. de France, tom. xii. p. 331-334), who quotes nobody, according to the last fashion of the French writers.

of Paris he was saluted by the chancellor and the parliament;
and Charles the Sixth, attended by his princes and nobles,
welcomed his brother with a cordial embrace. The successor
of Constantine was clothed in a robe of white silk and mounted
on a milk-white steed, a circumstance, in the French ceremonial,
of singular importance: the white colour is considered as the
symbol of sovereignty; and in a late visit the German emperor,
after a haughty demand and a peevish refusal, had been reduced
to content himself with a black courser. Manuel was lodged in
the Louvre: a succession of feasts and balls, the pleasures of the
banquet and the chase, were ingeniously varied by the politeness of the French to display their magnificence and amuse his
grief; he was indulged in the liberty of his chapel, and the
doctors of the Sorbonne were astonished, and possibly scandalised,
by the language, the rites, and the vestments of his Greek clergy.
But the slightest glance on the state of the kingdom must teach
him to despair of any effectual assistance. The unfortunate
Charles, though he enjoyed some lucid intervals, continually
relapsed into furious or stupid insanity; the reins of government were alternately seized by his brother and uncle, the dukes
of Orleans and Burgundy, whose factious competition prepared
the miseries of civil war. The former was a gay youth, dissolved
in luxury and love: the latter was the father of John count of
Nevers, who had so lately been ransomed from Turkish captivity;
and, if the fearless son was ardent to revenge his defeat, the more
prudent Burgundy was content with the cost and peril of the first
experiment. When Manuel had satiated the curiosity, and perhaps fatigued the patience of the French, he resolved on a visit
to the adjacent island. In his progress from Dover he was entertained at Canterbury with due reverence by the prior and monks
of St. Austin, and, on Blackheath, king Henry the Fourth, with
the English court, saluted the Greek hero (I copy our old
historian), who, during many days, was lodged and treated in
London as emperor of the East.[1] But the state of England was
still more adverse to the design of the holy war. In the same
year the hereditary sovereign had been deposed and murdered:

---

[1] A short note of Manuel in England is extracted by Dr. Hody from a
MS. at Lambeth (de Græcis illustribus, p. 14), C. P. Imperator, diu
variisque et horrendis Paganorum insultibus coarctatus, ut pro eisdem
resistentiam triumphalem perquireret, Anglorum Regem visitare decrevit,
etc. Rex (says Walsingham, p. 364) [cum] nobili apparatû . . . suscepit
(ut decuit) tantum Heroa, duxitque Londonias, et per multos dies ex-
hibuit gloriose, pro expensis hospitii sui solvens, et eum respiciens [dignis]
tanto fastigo donativis. He repeats the same in his Upodigma Neustriæ
(p. 556).

the reigning prince was a successful usurper, whose ambition
was punished by jealousy and remorse; nor could Henry of
Lancaster withdraw his person or forces from the defence of a
throne incessantly shaken by conspiracy and rebellion. He
pitied, he praised, he feasted, the emperor of Constantinople;
but if the English monarch assumed the cross, it was only to
appease his people, and perhaps his conscience, by the merit or
semblance of this pious intention.[1] Satisfied, however, with gifts
and honours, Manuel returned to Paris; and, after a residence of
two years in the West, shaped his course through Germany and
Italy, embarked at Venice, and patiently expected, in the Morea,
the moment of his ruin or deliverance. Yet he had escaped the
ignominious necessity of offering his religion to public or private
sale. The Latin church was distracted by the great schism:
the kings, the nations, the universities of Europe, were divided
in their obedience between the popes of Rome and Avignon;
and the emperor, anxious to conciliate the friendship of both
parties, abstained from any correspondence with the indigent
and unpopular rivals. His journey coincided with the year of
the jubilee; but he passed through Italy without desiring or
deserving the plenary indulgence which abolished the guilt or
penance of the sins of the faithful. The Roman pope was
offended by this neglect, accused him of irreverence to an image
of Christ, and exhorted the princes of Italy to reject and abandon
the obstinate schismatic.[2]

During the period of the crusades the Greeks beheld with
astonishment and terror the perpetual stream of emigration that
flowed, and continued to flow, from the unknown climates of the
West. The visits of their last emperors removed the veil of
separation, and they disclosed to their eyes the powerful nations
of Europe, whom they no longer presumed to brand with the
name of barbarians. The observations of Manuel and his more
inquisitive followers have been preserved by a Byzantine
historian of the times:[3] his scattered ideas I shall collect and

---

[1] Shakespeare begins and ends the play of Henry IV. with that prince's
vow of a crusade, and his belief that he should die in Jerusalem.

[2] This fact is preserved in the Historia Politica, A.D. 1391-1478, published
by Martin Crusius (Turco-Græcia, p. 1-43). The image of Christ, which
the Greek emperor refused to worship, was probably a work of sculpture.

[3] The Greek and Turkish history of Laonicus Chalcocondyles ends with
the winter of 1463, and the abrupt conclusion seems to mark that he laid
down his pen in the same year. We know that he was an Athenian, and
that some contemporaries of the same name contributed to the revival of
the Greek language in Italy. But in his numerous digressions the modest
historian has never introduced himself; and his editor Leunclavius, as

abridge; and it may be amusing enough, perhaps instructive, to contemplate the rude pictures of Germany, France, and England, whose ancient and modern state are so familiar to *our* minds. I. GERMANY (says the Greek Chalcocondyles) is of ample latitude from Vienna to the Ocean, and it stretches (a strange geography) from Prague, in Bohemia, to the river Tartessus and the Pyrenæan mountains.[1] The soil, except in figs and olives, is sufficiently fruitful; the air is salubrious, the bodies of the natives are robust and healthy, and these cold regions are seldom visited with the calamities of pestilence or earthquakes. After the Scythians or Tartars, the Germans are the most numerous of nations: they are brave and patient, and, were they united under a single head, their force would be irresistible. By the gift of the pope, they have acquired the privilege of choosing the Roman emperor;[2] nor is any people more devoutly attached to the faith and obedience of the Latin patriarch. The greatest part of the country is divided among the princes and prelates; but Strasburg, Cologne, Hamburg, and more than two hundred free cities, are governed by sage and equal laws, according to the will and for the advantage of the whole community. The use of duels, or single combats on foot, prevails among them in peace and war; their industry excels in all the mechanic arts; and the Germans may boast of the invention of gunpowder and cannon, which is now diffused over the greatest part of the world. II. The kingdom of FRANCE is spread above fifteen or twenty days' journey from Germany to Spain, and from the Alps to the British Ocean, containing many flourishing cities, and among these Paris, the seat of the king, which surpasses the rest in riches and luxury. Many princes and lords alternately wait in his palace and acknowledge him as their sovereign: the most powerful are the dukes of Bretagne and Burgundy, of whom the latter possesses the wealthy province of Flanders, whose harbours are frequented by the ships and

well as Fabricius (Biblioth. Græc. tom. vi. p. 474), seems ignorant of his life and character. For his descriptions of Germany, France, and England, see l. ii. p. 36, 37, 44-50 [p. 70-72, 85-96, ed. Bonn].

[1] I shall not animadvert on the geographical errors of Chalcocondyles. In this instance he perhaps followed, and mistook, Herodotus (l. ii. c. 33), whose text may be explained (Herodote de Larcher, tom. ii. p. 219, 220), or whose ignorance may be excused. Had these modern Greeks never read Strabo, or any of their lesser geographers?

[2] A citizen of new Rome, while new Rome survived, would have scorned to dignify the German ῾Ρήξ with the titles of Βασιλεύς or Αὐτοκράτωρ ῾Ρωμαίων; but all pride was extinct in the bosom of Chalcocondyles, and he describes the Byzantine prince and his subjects by the proper, though humble, names of Ἕλληνες and Βασιλεὺς Ἑλλήνων.

merchants of our own and the more remote seas. The French
are an ancient and opulent people, and their language and
manners, though somewhat different, are not dissimilar from
those of the Italians. Vain of the Imperial dignity of Charlemagne, of their victories over the Saracens, and of the exploits
of their heroes Oliver and Rowland,[1] they esteem themselves the
first of the western nations; but this foolish arrogance has been
recently humbled by the unfortunate events of their wars against
the English, the inhabitants of the British island. III. BRITAIN,
in the ocean and opposite to the shores of Flanders, may be considered either as one or as three islands; but the whole is united
by a common interest, by the same manners, and by a similar
government. The measure of its circumference is five thousand
stadia: the land is overspread with towns and villages; though
destitute of wine, and not abounding in fruit-trees, it is fertile
in wheat and barley, in honey and wool, and much cloth is manu-
factured by the inhabitants. In populousness and power, in
riches and luxury, London,[2] the metropolis of the isle, may claim
a pre-eminence over all the cities of the West. It is situate on
the Thames, a broad and rapid river, which at the distance of
thirty miles falls into the Gallic Sea; and the daily flow and ebb
of the tide affords a safe entrance and departure to the vessels
of commerce. The king is the head of a powerful and turbulent
aristocracy: his principal vassals hold their estates by a free
and unalterable tenure, and the laws define the limits of his
authority and their obedience. The kingdom has been often
afflicted by foreign conquest and domestic sedition; but the
natives are bold and hardy, renowned in arms and victorious in
war. The form of their shields or targets is derived from the
Italians, that of their swords from the Greeks; the use of the
long bow is the peculiar and decisive advantage of the English.
Their language bears no affinity to the idioms of the continent:
in the habits of domestic life they are not easily distinguished

---

[1] Most of the old romances were translated in the fourteenth century
into French prose, and soon became the favourite amusement of the
knights and ladies in the court of Charles VI. If a Greek believed in the
exploits of Rowland and Oliver, he may surely be excused, since the
monks of St. Denys, the national historians, have inserted the fables of
Archbishop Turpin in their Chronicles of France.

[2] Λονδρῶν δὲ ἡ πόλις δυνάμει τε προέχουσα τῶν ἐν τῇ νήσῳ ταύτῃ πασῶν
πόλεων, ὄλβῳ τε καὶ τῇ ἄλλῃ εὐδαιμονίᾳ οὐδεμιᾶς τῶν πρὸς ἑσπέραν λειπομένη
[l. ii. p. 93, ed. Bonn]. Even since the time of Fitzstephen (the twelfth
century), London appears to have maintained this pre-eminence of wealth
and magnitude; and her gradual increase has, at least, kept pace with the
general improvement of Europe.

from their neighbours of France; but the most singular circumstance of their manners is their disregard of conjugal honour and of female chastity. In their mutual visits, as the first act of hospitality, the guest is welcomed in the embraces of their wives and daughters: among friends they are lent and borrowed without shame; nor are the islanders offended at this strange commerce and its inevitable consequences.[1] Informed as we are of the customs of old England, and assured of the virtue of our mothers, we may smile at the credulity, or resent the injustice, of the Greek, who must have confounded a modest salute [2] with a criminal embrace. But his credulity and injustice may teach an important lesson, to distrust the accounts of foreign and remote nations, and to suspend our belief of every tale that deviates from the laws of nature and the character of man.[3]

After his return, and the victory of Timour, Manuel reigned many years in prosperity and peace. As long as the sons of Bajazet solicited his friendship and spared his dominions, he was satisfied with the national religion; and his leisure was

[1] If the double sense of the verb Κύω (osculor, and in utero gero) be equivocal, the context and pious horror of Chalcocondyles can leave no doubt of his meaning and mistake (p. 49 [p. 93, ed. Bonn]).

[It is certainly very difficult to detect the " pious horror " in Chalcocondyles of which Gibbon speaks. He says, οὐδὲ αἰσχύνην τοῦτο φέρει ἑαυτοῖς κυέσθαι τὰς τὲ γυναῖκας αὐτῶν καὶ τὰς θυγατέρας ; yet these are expressions beyond what would be used, if the ambiguous word κυέσθαι were taken in its more innocent sense. Nor can the phrase παρέχοντας τὰς ἑαυτῶν γυναῖκας ἐν τοῖς ἐπιτηδείοις, well bear a less coarse interpretation. " Gibbon is probably right as to the origin of this extraordinary mistake," says Milman. To this Dr. W. Smith adds that it may be observed that this idea of the unchastity of the English seems to have been prevalent amongst the Greeks. Finally, Prof. Bury says there is no ambiguity. Chalcocondyles uses the middle form κυεσθαι, instead of the active κυειν which is used in classical Greek: but there is no second sense. Neither Κύω nor Κυῶ is ever used in the sense of Κυνῶ to kiss. It is only in the aorist ἔκυσα : ἔκυσα that there would be a danger of confusion.—O. S.]

[2] Erasmus (Epist. Fausto Andrelino) has a pretty passage on the English fashion of kissing strangers on their arrival and departure, from whence, however, he draws no scandalous inferences.

[3] Perhaps we may apply this remark to the community of wives among the old Britons, as it is supposed by Cæsar [Bell. Gall. l. v. c. 14] and Dion (Dion Cassius, l. lxii. tom. ii [c. 6] p. 1007), with Reimar's judicious annotation. The Arreoy of Otaheite, so certain at first, is become less visible and scandalous in proportion as we have studied the manners of that gentle and amorous people.

[Manuel was a voluminous " Defender of the Faith." In twenty-six dialogues he wrote a defence of orthodox Christianity against Islam, having been suggested by certain conversations which he had at Ancyra in 1390 with a Turk. The dialogues are entitled Διάλογος περὶ τῆς τῶν Χριστιανῶν Θρησκείας πρὸς τινα Πέρσην.—O. S.]

employed in composing twenty theological dialogues for its
defence. The appearance of the Byzantine ambassadors at the
council of Constance [1] announces the restoration of the Turkish
power, as well as of the Latin church: the conquest of the sultans,
Mohammed and Amurath, reconciled the emperor to the
Vatican; and the siege of Constantinople almost tempted him
to acquiesce in the double procession of the Holy Ghost. When
Martin the Fifth ascended without a rival the chair of St. Peter,
a friendly intercourse of letters and embassies was revived
between the East and West. Ambition on one side, and distress
on the other, dictated the same decent language of charity and
peace: the artful Greek expressed a desire of marrying his six
sons to Italian princesses; and the Roman, not less artful,
despatched the daughter of the marquis of Montferrat, with a
company of noble virgins, to soften, by their charms, the
obstinacy of the schismatics. Yet under this mask of zeal a discerning eye will perceive that all was hollow and insincere in the
court and church of Constantinople. According to the vicissitudes of danger and repose, the emperor advanced or retreated;
alternately instructed and disavowed his ministers; and escaped
from an importunate pressure by urging the duty of inquiry,
the obligation of collecting the sense of his patriarchs and bishops,
and the impossibility of convening them at a time when the
Turkish arms were at the gates of his capital. From a review of
the public transactions it will appear that the Greeks insisted on
three successive measures, a succour, a council, and a final
reunion, while the Latins eluded the second, and only promised
the first as a consequential and voluntary reward of the third.
But we have an opportunity of unfolding the most secret intentions of Manuel, as he explained them in a private conversation
without artifice or disguise. In his declining age the emperor
had associated John Palæologus, the second of the name, and
the eldest of his sons, on whom he devolved the greatest part of
the authority and weight of government. One day, in the
presence only of the historian Phranza,[2] his favourite chamber-

---

[1] See Lenfant, Hist. du Concile de Constance, tom. ii. p. 576; and, for
the ecclesiastical history of the times, the Annals of Spondanus, the Bibliothèque of Dupin, tom. xii. and twenty-first and twenty-second volumes
of the History, or rather the Continuation, of Fleury.

[2] From his early youth, George Phranza, or Phranzes, was employed in
the service of the state and palace; and Hanckius (de Script. Byzant. P. i.
c. 40) has collected his life from his own writings. He was no more than
four-and-twenty years of age at the death of Manuel, who recommended
him in the strongest terms to his successor: Imprimis vero hunc Phranzen
tibi commendo, qui ministravit mihi fideliter et diligenter (Phranzes, l. ii.

lain, he opened to his colleague and successor the true principle
of his negotiations with the pope.[1] " Our last resource," said
Manuel, " against the Turks is their fear of our union with the
Latins, of the warlike nations of the West, who may arm for
our relief and for their destruction. As often as you are
threatened by the miscreants, present this danger before their
eyes. Propose a council; consult on the means; but ever delay
and avoid the convocation of an assembly, which cannot tend
either to our spiritual or temporal emolument. The Latins are
proud; the Greeks are obstinate; neither party will recede or
retract; and the attempt of a perfect union will confirm the
schism, alienate the churches, and leave us, without hope or
defence, at the mercy of the barbarians." Impatient of this
salutary lesson, the royal youth arose from his seat and departed
in silence; and the wise monarch (continues Phranza), casting
his eyes on me, thus resumed his discourse: " My son deems
himself a great and heroic prince; but, alas! our miserable age
does not afford scope for heroism or greatness. His daring spirit
might have suited the happier times of our ancestors; but the
present state requires not an emperor, but a cautious steward of
the last relics of our fortunes. Well do I remember the lofty
expectations which he built on our alliance with Mustapha; and
much do I fear that his rash courage will urge the ruin of our
house, and that even religion may precipitate our downfall."
Yet the experience and authority of Manuel preserved the peace
and eluded the council; till, in the seventy-eighth year of his
age, and in the habit of a monk, he terminated his career, dividing his precious movables among his children and the poor,
his physicians and his favourite servants. Of his six sons,[2]
Andronicus the Second was invested with the principality of
Thessalonica, and died of a leprosy soon after the sale of that
city to the Venetians and its final conquest by the Turks. Some
fortunate incidents had restored Peloponnesus, or the Morea, to
the empire; and in his more prosperous days, Manuel had fortified the narrow isthmus of six miles[3] with a stone wall and one

c. 1 [p. 125, ed. Bonn]). Yet the emperor John was cold, and he preferred
the service of the despots of Peloponnesus.
[1] See Phranzes, l. ii. c. 13 [p. 178, ed. Bonn]. While so many manuscripts of the Greek original are extant in the libraries of Rome, Milan, the
Escurial, etc., it is a matter of shame and reproach that we should be
reduced to the Latin version, or abstract, of James Pontanus (ad calcem
Theophylact. Simocattæ: Ingolstadt, 1604), so deficient in accuracy and
elegance (Fabric. Biblioth. Græc. tom. vi. p. 615-620).
[2] See Ducange, Fam. Byzant. p. 243-248.
[3] The exact measure of the Hexamilion, from sea to sea, was 3800 orgyiæ,

hundred and fifty-three towers. The wall was overthrown by
the first blast of the Ottomans; the fertile peninsula might have
been sufficient for the four younger brothers, Theodore and Constantine, Demetrius and Thomas; but they wasted in domestic
contests the remains of their strength; and the least successful of
the rivals were reduced to a life of dependence in the Byzantine
palace.

The eldest of the sons of Manuel, John Palæologus the Second,
was acknowledged, after his father's death, as the sole emperor
of the Greeks. He immediately proceeded to repudiate his wife,
and to contract a new marriage with the princess of Trebizond:
beauty was in his eyes the first qualification of an empress; and
the clergy had yielded to his firm assurance, that, unless he
might be indulged in a divorce, he would retire to a cloister and
leave the throne to his brother Constantine. The first, and in
truth the only victory of Palæologus, was over a Jew,[1] whom,
after a long and learned dispute, he converted to the Christian
faith; and this momentous conquest is carefully recorded in the
history of the times. But he soon resumed the design of uniting
the East and West; and, regardless of his father's advice,
listened, as it should seem with sincerity, to the proposal of
meeting the pope in a general council beyond the Adriatic. This
dangerous project was encouraged by Martin the Fifth, and
coldly entertained by his successor Eugenius, till, after a tedious
negotiation, the emperor received a summons from a Latin
assembly of a new character, the independent prelates of Basil,
who styled themselves the representatives and judges of the
Catholic church.

The Roman pontiff had fought and conquered in the cause of
ecclesiastical freedom; but the victorious clergy were soon
exposed to the tyranny of their deliverer; and his sacred character was invulnerable to those arms which they found so keen
and effectual against the civil magistrate. Their great charter,
the right of election, was annihilated by appeals, evaded by
trusts or commendams, disappointed by reversionary grants,

or *toises*, of six Greek feet (Phranzes, l. i. c. 35 [p. 108, ed. Bonn]), which
would produce a Greek mile still smaller than that of 660 French *toises*,
which is assigned by D'Anville as still in use in Turkey. Five miles are
commonly reckoned for the breadth of the isthmus. See the Travels of
Spon, Wheeler, and Chandler.

[1] The first objection of the Jews is on the death of Christ: if it were
voluntary, Christ was a suicide: which the emperor parries with a mystery.
They then dispute on the conception of the Virgin, the sense of the
prophecies, etc. (Phranzes, l. ii. c. 12, a whole chapter.)

and superseded by previous and arbitrary reservations.[1] A
public auction was instituted in the court of Rome: the cardinals
and favourites were enriched with the spoils of nations; and
every country might complain that the most important and
valuable benefices were accumulated on the heads of aliens and
absentees. During their residence at Avignon, the ambition of
the popes subsided in the meaner passions of avarice [2] and
luxury: they rigorously imposed on the clergy the tributes of
first-fruits and tenths; but they freely tolerated the impunity
of vice, disorder, and corruption. These manifold scandals
were aggravated by the great schism of the West, which continued above fifty years. In the furious conflicts of Rome and
Avignon, the vices of the rivals were mutually exposed; and
their precarious situation degraded their authority, relaxed their
discipline, and multiplied their wants and exactions. To heal
the wounds, and restore the monarchy, of the church, the synods
of Pisa and Constance [3] were successively convened; but these
great assemblies, conscious of their strength, resolved to vindicate
the privileges of the Christian aristocracy. From a personal
sentence against two pontiffs whom they rejected, and a third,
their acknowledged sovereign, whom they deposed, the fathers
of Constance proceeded to examine the nature and limits of the
Roman supremacy; nor did they separate till they had established the authority, above the pope, of a general council. It
was enacted, that, for the government and reformation of the
church, such assemblies should be held at regular intervals; and
that each synod, before its dissolution, should appoint the time
and place of the subsequent meeting. By the influence of the
court of Rome, the next convocation at Sienna was easily eluded;
but the bold and vigorous proceedings of the council of Basil [4]

[1] In the treatise delle Materie Beneficiarie of Fra Paolo (in the fourth
volume of the last, and best, edition of his works) the papal system is
deeply studied and freely described. Should Rome and her religion be
annihilated, this golden volume may still survive, a philosophical history
and a salutary warning.

[2] Pope John XXII. (in 1334) left behind him, at Avignon, eighteen
millions of gold florins, and the value of seven millions more in plate and
jewels. See the Chronicle of John Villani (l. xi. c. 20, in Muratori's Collection, tom. xiii. p. 765), whose brother received the account from the papal
treasurers. A treasure of six or eight millions sterling in the fourteenth
century is enormous, and almost incredible.

[3] A learned and liberal Protestant, M. Lenfant, has given a fair history
of the councils of Pisa, Constance, and Basil, in six volumes in quarto; but
the last part is the most hasty and imperfect, except in the account of the
troubles of Bohemia.

[4] The original acts or minutes of the council of Basil are preserved in the
public library, in twelve volumes in folio. Basil was a free city, con-

had almost been fatal to the reigning pontiff, Eugenius the
Fourth. A just suspicion of his design prompted the fathers to
hasten the promulgation of their first decree, that the representatives of the church-militant on earth were invested with a
divine and spiritual jurisdiction over all Christians, without
excepting the pope; and that a general council could not be
dissolved, prorogued, or transferred, unless by their free deliberation and consent. On the notice that Eugenius had fulminated
a bull for that purpose, they ventured to summon, to admonish,
to threaten, to censure, the contumacious successor of St. Peter.
After many delays, to allow time for repentance, they finally
declared, that, unless he submitted within the term of sixty days,
he was suspended from the exercise of all temporal and ecclesiastical authority. And to mark their jurisdiction over the
prince as well as the priest, they assumed the government of
Avignon, annulled the alienation of the sacred patrimony, and
protected Rome from the imposition of new taxes. Their boldness was justified, not only by the general opinion of the clergy,
but by the support and power of the first monarchs of Christendom: the emperor Sigismond declared himself the servant and
protector of the synod; Germany and France adhered to their
cause; the duke of Milan was the enemy of Eugenius; and he was
driven from the Vatican by an insurrection of the Roman people.
Rejected at the same time by his temporal and spiritual subjects,
submission was his only choice: by a most humiliating bull, the
pope repealed his own acts, and ratified those of the council;
incorporated his legates and cardinals with that venerable body;
and *seemed* to resign himself to the decrees of the supreme
legislature. Their fame pervaded the countries of the East:
and it was in their presence that Sigismond received the ambassadors of the Turkish sultan,[1] who laid at his feet twelve large
vases filled with robes of silk and pieces of gold. The fathers of
Basil aspired to the glory of reducing the Greeks, as well as the
Bohemians, within the pale of the church; and their deputies
invited the emperor and patriarch of Constantinople to unite
with an assembly which possessed the confidence of the Western
nations. Palæologus was not averse to the proposal; and his

veniently situate on the Rhine, and guarded by the arms of the neighbouring and confederate Swiss. In 1459 the university was founded by pope
Pius II. (Æneas Sylvius), who had been secretary to the council. But
what is a council, or a university, to the presses of Froben and the studies
of Erasmus?

[1] This Turkish embassy, attested only by Crantzius, is related with some
doubt by the annalist Spondanus, A.D. 1433, No. 25, tom. i. p. 824.

ambassadors were introduced with due honours into the Catholic senate. But the choice of the place appeared to be an insuperable obstacle, since he refused to pass the Alps, or the sea of Sicily, and positively required that the synod should be adjourned to some convenient city in Italy, or at least on the Danube. The other articles of this treaty were more readily stipulated: it was agreed to defray the travelling expenses of the emperor, with a train of seven hundred persons,[1] to remit an immediate sum of eight thousand ducats [2] for the accommodation of the Greek clergy; and in his absence to grant a supply of ten thousand ducats, with three hundred archers and some galleys, for the protection of Constantinople. The city of Avignon advanced the funds for the preliminary expenses; and the embarkation was prepared at Marseilles with some difficulty and delay.

In his distress the friendship of Palæologus was disputed by the ecclesiastical powers of the West; but the dexterous activity of a monarch prevailed over the slow debates and inflexible temper of a republic. The decrees of Basil continually tended to circumscribe the despotism of the pope, and to erect a supreme and perpetual tribunal in the church. Eugenius was impatient of the yoke; and the union of the Greeks might afford a decent pretence for translating a rebellious synod from the Rhine to the Po. The independence of the fathers was lost if they passed the Alps: Savoy or Avignon, to which they acceded with reluctance, were described at Constantinople as situate far beyond the Pillars of Hercules;[3] the emperor and his clergy were apprehensive of the dangers of a long navigation; they were offended by a haughty declaration, that, after suppressing the *new* heresy of the Bohemians, the council would soon eradicate the *old* heresy

---

[1] Syropulus, p. 19. In this list the Greeks appear to have exceeded the real numbers of the clergy and laity which afterwards attended the emperor and patriarch, but which are not clearly specified by the great ecclesiarch. The 75,000 florins which they asked in this negotiation of the pope (p. 9) were more than they could hope or want.

[2] I use indifferently the words *ducat* and *florin*, which derive their names, the former from the *dukes* of Milan, the latter from the republic of *Florence*. These gold pieces, the first that were coined in Italy, perhaps in the Latin world, may be compared in weight and value to one-third of the English guinea.

[3] At the end of the Latin version of Phranzes we read a long Greek epistle or declamation of George of Trebizond, who advises the emperor to prefer Eugenius and Italy. He treats with contempt the schismatic assembly of Basil, the barbarians of Gaul and Germany, who had conspired to transport the chair of St. Peter beyond the Alps; οἱ ἄθλιοι (says he) σε καὶ τὴν μετὰ σου σύνοδον ἔξω τῶν Ἡρακλείων στήλων καὶ περὰ Γαδήρων ἐξάξουσι. Was Constantinople unprovided with a map?

of the Greeks.[1]   On the side of Eugenius all was smooth, and
yielding, and respectful; and he invited the Byzantine monarch
to heal by his presence the schism of the Latin, as well as of the
Eastern, church.   Ferrara, near the coast of the Adriatic, was
proposed for their amicable interview: and with some indulgence
of forgery and theft, a surreptitious decree was procured, which
transferred the synod, with its own consent, to that Italian city.
Nine galleys were equipped for this service at Venice and in the
isle of Candia; their diligence anticipated the slower vessels of
Basil: the Roman admiral was commissioned to burn, sink, and
destroy;[2] and these priestly squadrons might have encountered
each other in the same seas where Athens and Sparta had formerly
contended for the pre-eminence of glory.   Assaulted by the
importunity of the factions, who were ready to fight for the possession of his person, Palæologus hesitated before he left his palace
and country on a perilous experiment.   His father's advice still
dwelt on his memory; and reason must suggest, that, since the
Latins were divided among themselves, they could never unite in
a foreign cause.   Sigismond dissuaded the unseasonable adventure; his advice was impartial, since he adhered to the council;
and it was enforced by the strange belief that the German Cæsar
would nominate a Greek his heir and successor in the empire of
the West.[3]   Even the Turkish sultan was a counsellor whom it
might be unsafe to trust, but whom it was dangerous to offend.
Amurath was unskilled in the disputes, but he was apprehensive
of the union, of the Christians.   From his own treasures he
offered to relieve the wants of the Byzantine court; yet he
declared with seeming magnanimity that Constantinople should
be secure and inviolate in the absence of her sovereign.[4]   The
resolution of Palæologus was decided by the most splendid gifts

[1] Syropulus (p. 26-31) attests his own indignation, and that of his
countrymen; and the Basil deputies, who excused the rash declaration,
could neither deny nor alter an act of the council.

[2] Condolmieri, the pope's nephew and admiral, expressly declared, ὅτι
ὁρισμον ἔχει παρὰ τοῦ Πάπα ἵνα πολεμήσῃ ὁποῦ ἂν εὕρῃ τὰ κάτεργα τῆς
Συνόδου, καὶ εἰ δυνήθη, καταδύσῃ, καὶ ἀφανίσῃ.   The naval orders of the
synod were less peremptory, and, till the hostile squadrons appeared, both
parties tried to conceal their quarrel from the Greeks.

[3] Syropulus mentions the hopes of Palæologus (p. 36), and the last advice
of Sigismond (p. 57).   At Corfu the Greek emperor was informed of his
friend's death; had he known it sooner, he would have returned home
(p. 79).

[4] Phranzes himself, though from different motives, was of the advice of
Amurath (l. ii. c. 13).   Utinam ne synodus ista unquam fuisset, si tantas
offensiones et detrimenta paritura erat.   This Turkish embassy is likewise
mentioned by Syropulus (p. 58); and Amurath kept his word.   He might
threaten (p. 125, 219), but he never attacked, the city.

and the most specious promises: he wished to escape for a while
from a scene of danger and distress; and after dismissing with
an ambiguous answer the messengers of the council, he declared
his intention of embarking in the Roman galleys.   The age of
the patriarch Joseph was more susceptible of fear than of hope;
he trembled at the perils of the sea, and expressed his apprehension that his feeble voice, with thirty perhaps of his orthodox
brethren, would be oppressed in a foreign land by the power and
numbers of a Latin synod.   He yielded to the royal mandate, to
the flattering assurance that he would be heard as the oracle of
nations, and to the secret wish of learning from his brother of the
West to deliver the church from the yoke of kings.[1]   The five
crossbearers, or dignitaries, of St. Sophia, were bound to attend
his person; and one of these, the great ecclesiarch or preacher,
Sylvester Syropulus,[2] has composed a free and curious history [3]
of the *false* union.[4]   Of the clergy that reluctantly obeyed the
summons of the emperor and the patriarch, submission was the
first duty, and patience the most useful virtue.   In a chosen list
of twenty bishops we discover the metropolitan titles of Heraclea
and Cyzicus, Nice and Nicomedia, Ephesus and Trebizond, and
the personal merit of Mark and Bessarion, who, in the confidence
of their learning and eloquence, were promoted to the episcopal
rank.   Some monks and philosophers were named to display the
science and sanctity of the Greek church; and the service of the
choir was performed by a select band of singers and musicians.

---

[1] The reader will smile at the simplicity with which he imparted these
hopes to his favourites: τοιαύτην πληροφορίαν σχήσειν ἤλπιζε καὶ διὰ τοῦ
Πάπα ἐθάρρει ἐλευθερῶσαι τὴν ἐκκλησίαν ἀπὸ τῆς ἀποτεθείσης αὐτοῦ δουλείας
παρὰ τοῦ βασιλέως (p. 92).   Yet it would have been difficult for him to
have practised the lessons of Gregory VII.

[2] The Christian name of Sylvester is borrowed from the Latin calendar,
In modern Greek, πουλός, as a diminutive, is added to the end of words:
nor can any reasoning of Creyghton, the editor, excuse his changing into
*Sguro*pulus (Sguros, fuscus) the Syropulus of his own manuscript, whose
name is subscribed with his own hand in the acts of the council of Florence.
Why might not the author be of Syrian extraction?

[3] From the conclusion of the history I should fix the date to the year
1444, four years after the synod, when the great ecclesiarch had abdicated
his office (sectio xii. p. 330-350).   His passions were cooled by time and
retirement; and, although Syropulus is often partial, he is never intemperate.

[4] *Vera historia unionis non veræ inter Græcos et Latinos* (*Hagæ Comitis*,
1660, in folio) was first published with a loose and florid version, by Robert
Creyghton, chaplain to Charles II. in his exile.   The zeal of the editor has
prefixed a polemic title, for the beginning of the original is wanting.
Syropulus may be ranked with the best of the Byzantine writers for the
merit of his narration, and even of his style; but he is excluded from the
orthodox collections of the councils.

The patriarchs of Alexandria, Antioch, and Jerusalem, appeared
by their genuine or fictitious deputies; the primate of Russia
represented a national church, and the Greeks might contend
with the Latins in the extent of their spiritual empire. The
precious vases of St. Sophia were exposed to the winds and
waves, that the patriarch might officiate with becoming splendour:
whatever gold the emperor could procure was expended in the
massy ornaments of his bed and chariot;[1] and while they
affected to maintain the prosperity of their ancient fortune, they
quarrelled for the division of fifteen thousand ducats, the first
alms of the Roman pontiff. After the necessary preparations,
John Palæologus, with a numerous train, accompanied by his
brother Demetrius and the most respectable persons of the
church and state, embarked in eight vessels with sails and oars,
which steered through the Turkish straits of Gallipoli to the
Archipelago, the Morea, and the Adriatic Gulf.[2]

After a tedious and troublesome navigation of seventy-seven
days, this religious squadron cast anchor before Venice; and
their reception proclaimed the joy and magnificence of that
powerful republic. In the command of the world the modest
Augustus had never claimed such honours from his subjects as
were paid to his feeble successor by an independent state.
Seated on the poop, on a lofty throne, he received the visit, or,
in the Greek style, the *adoration*, of the doge and senators.[3]
They sailed in the Bucentaur, which was accompanied by twelve
stately galleys: the sea was overspread with innumerable
gondolas of pomp and pleasure; the air resounded with music
and acclamations; the mariners, and even the vessels, were
dressed in silk and gold; and in all the emblems and pageants
the Roman eagles were blended with the lions of St. Mark. The
triumphal procession, ascending the great canal, passed under
the bridge of the Rialto; and the Eastern strangers gazed with

[1] Syropulus (p. 63) simply expresses his intention ἵν᾽ οὕτω πομπάων ἐν᾽
Ἰτάλοις μεγὰς βασιλεὺς παρ᾽ ἐκεινῶν νομίζοιτο; and the Latin of Creyghton
may afford a specimen of his florid paraphrase. Ut pompâ circumductus
noster Imperator Italiæ populis aliquis deauratus Jupiter crederetur, aut
Crœsus ex opulentâ Lydiâ.

[2] Although I cannot stop to quote Syropulus for every fact, I will observe
that the navigation of the Greeks from Constantinople to Venice and
Ferrara is contained in the fourth section (p. 67-100), and that the historian
has the uncommon talent of placing each scene before the reader's eye.

[3] At the time of the synod Phranzes was in Peloponnesus: but he
received from the despot Demetrius a faithful account of the honourable
reception of the emperor and patriarch both at Venice and Ferrara
(Dux . . . sedentem Imperatorem *adorat*), which are more slightly mentioned by the Latins (l. ii. c. 14, 15, 16).

admiration on the palaces, the churches, and the populousness
of a city that seems to float on the bosom of the waves.[1] · They
sighed to behold the spoils and trophies with which it had been
decorated after the sack of Constantinople. After an hospitable
entertainment of fifteen days, Palæologus pursued his journey
by land and water from Venice to Ferrara; and on this occasion
the pride of the Vatican was tempered by policy to indulge the
ancient dignity of the emperor of the East. He made his entry
on a *black* horse; but a milk-white steed, whose trappings were
embroidered with golden eagles, was led before him; and the
canopy was borne over his head by the princes of Este, the sons
or kinsmen of Nicholas, marquis of the city, and a sovereign
more powerful than himself.[2] Palæologus did not alight till he
reached the bottom of the staircase: the pope advanced to the
door of the apartment; refused his proffered genuflexion; and,
after a paternal embrace, conducted the emperor to a seat on his
left hand. Nor would the patriarch descend from his galley till
a ceremony, almost equal, had been stipulated between the
bishops of Rome and Constantinople. The latter was saluted
by his brother with a kiss of union and charity; nor would any
of the Greek ecclesiastics submit to kiss the feet of the Western
primate. On the opening of the synod, the place of honour in
the centre was claimed by the temporal and ecclesiastical chiefs;
and it was only by alleging that his predecessors had not assisted
in person at Nice or Chalcedon that Eugenius could evade the
ancient precedents of Constantine and Marcian. After much
debate it was agreed that the right and left sides of the church
should be occupied by the two nations; that the solitary chair
of St. Peter should be raised the first of the Latin line; and that
the throne of the Greek emperor, at the head of his clergy, should
be equal and opposite to the second place, the vacant seat of the
emperor of the West.[3]

[1] The astonishment of a Greek prince and a French ambassador
(Mémoires de Philippe de Comines, l. vii. c. 18) at the sight of Venice,
abundantly proves that in the fifteenth century it was the first and most
splendid of the Christian cities. For the spoils of Constantinople at Venice
see Syropulus (p. 87).

[2] Nicholas III. of Este reigned forty-eight years (A.D. 1393-1441), and
was lord of Ferrara, Modena, Reggio, Parma, Rovigo, and Commachio.
See his Life in Muratori (Antichità Estense, tom. ii. p. 159-201).

[3] The Latin vulgar was provoked to laughter at the strange dresses of
the Greeks, and especially the length of their garments, their sleeves, and
their beards; nor was the emperor distinguished, except by the purple
colour, and his diadem or tiara with a jewel on the top (Hody de Græcis
Illustribus, p. 31). Yet another spectator confesses that the Greek fashion
was più grave e più degna than the Italian (Vespasiano, in Vit. Eugen. IV.
in Muratori, tom. xxv. p. 261).

But as soon as festivity and form had given place to a more serious treaty, the Greeks were dissatisfied with their journey, with themselves, and with the pope. The artful pencil of his emissaries had painted him in a prosperous state, at the head of the princes and prelates of Europe, obedient at his voice to believe and to arm. The thin appearance of the universal synod of Ferrara betrayed his weakness; and the Latins opened the first session with only five archbishops, eighteen bishops, and ten abbots, the greatest part of whom were the subjects or countrymen of the Italian pontiff. Except the duke of Burgundy, none of the potentates of the West condescended to appear in person, or by their ambassadors; nor was it possible to suppress the judicial acts of Basil against the dignity and person of Eugenius, which were finally concluded by a new election. Under these circumstances a truce or delay was asked and granted, till Palæologus could expect from the consent of the Latins some temporal reward for an unpopular union; and, after the first session, the public proceedings were adjourned above six months. The emperor, with a chosen band of his favourites and *Janizaries*, fixed his summer residence at a pleasant spacious monastery, six miles from Ferrara; forgot, in the pleasures of the chase, the distress of the church and state; and persisted in destroying the game, without listening to the just complaints of the marquis or the husbandman.[1] In the meanwhile his unfortunate Greeks were exposed to all the miseries of exile and poverty; for the support of each stranger a monthly allowance was assigned of three or four gold florins, and, although the entire sum did not amount to seven hundred florins, a long arrear was repeatedly incurred by the indigence or policy of the Roman court.[2] They sighed for a speedy deliverance, but their escape was prevented by a triple chain; a passport from their superiors was required at the gates of Ferrara; the government

---

[1] For the emperor's hunting see Syropulus (p. 143, 144, 191). The pope had sent him eleven miserable hacks; but he bought a strong and swift horse that came from Russia. The name of *Janizaries* may surprise; but the name, rather than the institution, had passed from the Ottoman to the Byzantine court, and is often used in the last age of the empire.

[2] The Greeks obtained, with much difficulty, that, instead of provisions, money should be distributed, four florins *per* month to the persons of honourable rank, and three florins to their servants, with an addition of thirty more to the emperor, twenty-five to the patriarch, and twenty to the prince, or despot, Demetrius. The payment of the first month amounted to 691 florins, a sum which will not allow us to reckon above 200 Greeks of every condition (Syropulus, p. 104, 105). On the 20th October, 1438, there was an arrear of four months; in April, 1439, of three; and of five and a half in July, at the time of the union (p. 172, 225, 271).

of Venice had engaged to arrest and send back the fugitives, and inevitable punishment awaited them at Constantinople; excommunication, fines, and a sentence, which did not respect the sacerdotal dignity, that they should be stripped naked and publicly whipped.[1] It was only by the alternative of hunger or dispute that the Greeks could be persuaded to open the first conference, and they yielded with extreme reluctance to attend from Ferrara to Florence the rear of a flying synod. This new translation was urged by inevitable necessity: the city was visited by the plague; the fidelity of the marquis might be suspected; the mercenary troops of the duke of Milan were at the gates, and, as they occupied Romagna, it was not without difficulty and danger that the pope, the emperor, and the bishops explored their way through the unfrequented paths of the Apennine.[2]

Yet all these obstacles were surmounted by time and policy. The violence of the fathers of Basil rather promoted than injured the cause of Eugenius: the nations of Europe abhorred the schism, and disowned the election, of Felix the Fifth, who was successively a duke of Savoy, a hermit, and a pope; and the great princes were gradually reclaimed by his competitor to a favourable neutrality and a firm attachment. The legates, with some respectable members, deserted to the Roman army, which insensibly rose in numbers and reputation; the council of Basil was reduced to thirty-nine bishops and three hundred of the inferior clergy;[3] while the Latins of Florence could produce the subscriptions of the pope himself, eight cardinals, two patriarchs, eight archbishops, fifty-two bishops, and forty-five abbots or chiefs of religious orders. After the labour of nine months and the debates of twenty-five sessions, they attained the advantage and glory of the reunion of the Greeks. Four principal questions had been agitated between the two churches: 1. The use of unleavened bread in the communion of Christ's body. 2. The

---

[1] Syropulus (p. 141, 142, 204, 221) deplores the imprisonment of the Greeks and the tyranny of the emperor and patriarch.

[2] The wars of Italy are most clearly represented in the thirteenth volume of the Annals of Muratori. The schismatic Greek, Syropulus (p. 145), appears to have exaggerated the fear and disorder of the pope in his retreat from Ferrara to Florence, which is proved by the acts to have been somewhat more decent and deliberate.

[3] Syropulus is pleased to reckon seven hundred prelates in the council of Basil. The error is manifest, and perhaps voluntary. That extravagant number could not be supplied by *all* the ecclesiastics of every degree who were present at the council, nor by *all* the absent bishops of the West, who, expressly or tacitly, might adhere to its decrees.

nature of purgatory. 3. The supremacy of the pope. And,
4. The single or double procession of the Holy Ghost. The cause
of either nation was managed by ten theological champions:
the Latins were supported by the inexhaustible eloquence of
Cardinal Julian, and Mark of Ephesus and Bessarion of Nice were
the bold and able leaders of the Greek forces. We may bestow
some praise on the progress of human reason, by observing that
the first of these questions was *now* treated as an immaterial rite,
which might innocently vary with the fashion of the age and
country. With regard to the second, both parties were agreed in
the belief of an intermediate state of purgation for the venial
sins of the faithful; and whether their souls were purified by
elemental fire was a doubtful point, which in a few years might
be conveniently settled on the spot by the disputants. The
claims of supremacy appeared of a more weighty and substantial
kind, yet by the Orientals the Roman bishop had ever been
respected as the first of the five patriarchs; nor did they scruple
to admit that his jurisdiction should be exercised agreeably to
the holy canons: a vague allowance, which might be defined or
eluded by occasional convenience. The procession of the Holy
Ghost from the Father alone, or from the Father and the Son,
was an article of faith which had sunk much deeper into the
minds of men; and in the sessions of Ferrara and Florence the
Latin addition of *filioque* was subdivided into two questions,
whether it were legal, and whether it were orthodox. Perhaps
it may not be necessary to boast on this subject of my own
impartial indifference: but I must think that the Greeks were
strongly supported by the prohibition of the council of Chalcedon
against adding any article whatsoever to the creed of Nice, or
rather of Constantinople.[1] In earthly affairs it is not easy to
conceive how an assembly of legislators can bind their successors
invested with powers equal to their own. But the dictates of
inspiration must be true and unchangeable; nor should a private
bishop or a provincial synod have presumed to innovate against
the judgment of the Catholic church. On the substance of the
doctrine the controversy was equal and endless; reason is confounded by the procession of a deity; the Gospel, which lay on
the altar, was silent; the various texts of the fathers might be
corrupted by fraud or entangled by sophistry; and the Greeks

---

[1] The Greeks, who disliked the union, were unwilling to sally from this
strong fortress (p. 178, 193, 195, 202, of Syropulus). The shame of the
Latins was aggravated by their producing an old MS. of the second council
of Nice, with *filioque* in the Nicene creed. A palpable forgery! (p. 173).

were ignorant of the characters and writings of the Latin saints.[1] Of this at least we may be sure, that neither side could be convinced by the arguments of their opponents. Prejudice may be enlightened by reason, and a superficial glance may be rectified by a clear and more perfect view of an object adapted to our faculties. But the bishops and monks had been taught from their infancy to repeat a form of mysterious words: their national and personal honour depended on the repetition of the same sounds, and their narrow minds were hardened and inflamed by the acrimony of a public dispute.

While they were lost in a cloud of dust and darkness, the pope and emperor were desirous of a seeming union, which could alone accomplish the purposes of their interview; and the obstinacy of public dispute was softened by the arts of private and personal negotiation. The patriarch Joseph had sunk under the weight of age and infirmities; his dying voice breathed the counsels of charity and concord, and his vacant benefice might tempt the hopes of the ambitious clergy. The ready and active obedience of the archbishops of Russia and Nice, of Isidore and Bessarion, was prompted and recompensed by their speedy promotion to the dignity of cardinals. Bessarion, in the first debates, had stood forth the most strenuous and eloquent champion of the Greek church; and if the apostate, the bastard, was reprobated by his country,[2] he appears in ecclesiastical story a rare example of a patriot who was recommended to court favour by loud opposition and well-timed compliance. With the aid of his two spiritual coadjutors, the emperor applied his arguments to the general situation and personal characters of the bishops, and each was successively moved by authority and example. Their revenues were in the hands of the Turks, their persons in those of the Latins; an episcopal treasure, three robes and forty ducats, was soon exhausted;[3] the hopes of their return still depended on the ships of Venice and the alms of Rome; and such was their

[1] Ὡς ἔγω (said an eminent Greek) ὅταν εἰς νάον εἰσέλθω Λατίνων οὐ προσκυνῶ τινα τῶν ἐκεῖσε ἁγίων, ἔπει οὐδὲ γνωρίζω τινα (Syropulus, p. 109). See the perplexity of the Greeks (p. 217, 218, 252, 253, 273).

[2] See the polite altercation of Mark and Bessarion in Syropulus (p. 257), who never dissembles the vices of his own party, and fairly praises the virtues of the Latins.

[3] For the poverty of the Greek bishops, see a remarkable passage of Ducas (c. 31 [p. 216, ed. Bonn]). One had possessed, for his whole property, three old gowns, etc. By teaching one-and-twenty years in his monastery, Bessarion himself had collected forty gold florins; but of these the archbishop had expended twenty-eight in his voyage from Peloponnesus, and the remainder at Constantinople (Syropulus, p. 127).

indigence, that their arrears, the payment of a debt, would be
accepted as a favour, and might operate as a bribe.[1]   The danger
and relief of Constantinople might excuse some prudent and
pious dissimulation; and it was insinuated that the obstinate
heretics who should resist the consent of the East and West
would be abandoned in a hostile land to the revenge or justice of
the Roman pontiff.[2]   In the first private assembly of the Greeks
the formulary of union was approved by twenty-four, and
rejected by twelve, members; but the five *crossbearers* of St.
Sophia, who aspired to represent the patriarch, were disqualified
by ancient discipline, and their right of voting was transferred
to an obsequious train of monks, grammarians, and profane
laymen.   The will of the monarch produced a false and servile
unanimity, and no more than two patriots had courage to speak
their own sentiments and those of their country.   Demetrius,
the emperor's brother, retired to Venice, that he might not be
witness of the union; and Mark of Ephesus, mistaking perhaps
his pride for his conscience, disclaimed all communion with the
Latin heretics, and avowed himself the champion and confessor
of the orthodox creed.[3]   In the treaty between the two nations
several forms of consent were proposed, such as might satisfy the
Latins without dishonouring the Greeks; and they weighed the
scruples of words and syllables till the theological balance
trembled with a slight preponderance in favour of the Vatican.
It was agreed (I must entreat the attention of the reader) that
the Holy Ghost proceeds from the Father *and* the Son, as from
one principle and one substance; that he proceeds *by* the Son,
being of the same nature and substance; and that he proceeds
from the Father *and* the Son, by one *spiration* and production.
It is less difficult to understand the articles of the preliminary
treaty: that the pope should defray all the expenses of the Greeks
in their return home; that he should annually maintain two
galleys and three hundred soldiers for the defence of Constantinople; that all the ships which transported pilgrims to Jeru-

[1] Syropulus denies that the Greeks received any money before they had
subscribed the act of union (p. 283): yet he relates some suspicious circumstances; and their bribery and corruption are positively affirmed by
the historian Ducas [loc. cit.].

[2] The Greeks most piteously express their own fears of exile and perpetual slavery (Syropul. p. 196); and they were strongly moved by the
emperor's threats (p. 260).

[3] I had forgot another popular and orthodox protester: a favourite
hound, who usually lay quiet on the foot-cloth of the emperor's throne,
but who barked most furiously while the act of union was reading, without
being silenced by the soothing or the lashes of the royal attendants
(Syropul. p. 265, 266).

salem should be obliged to touch at that port; that as often as they were required, the pope should furnish ten galleys for a year, or twenty for six months; and that he should powerfully solicit the princes of Europe, if the emperor had occasion for land-forces.

The same year, and almost the same day, were marked by the deposition of Eugenius at Basil, and, at Florence, by his reunion of the Greeks and Latins. In the former synod (which he styled indeed an assembly of demons) the pope was branded with the guilt of simony, perjury, tyranny, heresy, and schism;[1] and declared to be incorrigible in his vices, unworthy of any title, and incapable of holding any ecclesiastical office. In the latter he was revered as the true and holy vicar of Christ, who, after a separation of six hundred years, had reconciled the Catholics of the East and West in one fold, and under one shepherd. The act of union was subscribed by the pope, the emperor, and the principal members of both churches; even by those who, like Syropulus,[2] had been deprived of the right of voting. Two copies might have sufficed for the East and West; but Eugenius was not satisfied unless four authentic and similar transcripts were signed and attested as the monuments of his victory.[3] On a memorable day, the sixth of July, the successors of St. Peter and Constantine ascended their thrones; the two nations assembled in the cathedral of Florence; their representatives, Cardinal Julian, and Bessarion archbishop of Nice, appeared in the pulpit, and, after reading in their respective tongues the act of union, they mutually embraced in the name and the presence of their applauding brethren. The pope and his ministers then officiated according to the Roman liturgy; the creed was chanted with the addition of *filioque*; the acquiescence of the Greeks was poorly excused by their ignorance of the harmonious but

---

[1] From the original Lives of the Popes, in Muratori's Collection (tom. iii. P. ii. tom. xxv.), the manners of Eugenius IV. appear to have been decent, and even exemplary. His situation, exposed to the world and to his enemies, was a restraint, and is a pledge.

[2] Syropulus, rather than subscribe, would have assisted, as the least evil, at the ceremony of the union. He was compelled to do both; and the great ecclesiarch poorly excuses his submission to the emperor (p. 290-292).

[3] None of these original acts of union can at present be produced. Of the ten MSS. that are preserved (five at Rome, and the remainder at Florence, Bologna, Venice, Paris, and London), nine have been examined by an accurate critic (M. de Brequigny), who condemns them for the variety and imperfections of the Greek signatures. Yet several of these may be esteemed as authentic copies, which were subscribed at Florence, before (26th of August, 1439) the final separation of the pope and emperor (Mémoires de l'Académie des Inscriptions, tom. xliii. p. 287-311).

inarticulate sounds;[1] and the more scrupulous Latins refused any public celebration of the Byzantine rite. Yet the emperor and his clergy were not totally unmindful of national honour. The treaty was ratified by their consent: it was tacitly agreed that no innovation should be attempted in their creed or ceremonies; they spared and secretly respected the generous firmness of Mark of Ephesus, and, on the decease of the patriarch, they refused to elect his successor, except in the cathedral of St. Sophia. In the distribution of public and private rewards the liberal pontiff exceeded their hopes and his promises: the Greeks, with less pomp and pride, returned by the same road of Ferrara and Venice; and their reception at Constantinople was such as will be described in the following chapter.[2] The success of the first trial encouraged Eugenius to repeat the same edifying scenes, and the deputies of the Armenians, the Maronites, the Jacobites of Syria and Egypt, the Nestorians, and the Æthiopians, were successively introduced to kiss the feet of the Roman pontiff, and to announce the obedience and the orthodoxy of the East. These Oriental embassies, unknown in the countries which they presumed to represent,[3] diffused over the West the fame of Eugenius; and a clamour was artfully propagated against the remnant of a schism in Switzerland and Savoy which alone impeded the harmony of the Christian world. The vigour of opposition was succeeded by the lassitude of despair; the council of Basil was silently dissolved; and Felix, renouncing the tiara, again withdrew to the devout or delicious hermitage of Ripaille.[4] A general peace was secured by mutual acts of oblivion and indemnity: all ideas of reformation subsided; the popes continued to exercise and abuse their ecclesiastical despotism; nor has Rome been since disturbed by the mischiefs of a contested election.[5]

---

[1] Ἡμῖν δὲ ὡς ἀσήμοι ἐδόκουν φῶναι (Syropul. p. 297).

[2] In their return the Greeks conversed at Bologna with the ambassadors of England; and after some questions and answers these impartial strangers laughed at the pretended union of Florence (Syropul. p. 307).

[3] So nugatory, or rather so fabulous, are these reunions of the Nestorians, Jacobites, etc., that I have turned over, without success, the Bibliotheca Orientalis of Assemannus, a faithful slave of the Vatican.

[4] Ripaille is situate near Thonon, in Savoy, on the southern side of the lake of Geneva. It is now a Carthusian abbey; and Mr. Addison (Travels into Italy, vol. ii. p. 147, 148, of Baskerville's edition of his works) has celebrated the place and the founder. Æneas Sylvius, and the fathers of Basil, applaud the austere life of the ducal hermit; but the French and Italian proverbs most unluckily attest the popular opinion of his luxury.

[5] In this account of the councils of Basil, Ferrara, and Florence, I have consulted the original acts, which fill the seventeenth and eighteenth tomes of the edition of Venice, and are closed by the perspicuous, though partial,

The journeys of three emperors were unavailing for their temporal, or perhaps their spiritual, salvation; but they were productive of a beneficial consequence, the revival of the Greek learning in Italy, from whence it was propagated to the last nations of the West and North. In their lowest servitude and depression, the subjects of the Byzantine throne were still possessed of a golden key that could unlock the treasures of antiquity, of a musical and prolific language that gives a soul to the objects of sense, and a body to the abstractions of philosophy. Since the barriers of the monarchy, and even of the capital, had been trampled under foot, the various barbarians had doubtless corrupted the form and substance of the national dialect; and ample glossaries have been composed, to interpret a multitude of words, of Arabic, Turkish, Sclavonian, Latin, or French origin.[1] But a purer idiom was spoken in the court and taught in the college, and the flourishing state of the language is described, and perhaps embellished, by a learned Italian,[2] who, by a long residence and noble marriage,[3] was naturalised at Constantinople about thirty years before the Turkish conquest. " The vulgar speech," says Philelphus,[4] " has been depraved by the people,

history of Augustin Patricius, an Italian of the fifteenth century. They are digested and abridged by Dupin (Bibliothèque Ecclés. tom. xii.), and the continuator of Fleury (tom. xxii.); and the respect of the Gallican church for the adverse parties confines their members to an awkward moderation.

[1] In the first attempt Meursius collected 3600 Græco-barbarous words, to which, in a second edition, he subjoined 1800 more; yet what plenteous gleanings did he leave to Portius, Ducange, Fabrotti, the Bollandists, etc.! (Fabric. Biblioth. Græc. tom. x. p. 101, etc.) Some Persic words may be found in Xenophon, and some Latin ones in Plutarch; and such is the inevitable effect of war and commerce; but the form and substance of the language were not affected by this slight alloy.

[2] The life of Francis Philelphus, a sophist, proud, restless, and rapacious, has been diligently composed by Lancelot (Mémoires de l'Academie des Inscriptions, tom. x. p. 691-751) and Tiraboschi (Istoria della Letteratura Italiana, tom. vii. p. 282-294), for the most part from his own letters. His elaborate writings, and those of his contemporaries, are forgotten: but their familiar epistles still describe the men and the times.

[3] He married, and had perhaps debauched, the daughter of John, and the granddaughter of Manuel Chrysoloras. She was young, beautiful, and wealthy; and her noble family was allied to the Dorias of Genoa and the emperors of Constantinople.

[4] Græci quibus lingua depravata non sit . . . ita loquuntur vulgo hâc etiam tempestate ut Aristophanes comicus, aut Euripides tragicus, ut oratores omnes, ut historiographi, ut philosophi . . . litterati autem homines et doctius et emendatius. . . . Nam viri aulici veterem sermonis dignitatem atque elegantiam retinebant in primisque ipsæ nobiles mulieres; quibus cum nullum esset omnino cum viris peregrinis commercium, merus ille ac purus Græcorum sermo servabatur intactus (Philelph. Epist. ad ann. 1451, apud Hodium, p. 188, 189). He observes in another passage, uxor illa mea Theodora locutione erat admodum moderatâ et suavi et maxime Atticâ.

and infected by the multitude of strangers and merchants, who
every day flock to the city and mingle with the inhabitants.   It
is from the disciples of such a school that the Latin language
received the versions of Aristotle and Plato, so obscure in sense,
and in spirit so poor.   But the Greeks, who have escaped the
contagion, are those whom *we* follow, and they alone are worthy
of our imitation.   In familiar discourse they still speak the
tongue of Aristophanes and Euripides, of the historians and
philosophers of Athens; and the style of their writings is still
more elaborate and correct.   The persons who, by their birth and
offices, are attached to the Byzantine court, are those who maintain, with the least alloy, the ancient standard of elegance and
purity; and the native graces of language most conspicuously
shine among the noble matrons, who are excluded from all intercourse with foreigners.   With foreigners do I say?   They live
retired and sequestered from the eyes of their fellow-citizens.
Seldom are they seen in the streets; and when they leave their
houses, it is in the dusk of evening, on visits to the churches and
their nearest kindred.   On these occasions they are on horseback, covered with a veil, and encompassed by their parents, their
husbands, or their servants." [1]

Among the Greeks a numerous and opulent clergy was
dedicated to the service of religion; their monks and bishops
have ever been distinguished by the gravity and austerity of
their manners, nor were they diverted, like the Latin priests, by
the pursuits and pleasures of a secular and even military life.
After a large deduction for the time and talents that were lost in
the devotion, the laziness, and the discord of the church and
cloister, the more inquisitive and ambitious minds would explore
the sacred and profane erudition of their native language.   The
ecclesiastics presided over the education of youth: the schools of
philosophy and eloquence were perpetuated till the fall of the
empire; and it may be affirmed that more books and more
knowledge were included within the walls of Constantinople
than could be dispersed over the extensive countries of the
West.[2]   But an important distinction has been already noticed:
the Greeks were stationary or retrograde, while the Latins were
advancing with a rapid and progressive motion.   The nations
were excited by the spirit of independence and emulation; and

---

[1] Philelphus, absurdly enough, derives this Greek or Oriental jealousy
from the manners of ancient Rome.

[2] See the state of learning in the thirteenth and fourteenth centuries in
the learned and judicious Mosheim (Institut. Hist. Eccles. p. 434-440,
490-494).

even the little world of the Italian states contained more people and industry than the decreasing circle of the Byzantine empire. In Europe the lower ranks of society were relieved from the yoke of feudal servitude; and freedom is the first step to curiosity and knowledge. The use, however rude and corrupt, of the Latin tongue had been preserved by superstition; the universities, from Bologna to Oxford,[1] were peopled with thousands of scholars; and their misguided ardour might be directed to more liberal and manly studies. In the resurrection of science Italy was the first that cast away her shroud; and the eloquent Petrarch, by his lessons and his example, may justly be applauded as the first harbinger of day. A purer style of composition, a more generous and rational strain of sentiment, flowed from the study and imitation of the writers of ancient Rome; and the disciples of Cicero and Virgil approached, with reverence and love, the sanctuary of their Grecian masters. In the sack of Constantinople, the French, and even the Venetians, had despised and destroyed the works of Lysippus and Homer; the monuments of art may be annihilated by a single blow, but the immortal mind is renewed and multiplied by the copies of the pen, and such copies it was the ambition of Petrarch and his friends to possess and understand. The arms of the Turks undoubtedly pressed the flight of the Muses: yet we may tremble at the thought that Greece might have been overwhelmed, with her schools and libraries, before Europe had emerged from the deluge of barbarism; that the seeds of science might have been scattered by the winds before the Italian soil was prepared for their cultivation.

The most learned Italians of the fifteenth century have confessed and applauded the restoration of Greek literature, after a long oblivion of many hundred years.[2] Yet in that country,

[1] At the end of the fifteenth century there existed in Europe about fifty universities, and of these the foundation of ten or twelve is prior to the year 1300. They were crowded in proportion to their scarcity. Bologna contained 10,000 students, chiefly of the civil law. In the year 1357 the number at Oxford had decreased from 30,000 to 6000 scholars (Henry's History of Great Britain, vol. iv. p. 478). Yet even this decrease is much superior to the present list of the members of the university.

[Rashdall, in his *Universities of Europe in the Middle Ages*, says that the maximum number of students at Oxford in the fourteenth century was from 1500 to 3000. By 1438 they had fallen to 1000. He thinks it unlikely that the numbers at Paris and Bologna exceeded 6000 or 7000.— O.S.]

[2] Of those writers who professedly treat of the restoration of the Greek learning in Italy, the two principal are Hodius, Dr. Humphrey Hody (de Graecis Illustribus, Linguae Graecae Literarumque humaniorum Instauratoribus; Londini, 1742, in large octavo), and Tiraboschi (Istoria della

and beyond the Alps, some names are quoted; some profound
scholars who, in the darker ages, were honourably distinguished
by their knowledge of the Greek tongue; and national vanity
has been loud in the praise of such rare examples of erudition.
Without scrutinising the merit of individuals, truth must observe
that their science is without a cause and without an effect; that
it was easy for them to satisfy themselves and their more
ignorant contemporaries; and that the idiom, which they had
so marvellously acquired, was transcribed in few manuscripts,
and was not taught in any university of the West.   In a corner
of Italy it faintly existed as the popular, or at least as the ecclesiastical, dialect.[1]   The first impression of the Doric and Ionic
colonies has never been completely erased; the Calabrian
churches were long attached to the throne of Constantinople;
and the monks of St. Basil pursued their studies in Mount Athos
and the schools of the East.   Calabria was the native country of
Barlaam, who has already appeared as a sectary and an ambassador; and Barlaam was the first who revived, beyond the Alps,
the memory, or at least the writings, of Homer.[2]   He is described,
by Petrarch and Boccace,[3] as a man of a diminutive stature,
though truly great in the measure of learning and genius: of a
piercing discernment, though of a slow and painful elocution.
For many ages (as they affirm) Greece had not produced his equal
in the knowledge of history, grammar, and philosophy; and his
merit was celebrated in the attestations of the princes and doctors
of Constantinople.   One of these attestations is still extant; and
the emperor Cantacuzene, the protector of his adversaries, is
forced to allow that Euclid, Aristotle, and Plato were familiar to
that profound and subtle logician.[4]   In the court of Avignon he
formed an intimate connection with Petrarch,[5] the first of the

Letteratura Italiana, tom. v. p. 364-377, tom. vii. p. 112-143).   The
Oxford professor is a laborious scholar, but the librarian of Modena enjoys
the superiority of a modern and national historian.

[1] In Calabria quæ olim Magna Græcia dicebatur, coloniis Græcis repleta,
remansit quædam linguæ veteris cognitio (Hodius, p. 2).   If it were eradicated by the Romans, it was revived and perpetuated by the monks of St.
Basil, who possessed seven convents at Rossano alone (Giannone, Istoria
di Napoli, tom. i. p. 520).

[2] Ii Barbari (says Petrarch, the French and Germans) vix, non dicam
libros sed nomen Homeri audiverunt.   Perhaps in that respect the thirteenth century was less happy than the age of Charlemagne.

[3] See the character of Barlaam, in Boccace de Genealog. Deorum, l. xv.
c. 6.

[4] Cantacuzen. l. ii. c. 36 [c. 39, tom. i. p. 543, ed. Bonn].

[5] For the connection of Petrarch and Barlaam, and the two interviews,
at Avignon in 1339, and at Naples in 1342, see the excellent Mémoires sur la
Vie de Pétrarque, tom. i. p. 406-410; tom. ii. p. 75-77.

Latin scholars; and the desire of mutual instruction was the principle of their literary commerce. The Tuscan applied himself with eager curiosity and assiduous diligence to the study of the Greek language, and in a laborious struggle with the dryness and difficulty of the first rudiments he began to reach the sense, and to feel the spirit, of poets and philosophers whose minds were congenial to his own. But he was soon deprived of the society and lessons of this useful assistant; Barlaam relinquished his fruitless embassy, and, on his return to Greece, he rashly provoked the swarms of fanatic monks, by attempting to substitute the light of reason to that of their navel. After a separation of three years the two friends again met in the court of Naples; but the generous pupil renounced the fairest occasion of improvement; and by his recommendation Barlaam was finally settled in a small bishopric of his native Calabria.[1] The manifold avocations of Petrarch, love and friendship, his various correspondence and frequent journeys, the Roman laurel, and his elaborate compositions in prose and verse, in Latin and Italian, diverted him from a foreign idiom; and as he advanced in life the attainment of the Greek language was the object of his wishes rather than of his hopes. When he was about fifty years of age, a Byzantine ambassador, his friend, and a master of both tongues, presented him with a copy of Homer, and the answer of Petrarch is at once expressive of his eloquence, gratitude, and regret. After celebrating the generosity of the donor, and the value of a gift more precious in his estimation than gold or rubies, he thus proceeds:—" Your present of the genuine and original text of the divine poet, the fountain of all invention, is worthy of yourself and of me; you have fulfilled your promise, and satisfied my desires. Yet your liberality is still imperfect: with Homer you should have given me yourself; a guide who could lead me into the fields of light, and disclose to my wondering eyes the specious miracles of the Iliad and Odyssey. But, alas! Homer is dumb, or I am deaf; nor is it in my power to enjoy the beauty which I possess. I have seated him by the side of Plato, the prince of poets near the prince of philosophers, and I glory in the sight of my illustrious guests. Of their immortal writings, whatever had been translated into the Latin idiom I had already acquired; but if there be no profit, there is

[1] The bishopric to which Barlaam retired was the old Locri, in the middle ages Scta. Cyriaca, and by corruption Hieracium, Gerace (Dissert. Chorographica Italiæ medii Ævi, p. 312). The dives opum of the Norman times soon lapsed into poverty, since even the church was poor: yet the town still contains 3000 inhabitants (Swinburne, p. 340).

some pleasure, in beholding these venerable Greeks in their proper
and national habit. I am delighted with the aspect of Homer;
and as often as I embrace the silent volume, I exclaim with a
sigh, Illustrious bard! with what pleasure should I listen to thy
song, if my sense of hearing were not obstructed and lost by the
death of one friend, and in the much lamented absence of another!
Nor do I yet despair, and the example of Cato suggests some
comfort and hope, since it was in the last period of age that he
attained the knowledge of the Greek letters." [1]

The prize which eluded the efforts of Petrarch was obtained
by the fortune and industry of his friend Boccace,[2] the father of
the Tuscan prose. That popular writer, who derives his reputation from the Decameron, a hundred novels of pleasantry and
love, may aspire to the more serious praise of restoring in Italy the
study of the Greek language. In the year one thousand three
hundred and sixty a disciple of Barlaam, whose name was Leo or
Leontius Pilatus, was detained in his way to Avignon by the
advice and hospitality of Boccace, who lodged the stranger in
his house, prevailed on the republic of Florence to allow him an
annual stipend, and devoted his leisure to the first Greek professor, who taught that language in the Western countries of
Europe. The appearance of Leo might disgust the most eager
disciple: he was clothed in the mantle of a philosopher or a
mendicant; his countenance was hideous; his face was overshadowed with black hair; his beard long and uncombed; his
deportment rustic; his temper gloomy and inconstant; nor
could he grace his discourse with the ornaments or even the perspicuity of Latin elocution. But his mind was stored with a
treasure of Greek learning: history and fable, philosophy and
grammar, were alike at his command; and he read the poems of
Homer in the schools of Florence. It was from his explanation
that Boccace composed and transcribed a literal prose version
of the Iliad and Odyssey, which satisfied the thirst of his friend
Petrarch, and which, perhaps in the succeeding century, was

[1] I will transcribe a passage from this epistle of Petrarch (Famil. ix. 2):
Donasti Homerum non in alienum sermonem violento alveo derivatum,
sed ex ipsis Græci eloquii scatebris, et qualis divino illi profluxit ingenio. . . . Sine tuâ voce Homerus tuus apud me mutus, immo vero ego
apud illum surdus sum. Gaudeo tamen vel adspectû solo, ac sæpe illum
amplexus atque suspirans dico, O magne vir, etc.

[2] For the life and writings of Boccace, who was born in 1313, and died in
1375, Fabricius (Biblioth. Latin. medii Ævi, tom. i. p. 248, etc.) and Tiraboschi (tom. v. p. 83, 439-451) may be consulted. The editions, versions,
imitations of his novels, are innumerable. Yet he was ashamed to communicate that trifling, and perhaps scandalous, work to Petrarch, his
respectable friend, in whose letters and memoirs he conspicuously appears.

clandestinely used by Laurentius Valla, the Latin interpreter.
It was from his narratives that the same Boccace collected the
materials for his treatise on the genealogy of the heathen gods,
a work, in that age, of stupendous erudition, and which he
ostentatiously sprinkled with Greek characters and passages, to
excite the wonder and applause of his more ignorant readers.[1]
The first steps of learning are slow and laborious; no more than
ten votaries of Homer could be enumerated in all Italy, and
neither Rome, nor Venice, nor Naples, could add a single name
to this studious catalogue. But their numbers would have
multiplied, their progress would have been accelerated, if the
inconstant Leo, at the end of three years, had not relinquished
an honourable and beneficial station. In his passage Petrarch
entertained him at Padua a short time: he enjoyed the scholar,
but was justly offended with the gloomy and unsocial temper of
the man. Discontented with the world and with himself, Leo
depreciated his present enjoyments, while absent persons and
objects were dear to his imagination. In Italy he was a Thes-
salian, in Greece a native of Calabria; in the company of the
Latins he disdained their language, religion, and manners: no
sooner was he landed at Constantinople than he again sighed for
the wealth of Venice and the elegance of Florence. His Italian
friends were deaf to his importunity: he depended on their
curiosity and indulgence, and embarked on a second voyage;
but on his entrance into the Adriatic the ship was assailed by a
tempest, and the unfortunate teacher, who like Ulysses had
fastened himself to the mast, was struck dead by a flash of
lightning. The humane Petrarch dropped a tear on his disaster;
but he was most anxious to learn whether some copy of Euripides
or Sophocles might not be saved from the hands of the mariners.[2]

But the faint rudiments of Greek learning, which Petrarch had
encouraged and Boccace had planted, soon withered and expired.
The succeeding generation was content for a while with the
improvement of Latin eloquence; nor was it before the end of
the fourteenth century that a new and perpetual flame was
rekindled in Italy.[3] Previous to his own journey, the emperor

[1] Boccace indulges an honest vanity: Ostentationis causâ Græca carmina adscripsi . . . jure utor meo; meum est hoc decus, mea gloria
scilicet inter Etruscos Græcis uti carminibus. Nonne ego fui qui Leontium
Pilatum, etc. (de Genealogiâ Deorum, l. xv. c. 7, a work which, though now
forgotten, has run through thirteen or fourteen editions).

[2] Leontius, or Leo Pilatus, is sufficiently made known by Hody (p. 2-11)
and the abbé de Sade (Vie de Pétrarque, tom. iii. p. 625-634, 670-673),
who has very happily caught the lively and dramatic manner of his original.

[3] Dr. Hody (p. 54) is angry with Leonard Aretin, Guarinus, Paulus

Manuel despatched his envoys and orators to implore the compassion of the Western princes. Of these envoys the most
conspicuous, or the most learned, was Manuel Chrysoloras,[1] of
noble birth, and whose Roman ancestors are supposed to have
migrated with the great Constantine. After visiting the courts
of France and England, where he obtained some contributions
and more promises, the envoy was invited to assume the office
of a professor; and Florence had again the honour of this second
invitation. By his knowledge, not only of the Greek but of the
Latin tongue, Chrysoloras deserved the stipend and surpassed
the expectation of the republic. His school was frequented by
a crowd of disciples of every rank and age; and one of these, in
a general history, has described his motives and his success. "At
that time," says Leonard Aretin,[2] "I was a student of the civil
law; but my soul was inflamed with the love of letters, and I
bestowed some application on the sciences of logic and rhetoric.
On the arrival of Manuel I hesitated whether I should desert my
legal studies or relinquish this golden opportunity; and thus, in
the ardour of youth, I communed with my own mind—Wilt
thou be wanting to thyself and thy fortune? Wilt thou refuse to
be introduced to a familiar converse with Homer, Plato, and
Demosthenes? with those poets, philosophers, and orators, of
whom such wonders are related, and who are celebrated by every
age as the great masters of human science? Of professors and
scholars in civil law, a sufficient supply will always be found in
our universities; but a teacher, and such a teacher of the Greek
language, if he once be suffered to escape, may never afterwards
be retrieved. Convinced by these reasons, I gave myself to
Chrysoloras, and so strong was my passion, that the lessons which
I had imbibed in the day were the constant subject of my nightly

Jovius, etc., for affirming that the Greek letters were restored in Italy *post
septingentos annos ;* as if, says he, they had flourished till the end of the
seventh century. These writers most probably reckoned from the last
period of thè exarchate; and the presence of the Greek magistrates and
troops at Ravenna and Rome must have preserved, in some degree, the use
of their native tongue.

[1] See the article of Emanuel, or Manuel Chrysoloras, in Hody (p. 12-54)
and Tiraboschi (tom. vii. p. 113-118). The precise date of his arrival
floats between the years 1390 and 1400, and is only confined by the reign
of Boniface IX.

[2] The name of *Aretinus* has been assumed by five or six natives of *Arezzo*
in Tuscany, of whom the most famous and the most worthless lived in the
sixteenth century. Leonardus Brunus Aretinus, the disciple of Chrysoloras, was a linguist, an orator, and an historian, the secretary of four
successive popes, and the chancellor of the republic of Florence, where he
died A.D. 1444, at the age of seventy-five (Fabric. Biblioth. medii Ævi,
tom. i. p. 190, etc.; Tiraboschi, tom. vii. p. 33-38).

dreams." [1]   At the same time and place the Latin classics were
explained by John of Ravenna, the domestic pupil of Petrarch: [2]
the Italians, who illustrated their age and country, were formed
in this double school, and Florence became the fruitful seminary
of Greek and Roman erudition. [3]   The presence of the emperor
recalled Chrysoloras from the college to the court; but he afterwards taught at Pavia and Rome with equal industry and
applause.   The remainder of his life, about fifteen years, was
divided between Italy and Constantinople, between embassies and
lessons.   In the noble office of enlightening a foreign nation,
the grammarian was not unmindful of a more sacred duty to
his prince and country; and Emanuel Chrysoloras died at
Constance on a public mission from the emperor to the council.

After his example, the restoration of the Greek letters in Italy
was prosecuted by a series of emigrants, who were destitute of
fortune and endowed with learning, or at least with language.
From the terror or oppression of the Turkish arms, the natives of
Thessalonica and Constantinople escaped to a land of freedom,
curiosity, and wealth.   The synod introduced into Florence the
lights of the Greek church and the oracles of the Platonic philosophy; and the fugitives who adhered to the union had the
double merit or renouncing their country, not only for the Christian but for the Catholic cause.   A patriot, who sacrifices his
party and conscience to the allurements of favour, may be
possessed however of the private and social virtues: he no longer
hears the reproachful epithets of slave and apostate, and the
consideration which he acquires among his new associates will
restore in his own eyes the dignity of his character.   The prudent
conformity of Bessarion was rewarded with the Roman purple:
he fixed his residence in Italy, and the Greek cardinal, the
titular patriarch of Constantinople, was respected as the chief
and protector of his nation: [4] his abilities were exercised in the

[1] See the passage in Aretin. Commentario Rerum suo Tempore in Italia
Gestarum, apud Hodium, p. 28-30.

[2] In this domestic discipline, Petrarch, who loved the youth, often complains of the eager curiosity, restless temper, and proud feelings, which
announce the genius and glory of a riper age (Mémoires sur Pétrarque,
tom. iii. p. 700-709).

[3] Hinc Græcæ Latinæque scholæ exortæ sunt, Guarino Philelpho,
Leonardo Aretino, Caroloque, ac plerisque aliis tanquam ex equo Trojano
prodeuntibus, quorum emulatione multa ingenia deinceps ad laudem exci-
tata sunt (Platina in Bonifacio IX.).   Another Italian writer adds the
names of Paulus Petrus Vergerius. Omnibonus Vincentius, Poggius, Franciscus Barbarus, etc.   But I question whether a rigid chronology would
allow Chrysoloras all these eminent scholars (Hodius, p. 25-27, etc.).

[4] See in Hody the article of Bessarion (p. 136-177).   Theodore Gaza,
George of Trebizond, and the rest of the Greeks whom I have named or

legations of Bologna, Venice, Germany, and France; and his election to the chair of St. Peter floated for a moment on the uncertain breath of a conclave.[1] His ecclesiastical honours diffused a splendour and pre-eminence over his literary merit and service: his palace was a school; as often as the cardinal visited the Vatican he was attended by a learned train of both nations;[2] of men applauded by themselves and the public, and whose writings, now overspread with dust, were popular and useful in their own times. I shall not attempt to enumerate the restorers of Grecian literature in the fifteenth century; and it may be sufficient to mention with gratitude the names of Theodore Gaza, of George of Trebizond, of John Argyropulus, and Demetrius Chalcocondyles, who taught their native language in the schools of Florence and Rome. Their labours were not inferior to those of Bessarion, whose purple they revered, and whose fortune was the secret object of their envy. But the lives of these grammarians were humble and obscure: they had declined the lucrative paths of the church; their dress and manners secluded them from the commerce of the world; and since they were confined to the merit, they might be content with the rewards of learning. From this character Janus Lascaris[3] will deserve an exception. His eloquence, politeness, and Imperial descent, recommended him to the French monarchs; and in the same cities he was alternately employed to teach and to negotiate. Duty and interest prompted them to cultivate the study of the Latin language, and the most successful attained the faculty of writing and speaking with fluency and elegance in a foreign idiom. But they ever retained the inveterate vanity

omitted, are inserted in their proper chapters of his learned work. See likewise Tiraboschi, in the first and second parts of the sixth tome.

[1] The cardinals knocked at his door, but his conclavist refused to interrupt the studies of Bessarion; " Nicholas," said he, " thy respect has cost thee a hat, and me the tiara."

[2] Such as George of Trebizond, Theodore Gaza, Argyropulus, Andronicus of Thessalonica, Philelphus, Poggius, Blondus, Nicholas Perrot, Valla, Campanus, Platina, etc. Viri (says Hody, with the pious zeal of a scholar) nullo ævo perituri (p. 156).

[For the study of the Renaissance period, see Symonds, *The Renaissance in Italy*; Burckhardt, *Italian Renaissance*; Oliphant Smeaton, *The Medici and the Italian Renaissance*.—O. S.]

[3] He was born before the taking of Constantinople, but his honourable life was stretched far into the sixteenth century (A.D. 1535). Leo X. and Francis I. were his noblest patrons, under whose auspices he founded the Greek colleges of Rome and Paris (Hody, p. 247-275). He left posterity in France; but the counts de Vintimille, and their numerous branches, derive the name of Lascaris from a doubtful marriage in the thirteenth century with the daughter of a Greek emperor (Ducange, Fam. Byzant. p. 224-230).

of their country: their praise, or at least their esteem, was reserved for the national writers to whom they owed their fame and subsistence; and they sometimes betrayed their contempt in licentious criticism or satire on Virgil's poetry and the oratory of Tully.[1] The superiority of these masters arose from the familiar use of a living language; and their first disciples were incapable of discerning how far they had degenerated from the knowledge and even the practice of their ancestors. A vicious pronunciation,[2] which they introduced, was banished from the schools by the reason of the succeeding age. Of the power of the Greek accents they were ignorant; and those musical notes, which, from an Attic tongue and to an Attic ear, must have been the secret soul of harmony, were to their eyes, as to our own, no more than mute and unmeaning marks, in prose superfluous and troublesome in verse. The art of grammar they truly possessed; the valuable fragments of Apollonius and Herodian were transfused into their lessons; and their treatises of syntax and etymology, though devoid of philosophic spirit, are still useful to the Greek student. In the shipwreck of the Byzantine libraries each fugitive seized a fragment of treasure, a copy of some author, who, without his industry, might have perished: the transcripts were multiplied by an assiduous and sometimes an elegant pen, and the text was corrected and explained by their own comments or those of the elder scholiasts. The sense, though not the spirit, of the Greek classics was interpreted to the Latin world: the beauties of style evaporate in a version; but the judgment of Theodore Gaza selected the more solid works of Aristotle and

[1] Two of his epigrams against Virgil, and three against Tully, are preserved and refuted by Franciscus Floridus, who can find no better names than Græculus ineptus et impudens (Hody, p. 274). In our own times an English critic has accused the Æneid of containing multa languida, nugatoria, spiritû et majestate carminis heroici defecta; many such verses as he, the said Jeremiah Markland, would have been ashamed of owning (præfat. ad Statii Sylvas, p. 21, 22).

[2] Manuel Chrysoloras and his colleagues are accused of ignorance, envy, or avarice (Sylloge, etc., tom. ii. p. 235). The modern Greeks pronounce the β as a V consonant, and confound three vowels (η ι υ) and several diphthongs. Such was the vulgar pronunciation which the stern Gardiner maintained by penal statutes in the university of Cambridge; but the monosyllable βη represented to an Attic ear the bleating of sheep, and a bellwether is better evidence than a bishop or a chancellor. The treatises of those scholars, particularly Erasmus, who asserted a more classical pronunciation, are collected in the Sylloge of Havercamp (2 vols. in octavo, Lugd. Bat. 1736, 1740); but it is difficult to paint sounds by words; and, in their reference to modern use, they can be understood only by their respective countrymen. We may observe that our peculiar pronunciation of the θ, th, is approved by Erasmus (tom. ii. p. 130).

Theophrastus, and their natural histories of animals and plants opened a rich fund of genuine and experimental science.

Yet the fleeting shadows of metaphysics were pursued with more curiosity and ardour. After a long oblivion, Plato was revived in Italy by a venerable Greek,[1] who taught in the house of Cosmo of Medicis. While the synod of Florence was involved in theological debate, some beneficial consequences might flow from the study of his elegant philosophy: his style is the purest standard of the Attic dialect, and his sublime thoughts are sometimes adapted to familiar conversation, and sometimes adorned with the richest colours of poetry and eloquence. The dialogues of Plato are a dramatic picture of the life and death of a sage; and, as often as he descends from the clouds, his moral system inculcates the love of truth, of our country, and of mankind. The precept and example of Socrates recommended a modest doubt and liberal inquiry; and if the Platonists, with blind devotion, adored the visions and errors of their divine master, their enthusiasm might correct the dry, dogmatic method of the Peripatetic school. So equal, yet so opposite, are the merits of Plato and Aristotle, that they may be balanced in endless controversy; but some spark of freedom may be produced by the collision of adverse servitude. The modern Greeks were divided between the two sects: with more fury than skill they fought under the banner of their leaders, and the field of battle was removed in their flight from Constantinople to Rome. But this philosophical debate soon degenerated into an angry and personal quarrel of grammarians; and Bessarion, though an advocate for Plato, protected the national honour by interposing the advice and authority of a mediator. In the gardens of the Medici the academical doctrine was enjoyed by the polite and learned; but their philosophic society was quickly dissolved; and if the writings of the Attic sage were perused in the closet, the more powerful Stagyrite continued to reign the oracle of the church and school.[2]

I have fairly represented the literary merits of the Greeks; yet it must be confessed that they were seconded and surpassed by the ardour of the Latins. Italy was divided into many inde-

[1] George Gemistus Pletho, a various and voluminous writer, the master of Bessarion, and all the Platonists of the times. He visited Italy in his old age, and soon returned to end his days in Peloponnesus. See the curious Diatribe of Leo Allatius de Georgiis, in Fabricius (Biblioth. Græc. tom. x. p. 739-756).

[2] The state of the Platonic philosophy in Italy is illustrated by Boivin (Mém. de l'Acad. des Inscriptions, tom. ii. p. 715-729) and Tiraboschi (tom. vi. P. i. p. 259-288).

pendent states; and at that time it was the ambition of princes and republics to vie with each other in the encouragement and reward of literature. The fame of Nicholas the Fifth[1] has not been adequate to his merits. From a plebeian origin he raised himself by his virtue and learning: the character of the man prevailed over the interest of the pope, and he sharpened those weapons which were soon pointed against the Roman church.[2] He had been the friend of the most eminent scholars of the age: he became their patron; and such was the humility of his manners, that the change was scarcely discernible either to them or to himself. If he pressed the acceptance of a liberal gift, it was not as the measure of desert, but as the proof of benevolence; and when modest merit declined his bounty, " Accept it," would he say, with a consciousness of his own worth: " you will not always have a Nicholas among ye." The influence of the holy see pervaded Christendom; and he exerted that influence in the search, not of benefices, but of books. From the ruins of the Byzantine libraries, from the darkest monasteries of Germany and Britain, he collected the dusty manuscripts of the writers of antiquity; and wherever the original could not be removed, a faithful copy was transcribed and transmitted for his use. The Vatican, the old repository for bulls and legends, for superstition and forgery, was daily replenished with more precious furniture; and such was the industry of Nicholas, that in a reign of eight years he formed a library of five thousand volumes. To his munificence the Latin world was indebted for the versions of Xenophon, Diodorus, Polybius, Thucydides, Herodotus, and Appian; of Strabo's Geography, of the Iliad, of the most valuable works of Plato and Aristotle, of Ptolemy and Theophrastus, and of the fathers of the Greek church. The example of the Roman pontiff was preceded or imitated by a Florentine merchant, who governed the republic without arms, and without a title. Cosmo of Medicis[3] was the father

[1] See the Life of Nicholas V. by two contemporary authors, Janottus Manettus (tom. iii. P. ii. p. 905-962) and Vespasian of Florence (tom. xxv. p. 267-290), in the collection of Muratori; and consult Tiraboschi (tom. vi. P. i. p. 46-52, 109) and Hody, in the articles of Theodore Gaza, George of Trebizond, etc.

[2] Lord Bolingbroke observes, with truth and spirit, that the popes in this instance were worse politicians than the muftis, and that the charm which had bound mankind for so many ages was broken by the magicians themselves (Letters on the Study of History, l. vi. p. 165, 166, octavo edition, 1779).

[3] See the literary history of Cosmo and Lorenzo of Medicis, in Tiraboschi (tom. vi. P. i. l. i. c. 2), who bestows a due measure of praise on Alphonso of Arragon, king of Naples, the dukes of Milan, Ferrara, Urbino, etc. The republic of Venice has deserved the least from the gratitude of scholars.

of a line of princes whose name and age are almost synonymous
with the restoration of learning: his credit was ennobled
into fame; his riches were dedicated to the service of mankind; he corresponded at once with Cairo and London; and
a cargo of Indian spices and Greek books was often imported in
the same vessel. The genius and education of his grandson
Lorenzo rendered him not only a patron but a judge and
candidate in the literary race. In his palace, distress was
entitled to relief, and merit to reward: his leisure hours were
delightfully spent in the Platonic academy; he encouraged the
emulation of Demetrius Chalcocondyles and Angelo Politian;
and his active missionary Janus Lascaris returned from the East
with a treasure of two hundred manuscripts, fourscore of which
were as yet unknown in the libraries of Europe.[1] The rest of
Italy was animated by a similar spirit, and the progress of the
nation repaid the liberality of her princes. The Latins held the
exclusive property of their own literature; and these disciples of
Greece were soon capable of transmitting and improving the
lessons which they had imbibed. After a short succession of
foreign teachers, the tide of emigration subsided; but the language of Constantinople was spread beyond the Alps, and the
natives of France, Germany, and England [2] imparted to their
country the sacred fire which they had kindled in the schools of
Florence and Rome.[3] In the productions of the mind, as in
those of the soil, the gifts of nature are excelled by industry and
skill: the Greek authors, forgotten on the banks of the Ilissus,
have been illustrated on those of the Elbe and the Thames; and
Bessarion or Gaza might have envied the superior science of the
barbarians, the accuracy of Budæus, the taste of Erasmus, the

---

[1] Tiraboschi (tom. vi. P. i. p. 104), from the preface of Janus Lascaris to
the Greek Anthology, printed at Florence 1494; Latebant (says Aldus, in
his preface to the Greek orators, apud Hodium, p. 249) in Atho Thraciæ
monte. Eas Lascaris . . . in Italiam reportavit. Miserat enim ipsum
Laurentius ille Medices in Græciam ad inquirendos simul, et quantovis
emendos pretio bonos libros. It is remarkable enough that the research
was facilitated by sultan Bajazet II.

[2] The Greek language was introduced into the university of Oxford in
the last years of the fifteenth century by Grocyn, Linacer, and Latimer,
who had all studied at Florence under Demetrius Chalcocondyles. See
Dr. Knight's curious Life of Erasmus. Although a stout academical
patriot, he is forced to acknowledge that Erasmus learned Greek at Oxford,
and taught it at Cambridge.

[3] The jealous Italians were desirous of keeping a monopoly of Greek
learning. When Aldus was about to publish the Greek scholiasts on
Sophocles and Euripides, Cave (said they), cave hoc facias, ne *Barbari* istis
adjuti domi maneant, et pauciores in Italiam ventitent (Dr. Knight, in his
Life of Erasmus, p. 365, from Beatus Rhenanus).

copiousness of Stephens, the erudition of Scaliger, the discernment of Reiske or of Bentley.   On the side of the Latins the discovery of printing was a casual advantage; but this useful art has been applied by Aldus and his innumerable successors to perpetuate and multiply the works of antiquity.[1]   A single manuscript imported from Greece is revived in ten thousand copies, and each copy is fairer than the original.   In this form Homer and Plato would peruse with more satisfaction their own writings; and their scholiasts must resign the prize to the labours of our Western editors.

Before the revival of classic literature the barbarians in Europe were immersed in ignorance; and their vulgar tongues were marked with the rudeness and poverty of their manners. The students of the more perfect idioms of Rome and Greece were introduced to a new world of light and science; to the society of the free and polished nations of antiquity; and to a familiar converse with those immortal men who spoke the sublime language of eloquence and reason.   Such an intercourse must tend to refine the taste and to elevate the genius of the moderns; and yet, from the first experiment, it might appear that the study of the ancients had given fetters, rather than wings, to the human mind.   However laudable, the spirit of imitation is of a servile cast; and the first disciples of the Greeks and Romans were a colony of strangers in the midst of their age and country.   The minute and laborious diligence which explored the antiquities of remote times might have improved or adorned the present state of society; the critic and metaphysician were the slaves of Aristotle; the poets, historians, and orators were proud to repeat the thoughts and words of the Augustan age: the works of nature were observed with the eyes of Pliny and Theophrastus; and some Pagan votaries professed a secret devotion to the gods of Homer and Plato.[2]   The Italians were oppressed by the

---

[1] The press of Aldus Manutius, a Roman, was established at Venice about the year 1494: he printed above sixty considerable works of Greek literature, almost all for the first time; several containing different treatises and authors, and of several authors two, three, or four editions (Fabric. Biblioth. Græc. tom. xiii. p. 605, etc.).   Yet his glory must not tempt us to forget that the first Greek book, the Grammar of Constantine Lascaris, was printed at Milan in 1476, and that the Florence Homer of 1488 displays all the luxury of the typographical art.   See the Annales Typographici of Mattaire, and the Bibliographie Instructive of De Bure, a knowing bookseller of Paris.

[2] I will select three singular examples of this classic enthusiasm.   1. At the synod of Florence, Gemistus Pletho said, in familiar conversation, to George of Trebizond, that in a short time mankind would unanimously renounce the Gospel and the Koran for a religion similar to that of the

strength and number of their ancient auxiliaries: the century after the deaths of Petrarch and Boccace was filled with a crowd of Latin imitators, who decently repose on our shelves; but in that era of learning it will not be easy to discern a real discovery of science, a work of invention or eloquence, in the popular language of the country.[1] But as soon as it had been deeply saturated with the celestial dew, the soil was quickened into vegetation and life; the modern idioms were refined; the classics of Athens and Rome inspired a pure taste and a generous emulation; and in Italy, as afterwards in France and England, the pleasing reign of poetry and fiction was succeeded by the light of speculative and experimental philosophy. Genius may anticipate the season of maturity; but in the education of a people, as in that of an individual, memory must be exercised before the powers of reason and fancy can be expanded: nor may the artist hope to equal or surpass, till he has learned to imitate, the works of his predecessors.

CHAPTER LXVII

Schism of the Greeks and Latins—Reign and Character of Amurath the Second—Crusade of Ladislaus, King of Hungary—His Defeat and Death—John Huniades—Scanderbeg—Constantine Palæologus, last Emperor of the East

THE respective merits of Rome and Constantinople are compared and celebrated by an eloquent Greek, the father of the Italian schools.[2] The view of the ancient capital, the seat of his ancestors,

Gentiles (Leo Allatius, apud Fabricium, tom. x. p. 751). 2. Paul II. persecuted the Roman academy, which had been founded by Pomponius Lætus; and the principal members were accused of heresy, impiety, and *paganism* (Tiraboschi, tom. vi. P. i. p. 81, 82). 3. In the next century some scholars and poets in France celebrated the success of Jodelle's tragedy of Cleopatra by a festival of Bacchus, and, as it is said, by the sacrifice of a goat (Bayle, Dictionnaire, JODELLE; Fontenelle, tom. iii. p. 56-61). Yet the spirit of bigotry might often discern a serious impiety in the sportive play of fancy and learning.

[1] The survivor Boccace died in the year 1375; and we cannot place before 1480 the composition of the Morgante Maggiore of Pulci, and the Orlando Inamorato of Boiardo (Tiraboschi, tom. vi. P. ii. p. 174-177).

[2] The epistle of Manuel Chrysoloras to the emperor John Palæologus will not offend the eye or ear of a classical student (ad calcem Codini de Antiquitatibus C. P. p. 107-126). The superscription suggests a chronological remark, that John Palæologus II. was associated in the empire before the year 1414, the date of Chrysoloras's death. A still earlier date, at least 1408, is deduced from the age of his youngest sons, Demetrius and Thomas, who were both *Porphyrogeniti* (Ducange, Fam. Byzant. p. 244, 247).

surpassed the most sanguine expectations of Manuel Chrysoloras; and he no longer blamed the exclamation of an old sophist, that Rome was the habitation, not of men, but of gods. Those gods, and those men, had long since vanished; but, to the eye of liberal enthusiasm, the majesty of ruin restored the image of her ancient prosperity. The monuments of the consuls and Cæsars, of the martyrs and apostles, engaged on all sides the curiosity of the philosopher and the Christian; and he confessed that in every age the arms and the religion of Rome were destined to reign over the earth. While Chrysoloras admired the venerable beauties of the mother, he was not forgetful of his native country, her fairest daughter, her Imperial colony; and the Byzantine patriot expatiates with zeal and truth on the eternal advantages of nature, and the more transitory glories of art and dominion, which adorned, or had adorned, the city of Constantine. Yet the perfection of the copy still redounds (as he modestly observes) to the honour of the original, and parents are delighted to be renewed, and even excelled, by the superior merit of their children. "Constantinople," says the orator," is situate on a commanding point between Europe and Asia, between the Archipelago and the Euxine. By her interposition the two seas and the two continents are united for the common benefit of nations; and the gates of commerce may be shut or opened at her command. The harbour, encompassed on all sides by the sea and the continent, is the most secure and capacious in the world. The walls and gates of Constantinople may be compared with those of Babylon: the towers are many; each tower is a solid and lofty structure; and the second wall, the outer fortification, would be sufficient for the defence and dignity of an ordinary capital. A broad and rapid stream may be introduced into the ditches; and the artificial island may be encompassed, like Athens,[1] by land or water." Two strong and natural causes are alleged for the perfection of the model of new Rome. The royal founder reigned over the most illustrious nations of the globe; and in the accomplishment of his designs the power of the Romans was combined with the art and science of the Greeks. Other cities have been reared to maturity by accident and time: their beauties are mingled with disorder and deformity; and the inhabitants, unwilling to remove from their natal spot, are incap-

---

[1] Somebody observed that the city of Athens might be circumnavigated (τις εἶπεν τὴν πόλιν τῶν Αθηναίων δύνασθαι καὶ παραπλεῖν καὶ περιπλεῖν). But what may be true in a rhetorical sense of Constantinople, cannot be applied to the situation of Athens, five miles from the sea, and not intersected or surrounded by any navigable streams.

able of correcting the errors of their ancestors and the original
vices of situation or climate.   But the free idea of Constantinople
was formed and executed by a single mind: and the primitive
model was improved by the obedient zeal of the subjects and
successors of the first monarch.   The adjacent isles were stored
with an inexhaustible supply of marble; but the various materials
were transported from the most remote shores of Europe and
Asia; and the public and private buildings, the palaces, churches,
aqueducts, cisterns, porticoes, columns, baths, and hippodromes,
were adapted to the greatness of the capital of the East.   The
superfluity of wealth was spread along the shores of Europe and
Asia; and the Byzantine territory, as far as the Euxine, the
Hellespont, and the long wall, might be considered as a populous
suburb and a perpetual garden.   In this flattering picture, the
past and the present, the times of prosperity and decay, are
artfully confounded: but a sigh and a confession escape from
the orator, that his wretched country was the shadow and
sepulchre of its former self.   The works of ancient sculpture had
been defaced by Christian zeal or barbaric violence; the fairest
structures were demolished; and the marbles of Paros or
Numidia were burnt for lime, or applied to the meanest uses.
Of many a statue, the place was marked by an empty pedestal;
of many a column, the size was determined by a broken capital;
the tombs of the emperors were scattered on the ground; the
stroke of time was accelerated by storms and earthquakes; and
the vacant space was adorned by vulgar tradition with fabulous
monuments of gold and silver.   From these wonders, which
lived only in memory or belief, he distinguishes, however, the
porphyry pillar, the column and colossus of Justinian,[1] and the
church, more especially the dome, of St. Sophia; the best conclusion, since it could not be described according to its merits,
and after it no other object could deserve to be mentioned.   But
he forgets that, a century before, the trembling fabrics of the
colossus and the church had been saved and supported by the
timely care of Andronicus the Elder.   Thirty years after the
emperor had fortified St. Sophia with two new buttresses or
pyramids, the eastern hemisphere suddenly gave way; and the

[1] Nicephorus Gregoras has described the colossus of Justinian (l. vii. 12):
but his measures are false and inconsistent.   The editor Boivin consulted
his friend Girardon; and the sculptor gave him the true proportions of an
equestrian statue.   That of Justinian was still visible to Peter Gyllius,
not on the column, but in the outward court of the seraglio; and he was
at Constantinople when it was melted down, and cast into a brass cannon
(de Topograph. C. P. l. ii. c. 17).

images, the altars, and the sanctuary were crushed by the falling
ruin. The mischief indeed was speedily repaired; the rubbish
was cleared by the incessant labour of every rank and age; and
the poor remains of riches and industry were consecrated by the
Greeks to the most stately and venerable temple of the East.[1]

The last hope of the falling city and empire was placed in the
harmony of the mother and daughter, in the maternal tenderness of Rome, and the filial obedience of Constantinople. In
the synod of Florence, the Greeks and Latins had embraced, and
subscribed, and promised; but these signs of friendship were
perfidious or fruitless;[2] and the baseless fabric of the union
vanished like a dream.[3] The emperor and his prelates returned
home in the Venetian galleys; but as they touched at the Morea
and the isles of Corfu and Lesbos, the subjects of the Latins
complained that the pretended union would be an instrument of
oppression. No sooner did they land on the Byzantine shore,
than they were saluted, or rather assailed, with a general
murmur of zeal and discontent. During their absence, above
two years, the capital had been deprived of its civil and
ecclesiastical rulers; fanaticism fermented in anarchy; the most
furious monks reigned over the conscience of women and bigots;
and the hatred of the Latin name was the first principle of nature
and religion. Before his departure for Italy the emperor had
flattered the city with the assurance of a prompt relief and a
powerful succour; and the clergy, confident in their orthodoxy
and science, had promised themselves and their flocks an easy
victory over the blind shepherds of the West. The double
disappointment exasperated the Greeks; the conscience of the
subscribing prelates was awakened; the hour of temptation was
past; and they had more to dread from the public resentment
than they could hope from the favour of the emperor or the pope.
Instead of justifying their conduct, they deplored their weakness,

---

[1] See the decay and repairs of St. Sophia, in Nicephorus Gregoras (l. vii.
12, l. xv. 2). The building was propped by Andronicus in 1317, the eastern
hemisphere fell in 1345. The Greeks, in their pompous rhetoric, exalt the
beauty and holiness of the church, an earthly heaven, the abode of angels,
and of God himself, etc.

[2] The genuine and original narrative of Syropulus (p. 312-351) opens
the schism from the first *office* of the Greeks at Venice to the general opposition at Constantinople of the clergy and people.

[3] On the schism of Constantinople, see Phranza (l. ii. c. 17), Laonicus
Chalcocondyles (l. vi. p. 155, 156 [p. 292-295, ed. Bonn]), and Ducas (c. 31);
the last of whom writes with truth and freedom. Among the moderns we
may distinguish the continuator of Fleury (tom. xxii. p. 338, etc., 401, 420,
etc.) and Spondanus (A.D. 1440-30). The sense of the latter is drowned
in prejudice and passion as soon as Rome and religion are concerned.

professed their contrition, and cast themselves on the mercy of God and of their brethren. To the reproachful question, what had been the event or the use of their Italian synod? they answered, with sighs and tears, " Alas! we have made a new faith; we have exchanged piety for impiety; we have betrayed the immaculate sacrifice; and we are become *Azymites*." (The Azymites were those who celebrated the communion with un-leavened bread; and I must retract or qualify the praise which I have bestowed on the growing philosophy of the times.) " Alas! we have been seduced by distress, by fraud, and by the hopes and fears of a transitory life. The hand that has signed the union should be cut off; and the tongue that has pronounced the Latin creed deserves to be torn from the root." The best proof of their repentance was an increase of zeal for the most trivial rites and the most incomprehensible doctrines; and an absolute separation from all, without excepting their prince, who preserved some regard for honour and consistency. After the decease of the patriarch Joseph, the archbishops of Heraclea and Trebizond had courage to refuse the vacant office; and Cardinal Bessarion preferred the warm and comfortable shelter of the Vatican. The choice of the emperor and his clergy was confined to Metrophanes of Cyzicus: he was consecrated in St. Sophia, but the temple was vacant. The crossbearers abdicated their service; the infection spread from the city to the villages; and Metrophanes discharged, without effect, some ecclesiastical thunders against a nation of schismatics. The eyes of the Greeks were directed to Mark of Ephesus, the champion of his country; and the sufferings of the holy confessor were repaid with a tribute of admiration and applause. His example and writings propagated the flame of religious discord; age and infirmity soon removed him from the world; but the gospel of Mark was not a law of forgiveness; and he requested with his dying breath that none of the adherents of Rome might attend his obsequies or pray for his soul.

The schism was not confined to the narrow limits of the Byzantine empire. Secure under the Mamaluke sceptre, the three patriarchs of Alexandria, Antioch, and Jerusalem assembled a numerous synod; disowned their representatives at Ferrara and Florence; condemned the creed and council of the Latins; and threatened the emperor of Constantinople with the censures of the Eastern church. Of the sectaries of the Greek communion, the Russians were the most powerful, ignorant, and superstitious. Their primate, the cardinal Isidore, hastened from Florence to Moscow,[1] to reduce the independent nation under the Roman yoke. But the Russian bishops had been educated at Mount Athos; and the prince and people embraced the theology of their priests. They were scandalised by the title, the pomp, the Latin cross of the legate, the friend of those impious men who shaved their beards, and performed the divine office with gloves on their hands and rings on their fingers: Isidore was condemned by a synod; his person was imprisoned in a monastery; and it was with extreme difficulty that the cardinal could escape from the hands of a fierce and fanatic people.[2] The Russians refused a passage to the missionaries of Rome who aspired to convert the Pagans beyond the Tanais;[3] and their refusal was justified by the maxim that the guilt of idolatry is less damnable than that of schism. The errors of the Bohemians were excused by their abhorrence for the pope; and a deputation of the Greek clergy solicited the friendship of those sanguinary enthusiasts.[4] While Eugenius triumphed in the union and orthodoxy of the Greeks, his party was contracted to the walls, or rather to the palace, of Constantinople. The zeal of Palæologus had been excited by interest; it was soon cooled by opposition: an attempt to violate the national belief might endanger his life and crown; nor could the pious rebels be destitute of foreign and domestic aid. The sword of his brother Demetrius, who in Italy had maintained a prudent and popular silence, was half unsheathed in the cause of religion; and Amurath, the Turkish sultan, was displeased and alarmed by the seeming friendship of the Greeks and Latins.

[1] Isidore was metropolitan of Kiow, but the Greeks subject to Poland have removed that see from the ruins of Kiow to Lemberg, or Leopold (Herbestein, in Ramusio, tom. ii. p. 127). On the other hand, the Russians transferred their spiritual obedience to the archbishop, who became, in 1588, the patriarch of Moscow (Levesque, Hist. de Russie, tom iii. p. 188, 190, from a Greek MS. at Turin, Iter et labores Archiepiscopi Arsenii).

[2] The curious narrative of Levesque (Hist. de Russie, tom..ii. p. 242-247) is extracted from the patriarchal archives. The scenes of Ferrara and Florence are described by ignorance and passion; but the Russians are credible in the account of their own prejudices.

[3] The Shamanism, the ancient religion of the Samanæans and Gymnosophists, has been driven by the more popular Bramins from India into the northern deserts: the naked philosophers were compelled to wrap themselves in fur; but they insensibly sunk into wizards and physicians. The Mordvans and Tcheremisses in the European Russia adhere to this religion, which is formed on the earthly model of one king or God, his ministers or angels, and the rebellious spirits who oppose his government. As these tribes of the Volga have no images, they might more justly retort on the Latin missionaries the name of idolaters (Levesque, Hist. des Peuples soumis à la Domination des Russes, tom. i. p. 194-237, 423-460).

[4] Spondanus, Annal. Eccles. tom. ii. A.D. 1451, No. 13. The epistle of the Greeks, with a Latin version, is extant in the college library at Prague.

" Sultan Murad, or Amurath, lived forty-nine, and reigned
thirty years, six months, and eight days. He was a just and
valiant prince, of a great soul, patient of labours, learned,
merciful, religious, charitable; a lover and encourager of the
studious, and of all who excelled in any art or science; a good
emperor, and a great general. No man obtained more or greater
victories than Amurath; Belgrade alone withstood his attacks.
Under his reign the soldier was ever victorious, the citizen rich
and secure. If he subdued any country, his first care was to
build mosques and caravanseras, hospitals and colleges. Every
year he gave a thousand pieces of gold to the sons of the Prophet,
and sent two thousand five hundred to the religious persons of
Mecca, Medina, and Jerusalem." [1] This portrait is transcribed
from the historian of the Othman empire: but the applause of a
servile and superstitious people has been lavished on the worst
of tyrants; and the virtues of a sultan are often the vices most
useful to himself, or most agreeable to his subjects. A nation
ignorant of the equal benefits of liberty and law must be awed by
the flashes of arbitrary power: the cruelty of a despot will assume
the character of justice; his profusion, of liberality; his obstinacy,
of firmness. If the most reasonable excuse be rejected, few acts
of obedience will be found impossible; and guilt must tremble,
where innocence cannot always be secure. The tranquillity of
the people, and the discipline of the troops, were best maintained
by perpetual action in the field: war was the trade of the Janizaries; and those who survived the peril, and divided the spoil,
applauded the generous ambition of their sovereign. To propagate the true religion was the duty of a faithful Musulman: the
unbelievers were *his* enemies, and those of the Prophet; and, in
the hands of the Turks, the scimitar was the only instrument of
conversion. Under these circumstances, however, the justice
and moderation of Amurath are attested by his conduct, and
acknowledged by the Christians themselves, who consider a
prosperous reign and a peaceful death as the reward of his singular
merits. In the vigour of his age and military power he seldom
engaged in war till he was justified by a previous and adequate
provocation: the victorious sultan was disarmed by submission;
and in the observance of treaties, his word was inviolate and
sacred.[2] The Hungarians were commonly the aggressors; he

[1] See Cantemir, History of the Othman Empire, p. 94. Murad, or
Morad, may be more correct: but I have preferred the popular name to
that obscure diligence which is rarely successful in translating an Oriental,
into the Roman, alphabet.
[2] See Chalcocondyles (l. vii. p. 186, 198 [p. 375, ed. Bonn]), Ducas (c. 33

was provoked by the revolt of Scanderbeg; and the perfidious Caramanian was twice vanquished, and twice pardoned, by the Ottoman monarch. Before he invaded the Morea, Thebes had been surprised by the despot: in the conquest of Thessalonica the grandson of Bajazet might dispute the recent purchase of the Venetians; and after the first siege of Constantinople, the sultan was never tempted, by the distress, the absence, or the injuries of Palæologus, to extinguish the dying light of the Byzantine empire.

But the most striking feature in the life and character of Amurath is the double abdication of the Turkish throne; and, were not his motives debased by an alloy of superstition, we must praise the royal philosopher,[1] who at the age of forty could discern the vanity of human greatness. Resigning the sceptre to his son, he retired to the pleasant residence of Magnesia; but he retired to the society of saints and hermits. It was not till the fourth century of the Hegira that the religion of Mohammed had been corrupted by an institution so adverse to his genius; but in the age of the crusades the various orders of dervishes were multiplied by the example of the Christian, and even the Latin, monks.[2] The lord of nations submitted to fast, and pray, and turn round in endless rotation with the fanatics, who mistook the giddiness of the head for the illumination of the spirit.[3] But he was soon awakened from this dream of enthusiasm by the Hungarian invasion; and his obedient son was the foremost to urge the public danger and the wishes of the people. Under the banner of their veteran leader, the Janizaries fought and conquered; but he withdrew from the field of Varna, again to pray, to fast, and to turn round with his Magnesian brethren. These pious occupations were again interrupted by the danger of the

[p. 228, ed. Bonn]), and Marinus Barletius (in Vit. Scanderbeg, p. 145, 146). In his good faith towards the garrison of Sfetigrade, he was a lesson and example to his son Mohammed.

[1] Voltaire (Essai sur l'Histoire Générale, c. 89, p. 283, 284) admires *le Philosophe Turc :* would he have bestowed the same praise on a Christian prince for retiring to a monastery? In his way, Voltaire was a bigot, an intolerant bigot.

[2] See the articles *Dervische, Fakir, Nasser, Rohbaniat,* in D'Herbelot's Bibliothèque Orientale. Yet the subject is superficially treated from the Persian and Arabian writers. It is among the Turks that these orders have principally flourished.

[3] Rycaut (in the Present State of the Ottoman Empire, p. 242-268) affords much information, which he drew from his personal conversation with the heads of the dervishes, most of whom ascribed their origin to the time of Orchan. He does not mention the *Zichidæ* of Chalcocondyles (l. vii. p. 186 [p. 352, ed. Bonn]), among whom Amurath retired: the *Seids* of that author are the descendants of Mohammed.

state. A victorious army disdained the inexperience of their
youthful ruler: the city of Adrianople was abandoned to rapine
and slaughter; and the unanimous divan implored his presence to
appease the tumult, and prevent the rebellion, of the Janizaries.
At the well-known voice of their master they trembled and
obeyed; and the reluctant sultan was compelled to support his
splendid servitude, till, at the end of four years, he was relieved
by the angel of death. Age or disease, misfortune or caprice,
have tempted several princes to descend from the throne; and
they have had leisure to repent of their irretrievable step. But
Amurath alone, in the full liberty of choice, after the trial of
empire and solitude, has *repeated* his preference of a private life.

After the departure of his Greek brethren, Eugenius had not
been unmindful of their temporal interest; and his tender regard
for the Byzantine empire was animated by a just apprehension
of the Turks, who approached, and might soon invade, the
borders of Italy. But the spirit of the crusades had expired;
and the coldness of the Franks was not less unreasonable than
their headlong passion. In the eleventh century a fanatic monk
could precipitate Europe on Asia for the recovery of the holy
sepulchre: but in the fifteenth, the most pressing motives of
religion and policy were insufficient to unite the Latins in the
defence of Christendom. Germany was an inexhaustible storehouse of men and arms:[1] but that complex and languid body
required the impulse of a vigorous hand; and Frederic the Third
was alike impotent in his personal character and his Imperial
dignity. A long war had impaired the strength, without satiat-
ing the animosity, of France and England;[2] but Philip duke of
Burgundy was a vain and magnificent prince; and he enjoyed,
without danger or expense, the adventurous piety of his subjects,
who sailed, in a gallant fleet, from the coast of Flanders to the
Hellespont. The maritime republics of Venice and Genoa were
less remote from the scene of action; and their hostile fleets

---

[1] In the year 1431 Germany raised 40,000 horse, men-at-arms, against
the Hussites of Bohemia (Lenfant, Hist. du Concile de Basle, tom. i. p. 318).
At the siege of Nuys, on the Rhine, in 1474, the princes, prelates, and
cities sent their respective quotas; and the bishop of Munster (qui n'est
pas des plus grands) furnished 1400 horse, 6000 foot, all in green, with
1200 waggons. The united armies of the king of England and the duke of
Burgundy scarcely equalled one-third of this German host (Mémoires de
Philippe de Comines, l. iv. c. 2). At present, six or seven hundred thousand
men are maintained in constant pay and admirable discipline by the powers
of Germany.

[2] It was not till the year 1444 that France and England could agree on a
truce of some months. (See Rymer's Fœdera, and the chronicles of both
nations.)

were associated under the standard of St. Peter. The kingdoms
of Hungary and Poland, which covered as it were the interior
pale of the Latin church, were the most nearly concerned to
oppose the progress of the Turks. Arms were the patrimony of
the Scythians and Sarmatians; and these nations might appear
equal to the contest, could they point, against the common foe,
those swords that were so wantonly drawn in bloody and domestic
quarrels. But the same spirit was adverse to concord and
obedience: a poor country and a limited monarch are incapable
of maintaining a standing force; and the loose bodies of Polish
and Hungarian horse were not armed with the sentiments and
weapons which, on some occasions, have given irresistible weight
to the French chivalry. Yet, on this side, the designs of the
Roman pontiff, and the eloquence of Cardinal Julian, his legate,
were promoted by the circumstances of the times;[1] by the
union of the two crowns on the head of Ladislaus,[2] a young and
ambitious soldier; by the valour of a hero, whose name, the
name of John Huniades, was already popular among the Christians, and formidable to the Turks. An endless treasure of
pardons and indulgences was scattered by the legate; many
private warriors of France and Germany enlisted under the holy
banner; and the crusade derived some strength, or at least some
reputation, from the new allies both of Europe and Asia. A
fugitive despot of Servia exaggerated the distress and ardour of
the Christians beyond the Danube, who would unaminously rise
to vindicate their religion and liberty. The Greek emperor,[3]
with a spirit unknown to his fathers, engaged to guard the
Bosphorus, and to sally from Constantinople at the head of his
national and mercenary troops. The sultan of Caramania[4]

[1] In the Hungarian crusade, Spondanus (Annal. Eccles. A.D. 1443, 1444)
has been my leading guide. He has diligently read, and critically compared, the Greek and Turkish materials, the historians of Hungary,
Poland, and the West. His narrative is perspicuous; and where he can
be free from a religious bias, the judgment of Spondanus is not contemptible.

[2] I have curtailed the harsh letter (Wladislaus) which most writers affix
to his name, either in compliance with the Polish pronunciation, or to distinguish him from his rival the infant Ladislaus of Austria. Their competition for the crown of Hungary is described by Callimachus (l. i. ii
p. 447-486), Bonfinius (Decad. iii. l. iv.), Spondanus, and Lenfant.

[3] The Greek historians, Phranza, Chalcocondyles, and Ducas, do not
ascribe to their prince a very active part in this crusade, which he seems to
have promoted by his wishes, and injured by his fears.

[4] Cantemir (p. 88) ascribes to his policy the original plan, and transcribes
his animating epistle to the king of Hungary. But the Mohammedan
powers are seldom informed of the state of Christendom; and the situation
and correspondence of the knights of Rhodes must connect them with the
sultan of Caramania.

announced the retreat of Amurath, and a powerful diversion in the heart of Anatolia; and if the fleets of the West could occupy at the same moment the straits of the Hellespont, the Ottoman monarchy would be dissevered and destroyed. Heaven and earth must rejoice in the perdition of the miscreants; and the legate, with prudent ambiguity, instilled the opinion of the invisible, perhaps the visible, aid of the Son of God and his divine mother.

Of the Polish and Hungarian diets a religious war was the unanimous cry; and Ladislaus, after passing the Danube, led an army of his confederate subjects as far as Sophia, the capital of the Bulgarian kingdom. In this expedition they obtained two signal victories, which were justly ascribed to the valour and conduct of Huniades. In the first, with a vanguard of ten thousand men, he surprised the Turkish camp; in the second, he vanquished and made prisoner the most renowned of their generals, who possessed the double advantage of ground and numbers. The approach of winter, and the natural and artificial obstacles of Mount Hæmus, arrested the progress of the hero, who measured a narrow interval of six days' march from the foot of the mountains to the hostile towers of Adrianople and the friendly capital of the Greek empire. The retreat was undisturbed; and the entrance into Buda was at once a military and religious triumph. An ecclesiastical procession was followed by the king and his warriors on foot: he nicely balanced the merits and rewards of the two nations; and the pride of conquest was blended with the humble temper of Christianity. Thirteen bashaws, nine standards, and four thousand captives, were unquestionable trophies; and as all were willing to believe, and none were present to contradict, the crusaders multiplied, with unblushing confidence, the myriads of Turks whom they had left on the field of battle.[1] The most solid proof, and the most salutary consequence, of victory, was a deputation from the divan to solicit peace, to restore Servia, to ransom the prisoners, and to evacuate the Hungarian frontier. By this treaty the rational objects of the war were obtained: the king, the despot, and Huniades himself, in the diet of Segedin, were satisfied with public and private emolument; a truce of ten years was concluded; and the followers of Jesus and Mohammed, who swore on the Gospel and the Koran, attested the word of

[1] In their letters to the emperor Frederic III. the Hungarians slay 30,000 Turks in one battle; but the modest Julian reduces the slaughter to 6000 or even 2000 infidels (Æneas Sylvius in Europ. c. 5, and epist. 44, 81, apud Spondanum).

God as the guardian of truth and the avenger of perfidy.   In the
place of the Gospel the Turkish ministers had proposed to substitute the Eucharist, the real presence of the Catholic Deity;
but the Christians refused to profane their holy mysteries; and
a superstitious conscience is less forcibly bound by the spiritual
energy than by the outward and visible symbols of an oath.[1]

During the whole transaction the cardinal legate had observed
a sullen silence, unwilling to approve, and unable to oppose,
the consent of the king and people.   But the diet was not dissolved before Julian was fortified by the welcome intelligence
that Anatolia was invaded by the Caramanian, and Thrace by
the Greek emperor; that the fleets of Genoa, Venice, and Burgundy were masters of the Hellespont; and that the allies, informed of the victory, and ignorant of the treaty, of Ladislaus,
impatiently waited for the return of his victorious army.   " And
is it thus," exclaimed the cardinal,[2] " that you will desert their
expectations and your own fortune?   It is to them, to your God,
and your fellow-Christians, that you have pledged your faith;
and that prior obligation annihilates a rash and sacrilegious
oath to the enemies of Christ.   His vicar on earth is the Roman
pontiff; without whose sanction you can neither promise nor
perform.   In his name I absolve your perjury and sanctify your
arms: follow my footsteps in the paths of glory and salvation;
and if still you have scruples, devolve on my head the punishment and the sin."   This mischievous casuistry was seconded
by his respectable character and the levity of popular assemblies:
war was resolved on the same spot where peace had so lately
been sworn; and, in the execution of the treaty, the Turks were
assaulted by the Christians, to whom, with some reason, they
might apply the epithet of Infidels.   The falsehood of Ladislaus
to his word and oath was palliated by the religion of the times:
the most perfect, or at least the most popular, excuse would have
been the success of his arms and the deliverance of the Eastern
church.   But the same treaty which should have bound his

[1] See the origin of the Turkish war, and the first expedition of Ladislaus,
in the fifth and sixth books of the third decad of Bonfinius, who, in his
division and style, copies Livy with tolerable success.   Callimachus (l. ii.
p. 487-496) is still more pure and authentic.

[2] I do not pretend to warrant the literal accuracy of Julian's speech,
which is variously worded by Callimachus (l. iii. p. 505-507), Bonfinius
(dec. iii. l. vi. p. 457, 458), and other historians, who might indulge their
own eloquence, while they represent one of the orators of the age.   But
they all agree in the advice and arguments for perjury, which in the field
of controversy are fiercely attacked by the Protestants, and feebly defended by the Catholics.   The latter are discouraged by the misfortune
of Varna.

conscience had diminished his strength. On the proclamation of
the peace the French and German volunteers departed with
indignant murmurs: the Poles were exhausted by distant warfare, and perhaps disgusted with foreign command; and their
palatines accepted the first licence, and hastily retired to their
provinces and castles. Even Hungary was divided by faction, or
restrained by a laudable scruple; and the relics of the crusade
that marched in the second expedition were reduced to an inadequate force of twenty thousand men. A Wallachian chief,
who joined the royal standard with his vassals, presumed to
remark that their numbers did not exceed the hunting retinue
that sometimes attended the sultan; and the gift of two horses
of matchless speed might admonish Ladislaus of his secret foresight of the event. But the despot of Servia, after the restoration of his country and children, was tempted by the promise
of new realms; and the inexperience of the king, the enthusiasm
of the legate, and the martial presumption of Huniades himself, were persuaded that every obstacle must yield to the invincible virtue of the sword and the cross. After the passage
of the Danube two roads might lead to Constantinople and the
Hellespont; the one direct, abrupt, and difficult, through the
mountains of Hæmus; the other more tedious and secure, over
a level country, and along the shores of the Euxine; in which
their flanks, according to the Scythian discipline, might always
be covered by a movable fortification of waggons. The latter
was judiciously preferred: the Catholics marched through the
plains of Bulgaria, burning, with wanton cruelty, the churches
and villages of the Christian natives; and their last station was
at Varna, near the sea-shore; on which the defeat and death of
Ladislaus have bestowed a memorable name.[1]

It was on this fatal spot that, instead of finding a confederate
fleet to second their operations, they were alarmed by the
approach of Amurath himself, who had issued from his Magnesian solitude and transported the forces of Asia to the defence
of Europe. According to some writers the Greek emperor had
been awed, or seduced, to grant the passage of the Bosphorus;
and an indelible stain of corruption is fixed on the Genoese, or

[1] Varna, under the Grecian name of Odessus, was a colony of the
Milesians, which they denominated from the hero Ulysses (Cellarius, tom. i.
p. 374; D'Anville, tom. i. p. 312). According to Arrian's Periplus of the
Euxine (p. 24, 25, in the first volume of Hudson's Geographers), it was
situate 1740 stadia, or furlongs, from the mouth of the Danube, 2140 from
Byzantium, and 360 to the north of a ridge or promontory of Mount
Hæmus, which advances into the sea.

the pope's nephew, the Catholic admiral, whose mercenary connivance betrayed the guard of the Hellespont.   From Adrianople
the sultan advanced by hasty marches at the head of sixty thousand men; and when the cardinal and Huniades had taken a
nearer survey of the numbers and order of the Turks, these
ardent warriors proposed the tardy and impracticable measure
of a retreat.   The king alone was resolved to conquer or die; and
his resolution had almost been crowned with a glorious and
salutary victory.   The princes were opposite to each other in
the centre; and the Beglerbegs, or generals of Anatolia and
Romania, commanded on the right and left against the adverse
divisions of the despot and Huniades.   The Turkish wings were
broken on the first onset: but the advantage was fatal; and the
rash victors, in the heat of the pursuit, were carried away far
from the annoyance of the enemy or the support of their friends.
When Amurath beheld the flight of his squadrons, he despaired
of his fortune and that of the empire: a veteran Janizary seized
his horse's bridle; and he had magnanimity to pardon and
reward the soldier who dared to perceive the terror, and arrest
the flight, of his sovereign.   A copy of the treaty, the monument
of Christian perfidy, had been displayed in the front of battle;
and it is said that the sultan in his distress, lifting his eyes and
his hands to heaven, implored the protection of the God of truth;
and called on the prophet Jesus himself to avenge the impious
mockery of his name and religion.[1]   With inferior numbers and
disordered ranks the king of Hungary rushed forwards in the
confidence of victory, till his career was stopped by the impenetrable phalanx of the Janizaries.   If we may credit the Ottoman
annals, his horse was pierced by the javelin of Amurath;[2] he
fell among the spears of the infantry; and a Turkish soldier proclaimed with a loud voice, " Hungarians, behold the head of your
king!"   The death of Ladislaus was the signal of their defeat.
On his return from an intemperate pursuit, Huniades deplored
his error and the public loss: he strove to rescue the royal body,
till he was overwhelmed by the tumultuous crowd of the victors
and vanquished; and the last efforts of his courage and conduct

[1] Some Christian writers affirm that he drew from his bosom the host or
wafer on which the treaty had *not* been sworn.   The Moslems suppose, with
more simplicity, an appeal to God and his prophet Jesus, which is likewise
insinuated by Callimachus (l. iii. p. 516; Spondan. A.D. 1444, No. 8).
[2] A critic will always distrust these *spolia opima* of a victorious general,
so difficult for valour to obtain, so easy for flattery to invent (Cantemir,
p. 90, 91).   Callimachus (l. iii. p. 517) more simply and probably affirms,
supervenientibus Janizaris, telorum multitudine, non tam confossus est,
quam obrutus.

were exerted to save the remnant of his Wallachian cavalry.
Ten thousand Christians were slain in the disastrous battle of
Varna: the loss of the Turks, more considerable in numbers, bore
a smaller proportion to their total strength; yet the philosophic
sultan was not ashamed to confess that his ruin must be the consequence of a second and similar victory. At his command a
column was erected on the spot where Ladislaus had fallen; but
the modest inscription, instead of accusing the rashness, recorded
the valour and bewailed the misfortune of the Hungarian youth.[1]

Before I lose sight of the field of Varna I am tempted to pause
on the character and story of two principal actors, the cardinal
Julian and John Huniades. Julian [2] Cæsarini was born of a
noble family of Rome: his studies had embraced both the Latin
and Greek learning, both the sciences of divinity and law; and
his versatile genius was equally adapted to the schools, the camp,
and the court. No sooner had he been invested with the Roman
purple than he was sent into Germany to arm the empire against
the rebels and heretics of Bohemia. The spirit of persecution
is unworthy of a Christian; the military profession ill becomes
a priest; but the former is excused by the times; and the latter
was ennobled by the courage of Julian, who stood dauntless and
alone in the disgraceful flight of the German host. As the pope's
legate he opened the council of Basil; but the president soon
appeared the most strenuous champion of ecclesiastical freedom;
and an opposition of seven years was conducted by his ability
and zeal. After promoting the strongest measures against the
authority and person of Eugenius, some secret motive of interest
or conscience engaged him to desert on a sudden the popular
party. The cardinal withdrew himself from Basil to Ferrara;
and, in the debates of the Greeks and Latins, the two nations
admired the dexterity of his arguments and the depth of his

---

[1] Besides some valuable hints from Æneas Sylvius, which are diligently
collected by Spondanus, our best authorities are three historians of the
fifteenth century, Philippus Callimachus (de Rebus a Vladislao Polonorum
atque Hungarorum Rege gestis, libri iii. in Bell. Script. Rerum Hungaricarum, tom. i. p. 433-518), Bonfinius (decad iii. l. v. p. 460-467), and Chalcocondyles (l. vii. p. 165-179 [p. 312, seq. ed. Bonn]). The two first were
Italians, but they passed their lives in Poland and Hungary (Fabric.
Biblioth. Latin. med. et infimæ Ætatis, tom. i. p. 324; Vossius, de Hist.
Latin. l. iii. c. 8, 11; Bayle, Dictionnaire, BONFINIUS). A small tract of
Fælix Petancius, chancellor of Segnia (ad calcem Cuspinian. de Cæsaribus,
p. 716, 722), represents the theatre of the war in the fifteenth century.

[2] M. Lenfant has described the origin (Hist. du Concile de Basle, tom. i.
p. 247, etc.) and Bohemian campaign (p. 315, etc.) of Cardinal Julian.
His services at Basil and Ferrara, and his unfortunate end, are occasionally
related by Spondanus and the continuator of Fleury.

theological erudition.[1] In his Hungarian embassy we have already seen the mischievous effects of his sophistry and eloquence, of which Julian himself was the first victim. The cardinal, who performed the duties of a priest and a soldier, was lost in the defeat of Varna. The circumstances of his death are variously related; but it is believed that a weighty incumbrance of gold impeded his flight, and tempted the cruel avarice of some Christian fugitives.

From a humble, or at least a doubtful, origin the merit of John Huniades promoted him to the command of the Hungariar armies. His father was a Wallachian, his mother a Greek: her unknown race might possibly ascend to the emperors of Constantinople; and the claims of the Wallachians, with the surname of Corvinus, from the place of his nativity, might suggest a thin pretence for mingling his blood with the patricians of ancient Rome.[2] In his youth he served in the wars of Italy, and was retained, with twelve horsemen, by the bishop of Zagrab: the valour of the *white knight* [3] was soon conspicuous; he increased his fortunes by a noble and wealthy marriage; and in the defence of the Hungarian borders he won in the same year three battles against the Turks. By his influence Ladislaus of Poland obtained the crown of Hungary; and the important service was rewarded by the title and office of Waivod of Transylvania. The first of Julian's crusades added two Turkish laurels on his brow; and in the public distress the fatal errors of Varna were forgotten. During the absence and minority of Ladislaus of Austria, the titular king, Huniades was elected supreme captain and governor of Hungary; and if envy at first was silenced by terror, a reign of twelve years supposes the arts of policy as well as of war. Yet the idea of a consummate general is not delineated in his campaigns; the white knight fought with the hand rather than the head, as the chief of desultory barbarians, who attack without fear and fly without shame; and his military life is composed of

---

[1] Syropulus honourably praises the talents of an enemy (p. 117): τοῖαυτα τινα εἶπεν ὁ Ἰουλιανὸς, πεπλατυσμένως ἀγὰν καὶ λογίκως, καὶ μετ' ἐπιστήμης καὶ δεινότητος ῥητορίκης.

[2] See Bonfinius, decad iii. l. iv. p. 423. Could the Italian historian pronounce, or the king of Hungary hear, without a blush, the absurd flattery which confounded the name of a Wallachian village with the casual, though glorious, epithet of a single branch of the Valerian family at Rome?

[3] Philip de Comines (Mémoires, l. vi. c. 13), from the tradition of the times, mentions him with high encomiums, but under the whimsical name of the Chevalier Blanc de Valaigne (Vallachia). The Greek Chalcocondyles, and the Turkish annals of Leunclavius, presume to accuse his fidelity or valour.

a romantic alternative of victories and escapes. By the Turks, who employed his name to frighten their perverse children, he was corruptly denominated *Jancus Lain*, or the Wicked: their hatred is the proof of their esteem; the kingdom which he guarded was inaccessible to their arms; and they felt him most daring and formidable when they fondly believed the captain and his country irrecoverably lost. Instead of confining himself to a defensive war, four years after the defeat of Varna he again penetrated into the heart of Bulgaria, and in the plain of Cossova sustained, till the third day, the shock of the Ottoman army, four times more numerous than his own. As he fled alone through the woods of Wallachia, the hero was surprised by two robbers; but while they disputed a gold chain that hung at his neck, he recovered his sword, slew the one, terrified the other, and, after new perils of captivity or death, consoled by his presence an afflicted kingdom. But the last and most glorious action of his life was the defence of Belgrade against the powers of Mohammed the Second in person. After a siege of forty days the Turks, who had already entered the town, were compelled to retreat; and the joyful nations celebrated Huniades and Belgrade as the bulwarks of Christendom.[1] About a month after this great deliverance the champion expired; and his most splendid epitaph is the regret of the Ottoman prince, who sighed that he could no longer hope for revenge against the single antagonist who had triumphed over his arms. On the first vacancy of the throne Matthias Corvinus, a youth of eighteen years of age, was elected and crowned by the grateful Hungarians. His reign was prosperous and long: Matthias aspired to the glory of a conqueror and a saint; but his purest merit is the encouragement of learning; and the Latin orators and historians, who were invited from Italy by the son, have shed the lustre of their eloquence on the father's character.[2]

In the list of heroes John Huniades and Scanderbeg are

---

[1] See Bonfinius (decad. iii. l. viii. p. 492) and Spondanus (A.D. 1456, No. 1-7). Huniades shared the glory of the defence of Belgrade with Capistran, a Franciscan friar; and in their respective narratives, neither the saint nor the hero condescends to take notice of his rival's merit.

[2] See Bonfinius, decad iii. l. viii.—decad iv. l. viii. The observations of Spondanus on the life and character of Matthias Corvinus are curious and critical (A.D. 1464, No. 1; 1475, No. 6; 1476, No. 14-16; 1490, No. 4, 5). Italian fame was the object of his vanity. His actions are celebrated in the Epitome Rerum Hungaricarum (p. 322-412) of Peter Ranzanus, a Sicilian. His wise and facetious sayings are registered by Galestus Martius of Narni (528-568), and we have a particular narrative of his wedding and coronation. These three tracts are all contained in the first vol. of Bel's Scriptores Rerum Hungaricarum.

commonly associated;[1] and they are both entitled to our notice,
since their occupation of the Ottoman arms delayed the ruin of
the Greek empire. John Castriot, the father of Scanderbeg,[2]
was the hereditary prince of a small district of Epirus, or Albania,
between the mountains and the Adriatic Sea. Unable to contend with the sultan's power, Castriot submitted to the hard
conditions of peace and tribute: he delivered his four sons as the
pledges of his fidelity; and the Christian youths, after receiving
the mark of circumcision, were instructed in the Mohammedan
religion and trained in the arms and arts of Turkish policy.[3]
The three elder brothers were confounded in the crowd of slaves;
and the poison to which their deaths are ascribed cannot be
verified or disproved by any positive evidence. Yet the suspicion is in a great measure removed by the kind and paternal
treatment of George Castriot, the fourth brother, who, from his
tender youth, displayed the strength and spirit of a soldier.
The successive overthrow of a Tartar and two Persians, who
carried a proud defiance to the Turkish court, recommended
him to the favour of Amurath, and his Turkish appellation of
Scanderbeg (*Iskender beg*), or the lord Alexander, is an indelible
memorial of his glory and servitude. His father's principality
was reduced into a province; but the loss was compensated by
the rank and title of Sanjiak, a command of five thousand horse,
and the prospect of the first dignities of the empire. He served
with honour in the wars of Europe and Asia; and we may smile
at the art or credulity of the historian, who supposes that in
every encounter he spared the Christians, while he fell with a
thundering arm on his Musulman foes. The glory of Huniades
is without reproach: he fought in the defence of his religion and
country; but the enemies who applaud the patriot have branded
his rival with the name of traitor and apostate. In the eyes of
the Christians the rebellion of Scanderbeg is justified by his

[1] They are ranked by Sir William Temple, in his pleasing Essay on Heroic
Virtue (Works, vol. iii. p. 385), among the seven chiefs who have deserved,
without wearing, a royal crown: Belisarius, Narses, Gonsalvo of Cordova,
William first prince of Orange, Alexander duke of Parma, John Huniades,
and George Castriot, or Scanderbeg.

[2] I could wish for some simple, authentic memoirs of a friend of Scanderbeg, which would introduce me to the man, the time, and the place. In
the old and national history of Marinus Barletius, a priest of Scodra (de
Vitâ, Moribus, et Rebus gestis Georgii Castrioti, etc., libri xiii. pp. 367,
Argentorat. 1537, in fol.), his gaudy and cumbersome robes are stuck with
many false jewels. See likewise Chalcocondyles, l. vii. p. 185, l. viii.
p. 229 [p. 350 and 432, ed. Bonn].

[3] His circumcision, education, etc., are marked by Marinus with brevity
and reluctance (l. i. p. 6, 7).

father's wrongs, the ambiguous death of his three brothers, his
own degradation, and the slavery of his country; and they adore
the generous, though tardy, zeal with which he asserted the faith
and independence of his ancestors.   But he had imbibed from
his ninth year the doctrines of the Koran: he was ignorant of
the Gospel; the religion of a soldier is determined by authority
and habit; nor is it easy to conceive what new illumination at the
age of forty [1] could be poured into his soul.   His motives would
be less exposed to the suspicion of interest or revenge, had he
broken his chain from the moment that he was sensible of its
weight: but a long oblivion had surely impaired his original
right; and every year of obedience and reward had cemented the
mutual bond of the sultan and his subject.   If Scanderbeg had
long harboured the belief of Christianity and the intention of
revolt, a worthy mind must condemn the base dissimulation that
could serve only to betray, that could promise only to be for-
sworn, that could actively join in the temporal and spiritual
perdition of so many thousands of his unhappy brethren.   Shall
we praise a secret correspondence with Huniades while he commanded the vanguard of the Turkish army?   Shall we excuse
the desertion of his standard, a treacherous desertion which
abandoned the victory to the enemies of his benefactor?   In the
confusion of a defeat, the eye of Scanderbeg was fixed on the
Reis Effendi, or principal secretary: with the dagger at his
breast, he extorted a firman or patent for the government of
Albania; and the murder of the guiltless scribe and his train prevented the consequences of an immediate discovery.   With some
bold companions, to whom he had revealed his design, he escaped
in the night by rapid marches from the field of battle to his
paternal mountains.   The gates of Croya were opened to the
royal mandate; and no sooner did he command the fortress
than George Castriot dropped the mask of dissimulation, abjured
the prophet and the sultan, and proclaimed himself the avenger
of his family and country.   The names of religion and liberty
provoked a general revolt: the Albanians, a martial race, were
unanimous to live and die with their hereditary prince; and the
Ottoman garrisons were indulged in the choice of martyrdom

---

[1] Since Scanderbeg died A.D. 1466, in the sixty-third year of his age
(Marinus, l. xiii. p. 370), he was born in 1403; since he was torn from his
parents by the Turks when he was *novennis* (Marinus, l. i. p. 1, 6), that
event must have happened in 1412, nine years before the accession of
Amurath II., who must have inherited, not acquired, the Albanian slave.
Spondanus has remarked this inconsistency, A.D. 1431, No. 31; 1443,
No. 14.

or baptism. In the assembly of the states of Epirus, Scanderbeg
was elected general of the Turkish war; and each of the allies
engaged to furnish his respective proportion of men and money.
From these contributions, from his patrimonial estate, and from
the valuable salt-pits of Selina, he drew an annual revenue of
two hundred thousand ducats; [1] and the entire sum, exempt from
the demands of luxury, was strictly appropriated to the public
use. His manners were popular; but his discipline was severe;
and every superfluous vice was banished from his camp: his
example strengthened his command; and under his conduct the
Albanians were invincible in their own opinion and that of their
enemies. The bravest adventurers of France and Germany
were allured by his fame and retained in his service: his standing militia consisted of eight thousand horse and seven thousand
foot; the horses were small, the men were active: but he viewed
with a discerning eye the difficulties and resources of the mountains; and, at the blaze of the beacons, the whole nation was
distributed in the strongest posts. With such unequal arms
Scanderbeg resisted twenty-three years the powers of the
Ottoman empire; and two conquerors, Amurath the Second and
his greater son, were repeatedly baffled by a rebel whom they
pursued with seeming contempt and implacable resentment. At
the head of sixty thousand horse and forty thousand Janizaries,
Amurath entered Albania: he might ravage the open country,
occupy the defenceless towns, convert the churches into mosques,
circumcise the Christian youths, and punish with death his
adult and obstinate captives: but the conquests of the sultan
were confined to the petty fortress of Sfetigrade; and the
garrison, invincible to his arms, was oppressed by a paltry
artifice and a superstitious scruple. [2] Amurath retired with
shame and loss from the walls of Croya, the castle and residence
of the Castriots; the march, the siege, the retreat, were harassed
by a vexatious, and almost invisible, adversary; [3] and the disappointment might tend to embitter, perhaps to shorten, the
last days of the sultan. [4] In the fulness of conquest Mohammed

[1] His revenue and forces are luckily given by Marinus (l. ii. p. 44).
[2] There were two Dibras, the upper and lower, the Bulgarian and
Albanian: the former, 70 miles from Croya (l. i. p. 17), was contiguous to
the fortress of Sfetigrade, whose inhabitants refused to drink from a well
into which a dead dog had traitorously been cast (l. v. p. 139, 140). We
want a good map of Epirus.
[3] Compare the Turkish narrative of Cantemir (p. 92) with the pompous
and prolix declamation in the fourth, fifth, and sixth books of the Albanian
priest, who has been copied by the tribe of strangers and moderns.
[4] In honour of his hero, Barletius (l. vi. p. 188-192) kills the sultan, by
disease indeed, under the walls of Croya. But this audacious fiction is

the Second still felt at his bosom this domestic thorn; his lieutenants were permitted to negotiate a truce, and the Albanian
prince may justly be praised as a firm and able champion of his
national independence. The enthusiasm of chivalry and religion
has ranked him with the names of Alexander and Pyrrhus; nor
would they blush to acknowledge their intrepid countryman:
but his narrow dominion and slender powers must leave him
at a humble distance below the heroes of antiquity, who
triumphed over the East and the Roman legions. His splendid
achievements, the bashaws whom he encountered, the armies that
he discomfited, and the three thousand Turks who were slain by
his single hand, must be weighed in the scales of suspicious
criticism. Against an illiterate enemy, and in the dark solitude
of Epirus, his partial biographers may safely indulge the latitude
of romance; but their fictions are exposed by the light of Italian
history, and they afford a strong presumption against their own
truth by a fabulous tale of his exploits, when he passed the
Adriatic with eight hundred horse to the succour of the king of
Naples.[1] Without disparagement to his fame, they might have
owned that he was finally oppressed by the Ottoman powers;
in his extreme danger he applied to pope Pius the Second for a
refuge in the ecclesiastical state; and his resources were almost
exhausted, since Scanderbeg died a fugitive at Lissus, on the
Venetian territory.[2] His sepulchre was soon violated by the
Turkish conquerors; but the Janizaries, who wore his bones
enchased in a bracelet, declared by this superstitious amulet
their involuntary reverence for his valour. The instant ruin of
his country may redound to the hero's glory; yet, had he balanced
the consequences of submission and resistance, a patriot perhaps
would have declined the unequal contest which must depend on
the life and genius of one man. Scanderbeg might indeed be
supported by the rational, though fallacious, hope that the pope,

disproved by the Greeks and Turks, who agree in the time and manner of
Amurath's death at Adrianople.

[1] See the marvels of his Calabrian expedition in the ninth and tenth
books of Marinus Barletius, which may be rectified by the testimony or
silence of Muratori (Annali d'Italia, tom. xiii. p. 291), and his original
authors (Joh. Simonetta de Rebus Francisci Sfortiæ, in Muratori, Script.
Rerum Ital. tom. xxi. p. 728, et alios). The Albanian cavalry, under the
name of *Stradiots*, soon became famous in the wars of Italy (Mémoires de
Comines, l. viii. c. 5).

[2] Spondanus, from the best evidence and the most rational criticism,
has reduced the giant Scanderbeg to the human size (A.D. 1461, No. 20;
1463, No. 9; 1465, No. 12, 13; 1467, No. 1). His own letter to the pope,
and the testimony of Phranza (l. iii. c. 28), a refugee in the neighbouring
isle of Corfu, demonstrate his last distress, which is awkwardly concealed
by Marinus Barletius (l. x.).

the king of Naples, and the Venetian republic would join in the defence of a free and Christian people, who guarded the sea-coast of the Adriatic and the narrow passage from Greece to Italy. His infant son was saved from the national shipwreck; the Castriots [1] were invested with a Neapolitan dukedom, and their blood continues to flow in the noblest families of the realm. A colony of Albanian fugitives obtained a settlement in Calabria, and they preserve at this day the language and manners of their ancestors.[2]

In the long career of the decline and fall of the Roman empire, I have reached at length the last reign of the princes of Constantinople, who so feebly sustained the name and majesty of the Cæsars. On the decease of John Palæologus, who survived about four years the Hungarian crusade,[3] the royal family, by the death of Andronicus and the monastic profession of Isidore, was reduced to three princes, Constantine, Demetrius, and Thomas, the surviving sons of the emperor Manuel. Of these, the first and the last were far distant in the Morea; but Demetrius, who possessed the domain of Selymbria, was in the suburbs, at the head of a party; his ambition was not chilled by the public distress, and his conspiracy with the Turks and the schismatics had already disturbed the peace of his country. The funeral of the late emperor was accelerated with singular and even suspicious haste; the claim of Demetrius to the vacant throne was justified by a trite and flimsy sophism, that he was born in the purple, the eldest son of his father's reign. But the empress-mother, the senate and soldiers, the clergy and people, were unanimous in the cause of the lawful successor; and the despot Thomas, who, ignorant of the change, accidentally returned to the capital, asserted with becoming zeal the interest of his absent brother. An ambassador, the historian Phranza, was immediately despatched to the court of Adrianople. Amurath received him with honour and dismissed him with gifts; but the gracious approbation of the Turkish sultan announced his supremacy, and the approaching downfall of the Eastern empire. By the hands of two illustrious deputies the Imperial crown was placed at Sparta on the head of Constantine. In the spring he

[1] See the family of the Castriots, in Ducange (Fam. Dalmaticæ, etc., xviii. p. 348-350).

[2] This colony of Albanese is mentioned by Mr. Swinburne (Travels into the Two Sicilies, vol. i. p. 350-354).

[3] The chronology of Phranza is clear and authentic; but instead of four years and seven months, Spondanus (A.D. 1445, No. 7) assigns seven or eight years to the reign of the last Constantine, which he deduces from a spurious epistle of Eugenius IV. to the king of Æthiopia.

sailed from the Morea, escaped the encounter of a Turkish squadron, enjoyed the acclamations of his subjects, celebrated the festival of a new reign, and exhausted by his donatives the treasure, or rather the indigence, of the state. The emperor immediately resigned to his brothers the possession of the Morea; and the brittle friendship of the two princes, Demetrius and Thomas, was confirmed in their mother's presence by the frail security of oaths and embraces. His next occupation was the choice of a consort. A daughter of the doge of Venice had been proposed, but the Byzantine nobles objected the distance between an hereditary monarch and an elective magistrate; and in their subsequent distress the chief of that powerful republic was not unmindful of the affront. Constantine afterwards hesitated between the royal families of Trebizond and Georgia; and the embassy of Phranza represents in his public and private life the last days of the Byzantine empire.[1]

The *protovestiare*, or great chamberlain, Phranza, sailed from Constantinople as the minister of a bridegroom, and the relics of wealth and luxury were applied to his pompous appearance. His numerous retinue consisted of nobles and guards, of physicians and monks: he was attended by a band of music; and the term of his costly embassy was protracted above two years. On his arrival in Georgia or Iberia the natives from the towns and villages flocked around the strangers; and such was their simplicity that they were delighted with the effects, without understanding the cause, of musical harmony. Among the crowd was an old man, above a hundred years of age, who had formerly been carried away a captive by the barbarians,[2] and who amused his hearers with a tale of the wonders of India,[3] from whence he had returned to Portugal by an unknown sea.[4] From this hospitable land Phranza proceeded to the court of Trebizond, where he was informed by the Greek prince of the recent decease

---

[1] Phranza (l. iii. c. 1-6) deserves credit and esteem.

[2] Suppose him to have been captured in 1394, in Timour's first war in Georgia (Sherefeddin, l. iii. c. 50), he might follow his Tartar master into Hindostan in 1398, and from thence sail to the Spice islands.

[3] The happy and pious Indians lived a hundred and fifty years, and enjoyed the most perfect productions of the vegetable and mineral kingdoms. The animals were on a large scale: dragons seventy cubits, ants (the *formica Indica*) nine inches long, sheep like elephants, elephants like sheep. Quidlibet audendi, etc.

[4] He sailed in a country vessel from the Spice islands to one of the ports of the exterior India; invenitque navem grandem *Ibericam*, quâ in *Portugalliam* est delatus. This passage, composed in 1477 (Phranza, l. iii. c. 30), twenty years before the discovery of the Cape of Good Hope, is spurious or wonderful. But this new geography is sullied by the old and incompatible error which places the source of the Nile in India.

of Amurath. Instead of rejoicing in the deliverance, the experienced statesman expressed his apprehension that an ambitious youth would not long adhere to the sage and pacific system of his father. After the sultan's decease his Christian wife, Maria,[1] the daughter of the Servian despot, had been honourably restored to her parents; on the fame of her beauty and merit she was recommended by the ambassador as the most worthy object of the royal choice; and Phranza recapitulates and refutes the specious objections that might be raised against the proposal. The majesty of the purple would ennoble an unequal alliance; the bar of affinity might be removed by liberal alms and the dispensation of the church; the disgrace of Turkish nuptials had been repeatedly overlooked; and, though the fair Maria was near fifty years of age, she might yet hope to give an heir to the empire. Constantine listened to the advice, which was transmitted in the first ship that sailed from Trebizond; but the factions of the court opposed his marriage, and it was finally prevented by the pious vow of the sultana, who ended her days in the monastic profession. Reduced to the first alternative, the choice of Phranza was decided in favour of a Georgian princess; and the vanity of her father was dazzled by the glorious alliance. Instead of demanding, according to the primitive and national custom, a price for his daughter,[2] he offered a portion of fifty-six thousand, with an annual pension of five thousand, ducats; and the services of the ambassador were repaid by an assurance that, as his son had been adopted in baptism by the emperor, the establishment of his daughter should be the peculiar care of the empress of Constantinople. On the return of Phranza the treaty was ratified by the Greek monarch, who with his own hand impressed three vermilion crosses on the golden bull, and assured the Georgian envoy that in the spring his galleys should conduct the bride to her Imperial palace. But Constantine embraced his faithful servant, not with the cold approbation of a sovereign, but with the warm confidence of a friend, who, after a long absence, is impatient to pour his secrets into the bosom of his friend. "Since the death of my mother and of Cantacuzene, who alone advised me without interest or passion,[3] I am sur-

[1] Cantemir (p. 83), who styles her the daughter of Lazarus Ogli, and the Helen of the Servians, places her marriage with Amurath in the year 1424. It will not easily be believed that, in six-and-twenty years' cohabitation, the sultan corpus ejus non tetigit. After the taking of Constantinople she fled to Mohammed II. (Phranza, l. iii. c. 22.)

[2] The classical reader will recollect the offers of Agamemnon (Iliad, I. v. 144), and the general practice of antiquity.

[3] Cantacuzene (I am ignorant of his relation to the emperor of that

rounded," said the emperor, " by men whom I can neither love,
nor trust, nor esteem.   You are not a stranger to Lucas Notaras,
the great admiral: obstinately attached to his own sentiments,
he declares, both in private and public, that his sentiments are
the absolute measure of my thoughts and actions.   The rest of
the courtiers are swayed by their personal or factious views;
and how can I consult the monks on questions of policy and
marriage?   I have yet much employment for your diligence and
fidelity.   In the spring you shall engage one of my brothers to
solicit the succour of the Western powers; from the Morea you
shall sail to Cyprus on a particular commission, and from thence
proceed to Georgia to receive and conduct the future empress."
" Your commands," replied Phranza, " are irresistible; but
deign, great sir," he added, with a serious smile, " to consider that,
if I am thus perpetually absent from my family, my wife may be
tempted either to seek another husband, or to throw herself
into a monastery."   After laughing at his apprehensions, the
emperor more gravely consoled him by the pleasing assurance
that *this* should be his last service abroad, and that he destined
for his son a wealthy and noble heiress; for himself, the important
office of great logothete, or principal minister of state.   The
marriage was immediately stipulated: but the office, however
incompatible with his own, had been usurped by the ambition
of the admiral.   Some delay was requisite to negotiate a consent
and an equivalent; and the nomination of Phranza was half
declared and half suppressed, lest it might be displeasing to an
insolent and powerful favourite.   The winter was spent in the
preparations of his embassy; and Phranza had resolved that the
youth his son should embrace this opportunity of foreign travel,
and be left, on the appearance of danger, with his maternal
kindred of the Morea.   Such were the private and public designs,
which were interrupted by a Turkish war, and finally buried in
the ruins of the empire.

name) was a great domestic, a firm asserter of the Greek creed, and a brother
of the queen of Servia, whom he visited with the character of ambassador.
(Syropulus, p. 37, 38, 45).

CHAPTER LXVIII

Reign and Character of Mohammed the Second—Siege, Assault, and Final Conquest of Constantinople by the Turks—Death of Constantine Palæologus—Servitude of the Greeks—Extinction of the Roman Empire in the East—Consternation of Europe—Conquests and Death of Mohammed the Second

THE siege of Constantinople by the Turks attracts our first attention to the person and character of the great destroyer. Mohammed the Second [1] was the son of the second Amurath; and though his mother has been decorated with the titles of Christian and princess, she is more probably confounded with the numerous concubines who peopled from every climate the harem of the sultan. His first education and sentiments were those of a devout Musulman; and as often as he conversed with an infidel he purified his hands and face by the legal rites of ablution. Age and empire appear to have relaxed this narrow bigotry: his aspiring genius disdained to acknowledge a power above his own; and in his looser hours he presumed (it is said) to brand the prophet of Mecca as a robber and impostor. Yet the sultan persevered in a decent reverence for the doctrine and discipline of the Koran: [2] his private indiscretion must have been sacred from the vulgar ear; and we should suspect the credulity of strangers and sectaries, so prone to believe that a mind which is hardened against truth must be armed with superior contempt for absurdity and error. Under the tuition of the most skilful masters Mohammed advanced with an early and rapid progress in the paths of knowledge; and besides his native tongue it is affirmed that he spoke or understood five languages,[3] the Arabic, the Persian, the Chaldæan or Hebrew, the Latin, and the Greek. The Persian might indeed contribute to his amusement, and the Arabic to his edification; and such studies are familiar to the Oriental youth. In the intercourse of the Greeks and Turks a

[1] For the character of Mohammed II. it is dangerous to trust either the Turks or the Christians. The most moderate picture appears to be drawn by Phranza (l. i. c. 32 [p. 93, ed. Bonn]), whose resentment had cooled in age and solitude. See likewise Spondanus (A.D. 1451, No. 11), and the continuator of Fleury (tom. xxii. p. 552), the *Elogia* of Paulus Jovius (l. iii. p. 164-166), and the Dictionnaire de Bayle (tom. iii. p. 272-279).

[2] Cantemir (p. 115), and the mosques which he founded, attest his public regard for religion. Mohammed freely disputed with the patriarch Gennadius on the two religions (Spond. A.D. 1453, No. 22).

[3] Quinque linguas præter suam noverat, Græcam, Latinam, Chaldaicam, Persicam. The Latin translator of Phranza has dropped the Arabic, which the Koran must recommend to every Musmulman.

conqueror might wish to converse with the people over whom
he was ambitious to reign: his own praises in Latin poetry [1]
or prose [2] might find a passage to the royal ear; but what
use or merit could recommend to the statesman or the scholar
the uncouth dialect of his Hebrew slaves? The history and
geography of the world were familiar to his memory: the lives
of the heroes of the East, perhaps of the West,[3] excited his
emulation: his skill in astrology is excused by the folly of the
times, and supposes some rudiments of mathematical science;
and a profane taste for the arts is betrayed in his liberal invitation
and reward of the painters of Italy.[4] But the influence of
religion and learning were employed without effect on his savage
and licentious nature. I will not transcribe, nor do I firmly
believe, the stories of his fourteen pages whose bellies were
ripped open in search of a stolen melon, or of the beauteous slave
whose head he severed from her body to convince the Janizaries
that their master was not the votary of love. His sobriety is
attested by the silence of the Turkish annals, which accuse three,
and three only, of the Ottoman line of the vice of drunkenness.[5]
But it cannot be denied that his passions were at once furious
and inexorable; that in the palace, as in the field, a torrent of
blood was spilt on the slightest provocation; and that the

[1] Philelphus, by a Latin ode, requested and obtained the liberty of his
wife's mother and sisters from the conqueror of Constantinople. It was
delivered into the sultan's hands by the envoys of the duke of Milan.
Philelphus himself was suspected of a design of retiring to Constantinople;
yet the orator often sounded the trumpet of holy war (see his Life by
M Lancelot, in the Mémoires de l'Académie des Inscriptions, tom. x.
p. 718, 724, etc.).

[2] Robert Valturio published at Verona, in 1483, his twelve books de Re
Militari, in which he first mentions the use of bombs. By his patron
Sigismond Malatesta, prince of Rimini, it had been addressed with a Latin
epistle to Mohammed II.

[3] According to Phranza, he assiduously studied the lives and actions of
Alexander, Augustus, Constantine, and Theodosius. I have read some-
where that Plutarch's Lives were translated by his orders into the Turkish
language. If the sultan himself understood Greek, it must have been for
the benefit of his subjects. Yet these Lives are a school of freedom as
well as of valour.

[4] The famous Gentile Bellino, whom he had invited from Venice, was
dismissed with a chain and collar of gold and a purse of 3000 ducats. With
Voltaire I laugh at the foolish story of a slave purposely beheaded to
instruct the painter in the action of the muscles.
[This story of the beautiful slave has been dramatised by Dr. Samuel
Johnson in his " Irene," which is the least satisfactory of the great lexi-
cographer's works.—O. S.]

[5] These Imperial drunkards were Soliman I., Selim II., and Amurath
IV. (Cantemir, p. 61). The sophis of Persia can produce a more regular
succession; and in the last age our European travellers were the witnesses
and companions of their revels.

noblest of the captive youth were often dishonoured by his unnatural lust. In the Albanian war he studied the lessons, and soon surpassed the example, of his father; and the conquest of two empires, twelve kingdoms, and two hundred cities, a vain and flattering account, is ascribed to his invincible sword. He was doubtless a soldier, and possibly a general; Constantinople has sealed his glory; but if we compare the means, the obstacles, and the achievements, Mohammed the Second must blush to sustain a parallel with Alexander or Timour. Under his command the Ottoman forces were always more numerous than their enemies, yet their progress was bounded by the Euphrates and the Adriatic, and his arms were checked by Huniades and Scanderbeg, by the Rhodian knights, and by the Persian king.

In the reign of Amurath he twice tasted of royalty, and twice descended from the throne: his tender age was incapable of opposing his father's restoration, but never could he forgive the vizirs who had recommended that salutary measure. His nuptials were celebrated with the daughter of a Turkman emir; and, after a festival of two months, he departed from Adrianople with his bride to reside in the government of Magnesia. Before the end of six weeks he was recalled by a sudden message from the divan which announced the decease of Amurath and the mutinous spirit of the Janizaries. His speed and vigour commanded their obedience: he passed the Hellespont with a chosen guard: and at the distance of a mile from Adrianople the vizirs and emirs, the imams and cadhis, the soldiers and the people, fell prostrate before the new sultan. They affected to weep, they affected to rejoice: he ascended the throne at the age of twenty-one years, and removed the cause of sedition by the death, the inevitable death, of his infant brothers.[1] The ambassadors of Europe and Asia soon appeared to congratulate his accession and solicit his friendship, and to all he spoke the language of moderation and peace. The confidence of the Greek emperor was revived by the solemn oaths and fair assurances with which he sealed the ratification of the treaty: and a rich domain on the banks of the Strymon was assigned for the annual payment of three hundred thousand aspers, the pension of an Ottoman prince who was detained at his request in the Byzantine court. Yet the neighbours of Mohammed might tremble at the

---

[1] Calapin, one of these royal infants, was saved from his cruel brother, and baptised at Rome under the name of Callistus Othomannus. The emperor Frederic III. presented him with an estate in Austria, where he ended his life; and Cuspinian, who in his youth conversed with the aged prince at Vienna, applauds his piety and wisdom (de Cæsaribus, p. 672, 673).

severity with which a youthful monarch reformed the pomp of his
father's household: the expenses of luxury were applied to those
of ambition, and a useless train of seven thousand falconers
was either dismissed from his service or enlisted in his troops.
In the first summer of his reign he visited with an army the
Asiatic provinces; but after humbling the pride Mohammed
accepted the submission of the Caramanian, that he might not
be diverted by the smallest obstacle from the execution of his
great design.[1]

The Mohammedan, and more especially the Turkish casuists,
have pronounced that no promise can bind the faithful against
the interest and duty of their religion, and that the sultan may
abrogate his own treaties and those of his predecessors. The
justice and magnanimity of Amurath had scorned this immoral
privilege; but his son, though the proudest of men, could stoop
from ambition to the basest arts of dissimulation and deceit.
Peace was on his lips while war was in his heart: he incessantly
sighed for the possession of Constantinople; and the Greeks, by
their own indiscretion, afforded the first pretence of the fatal
rupture.[2] Instead of labouring to be forgotten, their ambassadors pursued his camp to demand the payment, and even the
increase, of their annual stipend: the divan was importuned by
their complaints; and the vizir, a secret friend of the Christians,
was constrained to deliver the sense of his brethren. " Ye
foolish and miserable Romans," said Calil, " we know your
devices, and ye are ignorant of your own danger! the scrupulous
Amurath is no more; his throne is occupied by a young con-

---

[1] See the accession of Mohammed II. in Ducas (c. 33), Phranza (l. i. c. 33;
l. iii. c. 2), Chalcocondyles (l. vii. p. 199 [p. 376, ed. Bonn]), and Cantemir
(p. 96).
[2] Before I enter on the siege of Constantinople I shall observe that,
except the short hints of Cantemir and Leunclavius, I have not been able
to obtain any Turkish account of this conquest—such an account as we
possess of the siege of Rhodes by Soliman II. (Mémoires de l'Académie des
Inscriptions, tom. xxvi. p. 723-769). I must therefore depend on the
Greeks, whose prejudices, in some degree, are subdued by their distress.
Our standard texts are those of Ducas (c. 34-42), Phranza (l. iii. c. 7-20),
Chalcocondyles (l. viii. p. 201-214 [p. 380-403, ed. Bonn]), and Leonardus
Chiensis (Historia C. P. a Turco expugnatæ; Norimberghæ, 1544, in 4to,
20 leaves). The last of these narratives is the earliest in date, since it was
composed in the isle of Chios, the 16th of August, 1453, only seventy-nine
days after the loss of the city, and in the first confusion of ideas and
passions. Some hints may be added from an epistle of Cardinal Isidore
(in Farragine Rerum Turcicarum, ad calcem Chalcocondyl. Clauseri, Basil,
1556) to Pope Nicholas V., and a tract of Theodosius Zygomala, which he
addressed in the year 1581 to Martin Crusius (Turco-Græcia, l. i. p. 74-98,
Basil, 1584). The various facts and materials are briefly, though critically,
reviewed by Spondanus (A.D. 1453, No. 1-27). The hearsay relations of
Monstrelet and the distant Latins I shall take leave to disregard.

queror whom no laws can bind, and no obstacles can resist: and
if you escape from his hands, give praise to the divine clemency,
which yet delays the chastisement of your sins. Why do ye
seek to affright us by vain and indirect menaces? Release the
fugitive Orchan, crown him sultan of Romania, call the Hungarians from beyond the Danube, arm against us the nations of
the West, and be assured that you will only provoke and precipitate your ruin." But if the fears of the ambassadors were
alarmed by the stern language of the vizir, they were soothed
by the courteous audience and friendly speeches of the Ottoman
prince; and Mohammed assured them that on his return to
Adrianople he would redress the grievances, and consult the true
interests of the Greeks. No sooner had he repassed the Hellespont than he issued a mandate to suppress their pension, and to
expel their officers from the banks of the Strymon: in this
measure he betrayed a hostile mind; and the second order
announced, and in some degree commenced, the siege of Constantinople. In the narrow pass of the Bosphorus an Asiatic
fortress had formerly been raised by his grandfather; in the
opposite situation, on the European side, he resolved to erect a
more formidable castle, and a thousand masons were commanded
to assemble in the spring on a spot named Asomaton, about five
miles from the Greek metropolis.[1] Persuasion is the resource of
the feeble; and the feeble can seldom persuade: the ambassadors of the emperor attempted, without success, to divert
Mohammed from the execution of his design. They represented
that his grandfather had solicited the permission of Manuel to
build a castle on his own territories; but that this double fortification, which would command the strait, could only tend to
violate the alliance of the nations, to intercept the Latins who
traded in the Black Sea, and perhaps to annihilate the subsistence of the city. "I form no enterprise," replied the
perfidious sultan, "against the city; but the empire of Constantinople is measured by her walls. Have you forgot the
distress to which my father was reduced when you formed a
league with the Hungarians, when they invaded our country by
land, and the Hellespont was occupied by the French galleys?
Amurath was compelled to force the passage of the Bosphorus;

[1] The situation of the fortress and the topography of the Bosphorus are
best learned from Peter Gyllius (de Bosphoro Thracio, l. ii. c. 13), Leunclavius (Pandect. p. 445), and Tournefort (Voyage dans le Levant, tom. ii.
lettre xv. p. 443, 444); but I must regret the map or plan which Tournefort
sent to the French minister of the marine. The reader may turn back to
chap. xvii. of this History.

and your strength was not equal to your malevolence. I was then a child at Adrianople; the Moslems trembled, and for a while the *Gabours* [1] insulted our disgrace. But when my father had triumphed in the field of Varna, he vowed to erect a fort on the western shore, and that vow it is my duty to accomplish. Have ye the right, have ye the power, to control my actions on my own ground? For that ground *is* my own: as far as the shores of the Bosphorus Asia is inhabited by the Turks, and Europe is deserted by the Romans. Return, and inform your king that the present Ottoman is far different from his predecessors, that *his* resolutions surpass *their* wishes, and that *he* performs more than *they* could resolve. Return in safety; but the next who delivers a similar message may expect to be flayed alive." After this declaration, Constantine, the first of the Greeks in spirit as in rank,[2] had determined to unsheathe the sword, and to resist the approach and establishment of the Turks on the Bosphorus. He was disarmed by the advice of his civil and ecclesiastical ministers, who recommended a system less generous, and even less prudent, than his own, to approve their patience and long-suffering, to brand the Ottoman with the name and guilt of an aggressor, and to depend on chance and time for their own safety, and the destruction of a fort which could not long be maintained in the neighbourhood of a great and populous city. Amidst hope and fear, the fears of the wise and the hopes of the credulous, the winter rolled away; the proper business of each man and each hour was postponed; and the Greeks shut their eyes against the impending danger, till the arrival of the spring and the sultan decided the assurance of their ruin.

Of a master who never forgives, the orders are seldom disobeyed. On the twenty-sixth of March the appointed spot of Asomaton was covered with an active swarm of Turkish artificers; and the materials by sea and land were diligently transported from Europe and Asia.[3] The lime had been burnt in Cata-

---

[1] The opprobrious name which the Turks bestow on the infidels is expressed Καβουρ by Ducas, and *Giaour* by Leunclavius and the moderns. The former term is derived by Ducange (Gloss. Græc. tom. i. p. 530) from Καβουρον, in vulgar Greek a tortoise, as denoting a retrograde motion from the faith. But, alas! *Gabour* is no more than *Gheber*, which was transferred from the Persian to the Turkish language, from the worshippers of fire to those of the crucifix (D'Herbelot, Biblioth. Orient. p. 375).

[2] Phranza does justice to his master's sense and courage—Calliditatem hominis non ignorans Imperator prior arma movere constituit; and stigmatises the folly of the cum sacri tum profani proceres, which he had heard, amentes spe vanâ pasci. Ducas was not a privy counsellor.

[3] Instead of this clear and consistent account, the Turkish Annals (Cantemir, p. 97) revived the foolish tale of the ox's hide, and Dido's strata-

phrygia, the timber was cut down in the woods of Heraclea and
Nicomedia, and the stones were dug from the Anatolian quarries.
Each of the thousand masons was assisted by two workmen; and
a measure of two cubits was marked for their daily task. The
fortress [1] was built in a triangular form; each angle was flanked
by a strong and massy tower, one on the declivity of the hill, two
along the sea-shore; a thickness of twenty-two feet was assigned
for the walls, thirty for the towers; and the whole building was
covered with a solid platform of lead. Mohammed himself
pressed and directed the work with indefatigable ardour: his
three vizirs claimed the honour of finishing their respective
towers; the zeal of the cadhis emulated that of the Janizaries;
the meanest labour was ennobled by the service of God and the
sultan; and the diligence of the multitude was quickened by the
eye of a despot whose smile was the hope of fortune, and whose
frown was the messenger of death. The Greek emperor beheld
with terror the irresistible progress of the work, and vainly strove
by flattery and gifts to assuage an implacable foe, who sought,
and secretly fomented, the slightest occasion of a quarrel. Such
occasions must soon and inevitably be found. The ruins of
stately churches, and even the marble columns which had been
consecrated to Saint Michael the archangel, were employed
without scruple by the profane and rapacious Moslems; and
some Christians, who presumed to oppose the removal, received
from their hands the crown of martyrdom. Constantine had
solicited a Turkish guard to protect the fields and harvests of his
subjects: the guard was fixed; but their first order was to allow
free pasture to the mules and horses of the camp, and to defend
their brethren if they should be molested by the natives. The
retinue of an Ottoman chief had left their horses to pass the
night among the ripe corn: the damage was felt, the insult was
resented, and several of both nations were slain in a tumultuous
conflict. Mohammed listened with joy to the complaint; and a
detachment was commanded to exterminate the guilty village: the
guilty had fled; but forty innocent and unsuspecting reapers were
massacred by the soldiers. Till this provocation Constantinople
had been open to the visits of commerce and curiosity: on the
first alarm the gates were shut; but the emperor, still anxious

gem in the foundation of Carthage. These annals (unless we are swayed
by an anti-Christian prejudice) are far less valuable than the Greek
historians.
[1] In the dimensions of this fortress, the old castle of Europe, Phranza
does not exactly agree with Chalcocondyles, whose description has been
verified on the spot by his editor Leunclavius.

for peace, released on the third day his Turkish captives,[1] and expressed, in a last message, the firm resignation of a Christian and a soldier. " Since neither oaths, nor treaty, nor submission can secure peace, pursue," said he to Mohammed, " your impious warfare. My trust is in God alone: if it should please him to mollify your heart, I shall rejoice in the happy change; if he delivers the city into your hands, I submit without a murmur to his holy will. But until the Judge of the earth shall pronounce between us, it is my duty to live and die in the defence of my people." The sultan's answer was hostile and decisive: his fortifications were completed; and before his departure for Adrianople he stationed a vigilant Aga and four hundred Janizaries to levy a tribute on the ships of every nation that should pass within the reach of their cannon. A Venetian vessel, refusing obedience to the new lords of the Bosphorus, was sunk with a single bullet. The master and thirty sailors escaped in the boat; but they were dragged in chains to the *Porte :* the chief was impaled, his companions were beheaded; and the historian Ducas [2] beheld, at Demotica, their bodies exposed to the wild beasts. The siege of Constantinople was deferred till the ensuing spring; but an Ottoman army marched into the Morea to divert the force of the brothers of Constantine. At this era of calamity one of these princes, the despot Thomas, was blessed or afflicted with the birth of a son—" the last heir," says the plaintive Phranza, " of the last spark of the Roman empire."[3]

The Greeks and the Turks passed an anxious and sleepless winter: the former were kept awake by their fears, the latter by their hopes; both by the preparations of defence and attack; and the two emperors, who had the most to lose or to gain, were the most deeply affected by the national sentiment. In Mohammed that sentiment was inflamed by the ardour of his youth and temper: he amused his leisure with building at Adrianople [4] the lofty palace of Jehan Numa (the watch-tower of the world); but his serious thoughts were irrevocably bent

---

[1] Among these were some pages of Mohammed, so conscious of his inexorable rigour, that they begged to lose their heads in the city unless they could return before sunset.

[2] Ducas, c. 35 [p. 248, ed. Bonn]. Phranza (l. iii. c. 3), who had sailed in his vessel, commemorates the Venetian pilot as a martyr.

[3] Auctum est Palæologorum genus, et Imperii successor, parvæque Romanorum scintillæ hæres natus, Andreas, etc. (Phranza, l. iii. c. 3 [p. 236, ed. Bonn]). The strong expression was inspired by his feelings.

[4] Cantemir, p. 97, 98. The sultan was either doubtful of his conquest or ignorant of the superior merits of Constantinople. A city or a kingdom may sometimes be ruined by the Imperial fortune of their sovereign.

on the conquest of the city of Cæsar. At the dead of night, about the second watch, he started from his bed, and commanded the instant attendance of his prime vizir. The message, the hour, the prince, and his own situation, alarmed the guilty conscience of Calil Basha; who had possessed the confidence, and advised the restoration, of Amurath. On the accession of the son the vizir was confirmed in his office and the appearances of favour; but the veteran statesman was not insensible that he trod on a thin and slippery ice, which might break under his footsteps and plunge him in the abyss. His friendship for the Christians, which might be innocent under the late reign, had stigmatised him with the name of Gabour Ortachi, or foster-brother of the infidels; [1] and his avarice entertained a venal and treasonable correspondence, which was detected and punished after the conclusion of the war. On receiving the royal mandate, he embraced, perhaps for the last time, his wife and children; filled a cup with pieces of gold, hastened to the palace, adored the sultan, and offered, according to the Oriental custom, the slight tribute of his duty and gratitude.[2] " It is not my wish," said Mohammed, " to resume my gifts, but rather to heap and multiply them on thy head. In my turn I ask a present far more valuable and important—Constantinople." As soon as the vizir had recovered from his surprise, " The same God," said he, " who has already given thee so large a portion of the Roman empire, will not deny the remnant and the capital. His providence, and thy power, assure thy success; and myself, with the rest of thy faithful slaves, will sacrifice our lives and fortunes."—" Lala " [3] (or preceptor), continued the sultan, " do you see this pillow? all the night, in my agitation, I have pulled it on one side and the other; I have risen from my bed, again have I lain down, yet sleep has not visited these weary eyes. Beware of the gold and silver of the Romans: in arms we are superior; and with the aid

---

[1] Συντροφός, by the president Cousin, is translated *père* nourricier, most correctly indeed from the Latin version; but in his haste he has overlooked the note by which Ismael Boillaud (ad Ducam, c. 35 [p. 251, ed. Bonn]) acknowledges and rectifies his own error.

[2] The Oriental custom of never appearing without gifts before a sovereign or a superior is of high antiquity, and seems analogous with the idea of sacrifice, still more ancient and universal. See the examples of such Persian gifts, Ælian, Hist. Var. l. i. c. 31, 32, 33.

[3] The *Lala* of the Turks (Cantemir, p. 34) and the *Tata* of the Greeks (Ducas, c. 35) are derived from the natural language of children; and it may be observed that all such primitive words which denote their parents are the simple repetition of one syllable, composed of a labial or dental consonant and an open vowel (Des Brosses, Méchanisme des Langues, tom. i. p. 231-247).

of God, and the prayers of the prophet, we shall speedily become masters of Constantinople." To sound the disposition of his soldiers, he often wandered through the streets alone and in disguise; and it was fatal to discover the sultan when he wished to escape from the vulgar eye. His hours were spent in delineating the plan of the hostile city; in debating with his generals and engineers on what spot he should erect his batteries; on which side he should assault the walls; where he should spring his mines; to what place he should apply his scaling-ladders: and the exercises of the day repeated and proved the lucubrations of the night.

Among the implements of destruction, he studied with peculiar care the recent and tremendous discovery of the Latins; and his artillery surpassed whatever had yet appeared in the world. A founder of cannon, a Dane[1] or Hungarian, who had been almost starved in the Greek service, deserted to the Moslems, and was liberally entertained by the Turkish sultan. Mohammed was satisfied with the answer to his first question, which he eagerly pressed on the artist. "Am I able to cast a cannon capable of throwing a ball or stone of sufficient size to batter the walls of Constantinople? I am not ignorant of their strength; but were they more solid than those of Babylon, I could oppose an engine of superior power; the position and management of that engine must be left to your engineers." On this assurance a foundry was established at Adrianople: the metal was prepared; and at the end of three months Urban produced a piece of brass ordnance of stupendous and almost incredible magnitude; a measure of twelve palms is assigned to the bore; and the stone bullet weighed above six hundred pounds.[2] A vacant place before the new palace was chosen for the first experiment; but to prevent the sudden and mischievous effects of astonishment and fear, a proclamation was issued that the cannon would be discharged the ensuing day. The explosion was felt or heard in a circuit of a hundred furlongs: the ball, by the force of gunpowder, was driven above a mile; and on the spot where it fell, it buried itself a fathom deep in the ground.

[1] [Orban or Urban, the ordnance-founder, was not a Dane, but a Hungarian. Chalcocondyles describes him as a Dacian, which is also incorrect. —O. S.]

[2] The Attic talent weighed about sixty minæ, or avoirdupois pounds (see Hooper on Ancient Weights, Measures, etc.); but among the modern Greeks that classic appellation was extended to a weight of one hundred, or one hundred and twenty-five pounds (Ducange, τάλαντον). Leonardus Chiensis measured the ball or stone of the *second* cannon: Lapidem, qui palmis undecim ex meis ambibat in gyro.

For the conveyance of this destructive engine, a frame or carriage of thirty waggons was linked together and drawn along by a team of sixty oxen: two hundred men on both sides were stationed to poise and support the rolling weight; two hundred and fifty workmen marched before to smooth the way and repair the bridges; and near two months were employed in a laborious journey of one hundred and fifty miles. A lively philosopher [1] derides on this occasion the credulity of the Greeks, and observes, with much reason, that we should always distrust the exaggerations of a vanquished people. He calculates that a ball, even of two hundred pounds, would require a charge of one hundred and fifty pounds of powder; and that the stroke would be feeble and impotent, since not a fifteenth part of the mass could be inflamed at the same moment. A stranger as I am to the art of destruction, I can discern that the modern improvements of artillery prefer the number of pieces to the weight of metal; the quickness of the fire to the sound, or even the consequences, of a single explosion. Yet I dare not reject the positive and unanimous evidence of contemporary writers; nor can it seem improbable that the first artists, in their rude and ambitious efforts, should have transgressed the standard of moderation. A Turkish cannon, more enormous than that of Mohammed, still guards the entrance of the Dardanelles; and if the use be inconvenient, it has been found on a late trial that the effect was far from contemptible. A stone bullet of *eleven* hundred pounds' weight was once discharged with three hundred and thirty pounds of powder: at the distance of six hundred yards it shivered into three rocky fragments; traversed the strait; and, leaving the waters in a foam, again rose and bounded against the opposite hill. [2]

While Mohammed threatened the capital of the East, the Greek emperor implored with fervent prayers the assistance of earth and Heaven. But the invisible powers were deaf to his supplications; and Christendom beheld with indifference the fall of Constantinople, while she derived at least some promise of supply from the jealous and temporal policy of the sultan of Egypt. Some states were too weak, and others too remote; by

---

[1] See Voltaire (Hist. Générale, c. xci. p. 294, 295). He was ambitious of universal monarchy; and the poet frequently aspires to the name and style of an astronomer, a chemist, etc.

[2] The Baron de Tott (tom. iii. p. 85-89), who fortified the Dardanelles against the Russians, describes in a lively, and even comic, strain his own prowess, and the consternation of the Turks. But that adventurous traveller does not possess the art of gaining our confidence.

some the danger was considered as imaginary, by others as inevitable: the Western princes were involved in their endless and
domestic quarrels; and the Roman pontiff was exasperated by
the falsehood or obstinacy of the Greeks. Instead of employing
in their favour the arms and treasures of Italy, Nicholas the
Fifth had foretold their approaching ruin; and his honour was
engaged in the accomplishment of his prophecy. Perhaps he
was softened by the last extremity of their distress; but his
compassion was tardy; his efforts were faint and unavailing;
and Constantinople had fallen before the squadrons of Genoa
and Venice could sail from their harbours.[1] Even the princes
of the Morea and of the Greek islands affected a cold neutrality:
the Genoese colony of Galata negotiated a private treaty; and
the sultan indulged them in the delusive hope that by his
clemency they might survive the ruin of the empire. A plebeian
crowd and some Byzantine nobles basely withdrew from the
danger of their country; and the avarice of the rich denied the
emperor, and reserved for the Turks, the secret treasures which
might have raised in their defence whole armies of mercenaries.[2]
The indigent and solitary prince prepared however to sustain his
formidable adversary; but if his courage were equal to the peril,
his strength was inadequate to the contest. In the beginning of
the spring the Turkish vanguard swept the towns and villages
as far as the gates of Constantinople: submission was spared
and protected; whatever presumed to resist was exterminated
with fire and sword. The Greek places on the Black Sea,
Mesembria, Acheloum, and Bizon, surrendered on the first
summons; Selymbria alone deserved the honours of a siege or
blockade; and the bold inhabitants, while they were invested
by land, launched their boats, pillaged the opposite coast of
Cyzicus, and sold their captives in the public market. But on
the approach of Mohammed himself all was silent and prostrate:
he first halted at the distance of five miles; and, from thence

---

[1] Non audivit, indignum ducens, says the honest Antoninus; but, as the
Roman court was afterwards grieved and ashamed, we find the more courtly
expression of Platina, in animo fuisse pontifici juvare Græcos, and the
positive assertion of Æneas Sylvius, structam classem, etc. (Spond. A.D.
1453, No. 3.)
[2] Antonin. in Proem. — Epist. Cardinal. Isidor. apud Spondanum; and
Dr. Johnson, in the tragedy of Irene, has happily seized this characteristic
circumstance:—

> The groaning Greeks dig up the golden caverns,
> The accumulated wealth of hoarding ages;
> That wealth which, granted to their weeping prince,
> Had rang'd embattled nations at their gates.

advancing in battle array, planted before the gate of St. Romanus
the Imperial standard; and on the sixth day of April formed
the memorable siege of Constantinople.

The troops of Asia and Europe extended on the right and left
from the Propontis to the harbour; the Janizaries in the front
were stationed before the sultan's tent; the Ottoman line was
covered by a deep intrenchment; and a subordinate army
enclosed the suburb of Galata, and watched the doubtful faith
of the Genoese. The inquisitive Philelphus, who resided in
Greece about thirty years before the siege, is confident that all
the Turkish forces of any name or value could not exceed the
number of sixty thousand horse and twenty thousand foot; and
he upbraids the pusillanimity of the nations who had tamely
yielded to a handful of barbarians. Such indeed might be the
regular establishment of the *Capiculi*,[1] the troops of the Porte
who marched with the prince, and were paid from his royal
treasury. But the bashaws, in their respective governments,
maintained or levied a provincial militia; many lands were held
by a military tenure; many volunteers were attracted by the
hope of spoil; and the sound of the holy trumpet invited a swarm
of hungry and fearless fanatics, who might contribute at least to
multiply the terrors, and in a first attack to blunt the swords of
the Christians. The whole mass of the Turkish powers is magnified by Ducas, Chalcocondyles, and Leonard of Chios, to the
amount of three or four hundred thousand men; but Phranza
was a less remote and more accurate judge; and his precise
definition of two hundred and fifty-eight thousand does not
exceed the measure of experience and probability.[2] The navy of
the besiegers was less formidable: the Propontis was overspread
with three hundred and twenty sail; but of these no more than
eighteen could be rated as galleys of war; and the far greater
part must be degraded to the condition of store-ships and trans-

[1] The palatine troops are styled *Capiculi* ; the provincials, *Seratculi* ;
and most of the names and institutions of the Turkish militia existed
before the *Canon Nameh* of Soliman II., from which, and his own experience, Count Marsigli has composed his Military State of the Ottoman
Empire.

[2] The observation of Philelphus is approved by Cuspinian in the year
1508 (de Cæsaribus, in Epilog. de Militiâ Turcicâ, p. 697). Marsigli proves
that the effective armies of the Turks are much less numerous than they
appear. In the army that besieged Constantinople Leonardus Chiensis
reckons no more than 15,000 Janizaries.

[The estimates made by various writers as to the numbers of the forces
which Mohammed II. brought up against Constantinople are almost
ludicrously divergent. Suffice to say they vary from 160,000 to 450,000
men. One fact should be noted, that a large number of Christians fought
on the side of the Turks.—O. S.]

ports, which poured into the camp fresh supplies of men, ammunition, and provisions. In her last decay Constantinople was still peopled with more than a hundred thousand inhabitants; but these numbers are found in the accounts, not of war, but of captivity; and they mostly consisted of mechanics, of priests, of women, and of men devoid of that spirit which even women have sometimes exerted for the common safety. I can suppose, I could almost excuse, the reluctance of subjects to serve on a distant frontier, at the will of a tyrant; but the man who dares not expose his life in the defence of his children and his property has lost in society the first and most active energies of nature. By the emperor's command a particular inquiry had been made through the streets and houses, how many of the citizens, or even of the monks, were able and willing to bear arms for their country. The lists were intrusted to Phranza;[1] and after a diligent addition he informed his master, with grief and surprise, that the national defence was reduced to four thousand nine hundred and seventy *Romans*. Between Constantine and his faithful minister this comfortless secret was preserved; and a sufficient proportion of shields, cross-bows, and muskets, was distributed from the arsenal to the city bands. They derived some accession from a body of two thousand strangers, under the command of John Justiniani, a noble Genoese; a liberal donative was advanced to these auxiliaries; and a princely recompense, the isle of Lemnos, was promised to the valour and victory of their chief. A strong chain was drawn across the mouth of the harbour: it was supported by some Greek and Italian vessels of war and mechandise; and the ships of every Christian nation, that successively arrived from Candia and the Black Sea, were detained for the public service. Against the powers of the Ottoman empire, a city of the extent of thirteen, perhaps of sixteen, miles was defended by a scanty garrison of seven or eight thousand soldiers. Europe and Asia were open to the besiegers; but the strength and provisions of the Greeks must sustain a daily decrease; nor could they indulge the expectation of any foreign succour or supply.[2]

---

[1] Ego, eidem (Imp.) tabellas extribui non absque dolore et mœstitia, mansitque apud nos duos aliis occultus numerus (Phranza, l. iii. c. 3 [p. 241, ed. Bonn]). With some indulgence for national prejudices, we cannot desire a more authentic witness, not only of public facts, but of private counsels.

[2] [The Turks had a tremendous task before them in undertaking the siege of Constantinople. It must not be imagined that the enterprise was at all an easy one. The defences were enormously strong. From the fourth century onward almost every century saw some one of the emperors

The primitive Romans would have drawn their swords in the resolution of death or conquest. The primitive Christians might have embraced each other, and awaited in patience and charity the stroke of martyrdom. But the Greeks of Constantinople were animated only by the spirit of religion, and that spirit was productive only of animosity and discord. Before his death the emperor John Palæologus had renounced the unpopular measure of a union with the Latins; nor was the idea revived till the distress of his brother Constantine imposed a last trial of flattery and dissimulation.[1] With the demand of temporal aid his ambassadors were instructed to mingle the assurance of spiritual obedience: his neglect of the church was excused by the urgent cares of the state; and his orthodox wishes solicited the presence of a Roman legate. The Vatican had been too often deluded; yet the signs of repentance could not decently be overlooked; a legate was more easily granted than an army; and about six months before the final destruction, the cardinal Isidore of Russia appeared in that character with a retinue of priests and soldiers. The emperor saluted him as a friend and father; respectfully listened to his public and private sermons; and with the most obsequious of the clergy and laymen subscribed the act of union, as it had been ratified in the council of Florence. On the twelfth of December the two nations, in the church of St. Sophia, joined in the communion of sacrifice and prayer; and the names of the two pontiffs were solemnly commemorated; the names of Nicholas the Fifth, the vicar of Christ, and of the patriarch Gregory, who had been driven into exile by a rebellious people.

But the dress and language of the Latin priest who officiated at the altar were an object of scandal; and it was observed with horror that he consecrated a cake or wafer of *unleavened* bread, and poured cold water into the cup of the sacrament. A national historian acknowledges with a blush that none of his country-

---

strengthening the fortifications. For example, at the time of the Avar siege, Heraclius had strengthened the palace of Blachern on the west by a new wall running between the Tower of Anemas and the Xyloporta; while Leo V. erected another wall outside the wall of Heraclius. Then, as Bury points out, in the twelfth century Manuel Comnenus built a wall enclosing the quarter called the Caligaria, from the Tower of Anemas to the Xylokerkos. Then the siege of Constantinople in 1432 by Murad caused John Palæologus to repair and strengthen the whole of the outer line of wall.— O. S.]

[1] In Spondanus the narrative of the union is not only partial, but imperfect. The bishop of Pamiers died in 1642, and the history of Ducas, which represents these scenes (c. 36, 37) with such truth and spirit, was not printed till the year 1649.

men, not the emperor himself, were sincere in this occasional
conformity.[1] Their hasty and unconditional submission was
palliated by a promise of future revisal; but the best, or the
worst, of their excuses was the confession of their own perjury.
When they were pressed by the reproaches of their honest
brethren, " Have patience," they whispered, " have patience till
God shall have delivered the city from the great dragon who
seeks to devour us. You shall then perceive whether we are
truly reconciled with the Azymites." But patience is not the
attribute of zeal; nor can the arts of a court be adapted to the
freedom and violence of popular enthusiasm. From the dome
of St. Sophia the inhabitants of either sex, and of every degree,
rushed in crowds to the cell of the monk Gennadius,[2] to consult
the oracle of the church. The holy man was invisible; en-
tranced, as it should seem, in deep meditation, or divine rapture:
but he had exposed on the door of his cell a speaking tablet; and
they successively withdrew, after reading these tremendous
words: " O miserable Romans, why will ye abandon the truth;
and why, instead of confiding in God, will ye put your trust in
the Italians? In losing your faith you will lose your city. Have
mercy on me, O Lord! I protest in thy presence that I am innocent of the crime. O miserable Romans, consider, pause, and
repent. At the same moment that you renounce the religion of
your fathers, by embracing impiety, you submit to a foreign
servitude." According to the advice of Gennadius, the religious
virgins, as pure as angels, and as proud as demons, rejected the
act of union, and abjured all communion with the present and
future associates of the Latins; and their example was applauded
and imitated by the greatest part of the clergy and people.
From the monastery the devout Greeks dispersed themselves
in the taverns; drank confusion to the slaves of the pope;
emptied their glasses in honour of the image of the holy Virgin;
and besought her to defend against Mohammed the city which
she had formerly saved from Chosroes and the Chagan. In the

[1] Phranza, one of the conforming Greeks, acknowledges that the measure
was adopted only propter spem auxilii; he affirms with pleasure that those
who refused to perform their devotions in St. Sophia, extra culpam et in
pace essent (l. iii. c. 20).

[2] His primitive and secular name was George Scholarius, which he
changed for that of Gennadius, either when he became a monk or a
patriarch. His defence, at Florence, of the same union which he so
furiously attacked at Constantinople, has tempted Leo Allatius (Diatrib.
de Georgiis, in Fabric. Biblioth. Græc. tom. x. p. 760-786) to divide him
into two men; but Renaudot (p. 343-383) has restored the identity of his
person and the duplicity of his character.

double intoxication of zeal and wine, they valiantly exclaimed,
" What occasion have we for succour, or union, or Latins? far
from us be the worship of the Azymites! " During the winter
that preceded the Turkish conquest the nation was distracted
by this epidemical frenzy; and the season of Lent, the approach
of Easter, instead of breathing charity and love, served only to
fortify the obstinacy and influence of the zealots. The con-
fessors scrutinised and alarmed the conscience of their votaries,
and a rigorous penance was imposed on those who had received
the communion from a priest who had given an express or tacit
consent to the union. His service at the altar propagated the
infection to the mute and simple spectators of the ceremony:
they forfeited, by the impure spectacle, the virtue of the sacerdotal character; nor was it lawful, even in danger of sudden death,
to invoke the assistance of their prayers or absolution. No
sooner had the church of St. Sophia been polluted by the Latin
sacrifice than it was deserted as a Jewish synagogue, or a heathen
temple, by the clergy and people; and a vast and gloomy silence
prevailed in that venerable dome, which had so often smoked
with a cloud of incense, blazed with innumerable lights, and
resounded with the voice of prayer and thanksgiving. The
Latins were the most odious of heretics and infidels; and the
first minister of the empire, the great duke, was heard to declare
that he had rather behold in Constantinople the turban of
Mohammed than the pope's tiara or a cardinal's hat.[1] A sentiment so unworthy of Christians and patriots was familiar and
fatal to the Greeks: the emperor was deprived of the affection
and support of his subjects; and their native cowardice was
sanctified by resignation to the divine decree or the visionary
hope of a miraculous deliverance.

Of the triangle which composes the figure of Constantinople
the two sides along the sea were made inaccessible to an enemy;
the Propontis by nature, and the harbour by art. Between the
two waters, the basis of the triangle, the land side was protected
by a double wall and a deep ditch of the depth of one hundred
feet. Against this line of fortification, which Phranza, an eye-
witness, prolongs to the measure of six miles,[2] the Ottomans
directed their principal attack; and the emperor, after dis-

---

[1] Φακιόλιον, κάλυπτρα, may be fairly translated a cardinal's hat. The
difference of the Greek and Latin habits embittered the schism.

[2] We are obliged to reduce the Greek miles to the smallest measure
which is preserved in the wersts of Russia, of 547 French *toises*, and of $104\frac{2}{5}$
to a degree. The six miles of Phranza do not exceed four English miles
(D'Anville, Mesures Itinéraires, p. 61 123, etc.).

tributing the service and command of the most perilous stations,
undertook the defence of the external wall. In the first days of
the siege the Greek soldiers descended into the ditch, or sallied
into the field; but they soon discovered that, in the proportion
of their numbers, one Christian was of more value than twenty
Turks; and, after these bold preludes, they were prudently
content to maintain the rampart with their missile weapons.
Nor should this prudence be accused of pusillanimity. The
nation was indeed pusillanimous and base; but the last Constantine deserves the name of a hero: his noble band of
volunteers was inspired with Roman virtue; and the foreign
auxiliaries supported the honour of the Western chivalry. The
incessant volleys of lances and arrows were accompanied with
the smoke, the sound, and the fire of their musketry and cannon.
Their small arms discharged at the same time either five, or even
ten, balls of lead, of the size of a walnut; and, according to the
closeness of the ranks and the force of the powder, several breast-
plates and bodies were transpierced by the same shot. But the
Turkish approaches were soon sunk in trenches or covered with
ruins. Each day added to the science of the Christians; but
their inadequate stock of gunpowder was wasted in the operations of each day. Their ordnance was not powerful either in
size or number; and if they possessed some heavy cannon, they
feared to plant them on the walls, lest the aged structure should
be shaken and overthrown by the explosion.[1] The same destructive secret had been revealed to the Moslems; by whom it was
employed with the superior energy of zeal, riches, and despotism.
The great cannon of Mohammed has been separately noticed; an
important and visible object in the history of the times: but
that enormous engine was flanked by two fellows almost of
equal magnitude:[2] the long order of the Turkish artillery was
pointed against the walls; fourteen batteries thundered at once
on the most accessible places; and of one of these it is am-
biguously expressed that it was mounted with one hundred and
thirty guns, or that it discharged one hundred and thirty bullets.
Yet in the power and activity of the sultan we may discern the

[1] At indies doctiores nostri facti paravere contra hostes machinamenta,
quæ tamen avare dabantur. Pulvis erat nitri modica, exigua; tela
modica; bombardæ si aderant incommoditate loci primum hostes offendere,
maceriebus alveisque tectos, non poterant. Nam si quæ magnæ erant, ne
murus concuteretur noster, quiescebant. This passage of Leonardus
Chiensis is curious and important.

[2] According to Chalcocondyles and Phranza the great cannon burst; an
accident which, according to Ducas, was prevented by the artist's skill.
It is evident that they do not speak of the same gun.

infancy of the new science.   Under a master who counted the
moments the great cannon could be loaded and fired no more than
seven times in one day.[1]   The heated metal unfortunately burst;
several workmen were destroyed, and the skill of an artist was
admired who bethought himself of preventing the danger and
the accident, by pouring oil, after each explosion, into the mouth
of the cannon.

The first random shots were productive of more sound than
effect; and it was by the advice of a Christian that the engineers
were taught to level their aim against the two opposite sides of the
salient angles of a bastion.   However imperfect, the weight and
repetition of the fire made some impression on the walls; and
the Turks, pushing their approaches to the edge of the ditch,
attempted to fill the enormous chasm and to build a road to the
assault.[2]   Innumerable fascines, and hogsheads, and trunks of
trees, were heaped on each other; and such was the impetuosity
of the throng, that the foremost and the weakest were pushed
headlong down the precipice and instantly buried under the
accumulated mass.   To fill the ditch was the toil of the besiegers; to clear away the rubbish was the safety of the besieged;
and, after a long and bloody conflict, the web that had been
woven in the day was still unravelled in the night.   The next
resource of Mohammed was the practice of mines; but the soil
was rocky; in every attempt he was stopped and undermined
by the Christian engineers; nor had the art been yet invented
of replenishing those subterraneous passages with gunpowder
and blowing whole towers and cities into the air.[3]   A circumstance that distinguishes the siege of Constantinople is the reunion of the ancient and modern artillery.   The cannon were
intermingled with the mechanical engines for casting stones and
darts; the bullet and the battering-ram were directed against the
same walls; nor had the discovery of gunpowder superseded the

[1] Near a hundred years after the siege of Constantinople the French and
English fleets in the Channel were proud of firing 300 shot in an engage-
ment of two hours (Mémoires de Martin du Bellay, l. x. in the Collection
Générale, tom. xxi. p. 239).

[2] I have selected some curious facts, without striving to emulate the
bloody and obstinate eloquence of the Abbé de Vertot, in his prolix descriptions of the sieges of Rhodes, Malta, etc.   But that agreeable historian
had a turn for romance; and as he wrote to please the Order, he has
adopted the same spirit of enthusiasm and chivalry.

[3] The first theory of mines with gunpowder appears in 1480, in a MS. of
George of Sienna (Tiraboschi, tom. vi. P. i. p. 324).   They were first
practised at Sarzanella, in 1487; but the honour and improvement in 1503
is ascribed to Peter of Navarre, who used them with success in the wars of
Italy (Hist. de la Ligue de Cambray, tom. ii. p. 93-97).

use of the liquid and unextinguishable fire. A wooden turret of the largest size was advanced on rollers: this portable magazine of ammunition and fascines was protected by a threefold covering of bulls' hides; incessant volleys were securely discharged from the loopholes; in the front three doors were contrived for the alternate sally and retreat of the soldiers and workmen. They ascended by a staircase to the upper platform, and, as high as the level of that platform, a scaling-ladder could be raised by pulleys to form a bridge and grapple with the adverse rampart. By these various arts of annoyance, some as new as they were pernicious to the Greeks, the tower of St. Romanus was at length overturned: after a severe struggle the Turks were repulsed from the breach and interrupted by darkness; but they trusted that with the return of light they should renew the attack with fresh vigour and decisive success. Of this pause of action, this interval of hope, each moment was improved by the activity of the emperor and Justiniani, who passed the night on the spot, and urged the labours which involved the safety of the church and city. At the dawn of day the impatient sultan perceived, with astonishment and grief, that his wooden turret had been reduced to ashes: the ditch was cleared and restored, and the tower of St. Romanus was again strong and entire. He deplored the failure of his design, and uttered a profane exclamation, that the word of the thirty-seven thousand prophets should not have compelled him to believe that such a work, in so short a time, could have been accomplished by the infidels.

The generosity of the Christian princes was cold and tardy; but in the first apprehension of a siege Constantine had negotiated, in the isles of the Archipelago, the Morea, and Sicily, the most indispensable supplies. As early as the beginning of April, five [1] great ships, equipped for merchandise and war, would have sailed from the harbour of Chios, had not the wind blown obstinately from the north.[2] One of these ships bore the Imperial flag; the remaining four belonged to the Genoese; and they were laden with wheat and barley, with wine, oil, and vegetables, and, above all, with soldiers and mariners, for the service of the capital. After a tedious delay a gentle breeze, and

[1] It is singular that the Greeks should not agree in the number of these illustrious vessels; the *five* of Ducas, the *four* of Phranza and Leonardus, and the *two* of Chalcocondyles, must be extended to the smaller, or confined to larger, size. Voltaire, in giving one of these ships to Frederic III., confounds the emperors of the East and West.

[2] In bold defiance, or rather in gross ignorance, of language and geography, the president Cousin detains them at Chios with a south, and wafts them to Constantinople with a north, wind.

on the second day a strong gale from the south, carried them
through the Hellespont and the Propontis; but the city was
already invested by sea and land, and the Turkish fleet, at the
entrance of the Bosphorus, was stretched from shore to shore, in
the form of a crescent, to intercept, or at least to repel, these
bold auxiliaries. The reader who has present to his mind the
geographical picture of Constantinople will conceive and admire
the greatness of the spectacle. The five Christian ships continued to advance with joyful shouts, and a full press both of
sails and oars, against the hostile fleet of three hundred vessels;
and the rampart, the camp, the coasts of Europe and Asia, were
lined with innumerable spectators, who anxiously awaited the
event of this momentous succour. At the first view that event
could not appear doubtful; the superiority of the Moslems was
beyond all measure or account, and, in a calm, their numbers
and valour must inevitably have prevailed. But their hasty
and imperfect navy had been created, not by the genius of the
people, but by the will of the sultan: in the height of their prosperity the Turks have acknowledged that, if God had given them
the earth, he had left the sea to the infidels; [1] and a series of
defeats, a rapid progress of decay, has established the truth of
their modest confession. Except eighteen galleys of some force,
the rest of their fleet consisted of open boats, rudely constructed
and awkwardly managed, crowded with troops, and destitute of
cannon; and since courage arises in a great measure from the
consciousness of strength, the bravest of the Janizaries might
tremble on a new element. In the Christian squadron five stout
and lofty ships were guided by skilful pilots, and manned with
the veterans of Italy and Greece, long practised in the arts and
perils of the sea. Their weight was directed to sink or scatter
the weak obstacles that impeded their passage: their artillery
swept the waters; their liquid fire was poured on the heads of
the adversaries, who, with the design of boarding, presumed to
approach them; and the winds and waves are always on the side
of the ablest navigators. In this conflict the Imperial vessel,
which had been almost overpowered, was rescued by the
Genoese; but the Turks, in a distant and a closer attack, were
twice repulsed with considerable loss. Mohammed himself sat
on horseback on the beach, to encourage their valour by his voice
and presence, by the promise of reward, and by fear more potent

[1] The perpetual decay and weakness of the Turkish navy may be
observed in Rycaut (State of the Ottoman Empire, p. 372-378), Thévenot
(Voyages, P. i. p. 229-242), and Tott (Mémoires, tom. iii.); the last of
whom is always solicitous to amuse and amaze his reader.

than the fear of the enemy. The passions of his soul, and even the gestures of his body,[1] seemed to imitate the actions of the combatants; and, as if he had been the lord of nature, he spurred his horse with a fearless and impotent effort into the sea. His loud reproaches, and the clamours of the camp, urged the Ottomans to a third attack, more fatal and bloody than the two former; and I must repeat, though I cannot credit, the evidence of Phranza, who affirms, from their own mouth, that they lost above twelve thousand men in the slaughter of the day. They fled in disorder to the shores of Europe and Asia, while the Christian squadron, triumphant and unhurt, steered along the Bosphorus, and securely anchored within the chain of the harbour. In the confidence of victory, they boasted that the whole Turkish power must have yielded to their arms; but the admiral, or captain bashaw, found some consolation for a painful wound in his eye, by representing that accident as the cause of his defeat. Baltha Ogli was a renegade of the race of the Bulgarian princes: his military character was tainted with the unpopular vice of avarice; and under the despotism of the prince or people, misfortune is a sufficient evidence of guilt. His rank and services were annihilated by the displeasure of Mohammed. In the royal presence, the captain bashaw was extended on the ground by four slaves, and received one hundred strokes with a golden rod:[2] his death had been pronounced, and he adored the clemency of the sultan, who was satisfied with the milder punishment of confiscation and exile. The introduction of this supply revived the hopes of the Greeks, and accused the supineness of their Western allies. Amidst the deserts of Anatolia and the rocks of Palestine, the millions of the crusades had buried themselves in a voluntary and inevitable grave; but the situation of the Imperial city was strong against her enemies, and accessible to her friends; and a rational and moderate armament of the maritime states might have saved the relics of the Roman name, and maintained a Christian fortress in the heart of the Ottoman empire. Yet this was the sole and feeble attempt for the deliverance of Constantinople: the more distant powers were insensible of its danger; and the ambassador of Hungary, or at least of

---

[1] I must confess that I have before my eyes the living picture which Thucydides (l. vii. c. 71) has drawn of the passions and gestures of the Athenians in a naval engagement in the great harbour of Syracuse.

[2] According to the exaggeration or corrupt text of Ducas (c. 38 [p. 270, ed. Bonn]) this golden bar was of the enormous and incredible weight of 500 libræ, or pounds. Bouillaud's reading of 500 drachms, or five pounds, is sufficient to exercise the arm of Mohammed, and bruise the back of his admiral.

Huniades, resided in the Turkish camp, to remove the fears and to direct the operations of the sultan.[1]

It was difficult for the Greeks to penetrate the secret of the divan; yet the Greeks are persuaded that a resistance so obstinate and surprising had fatigued the perseverance of Mohammed. He began to meditate a retreat; and the siege would have been speedily raised, if the ambition and jealousy of the second vizir had not opposed the perfidious advice of Calil Bashaw, who still maintained a secret correspondence with the Byzantine court. The reduction of the city appeared to be hopeless, unless a double attack could be made from the harbour as well as from the land; but the harbour was inaccessible: an impenetrable chain was now defended by eight large ships, more than twenty of a smaller size, with several galleys and sloops; and, instead of forcing this barrier, the Turks might apprehend a naval sally and a second encounter in the open sea. In this perplexity the genius of Mohammed conceived and executed a plan of a bold and marvellous cast, of transporting by land his lighter vessels and military stores from the Bosphorus into the higher part of the harbour. The distance is about ten miles; the ground is uneven, and was overspread with thickets; and, as the road must be opened behind the suburb of Galata, their free passage or total destruction must depend on the option of the Genoese. But these selfish merchants were ambitious of the favour of being the last devoured, and the deficiency of art was supplied by the strength of obedient myriads. A level way was covered with a broad platform of strong and solid planks; and to render them more slippery and smooth, they were anointed with the fat of sheep and oxen. Fourscore light galleys and brigantines of fifty and thirty oars were disembarked on the Bosphorus shore, arranged successively on rollers, and drawn forwards by the power of men and pulleys. Two guides or pilots were stationed at the helm and the prow of each vessel: the sails were unfurled to the winds, and the labour was cheered by song and acclamation. In the course of a single night this Turkish fleet painfully climbed the hill, steered over the plain, and was launched from the declivity into the shallow waters of the harbour, far above the molestation of the deeper vessels of the Greeks. The real importance of this operation was magnified by

---

[1] Ducas, who confesses himself ill informed of the affairs of Hungary assigns a motive of superstition, a fatal belief that Constantinople would be the term of the Turkish conquests. See Phranza (l. iii. c. 20) and Spondanus.

the consternation and confidence which it inspired; but the notorious, unquestionable fact was displayed before the eyes, and is recorded by the pens, of the two nations.[1] A similar stratagem had been repeatedly practised by the ancients;[2] the Ottoman galleys (I must again repeat) should be considered as large boats; and, if we compare the magnitude and the distance, the obstacles and the means, the boasted miracle[3] has perhaps been equalled by the industry of our own times.[4] As soon as Mohammed had occupied the upper harbour with a fleet and army, he constructed in the narrowest part a bridge, or rather mole, of fifty cubits in breadth and one hundred in length: it was formed of casks and hogsheads, joined with rafters, linked with iron, and covered with a solid floor. On this floating battery he planted one of his largest cannon, while the fourscore galleys, with troops and scaling-ladders, approached the most accessible side, which had formerly been stormed by the Latin conquerors. The indolence of the Christians has been accused for not destroying these unfinished works; but their fire, by a superior fire, was controlled and silenced; nor were they wanting in a nocturnal attempt to burn the vessels as well as the bridge of the sultan. His vigilance prevented their approach: their foremost galliots were sunk or taken; forty youths, the bravest of Italy and Greece, were inhumanly massacred at his command; nor could the emperor's grief be assuaged by the just though cruel retaliation of exposing from the walls the heads of two hundred and sixty Musulman captives. After a siege of forty days the fate of Constantinople could no longer be averted. The diminutive garrison was exhausted by a double attack:

[1] The unanimous testimony of the four Greeks is confirmed by Cantemir (p. 96) from the Turkish annals; but I could wish to contract the distance of *ten* miles, and to prolong the term of *one* night.

[2] Phranza relates two examples of a similar transportation over the six miles of the isthmus of Corinth; the one fabulous, of Augustus after the battle of Actium; the other true, of Nicetas, a Greek general in the tenth century. To these he might have added a bold enterprise of Hannibal to introduce his vessels into the harbour of Tarentum (Polybius, l. viii. [c. 36] p. 749, edit. Gronov.).

[3] A Greek of Candia, who had served the Venetians in a similar undertaking (Spond. A.D. 1438, No. 37), might possibly be the adviser and agent of Mohammed.

[4] I particularly allude to our own embarkations on the lakes of Canada in the years 1776 and 1777, so great in the labour, so fruitless in the event. [There are other instances in history of this method of conveying vessels over the land. 1. The famous vessel, the Argo, in which the Argonauts made their marvellous voyage, was so conveyed from a river running south to one running north. 2. The dragging of the Syracusan fleet of Dionysius I. over the isthmus of Motya, a distance of two and a half miles. —O. S.]

the fortifications, which had stood for ages against hostile violence, were dismantled on all sides by the Ottoman cannon; many breaches were opened, and near the gate of St. Romanus four towers had been levelled with the ground. For the payment of his feeble and mutinous troops, Constantine was compelled to despoil the churches with the promise of a fourfold restitution; and his sacrilege offered a new reproach to the enemies of the union. A spirit of discord impaired the remnant of the Christian strength: the Genoese and Venetian auxiliaries asserted the pre-eminence of their respective service; and Justiniani and the great duke, whose ambition was not extinguished by the common danger, accused each other of treachery and cowardice.

During the siege of Constantinople the words of peace and capitulation had been sometimes pronounced; and several embassies had passed between the camp and the city.[1] The Greek emperor was humbled by adversity; and would have yielded to any terms compatible with religion and royalty. The Turkish sultan was desirous of sparing the blood of his soldiers; still more desirous of securing for his own use the Byzantine treasures; and he accomplished a sacred duty in presenting to the *Gabours* the choice of circumcision, of tribute, or of death. The avarice of Mohammed might have been satisfied with an annual sum of one hundred thousand ducats; but his ambition grasped the capital of the East: to the prince he offered a rich equivalent, to the people a free toleration, or a safe departure: but after some fruitless treaty, he declared his resolution of finding either a throne or a grave under the walls of Constantinople. A sense of honour, and the fear of universal reproach, forbade Palæologus to resign the city into the hands of the Ottomans; and he determined to abide the last extremities of war. Several days were employed by the sultan in the preparations of the assault; and a respite was granted by his favourite science of astrology, which had fixed on the twenty-ninth of May as the fortunate and fatal hour. On the evening of the twenty-seventh he issued his final orders; assembled in his presence the military chiefs; and dispersed his heralds through the camp to proclaim the duty and the motives of the perilous enterprise. Fear is the first principle of a despotic government; and his menaces were expressed in the Oriental style, that the fugitives and deserters,

---

[1] Chalcocondyles and Ducas differ in the time and circumstances of the negotiation; and as it was neither glorious nor salutary, the faithful Phranza spares his prince even the thought of a surrender.

had they the wings of a bird,[1] should not escape from his inexorable justice. The greatest part of his bashaws and Janizaries were the offspring of Christian parents: but the glories of the Turkish name were perpetuated by successive adoption; and in the gradual change of individuals, the spirit of a legion, a regiment, or an *oda*, is kept alive by imitation and discipline. In this holy warfare the Moslems were exhorted to purify their minds with prayer, their bodies with seven ablutions; and to abstain from food till the close of the ensuing day. A crowd of dervishes visited the tents, to instil the desire of martyrdom, and the assurance of spending an immortal youth amidst the rivers and gardens of paradise, and in the embraces of the black-eyed virgins. Yet Mohammed principally trusted to the efficacy of temporal and visible rewards. A double pay was promised to the victorious troops; "The city and the buildings," said Mohammed, "are mine; but I resign to your valour the captives and the spoil, the treasures of gold and beauty; be rich and be happy. Many are the provinces of my empire: the intrepid soldier who first ascends the walls of Constantinople shall be rewarded with the government of the fairest and most wealthy; and my gratitude shall accumulate his honours and fortunes above the measure of his own hopes." Such various and potent motives diffused among the Turks a general ardour, regardless of life and impatient for action: the camp re-echoed with the Moslem shouts of "God is God: there is but one God, and Mohammed is the apostle of God;"[2] and the sea and land, from

---

[1] These wings (Chalcocondyles, l. viii. p. 208 [p. 393, ed. Bonn]) are no more than an Oriental figure: but in the tragedy of Irene Mohammed's passion soars above sense and reason:—

> Should the fierce North, upon his frozen wings,
> Bear him aloft above the wondering clouds,
> And seat him in the Pleiads' golden chariot—
> Thence should my fury drag him down to tortures.

Besides the extravagance of the rant, I must observe, 1. That the operation of the winds must be confined to the *lower* region of the air. 2. That the name, etymology, and fable of the Pleiads are purely Greek (Scholiast ad Homer, Σ. 686; Eudocia in Ioniâ, p. 339; Apollodor. l. iii. c. 10; Heyne, p. 229; Not. 682), and had no affinity with the astronomy of the East (Hyde ad Ulugbeg, Tabul. in Syntagma Dissert. tom. i. p. 40, 42; Goguet, Origine des Arts, etc., tom. vi. p. 73-78; Gebelin, Hist. du Calendrier, p. 73), which Mohammed had studied. 3. The golden chariot does not exist either in science or fiction; but I much fear that Dr. Johnson has confounded the Pleiads with the great bear or waggon, the zodiac with a northern constellation:—

> Ἄρκτον θ' ἣν καὶ ἄμαξαν ἐπίκλησιν καλέουσιν. Il. Σ. 487.

[2] Phranza quarrels with these Moslem acclamations, not for the name of God, but for that of the prophet: the pious zeal of Voltaire is excessive, and even ridiculous.

Galata to the seven towers, were illuminated by the blaze of their nocturnal fires.

Far different was the state of the Christians; who, with loud and impotent complaints, deplored the guilt, or the punishment, of their sins. The celestial image of the Virgin had been exposed in solemn procession; but their divine patroness was deaf to their entreaties: they accused the obstinacy of the emperor for refusing a timely surrender; anticipated the horrors of their fate; and sighed for the repose and security of Turkish servitude. The noblest of the Greeks, and the bravest of the allies, were summoned to the palace, to prepare them, on the evening of the twenty-eighth, for the duties and dangers of the general assault. The last speech of Palæologus was the funeral oration of the Roman empire:[1] he promised, he conjured, and he vainly attempted to infuse the hope which was extinguished in his own mind. In this world all was comfortless and gloomy; and neither the Gospel nor the church have proposed any conspicuous recompense to the heroes who fall in the service of their country. But the example of their prince, and the confinement of a siege, had armed these warriors with the courage of despair; and the pathetic scene is described by the feelings of the historian Phranza, who was himself present at this mournful assembly. They wept, they embraced: regardless of their families and fortunes, they devoted their lives; and each commander, departing to his station, maintained all night a vigilant and anxious watch on the rampart. The emperor, and some faithful companions, entered the dome of St. Sophia, which in a few hours was to be converted into a mosque; and devoutly received, with tears and prayers, the sacrament of the holy communion. He reposed some moments in the palace, which resounded with cries and lamentations; solicited the pardon of all whom he might have injured;[2] and mounted on horseback to visit the guards, and explore the motions of the enemy. The distress and fall of the last Constantine are more glorious than the long prosperity of the Byzantine Cæsars.

In the confusion of darkness an assailant may sometimes

---

[1] I am afraid that this discourse was composed by Phranza himself; and it smells so grossly of the sermon and the convent, that I almost doubt whether it was pronounced by Constantine. Leonardus assigns him another speech, in which he addresses himself more respectfully to the Latin auxiliaries.

[2] This abasement, which devotion has sometimes extorted from dying princes, is an improvement of the Gospel doctrine of the forgiveness of injuries: it is more easy to forgive 490 times than once to ask pardon of an inferior.

succeed; but in this great and general attack, the military judgment and astrological knowledge of Mohammed advised him to expect the morning, the memorable twenty-ninth of May, in the fourteen hundred and fifty-third year of the Christian era. The preceding night had been strenuously employed: the troops, the cannon, and the fascines were advanced to the edge of the ditch, which in many parts presented a smooth and level passage to the breach; and his fourscore galleys almost touched, with the prows and their scaling ladders, the less defensible walls of the harbour. Under pain of death, silence was enjoined; but the physical laws of motion and sound are not obedient to discipline or fear: each individual might suppress his voice and measure his footsteps; but the march and labour of thousands must inevitably produce a strange confusion of dissonant clamours, which reached the ears of the watchmen of the towers. At daybreak, without the customary signal of the morning gun, the Turks assaulted the city by sea and land; and the similitude of a twined or twisted thread has been applied to the closeness and continuity of their line of attack.[1] The foremost ranks consisted of the refuse of the host, a voluntary crowd who fought without order or command; of the feebleness of age or childhood, of peasants and vagrants, and of all who had joined the camp in the blind hope of plunder and martyrdom. The common impulse drove them onwards to the wall; the most audacious to climb were instantly precipitated; and not a dart, not a bullet, of the Christians, was idly wasted on the accumulated throng. But their strength and ammunition were exhausted in this laborious defence: the ditch was filled with the bodies of the slain; they supported the footsteps of their companions; and of this devoted vanguard the death was more serviceable than the life. Under their respective bashaws and sanjaks, the troops of Anatolia and Romania were successively led to the charge: their progress was various and doubtful; but, after a conflict of two hours, the Greeks still maintained and improved their advantage; and the voice of the emperor was heard, encouraging his soldiers to achieve, by a last effort, the deliverance of their country. In that fatal moment the Janizaries arose, fresh, vigorous, and invincible. The sultan himself on horseback, with an iron mace in his hand, was the spectator and judge of their valour; he was surrounded by ten thousand of his domestic troops, whom he reserved for the

---

[1] Besides the 10,000 guards, and the sailors and the marines, Ducas numbers in this general assault 250,000 Turks, both horse and foot [c. 39, p. 283, ed. Bonn].

decisive occasion; and the tide of battle was directed and impelled by his voice and eye. His numerous ministers of justice were posted behind the line, to urge, to restrain, and to punish; and if danger was in the front, shame and inevitable death were in the rear, of the fugitives. The cries of fear and of pain were drowned in the martial music of drums, trumpets, and attaballs; and experience has proved that the mechanical operation of sounds, by quickening the circulation of the blood and spirits, will act on the human machine more forcibly than the eloquence of reason and honour. From the lines, the galleys, and the bridge, the Ottoman artillery thundered on all sides; and the camp and city, the Greeks and the Turks, were involved in a cloud of smoke, which could only be dispelled by the final deliverance or destruction of the Roman empire. The single combats of the heroes of history or fable amuse our fancy and engage our affections: the skilful evolutions of war may inform the mind, and improve a necessary, though pernicious, science. But in the uniform and odious pictures of a general assault, all is blood, and horror, and confusion; nor shall I strive, at the distance of three centuries and a thousand miles, to delineate a scene of which there could be no spectators, and of which the actors themselves were incapable of forming any just or adequate idea.

The immediate loss of Constantinople may be ascribed to the bullet, or arrow, which pierced the gauntlet of John Justiniani. The sight of his blood, and the exquisite pain, appalled the courage of the chief, whose arms and counsels were the firmest rampart of the city. As he withdrew from his station in quest of a surgeon, his flight was perceived and stopped by the indefatigable emperor. "Your wound," exclaimed Palæologus, "is slight; the danger is pressing: your presence is necessary; and whither will you retire?"—"I will retire," said the trembling Genoese, "by the same road which God has opened to the Turks;" and at these words he hastily passed through one of the breaches of the inner wall. By this pusillanimous act he stained the honours of a military life; and the few days which he survived in Galata, or the isle of Chios, were embittered by his own and the public reproach.[1] His example was imitated by

[1] In the severe censure of the flight of Justiniani, Phranza expresses his own feelings and those of the public. For some private reasons he is treated with more lenity and respect by Ducas; but the words of Leonardus Chiensis express his strong and recent indignation, gloriæ salutis suique oblitus. In the whole series of their Eastern policy, his countrymen, the Genoese, were always suspected, and often guilty.

[This condemnation of John Guistiniani is wholly undeserved. The fact that the great engineer only lived six days after the wound had been

the greatest part of the Latin auxiliaries, and the defence began
to slacken when the attack was pressed with redoubled vigour.
The number of the Ottomans was fifty, perhaps a hundred, times
superior to that of the Christians; the double walls were reduced
by the cannon to a heap of ruins: in a circuit of several miles
some places must be found more easy of access, or more feebly
guarded; and if the besiegers could penetrate in a single point,
the whole city was irrecoverably lost. The first who deserved
the sultan's reward was Hassan the Janizary, of gigantic stature
and strength. With his scimitar in one hand and his buckler
in the other, he ascended the outward fortification: of the thirty
Janizaries who were emulous of his valour, eighteen perished in
the bold adventure. Hassan and his twelve companions had
reached the summit: the giant was precipitated from the rampart: he rose on one knee, and was again oppressed by a shower of
darts and stones. But his success had proved that the achieve-
ment was possible: the walls and towers were instantly covered
with a swarm of Turks; and the Greeks, now driven from the
vantage ground, were overwhelmed by increasing multitudes.
Amidst these multitudes, the emperor,[1] who accomplished all the
duties of a general and a soldier, was long seen and finally lost.
The nobles, who fought round his person, sustained, till their last
breath, the honourable names of Palæologus and Cantacuzene:
his mournful exclamation was heard, " Cannot there be found
a Christian to cut off my head? " [2] and his last fear was that of
falling alive into the hands of the infidels.[3] The prudent despair
of Constantine cast away the purple: amidst the tumult he fell

received showed that the injury was not slight. The unfortunate man
suffers because of the untrustworthy character of his countrymen. They
were proverbially treacherous. But Guistiniani's services and valour
have been extolled by all the Greek writers, and this is sufficient answer to
the charge of cowardice.—O. S.]

[1] Ducas kills him with two blows of Turkish soldiers; Chalcocondyles
wounds him in the shoulder, and then tramples him in the gate. The
grief of Phranza, carrying him among the enemy, escapes from the precise
image of his death; but we may, without flattery, apply these noble lines
of Dryden:—

> As to Sebastian, let them search the field;
> And, where they find a mountain of the slain,
> Send one to climb, and, looking down beneath,
> There they will find him at his manly length,
> With his face up to heaven, in that red monument
> Which his good sword had digg'd.

[2] Spondanus (A.D. 1453, No. 10), who has hopes of his salvation, wishes
to absolve this demand from the guilt of suicide.

[3] Leonardus Chiensis very properly observes that the Turks, had they
known the emperor, would have laboured to save and secure a captive so
acceptable to the sultan.

by an unknown hand, and his body was buried under a mountain of the slain. After his death resistance and order were no more: the Greeks fled towards the city; and many were pressed and stifled in the narrow pass of the gate of St. Romanus. The victorious Turks rushed through the breaches of the inner wall; and as they advanced into the streets, they were soon joined by their brethren, who had forced the gate Phenar on the side of the harbour.[1] In the first heat of the pursuit about two thousand Christians were put to the sword; but avarice soon prevailed over cruelty; and the victors acknowledged that they should immediately have given quarter, if the valour of the emperor and his chosen bands had not prepared them for a similar opposition in every part of the capital. It was thus, after a siege of fifty-three days, that Constantinople, which had defied the power of Chosroes, the Chagan, and the caliphs, was irretrievably subdued by the arms of Mohammed the Second. Her empire only had been subverted by the Latins: her religion was trampled in the dust by the Moslem conquerors.[2]

The tidings of misfortune fly with a rapid wing; yet such was the extent of Constantinople, that the more distant quarters might prolong, some moments, the happy ignorance of their ruin.[3] But in the general consternation, in the feelings of selfish or social anxiety, in the tumult and thunder of the assault, a *sleepless* night and morning must have elapsed; nor can I believe that many Grecian ladies were awakened by the Janizaries from a sound and tranquil slumber. On the assurance of the public calamity, the houses and convents were instantly deserted; and the trembling inhabitants flocked together in the streets, like a herd of timid animals, as if accumulated weakness could be productive of strength, or in the vain hope that amid the crowd each individual might be safe and invisible. From every part of the capital they flowed into the church of St. Sophia: in the space of an hour, the sanctuary, the choir, the nave, the upper and lower galleries, were filled with the multitudes of fathers and husbands,

---

[1] Cantemir, p. 96. The Christian ships in the mouth of the harbour had flanked and retarded this naval attack.

[2] Chalcocondyles most absurdly supposes that Constantinople was sacked by the Asiatics in revenge for the ancient calamities of Troy [l. viii. p. 403, ed. Bonn]; and the grammarians of the fifteenth century are happy to melt down the uncouth appellation of Turks into the more classical name of *Teucri*.

[3] When Cyrus surprised Babylon during the celebration of a festival, so vast was the city, and so careless were the inhabitants, that much time elapsed before the distant quarters knew that they were captives. Herodotus (l. i. c. 191), and Usher (Annal. p. 78), who has quoted from the prophet Jeremiah a passage of similar import.

of women and children, of priests, monks, and religious virgins: the doors were barred on the inside, and they sought protection from the sacred dome which they had so lately abhorred as a profane and polluted edifice. Their confidence was founded on the prophecy of an enthusiast or impostor, that one day the Turks would enter Constantinople, and pursue the Romans as far as the column of Constantine in the square before St. Sophia: but that this would be the term of their calamities; that an angel would descend from heaven with a sword in his hand, and would deliver the empire, with that celestial weapon, to a poor man seated at the foot of the column. " Take this sword," would he say, " and avenge the people of the Lord." At these animating words the Turks would instantly fly, and the victorious Romans would drive them from the West, and from all Anatolia, as far as the frontiers of Persia. It is on this occasion that Ducas, with some fancy and much truth, upbraids the discord and obstinacy of the Greeks. " Had that angel appeared," exclaims the historian, " had he offered to exterminate your foes if you would consent to the union of the church, even then, in that fatal moment, you would have rejected your safety, or have deceived your God." [1]

While they expected the descent of the tardy angel, the doors were broken with axes; and as the Turks encountered no resistance, their bloodless hands were employed in selecting and securing the multitude of their prisoners. Youth, beauty, and the appearance of wealth, attracted their choice; and the right of property was decided among themselves by a prior seizure, by personal strength, and by the authority of command. In the space of an hour the male captives were bound with cords, the females with their veils and girdles. The senators were linked with their slaves; the prelates with the porters of the church; and young men of a plebeian class with noble maids whose faces had been invisible to the sun and their nearest kindred. In this common captivity the ranks of society were confounded; the ties of nature were cut asunder; and the inexorable soldier was careless of the father's groans, the tears of the mother, and the lamentations of the children. The loudest in their wailings were the nuns, who were torn from the altar with naked bosoms, outstretched hands, and dishevelled hair; and we should piously

[1] This lively description is extracted from Ducas (c. 39 [p. 291, ed. Bonn]), who, two years afterwards, was sent ambassador from the prince of Lesbos to the sultan (c. 44). Till Lesbos was subdued in 1463 (Phranza, l. iii. c. 27), that island must have been full of the fugitives of Constantinople, who delighted to repeat, perhaps to adorn, the tale of their misery.

believe that few could be tempted to prefer the vigils of the
harem to those of the monastery. Of these unfortunate Greeks,
of these domestic animals, whole strings were rudely driven
through the streets; and as the conquerors were eager to return
for more prey, their trembling pace was quickened with menaces
and blows. At the same hour a similar rapine was exercised in
all the churches and monasteries, in all the palaces and habitations, of the capital; nor could any place, however sacred or
sequestered, protect the persons or the property of the Greeks.
Above sixty thousand of this devoted people were transported
from the city to the camp and fleet; exchanged or sold according
to the caprice or interest of their masters, and dispersed in
remote servitude through the provinces of the Ottoman empire.
Among these we may notice some remarkable characters. The
historian Phranza, first chamberlain and principal secretary,
was involved with his family in the common lot. After suffering
four months the hardships of slavery, he recovered his freedom:
in the ensuing winter he ventured to Adrianople, and ransomed
his wife from the *mir bashi*, or master of the horse; but his two
children, in the flower of youth and beauty, had been seized for
the use of Mohammed himself. The daughter of Phranza died
in the seraglio, perhaps a virgin: his son, in the fifteenth year of
his age, preferred death to infamy, and was stabbed by the hand
of the royal lover.[1] A deed thus inhuman cannot surely be
expiated by the taste and liberality with which he released a
Grecian matron and her two daughters, on receiving a Latin ode
from Philelphus, who had chosen a wife in that noble family.[2]
The pride or cruelty of Mohammed would have been most sensibly
gratified by the capture of a Roman legate; but the dexterity of
Cardinal Isidore eluded the search, and he escaped from Galata
in a plebeian habit.[3] The chain and entrance of the outward
harbour was still occupied by the Italian ships of merchandise

---

[1] See Phranza, l. iii. c. 20, 21. His expressions are positive: Ameras
suâ manû jugulavit . . . volebat enim eo turpiter et nefarie abuti. Me
miserum et infelicem! Yet he could only learn from report the bloody
or impure scenes that were acted in the dark recesses of the seraglio.

[2] See Tiraboschi (tom. vi. P. i. p. 290) and Lancelot (Mém. de l'Académie
des Inscriptions, tom. x. p. 718). I should be curious to learn how he
could praise the public enemy, whom he so often reviles as the most corrupt
and inhuman of tyrants.

[3] The Commentaries of Pius II. suppose that he craftily placed his
cardinal's hat on the head of a corpse which was cut off and exposed in
triumph, while the legate himself was bought and delivered as a captive of
no value. The great Belgic Chronicle adorns his escape with new adventures, which he suppressed (says Spondanus, A.D. 1453, No. 15) in his own
letters, lest he should lose the merit and reward of suffering for Christ.

and war. They had signalised their valour in the siege: they embraced the moment of retreat, while the Turkish mariners were dissipated in the pillage of the city. When they hoisted sail, the beach was covered with a suppliant and lamentable crowd; but the means of transportation were scanty; the Venetians and Genoese selected their countrymen; and, notwithstanding the fairest promises of the sultan, the inhabitants of Galata evacuated their houses, and embarked with their most precious effects.

In the fall and the sack of great cities an historian is condemned to repeat the tale of uniform calamity: the same effects must be produced by the same passions; and when those passions may be indulged without control, small, alas! is the difference between civilised and savage man. Amidst the vague exclamations of bigotry and hatred, the Turks are not accused of a wanton or immoderate effusion of Christian blood: but according to their maxims (the maxims of antiquity), the lives of the vanquished were forfeited; and the legitimate reward of the conqueror was derived from the service, the sale, or the ransom of his captives of both sexes.[1] The wealth of Constantinople had been granted by the sultan to his victorious troops; and the rapine of an hour is more productive than the industry of years. But as no regular division was attempted of the spoil, the respective shares were not determined by merit; and the rewards of valour were stolen away by the followers of the camp, who had declined the toil and danger of the battle. The narrative of their depredations could not afford either amusement or instruction: the total amount, in the last poverty of the empire, has been valued at four millions of ducats;[2] and of this sum a small part was the property of the Venetians, the Genoese, the Florentines, and the merchants of Ancona. Of these foreigners the stock was improved in quick and perpetual circulation: but the riches of the Greeks were displayed in the idle ostentation of palaces and wardrobes, or deeply buried in treasures of ingots and old coin, lest it should be demanded at their hands for the defence of their country. The profanation and plunder of the monasteries and churches excited the most

[1] Busbequius expatiates with pleasure and applause on the rights of war and the use of slavery among the ancients and the Turks (de Legat. Turcicâ, Epist. iii. p. 161).

[2] This sum is specified in a marginal note of Leunclavius (Chalcocondyles, l. viii. p. 211); but, in the distribution to Venice, Genoa, Florence, and Ancona, of 50, 20, 20, and 15,000 ducats, I suspect that a figure has been dropped. Even with the restitution, the foreign property would scarcely exceed one-fourth.

tragic complaints. The dome of St. Sophia itself, the earthly heaven, the second firmament, the vehicle of the cherubim, the throne of the glory of God,[1] was despoiled of the oblations of ages; and the gold and silver, the pearls and jewels, the vases and sacerdotal ornaments, were most wickedly converted to the service of mankind. After the divine images had been stripped of all that could be valuable to a profane eye, the canvas, or the wood, was torn, or broken, or burnt, or trod under foot, or applied, in the stables or the kitchen, to the vilest uses. The example of sacrilege was imitated, however, from the Latin conquerors of Constantinople; and the treatment which Christ, the Virgin, and the saints had sustained from the guilty Catholic, might be inflicted by the zealous Musulman on the monuments of idolatry. Perhaps, instead of joining the public clamour, a philosopher will observe that in the decline of the arts the workmanship could not be more valuable than the work, and that a fresh supply of visions and miracles would speedily be renewed by the craft of the priest and the credulity of the people. He will more seriously deplore the loss of the Byzantine libraries, which were destroyed or scattered in the general confusion: one hundred and twenty thousand manuscripts are said to have disappeared;[2] ten volumes might be purchased for a single ducat; and the same ignominious price, too high perhaps for a shelf of theology, included the whole works of Aristotle and Homer, the noblest productions of the science and literature of ancient Greece. We may reflect with pleasure that an inestimable portion of our classic treasures was safely deposited in Italy; and that the mechanics of a German town had invented an art which derides the havoc of time and barbarism.

From the first hour[3] of the memorable twenty-ninth of May, disorder and rapine prevailed in Constantinople till the eighth hour of the same day, when the sultan himself passed in triumph through the gate of St. Romanus. He was attended by his viziers, bashaws, and guards, each of whom (says a Byzantine historian) was robust as Hercules, dexterous as Apollo, and equal in battle to any ten of the race of ordinary mortals. The conqueror[4] gazed with satisfaction and wonder on the strange though

[1] See the enthusiastic praises and lamentations of Phranza (l. iii. c. 17).

[2] See Ducas (c. 42 [p. 312, ed. Bonn]), and an epistle, July 15th, 1453, from Laurus Quirinus to Pope Nicholas V. (Hody de Græcis, p. 192, from a MS. in the Cotton library).

[3] The Julian calendar, which reckons the days and hours from midnight, was used at Constantinople. But Ducas seems to understand the natural hours from sunrise.

[4] See the Turkish Annals, p. 329, and the Pandects of Leunclavius, p. 448.

splendid appearance of the domes and palaces, so dissimilar from
the style of Oriental architecture. In the hippodrome, or
atmeidan, his eye was attracted by the twisted column of the
three serpents; and, as a trial of his strength, he shattered with
his iron mace or battle-axe the under jaw of one of these
monsters,[1] which in the eyes of the Turks were the idols or
talismans of the city. At the principal door of St. Sophia he
alighted from his horse and entered the dome; and such was
his jealous regard for that monument of his glory, that, on
observing a zealous Musulman in the act of breaking the marble
pavement, he admonished him with his scimitar that, if the spoil
and captives were granted to the soldiers, the public and private
buildings had been reserved for the prince. By his command
the metropolis of the Eastern church was transformed into a
mosque: the rich and portable instruments of superstition had
been removed; the crosses were thrown down; and the walls,
which were covered with images and mosaics, were washed and
purified, and restored to a state of naked simplicity. On the
same day, or on the ensuing Friday, the *muezin*, or crier,
ascended the most lofty turret, and proclaimed the *ezan*, or
public invitation, in the name of God and his prophet; the imam
preached; and Mohammed the Second performed the *namaz* of
prayer and thanksgiving on the great altar, where the Christian
mysteries had so lately been celebrated before the last of the
Cæsars.[2] From St. Sophia he proceeded to the august but
desolate mansion of a hundred successors of the great Constantine, but which in a few hours had been stripped of the
pomp of royalty. A melancholy reflection on the vicissitudes of
human greatness forced itself on his mind, and he repeated an
elegant distich of Persian poetry: " The spider has wove his web
in the Imperial palace, and the owl hath sung her watch-song on
the towers of Afrasiab." [3]

Yet his mind was not satisfied, nor did the victory seem
complete, till he was informed of the fate of Constantine—
whether he had escaped, or been made prisoner, or had fallen in

[1] I have had occasion (vol. ii. p. 82) to mention this curious relic of
Grecian antiquity.

[2] We are obliged to Cantemir (p. 102) for the Turkish account of the
conversion of St. Sophia, so bitterly deplored by Phranza and Ducas. It
is amusing enough to observe in what opposite lights the same object
appears to a Musulman and a Christian eye.

[3] This distich, which Cantemir gives in the original, derives new beauties
from the application. It was thus that Scipio repeated, in the sack of
Carthage, the famous prophecy of Homer. The same generous feeling
carried the mind of the conqueror to the past or the future.

the battle. Two Janizaries claimed the honour and reward of his death: the body, under a heap of slain, was discovered by the golden eagles embroidered on his shoes; the Greeks acknowledged with tears the head of their late emperor; and, after exposing the bloody trophy,[1] Mohammed bestowed on his rival the honours of a decent funeral. After his decease Lucas Notaras, great duke[2] and first minister of the empire, was the most important prisoner. When he offered his person and his treasures at the foot of the throne, " And why," said the indignant sultan, " did you not employ these treasures in the defence of your prince and country? "—" They were yours," answered the slave; " God had reserved them for your hands." —" If he reserved them for me," replied the despot, " how have you presumed to withhold them so long by a fruitless and fatal resistance? " The great duke alleged the obstinacy of the strangers, and some secret encouragement from the Turkish vizir; and from this perilous interview he was at length dismissed with the assurance of pardon and protection. Mohammed condescended to visit his wife, a venerable princess oppressed with sickness and grief; and his consolation for her misfortunes was in the most tender strain of humanity and filial reverence. A similar clemency was extended to the principal officers of state, of whom several were ransomed at his expense; and during some days he declared himself the friend and father of the vanquished people. But the scene was soon changed, and before his departure the hippodrome streamed with the blood of his noblest captives. His perfidious cruelty is execrated by the Christians: they adorn with the colours of heroic martyrdom the execution of the great duke and his two sons, and his death is ascribed to the generous refusal of delivering his children to the tyrant's lust. Yet a Byzantine historian has dropped an unguarded word of conspiracy, deliverance, and Italian succour: such treason may be glorious; but the rebel who bravely ventures, has justly forfeited his life; nor should we blame a conqueror for destroying the enemies whom he can no longer trust. On the eighteenth of June the victorious sultan returned to Adrianople, and smiled at

---

[1] I cannot believe with Ducas (see Spondanus, A.D. 1453, No. 13) that Mohammed sent round Persia, Arabia, etc., the head of the Greek emperor: he would surely content himself with a trophy less inhuman.

[2] Phranza was the personal enemy of the great duke; nor could time, or death, or his own retreat to a monastery, extort a feeling of sympathy or forgiveness. Ducas is inclined to praise and pity the martyr; Chalcocondyles is neuter, but we are indebted to him for the hint of the Greek conspiracy.

the base and hollow embassies of the Christian princes, who
viewed their approaching ruin in the fall of the Eastern empire.

Constantinople had been left naked and desolate, without a
prince or a people.   But she could not be despoiled of the incomparable situation which marks her for the metropolis of a great
empire; and the genius of the place will ever triumph over the
accidents of time and fortune.   Boursa and Adrianople, the
ancient seats of the Ottomans, sunk into provincial towns; and
Mohammed the Second established his own residence and that
of his successors on the same commanding spot which had been
chosen by Constantine.[1]   The fortifications of Galata, which
might afford a shelter to the Latins, were prudently destroyed;
but the damage of the Turkish cannon was soon repaired, and
before the month of August great quantities of lime had been
burnt for the restoration of the walls of the capital.   As the
entire property of the soil and buildings, whether public or
private, or profane or sacred, was now transferred to the conqueror, he first separated a space of eight furlongs from the point
of the triangle for the establishment of his seraglio or palace.   It
is here, in the bosom of luxury, that the *Grand Signor* (as he has
been emphatically named by the Italians) appears to reign over
Europe and Asia; but his person on the shores of the Bosphorus
may not always be secure from the insults of a hostile navy.
In the new character of a mosque, the cathedral of St. Sophia
was endowed with an ample revenue, crowned with lofty
minarets, and surrounded with groves and fountains for the
devotion and refreshment of the Moslems.   The same model was
imitated in the *jami*, or royal mosques; and the first of these was
built by Mohammed himself, on the ruins of the church of the
holy apostles and the tombs of the Greek emperors.   On the
third day after the conquest the grave of Abou Ayub, or Job, who
had fallen in the first siege of the Arabs, was revealed in a vision;
and it is before the sepulchre of the martyr that the new sultans
are girded with the sword of empire.[2]   Constantinople no longer

[1] For the restitution of Constantinople and the Turkish foundations, see
Cantemir (p. 102-109), Ducas (c. 42 [p. 317, ed. Bonn]), with Thévenot,
Tournefort, and the rest of our modern travellers.   From a gigantic
picture of the greatness, population, etc., of Constantinople and the Ottoman empire (Abrégé de l'Histoire Ottomane, tom. i. p. 16-21), we may
learn that, in the year 1586, the Moslems were less numerous in the capital
than the Christians, or even the Jews.

[2] The *Turbé*, or sepulchral monument of Abou Ayub, is described and
engraved in the Tableau Générale de l'Empire Ottoman (Paris, 1787, in
large folio), a work of less use, perhaps, than magnificence (tom. i. p. 305,
306).

appertains to the Roman historian; nor shall I enumerate the civil and religious edifices that were profaned or erected by its Turkish masters: the population was speedily renewed, and before the end of September five thousand families of Anatolia and Romania had obeyed the royal mandate, which enjoined them, under pain of death, to occupy their new habitations in the capital. The throne of Mohammed was guarded by the numbers and fidelity of his Moslem subjects; but his rational policy aspired to collect the remnant of the Greeks, and they returned in crowds as soon as they were assured of their lives, their liberties, and the free exercise of their religion. In the election and investiture of a patriarch the ceremonial of the Byzantine court was revived and imitated. With a mixture of satisfaction and horror, they beheld the sultan on his throne, who delivered into the hands of Gennadius the crosier or pastoral staff, the symbol of his ecclesiastical office; who conducted the patriarch to the gate of the seraglio, presented him with a horse richly caparisoned, and directed the vizirs and bashaws to lead him to the palace which had been allotted for his residence.[1] The churches of Constantinople were shared between the two religions: their limits were marked; and, till it was infringed by Selim, the grandson of Mohammed, the Greeks [2] enjoyed above sixty years the benefit of this equal partition. Encouraged by the ministers of the divan, who wished to elude the fanaticism of the sultan, the Christian advocates presumed to allege that this division had been an act, not of generosity, but of justice; not a concession, but a compact; and that, if one-half of the city had been taken by storm, the other moiety had surrendered on the faith of a sacred capitulation. The original grant had indeed been consumed by fire; but the loss was supplied by the testimony of three aged Janizaries who remembered the transaction, and their venal oaths are of more weight in the opinion of Cantemir than the positive and unanimous consent of the history of the times.[3]

[1] Phranza (l. iii. c. 19) relates the ceremony, which has possibly been adorned in the Greek reports to each other, and to the Latins. The fact is confirmed by Emanuel Malaxus, who wrote, in vulgar Greek, the History of the Patriarchs after the taking of Constantinople, inserted in the Turco-Græcia of Crusius (l. v. p. 106-184). But the most patient reader will not believe that Mohammed adopted the Catholic form, " Sancta Trinitas quæ mihi donavit imperium te in patriarcham novæ Romæ deligit."

[2] From the Turco-Græcia of Crusius, etc., Spondanus (A.D. 1453, No. 21; 1458, No. 16) describes the slavery and domestic quarrels of the Greek church. The patriarch who succeeded Gennadius threw himself in despair into a well.

[3] Cantemir (p. 101-105) insists on the unanimous consent of the Turkish

The remaining fragments of the Greek kingdom in Europe and
Asia I shall abandon to the Turkish arms; but the final extinction of the two last dynasties [1] which have reigned in Constantinople should terminate the decline and fall of the Roman
empire in the East.   The despots of the Morea, Demetrius and
Thomas,[2] the two surviving brothers of the name of PALÆOLOGUS,
were astonished by the death of the emperor Constantine and
the ruin of the monarchy.   Hopeless of defence, they prepared,
with the noble Greeks who adhered to their fortune, to seek a
refuge in Italy, beyond the reach of the Ottoman thunder.
Their first apprehensions were dispelled by the victorious sultan,
who contented himself with a tribute of twelve thousand ducats;
and while his ambition explored the continent and the islands in
search of prey, he indulged the Morea in a respite of seven years.
But this respite was a period of grief, discord, and misery.   The
hexamilion, the rampart of the isthmus, so often raised and so
often subverted, could not long be defended by three hundred
Italian archers: the keys of Corinth were seized by the Turks;
they returned from their summer excursions with a train of
captives and spoil, and the complaints of the injured Greeks
were heard with indifference and disdain.   The Albanians, a
vagrant tribe of shepherds and robbers, filled the peninsula with
rapine and murder: the two despots implored the dangerous
and humiliating aid of a neighbouring bashaw; and when he had
quelled the revolt, his lessons inculcated the rule of their future
conduct.   Neither the ties of blood, nor the oaths which they
repeatedly pledged in the communion and before the altar, nor
the stronger pressure of necessity, could reconcile or suspend
their domestic quarrels.   They ravaged each other's patrimony
with fire and sword; the alms and succours of the West were

historians, ancient as well as modern, and argues that they would not
have violated the truth to diminish their national glory, since it is
esteemed more honourable to take a city by force than by composition.
But, 1. I doubt this consent, since he quotes no particular historian; and
the Turkish Annals of Leunclavius affirm, without exception, that
Mohammed took Constantinople *per vim* (p. 329).   2. The same argument
may be turned in favour of the Greeks of the times, who would not have
forgotten this honourable and salutary treaty.   Voltaire, as usual, prefers
the Turks to the Christians.

[1] For the genealogy and fall of the Comneni of Trebizond, see Ducange
(Fam. Byzant. p. 195); for the last Palæologi, the same accurate antiquarian (p. 244, 247, 248).   The Palæologi of Montferrat were not extinct
till the next century, but they had forgotten their Greek origin and kindred.

[2] In the worthless story of the disputes and misfortunes of the two
brothers, Phranza (l. iii. c. 21-30) is too partial on the side of Thomas;
Ducas (c. 44, 45) is too brief, and Chalcocondyles (l. viii. ix. x.) too diffuse
and digressive.

consumed in civil hostility, and their power was only exerted in
savage and arbitrary executions. The distress and revenge of
the weaker rival invoked their supreme lord; and, in the season
of maturity and revenge, Mohammed declared himself the friend
of Demetrius, and marched into the Morea with an irresistible
force. When he had taken possession of Sparta, " You are too
weak," said the sultan, " to control this turbulent province; I
will take your daughter to my bed, and you shall pass the
remainder of your life in security and honour." Demetrius
sighed and obeyed; surrendered his daughter and his castles,
followed to Adrianople his sovereign and son, and received for
his own maintenance and that of his followers a city in Thrace,
and the adjacent isles of Imbros, Lemnos, and Samothrace. He
was joined the next year by a companion of misfortune, the last
of the COMNENIAN race, who, after the taking of Constantinople
by the Latins, had founded a new empire on the coast of
the Black Sea.[1] In the progress of his Anatolian conquests,
Mohammed invested with a fleet and army the capital of David,
who presumed to style himself emperor of Trebizond;[2] and the
negotiation was comprised in a short and peremptory question.
" Will you secure your life and treasures by resigning your kingdom? or had you rather forfeit your kingdom, your treasures,
and your life? " The feeble Comnenus was subdued by his own
fears, and the example of a Musulman neighbour, the prince of
Sinope,[3] who, on a similar summons, had yielded a fortified city
with four hundred cannon and ten or twelve thousand soldiers.
The capitulation of Trebizond was faithfully performed, and
the emperor, with his family, was transported to a castle in
Romania; but on a slight suspicion of corresponding with the
Persian king, David, and the whole Comnenian race, were
sacrificed to the jealousy or avarice of the conqueror. Nor
could the name of father long protect the unfortunate Demetrius

---

[1] See the loss or conquest of Trebizond in Chalcocondyles (l. ix. p. 263-
266 [p. 494-498, ed. Bonn]), Ducas (c. 45 [p. 343, ed. Bonn]), Phranza (l. iii.
c. 27), and Cantemir (p. 107).

[2] Though Tournefort (tom. iii. lettre xvii. p. 179) speaks of Trebizond
as mal peuplée, Peyssonel, the latest and most accurate observer, can find
100,000 inhabitants (Commerce de la Mer Noire, tom. ii. p. 72; and, for
the province, p. 53-90). Its prosperity and trade are perpetually disturbed
by the factious quarrels of two *odas* of Janizaries, in one of which 30,000
Lazi are commonly enrolled (Mémoires de Tott, tom. iii. p. 16, 17).

[3] Ismael Beg, prince of Sinope or Sinople, was possessed (chiefly from
his copper-mines) of a revenue of 200,000 ducats (Chalcocond. l. ix. p. 258-
259 [p. 489, ed. Bonn]). Peyssonel (Commerce de la Mer Noire, tom. ii.
p. 100) ascribes to the modern city 60,000 inhabitants. This account
seems enormous; yet it is by trading with a people that we become ac-
quainted with their wealth and numbers.

from exile and confiscation: his abject submission moved the
pity and contempt of the sultan; his followers were transplanted
to Constantinople, and his poverty was alleviated by a pension
of fifty thousand aspers, till a monastic habit and a tardy death
released Palæologus from an earthly master. It is not easy to
pronounce whether the servitude of Demetrius, or the exile of
his brother Thomas,[1] be the most inglorious. On the conquest
of the Morea the despot escaped to Corfu, and from thence to
Italy, with some naked adherents: his name, his sufferings, and
the head of the apostle St. Andrew, entitled him to the hospitality
of the Vatican; and his misery was prolonged by a pension of
six thousand ducats from the pope and cardinals. His two sons,
Andrew and Manuel, were educated in Italy; but the eldest,
contemptible to his enemies and burdensome to his friends, was
degraded by the baseness of his life and marriage. A title was
his sole inheritance; and that inheritance he successively sold to
the kings of France and Arragon.[2] During his transient prosperity, Charles the Eighth was ambitious of joining the empire of
the East with the kingdom of Naples: in a public festival he
assumed the appellation and the purple of *Augustus ;* the Greeks
rejoiced, and the Ottoman already trembled, at the approach of
the French chivalry.[3] Manuel Palæologus, the second son, was
tempted to revisit his native country: his return might be
grateful, and could not be dangerous, to the Porte; he was maintained at Constantinople in safety and ease, and an honourable
train of Christians and Moslems attended him to the grave. If
there be some animals of so generous a nature that they refuse
to propagate in a domestic state, the last of the Imperial race
must be ascribed to an inferior kind; he accepted from the sultan's
liberality two beautiful females, and his surviving son was lost in
the habit and religion of a Turkish slave.

The importance of Constantinople was felt and magnified in its
loss: the pontificate of Nicholas the Fifth, however peaceful and

---

[1] Spondanus (from Gobelin Comment. Pii II. l. v.) relates the arrival and
reception of the despot Thomas at Rome (A.D. 1461, No. 3).

[2] By an act dated A.D. 1494, Sept. 6, and lately transmitted from the
archives of the Capitol to the royal library of Paris, the despot Andrew
Palæologus, reserving the Morea, and stipulating some private advantages,
conveys to Charles VIII. king of France the empires of Constantinople and
Trebizond (Spondanus, A.D. 1495, No. 2). M. de Foncemagne (Mém. de
l'Académie des Inscriptions, tom. xvii. p. 539-578) has bestowed a dissertation on this national title, of which he had obtained a copy from Rome.

[3] See Philippe de Comines (l. vii. c. 14), who reckons with pleasure the
number of Greeks who were prepared to rise, 60 miles of an easy navigation, eighteen days' journey from Valona to Constantinople, etc. On this
occasion the Turkish empire was saved by the policy of Venice.

prosperous, was dishonoured by the fall of the Eastern empire; and the grief and terror of the Latins revived, or seemed to revive, the old enthusiasm of the crusades. In one of the most distant countries of the West, Philip duke of Burgundy entertained, at Lisle in Flanders, an assembly of his nobles; and the pompous pageants of the feast were skilfully adapted to their fancy and feelings.[1] In the midst of the banquet a gigantic Saracen entered the hall, leading a fictitious elephant with a castle on his back: a matron in a mourning robe, the symbol of religion, was seen to issue from the castle: she deplored her oppression, and accused the slowness of her champions: the principal herald of the golden fleece advanced, bearing on his fist a live pheasant, which, according to the rites of chivalry, he presented to the duke. At this extraordinary summons, Philip, a wise and aged prince, engaged his person and powers in the holy war against the Turks: his example was imitated by the barons and knights of the assembly: they swore to God, the Virgin, the ladies, and the *pheasant;* and their particular vows were not less extravagant than the general sanction of their oath. But the performance was made to depend on some future and foreign contingency; and during twelve years, till the last hour of his life, the duke of Burgundy might be scrupulously, and perhaps sincerely, on the eve of his departure. Had every breast glowed with the same ardour; had the union of the Christians corresponded with their bravery; had every country from Sweden [2] to Naples supplied a just proportion of cavalry and infantry, of men and money, it is indeed probable that Constantinople would have been delivered, and that the Turks might have been chased beyond the Hellespont or the Euphrates. But the secretary of the emperor, who composed every epistle, and attended every meeting, Æneas Sylvius,[3] a statesman and orator, describes from his own experience the repugnant state and spirit of Christendom. " It is a body," says he, " without a head; a republic without laws or magistrates. The pope and the emperor may shine as

---

[1] See the original feast in Olivier de la Marche (Mémoires, P. i. c. 29, 30), with the abstract and observations of M. de Ste. Palaye (Mémoires sur la Chevalerie, tom. i. P. iii. p. 182-185). The peacock and the pheasant were distinguished as royal birds.

[2] It was found, by an actual enumeration, that Sweden, Gothland, and Finland contained 1,800,000 fighting men, and consequently were far more populous than at present.

[3] In the year 1454 Spondanus has given, from Æneas Sylvius, a view of the state of Europe, enriched with his own observations. That valuable annalist, and the Italian Muratori, will continue the series of events from the year 1453 to 1481, the end of Mohammed's life and of this chapter.

lofty titles, as splendid images; but *they* are unable to command and none are willing to obey: every state has a separate prince, and every prince has a separate interest. What eloquence could unite so many discordant and hostile powers under the same standard? Could they be assembled in arms, who would dare to assume the office of general? What order could be maintained?—what military discipline? Who would undertake to feed such an enormous multitude? Who would understand their various languages, or direct their stranger and incompatible manners? What mortal could reconcile the English with the French, Genoa with Arragon, the Germans with the natives of Hungary and Bohemia? If a small number enlisted in the holy war, they must be overthrown by the infidels: if many, by their own weight and confusion." Yet the same Æneas, when he was raised to the papal throne, under the name of Pius the Second, devoted his life to the prosecution of the Turkish war. In the council of Mantua he excited some sparks of a false or feeble enthusiasm; but when the pontiff appeared at Ancona, to embark in person with the troops, engagements vanished in excuses; a precise day was adjourned to an indefinite term; and his effective army consisted of some German pilgrims, whom he was obliged to disband with indulgences and alms. Regardless of futurity, his successors and the powers of Italy were involved in the schemes of present and domestic ambition; and the distance or proximity of each object determined in their eyes its apparent magnitude. A more enlarged view of their interest would have taught them to maintain a defensive and naval war against the common enemy; and the support of Scanderbeg and his brave Albanians might have prevented the subsequent invasion of the kingdom of Naples. The siege and sack of Otranto by the Turks diffused a general consternation; and Pope Sixtus was preparing to fly beyond the Alps, when the storm was instantly dispelled by the death of Mohammed the Second, in the fifty-first year of his age.[1] His lofty genius aspired to the conquest of Italy: he

[1] Besides the two annalists, the reader may consult Giannone (Istoria Civile, tom. iii. p. 449-455) for the Turkish invasion of the kingdom of Naples. For the reign and conquests of Mohammed II. I have occasionally used the Memorie Istoriche de' Monarchi Ottomanni di Giovanni Sagredo (Venezia, 1677, in 4to). In peace and war the Turks have ever engaged the attention of the republic of Venice. All her despatches and archives were open to a procurator of St. Mark, and Sagredo is not contemptible either in sense or style. Yet he too bitterly hates the infidels: he is ignorant of their language and manners; and his narrative, which allows only seventy pages to Mohammed II. (p. 69-140), becomes more copious and authentic as he approaches the years 1640 and 1644, the term of the historic labours of John Sagredo.

was possessed of a strong city and a capacious harbour; and the
same reign might have been decorated with the trophies of the
New and the Ancient Rome.[1]

CHAPTER LXIX

State of Rome from the Twelfth Century—Temporal Dominion of the
Popes—Seditions of the City—Political Heresy of Arnold of Brescia—
Restoration of the Republic—The Senators—Pride of the Romans—
Their Wars—They are deprived of the Election and Presence of the
Popes, who retire to Avignon—The Jubilee—Noble Families of
Rome—Feud of the Colonna and Ursini

In the first ages of the decline and fall of the Roman empire our
eye is invariably fixed on the royal city, which had given laws to
the fairest portion of the globe. We contemplate her fortunes,
at first with admiration, at length with pity, always with attention; and when that attention is diverted from the Capitol to
the provinces, they are considered as so many branches which
have been successively severed from the Imperial trunk. The
foundation of a second Rome, on the shores of the Bosphorus,
has compelled the historian to follow the successors of Constantine; and our curiosity has been tempted to visit the most
remote countries of Europe and Asia, to explore the causes and
the authors of the long decay of the Byzantine monarchy. By
the conquests of Justinian we have been recalled to the banks
of the Tiber, to the deliverance of the ancient metropolis; but
that deliverance was a change, or perhaps an aggravation, of
servitude. Rome had been already stripped of her trophies, her
gods, and her Cæsars; nor was the Gothic dominion more inglorious and oppressive than the tyranny of the Greeks. In the

[1] As I am now taking an everlasting farewell of the Greek empire, I shall
briefly mention the great collection of Byzantine writers whose names and
testimonies have been successively repeated in this work. The Greek
presses of Aldus and the Italians were confined to the classics of a better
age; and the first rude editions of Procopius, Agathias, Cedrenus, Zonaras,
etc., were published by the learned diligence of the Germans. The whole
Byzantine series (thirty-six volumes in folio) has gradually issued (A.D.
1648, etc.) from the royal press of the Louvre, with some collateral aid
from Rome and Leipsic; but the Venetian edition (A.D. 1729), though
cheaper and more copious, is not less inferior in correctness than in magnificence to that of Paris. The merits of the French editors are various;
but the value of Anna Comnena, Cinnamus, Villehardouin, etc., is enhanced by the historical notes of Charles du Fresne du Cange. His supple-
mental works, the Greek Glossary, the Constantinopolis Christiana, the
Familiæ Byzantinæ, diffuse a steady light over the darkness of the Lower
Empire.

eighth century of the Christian era a religious quarrel, the worship of images, provoked the Romans to assert their independence: their bishop became the temporal, as well as the spiritual, father of a free people; and of the Western empire, which was restored by Charlemagne, the title and image still decorate the singular constitution of modern Germany. The name of Rome must yet command our involuntary respect: the climate (whatsoever may be its influence) was no longer the same:[1] the purity of blood had been contaminated through a thousand channels; but the venerable aspect of her ruins, and the memory of past greatness, rekindled a spark of the national character. The darkness of the middle ages exhibits some scenes not unworthy of our notice. Nor shall I dismiss the present work till I have reviewed the state and revolutions of the ROMAN CITY, which acquiesced under the absolute dominion of the popes about the same time that Constantinople was enslaved by the Turkish arms.

In the beginning of the twelfth century,[2] the era of the first crusade, Rome was revered by the Latins as the metropolis of the world, as the throne of the pope and the emperor, who, from the eternal city, derived their title, their honours, and the right or exercise of temporal dominion. After so long an interruption it may not be useless to repeat that the successors of Charlemagne and the Othos were chosen beyond the Rhine in a national diet; but that these princes were content with the humble names of kings of Germany and Italy till they had passed the Alps and the Apennine, to seek their Imperial crown on the banks of the Tiber.[3] At some distance from the city their approach was saluted by a long procession of the clergy and people with palms and crosses; and the terrific emblems of wolves and lions, of dragons and eagles, that floated in the military

---

[1] The abbé Dubos, who, with less genius than his successor Montesquieu, has asserted and magnified the influence of climate, objects to himself the degeneracy of the Romans and Batavians.   To the first of these examples he replies, 1. That the change is less real than apparent, and that the modern Romans prudently conceal in themselves the virtues of their ancestors.   2. That the air, the soil, and the climate of Rome have suffered a great and visible alteration (Réflexions sur la Poësie et sur la Peinture, part ii. sect. 16).

[2] The reader has been so long absent from Rome that I would advise him to recollect or review the xlixth chapter of this History.

[3] The coronation of the German emperors at Rome, more especially in the eleventh century, is best represented from the original monuments by Muratori (Antiquitat. Italiæ medii Ævi, tom. i. dissertat. ii. p. 99, etc.) and Cenni (Monument. Domin. Pontif. tom. ii. diss. vi. p. 261), the latter of whom I only know from the copious extract of Schmidt (Hist. des Allemands, tom. iii. p. 255-266).

banners, represented the departed legions and cohorts of the republic. The royal oath to maintain the liberties of Rome was thrice reiterated, at the bridge, the gate, and on the stairs of the Vatican;[1] and the distribution of a customary donative feebly imitated the magnificence of the first Cæsars. In the church of St. Peter the coronation was performed by his successor:[2] the voice of God was confounded with that of the people; and the public consent was declared in the acclamations of " Long life and victory to our lord the pope! long life and victory to our lord the emperor; long life and victory to the Roman and Teutonic armies!"[3] The names of Cæsar and Augustus, the laws of Constantine and Justinian, the example of Charlemagne and Otho, established the supreme dominion of the emperors: their title and image was engraved on the papal coins;[4] and their

[1] [Gregorovius says, with regard to the thrice repeated oath, " The emperor first took an oath to the Romans at the little bridge on the Neronian field faithfully to observe the rights and usages of the city. On the day of the coronation he made his entrance through the Porta Castella close to St. Angelo, and here repeated the oath. The clergy and the corporation of Rome greeted him at the church of St. Maria Traspontina on a legendary site called the Terebenthus of Nero.—O. S.]

[2] [Gregorovius thus describes the coronation of the kings of Germany and Italy, afterwards the emperors of the Holy Roman empire: " Having arrived at the steps, the king dismounted and stooped to kiss the pope's foot, tendered the oath to be an upright protector of the Church, and was adopted by him as the son of the Church. With solemn song both king and pope entered the church of St. Maria in Turri beside the steps of St. Peter's, and here the king was formally made canon of the cathedral. He then advanced, conducted by the Lateran count of the palace and by the primicerius of the judges to the silver door of the cathedral, where he prayed, and the bishop of Albano delivered the first oration. Innumerable mystic ceremonies awaited the king in St. Peter's itself. Here a short way from the entrance was the Rota Porphyretica, a round porphyry stone inserted in the pavement, on which the pope and king knelt. The imperial candidate here made his confession of faith; the cardinal - bishop of Portus placed himself in the middle of the rota and delivered the second oration. The king was then draped in new vestments, was made a cleric, in the sacristy by the pope, was clad with a tunic dalmatica, pluviale, mitre, and sandals, and was then led to the altar of St. Maurice, whither his wife, after similar but less fatiguing ceremonies, accompanied him. The bishop of Ostia here anointed the king on the right arm and the neck, and delivered the third oration. After this followed the chief ceremony. The pope placed a ring on the king's finger, girt him with a sword, and placed the crown on his head. Then the emperor, having taken off these symbols, ministered to the pope as sub-deacon at mass. The Count Palatine afterwards removed the sandals and put on the red imperial boots, with the spurs of St. Maurice, upon him."—O. S.]

[3] Exercitui Romano et Teutonico! The latter was both seen and felt; but the former was no more than magni nominis umbra.

[4] Muratori has given the series of the papal coins (Antiquitat. tom. ii. diss. xxvii. p. 548-554). He finds only two more early than the year 800: fifty are still extant from Leo III. to Leo IX. with the addition of the reigning emperor; none remain of Gregory VII. or Urban II.; but in those of Paschal II. he seems to have renounced this badge of dependence.

jurisdiction was marked by the sword of justice, which they delivered to the præfect of the city. But every Roman prejudice was awakened by the name, the language, and the manners of a barbarian lord. The Cæsars of Saxony or Franconia were the chiefs of a feudal aristocracy; nor could they exercise the discipline of civil and military power, which alone secures the obedience of a distant people, impatient of servitude, though perhaps incapable of freedom. Once, and once only, in his life, each emperor, with an army of Teutonic vassals, descended from the Alps. I have described the peaceful order of his entry and coronation; but that order was commonly disturbed by the clamour and sedition of the Romans, who encountered their sovereign as a foreign invader: his departure was always speedy, and often shameful; and, in the absence of a long reign, his authority was insulted and his name was forgotten. The progress of independence in Germany and Italy undermined the foundations of the Imperial sovereignty, and the triumph of the popes was the deliverance of Rome.

Of her two sovereigns, the emperor had precariously reigned by the right of conquest; but the authority of the pope was founded on the soft though more solid basis of opinion and habit. The removal of a foreign influence restored and endeared the shepherd to his flock. Instead of the arbitrary or venal nomination of a German court, the vicar of Christ was freely chosen by the college of cardinals, most of whom were either natives or inhabitants of the city. The applause of the magistrates and people confirmed his election; and the ecclesiastical power that was obeyed in Sweden and Britain had been ultimately derived from the suffrage of the Romans. The same suffrage gave a prince, as well as a pontiff, to the capital. It was universally believed that Constantine had invested the popes with the temporal dominion of Rome; and the boldest civilians, the most profane sceptics, were satisfied with disputing the right of the emperor and the validity of his gift. The truth of the fact, the authenticity of his donation, was deeply rooted in the ignorance and tradition of four centuries; and the fabulous origin was lost in the real and permanent effects. The name of *Dominus*, or Lord, was inscribed on the coin of the bishops: their title was acknowledged by acclamations and oaths of allegiance, and, with the free or reluctant consent of the German Cæsars, they had long exercised a supreme or subordinate jurisdiction over the city and patrimony of St. Peter. The reign of the popes, which gratified the prejudices, was not incompatible with the liberties of Rome; and a more critical inquiry would have revealed a still nobler source of their power—the gratitude of a nation whom they had rescued from the heresy and oppression of the Greek tyrant. In an age of superstition it should seem that the union of the royal and sacerdotal characters would mutually fortify each other, and that the keys of Paradise would be the surest pledge of earthly obedience. The sanctity of the office might indeed be degraded by the personal vices of the man. But the scandals of the tenth century were obliterated by the austere and more dangerous virtues of Gregory the Seventh and his successors; and in the ambitious contests which they maintained for the rights of the church, their sufferings or their success must equally tend to increase the popular veneration. They sometimes wandered in poverty and exile, the victims of persecution; and the apostolic zeal with which they offered themselves to martyrdom must engage the favour and sympathy of every Catholic breast. And sometimes, thundering from the Vatican, they created, judged, and deposed the kings of the world; nor could the proudest Roman be disgraced by submitting to a priest whose feet were kissed and whose stirrup was held by the successors of Charlemagne.[1] Even the temporal interest of the city should have protected in peace and honour the residence of the popes, from whence a vain and lazy people derived the greatest part of their subsistence and riches. The fixed revenue of the popes was probably impaired: many of the old patrimonial estates, both in Italy and the provinces, had been invaded by sacrilegious hands; nor could the loss be compensated by the claim, rather than the possession, of the more ample gifts of Pepin and his descendants. But the Vatican and Capitol were nourished by the incessant and increasing swarms of pilgrims and suppliants: the pale of Christianity was enlarged, and the pope and cardinals were overwhelmed by the judgment of ecclesiastical and secular causes. A new jurisprudence had established in the Latin church the right and practice of appeals;[2]

---

[1] See Ducange, Gloss. mediæ et infimæ Latinitat. tom. vi. p. 364, 365, STAFFA. This homage was paid by kings to archbishops, and by vassals to their lords (Schmidt, tom. iii. p. 262); and it was the nicest policy of Rome to confound the marks of filial and of feudal subjection.

[2] The appeals from all the churches to the Roman pontiff are deplored by the zeal of St. Bernard (de Consideratione, l. iii. tom. ii. p. 431-442, edit. Mabillon, Venet. 1750) and the judgment of Fleury (Discours sur l'Hist. Ecclésiastique, iv. et vii.). But the saint, who believed in the false decretals, condemns only the abuse of these appeals; the more enlightened historian investigates the origin and rejects the principles of this new jurisprudence.

and from the North and West the bishops and abbots were invited or summoned to solicit, to complain, to accuse, or to justify, before the threshold of the apostles. A rare prodigy is once recorded, that two horses, belonging to the archbishops of Mentz and Cologne, repassed the Alps, yet laden with gold and silver;[1] but it was soon understood that the success, both of the pilgrims and clients, depended much less on the justice of their cause than on the value of their offering. The wealth and piety of these strangers were ostentatiously displayed, and their expenses, sacred or profane, circulated in various channels for the emolument of the Romans.

Such powerful motives should have firmly attached the voluntary and pious obedience of the Roman people to their spiritual and temporal father. But the operation of prejudice and interest is often disturbed by the sallies of ungovernable passion. The Indian who fells the tree that he may gather the fruit,[2] and the Arab who plunders the caravans of commerce, are actuated by the same impulse of savage nature, which overlooks the future in the present, and relinquishes for momentary rapine the long and secure possession of the most important blessings. And it was thus that the shrine of St. Peter was profaned by the thoughtless Romans, who pillaged the offerings and wounded the pilgrims, without computing the number and value of similar visits, which they prevented by their inhospitable sacrilege. Even the influence of superstition is fluctuating and precarious; and the slave, whose reason is subdued, will often be delivered by his avarice or pride. A credulous devotion for the fables and oracles of the priesthood most powerfully acts on the mind of a barbarian; yet such a mind is the least capable of preferring imagination to sense, of sacrificing to a distant motive, to an invisible, perhaps an ideal object, the appetites and interests of the present world. In the vigour of health and youth, his practice will perpetually contradict his belief, till the pressure of age, or sickness, or calamity, awakens his terrors, and compels him to satisfy the double debt of piety and remorse. I have already observed that the modern times of religious indifference

[1] Germanici . . . summarii non levatis sarcinis onusti nihilominus repatriant inviti. Nova res! quando hactenus aurum Roma refudit? Et nunc Romanorum consilio id usurpatum non credimus (Bernard de Consideratione, l. iii. c. 3, p. 437). The first words of the passage are obscure, and probably corrupt.

[2] Quand les sauvages de la Louisiane veulent avoir du fruit, ils coupent l'arbre au pied et cueillent le fruit. Voilà le gouvernement despotique (Esprit des Loix, l. v. c. 13); and passion and ignorance are always despotic.

are the most favourable to the peace and security of the clergy.
Under the reign of superstition they had much to hope from the
ignorance, and much to fear from the violence, of mankind. The
wealth, whose constant increase must have rendered them the
sole proprietors of the earth, was alternately bestowed by the
repentant father and plundered by the rapacious son: their
persons were adored or violated; and the same idol, by the hands
of the same votaries, was placed on the altar or trampled in the
dust. In the feudal system of Europe, arms were the title of
distinction and the measure of allegiance; and amidst their
tumult the still voice of law and reason was seldom heard or
obeyed. The turbulent Romans disdained the yoke and insulted
the impotence of their bishop; [1] nor would his education or character allow him to exercise, with decency or effect, the power of
the sword. The motives of his election and the frailties of his
life were exposed to their familiar observation; and proximity
must diminish the reverence which his name and his decrees impressed on a barbarous world. This difference has not escaped
the notice of our philosophic historian: " Though the name and
authority of the court of Rome were so terrible in the remote
countries of Europe, which were sunk in profound ignorance and
were entirely unacquainted with its character and conduct, the
pope was so little revered at home, that his inveterate enemies
surrounded the gates of Rome itself, and even controlled his
government in that city; and the ambassadors, who from a
distant extremity of Europe carried to him the humble, or rather
abject, submissions of the greatest potentate of the age, found
the utmost difficulty to make their way to him and to throw
themselves at his feet." [2]

Since the primitive times the wealth of the popes was exposed

[1] In a free conversation with his countryman Adrian IV., John of Salisbury accuses the avarice of the pope and clergy: Provinciarum diripiunt
spolia, ac si thesauros Crœsi studeant reparare. Sed recte cum eis agit
Altissimus, quoniam et ipsi aliis et sæpe vilissimis hominibus dati sunt in
direptionem (de Nugis Curialium, l. vi. c. 24, p. 387). In the next page he
blames the rashness and infidelity of the Romans, whom their bishops
vainly strove to conciliate by gifts instead of virtues. It is pity that
this miscellaneous writer has not given us less morality and erudition, and
more pictures of himself and the times.

[2] Hume's History of England, vol. i. p. 419. The same writer has
given us from Fitz-Stephen a singular act of cruelty perpetrated on the
clergy by Geoffrey, the father of Henry II. " When he was master of
Normandy the chapter of Seez presumed, without his consent, to proceed
to the election of a bishop: upon which he ordered all of them, with the
bishop elect, to be castrated, and made all their testicles be brought him
in a platter." Of the pain and danger they might justly complain; yet,
since they had vowed chastity he deprived them of a superfluous treasure.

to envy, their power to opposition, and their persons to violence.
But the long hostility of the mitre and the crown increased the
numbers and inflamed the passions of their enemies. The deadly
factions of the Guelphs and Ghibelines, so fatal to Italy, could
never be embraced with truth or constancy by the Romans, the
subjects and adversaries both of the bishop and emperor; but
their support was solicited by both parties, and they alternately
displayed in their banners the keys of St. Peter and the German
eagle. Gregory the Seventh who may be adored or detested as
the founder of the papal monarchy, was driven from Rome, and
died in exile at Salerno. Six-and-thirty of his successors,[1] till
their retreat to Avignon, maintained an unequal contest with the
Romans: their age and dignity were often violated; and the
churches, in the solemn rites of religion, were polluted with
sedition and murder. A repetition [2] of such capricious brutality,
without connection or design, would be tedious and disgusting;
and I shall content myself with some events of the twelfth
century which represent the state of the popes and the city.
On Holy Thursday, while Paschal officiated before the altar, he
was interrupted by the clamours of the multitude, who imperi-
ously demanded the confirmation of a favourite magistrate.
His silence exasperated their fury: his pious refusal to mingle the
affairs of earth and heaven was encountered with menaces and
oaths that he should be the cause and the witness of the public
ruin. During the festival of Easter, while the bishop and the
clergy, barefoot and in procession, visited the tombs of the
martyrs, they were twice assaulted, at the bridge of St. Angelo
and before the Capitol, with volleys of stones and darts. The
houses of his adherents were levelled with the ground: Paschal
escaped with difficulty and danger; he levied an army in the
patrimony of St. Peter, and his last days were embittered by
suffering and inflicting the calamities of civil war. The scenes
that followed the election of his successor Gelasius the Second
were still more scandalous to the church and city. Cencio
Frangipani,[3] a potent and factious baron, burst into the assembly

---

[1] From Leo IX. and Gregory VII. an authentic and contemporary series
of the lives of the popes by the Cardinal of Arragon, Pandulphus Pisanus,
Bernard Guido, etc., is inserted in the Italian Historians of Muratori
(tom. iii. P. i. p. 277-685), and has been always before my eyes.

[2] The dates of years in the margin may throughout this chapter be
understood as tacit references to the Annals of Muratori, my ordinary and
excellent guide. He uses, and indeed quotes with the freedom of a master,
his great Collection of the Italian Historians in twenty-eight volumes;
and as that treasure is in my library, I have thought it an amusement, if
not a duty, to consult the originals.

[3] I cannot refrain from transcribing the high-coloured words of Pandul-

furious and in arms: the cardinals were stripped, beaten, and trampled under foot; and he seized, without pity or respect, the vicar of Christ by the throat. Gelasius was dragged by his hair along the ground, buffeted with blows, wounded with spurs, and bound with an iron chain in the house of his brutal tyrant. An insurrection of the people delivered their bishop: the rival families opposed the violence of the Frangipani; and Cencio, who sued for pardon, repented of the failure, rather than of the guilt, of his enterprise. Not many days had elapsed when the pope was again assaulted at the altar. While his friends and enemies were engaged in a bloody contest, he escaped in his sacerdotal garments. In this unworthy flight, which excited the compassion of the Roman matrons, his attendants were scattered or unhorsed; and, in the fields behind the church of St. Peter, his successor was found alone and half dead with fear and fatigue. Shaking the dust from his feet, the *apostle* withdrew from a city in which his dignity was insulted and his person was endangered; and the vanity of sacerdotal ambition is revealed in the involuntary confession that one emperor was more tolerable than twenty.[1] These examples might suffice; but I cannot forget the sufferings of two pontiffs of the same age, the second and third of the name of Lucius. The former, as he ascended in battle-array to assault the Capitol, was struck on the temple by a stone, and expired in a few days; the latter was severely wounded in the persons of his servants. In a civil commotion several of his priests had been made prisoners; and the inhuman Romans, reserving one as a guide for his brethren, put out their eyes, crowned them with ludicrous mitres, mounted them on asses with their faces to the tail, and extorted on oath that, in this wretched condition, they should offer themselves as a lesson to the head of the church. Hope or fear, lassitude or remorse, the characters of the men and the circumstances of the times, might sometimes obtain an interval of peace and obedience; and the pope was restored with joyful acclamations to the Lateran or Vatican, from whence he had been driven with threats and

phus Pisanus (p. 384): Hoc audiens inimicus pacis atque turbator jam fatus Centius Frajapane, more draconis immanissimi sibilans, et ab imis pectoribus trahens longa suspiria, accinctus retro gladio sine more cucurrit, valvas ac fores confregit. Ecclesiam furibundus introiit, inde custode remoto papam per gulam accepit, distraxit, pugnis calcibusque percussit, et tanquam brutum animal intra limen ecclesiæ acriter calcaribus cruentavit; et latro tantum dominum per capillos et brachia, Jesû bono interim dormiente, detraxit, ad domum usque deduxit, inibi catenavit et inclusit.

[1] Ego coram Deo et Ecclesiâ dico, si unquam possibile esset, mallem unum imperatorem quam tot dominos (Vit. Gelas. II. p. 398).

violence. But the root of mischief was deep and perennial; and a momentary calm was preceded and followed by such tempests as had almost sunk the bark of St. Peter. Rome continually presented the aspect of war and discord: the churches and palaces were fortified and assaulted by the factions and families; and, after giving peace to Europe, Calistus the Second alone had resolution and power to prohibit the use of private arms in the metropolis. Among the nations who revered the apostolic throne, the tumults of Rome provoked a general indignation; and, in a letter to his disciple Eugenius the Third, St. Bernard, with the sharpness of his wit and zeal, has stigmatised the vices of the rebellious people.[1] " Who is ignorant," says the monk of Clairvaux, " of the vanity and arrogance of the Romans? a nation nursed in sedition, cruel, untractable, and scorning to obey, unless they are too feeble to resist. When they promise to serve, they aspire to reign; if they swear allegiance, they watch the opportunity of revolt; yet they vent their discontent in loud clamours if your doors or your counsels are shut against them. Dexterous in mischief, they have never learnt the science of doing good. Odious to earth and heaven, impious to God, seditious among themselves, jealous of their neighbours, inhuman to strangers, they love no one, by no one are they beloved; and while they wish to inspire fear, they live in base and continual apprehension. They will not submit: they know not how to govern; faithless to their superiors, intolerable to their equals, ungrateful to their benefactors, and alike impudent in their demands and their refusals. Lofty in promise, poor in execution: adulation and calumny, perfidy and treason, are the familiar arts of their policy." Surely this dark portrait is not coloured by the pencil of Christian charity;[2] yet the features, however harsh and ugly, express a lively resemblance of the Romans of the twelfth century.[3]

The Jews had rejected the Christ when he appeared among

---

[1] Quid tam notum seculis quam protervia et cervicositas Romanorum? Gens insueta paci, tumultui assueta, gens immitis et intractabilis usque adhuc, subdi nescia, nisi cum non valet resistere (de Considerat. l. iv. c. 2, p. 441). The saint takes breath, and then begins again: Hi, invisi terræ et cœlo, utrique injecere manus, etc. (p. 443).

[2] As a Roman citizen, Petrarch takes leave to observe that Bernard, though a saint, was a man; that he might be provoked by resentment, and possibly repent of his hasty passion, etc. (Mémoires sur la Vie de Pétrarque, tom. i. p. 330.)

[3] Baronius, in his index to the twelfth volume of his Annals, has found a fair and easy excuse. He makes two heads, of Romani Catholici and Schismatici : to the former he applies all the good, to the latter all the evil, that is told of the city.

them in a plebeian character; and the Romans might plead their
ignorance of his vicar when he assumed the pomp and pride of
a temporal sovereign. In the busy age of the crusades some
sparks of curiosity and reason were rekindled in the Western
world: the heresy of Bulgaria, the Paulician sect, was successfully transplanted into the soil of Italy and France; the Gnostic
visions were mingled with the simplicity of the Gospel; and the
enemies of the clergy reconciled their passions with their conscience, the desire of freedom with the profession of piety.[1] The
trumpet of Roman liberty was first sounded by Arnold of
Brescia,[2] whose promotion in the church was confined to the
lowest rank, and who wore the monastic habit rather as a garb
of poverty than as a uniform of obedience. His adversaries
could not deny the wit and eloquence which they severely felt:
they confess with reluctance the specious purity of his morals;
and his errors were recommended to the public by a mixture of
important and beneficial truths. In his theological studies he
had been the disciple of the famous and unfortunate Abelard,[3]
who was likewise involved in the suspicion of heresy: but the
lover of Eloisa was of a soft and flexible nature; and his ecclesiastic judges were edified and disarmed by the humility of his
repentance. From this master Arnold most probably imbibed
some metaphysical definitions of the Trinity, repugnant to the
taste of the times; his ideas of baptism and the eucharist are
loosely censured; but a *political* heresy was the source of his
fame and misfortunes. He presumed to quote the declaration
of Christ, that his kingdom is not of this world: he boldly maintained that the sword and the sceptre were intrusted to the civil
magistrate; that temporal honours and possessions were lawfully
vested in secular persons; that the abbots, the bishops, and the
pope himself, must renounce either their state or their salvation;

[1] The heresies of the twelfth century may be found in Mosheim (Institut.
Hist. Eccles. p. 419-427), who entertains a favourable opinion of Arnold
of Brescia. I have already described the sect of the Paulicians, and
followed their migration from Armenia to Thrace and Bulgaria, Italy and
France.

[2] The original pictures of Arnold of Brescia are drawn by Otho bishop
of Frisingen (Chron. l. vii. c. 31, de Gestis Frederici I. l. i. c. 27, l. ii. c. 21),
and in the third book of the Ligurinus, a poem of Gunther, who flourished
A.D. 1200, in the monastery of Paris near Basil (Fabric. Biblioth. Latin.
med. et infimæ Ætatis, tom. iii. p. 174, 175). The long passage that relates
to Arnold is produced by Guilliman (de Rebus Helveticus, l. iii. c. 5, p. 108).

[3] The wicked wit of Bayle was amused in composing, with much levity
and learning, the articles of ABELARD, FOULQUES, HELOISE, in his Dictionnaire Critique. The dispute of Abelard and St. Bernard, of scholastic and
positive divinity, is well understood by Mosheim (Institut. Hist. Eccles.
p. 412-415).

and that, after the loss of their revenues, the voluntary tithes
and oblations of the faithful would suffice, not indeed for luxury
and avarice, but for a frugal life in the exercise of spiritual labours.
During a short time the preacher was revered as a patriot; and
the discontent, or revolt, of Brescia against her bishop, was the
first fruits of his dangerous lessons. But the favour of the people
is less permanent than the resentment of the priest; and after the
heresy of Arnold had been condemned by Innocent the Second,[1]
in the general council of the Lateran, the magistrates themselves
were urged by prejudice and fear to execute the sentence of the
church. Italy could no longer afford a refuge; and the disciple
of Abelard escaped beyond the Alps, till he found a safe and
hospitable shelter in Zürich, now the first of the Swiss cantons.
From a Roman station,[2] a royal villa, a chapter of noble virgins,
Zürich had gradually increased to a free and flourishing city;
where the appeals of the Milanese were sometimes tried by the
Imperial commissaries.[3] In an age less ripe for reformation the
precursor of Zuinglius was heard with applause: a brave and
simple people imbibed, and long retained, the colour of his
opinions; and his art, or merit, seduced the bishop of Constance,
and even the pope's legate, who forgot, for his sake, the interest
of their master and their order. Their tardy zeal was quickened
by the fierce exhortations of St. Bernard;[4] and the enemy of the
church was driven by persecution to the desperate measure of
erecting his standard in Rome itself, in the face of the successor
of St. Peter.

[1] —— Damnatus ab illo
Præsule, qui numeros vetitum contingere nostros
Nomen ab *innocuâ* ducit laudabile vitâ.

We may applaud the dexterity and correctness of Ligurinus, who turns the
unpoetical name of Innocent II. into a compliment.

[2] A Roman inscription of Statio Turicensis has been found at Zürich
(D'Anville, Notice de l'Ancienne Gaul, p. 642-644); but it is without sufficient warrant that the city and canton have usurped, and even monopolised,
the names of Tigurum and Pagus Tigurinus.

[3] Guilliman (de Rebus Helveticis, l. iii. c. 5, p. 106) recapitulates the
donation (A.D. 833) of the emperor Lewis the Pious to his daughter the
Abbess Hildegardis. Curtim nostram Turegum in ducatû Alamanniæ
in pago Durgaugensi, with villages, woods, meadows, waters, slaves,
churches, etc.—a noble gift. Charles the Bald gave the jus monetæ, the
city was walled under Otho I., and the line of the bishop of Frisingen,

Nobile Turegum multarum copiâ rerum,

is repeated with pleasure by the antiquaries of Zürich.

[4] Bernard, Epistol. cxcv. cxcvi. tom. i. p. 187-190. Amidst his invectives he drops a precious acknowledgment, qui, utinam quam sanæ esset
doctrinæ quam districtæ est vitæ. He owns that Arnold would be a valuable acquisition for the church.

Yet the courage of Arnold was not devoid of discretion: he
was protected, and had perhaps been invited, by the nobles and
people; and in the service of freedom his eloquence thundered
over the seven hills. Blending in the same discourse the texts
of Livy and St. Paul, uniting the motives of Gospel and of
classic enthusiasm, he admonished the Romans how strangely
their patience and the vices of the clergy had degenerated from
the primitive times of the church and the city. He exhorted
them to assert the inalienable rights of men and Christians; to
restore the laws and magistrates of the republic; to respect the
name of the emperor; but to confine their shepherd to the
spiritual government of his flock.[1] Nor could his spiritual
government escape the censure and control of the reformer;
and the inferior clergy were taught by his lessons to resist the
cardinals, who had usurped a despotic command over the
twenty-eight regions or parishes of Rome.[2] The revolution was
not accomplished without rapine and violence, the effusion of
blood and the demolition of houses: the victorious faction was
enriched with the spoils of the clergy and the adverse nobles.
Arnold of Brescia enjoyed, or deplored, the effects of his mission:
his reign continued above ten years, while two popes, Innocent
the Second and Anastasius the Fourth, either trembled in the
Vatican or wandered as exiles in the adjacent cities. They were
succeeded by a more vigorous and fortunate pontiff, Adrian the
Fourth,[3] the only Englishman who has ascended the throne of
St. Peter; and whose merit emerged from the mean condition of
a monk, and almost a beggar, in the monastery of St. Albans.
On the first provocation, of a cardinal killed or wounded in the
streets, he cast an interdict on the guilty people: and from
Christmas to Easter Rome was deprived of the real or imaginary
comforts of religious worship. The Romans had despised their
temporal prince; they submitted with grief and terror to the
censures of their spiritual father; their guilt was expiated by

[1] He advised the Romans,

> Consiliis armisque sua moderamina summa
> Arbitrio tractare suo: nil juris in hâc re
> Pontifici summo, modicum concedere regi
> Suadebat populo. Sic læsâ stultus utrâque
> Majestate, reum geminæ se fecerat aulæ.

Nor is the poetry of Gunther different from the prose of Otho.

[2] See Baronius (A.D. 1148, No. 38, 39) from the Vatican MSS. He
loudly condemns Arnold (A.D. 1141, No. 3) as the father of the political
heretics, whose influence then hurt him in France.

[3] The English reader may consult the Biographia Britannica, ADRIAN
IV.; but our own writers have added nothing to the fame or merits of
their countryman.

penance, and the banishment of the seditious preacher was the price of their absolution. But the revenge of Adrian was yet unsatisfied, and the approaching coronation of Frederic Barbarossa was fatal to the bold reformer, who had offended, though not in an equal degree, the heads of the church and state. In their interview at Viterbo, the pope represented to the emperor the furious, ungovernable spirit of the Romans: the insults, the injuries, the fears, to which his person and his clergy were continually exposed; and the pernicious tendency of the heresy of Arnold, which must subvert the principles of civil, as well as ecclesiastical, subordination. Frederic was convinced by these arguments, or tempted by the desire of the Imperial crown; in the balance of ambition the innocence or life of an individual is of small account; and their common enemy was sacrificed to a moment of political concord. After his retreat from Rome, Arnold had been protected by the viscounts of Campania, from whom he was extorted by the power of Cæsar: the præfect of the city pronounced his sentence: the martyr of freedom was burnt alive in the presence of a careless and ungrateful people; and his ashes were cast into the Tiber, lest the heretics should collect and worship the relics of their master.[1] The clergy triumphed in his death: with his ashes his sect was dispersed; his memory still lived in the minds of the Romans. From his school they had probably derived a new article of faith, that the metropolis of the Catholic church is exempt from the penalties of excommunication and interdict. Their bishops might argue that the supreme jurisdiction, which they exercised over kings and nations, more specially embraced the city and diocese of the prince of the apostles. But they preached to the winds, and the same principle that weakened the effect, must temper the abuse, of the thunders of the Vatican.

The love of ancient freedom has encouraged a belief that as early as the tenth century, in their first struggles against the Saxon Othos, the commonwealth was vindicated and restored by the senate and people of Rome; that two consuls were annually elected among the nobles, and that ten or twelve plebeian magistrates revived the name and office of the tribunes of the commons.[2] But this venerable structure disappears before the

---

[1] Besides the historian and poet already quoted, the last adventures of Arnold are related by the biographer of Adrian IV. (Muratori, Script. Rerum Ital. tom. iii. P. i. p. 441, 442.)

[2] Ducange (Gloss. Latinitatis mediæ et infimæ Ætatis, DECARCHONES, tom. ii. p. 726) gives me a quotation from Blondus (Decad. ii. l. ii.): Duo consules ex nobilitate quotannis fiebant, qui ad vetustum consulum

light of criticism. In the darkness of the middle ages the
appellations of senators, of consuls, of the sons of consuls, may
sometimes be discovered.[1] They were bestowed by the emperors,
or assumed by the most powerful citizens, to denote their rank,
their honours,[2] and perhaps the claim of a pure and patrician
descent: but they float on the surface, without a series or a
substance, the titles of men, not the orders of government;[3]
and it is only from the year of Christ one thousand one hundred
and forty-four that the establishment of the senate is dated, as
a glorious era, in the acts of the city. A new constitution was
hastily framed by private ambition or popular enthusiasm; nor
could Rome, in the twelfth century, produce an antiquary to
explain, or a legislator to restore, the harmony and proportions
of the ancient model. The assembly of a free, or an armed,
people, will ever speak in loud and weighty acclamations. But
the regular distribution of the thirty-five tribes, the nice balance
of the wealth and numbers of the centuries, the debates of the
adverse orators, and the slow operation of votes and ballots,
could not easily be adapted by a blind multitude, ignorant of the
arts, and insensible of the benefits, of legal government. It was
proposed by Arnold to revive and discriminate the equestrian
order; but what could be the motive or measure of such distinction?[4] The pecuniary qualification of the knights must have

exemplar summæ rerum præessent. And in Sigonius (de Regno Italiæ,
l. vi. Opp. tom. ii. p. 400) I read of the consuls and tribunes of the tenth
century. Both Blondus and even Sigonius too freely copied the classic
method of supplying from reason or fancy the deficiency of records.

[1] In the panegyric of Berengarius (Muratori, Script. Rer. Ital. tom. ii.
P. i. p. 408) a Roman is mentioned as consulis natus in the beginning of the
tenth century. Muratori (Dissert. v.) discovers, in the years 952 and 956,
Gratianus in Dei nomine consul et dux, Georgius consul et dux; and in
1015, Romanus, brother of Gregory VIII., proudly, but vaguely, styles
himself consul et dux et omnium Romanorum senator.

[2] As late as the tenth century the Greek emperors conferred on the dukes
of Venice, Naples, Amalphi, etc., the title of ὕπατος or consuls (see Chron.
Sagornini, *passim*); and the successors of Charlemagne would not abdicate
any of their prerogative. But in general the names of *consul* and *senator*,
which may be found among the French and Germans, signify no more
than count and lord (*Signeur*, Ducange, Glossar.). The monkish writers
are often ambitious of fine classic words.

[3] The most constitutional form is a diploma of Otho III. (A.D. 998),
Consulibus senatûs populique Romani; but the act is probably spurious.
At the coronation of Henry I., A.D. 1014, the historian Dithmar (apud
Muratori, Dissert. xxiii.) describes him, a senatoribus duodecim vallatum,
quorum sex rasi barbâ, alii prolixâ, mystice incedebant cum baculis. The
senate is mentioned in the panegyric of Berengarius (p. 406).

[4] In the ancient Rome the equestrian order was not ranked with the
senate and people as a third branch of the republic till the consulship of
Cicero, who assumes the merit of the establishment (Plin. Hist. Natur.
xxxiii. 3 [8]; Beaufort, République Romaine, tom. i. p. 144-155).

been reduced to the poverty of the times: those times no longer
required their civil functions of judges and farmers of the revenue;
and their primitive duty, their military service on horseback, was
more nobly supplied by feudal tenures and the spirit of chivalry.
The jurisprudence of the republic was useless and unknown; the
nations and families of Italy who lived under the Roman and
barbaric laws were insensibly mingled in a common mass; and
some faint tradition, some imperfect fragments, preserved the
memory of the Code and Pandects of Justinian. With their
liberty the Romans might doubtless have restored the appellation and office of consuls, had they not disdained a title so
promiscuously adopted in the Italian cities, that it has finally
settled on the humble station of the agents of commerce in a
foreign land. But the rights of the tribunes, the formidable
word that arrested the public counsels, suppose or must produce
a legitimate democracy. The old patricians were the subjects,
the modern barons the tyrants, of the state; nor would the
enemies of peace and order, who insulted the vicar of Christ,
have long respected the unarmed sanctity of a plebeian magistrate.[1]

In the revolution of the twelfth century, which gave a new
existence and era to Rome, we may observe the real and important events that marked or confirmed her political independence.
I. The Capitoline hill, one of her seven eminences,[2] is about four
hundred yards in length, and two hundred in breadth. A flight
of a hundred steps led to the summit of the Tarpeian rock;
and far steeper was the ascent before the declivities had been

---

[1] The republican plan of Arnold of Brescia is thus stated by Gunther:—

> Quin etiam titulos urbis renovare vetustos;
> Nomine plebeio secernere nomen equestre,
> Jura tribunorum, sanctum reparare senatum,
> Et senio fessas mutasque reponere leges.
> Lapsa ruinosis, et adhuc pendentia muris
> Reddere primævo Capitolia prisca nitori.

But of these reformations some were no more than ideas, others no more
than words.

[2] After many disputes among the antiquaries of Rome, it seems determined that the summit of the Capitoline hill next the river is strictly the
Mons Tarpeius, the Arx; and that on the other summit, the church and
convent of Araceli, the barefoot friars of St. Francis occupy the temple of
Jupiter (Nardini, Roma Antica, l. v. c. 11-16).
[This view is not correct. All the chief modern writers on Rome and
its topography maintain that the Arx was the north-eastern summit, now
occupied by the church of St. Maria in Aracoeli; while both the Tarpeian
Rock and the Temple of Jupiter were on the western height. The site of
the temple or the Capitolium is now occupied by the Palazzo Caffarelli, in
the gardens of which excavations have been carried on.—O. S.]

smoothed and the precipices filled by the ruins of fallen edifices.
From the earliest ages the Capitol had been used as a temple in
peace, a fortress in war: after the loss of the city it maintained
a siege against the victorious Gauls; and the sanctuary of the
empire was occupied, assaulted, and burnt, in the civil wars
of Vitellius and Vespasian.[1] The temples of Jupiter and his
kindred deities had crumbled into dust; their place was supplied
by monasteries and houses; and the solid walls, the long and
shelving porticoes, were decayed or ruined by the lapse of time.
It was the first act of the Romans, an act of freedom, to restore
the strength, though not the beauty, of the Capitol; to fortify
the seat of their arms and counsels; and as often as they ascended
the hill, the coldest minds must have glowed with the remembrance of their ancestors.   II. The first Cæsars had been invested
with the exclusive coinage of the gold and silver; to the senate
they abandoned the baser metal of bronze or copper: [2] the
emblems and legends were inscribed on a more ample field by
the genius of flattery; and the prince was relieved from the care
of celebrating his own virtues.   The successors of Diocletian
despised even the flattery of the senate: their royal officers at
Rome, and in the provinces, assumed the sole direction of the
mint; and the same prerogative was inherited by the Gothic
kings of Italy, and the long series of the Greek, the French, and
the German dynasties.   After an abdication of eight hundred
years the Roman senate asserted this honourable and lucrative
privilege; which was tacitly renounced by the popes, from
Paschal the Second to the establishment of their residence
beyond the Alps.   Some of these republican coins of the twelfth
and thirteenth centuries are shown in the cabinets of the curious.
On one of these, a gold medal, Christ is depictured holding in his
left hand a book with this inscription: " THE VOW OF THE
ROMAN SENATE AND PEOPLE: ROME THE CAPITAL OF THE
WORLD; " on the reverse, St. Peter delivering a banner to a
kneeling senator in his cap and gown, with the name and arms of
his family impressed on a shield.[3]   III. With the empire, the

---

[1] Tacit. Hist. iii. 69, 70.

[2] This partition of the noble and baser metals between the emperor and
senate must however be adopted, not as a positive fact, but as the probable
opinion of the best antiquaries (see the Science des Médailles of the Père
Joubert, tom. ii. p. 208-211, in the improved and scarce edition of the
Baron de la Bastie).

[3] In his twenty-seventh dissertation on the Antiquities of Italy (tom. ii.
p. 559-569), Muratori exhibits a series of the senatorian coins, which bore
the obscure names of *Affortiati, Infortiati, Provisini, Paparini*. During
this period, all the popes, without excepting Boniface VIII., abstained

præfect of the city had declined to a municipal officer; yet he
still exercised in the last appeal the civil and criminal jurisdiction; and a drawn sword, which he received from the successors of Otho, was the mode of his investiture and the emblem
of his functions.[1] The dignity was confined to the noble families
of Rome: the choice of the people was ratified by the pope; but
a triple oath of fidelity must have often embarrassed præfect
in the conflict of adverse duties.[2] A servant, in whom they
possessed but a third share, was dismissed by the independent
Romans: in his place they elected a patrician; but this title,
which Charlemagne had not disdained, was too lofty for a
citizen or a subject; and after the first fervour of rebellion, they
consented without reluctance to the restoration of the præfect.
About fifty years after this event, Innocent the Third, the most
ambitious or at least the most fortunate of the pontiffs, delivered
the Romans and himself from this badge of foreign dominion:
he invested the præfect with a banner instead of a sword, and
absolved him from all dependence of oaths or service to the
German emperors.[3] In his place an ecclesiastic, a present or
future cardinal, was named by the pope to the civil government
of Rome; but his jurisdiction has been reduced to a narrow
compass; and in the days of freedom the right or exercise was
derived from the senate and people. IV. After the revival of
the senate,[4] the conscript fathers (if I may use the expression)
were invested with the legislative and executive power; but
their views seldom reached beyond the present day; and that
day was most frequently disturbed by violence and tumult. In
its utmost plenitude the order or assembly consisted of fifty-six

from the right of coining, which was resumed by his successor Benedict
XI. and regularly exercised in the court of Avignon.

[1] A German historian, Gerard of Reicherspeg (in Baluz. Miscell. tom. v.
p. 64, apud Schmidt, Hist. des Allemands, tom. iii. p. 265), thus describes
the constitution of Rome in the eleventh century: Grandiora urbis et
orbis negotia spectant ad Romanum pontificem itemque ad Romanum
Imperatorem, sive illius vicarium urbis præfectum, qui de suâ dignitate
respicit utrumque, videlicet dominum papam cui facit hominium, et
dominum imperatorem a quo accipit suæ potestatis insigne, scilicet
gladium exertum.

[2] The words of a contemporary writer (Pandulph. Pisan. in Vit. Paschal.
II. p. 357, 358) describe the election and oath of the præfect in 1118, incon-
sultis patribus . . . loca præfectoria . . . Laudes præfectoriæ . . . comi-
tiorum applausum . . . juraturum populo in ambonem sublevant . . .
confirmari eum in urbe præfectum petunt.

[3] Urbis præfectum ad ligiam fidelitatem recepit, et per mantum quod illi
donavit de præfecturâ eum publice investivit, qui usque ad id tempus jura-
mento fidelitatis imperatori fuit obligatus et ab eo præfecturæ tenuit
honorem (Gesta Innocent. III. in Muratori, tom. iii. P. i. p. 487).

[4] See Otho Frising. Chron. vii. 31, de Gest. Frederic. I., l. i. c. 27.

senators,[1] the most eminent of whom were distinguished by the title of counsellors: they were nominated, perhaps annually, by the people; and a previous choice of their electors, ten persons in each region, or parish, might afford a basis for a free and permanent constitution. The popes, who in this tempest submitted rather to bend than to break, confirmed by treaty the establishment and privileges of the senate, and expected from time, peace, and religion, the restoration of their government. The motives of public and private interest might sometimes draw from the Romans an occasional and temporary sacrifice of their claims; and they renewed their oath of allegiance to the successor of St. Peter and Constantine, the lawful head of the church and the republic.[2]

The union and vigour of a public council was dissolved in a lawless city; and the Romans soon adopted a more strong and simple mode of administration. They condensed the name and authority of the senate in a single magistrate or two colleagues; and as they were changed at the end of a year, or of six months, the greatness of the trust was compensated by the shortness of the term. But in this transient reign the senators of Rome indulged their avarice and ambition: their justice was perverted by the interest of their family and faction; and as they punished only their enemies, they were obeyed only by their adherents. Anarchy, no longer tempered by the pastoral care of their bishop, admonished the Romans that they were incapable of governing themselves; and they sought abroad those blessings which they were hopeless of finding at home. In the same age, and from the same motives, most of the Italian republics were prompted to embrace a measure which, however strange it may seem, was adapted to their situation, and productive of the most salutary effects.[3] They chose, in some foreign but friendly

---

[1] Our countryman, Roger Hoveden, speaks of the single senators, of the *Capuzzi* family, etc., quorum temporibus melius regebatur Roma quam nunc (A.D. 1194) est temporibus lvi. senatorum (Ducange, Gloss. tom. vi. p. 191, SENATORES).

[2] Muratori (dissert. xlii. tom. iii. p. 785-788) has published an original treaty: Concordia inter D. nostrum papam Clementem III. et senatores populi Romani super regalibus et aliis dignitatibus urbis, etc., anno 44° senatûs. The senate speaks, and speaks with authority: Reddimus ad præsens . . . habebimus . . . dabitis presbyteria . . . jurabimus pacem et fidelitatem, etc. A chartula de Tenimentis Tusculani, dated in the forty-seventh year of the same era, and confirmed decreto amplissimi ordinis senatûs, acclamatione P. R. publice Capitolio consistentis. It is there we find the difference of senatores consiliarii and simple senators (Muratori, dissert. xlii. tom. iii. p. 787 789).

[3] Muratori (dissert. xlv. tom. iv. p. 64-92) has fully explained this mode of government; and the *Occulus Pastoralis*, which he has given at the end, is a treatise or sermon on the duties of these foreign magistrates.

city, an impartial magistrate of noble birth and unblemished
character, a soldier and a statesman, recommended by the voice
of fame and his country, to whom they delegated for a time
the supreme administration of peace and war. The compact
between the governor and the governed was sealed with oaths
and subscriptions; and the duration of his power, the measure
of his stipend, the nature of their mutual obligations, were
defined with scrupulous precision. They swore to obey him as
their lawful superior: he pledged his faith to unite the indifference of a stranger with the zeal of a patriot. At his choice,
four or six knights and civilians, his assessors in arms and
justice, attended the *Podestà*,[1] who maintained at his own
expense a decent retinue of servants and horses: his wife, his
son, his brother, who might bias the affections of the judge,
were left behind: during the exercise of his office he was not
permitted to purchase land, to contract an alliance, or even to
accept an invitation in the house of a citizen; nor could he
honourably depart till he had satisfied the complaints that
might be urged against his government.

It was thus, about the middle of the thirteenth century, that
the Romans called from Bologna the senator Brancaleone,[2]
whose fame and merit have been rescued from oblivion by the
pen of an English historian. A just anxiety for his reputation,
a clear foresight of the difficulties of the task, had engaged him
to refuse the honour of their choice: the statutes of Rome were
suspended, and his office prolonged to the term of three years.
By the guilty and licentious he was accused as cruel; by the
clergy he was suspected as partial; but the friends of peace
and order applauded the firm and upright magistrate by whom
those blessings were restored. No criminals were so powerful
as to brave, so obscure as to elude, the justice of the senator.
By his sentence two nobles of the Annibaldi family were executed
on a gibbet; and he inexorably demolished, in the city and
neighbourhood, one hundred and forty towers, the strong
shelters of rapine and mischief. The bishop, as a simple

---

[1] In the Latin writers, at least of the silver age, the title of *Potestas* was
transferred from the office to the magistrate:—

    Hujus qui trahitur prætextam sumere mavis;
    An Fidenarum Gabiorumque esse *Potestas*.

                 (Juvenal. Satir. x. 99.)

[2] See the life and death of Brancaleone, in the Historia Major of Matthew
Paris, p. 741, 757, 792, 797, 799, 810, 823, 833, 836, 840. The multitude
of pilgrims and suitors connected Rome and St. Alban's, and the resentment of the English clergy prompted them to rejoice whenever the popes
were humbled and oppressed.

bishop, was compelled to reside in his diocese; and the standard of Brancaleone was displayed in the field with terror and effect. His services were repaid by the ingratitude of a people unworthy of the happiness which they enjoyed. By the public robbers, whom he had provoked for their sake, the Romans were excited to depose and imprison their benefactor; nor would his life have been spared if Bologna had not possessed a pledge for his safety. Before his departure the prudent senator had required the exchange of thirty hostages of the noblest families of Rome: on the news of his danger, and at the prayer of his wife, they were more strictly guarded; and Bologna, in the cause of honour, sustained the thunders of a papal interdict. This generous resistance allowed the Romans to compare the present with the past; and Brancaleone was conducted from the prison to the Capitol amidst the acclamations of a repentant people. The remainder of his government was firm and fortunate; and as soon as envy was appeased by death, his head, enclosed in a precious vase, was deposited on a lofty column of marble.[1]

The impotence of reason and virtue recommended in Italy a more effectual choice: instead of a private citizen, to whom they yielded a voluntary and precarious obedience, the Romans elected for their senator some prince of independent power, who could defend them from their enemies and themselves. Charles of Anjou and Provence, the most ambitious and warlike monarch of the age, accepted at the same time the kingdom of Naples from the pope and the office of senator from the Roman people.[2] As he passed through the city in his road to victory he received their oath of allegiance, lodged in the Lateran palace, and smoothed in a short visit the harsh features of his despotic character. Yet even Charles was exposed to the inconstancy of the people, who saluted with the same acclamations the passage of his rival, the unfortunate Conradin; and a powerful avenger, who reigned in the Capitol, alarmed the fears and jealousy of

[1] Matthew Paris thus ends his account: Caput vero ipsius Brancaleonis in vase pretioso super marmoream columnam collocatum, in signum sui valoris et probitatis, quasi reliquias, superstitiose nimis et pompose sustulerunt. Fuerat enim superborum potentum et malefactorum urbis malleus et exstirpator, et populi protector et defensor, veritatis et justitiæ imitator et amator (p. 840). A biographer of Innocent IV. (Muratori, Script. tom. iii. P. i. p. 591, 592) draws a less favourable portrait of this Ghibeline senator.

[2] The election of Charles of Anjou to the office of perpetual senator of Rome is mentioned by the historians in the eighth vol ume of the Collection of Muratori, by Nicholas de Jamsilla (p. 592), the monk of Padua (p. 724), Sabas Malaspina (l. ii. c. 9, p. 808), and Ricordano Malespini (c. 177, p. 999).

the popes. The absolute term of his life was superseded by a renewal every third year; and the enmity of Nicholas the Third obliged the Sicilian king to abdicate the government of Rome. In his bull, a perpetual law, the imperious pontiff asserts the truth, validity, and use of the donation of Constantine, not less essential to the peace of the city than to the independence of the church; establishes the annual election of the senator, and formally disqualifies all emperors, kings, princes, and persons of an eminent and conspicuous rank.[1] This prohibitory clause was repealed in his own behalf by Martin the Fourth, who humbly solicited the suffrage of the Romans. In the presence, and by the authority, of the people two electors conferred, not on the pope, but on the noble and faithful Martin, the dignity of senator and the supreme administration of the republic,[2] to hold during his natural life, and to exercise at pleasure by himself or his deputies. About fifty years afterwards the same title was granted to the emperor Lewis of Bavaria; and the liberty of Rome was acknowledged by her two sovereigns, who accepted a municipal office in the government of their own metropolis.

In the first moments of rebellion, when Arnold of Brescia had inflamed their minds against the church, the Romans artfully laboured to conciliate the favour of the empire, and to recommend their merit and services in the cause of Cæsar. The style of their ambassadors to Conrad the Third and Frederic the First is a mixture of flattery and pride, the tradition and the ignorance of their own history.[3] After some complaint of his silence and neglect, they exhort the former of these princes to pass the Alps, and assume from their hands the Imperial crown. "We beseech your majesty not to disdain the humility of your sons and vassals, not to listen to the accusations of our common enemies, who calumniate the senate as hostile to your throne, who sow the seeds of discord that they may reap the harvest of destruction.

---

[1] The high-sounding bull of Nicholas III., which founds his temporal sovereignty on the donation of Constantine, is still extant; and as it has been inserted by Boniface VIII. in the *Sexte* of the Decretals, it must be received by the Catholics, or at least by the Papists, as a sacred and perpetual law.

[2] I am indebted to Fleury (Hist. Ecclés. tom. xviii. p. 306) for an extract of this Roman act, which he has taken from the Ecclesiastical Annals of Odericus Raynaldus, A.D. 1281, No. 14, 15.

[3] These letters and speeches are preserved by Otho bishop of Frisingen (Fabric. Biblioth. Lat. med. et infim. tom. v. p. 186, 187), perhaps the noblest of historians: he was son of Leopold marquis of Austria; his mother, Agnes, was daughter of the emperor Henry IV.; and he was half-brother and uncle to Conrad III. and Frederic I. He has left, in seven books, a Chronicle of the Times; in two, the Gesta Frederici I., the last of which is inserted in the sixth volume of Muratori's Historians.

The pope and the *Sicilian* are united in an impious league to oppose *our* liberty and *your* coronation. With the blessing of God our zeal and courage has hitherto defeated their attempts. Of their powerful and factious adherents, more especially the Frangipani, we have taken by assault the houses and turrets: some of these are occupied by our troops, and some are levelled with the ground. The Milvian bridge, which they had broken, is restored and fortified for your safe passage, and your army may enter the city without being annoyed from the castle of St. Angelo. All that we have done, and all that we design, is for your honour and service, in the loyal hope that you will speedily appear in person to vindicate those rights which have been invaded by the clergy, to revive the dignity of the empire, and to surpass the fame and glory of your predecessors. May you fix your residence in Rome, the capital of the world; give laws to Italy and the Teutonic kingdom; and imitate the example of Constantine and Justinian,[1] who, by the vigour of the senate and people, obtained the sceptre of the earth." [2] But these splendid and fallacious wishes were not cherished by Conrad the Franconian, whose eyes were fixed on the Holy Land, and who died without visiting Rome soon after his return from the Holy Land.

His nephew and successor, Frederic Barbarossa, was more ambitious of the Imperial crown; nor had any of the successors of Otho acquired such absolute sway over the kingdom of Italy. Surrounded by his ecclesiastical and secular princes, he gave audience in his camp at Sutri to the ambassadors of Rome, who thus addressed him in a free and florid oration: " Incline your ear to the queen of cities; approach with a peaceful and friendly mind the precincts of Rome, which has cast away the yoke of the clergy, and is impatient to crown her legitimate emperor. Under your auspicious influence may the primitive times be restored. Assert the prerogatives of the eternal city, and reduce under her monarchy the insolence of the world. You are not ignorant that in former ages, by the wisdom of the senate, by the valour and discipline of the equestrian order, she extended her victorious arms to the East and West, beyond the Alps, and over the islands of the ocean. By our sins, in the absence of our princes, the noble institution of the senate has sunk in oblivion;

---

[1] We desire (said the ignorant Romans) to restore the empire in eum statum, quo fuit tempore Constantini et Justiniani, qui totum orbem vigore senatûs et populi Romani suis tenuere manibus.

[2] Otho Frising. de Gestis Frederici I., l. i. c. 28, p. 662-664.

and with our prudence our strength has likewise decreased. We have revived the senate and the equestrian order: the counsels of the one, the arms of the other, will be devoted to your person and the service of the empire. Do you not hear the language of the Roman matron? You were a guest, I have adopted you as a citizen; a Transalpine stranger, I have elected you for my sovereign,[1] and given you myself, and all that is mine. Your first and most sacred duty is to swear and subscribe that you will shed your blood for the republic; that you will maintain in peace and justice the laws of the city and the charters of your predecessors; and that you will reward with five thousand pounds of silver the faithful senators who shall proclaim your titles in the Capitol. With the name assume the character of Augustus." The flowers of Latin rhetoric were not yet exhausted; but Frederic, impatient of their vanity, interrupted the orators in the high tone of royalty and conquest. " Famous indeed have been the fortitude and wisdom of the ancient Romans; but your speech is not seasoned with wisdom, and I could wish that fortitude were conspicuous in your actions. Like all sublunary things, Rome has felt the vicissitudes of time and fortune. Your noblest families were translated to the East, to the royal city of Constantine; and the remains of your strength and freedom have long since been exhausted by the Greeks and Franks. Are you desirous of beholding the ancient glory of Rome, the gravity of the senate, the spirit of the knights, the discipline of the camp, the valour of the legions? you will find them in the German republic. It is not empire, naked and alone; the ornaments and virtues of empire have likewise migrated beyond the Alps to a more deserving people:[2] they will be employed in your defence, but they claim your obedience. You pretend that myself or my predecessors have been invited by the Romans: you mistake the word; they were not invited, they were implored. From its foreign and domestic tyrants the city was rescued by Charlemagne and Otho, whose ashes repose in our country; and their dominion was the price of your deliverance. Under that dominion your ancestors lived and died. I claim by the right of inheritance and possession, and who shall dare to extort you from my hands? Is the hand of

---

[1] Hospes eras, civem feci. Advena fuisti ex Transalpinis partibus; principem constitui.

[2] Non cessit nobis nudum imperium, virtute sua amictum venit, ornamenta sua secum traxit. Penes nos sunt consules tui, etc. Cicero or Livy would not have rejected these images, the eloquence of a barbarian born and educated in the Hercynian forest.

the Franks [1] and Germans enfeebled by age? Am I vanquished? Am I a captive? Am I not encompassed with the banners of a potent and invincible army? You impose conditions on your master; you require oaths: if the conditions are just, an oath is superfluous; if unjust, it is criminal. Can you doubt my equity? It is extended to the meanest of my subjects. Will not my sword be unsheathed in the defence of the Capitol? By that sword the northern kingdom of Denmark has been restored to the Roman empire. You prescribe the measure and the objects of my bounty, which flows in a copious but a voluntary stream. All will be given to patient merit; all will be denied to rude importunity." [2] Neither the emperor nor the senate could maintain these lofty pretensions of dominion and liberty. United with the pope, and suspicious of the Romans, Frederic continued his march to the Vatican; his coronation was disturbed by a sally from the Capitol; and if the numbers and valour of the Germans prevailed in the bloody conflict, he could not safely encamp in the presence of a city of which he styled himself the sovereign. About twelve years afterwards he besieged Rome, to seat an antipope in the chair of St. Peter; and twelve Pisan galleys were introduced into the Tiber; but the senate and people were saved by the arts of negotiation and the progress of disease; nor did Frederic or his successors reiterate the hostile attempt. Their laborious reigns were exercised by the popes, the crusades, and the independence of Lombardy and Germany: they courted the alliance of the Romans; and Frederic the Second offered in the Capitol the great standard, the *Caroccio* of Milan.[3] After the extinction of

[1] Otho of Frisingen, who surely understood the language of the court and diet of Germany, speaks of the Franks in the twelfth century as the reigning nation (Proceres Franci, equites Franci, manus Francorum): he adds, however, the epithet of *Teutonici*.

[2] Otho Frising. de Gestis Frederici I., l. ii. c. 22, p. 720-723. These original and authentic acts I have translated and abridged with freedom, yet with fidelity.

[3] From the chronicles of Ricobaldo and Francis Pipin, Muratori (dissert. xxvi. tom. ii. p. 492) has transcribed this curious fact with the doggerel verses that accompanied the gift:—

Ave decus orbis, ave! victus tibi destinor, ave!
Currus ab Augusto Frederico Cæsare justo.
Væ Mediolanum! jam sentis spernere vanum
Imperii vires, proprias tibi tollere vires.
Ergo triumphorum urbs potes memor esse priorum
Quos tibi mittebant reges qui bella gerebant.

Ne si dee tacere (I now use the Italian Dissertations, tom. i. p. 444) che nell' anno 1727, una copia desso Caroccio in marmo dianzi ignoto si scopri, nel Campidoglio, presso alle carcere di quel luogo, dove Sisto V. l' avea falto rinchiudere. Stava esso posto sopra quatro colonne di marmo fino colla sequente inscrizione, etc.; to the same purpose as the old inscription

the house of Swabia, they were banished beyond the Alps; and
their last coronations betrayed the impotence and poverty of the
Teutonic Cæsars.[1]

Under the reign of Hadrian, when the empire extended from
the Euphrates to the ocean, from Mount Atlas to the Grampian
hills, a fanciful historian [2] amused the Romans with the picture
of their infant wars. " There was a time," says Florus, " when
Tibur and Præneste, our summer retreats, were the objects of
hostile vows in the Capitol, when we dreaded the shades of the
Arician groves, when we could triumph without a blush over
the nameless villages of the Sabines and Latins, and even Corioli
could afford a title not unworthy of a victorious general."   The
pride of his contemporaries was gratified by the contrast of the
past and the present: they would have been humbled by the
prospect of futurity; by the prediction that, after a thousand
years, Rome, despoiled of empire and contracted to her primæval
limits, would renew the same hostilities, on the same ground
which was then decorated with her villas and gardens.   The
adjacent territory on either side of the Tiber was always claimed,
and sometimes possessed, as the patrimony of St. Peter; but the
barons assumed a lawless independence, and the cities too faithfully copied the revolt and discord of the metropolis.   In the
twelfth and thirteenth centuries the Romans incessantly laboured
to reduce or destroy the contumacious vassals of the church
and senate; and if their headstrong and selfish ambition was
moderated by the pope, he often encouraged their zeal by the
alliance of his spiritual arms.   Their warfare was that of the
first consuls and dictators, who were taken from the plough.
They assembled in arms at the foot of the Capitol; sallied from
the gates, plundered or burnt the harvests of their neighbours,
engaged in tumultuary conflict, and returned home after an
expedition of fifteen or twenty days.   Their sieges were tedious
and unskilful: in the use of victory they indulged the meaner
passions of jealousy and revenge; and instead of adopting the
valour, they trampled on the misfortunes, of their adversaries.
The captives, in their shirts, with a rope round their necks,

---

[1] The decline of the Imperial arms and authority in Italy is related with
impartial learning in the Annals of Muratori (tom. x. xi. xii); and the
reader may compare his narrative with the Histoire des Allemands (tom.
iii. iv.) by Schmidt, who has deserved the esteem of his countrymen.

[2] Tibur nunc suburbanum, et æstivæ Præneste deliciæ, nuncupatis in
Capitolio votis petebantur.   The whole passage of Florus (l. i. c. 11) may
be read with pleasure, and has deserved the praise of a man of genius
(Œuvres de Montesquieu, tom. iii. p. 634, 635, quarto edition).

solicited their pardon: the fortifications, and even the buildings, of the rival cities were demolished, and the inhabitants were scattered in the adjacent villages. It was thus that the seats of the cardinal bishops, Porto, Ostia, Albanum, Tusculum, Præneste, and Tibur or Tivoli, were successively overthrown by the ferocious hostility of the Romans.[1] Of these,[2] Porto and Ostia, the two keys of the Tiber, are still vacant and desolate: the marshy and unwholesome banks are peopled with herds of buffaloes, and the river is lost to every purpose of navigation and trade. The hills, which afford a shady retirement from the autumnal heats, have again smiled with the blessings of peace; Frascati has arisen near the ruins of Tusculum; Tibur or Tivoli has resumed the honours of a city;[3] and the meaner towns of Albano and Palestrina are decorated with the villas of the cardinals and princes of Rome. In the work of destruction, the ambition of the Romans was often checked and repulsed by the neighbouring cities and their allies: in the first siege of Tibur they were driven from their camp; and the battles of Tusculum[4] and Viterbo[5] might be compared in their relative state to the memorable fields of Thrasymene and Cannæ. In the first of these petty wars thirty thousand Romans were overthrown by a thousand German horse, whom Frederic Barbarossa had detached to the relief of Tusculum; and if we number the slain at three, the prisoners at two, thousand, we shall embrace the most authentic and moderate account. Sixty-eight years afterwards they marched against Viterbo in the ecclesiastical state with the whole force of the city; by a rare coalition the Teutonic eagle was blended, in the adverse banners, with the keys of

[1] Ne a feritate Romanorum, sicut fuerant Hostienses, Portuenses, Tusculanenses, Albanenses, Labicenses, et nuper Tiburtini destruerentur (Matthew Paris, p. 757). These extracts are marked in the Annals and Index (the eighteenth volume) of Muratori.

[2] For the state or ruin of these suburban cities, the banks of the Tiber, etc., see the lively picture of the P. Labat (Voyage en Espagne et en Italie), who had long resided in the neighbourhood of Rome; and the more accurate description of which P. Eschinard (Roma, 1750, in octavo) has added to the topographical map of Cingolani.

[3] Labat (tom. iii. p. 233) mentions a recent decree of the Roman government, which has severely mortified the pride and poverty of Tivoli; in civitate Tiburtinâ non vivitur civiliter.

[4] I depart from my usual method of quoting only by the date the Annals of Muratori, in consideration of the critical balance in which he has weighed nine contemporary writers who mention the battle of Tusculum (tom. x. p. 42-44).

[5] Matthew Paris, p. 345. This bishop of Winchester was Peter de Rupibus, who occupied the see thirty-two years (A.D. 1206-1238), and is described, by the English historian, as a soldier and a statesman (p. 178, 399).

St. Peter; and the pope's auxiliaries were commanded by a
count of Toulouse and a bishop of Winchester. The Romans
were discomfited with shame and slaughter; but the English
prelate must have indulged the vanity of a pilgrim, if he
multiplied their numbers to one hundred, and their loss in the
field to thirty, thousand men. Had the policy of the senate and
the discipline of the legions been restored with the Capitol, the
divided condition of Italy would have offered the fairest opportunity of a second conquest. But in arms the modern Romans
were not *above*, and in arts they were far *below*, the common
level of the neighbouring republics. Nor was their warlike
spirit of any long continuance: after some irregular sallies they
subsided in the national apathy, in the neglect of military
institutions, and in the disgraceful and dangerous use of foreign
mercenaries.

Ambition is a weed of quick and early vegetation in the vineyard of Christ. Under the first Christian princes the chair of
St. Peter was disputed by the votes, the venality, the violence,
of a popular election: the sanctuaries of Rome were polluted
with blood; and, from the third to the twelfth century, the
church was distracted by the mischief of frequent schisms. As
long as the final appeal was determined by the civil magistrate,
these mischiefs were transient and local: the merits were tried
by equity or favour; nor could the unsuccessful competitor long
disturb the triumph of his rival. But after the emperors had
been divested of their prerogatives, after a maxim had been
established that the vicar of Christ is amenable to no earthly
tribunal, each vacancy of the holy see might involve Christendom
in controversy and war. The claims of the cardinals and inferior
clergy, of the nobles and people, were vague and litigious: the
freedom of choice was overruled by the tumults of a city that no
longer owned or obeyed a superior. On the decease of a pope,
two factions proceeded in different churches to a double election:
the number and weight of votes, the priority of time, the merit
of the candidates, might balance each other: the most respectable of the clergy were divided; and the distant princes, who
bowed before the spiritual throne, could not distinguish the
spurious from the legitimate idol. The emperors were often
the authors of the schism, from the political motive of opposing
a friendly to a hostile pontiff; and each of the competitors
was reduced to suffer the insults of his enemies, who were not
awed by conscience, and to purchase the support of his adherents,
who were instigated by avarice or ambition. A peaceful and

perpetual succession was ascertained by Alexander the Third,[1] who finally abolished the tumultuary votes of the clergy and people, and defined the right of election in the sole college of cardinals.[2] The three orders of bishops, priests, and deacons, were assimilated to each other by this important privilege; the parochial clergy of Rome obtained the first rank in the hierarchy: they were indifferently chosen among the nations of Christendom; and the possession of the richest benefices, of the most important bishoprics, was not incompatible with their title and office. The senators of the Catholic church, the coadjutors and legates of the supreme pontiff, were robed in purple, the symbol of martyrdom or royalty; they claimed a proud equality with kings; and their dignity was enhanced by the smallness of their number, which, till the reign of Leo the Tenth, seldom exceeded twenty or twenty-five persons. By this wise regulation all doubt and scandal were removed, and the root of schism was so effectually destroyed, that in a period of six hundred years a double choice has only once divided the unity of the sacred college. But as the concurrence of two-thirds of the votes had been made necessary, the election was often delayed by the private interest and passions of the cardinals; and while they prolonged their independent reign, the Christian world was left destitute of a head. A vacancy of almost three years had preceded the elevation of Gregory the Tenth, who resolved to prevent the future abuse; and his bull, after some opposition, has been consecrated in the code of the canon law.[3] Nine days are allowed for the obsequies of the deceased pope, and the arrival of the absent cardinals; on the tenth, they are imprisoned, each with one domestic, in a common apartment or *conclave*, without any separation of walls or curtains; a small window is reserved for the introduction of necessaries; but the door is locked on both sides, and guarded by the magistrates of the city, to seclude them from all correspondence with the world. If the election

---

[1] See Mosheim, Institut. Histor. Ecclesiast. p. 401, 403. Alexander himself had nearly been the victim of a contested election; and the doubtful merits of Innocent had only preponderated by the weight of genius and learning which St. Bernard cast into the scale (see his life and writings).

[2] The origin, titles, importance, dress, precedency, etc., of the Roman cardinals, are very ably discussed by Thomassin (Discipline de l'Eglise, tom. i. p. 1262-1287); but their purple is now much faded. The sacred college was raised to the definite number of seventy-two, to represent, under his vicar, the disciples of Christ.

[3] See the bull of Gregory X., approbante sacro concilio, in the *Sexte* of the Canon Law (l. i. tit. 6, c. 3), a supplement to the Decretals, which Boniface VIII. promulgated at Rome in 1298, and addressed to all the universities of Europe.

be not consummated in three days, the luxury of their table is
contracted to a single dish at dinner and supper; and after the
eighth day they are reduced to a scanty allowance of bread,
water, and wine. During the vacancy of the holy see the
cardinals are prohibited from touching the revenues, or assuming,
unless in some rare emergency, the government of the church:
all agreements and promises among the electors are formally
annulled; and their integrity is fortified by their solemn oath
and the prayers of the Catholics. Some articles of inconvenient
or superfluous rigour have been gradually relaxed, but the
principle of confinement is vigorous and entire: they are still
urged, by the personal motives of health and freedom, to
accelerate the moment of their deliverance; and the improvement of ballot or secret votes has wrapped the struggles of the
conclave [1] in the silky veil of charity and politeness.[2] By these
institutions the Romans were excluded from the election of
their prince and bishop; and in the fever of wild and precarious
liberty, they seemed insensible of the loss of this inestimable
privilege. The emperor Lewis of Bavaria revived the example
of the great Otho. After some negotiation with the magistrates,
the Roman people was assembled [3] in the square before St.
Peter's: the pope of Avignon, John the Twenty-second, was
deposed: the choice of his successor was ratified by their consent
and applause. They freely voted for a new law, that their
bishop should never be absent more than three months in the
year, and two days' journey from the city; and that, if he
neglected to return on the third summons, the public servant

---

[1] The genius of Cardinal de Retz had a right to paint a conclave (of 1655)
in which he was a spectator and an actor (Mémoires, tom. iv. p. 15-57);
but I am at a loss to appreciate the knowledge or authority of an anonymous Italian, whose history (Conclavi de' Pontifici Romani, in 4to, 1667)
has been continued since the reign of Alexander VII. The accidental
form of the work furnishes a lesson, though not an antidote, to ambition.
From a labyrinth of intrigues we emerge to the adoration of the successful
candidate; but the next page opens with his funeral.

[2] The expressions of Cardinal de Retz are positive and picturesque: On
y vécut toujours ensemble avec le même respect et la même civilité que
l'on observe dans le cabinet des rois, avec la même politesse qu'on avoit
dans la cour de Henri III., avec la même familiarité que l'on voit dans les
collèges; avec la même modestie qui se remarque dans les noviciats; et
avec la même charité, du moins en apparence, qui pourroit être entre des
frères parfaitement unis.

[3] Richiesti per bando (says John Villani) sanatori di Roma, e 52 del
popolo, et capitani de' 25, e consoli (consoli ?), et 13 buone huomini, uno
per rione. Our knowledge is too imperfect to pronounce how much of this
constitution was temporary, and how much ordinary and permanent.
Yet it is faintly illustrated by the ancient statutes of Rome.

should be degraded and dismissed.[1] But Lewis forgot his own debility and the prejudices of the times: beyond the precincts of a German camp, his useless phantom was rejected; the Romans despised their own workmanship; the antipope implored the mercy of his lawful sovereign;[2] and the exclusive right of the cardinals was more firmly established by this unseasonable attack.

Had the election been always held in the Vatican, the rights of the senate and people would not have been violated with impunity. But the Romans forgot, and were forgotten, in the absence of the successors of Gregory the Seventh, who did not keep as a divine precept their ordinary residence in the city and diocese. The care of that diocese was less important than the government of the universal church; nor could the popes delight in a city in which their authority was always opposed, and their person was often endangered. From the persecution of the emperors, and the wars of Italy, they escaped beyond the Alps into the hospitable bosom of France; from the tumults of Rome they prudently withdrew to live and die in the more tranquil stations of Anagni, Perugia, Viterbo, and the adjacent cities. When the flock was offended or impoverished by the absence of the shepherd, they were recalled by a stern admonition, that St. Peter had fixed his chair, not in an obscure village, but in the capital of the world; by a ferocious menace that the Romans would march in arms to destroy the place and people that should dare to afford them a retreat. They returned with timorous obedience; and were saluted with the account of a heavy debt, of all the losses which their desertion had occasioned, the hire of lodgings, the sale of provisions, and the various expenses of servants and strangers who attended the court.[3] After a short interval of peace, and perhaps of authority, they

[1] Villani (l. x. c. 68-71, in Muratori, Script. tom. xiii. p. 641-645) relates this law, and the whole transaction, with much less abhorrence than the prudent Muratori. Any one conversant with the darker ages must have observed how much the sense (I mean the nonsense) of superstition is fluctuating and inconsistent.

[2] In the first volume of the Popes of Avignon, see the second original Life of John XXII. p. 142-145; the confession of the antipope, p. 145-152; and the laborious notes of Baluze, p. 714, 715.

[3] Romani autem non valentes nec volentes ultra suam celare cupiditatem gravissimam, contra papam movere cœperunt questionem, exigentes ab eo urgentissime omnia quæ subierant per ejus absentiam damna et jacturas, videlicet in hospitiis locandis, in mercimoniis, in usuris, in redditibus, in provisionibus, et in aliis modis innumerabilibus. Quòd cum audisset papa, præcordialiter ingemuit, et se comperiens *muscipulatum*, etc. Matt. Paris, p. 757. For the ordinary history of the popes, their life and death, their residence and absence, it is enough to refer to the ecclesiastical annalists, Spondanus and Fleury.

were again banished by new tumults, and again summoned by
the imperious or respectful invitation of the senate. In these
occasional retreats the exiles and fugitives of the Vatican were
seldom long, or far, distant from the metropolis; but in the
beginning of the fourtenth century the apostolic throne was
transported, as it might seem for ever, from the Tiber to the
Rhône; and the cause of the transmigration may be deduced
from the furious contest beween Boniface the Eighth and the
king of France.[1] The spiritual arms of excommunication and
interdict were repulsed by the union of the three estates, and
the privileges of the Gallican church; but the pope was not
prepared against the carnal weapons which Philip the Fair had
courage to employ. As the pope resided at Anagni, without the
suspicion of danger, his palace and person were assaulted by
three hundred horse, who had been secretly levied by William
of Nogaret, a French minister, and Sciarra Colonna, of a noble
but hostile family of Rome. The cardinals fled; the inhabitants
of Anagni were seduced from their allegiance and gratitude;
but the dauntless Boniface, unarmed and alone, seated himself
in his chair, and awaited, like the conscript fathers of old, the
swords of the Gauls. Nogaret, a foreign adversary, was content
to execute the orders of his master: by the domestic enmity of
Colonna, he was insulted with words and blows; and during a
confinement of three days his life was threatened by the hardships which they inflicted on the obstinacy which they provoked.
Their strange delay gave time and courage to the adherents of
the church, who rescued him from sacrilegious violence; but
his imperious soul was wounded in a vital part; and Boniface
expired at Rome in a frenzy of rage and revenge. His memory
is stained with the glaring vices of avarice and pride; nor has
the courage of a martyr promoted this ecclesiastical champion
to the honours of a saint; a magnanimous sinner (say the
chronicles of the times), who entered like a fox, reigned like a
lion, and died like a dog. He was succeeded by Benedict the
Eleventh, the mildest of mankind. Yet he excommunicated the
impious emissaries of Philip, and devoted the city and people
of Anagni by a tremendous curse, whose effects are still visible
to the eyes of superstition.[2]

---

[1] Besides the general historians of the church of Italy and of France, we
possess a valuable treatise composed by a learned friend of Thuanus, which
his last and best editors have published in the appendix (Histoire particu-
lière du grand Différend entre Boniface VIII. et Philippe le Bel, par
Pierre du Puis, tom. vii. P. xi. p. 61-82).

[2] It is difficult to know whether Labat (tom. iv. p. 53-57) be in jest or in

After his decease, the tedious and equal suspense of the conclave was fixed by the dexterity of the French faction. A
specious offer was made and accepted, that, in the term of forty
days, they would elect one of the three candidates who should be
named by their opponents. The archbishop of Bordeaux, a
furious enemy of his king and country, was the first on the list;
but his ambition was known; and his conscience obeyed the
calls of fortune and the commands of a benefactor, who had been
informed by a swift messenger that the choice of a pope was now
in his hands. The terms were regulated in a private interview;
and with such speed and secrecy was the business transacted,
that the unanimous conclave applauded the elevation of Clement
the Fifth.[1] The cardinals of both parties were soon astonished
by a summons to attend him beyond the Alps; from whence, as
they soon discovered, they must never hope to return. He was
engaged by promise and affection to prefer the residence of
France; and, after dragging his court through Poitou and
Gascony, and devouring, by his expense, the cities and convents
on the road, he finally reposed at Avignon,[2] which flourished
above seventy years [3] the seat of the Roman pontiff and the
metropolis of Christendom. By land, by sea, by the Rhône, the
position of Avignon was on all sides accessible; the southern
provinces of France do not yield to Italy itself; new palaces
arose for the accommodation of the pope and cardinals; and the
arts of luxury were soon attracted by the treasures of the church.
They were already possessed of the adjacent territory, the

earnest, when he supposes that Anagni still feels the weight of this curse,
and that the corn-fields, or vineyards, or olive-trees, are annually blasted
by Nature, the obsequious handmaid of the popes.

[1] See in the Chronicle of Giovanni Villani (l. viii. c. 63, 64, 80, in Muratori,
tom. xiii.) the imprisonment of Boniface VIII. and the election of Clement
V., the last of which, like most anecdotes, is embarrassed with some
difficulties.

[2] The original lives of the eight popes of Avignon—Clement V., John
XXII., Benedict XII., Clement VI., Innocent VI., Urban V., Gregory XI.,
and Clement VII.—are published by Stephen Baluze (Vitæ Paparum
Avenionensium; Paris, 1693, 2 vols. in 4to) with copious and elaborate
notes, and a second volume of acts and documents. With the true zeal
of an editor and a patriot, he devoutly justifies or excuses the characters
of his countrymen.

[3] The exile of Avignon is compared by the Italians with Babylon, and
the Babylonish captivity. Such furious metaphors, more suitable to the
ardour of Petrarch than to the judgment of Muratori, are gravely refuted
in Baluze's preface. The abbé de Sade is distracted between the love of
Petrarch and of his country. Yet he modestly pleads that many of the
local inconveniences of Avignon are now removed; and many of the vices
against which the poet declaims had been imported with the Roman court
by the strangers of Italy (tom. i. p. 23-28).

Venaissin county,[1] a populous and fertile spot; and the sovereignty of Avignon was afterwards purchased from the youth
and distress of Jane, the first queen of Naples and countess of
Provence, for the inadequate price of fourscore thousand florins.[2]
Under the shadow of the French monarchy, amidst an obedient
people, the popes enjoyed an honourable and tranquil state, to
which they long had been strangers: but Italy deplored their
absence; and Rome, in solitude and poverty, might repent of
the ungovernable freedom which had driven from the Vatican
the successor of St. Peter. Her repentance was tardy and
fruitless: after the death of the old members, the sacred college
was filled with French cardinals,[3] who beheld Rome and Italy
with abhorrence and contempt, and perpetuated a series of
national, and even provincial, popes, attached by the most
indissoluble ties to their native country.

The progress of industry had produced and enriched the
Italian republics: the era of their liberty is the most flourishing
period of population and agriculture, of manufactures and
commerce; and their mechanic labours were gradually refined
into the arts of elegance and genius. But the position of Rome
was less favourable, the territory less fruitful: the character of
the inhabitants was debased by indolence and elated by pride;
and they fondly conceived that the tribute of subjects must for
ever nourish the metropolis of the church and empire. This
prejudice was encouraged in some degree by the resort of
pilgrims to the shrines of the apostles; and the last legacy of the
popes, the institution of the HOLY YEAR,[4] was not less beneficial

[1] The comtat Venaissin was ceded to the popes in 1273 by Philip III.,
king of France, after he had inherited the dominions of the count of
Toulouse. Forty years before, the heresy of Count Raymond had given
them a pretence of seizure, and they derived some obscure claim from the
eleventh century to some lands citra Rhodanum (Valesii Notitia Galliarum,
p. 459, 610; Longuerue, Description de la France, tom. i. p. 376-381.)

[2] If a possession of four centuries were not itself a title, such objection
might annul the bargain; but the purchase-money must be refunded, for
indeed it was paid. Civitatem Avenionem emit . . . per ejusmodi
venditionem pecuniâ redundans, etc. (iida. Vita Clement. VI. in Baluz.
tom. i. p. 272; Muratori, Script. tom. iii. P. ii. p. 565). The only temptation for Jane and her second husband was ready money, and without it
they could not have returned to the throne of Naples.

[3] Clement V. immediately promoted ten cardinals, nine French and one
English (Vita, ivta, p. 63, et Baluz. p. 625, etc.). In 1331 the pope refused
two candidates recommended by the king of France, quod xx. cardinales,
de quibus xvii. de regno Franciæ originem traxisse noscuntur in memorato
collegio existant (Thomassin, Discipline de l'Eglise, tom. i. p. 1281).

[4] Our primitive account is from Cardinal James Caietan (Maxima
Biblioth. Patrum, tom. xxv.); and I am at a loss to determine whether the
nephew of Boniface VIII. be a fool or a knave: the uncle is a much clearer
character.

to the people than to the clergy. Since the loss of Palestine, the gift of plenary indulgences, which had been applied to the crusades, remained without an object; and the most valuable treasure of the church was sequestered above eight years from public circulation. A new channel was opened by the diligence of Boniface the Eighth, who reconciled the vices of ambition and avarice; and the pope had sufficient learning to recollect and revive the secular games which were celebrated in Rome at the conclusion of every century. To sound without danger the depth of popular credulity, a sermon was seasonably pronounced, a report was artfully scattered, some aged witnesses were produced; and on the first of January of the year thirteen hundred the church of St. Peter was crowded with the faithful, who demanded the *customary* indulgence of the holy time. The pontiff, who watched and irritated their devout impatience, was soon persuaded by ancient testimony of the justice of their claim; and he proclaimed a plenary absolution to all Catholics who, in the course of that year, and at every similar period, should respectfully visit the apostolic churches of St. Peter and St. Paul. The welcome sound was propagated through Christendom; and at first from the nearest provinces of Italy, and at length from the remote kingdoms of Hungary and Britain, the highways were thronged with a swarm of pilgrims who sought to expiate their sins in a journey, however costly or laborious, which was exempt from the perils of military service. All exceptions of rank or sex, of age or infirmity, were forgotten in the common transport; and in the streets and churches many persons were trampled to death by the eagerness of devotion. The calculation of their numbers could not be easy nor accurate; and they have probably been magnified by a dexterous clergy, well apprised of the contagion of example: yet we are assured by a judicious historian, who assisted at the ceremony, that Rome was never replenished with less than two hundred thousand strangers; and another spectator has fixed at two millions the total concourse of the year. A trifling oblation from each individual would accumulate a royal treasure; and two priests stood night and day, with rakes in their hands, to collect, without counting, the heaps of gold and silver that were poured on the altar of St. Paul.[1] It was fortunately a season of peace and plenty; and if forage was scarce, if inns and lodgings were extravagantly dear, an

---

[1] See John Villani (l. viii. c. 36) in the twelfth, and the Chronicon Astense in the eleventh volume (p. 191, 192) of Muratori's Collection. Papa innumerabilem pecuniam ab eisdem accepit, nam duo clerici, cum rastris, etc.

inexhaustible supply of bread and wine, of meat and fish, was
provided by the policy of Boniface and the venal hospitality of
the Romans. From a city without trade or industry all casual
riches will speedily evaporate: but the avarice and envy of the
next generation solicited Clement the Sixth [1] to anticipate the
distant period of the century. The gracious pontiff complied
with their wishes; afforded Rome this poor consolation for his
loss; and justified the change by the name and practice of the
Mosaic Jubilee.[2] His summons was obeyed; and the number,
zeal, and liberality of the pilgrims did not yield to the primitive
festival. But they encountered the triple scourge of war,
pestilence, and famine: many wives and virgins were violated
in the castles of Italy; and many strangers were pillaged or
murdered by the savage Romans, no longer moderated by the
presence of their bishop.[3] To the impatience of the popes we
may ascribe the successive reduction to fifty, thirty-three, and
twenty-five years; although the second of these terms is com-
mensurate with the life of Christ. The profusion of indulgences,
the revolt of the Protestants, and the decline of superstition,
have much diminished the value of the jubilee; yet even the
nineteenth and last festival was a year of pleasure and profit
to the Romans; and a philosophic smile will not disturb the
triumph of the priest or the happiness of the people.[4]

In the beginning of the eleventh century Italy was exposed to
the feudal tyranny, alike oppressive to the sovereign and the
people. The rights of human nature were vindicated by her
numerous republics, who soon extended their liberty and
dominion from the city to the adjacent country. The sword of
the nobles was broken; their slaves were enfranchised; their
castles were demolished; they assumed the habits of society
and obedience; their ambition was confined to municipal
honours; and in the proudest aristocracy of Venice or Genoa,

[1] The two bulls of Boniface VIII. and Clement VI. are inserted in the
Corpus Juris Canonici (Extravagant. Commun. l. v. tit. ix. c. 1, 2).

[2] The sabbatic years and jubilees of the Mosaic law (Car. Sigon. de
Republicâ Hebræorum, Opp. tom. iv. l. iii. c. 14, 15, p. 151, 152), the suspension of all care and labour, the periodical release of lands, debts, servitude, etc., may seem a noble idea, but the execution would be impracticable in a *profane* republic; and I should be glad to learn that this ruinous
festival was observed by the Jewish people.

[3] See the Chronicle of Matteo Villani (l. i. c. 56) in the fourteenth volume
of Muratori, and the Mémoires sur la Vie de Pétrarque, tom. iii. p. 75-89.

[4] The subject is exhausted by M. Chais, a French minister at the Hague,
in his Lettres Historiques et Dogmatiques sur les Jubilés et les Indulgences;
la Haye, 1751, 3 vols. in 12mo; an elaborate and pleasing work, had not
the author preferred the character of a polemic to that of a philosopher.

each patrician was subject to the laws.[1] But the feeble and
disorderly government of Rome was unequal to the task of
curbing her rebellious sons, who scorned the authority of the
magistrate within and without the walls.   It was no longer a
civil contention between the nobles and plebeians for the government of the state: the barons asserted in arms their personal
independence; their palaces and castles were fortified against
a siege; and their private quarrels were maintained by the
numbers of their vassals and retainers.   In origin and affection
they were aliens to their country:[2] and a genuine Roman, could
such have been produced, might have renounced these haughty
strangers, who disdained the appellation of citizens, and proudly
styled themselves the princes of Rome.[3] After a dark series of
revolutions all records of pedigree were lost; the distinction of
surnames was abolished; the blood of the nations was mingled
in a thousand channels; and the Goths and Lombards, the
Greeks and Franks, the Germans and Normans, had obtained
the fairest possessions by royal bounty, or the prerogative of
valour.   These examples might be readily presumed; but the
elevation of a Hebrew race to the rank of senators and consuls
is an event without a parallel in the long captivity of these
miserable exiles.[4] In the time of Leo the Ninth a wealthy and
learned Jew was converted to Christianity; and honoured at his
baptism with the name of his godfather, the reigning pope.   The
zeal and courage of Peter the son of Leo were signalised in the
cause of Gregory the Seventh, who intrusted his faithful adherent
with the government of Hadrian's mole, the tower of Crescentius,
or, as it is now called, the castle of St. Angelo.   Both the father
and the son were the parents of a numerous progeny: their
riches, the fruits of usury, were shared with the noblest families
of the city; and so extensive was their alliance, that the grand-

---

[1] Muratori (Dissert. xlvii.) alleges the Annals of Florence, Padua, Genoa,
etc., the analogy of the rest, the evidence of Otho of Frisingen (de Gest.
Fred. I. l. ii. c. 13), and the submission of the marquis of Este.

[2] As early as the year 824 the emperor Lothaire I. found it expedient to
interrogate the Roman people, to learn from each individual by what
national law he chose to be governed (Muratori, Dissert. xxii.).

[3] Petrarch attacks these foreigners, the tyrants of Rome, in a declamation or epistle, full of bold truths and absurd pedantry, in which he applies
the maxims and even prejudices of the old republic to the state of the
fourteenth century (Mémoires, tom. iii. p. 157-169).

[4] The origin and adventures of this Jewish family are noticed by Pagi
(Critica, tom. iv. p. 435, A.D. 1124, No. 3, 4), who draws his information
from the Chronographus Maurigniacensis, and Arnulphus Sagiensis de
Schismate (in Muratori, Script. Ital. tom. iii. P. i. p. 423-432).   The fact
must in some degree be true; yet I could wish that it had been coolly
related before it was turned into a reproach against the antipope.

son of the proselyte was exalted by the weight of his kindred to
the throne of St. Peter. A majority of the clergy and people
supported his cause: he reigned several years in the Vatican;
and it is only the eloquence of St. Bernard, and the final triumph
of Innocent the Second, that has branded Anacletus with the
epithet of antipope. After his defeat and death the posterity
of Leo is no longer conspicuous; and none will be found of the
modern nobles ambitious of descending from a Jewish stock. It
is not my design to enumerate the Roman families which have
failed at different periods, or those which are continued in
different degrees of splendour to the present time.[1] The old
consular line of the *Frangipani* discover their name in the
generous act of *breaking* or dividing bread in a time of famine;
and such benevolence is more truly glorious than to have
enclosed, with their allies the *Corsi*, a spacious quarter of the
city in the chains of their fortifications; the *Savelli*, as it should
seem a Sabine race, have maintained their original dignity; the
obsolete surname of the *Capizucchi* is inscribed on the coins of
the first senators; the *Conti* preserve the honour, without the
estate, of the counts of Signia; and the *Annibaldi* must have
been very ignorant, or very modest, if they had not descended
from the Carthaginian hero.[2]

But among, perhaps above, the peers and princes of the city, I
distinguish the rival houses of COLONNA and URSINI, whose

---

[1] Muratori has given two dissertations (xli. and xlii.) to the names, surnames, and families of Italy. Some nobles, who glory in their domestic
fables, may be offended with his firm and temperate criticism; yet surely
some ounces of pure gold are of more value than many pounds of base
metal.

[2] The cardinal of St. George, in his poetical, or rather metrical, history
of the election and coronation of Boniface VIII. (Muratori, Script. Ital.
tom. iii. P. i. p. 641, etc.), describes the state and families of Rome at the
coronation of Boniface VIII. (A.D. 1295):—

> Interea titulis redimiti sanguine et armis
> Illustresque viri Romanâ a stirpe trahentes
> Nomen in emeritos tantæ virtutis honores
> Intulerant sese medios festumque colebant
> Auratâ fulgentes togâ sociante catervâ.
> Ex ipsis devota domus præstantis ab *Ursâ*
> Ecclesiæ, vultumque gerens demissius altum
> Festa *Columna* jocis, necnon *Sabellia* mitis;
> Stephanides senior, *Comites*, *Annibalica* proles,
> Præfectusque urbis magnum sine viribus nomen.
>
>   (l. ii. c. 5, 100, p. 647, 648.)

The ancient statutes of Rome (l. iii. c. 59, p. 174, 175) distinguish eleven
families of barons, who are obliged to swear in concilio communi, before
the senator, that they would not harbour or protect any malefactors, outlaws, etc.—a feeble security!

private story is an essential part of the annals of modern Rome.
I. The name and arms of Colonna [1] have been the theme of
much doubtful etymology; nor have the orators and antiquarians overlooked either Trajan's pillar, or the columns of
Hercules, or the pillar of Christ's flagellation, or the luminous
column that guided the Israelites in the desert. Their first
historical appearance in the year eleven hundred and four attests
the power and antiquity, while it explains the simple meaning,
of the name. By the usurpation of Cavæ the Colonna provoked
the arms of Paschal the Second; but they lawfully held in the
Campagna of Rome the hereditary fiefs of Zagarola and *Colonna;*
and the latter of these towns was probably adorned with some
lofty pillar, the relic of a villa or temple.[2] They likewise
possessed one moiety of the neighbouring city of Tusculum;
a strong presumption of their descent from the counts of
Tusculum, who in the tenth century were the tyrants of the
apostolic see. According to their own and the public opinion,
the primitive and remote source was derived from the banks of
the Rhine;[3] and the sovereigns of Germany were not ashamed
of a real or fabulous affinity with a noble race, which in the
revolutions of seven hundred years has been often illustrated by
merit and always by fortune.[4] About the end of the thirteenth
century the most powerful branch was composed of an uncle
and six brothers, all conspicuous in arms or in the honours of
the church. Of these, Peter was elected senator of Rome,
introduced to the Capitol in a triumphant car, and hailed in
some vain acclamations with the title of Cæsar; while John and

[1] It is pity that the Colonna themselves have not favoured the world
with a complete and critical history of their illustrious house. I adhere
to Muratori (Dissert. xlii. tom. iii. p. 647, 648).

[2] Pandulph. Pisan. in Vit. Paschal. II. in Muratori, Script. Ital. tom. iii.
P. i. p. 335. The family has still great possessions in the Campagna of
Rome; but they have alienated to the Rospigliosi this original fief of
Colonna (Eschinard, p. 258, 259).

[3] Te longinqua dedit tellus et pascua Rheni,

says Petrarch; and in 1417 a duke of Guelders and Juliers acknowledges
(Lenfant, Hist. du Concile de Constance, tom. ii. p. 539) his descent from
the ancestors of Martin V. (Otho Colonna): but the royal author of the
Memoirs of Brandenburg observes that the sceptre in his arms has been
confounded with the column. To maintain the Roman origin of the
Colonna it was ingeniously supposed (Diario di Monaldeschi, in the Script.
Ital. tom. xii. p. 533) that a cousin of the emperor Nero escaped from the
city and founded Mentz in Germany.

[4] I cannot overlook the Roman triumph or ovation of Marco Antonio
Colonna, who had commanded the pope's galleys at the naval victory of
Lepanto (Thuan. Hist. l. 7, tom. iii. p. 55, 56; Muret. Oratio x. Opp. i.
p. 180-190).

Stephen were declared marquis of Ancona and count of Romagna, by Nicholas the Fourth, a patron so partial to their family, that he has been delineated in satirical portraits, imprisoned as it were in a hollow pillar.[1] After his decease their haughty behaviour provoked the displeasure of the most implacable of mankind. The two cardinals, the uncle and the nephew, denied the election of Boniface the Eighth; and the Colonna were oppressed for a moment by his temporal and spiritual arms.[2] He proclaimed a crusade against his personal enemies; their estates were confiscated; their fortresses on either side of the Tiber were besieged by the troops of St. Peter and those of the rival nobles; and after the ruin of Palestrina or Præneste, their principal seat, the ground was marked with a ploughshare, the emblem of perpetual desolation. Degraded, banished, proscribed, the six brothers, in disguise and danger, wandered over Europe without renouncing the hope of deliverance and revenge. In this double hope the French court was their surest asylum: they prompted and directed the enterprise of Philip; and I should praise their magnanimity had they respected the misfortune and courage of the captive tyrant. His civil acts were annulled by the Roman people, who restored the honours and possessions of the Colonna; and some estimate may be formed of their wealth by their losses, of their losses by the damages of one hundred thousand gold florins which were granted them against the accomplices and heirs of the deceased pope. All the spiritual censures and disqualifications were abolished[3] by his prudent successors; and the fortune of the house was more firmly established by this transient hurricane. The boldness of Sciarra Colonna was signalised in the captivity of Boniface, and long afterwards in the coronation of Lewis of Bavaria; and by the gratitude of the emperor the pillar in their arms was encircled with a royal crown. But the first of the family in fame and merit was the elder Stephen, whom Petrarch loved and esteemed as a hero superior to his own times and not

[1] Muratori, Annali d'Italia, tom. x. p. 216, 220.

[2] Petrarch's attachment to the Colonna has authorised the abbé de Sade to expatiate on the state of the family in the fourteenth century, the persecution of Boniface VIII., the character of Stephen and his sons, their quarrels with the Ursini, etc. (Mémoires sur Pétrarque, tom. i. p. 98-110, 146-148, 174-176, 222-230, 275-280.) His criticism often rectifies the hearsay stories of Villani, and the errors of the less diligent moderns. I understand the branch of Stephen to be now extinct.

[3] Alexander III. had declared the Colonna who adhered to the emperor Frederic I. incapable of holding any ecclesiastical benefice (Villani, l. v. c. 1); and the last stains of annual excommunication were purified by Sixtus V. (Vita di Sisto V. tom. iii. p. 416). Treason, sacrilege, and proscription are often the best titles of ancient nobility.

unworthy of ancient Rome. Persecution and exile displayed to the nations his abilities in peace and war; in his distress he was an object, not of pity but of reverence; the aspect of danger provoked him to avow his name and country; and when he was asked, " Where is now your fortress? " he laid his hand on his heart, and answered, " Here." He supported with the same virtue the return of prosperity; and, till the ruin of his declining age, the ancestors, the character, and the children of Stephen Colonna exalted his dignity in the Roman republic and at the court of Avignon. II. The Ursini migrated from Spoleto; [1] the sons of Ursus, as they are styled in the twelfth century, from some eminent person who is only known as the father of their race. But they were soon distinguished among the nobles of Rome by the number and bravery of their kinsmen, the strength of their towers, the honours of the senate and sacred college, and the elevation of two popes, Celestin the Third and Nicholas the Third, of their name and lineage.[2] Their riches may be accused as an early abuse of nepotism: the estates of St. Peter were alienated in their favour by the liberal Celestin;[3] and Nicholas was ambitious for their sake to solicit the alliance of monarchs; to found new kingdoms in Lombardy and Tuscany; and to invest them with the perpetual office of senators of Rome. All that has been observed of the greatness of the Colonna will likewise redound to the glory of the Ursini, their constant and equal antagonists in the long hereditary feud which distracted above two hundred and fifty years the ecclesiastical state. The jealousy of pre-eminence and power was the true ground of

---

[1] ————— Vallis te proxima misit,
Appenninigenæ quâ prata virentia sylvæ
Spoletana metunt armenta gregesque protervi.

Monaldeschi (tom. xii. Script. Ital. p. 533) gives the Ursini a French origin which may be remotely true.

[2] In the metrical life of Celestin V. by the Cardinal of St. George (Muratori, tom. iii. P. i. p. 613, etc.) we find a luminous and not inelegant passage (l. i. c. 3, p. 203, etc.):—

————— genuit quem nobilis Ursæ (*Ursi ?*)
Progenies, Romana domus, veterataque magnis
Fascibus in clero, pompasque experta senatûs,
Bellorumque manû grandi stipata parentum
Cardineos apices necnon fastigia dudum
Papatûs *iterata* tenens.

Muratori (Dissert. xlii. tom. iii.) observes that the first Ursini pontificate of Celestin III. was unknown: he is inclined to read *Ursi* progenies.

[3] Filii Ursi, quondam Cœlestini papæ nepotes, de bonis ecclesiæ Romanæ ditati (Vit. Innocent. III. in Muratori, Script. tom. iii. P. i.). The partial prodigality of Nicholas III. is more conspicuous in Villani and Muratori. Yet the Ursini would disdain the nephews of a *modern* pope.

their quarrel; but as a specious badge of distinction, the Colonna
embraced the name of Ghibelines and the party of the empire;
the Ursini espoused the title of Guelphs and the cause of the
church. The eagle and the keys were displayed in their adverse
banners; and the two factions of Italy most furiously raged
when the origin and nature of the dispute were long since
forgotten.[1] After the retreat of the popes to Avignon they
disputed in arms the vacant republic; and the mischiefs of
discord were perpetuated by the wretched compromise of electing each year two rival senators. By their private hostilities
the city and country were desolated, and the fluctuating balance
inclined with their alternate success. But none of either family
had fallen by the sword till the most renowned champion of the
Ursini was surprised and slain by the younger Stephen Colonna.[2]
His triumph is stained with the reproach of violating the truce;
their defeat was basely avenged by the assassination, before the
church door, of an innocent boy and his two servants. Yet the
victorious Colonna, with an annual colleague, was declared
senator of Rome during the term of five years. And the muse
of Petrarch inspired a wish, a hope, a prediction, that the generous
youth, the son of his venerable hero, would restore Rome and
Italy to their pristine glory; that his justice would extirpate the
wolves and lions, the serpents and *bears*, who laboured to subvert
the eternal basis of the marble COLUMN.[3]

[1] In his fifty-first Dissertation on the Italian Antiquities Muratori
explains the factions of the Guelphs and Ghibelines.
[2] Petrarch (tom. i. p. 222-230) has celebrated this victory according to
the Colonna; but two contemporaries, a Florentine (Giovanni Villani l. x.
c. 220) and a Roman (Ludovico Monaldeschi, p. 533, 534), are less favourable to their arms.
[3] The Abbé de Sade (tom. i. Notes, p. 61-66) has applied the sixth
Canzone of Petrarch, *Spirto Gentil*, etc., to Stephen Colonna the younger:—

> *Orsi*, lupi, leoni, aquile e serpi
> Ad una gran marmorea *colonna*
> Fanno noja sovente e à se danno.

CHAPTER LXX

Character and Coronation of Petrarch—Restoration of the Freedom and
Government of Rome by the Tribune Rienzi—His Virtues and Vices,
his Expulsion and Death—Return of the Popes from Avignon—
Great Schism of the West—Reunion of the Latin Church—Last
Struggles of Roman Liberty—Statutes of Rome—Final Settlement of
the Ecclesiastical State

IN the apprehension of modern times Petrarch [1] is the Italian
songster of Laura and love. In the harmony of his Tuscan
rhymes Italy applauds, or rather adores, the father of her lyric
poetry; and his verse, or at least his name, is repeated by the
enthusiasm or affectation of amorous sensibility. Whatever may
be the private taste of a stranger, his slight and superficial knowledge should humbly acquiesce in the taste of a learned nation;
yet I may hope or presume that the Italians do not compare
the tedious uniformity of sonnets and elegies with the sublime
compositions of their epic muse, the original wildness of Dante,
the regular beauties of Tasso, and the boundless variety of the
incomparable Ariosto. The merits of the lover I am still less
qualified to appreciate: nor am I deeply interested in a metaphysical passion for a nymph so shadowy, that her existence has
been questioned; [2] for a matron so prolific, [3] that she was delivered
of eleven legitimate children, [4] while her amorous swain sighed

[1] The Mémoires sur la Vie de François Pétrarque (Amsterdam, 1764,
1767, 3 vols. in 4to) form a copious, original, and entertaining work, a
labour of love, composed from the accurate study of Petrarch and his contemporaries; but the hero is too often lost in the general history of the age,
and the author too often languishes in the affectation of politeness and
gallantry. In the preface to his first volume he enumerates and weighs
twenty Italian biographers, who have professedly treated of the same
subject.

[2] The allegorical interpretation prevailed in the fifteenth century; but
the wise commentators were not agreed whether they should understand,
by Laura, religion, or virtue, or the blessed Virgin, or ———. See the
prefaces to the first and second volume.

[3] Laure de Noves, born about the year 1307, was married in January,
1325, to Hugues de Sade, a noble citizen of Avignon, whose jealousy was
not the effect of love, since he married a second wife within seven months
of her death, which happened the 6th of April, 1348, precisely one-and-
twenty years after Petrarch had seen and loved her.

[4] Corpus crebris partubus exhaustum: from one of these is issued, in the
tenth degree, the abbé de Sade, the fond and grateful biographer of
Petrarch; and this domestic motive most probably suggested the idea of
his work, and urged him to inquire into every circumstance that could
affect the history and character of his grandmother (see particularly tom. i.
p. 122-133, notes, p. 7-58; tom. ii. p. 455-495, not. p. 76-82).

and sung at the fountain of Vaucluse.[1] But in the eyes of
Petrarch and those of his graver contemporaries his love was a
sin, and Italian verse a frivolous amusement. His Latin works
of philosophy, poetry, and eloquence established his serious
reputation, which was soon diffused from Avignon over France
and Italy: his friends and disciples were multiplied in every
city; and if the ponderous volume of his writings [2] be now
abandoned to a long repose, our gratitude must applaud the
man who, by precept and example, revived the spirit and study
of the Augustan age. From his earliest youth Petrarch aspired
to the poetic crown. The academical honours of the three
faculties had introduced a royal degree of master or doctor in
the art of poetry; [3] and the title of poet-laureat, which custom,
rather than vanity, perpetuates in the English court,[4] was first
invented by the Cæsars of Germany. In the musical games of
antiquity a prize was bestowed on the victor: [5] the belief that
Virgil and Horace had been crowned in the Capitol inflamed
the emulation of a Latin bard; [6] and the laurel was endeared to

[1] Vaucluse, so familiar to our English travellers, is described from the
writings of Petrarch, and the local knowledge of his biographer (Mémoires,
tom. i. p. 340-359). It was, in truth, the retreat of a hermit; and the
moderns are much mistaken if they place Laura and a happy lover in the
grotto.

[2] Of 1250 pages, in a close print, at Basil in the sixteenth century, but
without the date of the year. The abbé de Sade calls aloud for a new
edition of Petrarch's Latin works; but I much doubt whether it would
redound to the profit of the bookseller or the amusement of the public.

[3] Consult Selden's Titles of Honour, in his works (vol. iii. p. 457-466).
A hundred years before Petrarch, St. Francis received the visit of a poet
qui ab imperatore fuerat coronatus et exinde rex versuum dictus.

[4] From Augustus to Louis the muse has too often been false and venal;
but I much doubt whether any age or court can produce a similar establishment of a stipendiary poet, who, in every reign and at all events, is
bound to furnish twice a-year a measure of praise and verse, such as may
be sung in the chapel, and, I believe, in the presence, of the sovereign. I
speak the more freely, as the best time for abolishing this ridiculous custom
is while the prince is a man of virtue, and the poet a man of genius.

[5] Isocrates (in Panegyrico, tom. i. p. 116, 117, edit. Battie, Cantab.
1729) claims for his native Athens the glory of first instituting and recommending the ἀλῶνας—καὶ τὰ ἄθλα μέγιστα—μὴ μόνον τάχους καὶ
ῥώμης, ἀλλὰ καὶ λόγων καὶ γνώμης. The example of the Panathenæa was
imitated at Delphi; but the Olympic games were ignorant of a musical
crown, till it was extorted by the vain tyranny of Nero (Sueton. in Nerone,
c. 23; Philostrat. apud Casaubon ad locum; Dion Cassius, or Xiphilin,
l. lxiii. [c. 9, 20] p. 1032, 1041; Potter's Greek Antiquities. vol. i. p. 445,
450).

[6] The Capitoline games (certamen quinquennale, musicum, equestre,
gymnicum) were instituted by Domitian (Sueton. c. 4) in the year of
Christ 86 (Censorin. de Die Natali, c. 18, p. 100, edit. Havercamp.), and
were not abolished in the fourth century (Ausonius de Professoribus Burde-
gal. V.). If the crown were given to superior merit, the exclusion of Statius

the lover by a verbal resemblance with the name of his mistress.[1]
The value of either object was enhanced by the difficulties of
the pursuit; and if the virtue or prudence of Laura was inexorable,[2] he enjoyed, and might boast of enjoying, the nymph
of poetry.   His vanity was not of the most delicate kind, since
he applauds the success of his own *labours;* his name was popular;
his friends were active; the open or secret opposition of envy
and prejudice was surmounted by the dexterity of patient merit.
In the thirty-sixth year of his age he was solicited to accept the
object of his wishes; and on the same day, in the solitude of
Vaucluse, he received a similar and solemn invitation from the
senate of Rome and the university of Paris.   The learning of
a theological school, and the ignorance of a lawless city, were
alike unqualified to bestow the ideal though immortal wreath
which genius may obtain from the free applause of the public
and of posterity: but the candidate dismissed this troublesome reflection; and, after some moments of complacency and
suspense, preferred the summons of the metropolis of the world.

The ceremony of his coronation [3] was performed in the Capitol,
by his friend and patron the supreme magistrate of the republic.
Twelve patrician youths were arrayed in scarlet; six representatives of the most illustrious families, in green robes, with
garlands of flowers, accompanied the procession; in the midst
of the princes and nobles, the senator, count of Anguillara, a
kinsman of the Colonna, assumed his throne; and at the voice
of a herald Petrarch arose.   After discoursing on a text of Virgil,
and thrice repeating his vows for the prosperity of Rome, he
knelt before the throne and received from the senator a laurel
crown, with a more precious declaration, " This is the reward of
merit."   The people shouted, " Long life to the Capitol and the
poet! "   A sonnet in praise of Rome was accepted as the

(Capitolia nostræ inficiata lyræ, Silv. l. iii. v. 31) may do honour to the
games of the Capitol; but the Latin poets who lived before Domitian were
crowned only in the public opinion.

[1] Petrarch and the senators of Rome were ignorant that the laurel was
not the Capitoline, but the Delphic, crown (Plin. Hist. Natur. xv. 39; Hist.
Critique de la République des Lettres, tom. i. p. 150-220}.   The victors in
the Capitol were crowned with a garland of oak-leaves (Martial, l. iv.
epigram 54).

[2] The pious grandson of Laura has laboured, and not without success, to
vindicate her immaculate chastity against the censures of the grave and
the sneers of the profane (tom. ii. notes, p. 76-82).

[3] The whole process of Petrarch's coronation is accurately described by
the abbé de Sade (tom. i. p. 425-435; tom. ii. p. 1-6, notes, p. 1-13) from
his own writings, and the Roman diary of Ludovico Monaldeschi, without
mixing in this authentic narrative the more recent fables of Sannuccio
Delbene.

effusion of genius and gratitude; and after the whole procession had visited the Vatican the profane wreath was suspended before the shrine of St. Peter. In the act or diploma [1] which was presented to Petrarch, the title and prerogatives of poet-laureat are revived in the Capitol after the lapse of thirteen hundred years; and he receives the perpetual privilege of wearing, at his choice, a crown of laurel, ivy, or myrtle, of assuming the poetic habit, and of teaching, disputing, interpreting, and composing, in all places whatsoever, and on all subjects of literature. The grant was ratified by the authority of the senate and people; and the character of citizen was the recompense of his affection for the Roman name. They did him honour, but they did him justice. In the familiar society of Cicero and Livy he had imbibed the ideas of an ancient patriot; and his ardent fancy kindled every idea to a sentiment, and every sentiment to a passion. The aspect of the seven hills and their majestic ruins confirmed these lively impressions; and he loved a country by whose liberal spirit he had been crowned and adopted. The poverty and debasement of Rome excited the indignation and pity of her grateful son: he dissembled the faults of his fellow-citizens; applauded with partial fondness the last of their heroes and matrons; and in the remembrance of the past, in the hope of the future, was pleased to forget the miseries of the present time. Rome was still the lawful mistress of the world; the pope and the emperor, her bishop and general, had abdicated their station by an inglorious retreat to the Rhône and the Danube; but if she could resume her virtue, the republic might again vindicate her liberty and dominion. Amidst the indulgence of enthusiasm and eloquence,[2] Petrarch, Italy, and Europe were astonished by a revolution which realised for a moment his most splendid visions. The rise and fall of the tribune Rienzi will occupy the following pages: [3] the subject is interesting, the

---

[1] The original act is printed among the Pièces Justificatives in the Mémoires sur Pétrarque, tom. iii. p. 50-53.

[2] To find the proofs of his enthusiasm for Rome, I need only request that the reader would open, by chance, either Petrarch or his French biographer. The latter has described the poet's first visit to Rome (tom. i. p. 323-335). But, in the place of much idle rhetoric and morality, Petrarch might have amused the present and future age with an original account of the city and his coronation.

[3] It has been treated by the pen of a Jesuit, the P. du Cerçeau, whose posthumous work (Conjuration de Nicolas Gabrini, dit de Rienzi, Tyran de Rome, en 1347) was published at Paris, 1748, in 12mo. I am indebted to him for some facts and documents in John Hocsemius, canon of Liege, a contemporary historian (Fabricius, Biblioth. Lat. med. Ævi, tom. iii. p. 273; tom. iv. p. 85).

materials are rich, and the glance of a patriot bard [1] will sometimes vivify the copious, but simple, narrative of the Florentine,[2]
and more especially of the Roman,[3] historian.

In a quarter of the city which was inhabited only by mechanics
and Jews, the marriage of an innkeeper and a washerwoman
produced the future deliverer of Rome.[4] From such parents
Nicholas Rienzi Gabrini could inherit neither dignity nor fortune;
and the gift of a liberal education, which they painfully bestowed,
was the cause of his glory and untimely end. The study of
history and eloquence, the writings of Cicero, Seneca, Livy,
Cæsar, and Valerius Maximus, elevated above his equals and
contemporaries the genius of the young plebeian: he perused
with indefatigable diligence the manuscripts and marbles of
antiquity; loved to dispense his knowledge in familiar language,
and was often provoked to exclaim, "Where are now these
Romans? their virtue, their justice, their power? why was I
not born in those happy times?"[5] When the republic addressed
to the throne of Avignon an embassy of the three orders, the
spirit and eloquence of Rienzi recommended him to a place

---

[1] The abbé de Sade, who so freely expatiates on the history of the fourteenth century, might treat, as his proper subject, a revolution in which
the heart of Petrarch was so deeply engaged (Mémoires, tom. ii. p. 50, 51,
320-417, notes, p. 70-76; tom. iii. p. 221-243, 366-375). Not an idea or a
fact in the writings of Petrarch has probably escaped him.

[2] Giovanni Villani, l. xii. c. 89, 104, in Muratori, Rerum Italicarum
Scriptores, tom. xiii. p. 969, 970, 981-983.

[3] In his third volume of Italian Antiquities (p. 249-548) Muratori has
inserted the Fragmenta Historiæ Romanæ ab Anno 1327 usque ad Annum
1354, in the original dialect of Rome or Naples in the fourteenth century,
and a Latin version for the benefit of strangers. It contains the most
particular and authentic life of Colà (Nicholas) di Rienzi, which had been
printed at Bracciano, 1627, in 4to, under the name of Tomaso Fortifiocca,
who is only mentioned in this work as having been punished by the tribune
for forgery. Human nature is scarcely capable of such sublime or stupid
impartiality; but whosoever is the author of these Fragments, he wrote
on the spot and at the time, and paints, without design or art, the manners
of Rome and the character of the tribune.

[4] The first and splendid period of Rienzi, his tribunitian government, is
contained in the eighteenth chapter of the Fragments (p. 399-479), which,
in the new division, forms the second book of the history in thirty-eight
smaller chapters or sections.

[5] The reader may be pleased with a specimen of the original idiom: Fò
da soa juventutine nutricato di latte de eloquentia, bono gramatico,
megliore rettuorico, autorista bravo. Deh como et quanto era veloce
leitore! moito usava Tito Livio, Seneca, et Tullio, et Balerio Massimo,
moito li dilettava le magnificientie di Julio Cesare raccontare. Tutta la
die se speculava negl' intagli di marmo lequali iaccio intorno Roma. Non
era altri che esso, che sapesse lejere li antichi pataffii. Tutte scritture
antiche vulgarizzava; quesse fiure di marmo justamente interpretava.
Oh come spesso diceva, "Dove suono quelli buoni Romani? dove ene loro
somma justitia? poleramme trovare in tempo che quessi fiuriano!"

among the thirteen deputies of the commons. The orator had
the honour of haranguing Pope Clement the Sixth, and the satisfaction of conversing with Petrarch, a congenial mind; but his
aspiring hopes were chilled by disgrace and poverty, and the
patriot was reduced to a single garment and the charity of the
hospital. From this misery he was relieved by the sense of
merit or the smile of favour; and the employment of apostolic
notary afforded him a daily stipend of five gold florins, a more
honourable and extensive connection, and the right of contrast-
ing, both in words and actions, his own integrity with the vices
of the state. The eloquence of Rienzi was prompt and persuasive:
the multitude is always prone to envy and censure: he was
stimulated by the loss of a brother and the impunity of the
assassins; nor was it possible to excuse or exaggerate the public
calamities. The blessings of peace and justice, for which civil
society has been instituted, were banished from Rome: the
jealous citizens, who might have endured every personal or
pecuniary injury, were most deeply wounded in the dishonour
of their wives and daughters; [1] they were equally oppressed by
the arrogance of the nobles and the corruption of the magistrates;
and the abuse of arms or of laws was the only circumstance that
distinguished the lions from the dogs and serpents of the Capitol.
These allegorical emblems were variously repeated in the pictures
which Rienzi exhibited in the streets and churches; and while
the spectators gazed with curious wonder, the bold and ready
orator unfolded the meaning, applied the satire, inflamed their
passions, and announced a distant hope of comfort and deliverance. The privileges of Rome, her eternal sovereignty over her
princes and provinces, was the theme of his public and private
discourse; and a monument of servitude became in his hands
a title and incentive of liberty. The decree of the senate, which
granted the most ample prerogatives to the emperor Vespasian,
had been inscribed on a copper-plate still extant in the choir of
the church of St. John Lateran. [2] A numerous assembly of nobles
and plebeians was invited to this political lecture, and a convenient theatre was erected for their reception. The notary
appeared in a magnificent and mysterious habit, explained the
inscription by a version and commentary, [3] and descanted with

[1] Petrarch compares the jealousy of the Romans with the easy temper
of the husbands of Avignon (Mémoires, tom. i. p. 330).

[2] The fragments of the *Lex regia* may be found in the Inscriptions of
Gruter, tom. i. p. 242, and at the end of the Tacitus of Ernesti, with some
learned notes of the editor, tom. ii.

[3] I cannot overlook a stupendous and laughable blunder of Rienzi. The

eloquence and zeal on the ancient glories of the senate and people, from whom all legal authority was derived. The supine ignorance of the nobles was incapable of discerning the serious tendency of such representations: they might sometimes chastise with words and blows the plebeian reformer; but he was often suffered in the Colonna palace to amuse the company with his threats and predictions; and the modern Brutus [1] was concealed under the mask of folly and the character of a buffoon. While they indulged their contempt, the restoration of the *good estate*, his favourite expression, was entertained among the people as a desirable, a possible, and at length as an approaching, event; and while all had the disposition to applaud, some had the courage to assist, their promised deliverer.

A prophecy, or rather a summons, affixed on the church door of St. George, was the first public evidence of his designs—a nocturnal assembly of a hundred citizens on Mount Aventine, the first step to their execution. After an oath of secrecy and aid, he represented to the conspirators the importance and facility of their enterprise; that the nobles, without union or resources, were strong only in the fear of their imaginary strength; that all power, as well as right, was in the hands of the people; that the revenues of the apostolical chamber might relieve the public distress; and that the pope himself would approve their victory over the common enemies of government and freedom. After securing a faithful band to protect this first declaration, he proclaimed through the city, by sound of trumpet, that on the evening of the following day all persons should assemble without arms before the church of St. Angelo, to provide for the re-establishment of the good estate. The whole night was employed in the celebration of thirty masses of the Holy Ghost; and in the morning Rienzi, bareheaded, but in complete armour, issued from the church, encompassed by the hundred conspirators. The pope's vicar, the simple bishop of Orvieto, who had been persuaded to sustain a part in this singular ceremony, marched on his right hand, and three great standards were borne aloft

---

Lex regia empowers Vespasian to enlarge the Pomœrium, a word familiar to every antiquary. It was not so to the tribune; he confounds it with pomarium, an orchard, translates lo Jardino de Roma cioene Italia, and is copied by the less excusable ignorance of the Latin translator (p. 406) and the French historian (p. 33). Even the learning of Muratori has slumbered over the passage.

[1] Priori (*Bruto*) tamen similior, juvenis uterque, longe ingenio quam cujus simulationem induerat, ut sub hoc obtentû liberator ille P. R. aperiretur tempore suo. . . . Ille regibus, hic tyrannis contemptus (Opp. p. 536).

as the emblems of their design. In the first, the banner of *liberty*, Rome was seated on two lions, with a palm in one hand and a globe in the other; St. Paul, with a drawn sword, was delineated in the banner of *justice;* and in the third, St. Peter held the keys of *concord* and *peace*. Rienzi was encouraged by the presence and applause of an innumerable crowd, who understood little and hoped much; and the procession slowly rolled forwards from the castle of St. Angelo to the Capitol. His triumph was disturbed by some secret emotions which he laboured to suppress: he ascended without opposition, and with seeming confidence, the citadel of the republic; harangued the people from the balcony, and received the most flattering confirmation of his acts and laws. The nobles, as if destitute of arms and counsels, beheld in silent consternation this strange revolution; and the moment had been prudently chosen when the most formidable, Stephen Colonna, was absent from the city. On the first rumour he returned to his palace, affected to despise this plebeian tumult, and declared to the messenger of Rienzi that at his leisure he would cast the madman from the windows of the Capitol. The great bell instantly rang an alarm, and so rapid was the tide, so urgent was the danger, that Colonna escaped with precipitation to the suburb of St. Laurence: from thence, after a moment's refreshment, he continued the same speedy career till he reached in safety his castle of Palestrina, lamenting his own imprudence, which had not trampled the spark of this mighty conflagration. A general and peremptory order was issued from the Capitol to all the nobles that they should peaceably retire to their estates: they obeyed, and their departure secured the tranquillity of the free and obedient citizens of Rome.

But such voluntary obedience evaporates with the first transports of zeal; and Rienzi felt the importance of justifying his usurpation by a regular form and a legal title. At his own choice, the Roman people would have displayed their attachment and authority by lavishing on his head the names of senator or consul, of king or emperor: he preferred the ancient and modest appellation of tribune; the protection of the commons was the essence of that sacred office, and they were ignorant that it had never been invested with any share in the legislative or executive powers of the republic. In this character, and with the consent of the Romans, the tribune enacted the most salutary laws for the restoration and maintenance of the good estate. By the first he fulfils the wish of honesty and inexperience, that no civil suit

should be protracted beyond the term of fifteen days. The
danger of frequent perjury might justify the pronouncing against
a false accuser the same penalty which his evidence would have
inflicted: the disorders of the times might compel the legislator
to punish every homicide with death and every injury with equal
retaliation. But the execution of justice was hopeless till he had
previously abolished the tyranny of the nobles. It was formally
provided that none, except the supreme magistrate, should
possess or command the gates, bridges, or towers of the state;
that no private garrisons should be introduced into the towns or
castles of the Roman territory; that none should bear arms or
presume to fortify their houses in the city or country; that the
barons should be responsible for the safety of the highways and
the free passage of provisions; and that the protection of malefactors and robbers should be expiated by a fine of a thousand
marks of silver. But these regulations would have been impotent
and nugatory, had not the licentious nobles been awed by the
sword of the civil power. A sudden alarm from the bell of the
Capitol could still summon to the standard above twenty thousand volunteers: the support of the tribune and the laws required a more regular and permanent force. In each harbour
of the coast a vessel was stationed for the assurance of commerce:
a standing militia of three hundred and sixty horse and thirteen
hundred foot was levied, clothed, and paid in the thirteen
quarters of the city; and the spirit of a commonwealth may be
traced in the grateful allowance of one hundred florins, or
pounds, to the heirs of every soldier who lost his life in the
service of his country. For the maintenance of the public
defence, for the establishment of granaries, for the relief of
widows, orphans, and indigent convents, Rienzi applied, without
fear of sacrilege, the revenues of the apostolic chamber: the
three branches of hearth-money, the salt-duty, and the customs,
were each of the annual produce of one hundred thousand florins;[1]
and scandalous were the abuses, if in four or five months the
amount of the salt-duty could be trebled by his judicious
economy. After thus restoring the forces and finances of the
republic, the tribune recalled the nobles from their solitary independence, required their personal appearance in the Capitol,
and imposed an oath of allegiance to the new government, and of

---

[1] In one MS. I read (l. ii. c. 4, p. 409) perfumante quatro *solli* ; in another,
quatro *fiorini*—an important variety, since the florin was worth ten
Roman *solidi* (Muratori, dissert. xxviii.). The former reading would give
us a population of 25,000, the latter of 250,000, families; and I much fear
that the former is more consistent with the decay of Rome and her territory.

submission to the laws of the good estate. Apprehensive for their safety, but still more apprehensive of the danger of a refusal, the princes and barons returned to their houses at Rome in the garb of simple and peaceful citizens; the Colonna and Ursini, the Savelli and Frangipani, were confounded before the tribunal of a plebeian, of the vile buffoon whom they had so often derided, and their disgrace was aggravated by the indignation which they vainly struggled to disguise. The same oath was successively pronounced by the several orders of society, the clergy and gentlemen, the judges and notaries, the merchants and artisans, and the gradual descent was marked by the increase of sincerity and zeal. They swore to live and die with the republic and the church, whose interest was artfully united by the nominal association of the bishop of Orvieto, the pope's vicar, to the office of tribune. It was the boast of Rienzi that he had delivered the throne and patrimony of St. Peter from a rebellious aristocracy; and Clement the Sixth, who rejoiced in its fall, affected to believe the professions, to applaud the merits, and to confirm the title of his trusty servant. The speech, perhaps the mind, of the tribune, was inspired with a lively regard for the purity of the faith: he insinuated his claim to a supernatural mission from the Holy Ghost; enforced by a heavy forfeiture the annual duty of confession and communion; and strictly guarded the spiritual as well as temporal welfare of his faithful people.[1]

Never perhaps has the energy and effect of a single mind been more remarkably felt than in the sudden, though transient, reformation of Rome by the tribune Rienzi. A den of robbers was converted to the discipline of a camp or convent: patient to hear, swift to redress, inexorable to punish, his tribunal was always accessible to the poor and stranger; nor could birth, or dignity, or the immunities of the church, protect the offender or his accomplices. The privileged houses, the private sanctuaries in Rome, on which no officer of justice would presume to trespass, were abolished; and he applied the timber and iron of their barricades in the fortifications of the Capitol. The venerable father of the Colonna was exposed in his own palace to the double shame of being desirous and of being unable to protect a criminal. A mule, with a jar of oil, had been stolen near Capranica; and the lord of the Ursini family was condemned to restore the damage

---

[1] Hocsemius, p. 398, apud du Cerçeau, Hist. de Rienzi, p. 194. The fifteen tribunitian laws may be found in the Roman historian (whom for brevity I shall name) Fortifiocca, l. ii. c. 4.

and to discharge a fine of four hundred florins for his negligence in guarding the highways. Nor were the persons of the barons more inviolate than their lands or houses; and, either from accident or design, the same impartial rigour was exercised against the heads of the adverse factions. Peter Agapet Colonna, who had himself been senator of Rome, was arrested in the street for injury or debt; and justice was appeased by the tardy execution of Martin Ursini, who, among his various acts of violence and rapine, had pillaged a shipwrecked vessel at the mouth of the Tiber.[1] His name, the purple of two cardinals his uncles, a recent marriage, and a mortal disease, were disregarded by the inflexible tribune, who had chosen his victim. The public officers dragged him from his palace and nuptial bed: his trial was short and satisfactory; the bell of the Capitol convened the people: stripped of his mantle, on his knees, with his hands bound behind his back, he heard the sentence of death, and, after a brief confession, Ursini was led away to the gallows. After such an example, none who were conscious of guilt could hope for impunity, and the flight of the wicked, the licentious, and the idle, soon purified the city and territory of Rome. In this time (says the historian) the woods began to rejoice that they were no longer infested with robbers; the oxen began to plough; the pilgrims visited the sanctuaries; the roads and inns were replenished with travellers; trade, plenty, and good faith were restored in the markets; and a purse of gold might be exposed without danger in the midst of the highway. As soon as the life and property of the subject are secure, the labours and rewards of industry spontaneously revive: Rome was still the metropolis of the Christian world, and the fame and fortunes of the tribune were diffused in every country by the strangers who had enjoyed the blessings of his government.

The deliverance of his country inspired Rienzi with a vast and perhaps visionary idea of uniting Italy in a great federative republic, of which Rome should be the ancient and lawful head,

---

[1] Fortifiocca, l. ii. c. 11. From the account of this shipwreck we learn some circumstances of the trade and navigation of the age. 1. The ship was built and freighted at Naples for the ports of Marseilles and Avignon. 2. The sailors were of Naples and the isle of Œnaria, less skilful than those of Sicily and Genoa. 3. The navigation from Marseilles was a coasting voyage to the mouth of the Tiber, where they took shelter in a storm; but, instead of finding the current, unfortunately ran on a shoal: the vessel was stranded, the mariners escaped. 4. The cargo, which was pillaged, consisted of the revenue of Provence for the royal treasury, many bags of pepper and cinnamon, and bales of French cloth, to the value of 20,000 florins: a rich prize.

and the free cities and princes the members and associates. His
pen was not less eloquent than his tongue, and his numerous
epistles were delivered to swift and trusty messengers. On foot,
with a white wand in their hand, they traversed the forests
and mountains; enjoyed, in the most hostile states, the sacred
security of ambassadors; and reported, in the style of flattery
or truth, that the highways along their passage were lined with
kneeling multitudes, who implored Heaven for the success of
their undertaking. Could passion have listened to reason,
could private interest have yielded to the public welfare, the
supreme tribunal and confederate union of the Italian republic
might have healed their intestine discord, and closed the Alps
against the barbarians of the North. But the propitious season
had elapsed; and if Venice, Florence, Sienna, Perugia, and many
inferior cities, offered their lives and fortunes to the good estate,
the tyrants of Lombardy and Tuscany must despise or hate the
plebeian author of a free constitution. From them, however,
and from every part of Italy, the tribune received the most
friendly and respectful answers: they were followed by the
ambassadors of the princes and republics; and in this foreign
conflux, on all the occasions of pleasure or business, the low-born
notary could assume the familiar or majestic courtesy of a
sovereign.[1] The most glorious circumstance of his reign was an
appeal to his justice from Lewis king of Hungary, who complained that his brother and her husband had been perfidiously
strangled by Jane queen of Naples:[2] her guilt or innocence was
pleaded in a solemn trial at Rome; but after hearing the
advocates,[3] the tribune adjourned this weighty and invidious
cause, which was soon determined by the sword of the Hungarian.
Beyond the Alps, more especially at Avignon, the revolution

[1] It was thus that Oliver Cromwell's old acquaintance, who remembered
his vulgar and ungracious entrance into the House of Commons, were
astonished at the ease and majesty of the Protector on his throne (see
Harris's Life of Cromwell, p. 27-34, from Clarendon, Warwick, Whitelocke,
Waller, etc.). The consciousness of merit and power will sometimes
elevate the manners to the station.

[2] See the causes, circumstances, and effects of the death of Andrew, in
Giannone (tom. iii. l. xxiii. p. 220-229), and the Life of Petrarch (Mémoires,
tom. ii. p. 143-148, 245-250, 375-379, notes, p. 21-37). The abbé de Sade
wishes to extenuate her guilt.

[3] The advocate who pleaded against Jane could add nothing to the
logical force and brevity of his master's epistle. Johanna! inordinata
vita præcedens, retentio potestatis in regno, neglecta vindicta, vir alter
susceptus, et excusatio subsequens, necis viri tui te probant fuisse parti-
cipem et consortem. Jane of Naples and Mary of Scotland have a singular
conformity

was the theme of curiosity, wonder, and applause.[1] Petrarch
had been the private friend, perhaps the secret counsellor, of
Rienzi: his writings breathe the most ardent spirit of patriotism
and joy; and all respect for the pope, all gratitude for the
Colonna, was lost in the superior duties of a Roman citizen.
The poet-laureat of the Capitol maintains the act, applauds the
hero, and mingles with some apprehension and advice the most
lofty hopes of the permanent and rising greatness of the republic.[2]

While Petrarch indulged these prophetic visions, the Roman
hero was fast declining from the meridian of fame and power;
and the people, who had gazed with astonishment on the ascending meteor, began to mark the irregularity of its course, and the
vicissitudes of light and obscurity. More eloquent than judicious,
more enterprising than resolute, the faculties of Rienzi were not
balanced by cool and commanding reason; he magnified in a
tenfold proportion the objects of hope and fear; and prudence,
which could not have erected, did not presume to fortify, his
throne. In the blaze of prosperity, his virtues were insensibly
tinctured with the adjacent vices; justice with cruelty, liberality
with profusion, and the desire of fame with puerile and ostentatious vanity. He might have learned that the ancient tribunes,

[1] [In his letter to the archbishop of Prague, Rienzi thus describes the
effect of his elevation on Italy and the world: " Did I not restore real
peace among the cities that were distracted by factions; did I not cause all
the citizens exiled by party violence, with their wretched wives and
children, to be re-admitted? Had I not begun to extinguish the factious
names of Guelf and Ghibelline, for which countless thousands had perished,
body and soul, under the eyes of their pastors, by the reduction of the city
of Rome and all Italy into one amicable, peaceful, holy, and united confederacy? the consecrated standards and banners having been by me
collected and blended together, and, in witness to our holy association and
perfect union, offered up in the presence of the ambassadors of all the
cities of Italy on the day of the assumption of our Blessed Lady." In the
Libellus ad Cæsarem he goes on to say: " I received the homage and submission of all the sovereigns of Apulia, the barons and counts, and almost
all the people of Italy. I was honoured by solemn embassies and letters
by the emperor of Constantinople and the king of England. The queen
of Naples submitted herself and her kingdom to the protection of the
tribune. The king of Hungary, by two solemn embassies, brought his
cause against his queen and his nobles before my tribunal; and I venture
to say further, that the fame of the tribune alarmed the soldan of Babylon.
When the Christian pilgrims to the sepulchre of our Lord related to the
Christian and Jewish inhabitants of Jerusalem all the yet unheard-of and
wonderful circumstances of the reformation in Rome, both Jews and
Christians celebrated the event with unusual festivities. When the soldan
inquired the cause of these rejoicings, and received this intelligence about
Rome, he ordered all the havens and cities on the coast to be fortified."—
O. S.]

[2] See the Epistola Hortatoria de Capessenda Republica, from Petrarch
to Nicholas Rienzi (Opp. p. 535-540), and the fifth eclogue or pastoral, a
perpetual and obscure allegory.

so strong and sacred in the public opinion, were not distinguished in style, habit, or appearance, from an ordinary plebeian;[1] and that, as often as they visited the city on foot, a single viator, or beadle, attended the exercise of their office. The Gracchi would have frowned or smiled, could they have read the sonorous titles and epithets of their successor—" NICHOLAS, SEVERE AND MERCIFUL; DELIVERER OF ROME; DEFENDER OF ITALY;[2] FRIEND OF MANKIND, AND OF LIBERTY, PEACE, AND JUSTICE; TRIBUNE AUGUST:" his theatrical pageants had prepared the revolution; but Rienzi abused, in luxury and pride, the political maxim of speaking to the eyes, as well as the understanding, of the multitude. From nature he had received the gift of a handsome person,[3] till it was swelled and disfigured by intemperance: and his propensity to laughter was corrected in the magistrate by the affectation of gravity and sternness. He was clothed, at least on public occasions, in a parti-coloured robe of velvet or satin, lined with fur, and embroidered with gold: the rod of justice, which he carried in his hand, was a sceptre of polished steel, crowned with a globe and cross of gold, and enclosing a small fragment of the true and holy wood. In his civil and religious processions through the city, he rode on a white steed, the symbol of royalty: the great banner of the republic, a sun with a circle of stars, a dove with an olive-branch, was displayed over his head; a shower of gold and silver was scattered among the populace; fifty guards with halberds encompassed his person; a troop of horse preceded his march; and their tymbals and trumpets were of massy silver.

The ambition of the honours of chivalry[4] betrayed the mean-

[1] In his Roman Questions, Plutarch ([c. 81] Opuscul. tom. i. p. 505, 506, edit. Græc. Hen. Steph.) states, on the most constitutional principles, the simple greatness of the tribunes, who were not properly magistrates, but a check on magistracy. It was their duty and interest ὁμοιοῦσθαι καὶ σχήματι καὶ στολῇ καὶ διαίτῃ τοῖς ἐπιτυγχάνουσι τῶν πολιτῶν . . . . καταπατεῖσθαι δεῖ (a saying of C. Curio) καὶ μὴ σεμνὸν εἶναι τῇ ὄψει μηδὲ δυσπρόσοδον . . . . ὅσῳ δὲ μᾶλλον ἐκταπεινοῦται τῷ σώματι, τοσούτῳ μᾶλλον αὔξεται τῇ δυνάμει, etc. Rienzi, and Petrarch himself, were incapable perhaps of reading a Greek philosopher; but they might have imbibed the same modest doctrines from their favourite Latins, Livy and Valerius Maximus.

[2] I could not express in English the forcible, though barbarous, title of Zelator Italiæ, which Rienzi assumed.

[3] Era bell' homo (l. ii. c. 1, p. 399). It is remarkable that the riso sarcastico of the Bracciano edition is wanting in the Roman MS. from which Muratori has given the text. In his second reign, when he is painted almost as a monster, Rienzi travea una ventresca tonna trionfale, a modo de uno Abbate Asiano, or Asinino (l. iii. c. 18, p. 523).

[4] Strange as it may seem, this festival was not without a precedent. In the year 1327, two barons, a Colonna and an Ursini, the usual balance, were created knights by the Roman people: their bath was of rose-water,

ness of his birth and degraded the importance of his office; and
the equestrian tribune was not less odious to the nobles, whom
he adopted, than to the plebeians, whom he deserted. All that
yet remained of treasure, or luxury, or art, was exhausted on
that solemn day. Rienzi led the procession from the Capitol to
the Lateran; the tediousness of the way was relieved with
decorations and games; the ecclesiastical, civil, and military
orders marched under their various banners; the Roman ladies
attended his wife; and the ambassadors of Italy might loudly
applaud or secretly deride the novelty of the pomp. In the
evening, when they had reached the church and palace of Constantine, he thanked and dismissed the numerous assembly, with
an invitation to the festival of the ensuing day. From the
hands of a venerable knight he received the order of the Holy
Ghost; the purification of the bath was a previous ceremony;
but in no step of his life did Rienzi excite such scandal and
censure as by the profane use of the porphyry vase in which
Constantine (a foolish legend) had been healed of his leprosy by
Pope Sylvester.[1] With equal presumption the tribune watched
or reposed within the consecrated precincts of the baptistery;
and the failure of his state-bed was interpreted as an omen of his
approaching downfall. At the hour of worship he showed himself to the returning crowds in a majestic attitude, with a robe
of purple, his sword, and gilt spurs; but the holy rites were soon
interrupted by his levity and insolence. Rising from his throne,
and advancing towards the congregation, he proclaimed in a
loud voice, " We summon to our tribunal Pope Clement, and
command him to reside in his diocese of Rome: we also summon
the sacred college of cardinals.[2] We again summon the two

their beds were decked with royal magnificence, and they were served at
St. Maria of Araceli in the Capitol by the twenty-eight *buoni huomini*.
They afterwards received from Robert king of Naples the sword of
chivalry (Hist. Rom. l. i. c. 2, p. 259).
[Rienzi, on July 26, 1347, issued his famous edict affirming the sacred
majesty and supremacy of the Roman people, and declaring all the privileges assumed by the popes to be forfeited. This edict, after being submitted to a committee of jurists, was issued in the name of the Italian
nation.—O. S.]

[1] All parties believed in the leprosy and bath of Constantine (Petrarch,
Epist. Famil. vi. 2), and Rienzi justified his own conduct by observing to
the court of Avignon, that a vase which had been used by a pagan could
not be profaned by a pious Christian. Yet this crime is specified in the
bull of excommunication (Hocsemius, apud du Cerçeau, p. 189, 190).

[2] This *verbal* summons of Pope Clement VI., which rests on the authority
of the Roman historian and a Vatican MS., is disputed by the biographer
of Petrarch (tom. ii. not. p. 70-76) with arguments rather of decency than
of weight. The court of Avignon might not choose to agitate this delicate
question.

pretenders, Charles of Bohemia and Lewis of Bavaria, who style themselves emperors: we likewise summon all the electors of Germany to inform us on what pretence they have usurped the inalienable right of the Roman people, the ancient and lawful sovereigns of the empire." [1] Unsheathing his maiden sword, he thrice brandished it to the three parts of the world, and thrice repeated the extravagant declaration, " And this too is mine ! " The pope's vicar, the bishop of Orvieto, attempted to check this career of folly; but his feeble protest was silenced by martial music; and instead of withdrawing from the assembly, he consented to dine with his brother tribune at a table which had hitherto been reserved for the supreme pontiff. A banquet, such as the Cæsars had given, was prepared for the Romans. The apartments, porticoes, and courts of the Lateran were spread with innumerable tables for either sex and every condition; a stream of wine flowed from the nostrils of Constantine's brazen horse; no complaint, except of the scarcity of water, could be heard; and the licentiousness of the multitude was curbed by discipline and fear. A subsequent day was appointed for the coronation of Rienzi; [2] seven crowns of different leaves or metals were successively placed on his head by the most eminent of the Roman clergy; they represented the seven gifts of the Holy Ghost; and he still professed to imitate the example of the ancient tribunes. These extraordinary spectacles might deceive or flatter the people; and their own vanity was gratified in the vanity of their leader. But in his private life he soon deviated from the strict rule of frugality and abstinence; and the plebeians, who were awed by the splendour of the nobles, were provoked by the luxury of their equal. His wife, his son, his uncle (a barber in name and profession), exposed the contrast of vulgar manners

[1] The summons of the two rival emperors, a monument of freedom and folly, is extant in Hocsemius (Cerçeau, p. 163-166).

[2] It is singular that the Roman historian should have overlooked this sevenfold coronation, which is sufficiently proved by internal evidence, and the testimony of Hocsemius, and even of Rienzi (Cerçeau, p. 167-170, 229).

[It was on the occasion of his coronation that he made the impious comparison between himself and our Lord. In the midst of all the wild and joyous exultation of the people, one of his most zealous supporters, a monk, who was in high repute for his sanctity, stood apart in a corner of the church and wept bitterly. A domestic chaplain of Rienzi's inquired the cause of his grief. " Now," replied the man of God, " is thy master cast down from heaven; never saw I man so proud. By the aid of the Holy Ghost he has driven the tyrants from the city without drawing a sword: the citizens and the sovereigns of Italy have submitted to his power. Why is he so arrogant and ungrateful towards the Most High? . . . Tell your master that he can only atone for this offence by tears of penitence."—O. S.]

and princely expense; and without acquiring the majesty, Rienzi degenerated into the vices, of a king.

A simple citizen describes with pity, or perhaps with pleasure, the humiliation of the barons of Rome. " Bareheaded, their hands crossed on their breast, they stood with downcast looks in the presence of the tribune; and they trembled, good God, how they trembled! " [1] As long as the yoke of Rienzi was that of justice and their country, their conscience forced them to esteem the man whom pride and interest provoked them to hate: his extravagant conduct soon fortified their hatred by contempt; and they conceived the hope of subverting a power which was no longer so deeply rooted in the public confidence. The old animosity of the Colonna and Ursini was suspended for a moment by their common disgrace: they associated their wishes, and perhaps their designs; an assassin was seized and tortured; he accused the nobles; and as soon as Rienzi deserved the fate, he adopted the suspicions and maxims, of a tyrant. On the same day, under various pretences, he invited to the Capitol his principal enemies, among whom were five members of the Ursini and three of the Colonna name. But instead of a council or a banquet, they found themselves prisoners under the sword of despotism or justice; and the consciousness of innocence or guilt might inspire them with equal apprehensions of danger. At the sound of the great bell the people assembled; they were arraigned for a conspiracy against the tribune's life; and though some might sympathise in their distress, not a hand nor a voice was raised to rescue the first of the nobility from their impending doom. Their apparent boldness was prompted by despair; they passed in separate chambers a sleepless and painful night; and the venerable hero, Stephen Colonna, striking against the door of his prison, repeatedly urged his guards to deliver him by a speedy death from such ignominious servitude. In the morning they understood their sentence from the visit of a confessor and the tolling of the bell. The great hall of the Capitol had been decorated for the bloody scene with red and white hangings: the countenance of the tribune was dark and severe; the swords of the executioners were unsheathed; and the barons were interrupted in their dying speeches by the sound of trumpets. But in this decisive moment Rienzi was not less anxious or apprehensive than his captives: he dreaded the splendour of

[1] Puoi se faceva stare denante a se, mentre sedeva, li baroni tutti in piedi ritti co le vraccia piecate, e co li capucci tratti. Deh como stavano paurosi! (Hist. Rom. l. ii. c. 20, p. 439.) He saw them, and we see them.

their names, their surviving kinsmen, the inconstancy of the people, the reproaches of the world; and, after rashly offering a mortal injury, he vainly presumed that, if he could forgive, he might himself be forgiven. His elaborate oration was that of a Christian and a suppliant; and, as the humble minister of the commons, he entreated his masters to pardon these noble criminals, for whose repentance and future service he pledged his faith and authority. " If you are spared," said the tribune, " by the mercy of the Romans, will you not promise to support the good estate with your lives and fortunes? " Astonished by this marvellous clemency, the barons bowed their heads; and while they devoutly repeated the oath of allegiance, might whisper a secret, and more sincere, assurance of revenge. A priest, in the name of the people, pronounced their absolution; they received the communion with the tribune, assisted at the banquet, followed the procession; and, after every spiritual and temporal sign of reconciliation, were dismissed in safety to their respective homes, with the new honours and titles of generals, consuls, and patricians.[1]

During some weeks they were checked by the memory of their danger, rather than of their deliverance, till the most powerful of the Ursini, escaping with the Colonna from the city, erected at Marino the standard of rebellion. The fortifications of the castle were hastily restored; the vassals attended their lord; the outlaws armed against the magistrate; the flocks and herds, the harvests and vineyards from Marino to the gates of Rome, were swept away or destroyed; and the people arraigned Rienzi as the author of the calamities which his government had taught them to forget. In the camp Rienzi appeared to less advantage than in the rostrum; and he neglected the progress of the rebel barons till their numbers were strong, and their castles impregnable. From the pages of Livy he had not imbibed the art, or even the courage, of a general: an army of twenty thousand Romans returned without honour or effect from the attack of Marino; and his vengeance was amused by painting his enemies, their heads downwards, and drowning two dogs (at least they should have been bears) as the representatives of the Ursini. The belief of his incapacity encouraged their operations: they were invited by their secret adherents; and the barons attempted, with four thousand foot and sixteen hundred horse, to enter

---

[1] The original letter, in which Rienzi justifies his treatment of the Colonna (Hocsemius, apud Du Cerçeau, p. 222-229), displays, in genuine colours, the mixture of the knave and the madman.

Rome by force or surprise. The city was prepared for their reception; the alarm-bell rung all night; the gates were strictly guarded, or insolently open; and after some hesitation they sounded a retreat. The two first divisions had passed along the walls, but the prospect of a free entrance tempted the head-strong valour of the nobles in the rear; and after a successful skirmish, they were overthrown and massacred without quarter by the crowds of the Roman people. Stephen Colonna the younger, the noble spirit to whom Petrarch ascribed the restoration of Italy, were preceded or accompanied in death by his son John, a gallant youth, by his brother Peter, who might regret the ease and honours of the church, by a nephew of legitimate birth, and by two bastards of the Colonna race; and the number of seven, the seven crowns, as Rienzi styled them, of the Holy Ghost, was completed by the agony of the deplorable parent, of the veteran chief, who had survived the hope and fortune of his house. The vision and prophecies of St. Martin and Pope Boniface had been used by the tribune to animate his troops: [1] he displayed, at least in the pursuit, the spirit of a hero; but he forgot the maxims of the ancient Romans, who abhorred the triumphs of civil war. The conqueror ascended the Capitol; deposited his crown and sceptre on the altar; and boasted, with some truth, that he had cut off an ear which neither pope nor emperor had been able to amputate.[2] His base and implacable revenge denied the honours of burial; and the bodies of the Colonna, which he threatened to expose with those of the vilest malefactors, were secretly interred by the holy virgins of their name and family.[3] The people sympathised in their grief,

[1] Rienzi, in the above-mentioned letter, ascribes to St. Martin the tribune, Boniface VIII. the enemy of Colonna, himself, and the Roman people, the glory of the day, which Villani likewise (l. xii. c. 104) describes as a regular battle. The disorderly skirmish, the flight of the Romans, and the cowardice of Rienzi, are painted in the simple and minute narrative of Fortifiocca, or the anonymous citizen (l. ii. c. 34-37).

[2] In describing the fall of the Colonna, I speak only of the family of Stephen the elder, who is often confounded by the P. du Cerçeau with his son. That family was extinguished, but the house has been perpetuated in the collateral branches, of which I have not a very accurate knowledge. Circumspice (says Petrarch) familiæ tuæ statum. Columniensium *domos :* solito pauciores habeat columnas. Quid ad rem? modo fundamentum stabile, solidumque permaneat.

[3] The convent of St. Silvester was founded, endowed, and protected by the Colonna cardinals, for the daughters of the family who embraced a monastic life, and who, in the year 1318, were twelve in number. The others were allowed to marry with their kinsmen in the fourth degree, and the dispensation was justified by the small number and close alliances of the noble families of Rome (Mémoires sur Pétrarque, tom. i. p. 110, tom. ii. p. 401).

repented of their own fury, and detested the indecent joy of
Rienzi, who visited the spot where these illustrious victims had
fallen.   It was on that fatal spot that he conferred on his son the
honour of knighthood: and the ceremony was accomplished by
a slight blow from each of the horsemen of the guard, and by a
ridiculous and inhuman ablution from a pool of water, which
was yet polluted with patrician blood.[1]

A short delay would have saved the Colonna, the delay of a
single month, which elapsed between the triumph and the exile
of Rienzi.   In the pride of victory he forfeited what yet remained
of his civil virtues, without acquiring the fame of military
prowess.   A free and vigorous opposition was formed in the
city; and when the tribune proposed in the public council[2]
to impose a new tax, and to regulate the government of Perugia,
thirty-nine members voted against his measures, repelled the
injurious charge of treachery and corruption, and urged him to
prove, by their forcible exclusion, that, if the populace adhered
to his cause, it was already disclaimed by the most respectable
citizens.   The pope and the sacred college had never been dazzled
by his specious professions; they were justly offended by the
insolence of his conduct; a cardinal legate was sent to Italy,
and after some fruitless treaty, and two personal interviews, he
fulminated a bull of excommunication, in which the tribune is
degraded from his office, and branded with the guilt of rebellion,
sacrilege, and heresy.[3]   The surviving barons of Rome were
now humbled to a sense of allegiance; their interest and revenge
engaged them in the service of the church; but as the fate of
the Colonna was before their eyes, they abandoned to a private
adventurer the peril and glory of the revolution.   John Pepin,
count of Minorbino,[4] in the kingdom of Naples, had been con-

---

[1] Petrarch wrote a stiff and pedantic letter of consolation (Fam. l. vii.
epist. 13, p. 682, 683).   The friend was lost in the patriot.   Nulla toto
orbe principum familia carior; carior tamen respublica, carior Roma,
carior Italia.

Je rends grâces aux Dieux de n'être pas Romain.

[2] This council and opposition is obscurely mentioned by Pollistore, a
contemporary writer, who has preserved some curious and original facts
(Rer. Italicarum, tom. xxv. c. 31, p. 798-804).

[3] The briefs and bulls of Clement VI. against Rienzi are translated by
the P. du Cerçeau (p. 196, 232) from the ecclesiastical Annals of Odericus
Raynaldus (A.D. 1347, No. 15, 17, 21, etc.), who found them in the archives
of the Vatican.

[4] Matteo Villani describes the origin, character, and death of this count
of Minorbino, a man da natura inconstante e senza fede, whose grandfather, a crafty notary, was enriched and ennobled by the spoils of the
Saracens of Nocera (l. vii. c. 102, 103).   See his imprisonment, and the
efforts of Petrarch, tom. ii. p. 149-151.

demned for his crimes, or his riches, to perpetual imprisonment; and Petrarch, by soliciting his release, indirectly contributed to the ruin of his friend. At the head of one hundred and fifty soldiers the count of Minorbino introduced himself into Rome, barricaded the quarter of the Colonna, and found the enterprise as easy as it had seemed impossible. From the first alarm the bell of the Capitol incessantly tolled; but instead of repairing to the well-known sound, the people were silent and inactive; and the pusillanimous Rienzi, deploring their ingratitude with sighs and tears, abdicated the government and palace of the republic.

Without drawing his sword, Count Pepin restored the aristocracy and the church; three senators were chosen, and the legate, assuming the first rank, accepted his two colleagues from the rival families of Colonna and Ursini. The acts of the tribune were abolished, his head was proscribed; yet such was the terror of his name, that the barons hesitated three days before they would trust themselves in the city, and Rienzi was left above a month in the castle of St. Angelo, from whence he peaceably withdrew, after labouring, without effect, to revive the affection and courage of the Romans. The vision of freedom and empire had vanished: their fallen spirit would have acquiesced in servitude, had it been smoothed by tranquillity and order; and it was scarcely observed that the new senators derived their authority from the Apostolic See, that four cardinals were appointed to reform, with dictatorial power, the state of the republic. Rome was again agitated by the bloody feuds of the barons, who detested each other and despised the commons: their hostile fortresses, both in town and country, again rose, and were again demolished: and the peaceful citizens, a flock of sheep, were devoured, says the Florentine historian, by these rapacious wolves. But when their pride and avarice had exhausted the patience of the Romans, a confraternity of the Virgin Mary protected or avenged the republic: the bell of the Capitol was again tolled, the nobles in arms trembled in the presence of an unarmed multitude; and of the two senators, Colonna escaped from the window of the palace, and Ursini was stoned at the foot of the altar. The dangerous office of tribune was successively occupied by two plebeians, Cerroni and Baroncelli. The mildness of Cerroni was unequal to the times, and after a faint struggle he retired with a fair reputation and a decent fortune to the comforts of rural life. Devoid of eloquence or genius, Baroncelli was distinguished by a resolute spirit: he

spoke the language of a patriot, and trod in the footsteps of
tyrants; his suspicion was a sentence of death, and his own
death was the reward of his cruelties. Amidst the public misfortunes the faults of Rienzi were forgotten, and the Romans
sighed for the peace and prosperity of the good estate.[1]

After an exile of seven years, the first deliverer was again
restored to his country. In the disguise of a monk or a pilgrim
he escaped from the castle of St. Angelo, implored the friendship
of the king of Hungary at Naples, tempted the ambition of every
bold adventurer, mingled at Rome with the pilgrims of the
jubilee, lay concealed among the hermits of the Apennine, and
wandered through the cities of Italy, Germany, and Bohemia.
His person was invisible, his name was yet formidable; and the
anxiety of the court of Avignon supposes, and even magnifies,
his personal merit. The emperor Charles the Fourth gave
audience to a stranger, who frankly revealed himself as the tribune
of the republic, and astonished an assembly of ambassadors and
princes by the eloquence of a patriot and the visions of a prophet,
the downfall of tyranny and the kingdom of the Holy Ghost.[2]
Whatever had been his hopes, Rienzi found himself a captive;
but he supported a character of independence and dignity, and
obeyed, as his own choice, the irresistible summons of the
supreme pontiff. The zeal of Petrarch, which had been cooled
by the unworthy conduct, was rekindled by the sufferings and
the presence of his friend; and he boldly complains of the times

---

[1] The troubles of Rome, from the departure to the return of Rienzi, are
related by Matteo Villani (l. ii. c. 47, l. iii. c. 33, 57, 78) and Thomas Fortifiocca (l. iii. c. 1-4). I have slightly passed over these secondary characters,
who imitated the original tribune.

[2] These visions, of which the friends and enemies of Rienzi seem alike
ignorant, are surely magnified by the zeal of Pollistore, a Dominican in-
quisitor (Rer. Ital. tom. xxv. c. 36, p. 819). Had the tribune taught that
Christ was succeeded by the Holy Ghost, that the tyranny of the pope
would be abolished, he might have been convicted of heresy and treason,
without offending the Roman people.

[So far from having magnified these visions, Pollistore is more than confirmed by the documents published by Papencordt. The adoption of all
the wild doctrines of the Fratricelli, the Spirituals, in which, for the time
at least, Rienzi appears to have been in earnest, his magnificent offers to
the emperor, and the whole history of his life, from his first escape from
Rome to his imprisonment at Avignon, are among the most curious
chapters of his eventful life. The letters of Rienzi, as given in Papencordt's work, portray the state of Rome, indict the pope, and are
thoroughly Ghibelline in spirit, expressing the need of keeping the secular
and ecclesiastical powers apart. Gregorovius says, " The tribune in chains
at Prague was more dangerous to the papacy than he had been when at the
height of his power in the Capitol. He now expressed the necessity for
mankind of a reformation; and this it is which secures him a place in
history."—O. S.]

in which the saviour of Rome was delivered by her emperor into the hands of her bishop. Rienzi was transported slowly but in safe custody from Prague to Avignon: his entrance into the city was that of a malefactor; in his prison he was chained by the leg, and four cardinals were named to inquire into the crimes of heresy and rebellion. But his trial and condemnation would have involved some questions which it was more prudent to leave under the veil of mystery: the temporal supremacy of the popes, the duty of residence, the civil and ecclesiastical privileges of the clergy and people of Rome. The reigning pontiff well deserved the appellation of *Clement*: the strange vicissitudes and magnanimous spirit of the captive excited his pity and esteem; and Petrarch believes that he respected in the hero the name and sacred character of a poet.[1] Rienzi was indulged with an easy confinement and the use of books; and in the assiduous study of Livy and the Bible he sought the cause and the consolation of his misfortunes.

The succeeding pontificate of Innocent the Sixth opened a new prospect of his deliverance and restoration; and the court of Avignon was persuaded that the successful rebel could alone appease and reform the anarchy of the metropolis. After a solemn profession of fidelity, the Roman tribune was sent into Italy with the title of senator; but the death of Baroncelli appeared to supersede the use of his mission; and the legate, Cardinal Albornoz,[2] a consummate statesman, allowed him with reluctance, and without aid, to undertake the perilous experiment. His first reception was equal to his wishes: the day of his entrance was a public festival, and his eloquence and authority revived the laws of the good estate. But this momentary sunshine was soon clouded by his own vices and those of the people: in the Capitol he might often regret the prison of Avignon; and after a second administration of four months Rienzi was massacred in a tumult which had been fomented by the Roman barons. In the society of the Germans and Bohemians he is said to have contracted the habits of

---

[1] The astonishment, the envy almost, of Petrarch, is a proof, if not of the truth of this incredible fact, at least of his own veracity. The abbé de Sade (Mémoires, tom. iii. p. 242) quotes the sixth epistle of the thirteenth book of Petrarch, but it is of the royal MS. which he consulted, and not of the ordinary Basil edition (p. 920).

[2] Ægidius, or Giles Albornoz, a noble Spaniard, archbishop of Toledo, and cardinal legate in Italy (A.D. 1353-1367), restored, by his arms and counsels, the temporal dominion of the popes. His life has been separately written by Sepulveda; but Dryden could not reasonably suppose that his name, or that of Wolsey, had reached the ears of the Mufti in Don Sebastian.

intemperance and cruelty: adversity had chilled his enthusiasm
without fortifying his reason or virtue; and that youthful hope,
that lively assurance, which is the pledge of success, was now
succeeded by the cold impotence of distrust and despair. The
tribune had reigned with absolute dominion, by the choice, and
in the hearts, of the Romans; the senator was the servile minister
of a foreign court; and while he was suspected by the people,
he was abandoned by the prince. The legate Albornoz, who
seemed desirous of his ruin, inflexibly refused all supplies of men
and money: a faithful subject could no longer presume to touch
the revenues of the apostolical chamber; and the first idea of a
tax was the signal of clamour and sedition. Even his justice
was tainted with the guilt or reproach of selfish cruelty: the
most virtuous citizen of Rome was sacrificed to his jealousy;
and in the execution of a public robber, from whose purse
he had been assisted, the magistrate too much forgot, or too
much remembered, the obligations of the debtor.[1] A civil war
exhausted his treasures and the patience of the city: the
Colonna maintained their hostile station at Palestrina; and his
mercenaries soon despised a leader whose ignorance and fear
were envious of all subordinate merit. In the death, as in the
life, of Rienzi, the hero and the coward were strangely mingled.
When the Capitol was invested by a furious multitude, when he
was basely deserted by his civil and military servants, the
intrepid senator, waving the banner of liberty, presented himself
on the balcony, addressed his eloquence to the various passions
of the Romans, and laboured to persuade them that in the same
cause himself and the republic must either stand or fall. His
oration was interrupted by a volley of imprecations and stones;
and after an arrow had transpierced his hand, he sunk into
abject despair, and fled weeping to the inner chambers, from
whence he was let down by a sheet before the windows of the
prison. Destitute of aid or hope, he was besieged till the evening: the doors of the Capitol were destroyed with axes and fire;
and while the senator attempted to escape in a plebeian habit,
he was discovered and dragged to the platform of the palace,
the fatal scene of his judgments and executions. A whole hour,
without voice or motion, he stood amidst the multitude half
naked and half dead: their rage was hushed into curiosity and

---

[1] From Matteo Villani and Fortifiocca, the P. du Cerçeau (p. 344-394)
has extracted the life and death of the Chevalier Montreal, the life of a
robber and the death of a hero. At the head of a free company, the first
that desolated Italy, he became rich and formidable: he had money in all
the banks—60,000 ducats in Padua alone.

wonder: the last feelings of reverence and compassion yet struggled in his favour; and they might have prevailed, if a bold assassin had not plunged a dagger in his breast. He fell senseless with the first stroke; the impotent revenge of his enemies inflicted a thousand wounds; and the senator's body was abandoned to the dogs, to the Jews, and to the flames. Posterity will compare the virtues and failings of this extraordinary man; but in a long period of anarchy and servitude, the name of Rienzi has often been celebrated as the deliverer of his country, and the last of the Roman patriots.[1]

The first and most generous wish of Petrarch was the restoration of a free republic; but after the exile and death of his plebeian hero, he turned his eyes from the tribune to the king of the Romans. The Capitol was yet stained with the blood of Rienzi when Charles the Fourth descended from the Alps to obtain the Italian and Imperial crowns. In his passage through Milan he received the visit, and repaid the flattery, of the poet laureat; accepted a medal of Augustus; and promised, without a smile, to imitate the founder of the Roman monarchy. A false application of the names and maxims of antiquity was the source of the hopes and disappointments of Petrarch; yet he could not overlook the difference of times and characters; the immeasurable distance between the first Cæsars and a Bohemian prince, who by the favour of the clergy had been elected the titular head of the German aristocracy. Instead of restoring to Rome her glory and her provinces, he had bound himself by a secret treaty with the pope to evacuate the city on the day of his coronation; and his shameful retreat was pursued by the reproaches of the patriot bard.[2]

After the loss of liberty and empire, his third and more humble wish was to reconcile the shepherd with his flock; to recall the Roman bishop to his ancient and peculiar diocese. In the fervour of youth, with the authority of age, Petrarch addressed his exhortations to five successive popes, and his eloquence was always inspired by the enthusiasm of sentiment and the freedom of language.[3] The son of a citizen of Florence invariably

[1] The exile, second government, and death of Rienzi, are minutely related by the anonymous Roman, who appears neither his friend nor his enemy (l. iii. c. 12-25). Petrarch, who loved the *tribune*, was indifferent to the fate of the *senator*.

[2] The hopes and the disappointment of Petrarch are agreeably described in his own words by the French biographer (Mémoires, tom. iii. p. 375-413); but the deep, though secret, wound was the coronation of Zanubi, the poet laureat, by Charles IV.

[3] See, in his accurate and amusing biographer, the application of Petrarch

preferred the country of his birth to that of his education; and
Italy, in his eyes, was the queen and garden of the world.
Amidst her domestic factions she was doubtless superior to
France both in art and science, in wealth and politeness; but
the difference could scarcely support the epithet of barbarous,
which he promiscuously bestows on the countries beyond the
Alps. Avignon, the mystic Babylon, the sink of vice and
corruption, was the object of his hatred and contempt; but he
forgets that her scandalous vices were not the growth of the
soil, and that in every residence they would adhere to the power
and luxury of the papal court. He confesses that the successor
of St. Peter is the bishop of the universal church; yet it was not
on the banks of the Rhône, but of the Tiber, that the apostle
had fixed his everlasting throne: and while every city in the
Christian world was blessed with a bishop, the metropolis alone
was desolate and forlorn. Since the removal of the Holy See
the sacred buildings of the Lateran and the Vatican, their altars
and their saints, were left in a state of poverty and decay; and
Rome was often painted under the image of a disconsolate
matron, as if the wandering husband could be reclaimed by the
homely portrait of the age and infirmities of his weeping spouse.[1]
But the cloud which hung over the seven hills would be dispelled
by the presence of their lawful sovereign: eternal fame, the
prosperity of Rome, and the peace of Italy, would be the recompense of the pope who should dare to embrace this generous
resolution. Of the five whom Petrarch exhorted, the three first,
John the Twenty-second, Benedict the Twelfth, and Clement the
Sixth, were importuned or amused by the boldness of the orator;
but the memorable change which had been attempted by Urban
the Fifth was finally accomplished by Gregory the Eleventh.
The execution of their design was opposed by weighty and
almost insuperable obstacles. A king of France, who has
deserved the epithet of wise, was unwilling to release them from

and Rome to Benedict XII. in the year 1334 (Mémoires, tom. i. p. 261-265),
to Clement VI. in 1342 (tom. ii. p. 45-47), and to Urban V. in 1366 (tom.
iii. p. 677-691): his praise (p. 711-715) and excuse (p. 771) of the last of
these pontiffs. His angry controversy on the respective merits of France
and Italy may be found Opp. p. 1068-1085.

[1] Squalida sed quoniam facies, neglectaque cultû
    Cæsaries; multisque malis lassata senectus
    Eripuit solitam effigiem: vetus accipe nomen;
    Roma vocor.   (Carm. l. ii. p. 77.)

He spins this allegory beyond all measure or patience. The Epistles to
Urban V. in prose are more simple and persuasive (Senilium, l. vii. p. 811-
827; l. ix. epist. i. p. 844-854).

a local dependence: the cardinals, for the most part his subjects,
were attached to the language, manners, and climate of Avignon;
to their stately palaces; above all, to the wines of Burgundy.
In their eyes Italy was foreign or hostile; and they reluctantly
embarked at Marseilles, as if they had been sold or banished into
the land of the Saracens. Urban the Fifth resided three years
in the Vatican with safety and honour; his sanctity was protected
by a guard of two thousand horse; and the king of Cyprus, the
queen of Naples, and the emperors of the East and West,
devoutly saluted their common father in the chair of St. Peter.
But the joy of Petrarch and the Italians was soon turned into
grief and indignation. Some reasons of public or private
moment, his own impatience or the prayers of the cardinals,
recalled Urban to France; and the approaching election was
saved from the tyrannic patriotism of the Romans. The powers
of heaven were interested in their cause: Bridget of Sweden, a
saint and pilgrim, disapproved the return, and foretold the
death, of Urban the Fifth; the migration of Gregory the
Eleventh was encouraged by St. Catherine of Sienna, the spouse
of Christ and ambassadress of the Florentines; and the popes
themselves, the great masters of human credulity, appear to
have listened to these visionary females.[1] Yet those celestial
admonitions were supported by some arguments of temporal
policy. The residence of Avignon had been invaded by hostile
violence: at the head of thirty thousand robbers a hero had
extorted ransom and absolution from the vicar of Christ and
the sacred college; and the maxim of the French warriors, to
spare the people and plunder the church, was a new heresy of
the most dangerous import.[2] While the pope was driven from
Avignon, he was strenuously invited to Rome. The senate and
people acknowledged him as their lawful sovereign, and laid at
his feet the keys of the gates, the bridges, and the fortresses;[3]

[1] I have not leisure to expatiate on the legends of St. Bridget or St.
Catherine, the last of which might furnish some amusing stories. Their
effect on the mind of Gregory XI. is attested by the last solemn words of
the dying pope, who admonished the assistants, ut caverent ab hominibus,
sive viris, sive mulieribus, sub specie religionis loquentibus visiones sui
capitis, quia per tales ipse seductus, etc. (Baluz. Not. ad Vit. Pap. Avenionensium, tom. i. p. 1223).

[2] This predatory expedition is related by Froissard (Chronique, tom. i.
p. 230), and in the Life of Du Guesclin (Collection Générale des Mémoires
Historiques, tom. iv. c. 16, p. 107-113). As early as the year 1361 the
court of Avignon had been molested by similar freebooters, who afterwards passed the Alps (Mémoires sur Pétrarque, tom. iii. p. 563-569).

[3] Fleury alleges, from the annals of Odericus Raynaldus, the original
treaty which was signed the 21st of December, 1376, between Gregory XI.
and the Romans (Hist. Eccles. tom. xx. p. 275).

of the quarter at least beyond the Tiber. But this loyal offer was accompanied by a declaration they they could no longer suffer the scandal and calamity of his absence; and that his obstinacy would finally provoke them to revive and assert the primitive right of election. The abbot of Mount Cassin had been consulted whether he would accept the triple crown [1] from the clergy and people: " I am a citizen of Rome," [2] replied that venerable ecclesiastic, " and my first law is the voice of my country." [3]

If superstition will interpret an untimely death; [4] if the merit of counsels be judged from the event; the heavens may seem to frown on a measure of such apparent reason and propriety. Gregory the Eleventh did not survive above fourteen months his return to the Vatican; and his decease was followed by the great schism of the West, which distracted the Latin church above forty years. The sacred college was then composed of twenty-two cardinals: six of these had remained at Avignon; eleven Frenchmen, one Spaniard, and four Italians, entered the conclave in the usual form. Their choice was not yet limited to the purple; and their unanimous votes acquiesced in the archbishop of Bari, a subject of Naples, conspicuous for his zeal and learning, who ascended the throne of St. Peter under the name of Urban the Sixth. The epistle of the sacred college affirms his free and regular election, which had been inspired as usual by the Holy Ghost; he was adored, invested, and crowned, with the

---

[1] The first crown or regnum (Ducange, Gloss. Latin. tom. v. p. 702) on the episcopal mitre of the popes is ascribed to the gift of Constantine, or Clovis. The second was added by Boniface VIII., as the emblem not only of a spiritual, but of a temporal kingdom. The three states of the church are represented by the triple crown, which was introduced by John XXII. or Benedict XII. (Mémoires sur Pétrarque, tom. i. p. 258, 259).

[2] Baluze (Not. ad Pap. Avenion. tom. i. p. 1194, 1195) produces the original evidence which attests the threats of the Roman ambassadors, and the resignation of the abbot of Mount Cassin, qui, ultro se offerens, respondit se civem Romanum esse, et illud velle quod ipsi vellent.

[3] The return of the popes from Avignon to Rome, and their reception by the people, are related in the original Lives of Urban V. and Gregory XI. in Baluze (Vit. Paparum Avenionensium, tom. i. p. 363-486) and Muratori (Script. Rer. Italicarum, tom. iii. P. i. p. 610-712). In the disputes of the schism every circumstance was severely, though partially, scrutinised; more especially in the great inquest which decided the obedience of Castile, and to which Baluze, in his notes, so often and so largely appeals from a MS. volume in the Harley library (p. 1281, etc.).

[4] Can the death of a good man be esteemed a punishment by those who believe in the immortality of the soul? They betray the instability of their faith. Yet as a mere philosopher, I cannot agree with the Greeks, ὅν οἱ θέοι φιλοῦσιν ἀποθνήσκει νέος (Brunck, Poetæ Gnomici, p. 231). See in Herodotus (l. i. c. 31) the moral and pleasing tale of the Argive youths.

customary rites; his temporal authority was obeyed at Rome
and Avignon, and his ecclesiastical supremacy was acknowledged in the Latin world.   During several weeks the cardinals
attended their new master with the fairest professions of attachment and loyalty, till the summer heats permitted a decent
escape from the city.   But as soon as they were united at
Anagni and Fundi, in a place of security, they cast aside the
mask, accused their own falsehood and hypocrisy, excommunicated the apostate the antichrist of Rome, and proceeded
to a new election of Robert of Geneva, Clement the Seventh,
whom they announced to the nations as the true and rightful
vicar of Christ.   Their first choice, an involuntary and illegal
act, was annulled by the fear of death and the menaces of the
Romans; and their complaint is justified by the strong evidence
of probability and fact.   The twelve French cardinals, above
two-thirds of the votes, were masters of the election; and whatever might be their provincial jealousies, it cannot fairly be
presumed that they would have sacrificed their right and
interest to a foreign candidate, who would never restore them
to their native country.   In the various, and often inconsistent,
narratives,[1] the shades of popular violence are more darkly or
faintly coloured: but the licentiousness of the seditious Romans
was inflamed by a sense of their privileges, and the danger of
a second emigration.   The conclave was intimidated by the
shouts, and encompassed by the arms, of thirty thousand rebels;
the bells of the Capitol and St. Peter's rang an alarm; "Death,
or an Italian pope!" was the universal cry; the same threat was
repeated by the twelve bannerets or chiefs of the quarters, in the
form of charitable advice; some preparations were made for
burning the obstinate cardinals; and had they chosen a Transalpine subject, it is probable that they would never have departed
alive from the Vatican.   The same constraint imposed the
necessity of dissembling in the eyes of Rome and of the world;
the pride and cruelty of Urban presented a more inevitable
danger; and they soon discovered the features of the tyrant,
who could walk in his garden and recite his breviary while he
heard from an adjacent chamber six cardinals groaning on the
rack.   His inflexible zeal, which loudly censured their luxury

---

[1] In the first book of the Histoire du Concile de Pise, M. Lenfant has
abridged and compared the original narratives of the adherents of Urban
and Clement, of the Italians and Germans, the French and Spaniards.   The
latter appear to be the most active and loquacious, and every fact and
word in the original lives of Gregory XI. and Clement VII. are supported
in the notes of their editor Baluze.

and vice, would have attached them to the stations and duties
of their parishes at Rome; and had he not fatally delayed a
new promotion, the French cardinals would have been reduced
to a helpless minority in the sacred college. For these reasons,
and in the hope of repassing the Alps, they rashly violated the
peace and unity of the church; and the merits of their double
choice are yet agitated in the Catholic schools.[1] The vanity,
rather than the interest of the nation, determined the court and
clergy of France.[2] The states of Savoy, Sicily, Cyprus, Arragon,
Castile, Navarre, and Scotland, were inclined by their example
and authority to the obedience of Clement the Seventh, and,
after his decease, of Benedict the Thirteenth. Rome and the
principal states of Italy, Germany, Portugal, England,[3] the Low
Countries, and the kingdoms of the North, adhered to the prior
election of Urban the Sixth, who was succeeded by Boniface the
Ninth, Innocent the Seventh, and Gregory the Twelfth.

From the banks of the Tiber and the Rhône the hostile
pontiffs encountered each other with the pen and the sword·
the civil and ecclesiastical order of society was disturbed; and the
Romans had their full share of the mischiefs of which they may
be arraigned as the primary authors.[4] They had vainly flattered
themselves with the hope of restoring the seat of the ecclesiastical
monarchy, and of relieving their poverty with the tributes and
offerings of the nations; but the separation of France and Spain
diverted the stream of lucrative devotion; nor could the loss be
compensated by the two jubilees which were crowded into the
space of ten years. By the avocations of the schism, by foreign
arms, and popular tumults, Urban the Sixth and his three successors were often compelled to interrupt their residence in the

---

[1] The ordinal numbers of the popes seem to decide the question against
Clement VII. and Benedict XIII., who are boldly stigmatised as antipopes
by the Italians, while the French are content with authorities and reasons
to plead the cause of doubt and toleration (Baluz. in Præfat.). It is
singular, or rather it is not singular, that saints, visions, and miracles
should be common to both parties.

[2] Baluze strenuously labours (Not. p. 1271-1280) to justify the pure and
pious motives of Charles V., king of France: he refused to hear the arguments of Urban; but were not the Urbanists equally deaf to the reasons
of Clement, etc.?

[3] An epistle, or declamation, in the name of Edward III. (Baluz. Vit.
Pap. Avenion. tom. i. p. 553) displays the zeal of the English nation against
the Clementines. Nor was their zeal confined to words: the bishop of
Norwich led a crusade of 60,000 bigots beyond sea (Hume's History, vol. iii.
p. 57, 58).

[4] Besides the general historians, the Diaries of Delphinus Gentilis, Peter
Antonius, and Stephen Infessura, in the great Collection of Muratori,
represent the state and misfortunes of Rome.

Vatican. The Colonna and Ursini still exercised their deadly feuds: the bannerets of Rome asserted and abused the privileges of a republic: the vicars of Christ, who had levied a military force, chastised their rebellion with the gibbet, the sword, and the dagger; and, in a friendly conference, eleven deputies of the people were perfidiously murdered and cast into the street. Since the invasion of Robert the Norman, the Romans had pursued their domestic quarrels without the dangerous interposition of a stranger. But in the disorders of the schism, an aspiring neighbour, Ladislaus king of Naples, alternately supported and betrayed the pope and the people; by the former he was declared *gonfalonier*, or general, of the church, while the latter submitted to his choice the nomination of their magistrates. Besieging Rome by land and water, he thrice entered the gates as a barbarian conqueror; profaned the altars, violated the virgins, pillaged the merchants, performed his devotions at St. Peter's, and left a garrison in the castle of St. Angelo. His arms were sometimes unfortunate, and to a delay of three days he was indebted for his life and crown: but Ladislaus triumphed in his turn; and it was only his premature death that could save the metropolis and the ecclesiastical state from the ambitious conqueror, who had assumed the title, or at least the powers, of King of Rome.[1]

I have not undertaken the ecclesiastical history of the schism; but Rome, the object of these last chapters, is deeply interested in the disputed succession of her sovereigns. The first counsels for the peace and union of Christendom arose from the university of Paris, from the faculty of the Sorbonne, whose doctors were esteemed, at least in the Gallican church, as the most consummate masters of theological science.[2] Prudently waiving all invidious inquiry into the origin and merits of the dispute, they proposed, as a healing measure, that the two pretenders of Rome and Avignon should abdicate at the same time, after qualifying the cardinals of the adverse factions to join in a legitimate election; and that the nations should *subtract*[3] their obedience,

[1] It is supposed by Giannone (tom. iii. p. 292) that he styled himself Rex Romæ, a title unknown to the world since the expulsion of Tarquin. But a nearer inspection has justified the reading of Rex Ramæ, of Rama, an obscure kingdom annexed to the crown of Hungary.

[2] The leading and decisive part which France assumed in the schism is stated by Peter du Puis in a separate history, extracted from authentic records, and inserted in the seventh volume of the last and best edition of his friend Thuanus (P. xi. p. 110-184).

[3] Of this measure, John Gerson, a stout doctor, was the author or the champion. The proceedings of the university of Paris and the Gallican church were often prompted by his advice, and are copiously displayed in

if either of the competitors preferred his own interest to that of
the public. At each vacancy these physicians of the church
deprecated the mischiefs of a hasty choice; but the policy of the
conclave and the ambition of its members were deaf to reason
and entreaties; and whatsoever promises were made, the pope
could never be bound by the oaths of the cardinal. During
fifteen years the pacific designs of the university were eluded by
the arts of the rival pontiffs, the scruples or passions of their
adherents, and the vicissitudes of French factions, that ruled
the insanity of Charles the Sixth. At length a vigorous resolution was embraced; and a solemn embassy, of the titular
patriarch of Alexandria, two archbishops, five bishops, five
abbots, three knights, and twenty doctors, was sent to the courts
of Avignon and Rome, to require, in the name of the church and
king, the abdication of the two pretenders, of Peter de Luna, who
styled himself Benedict the Thirteenth, and of Angelo Corrario,
who assumed the name of Gregory the Twelfth. For the ancient
honour of Rome, and the success of their commission, the
ambassadors solicited a conference with the magistrates of the
city, whom they gratified by a positive declaration that the
most Christian king did not entertain a wish of transporting the
holy see from the Vatican, which he considered as the genuine
and proper seat of the successor of St. Peter. In the name of the
senate and people, an eloquent Roman asserted their desire to
co-operate in the union of the church, deplored the temporal and
spiritual calamities of the long schism, and requested the protection of France against the arms of the king of Naples. The
answers of Benedict and Gregory were alike edifying and alike
deceitful; and, in evading the demand of their abdication, the
two rivals were animated by a common spirit. They agreed on
the necessity of a previous interview; but the time, the place,
and the manner, could never be ascertained by mutual consent.
"If the one advances," says a servant of Gregory, "the other
retreats; the one appears an animal fearful of the land, the
other a creature apprehensive of the water. And thus, for a
short remnant of life and power, will these aged priests endanger
the peace and salvation of the Christian world." [1]

his theological writings, of which Le Clerc (Bibliothèque Choisie, tom. x.
p. 1-78) has given a valuable extract. John Gerson acted an important
part in the councils of Pisa and Constance.

[1] Leonardus Brunus Aretinus, one of the revivers of classic learning in
Italy, who, after serving many years as secretary in the Roman court,
retired to the honourable office of chancellor of the republic of Florence
(Fabric. Biblioth. medii Ævi, tom. i. p. 290). Lenfant has given the
version of this curious epistle (Concile de Pise, tom. i. p. 192-195)

The Christian world was at length provoked by their obstinacy and fraud: they were deserted by their cardinals, who embraced each other as friends and colleagues; and their revolt was supported by a numerous assembly of prelates and ambassadors. With equal justice, the council of Pisa deposed the popes of Rome and Avignon; the conclave was unanimous in the choice of Alexander the Fifth, and his vacant seat was soon filled by a similar election of John the Twenty-third, the most profligate of mankind. But instead of extinguishing the schism, the rashness of the French and Italians had given a third pretender to the chair of St. Peter. Such new claims of the synod and conclave were disputed; three kings, of Germany, Hungary, and Naples, adhered to the cause of Gregory the Twelfth: and Benedict the Thirteenth, himself a Spaniard, was acknowledged by the devotion and patriotism of that powerful nation. The rash proceedings of Pisa were corrected by the council of Constance; the emperor Sigismond acted a conspicuous part as the advocate or protector of the Catholic church; and the number and weight of civil and ecclesiastical members might seem to constitute the states-general of Europe. Of the three popes, John the Twenty-third was the first victim: he fled and was brought back a prisoner: the most scandalous charges were suppressed; the vicar of Christ was only accused of piracy, murder, rape, sodomy, and incest; and after subscribing his own condemnation, he expiated in prison the imprudence of trusting his person to a free city beyond the Alps. Gregory the Twelfth, whose obedience was reduced to the narrow precincts of Rimini, descended with more honour from the throne; and his ambassador convened the session in which he renounced the title and authority of lawful pope. To vanquish the obstinacy of Benedict the Thirteenth or his adherents, the emperor in person undertook a journey from Constance to Perpignan. The kings of Castile, Arragon, Navarre, and Scotland, obtained an equal and honourable treaty: with the concurrence of the Spaniards, Benedict was deposed by the council; but the harmless old man was left in a solitary castle to excommunicate twice each day the rebel kingdoms which had deserted his cause. After thus eradicating the remains of the schism, the synod of Constance proceeded with slow and cautious steps to elect the sovereign of Rome and the head of the church. On this momentous occasion the college of twenty-three cardinals was fortified with thirty deputies; six of whom were chosen in each of the five great nations of Christendom—the Italian, the German, the French, the Spanish, and

the *English :* [1] the interference of strangers was softened by their
generous preference of an Italian and a Roman; and the
hereditary, as well as personal, merit of Otho Colonna recommended him to the conclave. Rome accepted with joy and
obedience the noblest of her sons; the ecclesiastical state was
defended by his powerful family; and the elevation of Martin
the Fifth is the era of the restoration and establishment of the
popes in the Vatican.[2]

The royal prerogative of coining money, which had been
exercised near three hundred years by the senate, was *first*
resumed by Martin the Fifth,[3] and his image and superscription
introduce the series of the papal medals. Of his two immediate
successors, Eugenius the Fourth was the *last* pope expelled by

[1] I cannot overlook this great national cause, which was vigorously
maintained by the English ambassadors against those of France The
latter contended that Christendom was essentially distributed into the
four great nations and votes of Italy, Germany, France, and Spain; and
that the lesser kingdoms (such as England, Denmark, Portugal, etc.) were
comprehended under one or other of these great divisions. The English
asserted that the British islands, of which they were the head, should be
considered as a fifth and co-ordinate nation, with an equal vote; and
every argument of truth or fable was introduced to exalt the dignity of their
country. Including England, Scotland, Wales, the four kingdoms of
Ireland, and the Orkneys, the British islands are decorated with eight
royal crowns, and discriminated by four or five languages, English, Welsh,
Cornish, Scotch, Irish, etc. The greater island from north to south
measures 800 miles, or 40 days' journey; and England alone contains 32
counties and 52,000 parish churches (a bold account!) besides cathedrals,
colleges, priories, and hospitals. They celebrate the mission of St. Joseph
of Arimathea, the birth of Constantine, and the legatine powers of the two
primates, without forgetting the testimony of Bartholemy de Glanville
(A.D. 1360), who reckons only four Christian kingdoms—1, of Rome; 2, of
Constantinople; 3, of Ireland, which had been transferred to the English
monarchs; and, 4, of Spain. Our countrymen prevailed in the council,
but the victories of Henry V. added much weight to their arguments.
The adverse pleadings were found at Constance by Sir Robert Wingfield,
ambassador from Henry VIII. to the emperor Maximilian I., and by him
printed in 1517 at Louvain. From a Leipsic MS. they are more correctly
published in the Collection of Von der Hardt, tom. v.; but I have only
seen Lenfant's abstract of these acts (Concile de Constance, tom. ii. p. 447,
453, etc.).

[2] The histories of the three successive councils, Pisa, Constance, and
Basil, have been written with a tolerable degree of candour, industry, and
elegance, by a Protestant minister, M. Lenfant, who retired from France to
Berlin. They form six volumes in quarto; and as Basil is the worst, so
Constance is the best, part of the Collection.

[3] See the twenty-seventh Dissertation of the Antiquities of Muratori, and
the first Instruction of the Science des Médailles of the Père Joubert and
the Baron de la Bastie. The Metallic History of Martin V. and his successors has been composed by two monks, Moulinet a Frenchman, and
Bonanni an Italian: but I understand that the first part of the series is
restored from more recent coins.

the tumults of the Roman people,[1] and Nicholas the Fifth, the *last* who was importuned by the presence of a Roman emperor.[2] I. The conflict of Eugenius with the fathers of Basil, and the weight or apprehension of a new excise, emboldened and provoked the Romans to usurp the temporal government of the city. They rose in arms; elected seven governors of the republic, and a constable of the Capitol; imprisoned the pope's nephew; besieged his person in the palace; and shot volleys of arrows into his bark as he escaped down the Tiber in the habit of a monk. But he still possessed in the castle of St. Angelo a faithful garrison and a train of artillery: their batteries incessantly thundered on the city, and a bullet more dexterously pointed broke down the barricade of the bridge, and scattered with a single shot the heroes of the republic. Their constancy was exhausted by a rebellion of five months. Under the tyranny of the Ghibeline nobles, the wisest patriots regretted the dominion of the church; and their repentance was unanimous and effectual. The troops of St. Peter again occupied the Capitol; the magistrates departed to their homes; the most guilty were executed or exiled; and the legate, at the head of two thousand foot and four thousand horse, was saluted as the father of the city. The synods of Ferrara and Florence, the fear or resentment of Eugenius, prolonged his absence: he was received by a submissive people; but the pontiff understood, from the acclamations of his triumphal entry, that, to secure their loyalty and his own repose, he must grant without delay the abolition of the odious excise. II. Rome was restored, adorned, and enlightened, by the peaceful reign of Nicholas the Fifth. In the midst of these laudable occupations, the pope was alarmed by the approach of Frederic the Third of Austria; though his fears could not be justified by the character or the power of the Imperial candidate. After drawing his military force to the metropolis, and imposing the best security of oaths [3] and treaties, Nicholas received with a smiling countenance the faithful advocate and vassal of the

---

[1] Besides the Lives of Eugenius IV. (Rerum Italic. tom. iii. P. i. p. 869, and tom. xxv. p. 256), the Diaries of Paul Petroni and Stephen Infessura are the best original evidence for the revolt of the Romans against Eugenius IV. The former, who lived at the time and on the spot, speaks the language of a citizen, equally afraid of priestly and popular tyranny.

[2] The coronation of Frederic III. is described by Lenfant (Concile de Basle, tom. ii. p. 276-288) from Æneas Sylvius, a spectator and actor in that splendid scene.

[3] The oath of fidelity imposed on the emperor by the pope is recorded and sanctified in the Clementines (l. ii. tit. ix.); and Æneas Sylvius, who objects to this new demand, could not foresee that in a few years he should ascend the throne and imbibe the maxims of Boniface VIII.

church. So tame were the times, so feeble was the Austrian,
that the pomp of his coronation was accomplished with order
and harmony: but the superfluous honour was so disgraceful to
an independent nation, that his successors have excused themselves from the toilsome pilgrimage to the Vatican, and rest their
Imperial title on the choice of the electors of Germany.

A citizen has remarked, with pride and pleasure, that the king
of the Romans, after passing with a slight salute the cardinals
and prelates who met him at the gate, distinguished the dress
and person of the senator of Rome; and in this last farewell,
the pageants of the empire and the republic were clasped in a
friendly embrace.[1] According to the laws of Rome [2] her first
magistrate was required to be a doctor of laws, an alien, of a
place at least forty miles from the city, with whose inhabitants
he must not be connected in the third canonical degree of blood
or alliance. The election was annual: a severe scrutiny was
instituted into the conduct of the departing senator; nor could
he be recalled to the same office till after the expiration of two
years. A liberal salary of three thousand florins was assigned
for his expense and reward; and his public appearance represented the majesty of the republic. His robes were of gold
brocade or crimson velvet, or in the summer season of a lighter
silk: he bore in his hand an ivory sceptre; the sound of trumpets
announced his approach; and his solemn steps were preceded at
least by four lictors or attendants, whose red wands were
enveloped with bands or streamers of the golden colour or livery
of the city. His oath in the Capitol proclaims his right and duty,
to observe and assert the laws, to control the proud, to protect
the poor, and to exercise justice and mercy within the extent
of his jurisdiction. In these useful functions he was assisted by
three learned strangers; the two *collaterals* and the judge of
criminal appeals: their frequent trials of robberies, rapes, and
murders are attested by the laws; and the weakness of these
laws connives at the licentiousness of private feuds and armed
associations for mutual defence. But the senator was confined

[1] Lo senatore di Roma, vestito di brocarto con quella beretta, e con
quelle maniche, et ornamenti di pelle, co' quali va alle feste di Testaccio e
Nagone, might escape the eye of Æneas Sylvius, but he is viewed with
admiration and complacency by the Roman citizen (Diario di Stephano
Infessura, p. 1133).

[2] See in the statutes of Rome the *senator and three judges* (l. i. c. 3-14), the
conservators (l. i. c. 15, 16, 17, l. iii. c. 4), the *caporioni* (l. i. c. 18, l. iii. c. 8),
the *secret council* (l. iii. c. 2), the *common council* (l. iii. c. 3). The title of
feuds, defiances, acts of violence, etc., is spread through many a chapter
(c. 14-40) of the second book.

to the administration of justice: the Capitol, the treasury, and the government of the city and its territory were intrusted to the three *conservators*, who were changed four times in each year: the militia of the thirteen regions assembled under the banners of their respective chiefs, or *caporioni ;* and the first of these was distinguished by the name and dignity of the *prior*. The popular legislature consisted of the secret and the common councils of the Romans. The former was composed of the magistrates and their immediate predecessors, with some fiscal and legal officers, and three classes of thirteen, twenty-six, and forty counsellors; amounting in the whole to about one hundred and twenty persons. In the common council all male citizens had a right to vote; and the value of their privilege was enhanced by the care with which any foreigners were prevented from usurping the title and character of Romans. The tumult of a democracy was checked by wise and jealous precautions: except the magistrates, none could propose a question; none were permitted to speak, except from an open pulpit or tribunal; all disorderly acclamations were suppressed; the sense of the majority was decided by a secret ballot; and their decrees were promulgated in the venerable name of the Roman senate and people. It would not be easy to assign a period in which this theory of government has been reduced to accurate and constant practice, since the establishment of order has been gradually connected with the decay of liberty. But in the year one thousand five hundred and eighty the ancient statutes were collected, methodised in three books, and adapted to present use, under the pontificate, and with the approbation, of Gregory the Thirteenth: [1] this civil and criminal code is the modern law of the city; and, if the popular assemblies have been abolished, a foreign senator, with the three conservators, still resides in the palace of the Capitol.[2] The policy of the Cæsars has been repeated by the popes; and the bishop of Rome affected to maintain the form of a republic, while he reigned with the absolute powers of a temporal, as well as spiritual, monarch.

[1] *Statuta almæ Urbis Romæ Auctoritate S. D. N. Gregorii* XIII. *Pont. Max. a Senatû Populoque Rom. reformata et edita. Romæ*, 1580, *in folio*. The obsolete, repugnant statutes of antiquity were confounded in five books, and Lucas Pætus, a lawyer and antiquarian, was appointed to act as the modern Tribonian. Yet I regret the old code, with the rugged crust of freedom and barbarism.

[2] In my time (1765), and in M. Grosley's (Observations sur l'Italie, tom. ii. p. 361), the senator of Rome was M. Bielke, a noble Swede, and a proselyte to the Catholic faith. The pope's right to appoint the senator and the conservator is implied, rather than affirmed, in the statutes.

It is an obvious truth that the times must be suited to extraordinary characters, and that the genius of Cromwell or Retz might now expire in obscurity. The political enthusiasm of Rienzi had exalted him to a throne; the same enthusiasm, in the next century, conducted his imitator to the gallows. The birth of Stephen Porcaro was noble, his reputation spotless: his tongue was armed with eloquence, his mind was enlightened with learning; and he aspired, beyond the aim of vulgar ambition, to free his country and immortalise his name. The dominion of priests is most odious to a liberal spirit: every scruple was removed by the recent knowledge of the fable and forgery of Constantine's donation; Petrarch was now the oracle of the Italians; and as often as Porcaro revolved the ode which describes the patriot and hero of Rome, he applied to himself the visions of the prophetic bard. His first trial of the popular feelings was at the funeral of Eugenius the Fourth: in an elaborate speech he called the Romans to liberty and arms; and they listened with apparent pleasure till Porcaro was interrupted and answered by a grave advocate, who pleaded for the church and state. By every law the seditious orator was guilty of treason; but the benevolence of the new pontiff, who viewed his character with pity and esteem, attempted by an honourable office to convert the patriot into a friend. The inflexible Roman returned from Anagni with an increase of reputation and zeal; and, on the first opportunity, the games of the place Navona, he tried to inflame the casual dispute of some boys and mechanics into a general rising of the people. Yet the humane Nicholas was still averse to accept the forfeit of his life; and the traitor was removed from the scene of temptation to Bologna, with a liberal allowance for his support, and the easy obligation of presenting himself each day before the governor of the city. But Porcaro had learned from the younger Brutus that with tyrants no faith or gratitude should be observed: the exile declaimed against the arbitrary sentence; a party and a conspiracy was gradually formed; his nephew, a daring youth, assembled a band of volunteers; and on the appointed evening a feast was prepared at his house for the friends of the republic. Their leader, who had escaped from Bologna, appeared among them in a robe of purple and gold: his voice, his countenance, his gestures, bespoke the man who had devoted his life or death to the glorious cause. In a studied oration he expatiated on the motives and the means of their enterprise; the name and liberties of Rome; the sloth and pride of their ecclesiastical tyrants; the active or passive consent of their fellow-citizens; three hundred soldiers and four hundred exiles, long exercised in arms or in wrongs; the licence of revenge to edge their swords, and a million of ducats to reward their victory. It would be easy (he said) on the next day, the festival of the Epiphany, to seize the pope and his cardinals before the doors or at the altar of St. Peter's; to lead them in chains under the walls of St. Angelo; to extort, by the threat of their instant death, a surrender of the castle; to ascend the vacant Capitol; to ring the alarm-bell; and to restore in a popular assembly the ancient republic of Rome. While he triumphed, he was already betrayed. The senator, with a strong guard, invested the house: the nephew of Porcaro cut his way through the crowd; but the unfortunate Stephen was drawn from a chest, lamenting that his enemies had anticipated by three hours the execution of his design. After such manifest and repeated guilt even the mercy of Nicholas was silent. Porcaro, and nine of his accomplices, were hanged without the benefit of the sacraments; and, amidst the fears and invectives of the papal court, the Romans pitied, and almost applauded, these martyrs of their country.[1] But their applause was mute, their pity ineffectual, their liberty for ever extinct; and, if they have since risen in a vacancy of the throne or a scarcity of bread, such accidental tumults may be found in the bosom of the most abject servitude.

But the independence of the nobles, which was fomented by discord, survived the freedom of the commons, which must be founded in union. A privilege of rapine and oppression was long maintained by the barons of Rome: their houses were a fortress and a sanctuary; and the ferocious train of banditti and criminals, whom they protected from the law, repaid the hospitality with the service of their swords and daggers. The private interest of the pontiffs, or their nephews, sometimes involved them in these domestic feuds. Under the reign of Sixtus the Fourth, Rome was distracted by the battles and sieges of the rival houses: after the conflagration of his palace,

---

[1] Besides the curious, though concise, narrative of Machiavel (Istoria Fiorentina, l. vi. Opere, tom. i. p. 210, 211, edit. Londra, 1747, in 4to), the Porcarian conspiracy is related in the Diary of Stephen Infessura (Rer. Ital. tom. iii. P. ii. p. 1134, 1135), and in a separate tract by Leo Baptista Alberti (Rer. Ital. tom. xxv. p. 609-614). It is amusing to compare the style and sentiments of the courtier and citizen. Facinus profecto quo . . . neque periculo horribilius, neque audaciâ detestabilius, neque crudelitate tetrius, a quoquam perditissimo uspiam excogitatum sit. . . . Perdette la vita quell' huomo da bene, e amatore dello bene e libertà di Roma.

the protonotary Colonna was tortured and beheaded; and
Savelli, his captive friend, was murdered on the spot for refusing
to join in the acclamations of the victorious Ursini.[1] But the
popes no longer trembled in the Vatican: they had strength to
command, if they had resolution to claim, the obedience of their
subjects; and the strangers who observed these partial disorders
admired the easy taxes and wise administration of the ecclesiastical state.[2]

The spiritual thunders of the Vatican depend on the force of
opinion; and if that opinion be supplanted by reason or passion,
the sound may idly waste itself in the air; and the helpless
priest is exposed to the brutal violence of a noble or a plebeian
adversary. But after their return from Avignon, the keys of
St. Peter were guarded by the sword of St. Paul. Rome was
commanded by an impregnable citadel: the use of cannon is a
powerful engine against popular seditions: a regular force of
cavalry and infantry was enlisted under the banners of the pope:
his ample revenues supplied the resources of war; and, from the
extent of his domain, he could bring down on a rebellious city
an army of hostile neighbours and loyal subjects.[3] Since the
union of the duchies of Ferrara and Urbino, the ecclesiastical
state extends from the Mediterranean to the Adriatic, and from
the confines of Naples to the banks of the Po; and as early as the
sixteenth century the greater part of that spacious and fruitful
country acknowledged the lawful claims and temporal sovereignty
of the Roman pontiffs. Their claims were readily deduced from
the genuine or fabulous donations of the darker ages: the
successive steps of their final settlement would engage us too
far in the transactions of Italy, and even of Europe; the crimes

[1] The disorders of Rome, which were much inflamed by the partiality of
Sixtus IV., are exposed in the Diaries of two spectators, Stephen Infessura
and an anonymous citizen. See the troubles of the year 1484, and the
death of the protonotary Colonna, in tom. iii. P. ii. p. 1083, 1158.

[2] Est toute la terre de l'église troublée pour cette partialité (des Colonnes
et des Ursins), comme nous dirions Luce et Grammont, où en Hollande
Houc et Caballan; et quand ce ne seroit ce différend la terre de l'église
seroit la plus heureuse habitation pour les sujets qui soit dans tout le
monde (car ils ne payent ni tailles ni guères autres choses), et seroient toujours bien conduits (car toujours les papes sont sages et bien conseillés);
mais très souvent en advient de grands et cruels meurtres et pilleries.

[3] By the economy of Sixtus V. the revenue of the ecclesiastical state was
raised to two millions and a half of Roman crowns (Vita, tom. ii. p. 291-
296); and so regular was the military establishment, that in one month
Clement VIII. could invade the duchy of Ferrara with three thousand
horse and twenty thousand foot (tom. iii. p. 64). Since that time (A.D.
1597) the papal arms are happily rusted, but the revenue must have gained
some nominal increase.

of Alexander the Sixth, the martial operations of Julius the Second, and the liberal policy of Leo the Tenth, a theme which has been adorned by the pens of the noblest historians of the times.[1] In the first period of their conquests, till the expedition of Charles the Eighth, the popes might successfully wrestle with the adjacent princes and states, whose military force was equal or inferior to their own. But as soon as the monarchs of France, Germany, and Spain contended with gigantic arms for the dominion of Italy, they supplied with art the deficiency of strength, and concealed, in a labyrinth of wars and treaties, their aspiring views and the immortal hope of chasing the barbarians beyond the Alps. The nice balance of the Vatican was often subverted by the soldiers of the North and West, who were united under the standard of Charles the Fifth: the feeble and fluctuating policy of Clement the Seventh exposed his person and dominions to the conqueror; and Rome was abandoned seven months to a lawless army, more cruel and rapacious than the Goths and Vandals.[2] After this severe lesson the popes contracted their ambition, which was almost satisfied, resumed the character of a common parent, and abstained from all offensive hostilities, except in a hasty quarrel, when the vicar of Christ and the Turkish sultan were armed at the same time against the kingdom of Naples.[3] The French and Germans at length withdrew from the field of battle: Milan, Naples, Sicily, Sardinia, and the sea-coast of Tuscany, were firmly possessed by the Spaniards; and it became their interest to maintain the peace and dependence of Italy, which continued almost without disturbance from the middle of the sixteenth to the opening of the eighteenth century. The Vatican was swayed and protected by the religious policy of the Catholic king: his prejudice and interest disposed him in every dispute to support the prince against the people; and instead of the encouragement, the aid,

[1] More especially by Guicciardini and Machiavel; in the general history of the former; in the Florentine history, the " Prince," and the political discourses of the latter. These, with their worthy successors, Fra-Paolo and Davila, were justly esteemed the first historians of modern languages, till, in the present age, Scotland arose to dispute the prize with Italy herself.

[2] In the history of the Gothic siege I have compared the barbarians with the subjects of Charles V. (vol. iii. p. 258, 259)—an anticipation which, like that of the Tartar conquests, I indulged with the less scruple, as I could scarcely hope to reach the conclusion of my work.

[3] The ambitious and feeble hostilities of the Caraffa pope, Paul IV., may be seen in Thuanus (l. xvi.-xviii.) and Giannone (tom. iv. p. 149-163). Those Catholic bigots, Philip II. and the duke of Alva, presumed to separate the Roman prince from the vicar of Christ; yet the holy character, which would have sanctified his victory, was decently applied to protect his defeat.

and the asylum which they obtained from the adjacent states, the friends of liberty or the enemies of law were enclosed on all sides within the iron circle of despotism. The long habits of obedience and education subdued the turbulent spirit of the nobles and commons of Rome. The barons forgot the arms and factions of their ancestors, and insensibly became the servants of luxury and government. Instead of maintaining a crowd of tenants and followers, the produce of their estates was consumed in the private expenses which multiply the pleasures and diminish the power of the lord.[1] The Colonna and Ursini vied with each other in the decoration of their palaces and chapels; and their antique splendour was rivalled or surpassed by the sudden opulence of the papal families. In Rome the voice of freedom and discord is no longer heard; and, instead of the foaming torrent, a smooth and stagnant lake reflects the image of idleness and servitude.

A Christian, a philosopher,[2] and a patriot, will be equally scandalised by the temporal kingdom of the clergy; and the local majesty of Rome, the remembrance of her consuls and triumphs, may seem to embitter the sense and aggravate the shame of her slavery. If we calmly weigh the merits and defects of the ecclesiastical government, it may be praised in its present state as a mild, decent, and tranquil system, exempt from the dangers of a minority, the sallies of youth, the expenses of luxury, and the calamities of war. But these advantages are overbalanced by a frequent, perhaps a septennial, election of a sovereign, who is seldom a native of the country: the reign of a *young* statesman of threescore, in the decline of his life and abilities, without hope to accomplish, and without children to inherit, the labours of his transitory reign. The successful candidate is drawn from the church, and even the convent— from the mode of education and life the most adverse to reason, humanity, and freedom. In the trammels of servile faith he has learned to believe because it is absurd, to revere all that is contemptible, and to despise whatever might deserve the esteem of a rational being; to punish error as a crime, to reward mortification and celibacy as the first of virtues; to place the saints of

---

[1] This gradual change of manners and expense is admirably explained by Dr. Adam Smith (Wealth of Nations, vol. i. p. 495-504), who proves, perhaps too severely, that the most salutary effects have flowed from the meanest and most selfish causes.

[2] Mr. Hume (Hist. of England, vol. i. p. 389) too hastily concludes that, if the civil and ecclesiastical powers be united in the same person, it is of little moment whether he be styled prince or prelate, since the temporal character will always predominate.

the calendar [1] above the heroes of Rome and the sages of Athens; and to consider the missal, or the crucifix, as more useful instruments than the plough or the loom. In the office of nuncio, or the rank of cardinal, he may acquire some knowledge of the world; but the primitive stain will adhere to his mind and manners: from study and experience he may suspect the mystery of his profession; but the sacerdotal artist will imbibe some portion of the bigotry which he inculcates. The genius of Sixtus the Fifth [2] burst from the gloom of a Franciscan cloister. In a reign of five years he exterminated the outlaws and banditti, abolished the *profane* sanctuaries of Rome,[3] formed a naval and military force, restored and emulated the monuments of antiquity, and, after a liberal use and large increase of the revenue, left five millions of crowns in the castle of St. Angelo. But his justice was sullied with cruelty, his activity was prompted by the ambition of conquest: after his decease the abuses revived; the treasure was dissipated; he entailed on posterity thirty-five new taxes and the venality of offices; and, after his death, his statue was demolished by an ungrateful or an injured people.[4] The wild and original character of Sixtus the Fifth stands alone in the series of the pontiffs: the maxims and effects of their temporal government may be collected from the positive and comparative view of the arts and philosophy, the agriculture

[1] A Protestant may disdain the unworthy preference of St. Francis or St. Dominic, but he will not rashly condemn the zeal or judgment of Sixtus V., who placed the statues of the apostles St. Peter and St. Paul on the vacant columns of Trajan and Antonine.

[2] A wandering Italian, Gregorio Leti, has given the Vita di Sisto Quinto (Amstel. 1721, three vols. in 12mo), a copious and amusing work, but which does not command our absolute confidence. Yet the character of the man, and the principal facts, are supported by the annals of Spondanus and Muratori (A.D. 1585-1590) and the contemporary history of the great Thuanus (l. lxxxii. c. 1, 2; l. lxxxiv. c. 10; l. c. c. 8).

[3] These privileged places, the *quartieri* or *franchises*, were adopted from the Roman nobles by the foreign ministers. Julius II. had once abolished the abominandum et detestandum franchitiarum hujusmodi nomen; and after Sixtus V. they again revived. I cannot discern either the justice or magnanimity of Louis XIV., who, in 1687, sent his ambassador, the marquis de Lavardin, to Rome, with an armed force of a thousand officers, guards, and domestics, to maintain this iniquitous claim, and insult Pope Innocent XI. in the heart of his capital (Vita di Sisto V. tom. iii. p. 260-278; Muratori, Annali d'Italia, tom. xv. p. 494-496; and Voltaire, Siècle de Louis XIV. tom. ii. c. 14, p. 58, 59).

[4] This outrage produced a decree, which was inscribed on marble, and placed in the Capitol. It is expressed in a style of manly simplicity and freedom: Si quis, sive privatus, sive magistratum gerens de collocandâ *vivo* pontifici statuâ mentionem facere ausit, legitimo S. P. Q. R. decreto in perpetuum infamis et publicorum munerum expers esto. MDXC. mense Augusto (Vita di Sisto V. tom. iii. p. 469). I believe that this decree is still observed, and I know that every monarch who deserves a statue should himself impose the prohibition.

and trade, the wealth and population, of the ecclesiastical state
For myself, it is my wish to depart in charity with all mankind,
nor am I willing, in these last moments, to offend even the pope
and clergy of Rome.[1]

[1] The histories of the church, Italy, and Christendom, have contributed
to the chapter which I now conclude. In the original Lives of the Popes
we often discover the city and republic of Rome; and the events of the
fourteenth and fifteenth centuries are preserved in the rude and domestic
chronicles which I have carefully inspected, and shall recapitulate in the
order of time.

1. Monaldeschi (Ludovici Boncomitis) Fragmenta Annalium Roman. (A.D.
1328), in the Scriptores Rerum Italicarum of Muratori, tom. xii. p. 525.
N.B. The credit of this fragment is somewhat hurt by a singular interpola-
tion, in which the author relates *his own death* at the age of 115 years.
2. Fragmenta Historiæ Romanæ (vulgo Thomas Fortifioccæ), in Romana
Dialecto vulgari (A.D. 1327-1354, in Muratori, Antiquitat. medii Ævi
Italiæ, tom. iii. p. 247-548); the authentic groundwork of the history of
Rienzi.
3. Delphini (Gentilis) Diarium Romanum (A.D. 1370-1410), in the Rerum
Italicarum, tom. iii. P. ii. p. 846.
4. Antonii (Petri) *Diarium* Rom. (A.D. 1404-1417), tom. xxiv. p. 969.
5. Petroni (Pauli) Miscellanea Historica Romana (A.D. 1433-1446), tom.
xxiv. p. 1101.
6. Volaterrani (Jacob.) Diarium Rom. (A.D. 1472-1484), tom. xxiii. p. 81.
7. Anonymi Diarium Urbis Romæ (A.D. 1481-1492), tom. iii. P. ii. p. 1069.
8. Infessuræ (Stephani) Diarium Romanum (A.D. 1294, or 1378-1494),
tom. iii. P. ii. p. 1109.
9. Historia Arcana Alexandri VI. sive Excerpta ex Diario Joh. Burcardi
(A.D. 1492-1503), edita a Godefr. Gulielm. Leibnizio, Hanover, 1697, in
4to.   The large and valuable Journal of Burcard might be completed from
the MSS. in different libraries of Italy and France (M. de Foncemagne,
in the Mémoires de l'Acad. des Inscrip. tom. xvii. p. 597-606).
Except the last, all these fragments and diaries are inserted in the Collections of Muratori, my guide and master in the history of Italy. His
country, and the public, are indebted to him for the following works on
that subject:—1. *Rerum Italicarum Scriptores* (A.D. 500-1500), *quorum
potissima pars nunc primum in lucem prodit*, etc., twenty-eight vols. in folio,
Milan, 1723-1738, 1751. A volume of chronological and alphabetical
tables is still wanting as a key to this great work, which is yet in a disorderly and defective state. 2. *Antiquitates Italiæ medii Ævi*, six vols., in
folio, Milan, 1738-1743, in seventy-five curious dissertations, on the manners,
government, religion, etc., of the Italians of the darker ages, with a large
supplement of charters, chronicles, etc. 3. *Dissertazioni sopra le Antiquità Italiane*, three vols. in 4to, Milano, 1751, a free version by the author,
which may be quoted with the same confidence as the Latin text of the
Antiquities. 4. *Annali d' Italia*, eighteen vols. in octavo, Milan, 1753-
1756, a dry, though accurate and useful, abridgment of the history of
Italy, from the birth of Christ to the middle of the eighteenth century.
5. *Dell' Antichità Estense ed Italiane*, two vols. in folio, Modena, 1717,
1740. In the history of this illustrious race, the parent of our Brunswick
kings, the critic is not seduced by the loyalty or gratitude of the subject.
In all his works Muratori approves himself a diligent and laborious writer,
who aspires above the prejudices of a Catholic priest. He was born in the
year 1672, and died in the year 1750, after passing near sixty years in the
libraries of Milan and Modena (Vita del Proposto Ludovico Antonio Muratori, by his nephew and successor Gian. Francesco Soli Muratori, Venezia,
1756, in 4to).

CHAPTER LXXI

Prospect of the Ruins of Rome in the Fifteenth Century—Four Causes of Decay and Destruction—Example of the Coliseum—Renovation of the City—Conclusion of the whole Work

IN the last days of Pope Eugenius the Fourth, two of his servants, the learned Poggius [1] and a friend, ascended the Capitoline hill, reposed themselves among the ruins of columns and temples, and viewed from that commanding spot the wide and various prospect of desolation.[2] The place and the object gave ample scope for moralising on the vicissitudes of fortune, which spares neither man nor the proudest of his works, which buries empires and cities in a common grave; and it was agreed that, in proportion to her former greatness, the fall of Rome was the more awful and deplorable. " Her primeval state, such as she might appear in a remote age, when Evander entertained the stranger of Troy,[3] has been delineated by the fancy of Virgil. This Tarpeian rock was then a savage and solitary thicket: in the time of the poet it was crowned with the golden roofs of a temple; the temple is overthrown, the gold has been pillaged, the wheel of fortune has accomplished her revolution, and the sacred ground is again disfigured with thorns and brambles. The hill of the Capitol, on which we sit, was formerly the head of the Roman empire, the citadel of the earth, the terror of kings; illustrated by the footsteps of so many triumphs, enriched with the spoils and tributes of so many nations. This spectacle of the world, how is it fallen! how changed! how defaced! the path of victory is obliterated by vines, and the benches of the senators are concealed by a dunghill. Cast your eyes on the Palatine hill, and seek among the shapeless and enormous fragments the marble theatre, the obelisks, the colossal statues, the porticoes of Nero's palace: survey the other hills of the city, the vacant space is interrupted only by ruins and gardens.

[1] I have already (notes 4, p. 327, and 1, p. 328) mentioned the age, character, and writings of Poggius; and particularly noticed the date of this elegant moral lecture on the varieties of fortune.

[2] Consedimus in ipsis Tarpeiæ arcis ruinis, pone ingens portæ cujusdam, ut puto, templi, marmoreum limen, plurimasque passim confractas columnas, unde magnâ ex parte prospectus urbis patet (p. 5).

[3] Æneid viii. 97-369. This ancient picture, so artfully introduced, and so exquisitely finished, must have been highly interesting to an inhabitant of Rome; and our early studies allow us to sympathise in the feelings of a Roman.

The forum of the Roman people, where they assembled to enact
their laws and elect their magistrates, is now enclosed for the
cultivation of pot-herbs, or thrown open for the reception of
swine and buffaloes. The public and private edifices, that were
founded for eternity, lie prostrate, naked, and broken, like the
limbs of a mighty giant; and the ruin is the more visible, from
the stupendous relics that have survived the injuries of time and
fortune." [1]

These relics are minutely described by Poggius, one of the first
who raised his eyes from the monuments of legendary to those
of classic superstition.[2] 1. Besides a bridge, an arch, a sepulchre,
and the pyramid of Cestius, he could discern, of the age of the
republic, a double row of vaults in the salt-office of the Capitol,
which were inscribed with the name and munificence of Catulus.
2. Eleven temples were visible in some degree, from the perfect
form of the Pantheon to the three arches and a marble column
of the temple of Peace, which Vespasian erected after the civil
wars and the Jewish triumph. 3. Of the number, which he
rashly defines, of seven *thermæ*, or public baths, none were
sufficiently entire to represent the use and distribution of the
several parts; but those of Diocletian and Antoninus Caracalla
still retained the titles of the founders, and astonished the curious
spectator, who, in observing their solidity and extent, the
variety of marbles, the size and multitude of the columns,
compared the labour and expense with the use and importance.
Of the baths of Constantine, of Alexander, of Domitian, or
rather of Titus, some vestige might yet be found.[3] 4. The
triumphal arches of Titus, Severus, and Constantine, were entire,
both the structure and the inscriptions: a falling fragment was
honoured with the name of Trajan; and two arches, then
extant, in the Flaminian way, have been ascribed to the base
memory of Faustina and Gallienus. 5. After the wonder of the
Coliseum, Poggius might have overlooked a small amphitheatre

---

[1] Capitolium adeo . . . immutatum ut vineæ in senatorum subsellia suc-
cesserint, stercorum ac purgamentorum receptaculum factum. Respice
ad Palatinum montem . . . vasta rudera . . . cæteros colles perlustra
omnia vacua ædificiis, ruinis vineisque oppleta conspicies (Poggius de
Varietat. Fortunæ, p. 21).

[2] See Poggius, p. 8-22.

[3] [With regard to the baths of Titus, Bury says, " It has been proved
only quite recently (by excavations in 1895) that the baths of Titus and
Trajan were distinct. It was not a case of baths built by Titus and
restored or improved by Trajan. The Propylæa of the Thermæ of Titus
have been found on the north side of the Coliseum: the baths of Trajan
were to the north-east, almost adjoining. Lanciani says that on the Aventine there were large baths called the Thermæ Decianæ.—O. S.]

of brick, most probably for the use of the prætorian camp: the theatres of Marcellus and Pompey were occupied in a great measure by public and private buildings; and in the Circus. Agonalis and Maximus, little more than the situation and the form could be investigated. 6. The columns of Trajan and Antonine were still erect; but the Egyptian obelisks were broken or buried. A people of gods and heroes, the workmanship of art, was reduced to one equestrian figure of gilt brass and to five marble statues, of which the most conspicuous were the two horses of Phidias and Praxiteles. 7. The two mausoleums or sepulchres of Augustus and Hadrian could not totally be lost; but the former was only visible as a mound of earth, and the latter, the castle of St. Angelo, had acquired the name and appearance of a modern fortress. With the addition of some separate and nameless columns, such were the remains of the ancient city; for the marks of a more recent structure might be detected in the walls, which formed a circumference of ten miles, included three hundred and seventy-nine turrets, and opened into the country by thirteen gates.

This melancholy picture was drawn above nine hundred years after the fall of the Western empire, and even of the Gothic kingdom of Italy. A long period of distress and anarchy, in which empire, and arts, and riches had migrated from the banks of the Tiber, was incapable of restoring or adorning the city; and, as all that is human must retrograde if it do not advance, every successive age must have hastened the ruin of the works of antiquity. To measure the progress of decay, and to ascertain, at each era, the state of each edifice, would be an endless and a useless labour; and I shall content myself with two observations which will introduce a short inquiry into the general causes and effects. 1. Two hundred years before the eloquent complaint of Poggius, an anonymous writer composed a description of Rome.[1] His ignorance may repeat the same objects under strange and fabulous names. Yet this barbarous topographer had eyes and ears; he could observe the visible remains; he could listen to the tradition of the people; and he distinctly enumerates

[1] Liber de Mirabilibus Romæ, ex Registro Nicolai Cardinalis de Arragoniâ, in Bibliothecâ St. Isidori Armario IV. No. 69. This treatise, with some short but pertinent notes, has been published by Montfaucon (Diarium Italicum, p. 283-301), who thus delivers his own critical opinion: Scriptor xiiimi. circiter sæculi, ut ibidem notatur; antiquariæ rei imperitus, et, ut ab illo ævo, nugis et anilibus fabellis refertus: sed, quia monumenta quæ iis temporibus Romæ supererant pro modulo recenset, non parum inde lucis mutuabitur qui Romanis antiquitatibus indagandis operam navabit (p. 283).

seven theatres, eleven baths, twelve arches, and eighteen palaces, of which many had disappeared before the time of Poggius. It is apparent that many stately monuments of antiquity survived till a late period,[1] and that the principles of destruction acted with vigorous and increasing energy in the thirteenth and fourteenth centuries. 2. The same reflection must be applied to the three last ages; and we should vainly seek the Septizonium of Severus,[2] which is celebrated by Petrarch and the antiquarians of the sixteenth century. While the Roman edifices were still entire, the first blows, however weighty and impetuous, were resisted by the solidity of the mass and the harmony of the parts; but the slightest touch would precipitate the fragments of arches and columns, that already nodded to their fall.

After a diligent inquiry I can discern four principal causes of the ruin of Rome, which continued to operate in a period of more than a thousand years. I. The injuries of time and nature. II. The hostile attacks of the barbarians and Christians. III. The use and abuse of the materials. And, IV. The domestic quarrels of the Romans.

I. The art of man is able to construct monuments far more permanent than the narrow span of his own existence: yet these monuments, like himself, are perishable and frail; and in the boundless annals of time his life and his labours must equally be measured as a fleeting moment. Of a simple and solid edifice it is not easy however to circumscribe the duration. As the wonders of ancient days, the pyramids [3] attracted the curiosity of the ancients: a hundred generations, the leaves of autumn,[4] have dropped into the grave; and after the fall of the Pharaohs and Ptolemies, the Cæsars and caliphs, the same pyramids stand erect and unshaken above the floods of the Nile. A complex figure of various and minute parts is more accessible to injury and decay; and the silent lapse of time is often accelerated by

---

[1] The Père Mabillon (Analecta, tom. iv. p. 502) has published an anonymous pilgrim of the ninth century, who, in his visit round the churches and holy places of Rome, touches on several buildings, especially porticoes, which had disappeared before the thirteenth century.

[2] On the Septizonium, see the Mémoires sur Pétrarque (tom. i. p. 325), Donatus (p. 338), and Nardini (p. 117, 414).

[3] The age of the pyramids is remote and unknown, since Diodorus Siculus (tom. i. l. i. c. 44, p. 72) is unable to decide whether they were constructed 1000 or 3400 years before the clxxxth Olympiad. Sir John Marsham's contracted scale of the Egyptian dynasties would fix them about 2000 years before Christ (Canon. Chronicus, p. 47).

[4] See the speech of Glaucus in the Iliad (Z. 146). This natural but melancholy image is familiar to Homer.

hurricanes and earthquakes, by fires and inundations. The air
and earth have doubtless been shaken; and the lofty turrets of
Rome have tottered from their foundations; but the seven hills
do not appear to be placed on the great cavities of the globe;
nor has the city, in any age, been exposed to the convulsions of
nature, which, in the climate of Antioch, Lisbon, or Lima, have
crumbled in a few moments the works of ages into dust. Fire
is the most powerful agent of life and death: the rapid mischief
may be kindled and propagated by the industry or negligence of
mankind; and every period of the Roman annals is marked by
the repetition of similar calamities. A memorable conflagration,
the guilt or misfortune of Nero's reign, continued, though with
unequal fury, either six or nine days.[1] Innumerable buildings,
crowded in close and crooked streets, supplied perpetual fuel
for the flames; and when they ceased, four only of the fourteen
regions were left entire; three were totally destroyed, and seven
were deformed by the relics of smoking and lacerated edifices.[2]
In the full meridan of empire the metropolis arose with fresh
beauty from her ashes; yet the memory of the old deplored their
irreparable losses, the arts of Greece, the trophies of victory, the
monuments of primitive or fabulous antiquity. In the days of
distress and anarchy every wound is mortal, every fall irretrievable; nor can the damage be restored either by the public
care of government, or the activity of private interest. Yet two
causes may be alleged which render the calamity of fire more
destructive to a flourishing than a decayed city. 1. The more
combustible materials of brick, timber, and metals, are first
melted or consumed; but the flames may play without injury
or effect on the naked walls and massy arches that have been
despoiled of their ornaments. 2. It is among the common and
plebeian habitations that a mischievous spark is most easily
blown to a conflagration; but as soon as they are devoured, the

---

[1] The learning and criticism of M. des Vignoles (Histoire Critique de la
République des Lettres, tom. viii. p. 74-118; ix. p. 172-187) dates the
fire of Rome from A.D. 64, July 19, and the subsequent persecution of the
Christians from November 15 of the same year.
[2] Quippe in regiones quatuordecim Roma dividitur, quarum quatuor
integræ manebant, tres solo tenus dejectæ: septem reliquis pauca tec-
torum vestigia supererant, lacera et semiusta. Among the old relics that
were irreparably lost, Tacitus enumerates the temple of the Moon of
Servius Tullius; the fane and altar consecrated by Evander præsenti
Herculi; the temple of Jupiter Stator, a vow of Romulus; the palace of
Numa; the temple of Vesta cum Penatibus pópuli Romani. He then
deplores the opes tot victoriis quæsitæ et Græcarum artium decora . . .
multa quæ seniores meminerant, quæ reparari nequibant (Annal. xv. 40,
41).

greater edifices which have resisted or escaped are left as so
many islands in a state of solitude and safety. From her
situation, Rome is exposed to the danger of frequent inundations.
Without excepting the Tiber, the rivers that descend from either
side of the Apennine have a short and irregular course; a shallow
stream in the summer heats; an impetuous torrent when it is
swelled in the spring or winter, by the fall of rain and the melt-
ing of the snows. When the current is repelled from the sea by
adverse winds, when the ordinary bed is inadequate to the
weight of waters, they rise above the banks, and overspread,
without limits or control, the plains and cities of the adjacent
country. Soon after the triumph of the first Punic war the
Tiber was increased by unusual rains; and the inundation,
surpassing all former measure of time and place, destroyed all
the buildings that were situate below the hills of Rome. According to the variety of ground, the same mischief was produced by
different means; and the edifices were either swept away by the
sudden impulse, or dissolved and undermined by the long continuance, of the flood.[1] Under the reign of Augustus the same
calamity was renewed: the lawless river overturned the palaces
and temples on its banks;[2] and, after the labours of the
emperor in cleansing and widening the bed that was encumbered
with ruins,[3] the vigilance of his successors was exercised by
similar dangers and designs. The project of diverting into new
channels the Tiber itself, or some of the dependent streams, was
long opposed by superstition and local interests;[4] nor did the

[1] A.U.C. 507, repentina subversio ipsius Romæ prævenit triumphum
Romanorum . . . diversæ ignium aquarumque clades pene absumsere
urbem. Nam Tiberis insolitis auctus imbribus et ultra opinionem, vel
diuturnitate vel magnitudine redundans, *omnia* Romæ ædificia in plano
posita delevit. Diversæ qualitates locorum ad unam convenere perniciem:
quoniam et quæ segnior inundatio tenuit madefacta dissolvit, et quæ cursus
torrentis invenit impulsa dejecit (Orosius, Hist. l. iv. c. 11, p. 244, edit.
Havercamp). Yet we may observe that it is the plan and study of the
Christian apologist to magnify the calamities of the pagan world.

[2] Vidimus flavum Tiberim, retortis
  Littore Etrusco violenter undis,
  Ire dejectum monumenta Regis
    Templaque Vestæ.   (Horat. Carm. i. 2.)
If the palace of Numa and temple of Vesta were thrown down in Horace's
time, what was consumed of those buildings by Nero's fire could hardly
deserve the epithets of vetustissima or incorrupta.

[3] Ad coercendas inundationes alveum Tiberis laxavit ac repurgavit,
completum olim ruderibus, et ædificiorum prolapsionibus coarctatum
(Suetonius in Augusto, c. 30).

[4] Tacitus (Annal. i. 79) reports the petitions of the different towns of
Italy to the senate against the measure; and we may applaud the progress of
reason. On a similar occasion local interests would undoubtedly be consulted; but an English House of Commons would reject with contempt the

use compensate the toil and cost of the tardy and imperfect execution. The servitude of rivers is the noblest and most important victory which man has obtained over the licentiousness of nature; [1] and if such were the ravages of the Tiber under a firm and active government, what could oppose, or who can enumerate, the injuries of the city after the fall of the Western empire? A remedy was at length produced by the evil itself: the accumulation of rubbish and the earth that has been washed down from the hills is supposed to have elevated the plain of Rome fourteen or fifteen feet, perhaps, above the ancient level; [2] and the modern city is less accessible to the attacks of the river. [3]

II. The crowd of writers of every nation, who impute the destruction of the Roman monuments to the Goths and the Christians, have neglected to inquire how far they were animated by a hostile principle, and how far they possessed the means and the leisure to satiate their enmity. In the preceding volumes of this History I have described the triumph of barbarism and religion; and I can only resume, in a few words, their real or imaginary connection with the ruin of ancient Rome. Our fancy may create, or adopt, a pleasing romance, that the Goths and Vandals sallied from Scandinavia, ardent to avenge the flight of Odin; [4] to break the chains, and to chastise the oppressors, of mankind; that they wished to burn the records of classic literature, and to found their national architecture on the broken members of the Tuscan and Corinthian orders. But in simple truth, the northern conquerors were neither sufficiently savage, nor sufficiently refined, to entertain such aspiring ideas of destruction and revenge. The shepherds of Scythia and Germany had been educated in the armies of the empire, whose discipline they acquired, and whose weakness they invaded:

arguments of superstition, " that nature had assigned to the rivers their proper course," etc.

[1] See the Epoques de la Nature of the eloquent and philosophic Buffon. His picture of Guyana, in South America, is that of a new and savage land, in which the waters are abandoned to themselves, without being regulated by human industry (p. 212, 561, quarto edition).

[2] In his Travels in Italy, Mr. Addison (his Works, vol. ii. p. 98, Baskerville's edition) has observed this curious and unquestionable fact.

[3] Yet in modern times the Tiber has sometimes damaged the city, and in the years 1530, 1557, 1598, the Annals of Muratori record three mischievous and memorable inundations (tom. xiv. p. 268, 429; tom. xv. p. 99, etc.).

[4] I take this opportunity of declaring that. in the course of twelve years, I have forgotten, or renounced, the flight of Odin from Azoph to Sweden, which I never very seriously believed. The Goths are apparently Germans; but all beyond Cæsar and Tacitus is darkness or fable in the antiquities of Germany.

with the familiar use of the Latin tongue they had learned to reverence the name and titles of Rome; and, though incapable of emulating, they were more inclined to admire than to abolish the arts and studies of a brighter period. In the transient possession of a rich and unresisting capital, the soldiers of Alaric and Genseric were stimulated by the passions of a victorious army; amidst the wanton indulgence of lust or cruelty, portable wealth was the object of their search: nor could they derive either pride or pleasure from the unprofitable reflection that they had battered to the ground the works of the consuls and Cæsars. Their moments were indeed precious: the Goths evacuated Rome on the sixth,[1] the Vandals on the fifteenth day;[2] and, though it be far more difficult to build than to destroy, their hasty assault would have made a slight impression on the solid piles of antiquity. We may remember that both Alaric and Genseric affected to spare the buildings of the city; that they subsisted in strength and beauty under the auspicious government of Theodoric;[3] and that the momentary resentment of Totila[4] was disarmed by his own temper and the advice of his friends and enemies. From these innocent barbarians the reproach may be transferred to the Catholics of Rome. The statues, altars, and houses of the demons were an abomination in their eyes; and in the absolute command of the city, they might labour with zeal and perseverance to erase the idolatry of their ancestors. The demolition of the temples in the East[5] affords to *them* an example of conduct, and to *us* an argument of belief; and it is probable that a portion of guilt or merit may be imputed with justice to the Roman proselytes. Yet their abhorrence was confined to the monuments of heathen superstition; and the civil structures that were dedicated to the business or pleasure of society might be preserved without injury or scandal. The change of religion was accomplished, not by a popular tumult, but by the decrees of the emperors, of the senate, and of time. Of the Christian hierarchy, the bishops of Rome were commonly the most prudent and least fanatic; nor can any positive charge be opposed to the meritorious act of saving and converting the majestic structure of the Pantheon.[6]

---

[1] History of the Decline, etc., vol. iii. p. 258.   [2] Ibid. vol. iv. p. 411.
[3] Ibid. vol. iv. p. 131-133.   [4] Ibid. vol. iv. p. 338, 339.
[5] Ibid. vol. iii. p. 126-129.

[6] Eodem tempore petiit a Phocate principe templum, quod appellatur *Pantheon*, in quo fecit ecclesiam Sanctæ Mariæ semper Virginis, et omnium martyrum; in quâ ecclesia princeps multa bona obtulit (Anastasius vel potius Liber Pontificalis in Bonifacio IV. in Muratori, Script. Rerum Italicarum, tom. iii. P. i. p. 135). According to the anonymous writer in

III. The value of any object that supplies the wants or pleasures of mankind is compounded of its substance and its form, of the materials and the manufacture. Its price must depend on the number of persons by whom it may be acquired and used; on the extent of the market; and consequently on the ease or difficulty of remote exportation, according to the nature of the commodity, its local situation, and the temporary circumstances of the world. The barbarian conquerors of Rome usurped in a moment the toil and treasure of successive ages; but, except the luxuries of immediate consumption, they must view without desire all that could not be removed from the city in the Gothic waggons or the fleet of the Vandals.[1] Gold and silver were the first objects of their avarice; as in every country, and in the smallest compass, they represent the most ample command of the industry and possessions of mankind. A vase or a statue of those precious metals might tempt the vanity of some barbarian chief; but the grosser multitude, regardless of the form, was tenacious only of the substance; and the melted ingots might be readily divided and stamped into the current coin of the empire. The less active or less fortunate robbers were reduced to the baser plunder of brass, lead, iron, and copper: whatever had escaped the Goths and Vandals was pillaged by the Greek tyrants; and the emperor Constans, in his rapacious visit, stripped the bronze tiles from the roof of the Pantheon.[2] The edifices of Rome might be considered as a vast and various mine; the first labour of extracting the materials was already performed; the metals were purified and cast; the marbles were hewn and polished; and after foreign and domestic rapine had been satiated, the remains of the city, could a purchaser have been found, were still venal. The monuments of antiquity had been left naked of their precious ornaments; but the Romans would demolish with their own hands the arches

Montfaucon, the Pantheon had been vowed by Agrippa to Cybele and Neptune, and was dedicated by Boniface IV. on the calends of November to the Virgin, quæ est mater omnium sanctorum (p. 297, 298).

[1] Flaminius Vacca (apud Montfaucon, p. 155, 156: his memoir is likewise printed. p. 21, at the end of the Roma Antica of Nardini) and several Romans, doctrinâ graves, were persuaded that the Goths buried their treasures at Rome, and bequeathed the secret marks filiis nepotibusque. He relates some anecdotes to prove that, in his own time, these places were visited and rifled by the Transalpine pilgrims, the heirs of the Gothic conquerors.

[2] Omnia quæ erant in ære ad ornatum civitatis deposuit; sed et ecclesiam B. Mariæ ad martyres quæ de tegulis æreis cooperta discooperuit (Anast. in Vitalian. p. 141). The base and sacrilegious Greek had not even the poor pretence of plundering a heathen temple; the Pantheon was already a Catholic church.

and walls, if the hope of profit could surpass the cost of the
labour and exportation. If Charlemagne had fixed in Italy
the seat of the Western empire, his genius would have aspired
to restore, rather than to violate, the works of the Cæsars; but
policy confined the French monarch to the forests of Germany;
his taste could be gratified only by destruction; and the new
palace of Aix-la-Chapelle was decorated with the marbles of
Ravenna [1] and Rome.[2] Five hundred years after Charlemagne,
a king of Sicily, Robert, the wisest and most liberal sovereign
of the age, was supplied with the same materials by the easy
navigation of the Tiber and the sea; and Petrarch sighs an
indignant complaint, that the ancient capital of the world should
adorn from her own bowels the slothful luxury of Naples.[3] But
these examples of plunder or purchase were rare in the darker
ages; and the Romans, alone and unenvied, might have applied
to their private or public use the remaining structures of
antiquity, if in their present form and situation they had not
been useless in a great measure to the city and its inhabitants.
The walls still described the old circumference, but the city had
descended from the seven hills into the Campus Martius; and

[1] For the spoils of Ravenna (musiva atque marmora) see the original
grant of Pope Adrian I. to Charlemagne (Codex Carolin. epist. lxvii. in
Muratori, Script. Ital. tom. iii. P. ii. p. 223).

[2] I shall quote the authentic testimony of the Saxon poet (A.D. 887-899),
de Rebus gestis Caroli Magni, l. v. 437-440, in the Historians of France
(tom. v. p. 180):—

> Ad quæ marmoreas præstabat ROMA columnas,
>   Quasdam præcipuas pulchra Ravenna dedit.
> De tam longinquâ poterit regione vetustas
>   Illius ornatum, Francia, ferre tibi.

And I shall add, from the chronicle of Sigebert (Historians of France, tom.
v. p. 378) extruxit etiam Aquisgrani basilicam plurimæ pulchritudinis, ad
cujus structuram a ROMA et Ravenna columnas et marmora devehi fecit.

[3] I cannot refuse to transcribe a long passage of Petrarch (Opp. p. 536,
537) in Epistolâ hortatoriâ ad Nicolaum Laurentium; it is so strong and
full to the point: Nec pudor aut pietas continuit quominus impii spoliata
Dei templa, occupatas arces, opes publicas, regiones urbis, atque honores
magistratûum inter se divisos; (habeant ?) quam unâ in re, turbulenti ac
seditiosi homines et totius reliquæ vitæ consiliis et rationibus discordes,
inhumani fœderis stupendâ societate convenirent, in pontes et mœnia
atque immeritos lapides desævirent. Denique post vi vel senio collapsa
palatia, quæ quondam ingentes tenuerunt viri, post diruptos arcus trium-
phales (unde majores horum forsitan corruerunt), de ipsius vetustatis ac
propriæ impietatis fragminibus vilem quæstum turpi mercimonio captare
non puduit. Itaque nunc, heu dolor! heu scelus indignum! de vestris
marmoreis columnis, de liminibus templorum (ad quæ nuper ex orbe toto
concursus devotissimus fiebat), de imaginibus sepulchrorum sub quibus
patrum vestrorum venerabilis civis (cinis ?) erat, ut reliquas sileam,
desidiosa Neapolis adornatur. Sic paullatim ruinæ ipsæ deficiunt. Yet
king Robert was the friend of Petrarch.

some of the noblest monuments which had braved the injuries
of time were left in a desert far remote from the habitations of
mankind. The palaces of the senators were no longer adapted
to the manners or fortunes of their indigent successors: the use
of baths [1] and porticoes was forgotten: in the sixth century the
games of the theatre, amphitheatre, and circus had been interrupted: some temples were devoted to the prevailing worship;
but the Christian churches preferred the holy figure of the cross;
and fashion, or reason, had distributed after a peculiar model
the cells and offices of the cloister. Under the ecclesiastical
reign the number of these pious foundations was enormously
multiplied; and the city was crowded with forty monasteries of
men, twenty of women, and sixty chapters and colleges of
canons and priests,[2] who aggravated, instead of relieving, the
depopulation of the tenth century. But if the forms of ancient
architecture were disregarded by a people insensible of their use
and beauty, the plentiful materials were applied to every call of
necessity or superstition; till the fairest columns of the Ionic
and Corinthian orders, the richest marbles of Paros and Numidia,
were degraded, perhaps to the support of a convent or a stable.
The daily havoc which is perpetrated by the Turks in the cities
of Greece and Asia may afford a melancholy example; and in
the gradual destruction of the monuments of Rome, Sixtus the
Fifth may alone be excused for employing the stones of the
Septizonium in the glorious edifice of St. Peter's.[3] A fragment,
a ruin, howsoever mangled or profaned, may be viewed with
pleasure and regret; but the greater part of the marble was
deprived of substance, as well as of place and proportion; it
was burnt to lime for the purpose of cement. Since the arrival
of Poggius the temple of Concord [4] and many capital structures
had vanished from his eyes; and an epigram of the same age
expresses a just and pious fear that the continuance of this

---

[1] Yet Charlemagne washed and swam at Aix-la-Chapelle with a hundred
of his courtiers (Eginhart, c. 22, p. 108, 109); and Muratori describes, as
late as the year 814, the public baths which were built at Spoleto in Italy
(Annali, tom. vi. p. 416).

[2] See the Annals of Italy, A.D. 988. For this and the preceding fact
Muratori himself is indebted to the Benedictine history of Père Mabillon.

[3] Vita di Sisto Quinto, da Gregorio Leti, tom. iii. p. 50.

[4] Porticus ædis Concordiæ, quam cum primum ad urbem accessi vidi fere
integram opere marmoreo admodum specioso: Romani postmodum ad
calcem ædem totam et porticûs partem disjectis columnis sunt demoliti
(p. 12). The temple of Concord was therefore *not* destroyed by a sedition
in the thirteenth century, as I have read in a MS. treatise del' Governo
civile di Roma, lent me formerly at Rome, and ascribed (I believe falsely)
to the celebrated Gravina. Poggius likewise affirms that the sepulchre of
Cæcilia Metella was burnt for lime (p. 19, 20).

practice would finally annihilate all the monuments of antiquity.[1]
The smallness of their numbers was the sole check on the
demands and depredations of the Romans.   The imagination of
Petrarch might create the presence of a mighty people; [2] and I
hesitate to believe that, even in the fourteenth century, they
could be reduced to a contemptible list of thirty-three thousand
inhabitants.   From that period to the reign of Leo the Tenth,
if they multiplied to the amount of eighty-five thousand,[3] the
increase of citizens was in some degree pernicious to the ancient
city.

IV. I have reserved for the last the most potent and forcible
cause of destruction, the domestic hostilities of the Romans
themselves.   Under the dominion of the Greek and French
emperors the peace of the city was disturbed by accidental,
though frequent, seditions: it is from the decline of the latter,
from the beginning of the tenth century, that we may date the
licentiousness of private war, which violated with impunity the
laws of the Code and the Gospel, without respecting the majesty
of the absent sovereign, or the presence and person of the vicar
of Christ.   In a dark period of five hundred years Rome was
perpetually afflicted by the sanguinary quarrels of the nobles
and the people, the Guelphs and Ghibelines, the Colonna and
Ursini; and if much has escaped the knowledge, and much is
unworthy of the notice, of history, I have exposed in the two
preceding chapters the causes and effects of the public disorders.
At such a time, when every quarrel was decided by the sword,
and none could trust their lives or properties to the impotence of
law, the powerful citizens were armed for safety, or offence,
against the domestic enemies whom they feared or hated.
Except Venice alone, the same dangers and designs were common
to all the free republics of Italy; and the nobles usurped the

---

[1] Composed by Æneas Sylvius, afterwards Pope Pius II., and published
by Mabillon, from a MS. of the queen of Sweden (Musæum Italicum, tom. i.
p. 97).

> Oblectat me, Roma, tuas spectare ruinas;
>   Ex cujus lapsû gloria prisca patet.
> Sed tuus hic populus muris defossa vetustis
>   Calcis in obsequium marmora dura coquit.
> Impia tercentum si sic gens egerit annos
>   Nullum hinc indicium nobilitatis erit.

[2] Vagabamur pariter in illâ urbe tam magnâ; quæ, cum propter spatium
vacua videretur, populum habet immensum (Opp. p. 605, Epist. Fami-
liares, ii. 14).

[3] These states of the population of Rome at different periods are derived
from an ingenious treatise of the physician Lancisi, de Romani Cœli
Qualitatibus (p. 122).

prerogative of fortifying their houses, and erecting strong towers [1] that were capable of resisting a sudden attack. The cities were filled with these hostile edifices; and the example of Lucca, which contained three hundred towers; her law, which confined their height to the measure of fourscore feet, may be extended with suitable latitude to the more opulent and populous states. The first step of the senator Brancaleone in the establishment of peace and justice was to demolish (as we have already seen) one hundred and forty of the towers of Rome; and, in the last days of anarchy and discord, as late as the reign of Martin the Fifth, forty-four still stood in one of the thirteen or fourteen regions of the city. To this mischievous purpose the remains of antiquity were most readily adapted: the temples and arches afforded a broad and solid basis for the new structures of brick and stone; and we can name the modern turrets that were raised on the triumphal monuments of Julius Cæsar, Titus, and the Antonines.[2] With some slight alterations, a theatre, an amphitheatre, a mausoleum, was transformed into a strong and spacious citadel. I need not repeat that the mole of Hadrian has assumed the title and form of the castle of St. Angelo;[3] the Septizonium of Severus was capable of standing against a royal army;[4] the sepulchre of Metella has sunk under its outworks;[5] the theatres of Pompey and Marcellus were occupied by the

[1] All the facts that relate to the towers at Rome, and in other free cities of Italy, may be found in the laborious and entertaining compilation of Muratori, Antiquitates Italiæ medii Ævi, dissertat. xxvi. (tom. ii. p. 493-496, of the Latin; tom. i. p. 446, of the Italian work).

[2] As for instance, Templum Jani nunc dicitur, turris Centii Frangapanis; et sane Jano impositæ turris lateritiæ conspicua hodieque vestigia super-sunt (Montfaucon Diarium Italicum, p. 186). The anonymous writer (p. 285) enumerates arcus Titi, turris Cartularia; arcus Julii Cæsaris et Senatorum, turres de Bratis; arcus Antonini, turris de Cosectis, etc.

[3] Hadriani molem . . . magna ex parte Romanorum injuria . . . disturbavit: quod certe funditus evertissent, si eorum manibus pervia, absumptis grandibus saxis, reliqua moles exstitisset (Poggius de Varietate Fortunæ, p. 12).

[4] Against the emperor Henry IV. (Muratori, Annali d'Italia, tom. ix. p. 147).

[5] I must copy an important passage of Montfaucon: Turris ingens rotunda . . . Cæciliæ Metellæ . . . sepulchrum erat, cujus muri tam solidi, ut spatium perquam minimum intus vacuum supersit: et *Torre di Bove* dicitur, a boum capitibus muro inscriptis. Huic sequiori ævo, tempore intestinorum bellorum, ceu urbecula adjuncta fuit, cujus mœnia et turres etiamnum visuntur; ita ut sepulchrum Metellæ quasi arx oppiduli fuerit. Ferventibus in urbe partibus, cum Ursini atque Columnenses mutuis cladibus perniciem inferrent civitati, in utriusve partis ditionem cederet magni momenti erat (p. 142).

[The tomb of Cæcilia Metella still adorns the Appian Way in Rome, and is one of the most conspicuous objects which meets the eye of the traveller along that famous thoroughfare.—O. S.]

Savelli and Ursini families;[1] and the rough fortress has been
gradually softened to the splendour and elegance of an Italian
palace. Even the churches were encompassed with arms and
bulwarks, and the military engines on the roof of St. Peter's
were the terror of the Vatican and the scandal of the Christian
world. Whatever is fortified will be attacked; and whatever
is attacked may be destroyed. Could the Romans have wrested
from the popes the castle of St. Angelo, they had resolved by a
public decree to annihilate that monument of servitude. Every
building of defence was exposed to a siege; and in every siege
the arts and engines of destruction were laboriously employed.
After the death of Nicholas the Fourth, Rome, without a
sovereign or a senate, was abandoned six months to the fury of
civil war. " The houses," says a cardinal and poet of the times,[2]
" were crushed by the weight and velocity of enormous stones;[3]
the walls were perforated by the strokes of the battering-ram;
the towers were involved in fire and smoke; and the assailants
were stimulated by rapine and revenge." The work was consummated by the tyranny of the laws; and the factions of Italy
alternately exercised a blind and thoughtless vengeance on their
adversaries, whose houses and castles they razed to the ground.[4]

[1] See the testimonies of Donatus, Nardini, and Montfaucon. In the
Savelli palace the remains of the theatre of Marcellus are still great and
conspicuous.

[Towards the close of the eleventh century the theatre of Marcellus was
transformed by the Pierleoni family into a fortress, and seven hundred years
later was purchased by the Orsini family. Lanciani says, " The section
of the outside shell visible at present, a magnificent ruin, in outline and
colour, is buried fifteen feet in modern soil, and supports the Orsini palace,
erected upon its stage and ranges of seats. What stands above ground of
the lower or Doric arcades is rented by the prince for the most squalid and
ignoble class of shops.—O. S.]

[2] James, cardinal of St. George, ad velum aureum, in his metrical Life
of Pope Celestin V. (Muratori, Script. Ital. tom. i. P. iii. p. 621, l. i. c. 1,
ver. 132, etc.)

> Hoc dixisse sat est, Romam caruisse Senatû
> Mensibus exactis heu sex; belloque vocatum (vocatos)
> In scelus, in socios fraternaque vulnera patres;
> Tormentis jecisse viros immania saxa;
> Perfodisse domus trabibus, fecisse ruinas
> Ignibus; incensas turres, obscuraque fumo
> Lumina vicino, quo sit spoliata supellex.

[3] Muratori (Dissertazione sopra le Antiquità Italiane, tom. i. p. 427-431)
finds that stone bullets of two or three hundred pounds' weight were not
uncommon; and they are sometimes computed at twelve or eighteen can-
tari of Genoa, each cantaro weighing 150 pounds.

[4] The sixth law of the Visconti prohibits this common and mischievous
practice; and strictly enjoins that the houses of banished citizens should
be preserved pro communi utilitate (Gualvaneus de la Flamma, in Muratori, Script. Rerum Italicarum, tom. xii. p. 1041).

In comparing the *days* of foreign with the *ages* of domestic
hostility, we must pronounce that the latter have been far more
ruinous to the city; and our opinion is confirmed by the evidence
of Petrarch. " Behold," says the laureate, " the relics of Rome,
the image of her pristine greatness! neither time nor the barbarian
can boast the merit of this stupendous destruction: it was
perpetrated by her own citizens, by the most illustrious of her
sons; and your ancestors (he writes to a noble Annibaldi) have
done with the battering-ram what the Punic hero could not
accomplish with the sword." [1] The influence of the two last
principles of decay must in some degree be multiplied by each
other; since the houses and towers which were subverted by
civil war required a new and perpetual supply from the
monuments of antiquity.

These general observations may be separately applied to the
amphitheatre of Titus, which has obtained the name of the
COLISEUM,[2] either from its magnitude, or from Nero's colossal
statue: an edifice, had it been left to time and nature, which
might perhaps have claimed an eternal duration. The curious
antiquaries, who have computed the numbers and seats, are
disposed to believe that above the upper row of stone steps the
amphitheatre was encircled and elevated with several stages of
wooden galleries, which were repeatedly consumed by fire, and
restored by the emperors. Whatever was precious, or portable,
or profane, the statues of gods and heroes, and the costly
ornaments of sculpture, which were cast in brass, or overspread
with leaves of silver and gold, became the first prey of conquest
or fanaticism, of the avarice of the barbarians or the Christians.
In the massy stones of the Coliseum many holes are discerned;

---

[1] Petrarch thus addresses his friend, who, with shame and tears, had
shown him the mœnia, laceræ specimen miserabile Romæ, and declared
his own intention of restoring them (Carmina Latina, l. ii. epist. Paulo
Annibalensi, xii. p. 97, 98).

> Nec te parva manet servatis fama ruinis
> Quanta quod integræ fuit olim gloria Romæ
> Reliquiæ testantur adhuc; quas longior ætas
> Frangere non valuit; non vis aut ira cruenti
> Hostis, ab egregiis franguntur civibus, heu! heu!
> ——— Quod *ille* nequivit (*Hannibal*)
> Perficit hic aries.

[2] The fourth part of the Verona Illustrata of the Marquis Maffei professedly treats of amphitheatres, particularly those of Rome and Verona,
of their dimensions, wooden galleries, etc. It is from magnitude that he
derives the name of *Colosseum*, or *Coliseum :* since the same appellation
was applied to the amphitheatre of Capua, without the aid of a colossal
statue; since that of Nero was erected in the court (*in atrio*) of his palace,
and not in the Coliseum (p. iv. p. 15-19, l. i. c. 4).

and the two most probable conjectures represent the various
accidents of its decay. These stones were connected by solid
links of brass or iron, nor had the eye of rapine overlooked the
value of the baser metals; [1] the vacant space was converted into
a fair or market; the artisans of the Coliseum are mentioned in
an ancient survey; and the chasms were perforated or enlarged
to receive the poles that supported the shops or tents of the
mechanic trades.[2] Reduced to its naked majesty, the Flavian
amphitheatre was contemplated with awe and admiration by
the pilgrims of the North; and their rude enthusiasm broke
forth in a sublime proverbial expression, which is recorded in
the eighth century, in the fragments of the venerable Bede:
" As long as the Coliseum stands, Rome shall stand; when the
Coliseum falls, Rome will fall; when Rome falls, the world will
fall." [3]   In the modern system of war, a situation commanded
by three hills would not be chosen for a fortress; but the strength
of the walls and arches could resist the engines of assault; a
numerous garrison might be lodged in the enclosure; and while
one faction occupied the Vatican and the Capitol, the other was
intrenched in the Lateran and the Coliseum.[4]

The abolition at Rome of the ancient games must be understood with some latitude; and the carnival sports, of the Testa-
cean mount and the Circus Agonalis,[5] were regulated by the
law [6] or custom of the city.   The senator presided with dignity

[1] Joseph Maria Suarés, a learned bishop, and the author of a history of
Præneste, has composed a separate dissertation on the seven or eight
probable causes of these holes, which has been since reprinted in the Roman
Thesaurus of Sallengre. Montfaucon (Diarium, p. 233) pronounces the
rapine of the barbarians to be the unam germanamque causam foraminum.

[2] Donatus, Roma Vetus et Nova, p. 285.

[3] Quamdiu stabit Colyseus, stabit et Roma; quando cadet Colyseus,
cadet Roma; quando cadet Roma, cadet et mundus (Beda in Excerptis seu
Collectaneis apud Ducange Glossar. med. et infimæ Latinitatis, tom. ii.
p. 407, edit. Basil). This saying must be ascribed to the Anglo-Saxon
pilgrims who visited Rome before the year 735, the era of Bede's death;
for I do not believe that our venerable monk ever passed the sea.

[4] I cannot recover, in Muratori's original Lives of the Popes (Script.
Rerum Italicarum, tom. iii. P. i.), the passage that attests this hostile partition, which must be applied to the end of the eleventh or the beginning of
the twelfth century.

[5] Although the structure of the Circus Agonalis be destroyed, it still
retains its form and name (Agona, Nagona, Navona); and the interior
space affords a sufficient level for the purpose of racing. But the Monte
Testaceo, that strange pile of broken pottery, seems only adapted for the
annual practice of hurling from top to bottom some waggon-loads of live
hogs for the diversion of the populace (Statuta Urbis Romæ, p. 186).

[6] See the Statuta Urbis Romæ, l. iii. c. 87, 88, 89, p. 185, 186. I have
already given an idea of this municipal code. The races of Nagona and
Monte Testaceo are likewise mentioned in the Diary of Peter Antonius
from 1404 to 1417 (Muratori, Script. Rerum Italicarum, tom. xxiv. p. 1124)

and pomp to adjudge and distribute the prizes, the gold ring, or the *pallium*,[1] as it was styled, of cloth or silk. A tribute on the Jews supplied the annual expense;[2] and the races, on foot, on horseback, or in chariots, were ennobled by a tilt and tournament of seventy-two of the Roman youth. In the year one thousand three hundred and thirty-two, a bull-feast, after the fashion of the Moors and Spaniards, was celebrated in the Coliseum itself; and the living manners are painted in a diary of the times.[3] A convenient order of benches was restored; and a general proclamation, as far as Rimini and Ravenna, invited the nobles to exercise their skill and courage in this perilous adventure. The Roman ladies were marshalled in three squadrons, and seated in three balconies, which on this day, the third of September, were lined with scarlet cloth. The fair Jacova di Rovere led the matrons from beyond the Tiber, a pure and native race, who still represent the features and character of antiquity. The remainder of the city was divided as usual between the Colonna and Ursini: the two factions were proud of the number and beauty of their female bands: the charms of Savella Ursini are mentioned with praise; and the Colonna regretted the absence of the youngest of their house, who had sprained her ankle in the garden of Nero's tower. The lots of the champions were drawn by an old and respectable citizen; and they descended into the arena, or pit, to encounter the wild bulls, on foot as it should seem, with a single spear. Amidst the crowd, our annalist has selected the names, colours, and devices of twenty of the most conspicuous knights. Several of the names are the most illustrious of Rome and the ecclesiastical state: Malatesta, Polenta, della Valle, Cafarello, Savelli, Capoccio, Conti, Annibaldi, Altieri, Corsi: the colours were adapted to their taste and situation; the devices are expressive of hope or despair, and breathe the spirit of gallantry and arms. " I am alone, like the youngest of the Horatii," the

---

[1] The *Pallium*, which Menage so foolishly derives from *Palmarium*, is an easy extension of the idea and the words, from the robe or cloak to the materials, and from thence to their application as a prize (Muratori, dissert. xxxiii.).

[2] For these expenses the Jews of Rome paid each year 1130 florins, of which the odd thirty represented the pieces of silver for which Judas had betrayed his Master to their ancestors. There was a foot-race of Jewish as well as of Christian youths (Statuta Urbis, ibidem).

[3] This extraordinary bull-feast in the Coliseum is described, from tradition rather than memory, by Ludovico Buonconte Monaldesco, in the most ancient fragments of Roman annals (Muratori, Script. Rerum Italicarum, tom. xii. p. 535, 536); and however fanciful they may seem, they are deeply marked with the colours of truth and nature.

confidence of an intrepid stranger: " I live disconsolate," a weeping widower: " I burn under the ashes," a discreet lover: " I adore Lavinia, or Lucretia," the ambiguous declaration of a modern passion: " My faith is as pure," the motto of a white livery: " Who is stronger than myself?" of a lion's hide: " If I am drowned in blood, what a pleasant death!" the wish of ferocious courage. The pride or prudence of the Ursini restrained them from the field, which was occupied by three of their hereditary rivals, whose inscriptions denoted the lofty greatness of the Colonna name: " Though sad, I am strong:" " Strong as I am great:" " If I fall," addressing himself to the spectators, " you fall with me:"—intimating (says the contemporary writer) that, while the other families were the subjects of the Vatican, they alone were the supporters of the Capitol. The combats of the amphitheatre were dangerous and bloody. Every champion successively encountered a wild bull; and the victory may be ascribed to the quadrupeds, since no more than eleven were left on the field, with the loss of nine wounded and eighteen killed on the side of their adversaries. Some of the noblest families might mourn, but the pomp of the funerals, in the churches of St. John Lateran and Sta. Maria Maggiore, afforded a second holiday to the people. Doubtless it was not in such conflicts that the blood of the Romans should have been shed; yet, in blaming their rashness, we are compelled to applaud their gallantry; and the noble volunteers, who display their magnificence, and risk their lives, under the balconies of the fair, excite a more generous sympathy than the thousands of captives and malefactors who were reluctantly dragged to the scene of slaughter.[1]

This use of the amphitheatre was a rare, perhaps a singular, festival: the demand for the materials was a daily and continual want, which the citizens could gratify without restraint or remorse. In the fourteenth century a scandalous act of concord secured to both factions the privilege of extracting stones from the free and common quarry of the Coliseum;[2] and Poggius laments that the greater part of these stones had been burnt to lime by the folly of the Romans.[3] To check this abuse, and to

[1] Muratori has given a separate dissertation (the xxixth) to the games of the Italians in the middle ages.

[2] In a concise but instructive memoir, the abbé Barthelemy (Mémoires de l'Académie des Inscriptions, tom. xxviii. p. 585) has mentioned this agreement of the factions of the fourteenth century de Tiburtino faciendo in the Coliseum, from an original act in the archives of Rome.

[3] Coliseum . . . ob stultitiam Romanorum *majori ex parte* ad calcem

prevent the nocturnal crimes that might be perpetrated in the vast and gloomy recess, Eugenius the Fourth surrounded it with a wall; and, by a charter, long extant, granted both the ground and edifice to the monks of an adjacent convent.[1]   After his death the wall was overthrown in a tumult of the people; and had they themselves respected the noblest monument of their fathers, they might have justified the resolve that it should never be degraded to private property. The inside was damaged; but in the middle of the sixteenth century, an era of taste and learning, the exterior circumference of one thousand six hundred and twelve feet was still entire and inviolate; a triple elevation of fourscore arches, which rose to the height of one hundred and eight feet. Of the present ruin the nephews of Paul the Third are the guilty agents; and every traveller who views the Farnese palace may curse the sacrilege and luxury of these upstart princes.[2]   A similar reproach is applied to the Barberini; and the repetition of injury might be dreaded from every reign, till the Coliseum was placed under the safeguard of religion by the most liberal of the pontiffs, Benedict the Fourteenth, who consecrated a spot which persecution and fable had stained with the blood of so many Christian martyrs.[3]

When Petrarch first gratified his eyes with a view of those monuments whose scattered fragments so far surpass the most eloquent descriptions, he was astonished at the supine indifference[4]

deletum, says the indignant Poggius (p. 17): but his expression, too strong for the present age, must be very tenderly applied to the fifteenth century.

[The injury which the Coliseum has received has been less from the tooth of time than from earthquakes and the vandalism of man. The earthquake of 1348 destroyed the whole western side, after which the ruins were freely used as a quarry. Gibbon has followed Donatus in believing that a silk manufactory was established in the Coliseum in the thirteenth century. The Bandonarii or Bandererii were the officers who carried the standards of their school before the pope.—O. S.]

[1] Of the Olivetan monks. Montfaucon (p. 142) affirms this fact from the memorials of Flaminius Vacca (No. 72). They still hoped, on some future occasion, to revive and vindicate their grant.

[2] After measuring the priscus amphitheatri gyrus, Montfaucon (p. 142) only adds that it was entire under Paul III.; tacendo clamat. Muratori (Annali d' Italia, tom. xiv. p. 371) more freely reports the guilt of the Farnese pope, and the indignation of the Roman people. Against the nephews of Urban VIII. I have no other evidence than the vulgar saying, " Quod non fecerunt Barbari, fecere Barberini," which was perhaps suggested by the resemblance of the words.

[3] As an antiquarian and a priest, Montfaucon thus deprecates the ruin of the Coliseum: Quòd si non suopte merito atque pulchritudine dignum fuisset quod improbas arceret manus, indigna res utique in locum tot martyrum cruore sacrum tantopere sævitum esse.

[4] Yet the Statutes of Rome (l. iii. c. 81, p. 182) impose a fine of 500 aurei on whosoever shall demolish any ancient edifice, ne ruinis civitas deformetur, et ut antiqua ædificia decorem urbis perpetuo representent.

of the Romans themselves;[1] he was humbled rather than
elated by the discovery that, except his friend Rienzi, and one of
the Colonna, a stranger of the Rhône was more conversant with
these antiquities than the nobles and natives of the metropolis.[2]
The ignorance and credulity of the Romans are elaborately displayed in the old survey of the city which was composed about
the beginning of the thirteenth century; and, without dwelling
on the manifold errors of name and place, the legend of the
Capitol[3] may provoke a smile of contempt and indignation.
"The Capitol," says the anonymous writer, "is so named as
being the head of the world; where the consuls and senators
formerly resided for the government of the city and the globe.
The strong and lofty walls were covered with glass and gold, and
crowned with a roof of the richest and most curious carving.
Below the citadel stood a palace, of gold for the greatest part,
decorated with precious stones, and whose value might be
esteemed at one third of the world itself. The statues of all the
provinces were arranged in order; each with a small bell suspended from its neck; and such was the contrivance of art
magic,[4] that, if the province rebelled against Rome, the statue
turned round to that quarter of the heavens, the bell rang, the
prophet of the Capitol reported the prodigy, and the senate was
admonished of the impending danger." A second example, of
less importance, though of equal absurdity, may be drawn from

---

[1] In his first visit to Rome (A.D. 1337; see Mémoires sur Pétrarque, tom.
i. p. 322, etc.) Petrarch is struck mute miraculo rerum tantarum, et stuporis
mole obrutus. . . . Præsentia vero, mirum dictû, nihil imminuit: vere
major fuit Roma majoresque sunt reliquiæ quam rebar. Jam non orbem
ab hâc urbe domitum, sed tam sero domitum, miror (Opp. p. 605, Fami-
liares, ii. 14, Joanni Columnæ).

[2] He excepts and praises the *rare* knowledge of John Colonna. Qui enim
hodie magis ignari rerum Romanarum, quam Romani cives? Invitus
dico, nusquam minus Roma cognoscitur quam Romæ.

[3] After the description of the Capitol, he adds, statuæ erant quot sunt
mundi provinciæ; et habebat quælibet tintinnabulum ad collum. Et
erant ita per magicam artem dispositæ, ut quándo aliqua regio Romano
Imperio rebellis erat, statim imago illius provinciæ vertebat se contra
illam; unde tintinnabulum resonabat quod pendebat ad collum; tuncque
vates Capitolii qui erant custodes senatui, etc. He mentions an example
of the Saxons and Suevi, who, after they had been subdued by Agrippa,
again rebelled: tintinnabulum sonuit; sacerdos qui erat in speculo in heb-
domadâ senatoribus nuntiavit: Agrippa marched back and reduced
the —— Persians (Anonym. in Montfaucon, p. 297, 298).

[4] The same writer affirms that Virgil captus a Romanis invisibiliter exiit,
ivitque Neapolim. A Roman magician, in the eleventh century, is introduced by William of Malmesbury (de Gestis Regum Anglorum, l. ii. p. 86);
and in the time of Flaminius Vacca (No. 81, 103) it was the vulgar belief
that the strangers (the *Goths*) invoked the demons for the discovery of
hidden treasures.

the two marble horses, led by two naked youths, which have
since been transported from the baths of Constantine to the
Quirinal hill. The groundless application of the names of
Phidias and Praxiteles may perhaps be excused; but these
Grecian sculptors should not have been removed above four
hundred years from the age of Pericles to that of Tiberius; they
should not have been transformed into two philosophers or
magicians, whose nakedness was the symbol of truth and knowledge, who revealed to the emperor his most secret actions; and,
after refusing all pecuniary recompense, solicited the honour of
leaving this eternal monument of themselves.[1] Thus awake to
the power of magic, the Romans were insensible to the beauties
of art: no more than five statues were visible to the eyes of
Poggius; and of the multitudes which chance or design had
buried under the ruins, the resurrection was fortunately delayed
till a safer and more enlightened age.[2] The Nile, which now
adorns the Vatican, had been explored by some labourers, in
digging a vineyard near the temple, or convent, of the Minerva;
but the impatient proprietor, who was tormented by some visits
of curiosity, restored the unprofitable marble to its former grave.[3]
The discovery of a statue of Pompey, ten feet in length, was the
occasion of a lawsuit. It had been found under a partition wall:
the equitable judge had pronounced, that the head should be
separated from the body to satisfy the claims of the contiguous
owners; and the sentence would have been executed if the intercession of a cardinal, and the liberality of a pope, had not rescued
the Roman hero from the hands of his barbarous countrymen.[4]

But the clouds of barbarism were gradually dispelled; and the
peaceful authority of Martin the Fifth and his successors restored
the ornaments of the city as well as the order of the ecclesiastical

---

[1] Anonym. p. 289. Montfaucon (p. 191) justly observes that, if Alexander be represented, these statues cannot be the work of Phidias (Olympiad lxxxiii.) or Praxiteles (Olympiad civ.), who lived before that conqueror
(Plin. Hist. Natur. xxxiv. 19).

[2] William of Malmesbury (l. ii. p. 86, 87) relates a marvellous discovery
(A.D. 1046) of Pallas, the son of Evander, who had been slain by Turnus;
the perpetual light in his sepulchre, a Latin epitaph, the corpse, yet entire,
of a young giant, the enormous wound in his breast (pectus perforat ingens),
etc. If this fable rests on the slightest foundation, we may pity the bodies,
as well as the statues, that were exposed to the air in a barbarous age.

[3] Prope porticum Minervæ, statua est recubantis, cujus caput integrâ
effigie tantæ magnitudinis, ut signa omnia excedat. Quidam ad plan-
tandas arbores scrobes faciens detexit. Ad hoc visendum cum plures in
dies magis concurrerent, strepitum adeuntium fastidiumque pertæsus,
horti patronus congestâ humo texit (Poggius de Varietate Fortunæ, p. 12).

[4] See the memorials of Flaminius Vacca, No. 57, p. 11, 12, at the end of
the Roma Antica of Nardini (1704, in 4to).

state. The improvements of Rome, since the fifteenth century, have not been the spontaneous produce of freedom and industry. The first and most natural root of a great city is the labour and populousness of the adjacent country, which supplies the materials of subsistence, of manufactures, and of foreign trade. But the greater part of the Campagna of Rome is reduced to a dreary and desolate wilderness: the overgrown estates of the princes and the clergy are cultivated by the lazy hands of indigent and hopeless vassals; and the scanty harvests are confined or exported for the benefit of a monopoly. A second and more artificial cause of the growth of a metropolis is the residence of a monarch, the expense of a luxurious court, and the tributes of dependent provinces. Those provinces and tributes had been lost in the fall of the empire; and if some streams of the silver of Peru and the gold of Brazil have been attracted by the Vatican, the revenues of the cardinals, the fees of office, the oblations of pilgrims and clients, and the remnant of ecclesiastical taxes, afford a poor and precarious supply, which maintains, however, the idleness of the court and city. The population of Rome, far below the measure of the great capitals of Europe, does not exceed one hundred and seventy thousand inhabitants;[1] and within the spacious enclosure of the walls, the largest portion of the seven hills is overspread with vineyards and ruins. The beauty and splendour of the modern city may be ascribed to the abuses of the government, to the influence of superstition. Each reign (the exceptions are rare) has been marked by the rapid elevation of a new family, enriched by the childless pontiff at the expense of the church and country. The palaces of these fortunate nephews are the most costly monuments of elegance and servitude: the perfect arts of architecture, painting, and sculpture, have been prostituted in their service; and their galleries and gardens are decorated with the most precious works of antiquity, which taste or vanity has prompted them to collect. The ecclesiastical revenues were more decently employed by the popes themselves in the pomp of the Catholic worship; but it is superfluous to enumerate their pious foundations of altars, chapels, and churches, since these lesser stars are eclipsed by the sun of the Vatican, by the dome of St. Peter, the most glorious structure that ever has been applied to the use of religion. The

[1] In the year 1709 the inhabitants of Rome (without including eight or ten thousand Jews) amounted to 138,568 souls (Labat, Voyages en Espagne et en Italie, tom iii. p. 217, 218). In 1740 they had increased to 146,080; and in 1765 I left them, without the Jews, 161,899. I am ignorant whether they have since continued in a progressive state.

fame of Julius the Second, Leo the Tenth, and Sixtus the Fifth, is accompanied by the superior merit of Bramante and Fontana, of Raphael and Michael Angelo; and the same munificence which had been displayed in palaces and temples was directed with equal zeal to revive and emulate the labours of antiquity. Prostrate obelisks were raised from the ground, and erected in the most conspicuous places; of the eleven aqueducts of the Cæsars and consuls, three were restored; the artificial rivers were conducted over a long series of old or of new arches, to discharge into marble basins a flood of salubrious and refreshing waters: and the spectator, impatient to ascend the steps of St. Peter's, is detained by a column of Egyptian granite, which rises between two lofty and perpetual fountains to the height of one hundred and twenty feet. The map, the description, the monuments of ancient Rome, have been elucidated by the diligence of the antiquarian and the student; [1] and the footsteps of heroes, the relics, not of superstition, but of empire, are devoutly visited by a new race of pilgrims from the remote and once savage countries of the North.

Of these pilgrims, and of every reader, the attention will be excited by a History of the Decline and Fall of the Roman Empire; the greatest, perhaps, and most awful scene in the history of mankind. The various causes and progressive effects are connected with many of the events most interesting in human annals: the artful policy of the Cæsars, who long maintained the name and image of a free republic; the disorders of military despotism; the rise, establishment, and sects of Christianity; the foundation of Constantinople; the division of the monarchy; the invasion and settlements of the barbarians of Germany and Scythia; the institutions of the civil law; the character and

[1] The Père Montfaucon distributes his own observations into twenty days, he should have styled them weeks, or months, of his visits to the different parts of the city (Diarium Italicum, c. 8-20, p. 104-301). That learned Benedictine reviews the topographers of ancient Rome; the first efforts of Blondus, Fulvius, Martianus, and Faunus, the superior labours of Pyrrhus Ligorius, had his learning been equal to his labours; the writings of Onuphrius Panvinius, qui omnes obscuravit, and the recent but imperfect books of Donatus and Nardini. Yet Montfaucon still sighs for a more complete plan and description of the old city, which must be attained by the three following methods:—1. The measurement of the space and intervals of the ruins. 2. The study of inscriptions and the places where they were found. 3. The investigation of all the acts, charters, diaries of the middle ages, which name any spot or building of Rome. The laborious work, such as Montfaucon desired, must be promoted by princely or public munificence: but the great modern plan of Nolli (A.D. 1748) would furnish a solid and accurate basis for the ancient topography of Rome.

religion of Mohammed; the temporal sovereignty of the popes; the restoration and decay of the Western empire of Charlemagne; the crusades of the Latins in the East; the conquests of the Saracens and Turks; the ruin of the Greek empire; the state and revolutions of Rome in the middle age. The historian may applaud the importance and variety of his subject; but, while he is conscious of his own imperfections, he must often accuse the deficiency of his materials. It was among the ruins of the Capitol that I first conceived the idea of a work which has amused and exercised near twenty years of my life, and which, however inadequate to my own wishes, I finally deliver to the curiosity and candour of the public.

LAUSANNE,
    June 27, 1787.

INDEX

Letters following numerals refer to the four quarters of the page reading from top to bottom.

ABAN, v. 317*a*

Abbas, v. 266*c*, 289*b*, 383*a*

Abbassides, v. 385*a*, 402*c*, 417*a*, 433*a*, 436*c*–437; vi. 116, 29*b*, 105*b*–109, 283*b*

Abdallah, v. 222*b*, 321*d*–322, 352*a*, 359*c*

Abdalmalek, v. 359*c*

Abdalrahman, v. 397*c*–400

Abelard, vi. 471*c*

Abgarus, i. 202*a*, 494 n.[2]; v. 144*c*

Abrahah, v. 229*b*

Abraham, ii. 42*a*; iv. 168*a*; v. 228*a*

Abubeker, v. 240*a*, 249*a*, 252*c*, 269*a*–295, 308*c*

Abulpharagius, v. 345*c*, 410*c*

Abundantius, iii. 292*a*

Abu Obeidah, v. 318*a*, 326*c*, 334*d*

Abu Sophian, v. 252*b*, 259*b*, 264*b*, 283*d*, 285*a*

Abu Taher, v. 431*c*–432

Abu Taleb, v. 231*a*, 249*a*, 251*a*, *c*, 278*b*

Abyssinia, ii. 243*a*; iv. 173*d*, 481*b*; v. 67*b*, 68*b*–71, 229*b*

Abyssinians, iv. 322*c*–325; v. 1*b*

Acacius, iii. 319*d*–320

Academies, i. 30*c*; ii. 476*c*; iv. 398*c*

Academy, ii. 185*c*, 265*c*, 267*a*, 324*d*, 455*c*; iv. 140*b*, 202*c*; v. 413*a*

Acatzires, iii. 357*b*, 402*c*

Acesius, bishop, ii. 261*c*

Achilleus, i. 352*d*

Acholius, iii. 74*a*

Achrida, v. 506*c*

Acilius, iii. 226*a*

Acra, ii. 380*c*–381

Acre, vi. 118*a*–119, 132*b*–133

Acroceraunian rocks, v. 564*b*

Acropolita, vi. 219*c*

Actium, i. 19*a*

Adauctus, ii. 60*a*

Addua, iii. 182*c*, 183*b*

Adhemar, vi. 53*d*–54, 78*d*

Adiabene, ii. 416*b*

Adige, iii. 182*c*; iv. 120*c*

Adolius, iii. 341*b*

Adolphus, iii. 242*d*, 248*a*, 250*d*, 261*a*–265, 273*a*, 276*b*–277

Adrian, Pope, vi. 473*c*

Adulis, iv. 174*a*, 324*b*

Ædesius, ii. 364*a*, 367*a*

Ægæ, iii. 340*b*

Ægean, iii. 173*c*

Ægidius, iii. 431*b*–432, 444*a*

Ælia Capitolina, i. 439*a*

Æmilia, iii. 461*a*

Æmilianus, Emperor, i. 246*b*–247

Æmilian way, i. 289*c*; ii. 190*c*; iv. 355*b*

Æmilius Paulus, iii. 219*b*

Æmona, iii. 95*a*, 96*d*, 97*c*, 206*a*

Æneas, philosopher, iv. 35*d*–36; vi. 459*d*, 558 n.[1] (Sylvius)

Æsculapius, i. 33*a*; ii. 48 n.[3], 147 n.[1]; iii. 447*c*; iv. 205*c*

Æstians, iv. 126*d*

Æstii, ii. 514*a*

Æthiopia, i. 155*c*, 440 n.[2]; ii. 243*a*, 245*a*, 292*b*; iii. 166*c*, 288*b*; iv. 195*c*, 371*a*

Æthiopians, iv. 173*d*, 278*c*, 322*c*–325; v. 69*a*

Aëtius, atheist, ii. 280*b*, 289*a*, 302 n.[3]

Aëtius, general, iii. 216*c*, 266*b*, 322*c*, 326*c*–328, 332*c*, 333*a*, 336*c*, 344*c*, 361*c*, 373*a*–393, 398*c*, 403*d*–405, 421*c*, 431*c*.

Afrasiabs, iii. 13*a*

Africa, i. 26*c*, 156*a*, 171*b*, 352*c*, 491*b*; ii. 174*b*, 245*d*, 251*c*, 252*b*–264, 317*b*, 486*d*–508; iii. 53*a*,

73b, 147d, 158b–164, 262a–268,
322c, 327a, 407c; iv. 325c; v.
293a, 352a
Africans, iii. 218c, 408b; iv. 32c
Agathias, iii. 311c; iv. 301a, 358c
Aglabites, v. 433d
Agria, iii. 365a
Agricola, i. 4b; ii. 94 n.[3]
Agrippa, iii. 233c
Agrippina, i. 131c, 146a
Ahriman, i. 193b
Akbah, v. 356c, 357b–359
Aladin, vi. 82b, 292a, 293b
Alani, i. 314b; iii. 23b, 40a, 59b,
68d–69, 184c–199, 270b–330,
377a, 388a, 390b; iv. 291c
Alaric, iii. 113b, 157a, 171c–187,
195a–217a, 239a–264, 295c,
329b, 394c, 400b
Alaric II, iv. 22b, 57a, 59d
Alatheus, iii. 30d, 32c, 39c, 45a,
61a–62
Alavivus, ii. 513b; iii. 27a, 32d,
33c
Albania (Asia), iv. 200b
Albanians, ii. 199c; vi. 409a–413
Alberic, v. 196d–197
Albigeois, v. 500c; vi. 193b
Albinus, i. 106c, 113c, 115a, 117c–
119 (Clodius); iii. 267c; iv. 142b
Alboin, iv. 283a, 447b–455, 466c
Alcantara, i. 44c
Alemanni, i. 248c, 252a, 286d–
289, 322c, 388c, 401b; ii. 203c–
213, 325a, 334a, 487a–510; iii.
40a, 41a, 44a, 181d, 198c, 199d,
271c; iv. 42c, 48a, 49a, 325c,
355a–358
Aleppo, v. 330c, 440a; vi. 320c–322
Alexander, Archbishop of Alexandria, ii. 273c, 283d
Alexander III, Pope, v. 583c
Alexander Severus, i. 144a–145,
158a, 161c–167, 203a–204,
252b; ii. 41d–42
Alexandria, i. 50b, 55b, 132b,
272b–274, 353b, 354 n.[3], 438a,
488c, 489b; ii. 29a, 251c–258,
273a, 298c, 304c–305, 397c–402;
iii. 1d, 75c, 129d, 130b–134,
137c, 214 n.[1]; v. 12d, 342c–345
Alexandria, school of, ii. 266a,
267a, 269b

Alexius I., Comnenus, v. 119,
123a–126, 498c–499, 565c–568;
vi. 33d, 36b, 49c, 60c–65, 69a,
76d, 93c, 98a
Alexius II., Comnenus, v. 119,
130a, 136b
Alexius Angelus, vi. 134a, 143d–
144, 157d–162
Alexius Strategopulus, vi. 203a,
224d
Alexius the Great, son of Manuel,
vi. 185a
Alexius, Younger, vi. 153c–154,
163c–167
Alfred, King, iv. 40c, 144a; v. 55a
Algardi, iii. 400c
Ali, v. 207a, 249a–250, 262d–303
Aligern, iv. 353a, 354b, 355c, 357d
Allectus, i. 349a
Allier, iv. 78a
Allobich, iii. 255c
Almanon, v. 432d
Almansor, v. 410b
Almohades, v. 578c
Almondar, iv. 303a
Alp Arslan, vi. 1b, 12a, c, 15d–19
Alps, i. 405c; ii. 233a, 326c, 328a,
338a; iii. 73b, 94a, 199c, 200b,
203c, 427d
Alps, Cottian, ii. 174c, 336b; iv.
268a
Alps, Julian, i. 109c; ii. 172b; iii.
49b, 97c, 113c, 179a; iv. 120b
Alps, Rhætian, iii. 186d, 422 n.[1]
Alsace, ii. 204a; iv. 48b
Amala, i. 238b
Amalaric, iv. 145c
Amalasontha, iv. 145c, 146a,
240a–242
Amalfi, v. 558c; vi. 139c
Amali, ii. 513a; iii. 59c, 171c; iv.
112c, 240a
Amantius, eunuch, iv. 147c–148
Amazons, i. 302b
Amboise, iv. 57a
Ambrose, bishop, ii. 244 n.[3],
252 n.[4], 276c, 386c; iii. 87b–92,
105c–124, 141b, 195c
Amelius, i. 382b
America, iv. 109c
Amida, ii. 198c–202, 424c, 453a;
iii. 319d–320; iv. 197a, 199a
Amir, Prince of Ionia, vi. 295c

Ammianus, historian, ii. 197c, 288a, 318d–319, 372c, 387a, 452d, 473d–474, 484c, 506b; iii. 56a, 224c–231

Ammonius, i. 382b; mathematician, iii. 236c, 382b; martyr, v. 14b

Amorium, v. 427b

Amphilochus, iii. 75a

Amphitheatre, iii. 188c; vi. 564b

Ampsaga, iii. 337c

Amrou, v. 284d, 285d, 313d, 316b, 337a–338, 343c–348

Amurath I., vi. 273a, 299a–300, 343c, 346a, 366c

Amurath II., iv. 308c, 392c, 397c–400, 404d, 411c, 413d

Anabaptists, v. 503c

Anachorets, iv. 2a, 4b, 5c, 6c, 16c–20

Anacletus, Pope, v. 577c–578; vi. 498a

Anah or Anatho, ii. 420c

Anas, iii. 329d

Anastasius I., iv. 52a, 61b, 112b, 116b, 127c, 150c, 176a, b, 183b, 193c, 194c, 198b, 199b, 296c

Anatolius, iii. 371b

Anchialus, i. 260b

Ancyra, ii. 460a

Anderida, iv. 86b

Andragathius, iii. 71c

Andrew, St., iii. 140c; v. 451c

Andronicus I., Comnenus, v. 119, 130c–139

Andronicus of Libya, ii. 255b–256

Andronicus the Elder, vi. 230a, 234b, 240b, 247a, 249b–253, 347b

Andronicus, the last, vi. 141c

Andronicus the Younger, vi. 247a, 249a–255

Angamala, v. 56b

Angara, iii. 16b

Angelo, St., iii. 450d; vi. 549b

Angles, iv. 90a, b, 93a, 94b, 97c, 101d

Anglo-Saxons, iv. 99a, 477c

Angora, vi. 323c–324

Angoulême, iv. 60c

Anianus, bishop, iii. 386a, b

Anician family, iii. 220a, 221a, c, 238a, 257b, 405b, 449d; iv. 139c

Anicius, iii. 220a; Anicius Julian, iii. 221a

Anna Comnena, v. 119, 124b, 126b, 485b, 565c–568; vi. 66c

Anne of Savoy, vi. 255a–258, 260d–262, 351a

Annian house, iii. 220c

Annibalianus, i. 319b

Antala, iii. 394c

Anthemius, architect, iv. 183a–185

Anthemius, Emperor, iii. 407c, 431a, 436c–451, 457b

Anthemius, præfect, iii. 312b

Anthropomorphites, v. 7b

Antichrist, ii. 309b; iii. 259d

Antioch, i. 50b, 128b, 139a, 151c–152, 204c, 264a, 359a, 438a, 488c; ii. 44b–46, 181a, 251c–295, 310a, 394a, 395b, 408b–411, 453c, 459b; iii. 100c–103, 317c; iv. 280b, 305c, 370a; v. 52b, 441c; vi. 33d, 51c, 72b–75, 77a–79

Antioch, council of, ii. 277c, 296a

Antiochus, i. 432a; iii. 226a; proconsul, iii. 172b

Antonina, iv. 214d, 218c, 259c–260, 273b–278, 342c, 364a

Antonines, the, i. 20a, 21c, 31b, 37a, 40b, 57 n.[1], 58d–82

Antoninus, Marcus Aurelius, i. 9c, 77b, 82c; ii. 39b, 406b–407, 518c

Antoninus Pius, i. 8b, 76c, 77a; ii. 3d, 25c

Antoninus, Roman refugee, ii. 197b–198

Antoninus, wall of, i. 21d, 50b; ii. 499c; iii. 204d, 269b; iv. 92d

Antony, hermit, ii. 292 n.[3], 304 n.[1], 368c, 507 n.[1], [3]; iv. 2 n.[1], 3a–4, 12a

Apamea, i. 257c; iii. 128b, 129a; iv. 482c; v. 52b

Apennine, ii. 233a; iii. 186b, 194c, 198b, 217b; iv. 263d

Aper, Arrius, i. 338a

Apharban, i. 362a

Apocaucus, admiral, vi. 256c–260

Apollinaris of Alexandria, v. 64c; of Laodicea, v. 9c–10, 11c. See also Sidonius

Apollo, ii. 82*a*, 220*c*, 221*a*, 362*c*, 363*a*, 368*c*, 393*b*, 395*a*, 396*b*, 414*c*; iii. 136*d*

Apollonius of Tyana, i. 296*c*; ii. 42*a*, 48 n.[3]

Apostles, ii. 241*a*, 259*a*; iii. 74*b*, 89*c*

Appian way, iii. 226 n.[1], 259*d*; iv. 249*b*, 250*c*

Apsimar, v. 82*c*–83

Apulia, iii. 219*c*, 267*a*, 433*a*; v. 552*c*–557, 561*c*, 565*b*, 576*a*, *c*, 590*b*

Aquileia, i. 178*c*–180; ii. 172*c*, 342*c*, 344*c*; iii. 94*c*, 97*c*, 114*a*, 179*a*, 180*a*, 216*d*, 324*c*, *d*, 394*a*–396, 437*d*

Aquitain, iii. 279*a*, 285*c*, 417*c*; iv. 27*a*, 58*a*, 60*b*, 61*a*, 86*c*; v. 184*b*

Arabia, i. 55*a*, *c*, 158*a*, 272*c*, 302*a*; ii. 243*a*, 420*a*; iv. 323*a*, 324*a*; v. 207*a*–228; A. Felix, i. 2*b*; iv. 481*a*; v. 209*b*

Arabissus, iii. 308*d*

Arabs, i. 26*a*, 298*c*, 355*a*; ii. 202*a*, 417*d*, 506*c*; iii. 48*c*, 113*b*, 266*c*, 319*d*, 440*b*; iv. 108*b*, 197*d*; v. 75*c*, 214*b*–226, 277*a*, 293*a*, 299*a*, 352*a*–355, 385*a*, 442*a*

Araric, ii. 149*a*, 150*c*

Araxes, i. 199*a*, 364*b*

Arbela, ii. 434*b*

Arbetio, ii. 350*c*, 470*b*

Arbogastes, iii. 96*c*, 98*a*, 109*d*–115

Arcadia, iii. 175*c*, 313*b*

Arcadius, Emperor, iii. 75*a*, 101*c*, 116*c*, 141*b*, 147*c*–163, 171*c*, 176*c*, 208*c*, 287*a*–315, 321*a*

Ardaburius, iii. 324*b*, *c*, 372*d*, 435*b*

Ardaric, iii. 349*a*, 390*b*, 402*b*, *d*

Areopagus. i. 267*a*; ii. 341*b*

Argentaria, iii. 41*a*, 256*c*

Argos, i. 259*c*; ii. 355*c*; iii. 174*a*, 185*a*

Ariadne, iv. 115*b*, 116*a*

Arians, ii. 268 n.[3], 276*a*, 280*c*–283, 287*c*, 289*c*–313, 399*c*, 400*a*, 409*b*, 480*a*; iii. 90*b*, 300*b*, *d*; iv. 26*d*, 27*c*, 31*d*, 35*b*, 54*a*, 326*d*

Arii, i. 320*a*

Arintheus, ii. 419*a*, 470*a*, 510*a*, 516*b*, *d*

Ariovistus, iv. 72*a*

Aristobulus, i. 341*c*

Aristotle, i. 57*c*, 197*c*, 382*c*, 495*c*, 496*a*; ii. 215*d*, 280*c*, 345*c*, 349*b*; iv. 140*b*, *c*, 203*a*, 301*b*, 391*c*; v. 412*c*; vi. 206*d*, 388*c*

Arius, ii. 273*b*, 274*b*, 276*a*, 279*c*, 280*a*–285, 292*c*, 310 n.[1]

Arles, ii. 288*c*; iii. 183*a*, 204*c*, 269*c*, 285*c*, 377*b*, 387*a*, 444*a*; iv. 44*b*, 61*a*, 62*c*, 63*a*; v. 189*c*; council, ii. 258*c*, 262*d*, 301*d*

Armenia, i. 191*b*, 204*a*, 262*b*, 355*c*–360, 365*c*; ii. 157*c*, 242 n.[3], 416*c*, 432*c*, 447*d*, 508*a*–512; iii. 37*a*, 38*b*, 308*c*, 319*b*, 320*b*, *c*, 322*a*; iv. 521*b*; v. 488*b*; vi. 13*a*, 14*c*

Armenians, i. 201*c*; ii. 119*a*, 509*c*, 511*a*; v. 1*b*, 49*b*, 61*b*

Armorica, ii. 495*a*; iii. 281*d*, 285*c*, 407*b*; iv. 52*b*, 93*b*–100

Armoricans, iii. 388*a*; iv. 52*c*

Arnold of Brescia, vi. 461*b*, 471*b*–474, 482*a*

Arrian, iv. 314*a*

Arsaces, i. 262*b*; ii. 508 n.[3]; iii. 320*c*–322

Arsacides, i. 191*c*, 198*b*, 199*c*; ii. 508*b*; v. 101*c*

Arsacius, iii. 308*a*

Arsenius, bishop, ii. 293*a*; iii. 154*a*; vi. 220*b*, 224*c*–229

Artaban, i. 191*b*; iv. 343*b*, 345*d*

Artasires, iii. 321*b*–322

Artavasdes, v. 151*d*

Artaxata, iii. 321*b*

Artaxerxes, i. 190*b*, 197*c*, 205*b*, 262*a*, 330; ii. 509*c*; iv. 299*a*

Artemius, ii. 351*d*; v. 85*c*

Arthur, King, iv. 94*b*–96

Artogerassa, ii. 508*c*, 511*a*

Artois, iii. 381*b*

Arvandus, iii. 445*c*–447

Arzema, v. 300*a*

Ascalon, vi. 85*c*

Ascetics, iv. 1*c*, 9*a*–12, 17*a*

Asclepiodotus, i. 319*b*

Asfendiar, iii. 13*a*

Asgard, i. 236*a*

Asia, i. 24*d*–25, 36*a*, 38*c*, 49*c*, 155*b*, 189*d*; ii. 245*d*, 281*a*, 468*d*;

iii. 4*a*, 5*c*, 11*b*, 13*b*, 52*c*, 101*a*, 305*c*; vi. 330*a*

Asia Minor, i. 25*a*, 254*b*; iii. 147*d*, 296*a*, 308*c*; iv. 193*c*; v. 493*a*; vi. 1*b*, 24*c*, 25*c*

Asia, Upper, i. 198*c*, 200*b*

Asiarchs, i. 484 n.²

Asiatics, iii. 232*c*

Aspacuras, ii. 508*c*, 509*d*

Aspar, iii. 324*b*, *d*, 336*a*, 372*d*, 435*b*; iv. 115*a*

Assassins, vi 282*d*–283

Assyria, ii. 245*a*, 420*a*–423, 426*c*, 463*b*

Assyrians, ii. 422*b*, 423*b*

Asta, iii. 179 n.³, 183*a*, *c*

Astarte, i. 142*b*

Asterius, Count, iii. 328*d*

Astorga, iii. 418*b*, *d*

Athalaric, iv. 145*b*, 240*b*–242

Athanaric, ii. 513*b*, 516*a*, *c*, 517*a*; iii. 26*c*, 27*b*, 59*d*, 60*a*; iv. 21*c*

Athanasius, ii. 255*b*, 269*c*, 277*c*, 278*a*, *c*, 286*a*, 290*c*–309, 401*a*–403, 409*b*, 457*c*–458, 479*c*, 480*c*; iii. 81*a*; iv. 3 n.⁴, 4*a*, 5*a*

Athanasius of Constantinople, vi. 247*c*

Athenais, iii. 316*b*–318, 325*c*

Athenians, iv. 203*c*

Athens, i. 31*d*, 33*b*, 46*b*, 56*b*, 57 n.¹, 259*a*, 261*d*, 425*c*, 487*d*; ii. 185*b*, 187*b*, 256*c*, 341*a*, 355*c*, 367*b*; iii. 76*c*, 173*a*–175; iv. 5*c*, 192*c*, 371*b*, 372*d*, 415*c*; v. 73*a*; vi. 216*c*, 243*a*–246; schools, iv. 140*a*, 146*c*, 201*c*–206

Athos, Mount, vi. 265*a*

Atlantic, iii. 2*d*, 277*b*; iv. 22*b*

Atlantis (Plato), i. 212*b*

Atlas, Mount, i. 27*b*; ii. 466*a*, 504*d*; iii. 330*a*, 331*b*, 408*b*

Attacotti, ii. 500*a*

Attalus, præfect, iii. 248*a*–250, 265*b*, 269*a*, 273*a*–274

Attalus of Auvergne, iv. 79*c*–81

Attica, iii. 173*b*

Attila, i. 226 n.¹; iii. 26*b*, 314*c*, 327*a*, 329*b*, 343–401

Atys, ii. 364*b*, *d*

Audians, iii. 85*c*

Augurs, iii. 120*a*

Augusta (title), iii. 313*a*, 383*a*

Augustine, ii. 435*a*; iii. 93*a*, 141 n.³, 143*b*, *c*, 196*a*, *b*, 200 n.³, 252*d*–253, 327*a*, 331*d*, 334*c*–335

Augustulus, iii. 407*c*, 454*a*–458

Augustus (title), ii. 146*a*, 155*c*, 329*c*, 332*c*; iii. 52*c*, 310*b*, 323*b*, 326*b*

Augustus, i. 2*a*, 3*a*, 8*a*, 19*a*, 20*b*, *d*, 22*c*, 32 n.⁷, 34*b*, 44*a*, 59*b*–61, 62*d*–73, 156*c*, 157*d*, 158*b*, 254*c*; ii. 406*b*; iii. 233*a*–237, 280*c*; v. 206*b*

Aurasius, Mount, iv. 236*c*–237, 327*a*

Aurelian, iii. 299*b*, 300*a*; Ambrosius A., iv. 94*b*

Aurelian, Emperor, i. 275*a*, 282*c*, 283*b*–307, 308*a*; ii. 44*b*, 46*b*; iii. 234*a*; iv. 170*c*

Aurungzebe, i. 200 n.⁵

Ausonius, iii. 260 n.⁴

Austin, ii. 254*c*

Austrasia, iv. 37*a*, 71*c*, 78*b*, 355*a*

Autharis, iv. 463*c*–464, 469*b*–470

Autun, i. 293*a*, 400*d*–401; ii. 129*b*, 164*c*, 206*a*; iv. 43*c*, 82*b*

Auvergne, iii. 387*a*, 420*b*, 444*c*–447; iv. 42*b*, 60*a*, 77*b*–79

Auxerre, iii. 385*c*

Avars, iii. 403*b*; iv. 278*b*, 291*b*–294, 444*b*–450, 480*a*, 494*a*, 501*a*–516, 525*a*–526; v. 186*c*

Aventine hill, iv. 132*c*

Avernus, iii. 227 n.²

Avienus, iii. 399*b*

Avignon, iv. 55*a*; v. 204*a*; vi. 349*a*, 352*a*, *b*, 363*a*–364, 461*a*, 493*c*, 503*a*, 529*c*

Avila, iii. 86*a*

Avitus, iii. 387*a*, 407*c*, 413*d*–420; Bishop of Vienne, iv. 54*b*, 71*a*

Axuch, v. 126*d*

Axume (Abyssinia), iv. 324*b*; v. 69*c*

Ayesha, v. 271*c*, 276*a*–279, 283*a*

Azimuntium, iii. 359*b*–360

Azymites, vi. 396*a*, 432*a*

Baalbec. *See* Heliopolis

Babylas, bishop, ii. 395*c*, 409*c*; iii. 259*d*

Babylon, i. 201*b*, 455*b*; ii. 422*a*, *d*, 435*b*; v. 53*a*, 54*a*, 226*c*, 227*b*

Bacchus, iii. 132a
Bactriana, i. 302a; iii. 21 n.²; v. 305a
Bacurius, iii. 45a, 114b
Bætica, iii. 276a, 278b, 328d; iv. 38d; v. 368b
Bafina, iv. 44d–45
Bagaudæ, iii. 407b, 428a
Bagdad, ii. 422a, 429a, 437a; v. 406c; vi. 2a, 10d, 11a, c, 12a, 278d, 283b, 313c
Bahram or Varanes, i. 330a; iii. 319b, 322a; iv. 480a, 486a–487, 489b–492
Bahrein, v. 431c
Baiæ, iv. 134a
Baikal, iii. 16b
Bajazet I., vi. 273a, 300d–305, 308c–320, 323a–330
Balbinus, i. 175c–176
Baldwin I., Emperor, vi. 65a, 71a–72, 85a, 146b, 147a, 158d, 171c, 179b, c, 187d–190
Baldwin II., Emperor, vi. 194c–204, 225b, 230d
Balista, pretender, i. 268b
Balti, iii. 171c, 250d, 273c
Baltic, i. 209 n.¹; ii. 493b, 514a; iii. 24a, b, 192c, 193b, d, 201c; iv. 22d
Ban, v. 538c–540
Banditti, i. 272a
Bangor or Banchor, iv. 6c
Barbatio, ii. 207d–208
Barcelona, iii. 276c, d, 277b
Barchochebas, ii. 3c
Bardanes, v. 85b
Bardas, v. 103b, 483b
Bards, iv. 99c
Barlaam, vi. 266a, 347c–348, 380b–381
Basel, ii. 208a, 333c; council, vi. 363c–364
Basil I., Emperor, v. 73d, 101c–105, 496c, 538c
Basil II., Emperor, v. 106, 111a, 113b–115, 511a
Basil of Cæsarea, ii. 404 n.¹, 481c; iii. 76c; iv. 5c; v. 10c
Basileus (title), i. 371b; v. 510c
Basiliscus, iii. 441c–443; iv. 115c
Basra, ii. 422a
Bassianus, i. 138a

Bassora, v. 301d
Bastarnæ, i. 238d, 323d, 352b; iii. 157b
Batavians, i. 227c, 319d; ii. 204a, 487c, d, 500c; iv. 45a
Bath, i. 48d; iv. 92d
Batou, vi. 284b–286
Bavarians, iii. 326a, 345a; iv. 66b, 127b, 451a, 469b, 520a, 521a
Bayeux, ii. 494 n.²
Beauvais, iv. 46c
Bede, ii. 497d; iii. 282 n.⁴; iv. 87c, 91 n.¹, 97c
Beder, v. 258c, 284a
Bedouins, v. 210c, 212a, 222a, 431b
Belgic provinces, iii. 377c, 385a
Belgrade, iv. 190c, 280d; v. 516c. See also Singidunum
Belisarius, iv. 28c, 151a–153, 167b, 182a, 212b–364
Benedict XII., Pope, vi. 347c, 349a
Benedict XIV., vi. 565c
Benedictines, iv. 10c, 12b, 14 n.³
Benevento, v. 577a; vi. 235b
Beneventum, iv. 249a; v. 538a, 542a
Bengal Sea, iv. 288b
Bernard, St., vi. 93b, 102c–105, 470b, 472c
Berry, iii. 444c, 445b
Berytus, iv. 170c, 179b, 203b, 370b; school, ii. 104c; iv. 398c
Bessarion, Cardinal, vi. 375c, 385c–386, 396c
Bessas, iv. 336a–339
Bethlehem, iii. 257c; iv. 8a
Bezabde, ii. 201b, 203a
Bindoes, iv. 488a
Bishops, ii. 245c–249, 252c–255, 258c; iv. 108d
Bithynia, i. 257d; ii. 271b, 316a, 467b, 468d; iii. 2a, 291c; iv. 159c; synod, ii. 274a
Black Forest, ii. 338c
Black Sea, iv. 6a; v. 526c; vi. 267c
Bleda, iii. 345c, 348a, 364c
Blemmyes, i. 301b, 352c, 353c–354; v. 25a
Boccaccio, vi. 382b–383

Index

Boethius, ii. 275 n.³, 498a; iii. 404a; iv. 112b, 131a, 137c, 139c–144

Bohemia, iv. 49c; v. 204a–206, 520a

Bohemond (Guiscard), v. 569d–571, 576a; vi. 54c–55, 59d, 63a, 64a, 67c, 70a, 94c–95

Bologna, iii. 209a, c, 248d

Boniface, Apostle of Germany, iv. 23 n.¹

Boniface, Count, iii. 263c, 322c–336

Boniface, Marquis of Montserrat, vi. 151d, 153c, 159a, 170c, 179b

Boniface VIII., Pope, vi. 492a

Bonosus, i. 325c

Borani, i. 239a

Bordeaux, iii. 86b, 263c, 279a, 280c; iv. 43c, 60c; v. 397b

Borderers, ii. 108d

Borysthenes, i. 238c, 239b, 253d, 257a; iii. 4b, 403c

Bosphorus, i. 254c, 257a, 280b; ii. 72a–73; iii. 48c, 141a, 307b; v. 528a; kingdom, i. 254c; ii. 467a

Bosra, v. 311a–312

Botheric, iii. 104a, 105a

Boucicault, Marshal, vi. 307c, 354b

Boulogne, i. 348b; ii. 498b; iii. 202d

Bowides, v. 435d

Brabant, ii. 204b; iii. 280a

Bracara, iii. 274d

Braga, iii. 418b; iv. 85c

Brancaleone, vi. 480c, 559a

Bregetio, ii. 522b

Britain, i. 3c, 9 n.¹, 21b, 36 n.³, 48d, 81c, 106c–107, 126c, 227a, 346c–350, 388a; ii. 175c, 214b, 327c, 385c, 486d–506; iii. 53a, 69c, 70a, c, 147d, 182a, 201d–203, 269b, 282a–285; iv. 22c, 42a, c, 87b, 91b, 477b; vi. 358b–359

British Channel, ii. 494a, 500b; island, ii. 492d; iii. 281c; iv. 92a; tribes, ii. 496a

Britons, iii. 281c; iv. 86b, 89a, 91c, 92b, 100b, 101d; v. 184a

Bructeri, i. 228c
*T 476

Brunechild, iv. 37a

Brussels, iii. 381a

Bruttium, iii. 267a, 433a; iv. 134c

Buccelin, iv. 355a–357

Buda, ii. 195b

Bulgaria, iv. 146c; v. 114d, 530c–532; vi. 137d

Bulgarians, iv. 120a, 283a–286, 360b, 361d–362, 451a; v. 75d, 500b, 505a–514; vi. 134a, 142c, 178a

Burgundians, i. 237b, 319d; ii. 491a, c; iii. 192d, 198a, 199c, 272c, 279c, 348c, 377c, 388a, 390a; iv. 42c, 53b

Burgundy, i. 53a; iii. 279c; iv. 54c, 55b, 56b

Busiris, i. 353b

Buzurg, iv. 484b

Byzacium, iii 339b

Byzantine palace, iv. 190a

Byzantium, i. 116d, 414b, 427a; ii. 71c, 76b

Caaba, v. 223d–225, 229c, 242c, 243b, 265b

Cabades, iv. 198b–201

Cadesia, battle of, v. 300b–301

Cadijah, v. 231a, 249a, 252b

Cæcilian, ii. 251a, 262a

Cæcilius, ii. 231b–232

Cæsar (title), i. 373d; ii. 143c, 155b, 178b; iii. 225b, 310b

Cæsar, Julius, i. 3c, 70b; ii. 212b, 347 n.¹, 406b, 450 n.¹, 455c, 496 n.¹; iii. 196c, 205c, 280c, 390c; iv. 368b

Cæsarea, i. 264c; ii. 36a, 404a, 482a; iii. 77a; v. 333d; council, ii. 293a

Cahina, moorish queen, v. 361b, 362

Cairo, vi. 107b

Cairoan, v. 358d, 359a

Calabria, iii. 267a, 433a; iv. 121c

Caled, v. 264a, c, 268c, 294c

Caledonia, i. 388b; ii. 496b, c, 497a, c, d, 500a; iii. 281c; rampart, ii. 466a

Caledonians, i. 5a, 125c–126; ii. 499c, 501b; iii. 147d, 182a; iv. 88c

Caledonian war, i. 125c–126

Caliphs, v. 293*a*, 295*b*–297, 299*a*, 384*a*, 385*a*, 406*b*, 410*b*, 432*d*; vi. 1*b*, 283*b*
Callinicum, iii. 105*d*
Callinicus, v. 393*a*
Calmucks, iii. 22*b*, 346*a*; iv. 108*a*, 289*b*
Calo-Johannes (Comnenus), v. 126*c*
Calo-John, King of Bulgaria, vi. 186*d*–192
Calvary, ii. 268*c*, 382*a*, 385*b*; v. 5*c*
Calvin, v. 501*c*–504
Cambray, iii. 381*a*
Camillus, iii. 194*b*
Camisards, ii. 317*d*–318
Campania, ii. 125*c*; iii. 234*a*, 256*c*, 260*a*–263, 267*a*, 426*d*, 433*a*, 458*b*
Canaan, i. 434*b*, 441*b*
Candidian, v. 21*a*
Candidianus, i. 415*b*, *c*, *d*
Cannæ, iii. 46*a*; v. 538*b*
Cantacuzene, John, vi. 247*a*–272, 298*a*, 349*a*–350
Canton, iii. 18*c*
Capelianus, i. 174*c*
Caphgamala, iii. 142*b*, 143*a*
Capito, iv. 390*b*, 393*b*
Capitol, ii. 19*c*; iii. 123*c*, 126*a*, 130*c*, 241*a*, 281*b*, 411*d*, 446*a*; vi. 476*c*, 547*c*, 566*a*
Cappadocia, ii. 118*b*, 178*c*, 243*b*, 255*b*, 361*a*, 398*a*, 466*c*; iii. 57*a*, 76*c*
Capraria, iii. 165*c*–166
Capua, iii. 218*d*, 260*a*; iv. 250*c*
Caracalla, i. 124*b*–125, 126*d*, 127*b*–134, 160*d*–161, 167*c*; ii. 40*b*; baths, ii. 191*c*; iii. 234*b*; vi. 548*c*
Caracorum, vi. 287*c*
Carausius, i. 346*c*–349
Carbeas, v. 495*c*
Carbonarian forest, iii. 381*a*
Carinus, i. 328*c*–336, 339*d*
Carizme, iii. 21*a*; v. 308*b*; vi. 6*d*, 278*d*, 279*b*
Carizmians, vi. 127*c*
Carlscrona, i. 236*c*
Carmania, ii. 510*c*
Carmath, v. 431*a*
Carmelites, iv. 2 n.[3]

Carpathians, i. 238*d*; ii. 193*c*; iii. 365*a*, 402*d*
Carpi, i. 239*a*, 352*b*
Carrhæ, i. 134*b*, 262*c*; ii. 415*c*–416, 417*b*, 451 n.[1], 466*c*
Carthage, i. 49*b*, 155*c*–174, 352*c*, 401*d*, 496*c*; ii. 29*a*, 250*a*–262, 507*a*; iii. 129*c*, 224*a*, 268*c*, 331*b*–340, 408*c*, 429*a*, 432*c*, 442*b*; iv. 29*c*–34, 219*a*–225, 328*a*–330, 512*a*; v. 359*d*–361; synod, iv. 229*a*
Carthagena, i. 156*b*; iii. 275*d*, 329*a*, 428*c*–430, 447*c*
Carun, i. 126*a*
Carus, Emperor, i. 319*b*, 328*a*–329
Cashmir, vi. 3*a*
Caspian, i. 358*a*; ii. 198*a*; iii. 8*a*, 13*a*, 21*a*, 192*b*, 349*d*; iv. 198*a*, 483*c*; vi. 280*c*; gates, iii. 403*c*
Cassian, ii. 195*d*
Cassians, iv. 394*a*
Cassiodorus, i. 233*d*; iii. 390*d*, 397*a*, 398*b*; iv. 123*a*, 130*a*, 131*a*, 239*b*
Castilians, iii. 259*b*
Castinus, iii. 328*d*
Catalans, vi. 216*c*, 239*d*–242, 244*a*, 271*c*
Catalaunia, ii. 488*c*; iii. 388*c*, 390*b*
Catana, iv. 243*d*; v. 588*a*
Catholics, ii. 309*d*, 398*b*, 480*c*; v. 10*d*; iii. 74*c*, 79*a*, 84*a*, 109*c*, 308*a*, 310*c*, 331*b*, 337*c*, 460*c*; iv. 26*d*, 31*c*–37, 135*c*, 149*c*
Cato, iii. 230*a*, 440*b*; iv. 20*a*, 142*a*, 399*c*; the Censor, iv. 411*b*
Catti, i. 249*b*
Caucaland, iii. 27*b*, 59*d*
Caucasus, iii. 12*a*, 24*a*; iv. 174*c*, 200*b*, 309*a*, 315*b*
Ceaulin, iv. 92*d*
Celestine, Pope, v. 18*c*, 589*a*
Celsus, i. 496 n.[1]; ii. 6 n.[1], 8 n.[1], 66 n.[1], 407*a*
Censor, i. 242*c*–243; iii. 218*a*; iv. 414*a*
Ceos, iv. 169*b*
Cerca, Queen, iii. 366*a*
Ceres, iii. 175*a*
Cerinthus, v. 7*c*, 10*d*, 11*d*
Ceuta, iv. 228*c*–238*a*; 363*c*

Cevennes, iv. 77d

Ceylon, iv. 173a, c, d, 174a; v. 53a

Chaboras, ii. 418b, 420a, 437c

Chagan, iv. 480a, 494a–497, 525a; v. 522a

Chalcedon, i. 257b; ii. 73b, 350b, 351c; iii. 150d, 299b, d, 306b; iv. 42b; v. 1b, 28d–31 (4th council)

Chaldæans, iv. 196b; v. 226c

Chaled, v. 299a, 310c–314, 315c–321, 326b–332, 333c, 335b, 337c

Châlons, ii. 129b, 488c; iii. 388b, c, 390c, 392b

Chamavians, ii. 211c–212

Charlemagne, ii. 492d; iv. 22c, 66a, 69a; v. 75b, 141d, 165b, 168a, 171c, 178a, 179d–188, 477a; vi. 462a

Charles, Emperor, v. 204a–206; vi. 524b, 527b

Charles V., Emperor, i. 375b; ii. 69a; iii. 201c, 258c; vi. 543b

Charles VI. of France, vi. 355a

Charles Martel, v. 163c, 167c, 385a, 399a–401

Charles of Anjou, vi. 216c, 235a–239, 481c–482

Charles the Fat, v. 189c

Chauci, i. 249a

Chazars, v. 512c–513

Chersonesus, Taurica, i. 254b; ii. 149c; iii. 301a; Thracian, iii. 353c; iv. 192d, 193a, 286c

Chersonites, v. 82d, 84d

Cherusci, i. 249b

Childebert, iv. 77c–79, 463b

Childeric, iii. 432b; iv. 44d; v. 166b, c

China, i. 357b; iii. 7c–23, 191b, c, d, 344a, 349a, 354b, 383d; iv. 107c, 109c, 169a–170, 171c, 172c–173, 174b–175; v. 54a, 306b, 513b; vi. 273a, 281a; wall, iii. 14b, 16c; vi. 278a

Chinese, iii. 12a–22

Chnodomar, ii. 208c–210

Chorazan, vi. 7b, 279c

Chosroes II., iv. 480a, d, 488b–493, 511a–531

Chosroes of Armenia, i. 204a, 262b; iii. 321a, b

Chosroes or Nushirvan, iv. 201b, 206c, 278b, 295b, 297a–310, 316d–322, 480a, d, 482a–484

Chosroes, son of Tiridates, ii. 158a, 416c

Chozars, iv. 526c

Christ, i. 438a–442, 453a; ii. 15a, 42a, 65b, 219b–240, 268a; iii. 80d, 253a, 317b; iv. 42a, 51a; v. 6c, 8a, 237c–239

Christians, i. 447c–448, 462a–469; ii. 1–2, 5a–69, 220a–245, 389c–404; iii. 119a; iv. 1c, 411c; v. 226c, 228a, 293a; vi. 43a

Chrysaphius, iii. 369d–372

Chrysoloras, vi. 384a–385, 392c, 393a

Chrysostom, i. 489a; ii. 239 n.[3], 257d, 386c; iii. 102d–103, 287b, 298b, 302b–309; iv. 7 n.[1]

Cibalis, i. 418d; ii. 461c

Cicero, i. 30 n.[3], 31a, 35b, 71a, 82b, 148a, 160a, 448b; iii. 121a, 261c, 368b, 406b; iv. 24d, 379d, 391a

Cilicia, i. 273d; ii. 397d, 511c, d; iii. 340b

Cimbri, ii. 492 n.[2]; iii. 185b, 193b

Cimmerians, iii. 227c

Circassia, i. 255d; iv. 312a

Circassians, iv. 291c

Circesium, ii. 417c, 418b, 421c; iv. 196a

Circumcellions, ii. 316a–317; iii. 332a

Circus, ii. 347a; iii. 235a; iv. 131c, 146c, 160b–161, 306b–345a; vi. 562c–563

Cirta, iii. 333b, 337c

Citizens, iii. 218a, 236c–237

City, the Eternal, iii. 232c, 400b; the Venerable, 225b

Cius, i. 257c

Civilians (law), iv. 392c–395

Civilis, i. 227c

Clairvaux, vi. 103a, 105a

Claudian, iii. 155c, d, 168c–169, 180b, 184c, 185c, 188c, 205a, 212a–214, 220a, 291a

Claudius, Emperor, i. 42c, 72a, 187b, 275–282; iii. 247a

Cleander, i. 88c–90

Clematius of Alexandria, ii. 180 n.[1]

Clemens, Flavius, ii. 21b
Clement VI., Pope, vi. 349c, 512b
Clement VII., Pope, vi. 531a–532, 543b
Clergy, ii. 248c, 249b–250; iii. 73c, 81b–82; iv. 82c
Clitumnus, iii. 217b
Clodion, King, iii. 380c–381, 382a
Clotilda, iv. 49d, 53c, 56c, 57c
Clovis, iii. 266a, 393c; iv. 22c, 40b, 42c, 44d–62, 72c–74, 83c–84, 93c, 128b
Cniva, i. 240d, 241b
Cochin, v. 55b
Codrus, iii. 238a
Cœnobites, iv. 2 n.¹, 16c–17
Colchis, i. 256a; iv. 309c–315
Colchos, iv. 195c
Coliseum, i. 44c, 47b; vi. 561b
Colmar, iii. 41a, 66c
Cologne, ii. 24b, 190a, 203d, 206d; iii. 382a
Colonna family, vi. 461a, 498c–501, 512a–513, 519b–526, 533a; Stephen, vi. 510b, 519d
Columba, iv. 6 n.⁸
Columbanus, iv. 9 n.⁵, 12 n.¹
Comana, ii. 118b; iii. 309b
Comans, vi. 187d–189, 285c
Commentiolus, iv. 499a
Commodus, i. 82c–95; ii. 39d–40; iii. 68b
Comnenian family, v. 74a, 118a, 119; vi. 457b
Comum, iii. 395c; iv. 134b
Conrad III., vi. 95c, 97a, 99c
Conrad of Montferrat, vi. 117a, 120
Conradin, vi. 235c, 237b
Constance, ii. 336b; lake, iii. 40b; treaty, v. 200d
Constans, Emperor, ii. 136d, 137, 143c, 145c, 155c, 163a–165, 296b, 297c, 298c, 498a
Constans II., Emperor, v. 78c–80
Constantia, Princess, ii. 469a, 518d, 522a
Constantina, daughter of Constantine I., ii. 165d–166, 179c, 182d; widow of Maurice, iv. 505c–506
Constantine, Emperor (Britain), iii. 202c–204, 269b–272, 282a
Constantine I., i. 386b–394, 397a–414, 417c–429; ii. 59c, 70a, 71c, 95a, d, 104a–111, 113b, 133a–154, 218–240, 283c–286, 319c–320; iii. 141a; iv. 106d; vi. 464c
Constantine II., ii. 137, 145c, 155d, 163a
Constantine III., v. 77c–78
Constantine IV. (Pogonatus), v. 80b–81
Constantine V. (Copronymus), v. 88a–89, 173a, 497c
Constantine VI., v. 90a–92
Constantine VII. (Porphyrogenitus), v. 106, 107d–110, 442a
Constantine VIII. (Romanus II.), v. 110c
Constantine IX., v. 106, 111a, 113d–114
Constantine X. (Monomachus), v. 106, 117a
Constantine XI. (Ducas), v. 120c
Constantine XII. (Comnenus), v. 120d
Constantine Palæologus, vi. 413b
Constantine Sylvanus, v. 492c
Constantinople, i. 429c; ii. 70c–88, 183a, 241c, 250a–258, 288c, 312c, 320d, 344a–348, 355a, 464c, 510d–517; iii. 42a, 48a, 60a, 75c, 147c, 287b, 300c, 304c–305, 312d, 437a; iv. 161c–167, 183a–190; v. 73a, 385a–386, 390d–392, 448d–449, 455b, 456d–457; vi. 33d–216, 224d, 247a, 273a, 346d, 393c–395, 417a
Constantius I. (Chlorus), i. 319c, 333c, 343d–344, 348c–349, 351c, 383d–386, 389d; ii. 58c–59, 137
Constantius II., ii. 137, 144c–145, 154c, 155c, 163a, 166a–175, 176a, 190c–192, 214c, 286c–290, 295c–324, 325a, 332a–337, 343a, 352a, 499a; iii. 268c, 271a–272, 276b
Constantius, general of Honorius, iii. 323a, b
Constantius, secretary of Attila, iii. 361b, 369c
Consul, i. 61d, 64c; ii. 93a; iii.

218*a*; iv. 129*c*, 141*a*, *b*, 201*c*, 207*b*–208

Copts, v. 1*b*, 49*b*, 67*a*, 341*a*–342, 348*a*

Cordova, Corduba, iii. 274*d*; iv. 37*c*; v. 376*c*, 411*d*

Corea, iii. 15*b*, 192*b*

Corinth, i. 259*c*, 438*a*; ii. 355*c*; iii. 173*c*–176, 185*a*; iv. 192*c*; v. 580*b*

Corsica, iii. 166*c*; iv. 29*c*, 30*b*

Corvinus, Matthias, vi. 408*c*

Cosmo of Medicis, vi. 389*d*–390

Courtenay, family of, vi. 208*d*–216

Crassus, i. 2*b*

Cremona, iii. 216*d*

Crescentius, v. 197*d*

Crete, v. 385*a*, 419*d*, 420*c*, 438*a*; vi. 181*c*

Crim Tartary, i. 254*b*

Crimea, iii. 10*c*; iv. 195*c*; vi. 268*c*

Crispus, patrician, iv. 506*c*, 508*a*

Crispus, son of Constantine, i. 427*b*; ii. 138*d*–139, 240*b*

Croatia, v. 508*a*

Ctesiphon, ii. 200*c*–201, 330*c*; ii. 416*b*, 423*d*, 424*d*, 428*d*–434; iv. 306*c*, 307*c*, 484*c*; v. 303*c*

Cublai Khan, vi. 280*d*, 281*c*–282, 288*c*–289

Cucusus, iii. 308*c*, *d*

Cufa, v. 303*d*–304

Cumæ, iv. 353*a*, 354*b*

Cunimund, iv. 447*d*–448, 449*c*, 454*c*

Curds, vi. 110*a*

Cybele, i. 33*a*, 88*b*; ii. 363*b*, 364*b*, 404*a*

Cynics, ii. 520*a*; iv. 3*b*

Cyprian, i. 476*a*, 479*d*, 495*d*; ii. 29*a*–34, 37 n.³, 246 n.², 263 n.¹

Cyprus, ii. 146*a*; iii. 169*a*, 299*a*, 309*a*; iv. 6*c*, 483*d*; vi. 142*b*

Cyrene, i. 26*b*; ii. 255*b*, 262*a*

Cyriades, i. 263*d*

Cyril of Alexandria, ii. 370*b*; v. 1*b*, 10*d*–15, 18*a*, 19*b*–28

Cyril of Jerusalem, ii. 287*c*, 384*b*

Cyrus, i. 202*b*; ii. 177 n.¹, 420*b*; iii. 13*b*; iv. 196*b*

Cyzicus, i. 257*d*–258, 259*a*; ii.

74*c*, 316*a*, 468*d*; iii. 308*c*; iv. 182*c*

Dacia, i. 6*b*, 240*a*, 286*a*; ii. 340*b*; iii. 53*a*, 148*a*, 172*a*; iv. 120*a*, 146*c*

Dacians, i. 6*a*, 286*a*; ii. 148*a*

Dagisteus, iv. 316*d*, 348*c*

Dagobert, iii. 266*b*; iv. 66*a*

Daimbert, vi. 86*a*

Dalmatia, i. 23*d*; iii. 1*d*, 148*a*, 171*a*, 243*c*, 245*a*, 323*d*, 326*a*, 433*a*, 452*a*

Dalmatius, ii. 137, 153*c*; v. 23*a*

Damascus, iv. 194*a*, 510*d*; v. 288*c*, 296*d*, 312*c*, 316*a*–319, 389*a*; vi. 322*b*

Damasus, ii. 483*a*, 484*b*–486; iii. 74*b*

Dames the Arab, v. 331*b*–332

Damietta, vi. 124*c*, 129*a*

Damophilus, iii. 75*c*, 79*a*

Dandalo, vi. 149*c*–150, 154*a*, 179*a*, 180*d*–181

Danes, iv. 90*c*

Dantzic, i. 237*a*

Danube, i. 3*a*, 18*b*–24*a*, 209*a*, *c*, 240*b*, *c*, 253*d*; ii. 147*b*, 186*b*; iii. 13*a*, 26*d*, 29*c*, 193*d*; v. 505*a*

Daphne, ii. 394*a*–395, 396*b*; iv. 306*a*

Dara, iv. 199*c*, 213*a*, 214*a*, 482*b*

Dastagerd, iv. 530*a*

Datius, bishop, iv. 262*a*, 266*b*

David, King (Hebrew), ii. 225*c*, 381*a*; iii. 107*d*; v. 134*c*

Dead Sea, iv. 2*c*

Decemvirs, iv. 374*c*, 377*a*–383, 388*c*

Decius, Emperor, i. 232*c*–233, 240*d*–244, 478*b*; ii. 29*c*, 43*a*; iii. 136*c*, 340*d*–342

Delators, i. 86*c*, 98*c*

Delphi, ii. 82*b*, 355*c*; iii. 112*b*

Denmark, iv. 107*d*

Deogratias, bishop, iii. 413*a*

Derar, v. 313*a*, 314*c*–315

Despot (title), v. 460*d*; vi. 224*b*

Diana, i. 254*b*, 261*a*; iii. 343*a*

Dictator, iii. 218*a*, 285*b*

Dijon, iv. 54*d*

Diocletian, Emperor, i. 275*a*, 319*b*, 338*d*–339, 340*a*–384*d*,

372*a*–379, 384*c*, 416*d*–417; ii.
46*d*–58, 176*b*, 353*d*; iii. 136*c*
Dion Cassius, i. xv*a*, 2 n.[1], etc.,
151*a*
Dioscuros, v. 26*c*–30
Disabul, great Khan, iv. 294*a*, *c*
Dniester, i. 240*b*, 280*a*; iii. 26*c*
Docetes, ii. 268*b*; v. 5*c*, 6*a*
Dominus (title), i. 370*d*; ii. 354*a*;
v. 161*b*; vi. 464*d*
Domitian, Emperor, i. 131*d*–132,
187*b*; ii. 21*b*; baths, ii. 191*c*
Donatists, ii. 262 n.[1], 263*d*, *c*,
316*a*–319, 372*a*; iii. 331*b*–337;
iv. 32*b*, 35*b*
Donatus, ii. 262*a*
Dorylæum, battle of, vi. 69*c*–70
Druids, i. 32*c*; iv. 99*c*
Dura, ii. 445*c*, 447 n.[2], 448*c*; iv.
304*c*
Durazzo, v. 564*a*–569; vi. 185*c*
Dyrrachium, iii. 196*c*; iv. 241*d*

East, the, ii. 486*d*, 509*d*, 511*a*,
515*b*; iii. 19*a*
Ebionites, i. 439*c*–440, 441*a*; ii.
267*c*–268; v. 2*a*, 3*c*
Ecbatana, i. 201*b*; ii. 437*a*, 450*c*,
508*c*; v. 441*a*
Edecon, Attila's ambassador, iii.
362*a*–363, 369*d*, 455*a*
Edessa, i. 201*c*–202, 263*a*, 494*a*;
ii. 202*c*, 400*a*, 415*c*, 457*a*; iv.
176*b*, 197*a*, *c*, 199*c*; v. 50*c*,
144*c*–148; vi. 51*c*, 72*a*, 208*d*
Egeria, iv. 376*b*
Egypt, i. 26*a*, 155*c*, 326*c*, 353*a*–
354; ii. 192*a*, 245*a*–292, 398*b*,
440*b*; iii. 1*d*, 52*c*, 87*a*, 130*a*,
147*d*; iv. 3*a*, 371*a*, 415*b*, 511*c*;
v. 293*a*, 337*a*, 349*a*–351; vi.
320*b*
Egyptians, i. 301*b*; ii. 352*b*, 495*d*;
iii. 232*c*; iv. 5*a*
Elagabalus, i. 138*a*–145; iii.
236*b*; iv. 170*c*
Elbe, i. 321*a*; ii. 491*a*–493; iii.
261*c*, 330*a*; iv. 22*d*, 90*a*
Elephantine, i. 354*b*
Eleusis, mysteries, ii. 367*b*, 478*d*;
temple, iii. 174 n.[1], 175*b*
Elis, ii. 355*c*, 394*a*; iii. 175*c*
Elysian Fields, i. 212*b*

Emesa, i. 138*a*, 141*b*, 264*b*; v.
323*c*, 325*b*
Emir, ii. 420*c*, 421*b*; v. 217*a*, 462*c*
Empire, Holy Roman, v. 188*c*–
206
England, iv. 22*c*, 98*c*; vi. 208*d*
Ephesus, i. 50*b*, 261*a*, 438*a*; ii.
367*b*, 369*d*; iii. 340*d*, 341*b*, *c*;
council, iv. 42*b*; v. 1*b*, 19*a*–22
Epicureans, i. 30*c*; ii. 375*a*
Epicurus, i. 59*d*; iv. 204*a*
Epirus, ii. 355*c*, 520*a*; iii. 96*c*,
176*c*, 178*a*, 206*a*, 433*a*
Equitius, ii. 517*d*, 519*b*, 520*c*,
522*b*
Erasmus, iii. 302 n.[3]; 303 n.[1]; v.
504*a*
Erdaviraph, i. 192*b*
Essenians (Essenes), iv. 2*c*
Esthonia, ii. 514*a*
Ethiopia. *See* Æthiopia
Etruscans, i. 22*b*
Eucherius, iii. 208*b*, 210*c*, 211*b*, *c*
Eudocia, wife of Constantine XI.,
v. 121*a*–122; wife of Theodosius,
iii. 317*a*–318, 326*b*
Eudoxia, daughter of Valentinian,
iii. 404*a*, 449*d*; wife of Arcadius,
iii. 153*a*–154, 161*b*, 298*a*–310,
405*a*, 410*a*
Eudoxus, bishop, ii. 479*d*, 480*a*;
iii. 75*c*
Eugenius, Emperor, iii. 111*c*,
114*c*, 115*b*, *d*, 157*c*, 165*b*
Eugenius, Pope, vi. 364*a*–370,
375*a*, 400*b*, 540*d*, 547*a*
Eunomians, ii. 372*a*; iii. 85*b*
Eunomius, ii. 280*b*, 467 n.[1]; iii. 74*d*
Eunuchs, ii. 176*a*–177, 286*c*,
288*d*, 348*a*; iii. 228*b*, 289*a*; iv.
108*d*
Euric, iii. 444*b*; iv. 27*b*, 44*a*, 66*b*,
86*c*
Europe, i. 209*b*; ii. 263*d*, 508*a*; iii.
4*a*, 5*c*, 11*b*, 22*c*, 147*c*; iv. 107*a*,
371*b*
Eusebia, wife of Constantius, ii.
185*a*–189, 207*c*, 334*d*–335
Eusebius, chamberlain, ii. 177*b*,
183*d*, 343*c*, 350*d*; iii. 245*c*
Eusebius of Cæsarea, ii. 65*a*, 67*b*,
218*c*, 226*c*, 233*c*–237, 274*a*,
285*a*, *c*, 293*c*; v. 145*a*

Eusebius of Nicomedia, ii. 274a, 276c, 284d-286, 360b

Eustathius, bishop, ii. 286a, 310c

Eutropius, eunuch, iii. 112c, 153c-155, 161b, 288d-299, 302c

Eutyches, iii. 314a; v. 1b, 23a, 26a, 44b

Euxine Sea, i. 254a-258; ii. 72a, 80b, 467a; iii. 8a, 12a, 24b; iv. 193c, 195c, 283a, 286a, 309a

Exarchs, iii. 191a; iv. 229d, 358b, 359c, 444b, 464b; v. 169a-171

Falcandus, Hugh, v. 587a

Fathers, iv. 406b 409

Fatima, v. 277b, 179d, 281c, 287a

Fatimites, v. 85c, 107a, 287a, 289b, 402a, 411a; vi. 29b, 32a, 80a

Faunus, i. 329b; iii. 439a

Fausta, Empress, i. 394a, 398a, 399c; ii. 142b-143

Faustina, Empress, i. 76c, 83a; ii. 469a

Felix, bishop, ii. 311c-312; iii. 260b, c

Fingal, i. 126a, 493 n.[4]

Finland, iv. 108a

Firmus (Moor), ii. 503c-505, 518c, iii. 162b

Flacilla, Empress, iii. 75a, 101c

Flaminian way, i. 289c; ii. 190c; iii. 217b, 246c; iv. 250a, 251c, 349c

Flavian of Constantinople, v. 27c

Florence, iii. 195a-198, 211b; vi. 346d, 395a

Florentius, ii. 327c, 333a, 340c, 351b

Fortune, goddess, iv. 103c; temple, ii. 404a

France, ii. 128c; iv. 74a, 77a, 85a, 404c; v. 184a, 385a, 396a; vi. 208d, 357c-388

Frangipani, Cencio, vi. 468d-469

Franks, i. 248c-251, 319d-324, 401b; ii. 113c, 203c-211, 325a, 333c; iii. 41a, 71c, 109d, 110b, 198c-199, 266a-279, 380a-390, 413c; iv. 49c, 64c-87, 325c, 355a; v. 75b, 141d, 442a, 477a, 537b, 538d

Franks, Empire of, v. 470c, 477a

Fravitta, iii. 65b, d, 301a-302

Frederic I. (Barbarossa), v. 200b, 582d-583; vi. 96a, 99b, c, 101c-102, 483c-485

Frederic II., v. 200d-201, 501a, 589c, 590a; vi. 93c, 125c, 286b

French, vi. 134a, 172c, 178a

Frisians, iv. 90b, 101d

Fritigern, ii. 513b; iii. 27a, 32b-44, 58d-59; iv. 21b

Fulk of Neuilly, vi. 144d-145

Gabinius, ii. 518a, 520a

Gætulia, ii. 502b, 504d; iii. 166c, 339b

Gainas, iii. 159c, 160a, 161b, 296c, 297b, 299c-302

Galata, vi. 247a, 267a

Galatia, ii. 316a; iii. 291c, 448 n.[3]

Galen, i. 57d, 496a; iv. 353b

Galerius, i. 319b, 343c, 344b, 351c, 356a, 359b, 360c-363, 383d-386, 389c-400; ii. 49c-51, 52c, 55a, 61c-63, 226a

Galilæans, ii. 18c-19, 388b, 397a, 400b, 402a

Gallicia, iii. 275d, 276a, 278c, 328c, 417c; iv. 84c

Gallienus, 231c, 248b, 250a-253, 259d, 266c-271, 275a, d, 276b; ii. 44a

Gallipoli, ii. 74b; iv. 193a; vi. 242a

Gallus, Emperor, i. 245a-246

Gallus, nephew of Constantine, ii. 137, 178a-184, 289a, 361a, 362b

Gannys, eunuch, i. 139c

Garonne, iii. 279a; iv. 44c

Gaudentius, ii. 351c; iii. 127b

Gaul, i. 20c, 35c, 48d-49, 291c-293, 319c, 345a-346, 491c-492; ii. 126b-130, 174b, 186a, 203c-204, 213d-216, 245a, d, 326d, 401d, 466a, 490c-496; iii. 24a, 40a, 41d, 69a, 147d, 186d, 199c-201, 385a, 445a

Gauls, iii. 97a, 114b, 115b, 123c, 232c, 279b, 447b; iv. 11d, 42d, 43c

Gaza, iv. 5c, 35d

Gelasius, Pope, iii. 439d, 461c

Gelasius II., Pope, vi. 468b-469

Gelimer, iv. 210c–211, 219a, 221b, 225a–227, 230a, 233a–234, 238b, 245a

Geneva, iv. 34b, 53c, 54c

Gennerid, general, iii. 244c–245

Genoa, iv. 267b; vi. 267b

Genoese, vi. 267a–272

Genseric, 329b–339, 351d, 375c, 379c, 407c–450; iv. 27b, 30b, 32a

Gentoos, vi. 2c, 4b

George of Cappadocia, St. George (England), ii. 305b, 397c–399; vi. 56c

Georgia, iv. 200c, 201a, 312a

Geougen, iii. 191a–193, 349a, 403b; iv. 280b

Gepidæ, i. 237a, 323c; iii. 349a, 388c, 390b; iv. 120a, 447c–450, 455d

Germans, i. 208a–231, 240d, 249a–253, 284a, 321c; ii. 112b, 174c, 204b, 207a, 213b, 520a; iii. 9b, 69b, 97a, 194a, 197c, 259a, c, 275a, 337c

Germanus, iv. 346a, 501d–503

Germany, i. 2c, 208–231, 321a–323; ii. 486d, 491a, 493a, 514b, 518a; iii. 2d, 7c, 24a, 199c, 279c, 280a, 348b; v. 185c, 519a; vi. 357a

Gerontius, iii. 172b, 269c–271

Geta, brother of Caracalla, i. 124b, 127b–129, 131b

Ghibelins and Guelfs, v. 201a; vi. 468a, 502a

Gibraltar, iii. 277c, 329d; v. 366c, 367a

Gildas, iv. 87c, 91a

Gildo the Moor, iii. 158b, 162b–167

Glycerius, Emperor, iii. 407c, 452b–453

Gnostics, i. 441a–444; ii. 260d, 268a; iii. 87a; iv. 42a; v. 6a, 489c

Godfrey of Bouillon, vi. 33d, 51b–52, 58c–59, 62a, 63a, 70a, 73b, 80c–92

Gog and Magog, iv. 201a; v. 511b

Golden Horn, ii. 73b

Gonderic, iii. 328c, 329b, 337b, d

Gordian, the third, i. 176c, 183d–186

Gordianus, Emperor, 170b–174

Goths, i. 233b–245, 248c, 253d–254, 259d, 280a–285, 302a, 423b–424; ii. 112b, 148b–150, 194c, 501c, 513a–517; iii. 2d, 25a–65, 91b, 97b, 113b–379; iv. 20b–22, 84c, 116c–146, 237d, 238d, 330c, 352d; v. 365a (Spanish); vi. 553b

Gratian, ii. 137, 461c–462, 489c, 521c–523; iii. 37a, 40b–44, 51c, 55b, 61b, 66b–73, 88d, 121b, 202b

Greece, i. 24d, 30b, 35c, 39a, 425c; ii. 176b, 265d, 362b, 401a, 466a; iii. 1d, 6b, 21a, 96c, 169a, 172b, d, 433a; vi. 216c

Greek empire, v. 470c, 505a; vi. 93b, 273a

Greek fire, v. 151d, 392a, 393a–395, 473a, 528c

Greek language, i. 38b; ii. 476d

Greek refugees, vi. 385b–392

Greeks, i. 38b; ii. 281d, 295c, 376b, 389d, 408c, 411b; iii. 12a, 13b, 162a, 172c–174; iv. 103c, 279b; v. 76b, 442a, 537b; vi. 24a, 174d, 178a, 392c, 417a

Gregory I., Pope, iv. 36a, 39c, 444b, 473b, 474b–479, 504c

Gregory II., Pope, v. 155a–157, 162b

Gregory VII., Pope, v. 381b, 571c–573; vi. 35b, 465b, 468a, 491b

Gregory X., Pope, vi. 231a, 232a, 236b

Gregory XII., Pope, vi. 532b, 534b, 535b

Gregory Nazianzen, ii. 178 n.[1], 186 n.[1], 257d, 277c, 319a, 360a, 386c, 435a; iii. 76c–80, 83a–84, 88a, 302c

Gregory of Tours, iii. 341d; iv. 81a

Guelfs and Ghibelins, v. 201a; vi. 468a, 502a

Guiscard, Robert, v. 537c, 551c, 552c–575

Gundobald, iii. 451c, 452b; iv. 53c–55, 71a

Guy de Lusignan, vi. 113b, 114a, 118a

Hadrian, Emperor, i. 7d–8, 12c, 17d, 36c, 40b, 44b, 45 n.¹, 70d, 75c, 438d–439, 489c; ii. 24a, 25c, 380c; iii. 232c; iv. 384a, b

Hadrianople, i. 426a; ii. 183b; iii. 35b–47, 353c; battle of, iii. 56c–57

Hadriatic, iii. 48c, 57d, 94d, 114a, 159b, 216d, 394c

Hakem, Caliph, vi. 29b–31

Hamadanites, v. 435c

Hannibal, i. 227d, 289c, 326d, 405b; iii. 123c, 217c–219

Hannibalianus, ii. 136d, 137, 144b, 145d, 154c

Hanse merchants, iv. 107d

Harran, i. 134 n.¹; v. 227a. See also Carrhæ

Harun al Rashid, v. 187c, 417a–419; vi. 28c

Hassan, v. 282d, 359d–360; the Janizary, vi. 446b

Hebrides, ii. 497b; iv. 6c

Helena, i. 386c; ii. 137, 142c, 382c, 383 n.²; mother of Constantine I., iii. 317d; wife of Constantine VII., v. 109d–110; wife of Julian, ii. 137, 187a, 334c

Heliopolis (Syria), v. 323c–324

Hellespont, i. 427b; ii. 74a–75; iii. 35b, 39b, 50c, 296c

Hengist, iv. 88c, d, 89b, 90a, 92b, 97c

Henry, Emperor of Constantinople, vi. 189a–193

Henry II. (England), iv. 100c

Henry IV. (England), vi. 355d

Henry I. (France), v. 111a

Henry IV. (France), iv. 53b

Henry III. (Germany), v. 550c

Henry IV. (Germany), v. 571a–572

Henry VI. (Germany), v. 587a, 588c–590

Henry the Fowler, v. 519a

Heracleonas, Emperor, v. 77b–78

Heraclian, Count, iii. 210b, c, 250a, 257c, 268a, c, 269a

Heraclius, Emperor, iv. 480a, 507a–508, 510c, 514c, 534; v. 44c, 76d–77, 314a, 332c–333

Heraclius, eunuch, iii. 403d, 405d; præfect, iii. 440b, 442a, 443b

Herat, iii. 355b; v. 379a

Hercules, i. 91d; ii. 220c, 368c; iii. 137a, 231b, 343a; Columns of, i. 27b; ii. 262a, 493b; iii. 204d, 269b, 433b; iv. 228c

Hercynian forest, i. 210a, 211b; ii. 338 n.²; iii. 200a, 385a

Heretics, ii. 260b; iii. 74c, 76a, 84a

Hermanric, ii. 513a–515; iii. 24b–26, 329c

Hermenegild, iv. 37a–38

Hermits, iv. 2a, 7c, 17a

Herodes Atticus, i. 45a–46

Heruli, i. 237b, 259d; ii. 487c, 500c, 513c; iii. 390a, 453b; iv. 125c, 265c, 282a, 357a

Hierapolis, ii. 342a, 410c, 414c–415

Hieronymus. See Jerome

Hilarion, iv. 5c, 6c

Hilary, Pope, iii. 438c

Hilary of Poitiers, ii. 279a, 281c, 282a, 300 n.², 301d

Hilderic, iv. 28c, 30a, 33a, 210a, 222d, 234a

Hindostan, vi. 1b, 2c, 3d, 282d

Hippo, iii. 143b, c, 333b–337; iv. 227d

Hippodrome, ii. 82b; iii. 42a, 325a, 403a; iv. 161c–167

Holy Land, iii. 317d; v. 227c; vi. 27c, 29b

Holy Sepulchre, vi. 1b, 33b

Homer, i. 57b, 446c; ii. 188c, 357a, 362b, 390a, 431c; iii. 92 n.², 175a, 317b; v. 73c

Homerites, ii. 243b; iv. 323a, 325a, 481a; v. 212c, 220d

Homoiousians, ii. 281c

Homoousians, ii. 479c, 480a; iii. 76b

Honoria, sister of Valentinian III., iii. 323a, 382c–384, 394a, 400a, c

Honorius, Emperor, iii. 62c, 101c, 116c–117, 147c–323; iv. 91b

Hordes, iii. 9c, 10a, 15b; vi. 274a

Hormisdas, ii. 419a–425, 433d–434, 468d–469

Hormouz, i. 358c; ii. 155d, 156a; iv. 480a, 484a–490

Hosein, v. 286c–288

Hostilianus, i. 245a

Hugh of Burgundy, v. 196*c*
Hugh of Vermandois, vi. 52*c*–53, 60*a, b,* 61*c,* 70*a,* 76*c,* 96*c*
Hungarians, iii. 344*b,* 355 n.[4]; v. 75*d,* 505*a,* 511*b*–521
Hungary, iii. 22*a,* 344*b,* 364*a,* 365*a,* 384*c;* iv. 280*c;* v. 516*c;* vi. 58*c*–59
Huniades, John, vi. 392*c,* 401*c*–409.
Hunneric, iii. 337*a,* 434*a;* iv. 27*d*–35
Huns, ii. 510*c;* iii. 2*d,* 11 n.[1], 15*a*–27, 40*a,* 49*b,* 97*a,* 118*c,* 191*c*–192, 242*d,* 245*b,* 312*c,* 336*d,* 343*c*–403; iv. 107*c,* 113*a,* 198*a*
Hypatia, v. 14*c*–15
Hyrcania, ii. 437*b;* iv. 322*b,* 483*d,* 485*d*

Iamblichus, ii. 364*a,* 366 n.[2]; iii. 341*b*
Iberia, i. 365*d*–366; ii. 508*a,* 510*a, d;* iv. 200*d*
Iberians, ii. 508*c,* 509*c, d;* iii. 113*b,* 114*b;* vi. 13*b*
Iconoclasts, v. 86*b,* 149*c*–153, 174*a*–176, 494*c*–495
Idatius, bishop, iii. 330 n.[1]
Ignatius, Bishop of Antioch, ii. 28 n.[1], 34*c;* patron of Constantinople, vi. 136*c*
Igours, iii. 15*c,* 403*c;* v. 513*b;* vi. 276*b*
Illyrian provinces, i. 245*a,* 246*b;* ii. 193*a,* 517*c*–519; iii. 49*c,* 103*c*
Illyricum, i. 22*d,* 23*c,* 394*b,* 413*d,* 419*b,* 423*c;* ii. 61*d,* 165*b,* 282*d,* 285*a,* 336*c,* 466*a,* 489*c,* 519*c;* iii. 73*b,* 147*d,* 177*d,* 178*c,* 205*c,* 312*d,* 325*d*–326, 352*c;* iv. 191*c,* 286*d*
Immortals (Persian), ii. 445*a;* iii. 319*c*
India, i. 7*b,* 55*a, c,* 155*c,* 158*a,* 272*c,* 302*a;* ii. 151*d,* 243*a,* 245*a,* 407*a,* 433*b,* 437*b,* 511*a;* iii. 23*c;* iv. 109*c,* 198*a;* v. 54*c;* vi. 316*a*
Indies, iv. 371*a*
Indus, i. 199*a;* iv. 290*c*
Ingenuus, i. 268*b* (pretender); iii. 265*a*
Innocent, bishop, iii. 240*c,* 244*b*

Innocent II., Pope, v. 577*c;* vi. 103*c,* 472*a*
Innocent III., Pope, v. 501*a;* vi. 93*c,* 124*a,* 125*b, c,* 143*b*–145, 171*a,* 180*b,* 428*b*
Innocent VI., Pope, vi. 351*b,* 525*c*
Innocent VII., Pope, vi. 532*b*
Inquisitors, iii. 85*c;* v. 501*b*
Iona, iv. 6*c*
Ionian Sea, iii. 94*d,* 173*c,* 175*c;* iv. 218*c*
Iran, iii. 13*a;* vi. 282*d*
Ireland, ii. 496*c,* 497*c, d;* iii. 201*d,* 287*c;* iv. 6*c*
Irene, Empress, v. 90*a*–93, 173*b*–175; wife of Vataces, vi. 218*b*–219
Irtish, iii. 15*c,* 192*b;* v. 513*b*
Isaac, Archbishop of Armenia, iii. 321*c*
Isaac I., Comnenus, v. 118*b*–120
Isaac II., Angelus, v. 138*b;* vi. 98*b,* 99*b*–100, 134*a,* 141*c*–144, 162*d*–167
Isaac Sebastocrator, v. 119, 130*b*
Isauria, i. 273*b*
Isaurians, i. 273*b,* 319*a;* ii. 186*b;* iii. 27*b,* 308*c,* 310*c;* iv. 118*c,* 193*c*–195, 243*c*
Isidore, Cardinal, v. 171*b;* vi. 396*d*–397, 431*c,* 449*d*
Isis, i. 32*d;* ii. 368*a;* iii. 130*b*
Istria, iii. 94*d,* 179*b;* iv. 134*a*
Italians, iii. 225*a* (tribes), 259*a, c,* 434*b,* 459*c*
Italy, i. 22*a,* 34*c,* 37*c,* 48*c,* 51*c;* ii. 100 n.[1], 245*d,* 252*b,* 257*b,* 401*d,* 466*a;* iii. 6*b,* 42*c,* 73*b,* 93*c,* 147*d,* 178*c,* 215*c,* 432*c,* 448*b,* 454*c,* 457*a,* 460*a*–462; v. 141*d,* 185*b,* 537*b;* vi. 346*d*

Jacobites, v. 1*b,* 43*d,* 44*d,* 52*a,* 57*c*–59, 66*d,* 342*b,* 382*d*
Janizaries, vi. 300*a,* 323*b*
Janus, i. 185*b;* iv. 255*a*
Japan, iii. 14*a;* vi. 282*c*
Jaxartes, iii. 13*a;* iv. 172*a;* v. 306*a*
Jericho, ii. 228*c;* iv. 60*c*
Jerome, ii. 283*b,* 484*b;* iii. 49*b,* 141*b,* 219*a,* 220*a,* 257*c,* 262*d;* iv. 8*a*

Jerusalem, i. 50c, 432b–439; ii. 3a, 19c, 251c, 380c–384; iii. 142b, d, 317c, 318b, c, 412a; iv. 16b, 511a; v. 261b, 328b–330; vi. 1b, 27b, 33d, 51c, 80c, 81d–84, 115d; synod, ii. 285c; temple, ii. 379d, 384b, 385c–386, 387 n.[2], 388a

Jesus, i. 437a; ii. 7d–8, 16 n.[4], 20 n.[3], 267b, c, 275d; v. 3a, 6d, 8a, 16c, 235c

Jews, i. 431d–439, 440 n.[2], 441 n.[2], 451a–452; ii. 3a–4, 18b, 19c–20, 243a, 266a, 379d–380, 478c; iii. 108d, 232c; iv. 40c–41, 138b, 511a; v. 40a, 261c, 263a, 369a; vi. 48a

John XII., Pope, v. 195a, 197a

John XXII., Pope, vi. 490c

John XXIII., Pope, vi. 535a

John Comnenus, brother of Isaac I., v. 118b, 120b, 122d

John Comnenus II., v. 119, 126b–127 (Calo-Joannes)

John of Alexandria, iv. 511c; v. 65a

John of Antioch, v. 20a, 21a–22

John of Apri, vi. 257b, 266c

John of Brienne, Emperor, vi. 196a–197

John of Cappadocia, iv. 181a–182, 211d–212

John of Lycopolis, iii. 112c–113

John of Procida, vi. 236d

John of Selymbria, vi. 306d–308

John, St., apostle, ii. 267 n.[2], 268a, 169a; iv. 189a

John the Sanguinary, iv. 262a–263

John the tribune, iii. 241b

John, usurper after Honorius, iii. 324a, d, 344c

John Zimisces, v. 112b–113, 531d–533

Jordanes, i. 233d; iii. 60 n.[1], 264c, 388c

Josephus, ii. 16 n.[4], 265 n.[1]

Jovian, Emperor, ii. 444a–460, 508a

Jovians, legion, ii. 468d, 500c

Jovinian of Verona, iii. 180a and n.[2]

Jovinus, ii. 488a, 489c, 500b

Jovinus, Emperor, iii. 272c, 273b, 276b, 279c

Jovius, prætorian præfect, iii. 127b, 244b–250

Judæa, i. 73c; ii. 245a

Jude the apostle, ii. 20c–21

Julia Domna, i. 123d–124, 128c–129, 137c

Julia Mæsa, i. 137d–138, 144a

Julian, Emperor, ii. 137, 155a, 178a–179, 184b–189, 203b–217, 324b–442, 453d–455, 499a, 515c; iii. 121c

Julian, notary, iii. 249a; Count, v. 367c–368, 370c; legate, vi. 401b–403, 406b–407

Jupiter, i. 31c, 39d; ii. 20b, 131c, 220c, 238c; iii. 120b, 124c, 125a, 128b, 133c, 136d, 137d, 195c

Justin II., Emperor, iv. 444b–447, 456d–459

Justin Martyr, i. 440a, 454c, 493b, 495c; ii. 268a

Justin the Elder, iv. 146c, 147a–148, 150d

Justina, ii. 521b, 522b; iii. 88d–96, 108c, 109b

Justinian, advocate, iii. 208c; general, iii. 203c; iv. 483c

Justinian, Emperor, ii. 104b; iii. 295b, 311c; iv. 36a, 62c, 112c, 139a, 146c, 148c–366, 369c, 372a–444; v. 1b, 37a–39, 41b–44, 105c, 481a

Justinian II., Emperor, v. 81c–85, 494c

Justiniani, vi. 445c

Kent, ii. 496a, 499c; iv. 90a, 92b, 477c

Kerboga VI., vi. 74c

Khan, title of, iii. 10b, 192b, 193a

Kiow, v. 525a, 528a, 530b, 533c; vi. 284d

Knights, vi. 55b–57; of St. John, vi. 88a, 295b

Koran, i. 80c; iii. 342a; v. 147b, 207b, 234b–241, 410a, 431a; vi. 10a, b

Koreish, v. 217c, 224b, 229a, 251c–279

Labarum, ii. 230*a*, 379*a*, 456*c*
Labeo, iv. 390*b*, 393*b*
Lactantius, i. xv*d*, 384 n.³; ii. 65*a*, 138*c*, 218*c*, 224*a*, 226*a*, 236*c*–237; iii. 145*c*
Ladislaus, King of Hungary, vi. 392*c*, 401*b*–406, 407*c*
Ladislaus, King of Naples, vi. 533*b*
Læta, wife of Emperor Gratian, iii. 239*d*; daughter of Proba, iii. 257*b*
Langres, iv. 54*d*, 79*c*, 80*d*
Larian lake, iii. 181*c*; iv. 134*c*
Lascaris, Janus, vi. 386*c*; John, vi. 224*a*, *c*, 227*a*; Theodore, vi. 184*b*, 216*d*–217
Lateran, iv. 478*b*; v. 171*b*; fourth council, ii. 282 n.³
Latin empire, vi. 178–208
Latin tongue, i. 37*c*; ii. 476*d*; iv. 83*a*, 103*a*, 140*a*; v. 481*a*
Latins, v. 75*d*; vi. 41*b*–207, 226*a*, 346*d*, 392*c*
Laurentius Valla, v. 172*b*
Lazi, iv. 309*a*, 314*c*–320
Leander, ii. 75*a*; Archbishop of Seville, iv. 37*c*, *d*
Lebanon, iv. 189*c*. See also Libanus
Legion, Roman, i. 12*d*–14; iii. 165*b*
Leo, favourite of Eutropius, iii. 296*d*; slave, iv. 79*d*–80
Leo I., Emperor, iii. 434*d*, 435*c*, 440*a*, 450*b*, 452*a*; iv. 113*b*, 115*a*, 155*b*–160, 390*c*
Leo III., the Isaurian, v. 86*b*–88, 148*c*–153, 155*b*–160, 390*c*
Leo IV., v. 90*a*, 173*b*
Leo V., the Armenian, v. 94*c*–96
Leo VI., the philosopher, v. 105*d*–107, 469*a*, 484*b*
Leo III., Pope, v. 179*a*–180; vi. 135*c*
Leo IV., Pope, v. 423*c*–426
Leo IX., Pope, v. 550*b*–552
Leo Pilatus, vi. 382*b*–383
Leo the Great, Bishop of Rome, iii. 399*c*, 400*b*, 411*b*–412; v. 28*a*, 31*a*, 41*a*
Leonidas, iii. 172*c*; iv. 278*d*
Leonigild, iv. 36*c*–38
Leontius, iii. 316*b*, *c*; v. 81*d*–83

Leptis, ii. 502*a*; iv. 329*a*
Lewis II., v. 189*c*, 192*c*, 538*d*–539
Lewis IX. (France), vi. 93*c*, 127*d*–130
Lewis of Bavaria, vi. 490*c*–491
Lewis the Pious, Emperor, v. 188*d*–189
Libanius, ii. 66 n.¹, 178 n.², 186 n.¹, 355*b*, 356*c*, 368*b*, 369*c*, 373*d*–374, 412*a*–413, 415*b*, 448*a*, 454*d*; iii. 46*c*–47, 101*d*, 138*a*, *c*, 303*b*
Libanus, iv. 369*d*; v. 333*c*
Liberius, Bishop of Rome, ii. 301*d*–302, 311*b*–312
Libya, ii. 255*b*; iii. 293*a*, *b*, 440*b*; iv. 4*a*
Licinius, i. 355*d*–356, 378*d*, 396*c*, 397*a*, 400*b*, 413*d*–421, 424*c*–429; ii. 134*d*, 137, 138*b*, 221*a*, 226*a*, 228*a*
Liguria, iii. 88*b*, 183*a*, 427*d*, 433*a*, 448*b*
Lipari, iii. 274*b*; iv. 6*b*, 146*b*
Lithuania, iv. 283*a*; v. 536*a*
Liutprand, v. 162*b*–163, 463*b*
Loire, iii. 279*a*, 281*d*, 376*c*, 386*a*; iv. 57*a*
Lombards, i. 237*b*; iv. 40*a*, 278*b*, 281*b*–283, 447*b*–456, 462*c*–472; v. 162*b*–164, 199*c*–200
Lombardy, i. 22*a*; iii. 395*c*; iv. 452*a*
London, i. 48*d*; ii. 501*a*; vi. 358*c*
Longinus, i. 58*b*, 300*c*; exarch, iv. 452*a*, 456*b*
Lorraine, ii. 204*a*; iv. 48*b*; v. 189*c*
Lothair, iv. 355*a*–356; Emperor, v. 189*a*
Louis VII., v. 138*c*, 580*d*; vi. 95*c*, 100*c*–101, 104*a*, 139*a*
Louis IX., vi. 93*c*, 127*d*–130, 200*d*, 235*a*, *c*
Lucania, iii. 233*b*, 267*a*, 408*c*, 433*a*; iv. 134*b*
Lucian, i. 31*a*, 57*c*, 488*a*; ii. 7*a*; iii. 142*b*, *d*, 152*c*–153
Luke, St., ii. 390*a*; iii. 140*c*, 317*b*; v. 146*c*
Lupicinus, general, ii. 327*c*, 333*a*, 470*a*; governor, iii. 31*b*–34
Lyceum, ii. 267*b*; iv. 203*c*; v. 413*a*

Lycus, ii. 75c–76; iii. 371d
Lydia, ii. 377a; iii. 63a, 291c, 299c, 305d
Lyons, i. 293b; ii. 174b; iii. 71b, 387a, 427d; iv. 53c, 55a; battle, i. 115c

Macarius of Antioch, v. 46b–47, 60a
Macedonia, i. 24c, 391b; ii. 355a; iii. 53c, 64c, 148a, 172b, 353c; iv. 109c
Macedonians, ii. 265d; iv. 202b; sect, ii. 372a; iii. 81c
Macedonius, bishop, ii. 312d–315; iii. 75c; heretic, v. 34c–36
Machiavel, i. 218a; iii. 195a
Macrianus, pretender, i. 268; prince, ii. 492b
Macrinus, Emperor, i. 133c, 135b, 200a; præfect, i. 263b
Mæotis, lake, iii. 513c; iii. 12a, 350b; iv. 278d, 283a
Mæsia, i. 232a, 240b, 260a; ii. 519b; iii. 30d, 53c, 352a
Magi, i. 191c–192, 195b–197; ii. 156a, 243a, 509c; iii. 319a; iv. 198a, 199a, 206c, 300c, 315a, 316c, 481b, 491b, 493a, 512c, 522c; v. 226c, 227b, 378b–380
Magnentius, ii. 164a–167, 169b–175; iii. 96d
Mahmud the Gaznevide, vi. 1b–7; sultan, vi. 316b–317
Mahomet, iii. 323 n.[1]; iv. 108b, 197d, 301a
Mahometans, iii. 356 n.[1]; iv. 311d
Majorian, Emperor, iii. 412a–430
Majorca and Minorca, iii. 329a; iv. 228b
Malabar, iv. 172a, 174a; v. 53a, 55a, c, 56b
Malek-Shah, Turkish sultan, vi. 20a–23, 32a
Malta, v. 578d; vi. 88c
Mamæa, i. 138 n.[2], 144a, 145b–147, 153b, 167b; ii. 41c
Mamelukes, v. 76a; vi. 93c, 130a, 131b, 268b, 284a, 320b
Mamgo, i. 357b–358
Manichæans, ii. 260d–261; iii. 85b, 87a, 335a; iv. 29b, 42a; v. 5c, 6b, 228a, 489b, d, 492d

Manuel Comnenus, v. 118a, 119, 127d–135, 537c, 581a–585; vi. 98b, 99b, 100b, 306a–308, 340a–342
Maogamalcha, ii. 424c–425, 427b, 428c
Marcellinus, ii. 518a, c; iii. 97b, 431b–443, 452a
Marcellinus, Count, ii. 164a, 173 n.[2], 175b; iv. 36a
Marcellus, i. 82b; ii. 50b, 207b, 353b; iii. 227b; iv. 363a
Marcellus, bishops, ii. 60c, 278a; iii. 128b–129
Marcian, Emperor, iii. 313b, 343b, 372b–373, 435a–437
Marcianopolis, i. 240c; ii. 516c; iii. 33b, d, 34b, 352d, 353b; v. 532a
Marcionites, ii. 260d; v. 5c, 228a, 487c
Marcomanni, i. 84d, 229c, 253c; iii. 204b
Marcus Aurelius Antoninus, i. 9c, 76c–78, 82c–83, 229c–230
Margus, i. 339c; iii. 178b, 345c, 351d, 352a; iv. 127c
Maria, wife of Honorius, iii. 168c, 169b, 210d; wife of Manuel I., v. 135b, 136d–137
Marius, i. 35b, 67b; iii. 99c, 185b, 230b, 458b
Mark, Bishop of Ephesus, vi. 372a, 374b, 396c
Maronites, v. 1b, 49b, 59c–61
Marozia, v. 194b–195, 196c–197
Mars, ii. 220c, 331a, 365c; iii. 120b, 347b, 348a; field, ii. 455c; iii. 159d, 405d, 427b
Marseilles, i. 398d–399; iii. 263c, 327a; iv. 6 n.[2], 44b, 62c
Martin IV., Pope, vi. 234b, 236b, 482b
Martin V., Pope, v. 45d–46; vi. 360a, 362c, 536a
Martin of Tours, ii. 244 n.[4]; iii. 87b, 88a, 128a, 144c; iv. 6a, 51c, 58c
Martyrs, ii. 59a, 60a, 64d–69; iii. 139d–146
Mascezel, iii. 165a–168
Massagetæ, ii. 162c; iv. 221b, 226c
Masters General, ii. 107b

Matthew, St., ii. 390a; v. 3c

Maurice, Emperor, iv. 444b, 461a–462, 480a, 487c–504

Mauritania, i. 251a, 353a; ii. 251c, 264c, 316b, 504a, 506c; iii. 330a, c, 337a, 429b; iv. 35a; v. 357a

Maxentius, i. 391b–414; ii. 60b, 134d, 226a–234

Maximian, Emperor, i. 319b, 340b–346, 353a, 366b–371, 377b, 378a, 392c–399; ii. 49c–50c, 59c

Maximin, chamberlain, iii. 362a–369, 370b, 376b

Maximin, minister of Valentinian, ii. 475c, 517d

Maximin, rival of Alexander Severus, i. 164c–180; ii. 42b

Maximin Daza, nephew of Galerius, i. 385c, 396d–397, 400b, 414a–417; ii. 62a–65, 226a

Maximus and Albinus, i. 175c–183

Maximus, Emperor, ii. 244 n.⁴; iii. 31b, 32b, 64c, 69d–73, 78c, 85b, 89a, 93b–99, 108c–109

Maximus, philosopher, ii. 376c–377, 442c, 465 n.³, 473 n.²; of Tarragona, iii. 269d–270

Maximus, Petronius, iii. 405b; reign, iii. 407c–411, 413c

Mecca, iv. 481a; v. 207a, 213a–214, 224c–253, 265a, b, 294a

Media, i. 201b, 204a; ii. 416b, 421c, 436b; iii. 351a, b

Medina, v. 207a, 213a, 214b, 253a–256, 261c–272, 309a

Mediterranean, i. 27c; iii. 1c, 408c; iv. 87a

Mercury, ii. 365c, 368a, 369d, 405b; iii. 195c, 231c

Mervan, Caliph, v. 403c–405

Mesopotamia, i. 201c–205, 364b; ii. 160d, 198b, 408a, 420b, 449d–453; iii. 319b; iv. 17c

Messiah, i. 436b, 437a; ii. 268a; v. 2a, 4c, 261c

Messina, iii. 262a; iv. 246c

Metz, ii. 488a; iii. 385b

Meuse, ii. 210d; iii. 280a; iv. 45b, 80c

Michaels of Constantinople: I., v. 93b; II., v. 94c–97; III., v. 99d–101, 103a; IV., v. 115d–116; V., v. 116c; VI., v. 117c; VII., v. 120d–122

Milan, i. 276a, 278b, 361d, 390c, 406d; ii. 183b, 184b, 258c, 288c, 296b, 522d; iii. 88c, 94a, 98b, 181b–182, 189c, 248d, 395b, 453a; iv. 265d, 266c, 355a, 453b, c; council, ii. 300a, 301b; edict, ii. 222a, 226c, 250b, 260b

Milvian bridge, i. 410d; ii. 231c; iii. 187d, 450c; iv. 251c, 263b

Mingrelia, iv. 312a–313

Misenum, i. 198b; iii. 428b, 458b, 459a

Mithridates, i. 36a, 62c, 254c, 257d; iv. 313c

Moawiyah, v. 283d, 356b, 386a

Moguls, iii. 18b, 346c, 347a, 354b, c, 355a; v. 76b; vi. 127c, 273a–308

Mohammed, prophet, iv. 480d, 514b, 534a; v. 207a, 217c, 226a, 228c–243, 248d–278, 290b–295

Mohammed, son of Bajazet, vi. 338a

Mohammed, sultan, v. 76c; vi. 408b, 411d–412, 417a–461

Monks, ii. 307c, 310b, 482b; iii. 128a, 129b, 139d–140, 165d–166, 305a, 318c; iv. 2a, 6a–20; v. 152a–153, 585c

Monophysites, v. 32a, 48b, 49a, 56d–59, 71d

Monothelites, v. 45b, 47a, 59c–60

Montanists, ii. 260d; v. 39a

Moors, ii. 505b, 506c; iii. 53b, 99d, 139 n.³, 147d, 204b, 330c–337, 408b, d, 433c, 442c; iv. 31a, 235b–237, 328c–330; v. 357c–358, 361b

Moscow, v. 512c, 524a; vi. 284d

Moseilama, v. 294b–295

Moselle, ii. 488b, 519d; iv. 45b, 48b

Moses, i. 432a, 440c, 450 n.⁴; ii. 225c, 384c; iii. 119c; v. 237c, 256c; law, i. 431c, 433a, 436a, 441a, 451a, 452a; ii. 20b

Moslems, v. 282c, 283b, 300b, 302c, 334a

Motassem, v. 426b–429; vi. 283c

Mourzoufle, **vi.** 167*b*–170, 183*b*–184
Mursa, ii. 170*d*–172, 287*a*
Musa, v. 363*d*–374
Mustapha, vi. 336*c*–338
Muta, battle of, v. 268*b*

Nabal, ii. 503*c*; iii. 164*d*
Naissus, i. 386*c*; ii. 340*d*, 465*d*; iii. 178*b*, 352*d*, 363*b*; battle of, i. 281*b*
Naples, iii. 458*b*–459; iv. 133*c*, 134*a*, 247*b*–248, 332*b*, 334*a*, 465*c*, *d*; v. 538*b*, 539*d*, 557*a*
Narbonne, iii. 262*d*, 263*c*, 265*a*, *c*, 285*c*, 377*c*, 378*a*, 444*a*; iv. 85*c*; v. 397*b*
Narses, ambassador, ii. 196*a*–197; general, iv. 491*a*, 509*c*–510; Persarmenian, iv. 491 n.
Narses, Persian king, i. 358*d*, 361*b*, 363*b*; ii. 155*d*
Narses the eunuch, iv. 153*a*, 263*d*, 265*a*, 325*c*, 347*b*–360, 451*c*–452, 491*b*
Nazarenes, i. 438*b*; ii. 267*c*; v. 2*a*, 3*c*
Neckar, i. 321*a*; iii. 384*c*
Nephthalites, iii. 21*a*; iv. 198*a*, 290*b*
Nepos, Julius, iii. 407*c*, 452*a*–457
Nero, i. 47*a*, 70*c*, 73*a*, 131*d*–132, 160*b*; ii. 14*a*–16, 18*b*, 224*d*; iii. 68*b*, 237*a*; iv. 473*d*; v. 99*d*, 100*b*; vi. 551*b*
Nerva, Emperor, i. 45*b*, 74*c*; ii. 17*b*
Nestorians, iii. 356 n.[1]; v. 1*b*, 16*a*–26, 31*b*, 32*a*, 48*b*, 49*a*–56, 382*b*
Nestorius, iii. 314*a*; v. 10*c*, 16*a*–26, 42*b*, 44*b*, 49*c*
Nice or Nicæa, i. 257*c*; ii. 461*a*, 464*c*; vi. 25*d*–26, 33*d*, 50*a*, 66*d*, 68*b*–69, 216*d*; council, ii. 240*b*, 253*b*, 258*c*–259, 261*c*, 274*a*, 276*c*–277, 284*d*–285, 286*b*, 372*a*; iii. 80*b*, 81*a*, 109*c*, 435*b*; iv. 32*a*, 37*c*
Nicephorus I., Emperor, v. 93*b*, 191*b*, 418*a*, 419*c*, 509*a*, 530*c*–531
Nicephorus II., v. 111*c*–113, 437*d*–438

Nicephorus III., v. 122*c*; vi. 24*d*–25
Nicephorus (Bryennius), v. 122*c*; vi. 24*d*–25
Nicetus, vi. 170*a*–175
Nicholas III., Pope, vi. 236*b*, 237*c*, 482*a*
Nicholas V., Pope, vi. 389*a*, 458*d*–459
Nicomedia, i. 257*a*, 368*a*, 390*c*, 400*a*, 414*d*; ii. 52*b*, 54*b*, 152*a*, 220*c*, 240*c*, 289*c*; iii. 308*c*
Nicopolis, iii. 223*a*; vi. 303*c*
Nile, i. 29*c*; ii. 245*d*; iii. 131*a*, 134*c*, 433*b*; iv. 4*a*
Nineveh, iv. 528*a*
Nisibis, i. 201*b*, 262*c*, 363*c*; ii. 157*b*, 160*d*–162, 416*a*, 417*b*, 447*b*, 450*b*, 451*b*, 452*a*–453; iii. 319*c*
Nitria, ii. 482*c*; iv. 4*b*; v. 12*a*, 14*a*
Noricum, i. 23*b*; ii. 338*a*; iii. 148*a*, 243*c*, 245*a*, 326*a*, 376*b*, 455*c*, 461*a*
Normans, iv. 95*c*; v. 75*d*, 188*c*, 454*a*, 506*a*, 522*c*, 537*c*, 543*c*–590
Noureddin, v. 134*b*; vi. 106*b*–109
Novatians, ii. 260*d*–261, 315*b*, 372*a*; v. 13*b*
Numa, i. 142*a*; ii. 244*b*, 322*c*; iii. 119*d*, 120*c*, 123*b*, 225*c*; iv. 376*a*, *b*, 408*a*, 410*a*
Numerian, Emperor, i. 328*c*–332, 337*b*
Numidia, ii. 251*c*, 262*a*, 264*b*, 316*b*, 504*a*, 506*c*; iii. 234*b*, 334*c*, 337*c*, 339*b*; iv. 237*a*

Odenathus, i. 265*a*, 270*c*, 294*b*–295, 301*b*
Odin, i. 218 n.[5], 235*c*–236. *See also* Woden
Odoacer, iii. 407*c*, 454*c*–462; iv. 43*d*, 120*a*–122, 137*b*
Olybrius, iii. 220*c*, 407*c*, 449*d*–451
Olympic games, ii. 394*a*; iv. 160*a*
Olympius, iii. 132*a*, 208*a*–210, 215*a*, 243*d*, 244*b*, *c*
Olympus, ii. 74*b*, 220*c*, 362*c*, 406*a*
Omar, v. 250*d*, 260*a*, 279*c*, 280*a*, 285*b*, 295*c*, 297*c*, 302*c*, 305*c*, 329*a*–330, 334*d*–335, 338*b*, 343*c*, 345*d*–346, 349*a*; vi. 116*c*

Ommiades, v. 376*b*, 384*b*, 385*a*, 402*d*, 405*a*, 410*a*, 417*a*

Ommiyah, house of, v. 283*d*, 296*d*, 335*c*, 355*d*, 359*c*, 388*a*, 403*d*

Orchan, emir, v. 273*a*, 293*c*–299

Orestes, father of Augustulus, iii. 362*a*–363, 370*d*–371, 452*c*–455, 457–458; prætor of Egypt, v. 14*a*

Origen, i. 467*a*, 468 n.⁴, 490*b*, 494*b*, 495*d*; ii. 28*b*, 41*c*, 42*b*; v. 42*a*

Orleans, iii. 376, 385*c*, 386*a*, *c*, 388*c*, 444*a*; iv. 56*c*, 58*c*, 77*c*

Ormuzd, i. 193*b*–194, 356*c*; ii. 425*b*

Osius, Bishop of Cordova, ii. 236 n.¹, 244 n.¹, 263*b*, 284*d*, 301*d*–302

Osrhoene, i. 201*c*–202; ii. 419*c*

Ossian, i. 5 n.⁵, 126*b*, 493 n.⁴; ii. 499*d*

Ostia, i. 51*c*; iii. 242*c*, 246*d*–247, 411*b*

Ostrogoths, i. 237*a*; ii. 513*a*; iii. 26*b*–39, 59*b*–63, 149*b*, 291*a*, 295*b*, 296*a*, 349*a*, 390*b*, 391*b*; iv. 325*c*

Othman, v. 205*a*, 280*c*–282, 295*c*, 352*a*; vi. 273*a*, 292*a*

Otho I., v. 190, 192*c*, 193*d*, 197*c*, 519*a*–521

Otranto, iv. 355*d*; v. 563*b*

Ottomans, v. 76*c*; vi. 260*b*, 273*b*, 293*a*, 336*b*, 342*d*; 273*a* (Turks)

Oxus, i. 199*a*; ii. 195*d*; iii. 13*a*, 20*d*; iv. 296*a*

Pachomius, ii. 307*b*, 368*c*; iv. 3 n.⁴, 4*b*, 12*a*

Pagans, ii. 371*a*, 378*a*, 398*c*, 456*b*, 478*c*; iii. 126*b*–129, 135*c*–137, 438*c*

Palæologus family, vi. 221*a*; Constantine, vi. 392*c*, 413*b*–416, 417*a*, 427*d*, 433*d*, 443*b*, 446*c*–447; Demetrius, vi. 456*a*–458; George, v. 564*a*, 569*a*, 581*b*; John I., vi. 247*a*, 255*b*, 258*b*, 262*b*–264, 305*c*–306, 342*b*, 346*d*, 351*a*–356; John II., vi. 346*d*, 360*d*–361, 362*b*, 364*d*–376, 395*b*–396, 413*b*; Manuel,

vi. 354*a*–356, 359*b*–361; Michael, vi. 202*a*–204, 216*c*–236, 239*a*

Palatines, ii. 108*d*–109; iii. 201*a*

Palermo, iii. 408*c*; iv. 244*a*; v. 421*d*, 422*a*, 538*b*, 576*a*–577; vi. 237*d*–238

Palestine, i. 25*d*; ii. 67*c*–68, 380*c*, 385*c*; iii. 2*a*, 141*a*, 310*c*, 318*c*; iv. 5*c*; synod, ii. 274*a*

Palmyra, i. 265*a*, 294*d*, 295*b*, 297*a*, *c*, *d*, 298*b*, *c*, 299*c*, 301*a*

Pan, ii. 368*a*; iii. 175*c*, 409*a*, *b*; iv. 205*c*

Pannonia, i. 23*b*, 108*c*, 399*d*; ii. 169*c*, 287*c*, 462*a*, 518*c*, 519*b*; iii. 40*d*, 49*b*, 94*a*, 96*d*, 113*c*, 148*a*, 179*a*, 245*a*, 326*a*, 336*d*, 453*c*; iv. 120*a*

Papinian, i. 121*b*, 131*a*; iv. 390*a*, 395*a*

Para, ii. 509*c*, 511*a*–512, 518*c*

Paris, i. 49*a*; ii. 211*b*, 216*d*–217, 326*a*–330; iii. 71*a*, *b*, 201*c*, 237*c*, 238*d*, 385*b*; iv. 57*b*, 58*c*, 77*c*, 83*b*; vi. 533*c*

Parthians, i. 190*b*, 191*a*, 197*c*, 198*a*, 200*c*, 420*a*, 365*c*; iii. 16*a*

Patricians, ii. 93*c*–95

Paul, Archbishop of Constantinople. ii. 286*a*, 312*d*–313

Paul of Samosata, ii. 44*b*–46, 260*d*

Paul, St., ii. 252*b*; iii. 140*c*, 151*a*, 251*d*, 400*c*; iv. 474*a*; v. 490*a*, 502*b*

Paula, iii. 219*a*, 223*a*; iv. 8*a*, 14*a*

Paulicians, v. 488*b*–501

Paulinus, ii. 409*b*; iii. 82*b*, 93*a*, 318*a*

Paulinus of Nola, i. xviib; iii. 260*a*, *c*

Pavia, i. 289*c*; ii. 173*d*; iii. 194*c*, 208*c*–210, 395*b*, 454*d*; iv. 133*c*, 136*a*, 142*d*, 143*a*, 454*a*, 456*d*; v. 517*c*

Pekin, vi. 278*a*, *c*, 281*a*, 288*d*

Pelagius, archdeacon, iv. 339*c*; heretic, iii. 200*c*, 285*b*, 335*a*

Peloponnesus, ii. 355*c*; iii. 94*d*, 173*d*, 176*b*; v. 450*b*, 452*b*

Pelusium, iv. 371*a*; v. 339*b*

Pepin, count, vi. 522*c*–523; king, v. 163*d*–165

Perisabor, ii. 423*d*–424, 427*b*

Perozes, King of Persia, iv. 197*d*–198; v. 51*b*

Persia, i. 79*d*, 190*b*, 199*a*, 201*b*, 204*a*, 206*a*, 262*a*, 302*a*, 330*a*, 331*a*, 364*a*; ii. 245*a*, 260*d*, 326*a*, 335*a*, 407*c*–408, 424*d*, 425*d*, 448*b*, 510*c*; iii. 21*b*, 96*b*, 309*a*; iv. 213*b*, 293*c*, 480*a*; v. 50*c*, 293*a*, 304*c*; vi. 1*b*, 282*d*

Persians, i. 185*a*, 190*a*, 205*c*–206, 248*c*, 330*b*, 331*c*, 355*c*, 364*b*; ii. 426*b*, 427*b*, 438*a*, 445*b*, 508*a*, 509*a*; iii. 12*a*, 13*b*, 319*c*; iv. 171*b*, 173*c*, 198*a*, 296*a*–318*a*, 480*c*; vi. 9*d*

Pertinax, Emperor, i. 95*b*–101, 106*a*, 107 n.², 108*a*, 109*b*, 112*d*–113

Pescennius, Niger, i. 107*d*–108, 114*b*, 115*b*, 117*c*

Peter, of Arragon, vi. 237*b*–239; Bartholemy, vi. 77*c*–79; of Courtenay, Emperor, vi. 193*a*–194; the Hermit, vi. 33*d*, 47*b*, 49*c*, 76*c*

Peter, St., ii. 43*c*, 252*b*; iii. 74*b*, 140*c*, 151*a*, 240*c*; iv. 39*d*, 136*a*, *c*, 251*a*, 254*a*; v. 193*c*, 490*c*; vi. 463*a*

Petra, iv. 315*c*–318

Petrarch, v. 205*a*; vi. 272*a*, 380*c*–386, 503*a*–507, 515*a*, 524*c*, 527*b*–528, 540*b*–541, 565*b*–566

Pharas, iv. 230*b*–232

Philip, Emperor, i. 185*c*–187, 232*a*–233; ii. 42*c*–43

Philip Augustus, vi. 119*c*–120, 145*c*

Philippopolis, i. 241*a*; ii. 297*a*

Phocas, Emperor, iv. 480*a*, 501*c*–507, 514*c*

Phœnicia, i. 25*d*; ii. 320*d*; iii. 309*a*; iv. 370*a*, *b*

Phœnicians, i. 156*a*; iv. 169*a*, 172*c*

Photius, patriarch, v. 483*c*–484, 533*b*; vi. 136*c*–137; patrician, v. 39*c*; son of Antonina, iv. 273*c*–276

Phranza, vi. 413*d*–416, 424*c*, 429*c*, 430*b*, 449*b*

Phrygia, ii. 57*a*, 260*d*, 470*c*; iii. 63*a*, 291*c*, 295*c*, 305*d*; iv. 194*d*

Pilate, Pontius, ii. 15*a*, 38 n.², 39*a*, 268*c*

Piræus, i. 259*a*; iii. 173*a*

Pityus, i. 255*d*–256; iii. 292*b*, 309*b*

Placidia, iii. 264*a*–265, 277*a*, *d*, 322*c*–326*b*, 333*a*, 336*a*, *d*, 374*b*, 383*a*, 434*b*, 449*d*, 450*a*, 481*c*; iv. 32*c*

Plato, i. 30*c*, 57*c*, 148*a*, 382*c*, 449*a*, 477*b*; ii. 205*a*, 215*d*, 265*a*–269, 281*d*, 345*b*, 365*a*, 375*b*, 455*c*; iii. 138*c*; iv. 140*b*, *c*, 141*c*, 202*a*; v. 412*c*; vi. 388*a*

Platonists, i. 30*b*, 382*b*–383; ii. 364*c*, 366*a*, *c*; iv. 205*b*

Plebeians, ii. 93*c*–94; iii. 461*c*

Pliny, i. 49*b*, 355*a*, 499*c*; iii. 224*a*; iv. 2*c*, 134*b*, 170*a*

Pliny the Younger, i. 44*c*, 51 n.⁴, 463*c*, 488*a*, 496*b*; ii. 9*a*, 22*c*, 271*b*

Plotinus, i. 267*a*, 382*b*; ii. 364*a*

Po, iii. 183*a*, *c*, 186*c*, 189*c*, 190*a*, 194*c*, 216*d*, 269*c*, 324*d*

Poitiers, battle, iv. 59*a*, *c*, *d*, 77*c*

Poland, i. 220*a*, 238*c*; ii. 193*c*, 513*d*; iv. 107*d*, 283*a*, 284*b*; vi. 273*a*

Pollentia, iii. 184*b*–188, 205*a*, 211*b*

Pompey the Great, i. 62*c*, 155*b*, 170*c*; iii. 121*a*; iv. 278*d*–279; theatre, ii. 191*c*; iv. 132*c*; vi. 547*a*

Pontiff, Supreme, i. 31*d*, 65*d*, 176*b*, 318*b*; ii. 244*b*, 322*c*; iii. 121*a*

Pontus, i. 256*d*–258; ii. 22*c*, 246*a*; iii. 76*c*, 130*a*, 291*c*, 309*b*, 310*c*; iv. 6*a*

Popes, election, v. 141*d*, 153*a*–154; vi. 488*b*–490; temporal dominion, vi. 461*a*; title, iv. 135*c*

Porcaro, Stephen, vi. 540*a*–541

Porphyrians, ii. 285*b*

Porphyry, i. 382*b*; ii. 364*a*, 370*c*; iv. 140*d*

Posthumus, i. 250*b*, 268*b*, 291*c*

Præneste, iii. 220*a*; iv. 134*a*

Prætorian Guards, i. 18*c*, 72*a*, 74*b*, 90*a*, 99*d*–101, 101*d*–105, 112*b*, 120*c*–121, 139*b*, 144*c*, 145*a*, 150*b*, 181*d*–182, 183*b*, 369*c*, 393*a*, 404*b*, 410*c*, 412*c*

Prætorian præfect, i. 121 n.[1], 150c, 185a, 186c, 263b; ii. 56a, 95b–97, 102 f., 105a, 215c, 357a; iii. 88b, 209b, 212b, 221a, 286a, 409b, 414a, 424a, 441a, 445c, 460c; iv. 130a

Prester John, v. 53c; vi. 274c

Priscillian, bishop, iii. 86a

Priscillianists, ii. 399 n.[3]; iii. 85d–87

Probus, Emperor, i. 275a, 291a, 315d–328

Probus, Prætorian præfect, ii. 519a, d; iii. 221a

Proclus, mathematician, iv. 183a–184; philosopher, iv. 205c

Proconsul, i. 63a; ii. 100b

Procopius, ii. 432c, 448b, 450a, 453c, 466b, 470c, 514c, 515a, 518d; iii. 249c, 292d, 311a, 436c

Procopius, historian, iii. 428c; iv. 101a, 151b–153, 177a–180c, 193a, 213b, 215c–216, 287c, 365b, 371b; v. 145b

Proculus, i. 325c; iii. 149c–150

Propontis, ii. 74a; iv. 193c

Prusa, i. 257c, 258a; vi. 293a

Prussia, i. 237b, 253d

Prussians, iv. 90c; v. 524b

Ptolemy, geographer, ii. 492c; iv. 173a

Pulcheria, iii. 313a–318a, 326b, 372a, 434d

Puteoli, i. 52 n.[1]; iii. 227c

Pyrenees, ii. 174b; iii. 200b–204, 275b

Pythagoras, ii. 375a; iv. 2b, 140c, 378b

Quadi, i. 84d, 229c; ii. 193a, 517d, 518b, c, 520b, c

Quæstors, ii. 115c, 117

Quintianus, bishop, iv. 58a

Quintilius, i. 283a

Quirinal, iii. 120b, 252c

Radagaisus, iii. 167a, 193a–198, 205c

Ragusa, i. 23 n.

Ravenna, i. 19a, b, 179b, 393a, 425d; iii. 189c–216, 246c 269c, 272b, 323c, 324c; iv. 121c–122, 125b, 126a, 130a, 133b, 146a,

251c, 268b, 270c, 358b, 359c, 444b, 465c; court, iii. 240c–245, 251a, 269c, 271b, 278c; v. 157c, 158c; exarchs, iv. 464b. See also Exarchs

Raymond, of Poitou, v. 133d; of Tripoli, vi. 113c

Raymond of Toulouse, vi. 39c, 53d–54, 59b, 63d–64, 68c, 81c–84

Recared, iv. 38b, 85c, 87a

Red Sea, i. 55a; ii. 243b; iv. 3a, 173c, 278d; v. 210a

Reformers, v. 501c–504

Remigius, Bishop of Rheims, iv. 50a; master of offices, ii. 502c

Rhætia, i. 23a; ii. 190c, 338a; iii. 181c, d, 245a; provinces, ii. 517c

Rheims, ii. 206c; iii. 200b; iv. 46c, 50a, 80d, 90a

Rhine, i. 3a, 18b, 19c, 21b, 22d, 209a, c; ii. 204b, 208a, 214c, 490b, 495a; iii. 40c

Rhodes, vi. 295b; colossus, v. 336c–337

Rhône, ii. 495a; iii. 376c, 378d; iv. 53c, 61b

Richard I. (England), vi. 93b, 116d, 119b, 120a–123, 142c, 145c

Ricimer, iii. 419c–451, 460a

Rienzi, vi. 503a, 507a–527

Rimini, iii. 91d, 216d, 245d–246, 250c; iv. 262d, 264a; council, ii. 253a, 282c, 289d, 308d

Robert of Courtenay, Emperor, vi. 194c–196

Robert, of Flanders, vi. 53c; of Normandy, vi. 53a, 63c, 70a, 73c; of Paris, vi. 64d–65

Roderic, iv. 85c; v. 364b–368

Roger, Count of Sicily, v. 454a, 537c, 559b, 561b, 573a

Roger, son of former, v. 576a–579; de Flor, vi. 240b–242

Roman army, i. 9d–18, 72b

Roman empire, i. 1–27; iii. 286b; iv. 108b; vi. 417a

Roman pontiff, ii. 258d, 282c, 296b, 311b; iii. 119d, 309a, c, 460c; iv. 36a, 99c, 135c, 139b, 149d, 477a; v. 194b, 503c

Romans, ii. 512c–515c; iii. 22c,
29a, 75c, 113b, 126a, 241c, 433c,
459d–460; iv. 66c, 279b; v.
160c, 482b; vi. 461a

Romanus I., v. 108c–109; II., v.
106, 110c–111; III. (Argyros),
v. 115d–116; IV (Diogenes), v.
121a; vi. 1b, 14a–18; Count, ii.
502a–506

Rome, i. 32c–34, 56b, 290b–291,
491a; ii. 15a, 97b, 176b, 190d,
223c, 246b, 252b, c, 256c, 258a,
311b, 518c; iii. 122a, 123b, 164d,
199d, 206d, 217c–238, 251c–
258, 425b; iv. 103c–105, 253a–
254, 332d, 336a–340, 352a,
359c, 376c, 444b, 472a–473; v.
76d, 141d, 160a, 193a, 385a,
422d–425, 572a; vi. 461a–502,
547a–569; council, ii. 262d

Romulus, i. 309b; ii. 405c; iii.
406b, 439c; iv. 352c, 376a, b,
406c, 420a

Rosamond; iv. 448c, 454c–456

Rufinus, iii. 104c, 148c–160, 171b,
172b, iii. 288d, 290c, 297b,
306b; heretic, iii. 180a

Rugians, iii. 390a, 427c, 453b,
461a; iv. 90c

Ruric, v. 523a–524

Russia, i. 238c; iii. 22b, 26c; iv.
108a, 283a, 284b; v. 505a; vi.
315a

Russians, v. 75d, 505a, 521b–537

Sabæans, ii. 243b; v. 223d

Sabellians, ii. 273a, 276 n.[1], 277a,
278a

Sabellius, ii. 272c

Saladin, v. 76a, 134b; the Great,
vi. 93b, 110b–123

Salerno, v. 541c, 557c–558, 577a;
vi. 236d; medical school, v. 414b

Salians, ii. 211c; iii. 120c

Sallust, councillor of Julian, ii.
327b, 337c; historian, iii. 255c;
officer, ii. 206a; præfect of
East, ii. 350c, 440d–443, 447a,
461b–469; præfect of Gaul, ii.
350 n.[2]

Samarcand, iv. 171c, 172a; vi.
1d, 8c, 308c

Samaritans, v. 40a, c

Samoiedes, iii. 15a; vi. 287a

Saphrax, iii. 30d, 32c, 37a, 39c,
45a, 61a, 320c

Sapor, i. 262c–266; ii. 196b–202,
341c, 408a, 416a, 417b, 419b,
425d, 433b–437, 445a–448,
453b, 508a–510

Saracens, ii. 417d, 445c, 449b;
iii. 27b, 48b; iv. 19a, 108b, 303a;
v. 75c, 97a, 184d–185, 216c–
441, 505b, 537b–540, 546a,
573a; vi. 82b

Sardica, iii. 352d, 361c, 362c; iv.
146c; council, ii. 296c, 301a

Sardinia, iii. 166c, 218b, 433b,
440c, 443c; iv. 30a, b, c, 219a–
222, 225c

Sarmatia, i. 229c, 255a; iii. 192d

Sarmatians, i. 209a, 239a, 240d,
253d, 302a, 329d, 352b, 423c;
ii. 146b–148, 150d–151, 186b,
193a, 194c, 518c, 519c, d; iii
40a, 53c, 388a; iv. 120a, 178b,
451a

Sarus the Goth, iii. 194c, 203b,
209d, 214c, 250d, 273b, 276c

Sassan, house of, i. 199b; iii. 320c,
351b

Sassanides, i. 190b, 207; ii. 419b,
429b; v. 307b

Saturninus, i. 268b, 270a, 324d–
325; iii. 39a, 292d, 300a, 318b,
361c

Save, iii. 96d, 97b; iv. 191a

Saxons, ii. 492c–495, 499c, 501c;
iii. 53c, 281c, 282c, 388a, 413c;
iv. 42c, 87b–97, 466c; v. 193d,
197b–198, 519a

Scanderbeg, vi. 392c, 399a, 408d–
413

Scandinavia, i. 234a, 253d; ii.
495d; iii. 342b, 348c; iv. 126b

Scheldt, iii. 280a; iv. 45b

Scipio, i. 171d; iii. 224a, 458b

Sclavonians, iv. 191c, 278b, 283a–
287, 360b; v. 186b

Scots, ii. 327c, 496b–499; iii. 53c,
204b

Scourge of God, iii. 355c

Scythia, i. 424b; ii. 433b, 514b,
515b; iii. 2d–14, 21a–27, 38d,
48b, 69a, 170d, 177a, 261c,
309a, 348b; v. 505c, 524a

Scythians, i. 208a, 260d, 357b, 358a; ii. 112b, 517c; iii. 3a–14

Sebastian, Count, ii. 489c, 490a; iii. 42c, 43a, c, 46a; iv. 32a

Sebastian, brother of Jovinus, iii. 273b, 276b; son-in-law of Boniface, iii. 374b

Sebastocrator, v. 126c, 460a

Segestans, ii. 199c; v. 305a

Seine, ii. 217a, 495a; iii. 69b, 281d, 385c, 388b, 413c

Seleucia (on Tigris), i. 200b–201, 330c; ii. 429a

Seleucia, council of, ii. 281b, 289d, 308d

Seljuk, vi. 1b, 7a, 8b, 32c

Senators, ii. 355a; iii. 206d, 218a–228c, 261c, 407c, 437c, 450c, 460b; iv. 134a, 160b, 352b, c; vi. 461a, 477c

Seneca, i. 36a, 131b, 146a, 497c, 499c; ii. 282 n.²; iii. 223a; iv. 30a; vi. 507a

Serapeum, iii. 131 n.¹, 132 n.²

Serapion, deacon, iii. 305c; monk, v. 7b

Serapis, i. 32d, 132b; ii. 400d, 402d; iii. 129d, 130b–134

Serena, daughter of Honorius, iii. 156c, 169b, 207b, 211c, 239b, 264b

Servius Tullius, i. 33c; iv. 376a, 381a

Severus, Alexander. See Alexander

Severus, Cæsar, i. 385d–386, 389d, 392d–393

Severus, Libius, Emperor, iii., 407c, 430c–431

Severus, Septimius, i. 107d, 109b–127, 187b, 200a; ii. 40c–41

Severus, general, ii. 207c, 489c, 495b, 500b; Patriarch of Antioch, v. 57a, 62a; philosopher, iii. 438c

Seville, iii. 274d, 329a; iv. 37c, 38b, 85c; v. 370d

Shepherds, iii. 3c–8, 11b, 354a; vi. 1d

Siberia, iii. 7a, 14b, 16a, 21c, 23c, 403c; vi. 286c–287

Sibylline books, i. 289d–290, 409c, 498 n.³; ii. 237c; iii. 120a, 211c

Sicilian Vespers, vi. 238a

Sicily, i. 272a; iii. 1d, 180c, 262a, 351d, 408c, 433a, 443c; iv. 30c, 243d–244; v. 385a, 419d, 421b, 537c, 546a, 543d–590; vi. 216c, 237a

Sidon, iii. 190 n.¹, 292b; iv. 168a

Sidonius Apollinaris, ii. 127c; iii. 384b, 408 n., 419a–421, 437d–438, 445c, 446d, 460b; iv. 81a

Sigismond, Hungarian king, vi. 302a; son of Gundobald, iv. 55d–56

Sigismund, Emperor, vi. 364c, 366c

Simeon, (Greek) v. 493c–494, (Bulgarian) 509d–510

Simeon Stylites, iv. 18a, 20a

Singara, ii. 159b, 201b, 447c, 453b

Singidunum, iii. 352d, 358b; iv. 495d–496

Sion, Mount, i. 439a; ii. 380c–381, 382a; iii. 143a

Sirmium, i. 282c, 327a, 342c, 379a; ii. 288c, 340a, d, 519a, b, d; iii. 52c, 352d

Slaves, i. 39d–42; iii. 197c, 223a, 224b, 228a, c, 232b, 238 n.³, 256a

Sleepers, Seven, iii. 340c–342

Soæmias, i. 138 n.³, 146b

Socrates, i. 456c; ii. 411b; iv. 372d; v. 3a, 273c

Socrates, ecclesiastic, i. xvid; ii. 178 n.³; iii. 305 n.¹

Sogdiana, iii. 21a; iv. 171b

Soissons, iv. 46c, 47b, 71c, 72c

Soliman, (Kilidge Arslan), vi. 24b–26, 68a; son of Bajazet I., vi. 325a, 330c, 337b; sultan, v. 389b, 391c

Solomon, ii. 266b, 385a; iii. 266 n.¹, n⁴; iv. 186a; knights of temple of, vi. 88a

Solomon the eunuch, iv. 236b, 327a–329

Sophia, widow of Justin, iv. 452a, 457c–460

Sophia (town), iv. 191c; vi. 420b

Sophia, St. (church), iii. 78b, 79b, 304b, 307c, 308a, 443b; iv. 146c, 165b, 185b–188, 366c; v. 291b; vi. 1d, 394d–395, 447d–448, 451a–454

South, the, iii. 7*a*, *c*, 12*a*, 16*c*, 23*a*, 48*c*, 353*d*

Spain, i. 20*a*, 36 n.⁸, 38 n.⁴, 49*b*, 156*a*, 250*c*–251, 482*c*, 492*c*–493; ii. 174*b*, 246*a*, 401*d*; iii. 24*a*, 53*c*, 57*a*, 69*d*, 86*a*, 87*a*, 147*c*, 203*d*, 204*c*, 218*c*, 266*c*, 274*c*–276, 407*b*, 433*a*; iv. 85*c*–86; v. 185*a*, 293*a*, 363*b*–377

Spaniards, ii. 495*d*; iii. 53*a*, 257*a*, *b*, 275*a*, 329*d*

Spoleto, iii. 230*c*; iv. 133*a*, 134*c*, 264*b*

Stephen, Count of Chartres, vi. 53*c*, 60*a*, 63*d*, 76*c*, 96*c*

Stephen, St., iii. 142*c*, 143*a*, *b*, 144*c*, 317*d*

Stephen III., Pope, v. 164*a*

Stilicho, iii. 113*a*, 155*b*–216, 239*b*, 244*c*

Stoics, i. 251*a*; ii. 375*b*; iv. 2*b*, 391*c*

Stoza, iv. 327*c*–328

Strasburg, battle of, ii. 208*c*–209

Suetonius, i. 3 n.⁸; ii. 16*c*

Suevi, i. 251*a*; iii. 192*d*, 193*a*, 198*a*, 199*c*, 275*b*, *d*, 278*b*, 328*c*, 329*c*, 379*b*, 417*c*, 427*c*, 444*c*

Sulpicius, iv. 390*d*, 399*c*

Susa, (near Mt. Cenis) i. 406*a*; (Persia) ii. 437*a*, 450*c*; iii. 319*a*; iv. 300*a*; v. 305*c*

Swatoslaus, v. 530*c*–532

Sweden, i. 209 n.¹, 218 n.⁸, 234*b*–235, 236*b*; iv. 107*d*, 126*a*

Syagrius, King of Franks, iv. 46*b*–47

Sylla, iii. 99*c*, 458*b*; iv. 435*a*, 440*d*

Sylvanus, ii. 189*c*–190; v. 490*c*, 492*c*–493

Symmachus, ii. 322*b*, 495*c*; iii. 122*b*–123, 125*a*, 138*c*, 164*c*; iv. 136*c*, 140*c*, 144*b*

Synesius, bishop, i. xvi*d*–xvii; ii. 255*b*–256; iii. 64 n.², 176*d*–177

Syracuse, i. 324*c*; iii. 227*b*; iv. 244*b*; v. 588*a*

Syria, i. 25*c*, 107*d*–108, 137*b*, 139*a*, 153*b*, 264*b*; ii. 397*a*; iii. 16*a*, 102*b*, 128*b*, 137*c*, 147*d*, 296*c*; v. 293*c*, 309*b*–337; vi. 1*b*

Syrians, ii. 408*c*–409; iii. 232*c*

Tacitus, Emperor, i. 310*c*–315; ii. 259*b*

Tacitus, historian, i. 3 n², 211*a*, 214*a*, 218*a*, *b*, 228*c*, 230*b*, 490*c*; ii. 15*a*, 16*c*–19, 473*d*; iv. 42*d*

Tamerlane, iii. 10 n.¹, 11 n.¹, 355*b*; vi. 308*c*–336,

Tanais, ii. 146*b*; iii. 23*b*, 24*a*, 349*c*

Tancred, v. 553*a*, 572*d*; vi. 55*a*, 59*d*, 64*b*, 70*a*, 76*b*, 84*a*, *b*, 94*c*

Tangier, iii. 331*c*, 408*a*; v. 356*d*

Tarik, v. 366*b*–374

Tarragona, i. 250*c*; iii. 269*d*, 274*d*, 328*d*, 417*c*, 444*c*; iv. 85*c*

Tarsus, i. 264*b*; ii. 343*b*, 412*a*, 453*d*, 455*b*, 511*c*, 512*a*; iv. 194*a*

Tartars, iii. 3*a*–14, 22*b*, 191*c*, 354*b*–355; v. 76*b*; vi. 275*a*, 276*a*, 279*a*, 284*d*

Taurus, i. 264*b*; ii. 313*a*, 459*d*; iii. 296*a*, *c*, 308*c*; iv. 195*b*

Teias, King of Goths, iv. 352*d*–353, 354*c*

Telemachus the Monk, iii. 189*a*

Terminus (god), i. 7*c*, 52 n.¹; ii. 453*c*

Tertullian, i. 457*b*, 463*c*, 496*c*; ii. 38*d*–39, 267 n.¹, 270*c*

Tetricus, i. 268*b*, 279*d*, 284*a*, 292*b*–293, 302*d*, 303*b*

Thebais, ii. 307*a*, 479*b*; iii. 112*c*, 440*b*; iv. 3*a*, 4*a*, 6*a*, 13*c*, 17*c*

Theodatus, iv. 242*a*–246, 249*a*

Theodebert, iv. 266*a*–268

Theodemir, iv. 113*a*–114; v. 372*b*

Theodora, daughter of Constantine IX., v. 106, 115*c*, 116*d*, 117*c*

Theodora, wife of Baldwin, iii. 134*a*, *d*; wife of Constantine I., ii. 137; wife of Emperor Theophilus, v. 99*a*–100, 175, 495*a*

Theodora, wife of Emperor Justinian, iv. 146*c*, 152*b*, 153*a*–160, 166*d*–167, 181*d*–182, 260*a*, 273*c*, 276*a*, 277*c*, 343*c*; v. 41*b*

Theodore, of Mopsuestia, v. 42*a*, 50*c*; Angelus, vi. 194*a*–195

Theodoret, i. xvi*d*; iii. 128*b*, 339*c*, 340*b*; of Cyrrhus, v. 42*a*

Theodoric II., iii. 414*c*–418, 444*a*, *b*

Theodoric the Goth, i. 226 n.[1], 238b; iii. 377b–380, 386c–390

Theodoric the Ostrogoth, iii. 462c; iv. 49a, 58b, 61a, 112b–146, 240a; v. 506a

Theodosian Code, ii. 88c; iii. 131a, 233 n.[1], 295b, 326 n.[2]; iv. 81c, 82c

Theodosius, lover of Antonina, iv. 273d–276; patriarch of Alexandria, v. 65b

Theodosius III., v. 85d–86

Theodosius the Great, i. 488c; ii. 132 n.[2], 244 n.[3], 510d, 519c; iii. 52c–66, 70a, 72a–75, 79a–80, 84a–85, 93b–119, 124b–139, 147b–157, 170c, 171a

Theodosius the Younger, ii. 79b, 84 n.[4], 254c, 255b; iii. 54, 142b, 309c, 311a, 314c–316, 319a, 324c–325, 342c, 343b, 349c, 353a, d, 358a, d, 371a, d–372; iv. 19a, 387b

Theophilus, Archbishop of Alexandria, ii. 255 n.[4]; iii. 131a–133, 306a, 308a, 309 n.[2]

Theophilus, bishop, ii. 243b; time of Justinian, iv. 385c

Theophilus, Emperor, v. 97a–99, 175d, 426a, 521b

Thermopylæ, iii. 172c, d, 174c, 353c; iv. 27d, 192b

Thessalonica, i. 280c; ii. 252c; iii. 57c, 74a, 94d, 95a, 100c, 103c–108, 178b, 189c, 325c; iv. 192b

Thibaut of Champagne, vi. 145d–146, 151b

Thibet, iv. 172a; vi. 3a

Thomas, St., iii. 319c; iv. 174a; v. 54c, 55c

Thomas the Cappadocian, v. 94c, 96c

Thor, iii. 195 n.[2]; iv. 21c

Thrace, i. 164d; ii. 246a, 340b, 344a, 468c, 515a; iii. 28d, 31b, 35a, 36a, 37b, 43d, 52c, 61c, 63a, 147d, 172a, 296c, 301d, 313c; iv. 116c; v. 488b, 497c

Thrasimund, iv. 28a, 30a

Thule, ii. 501c; iv. 126b; v. 523d, 566b

Thuringia, ii. 491a, 513b; iii. 390a, 393c

Thyatira, ii. 470c; iii. 299c

Tiber, i. 22b, 29c; iii. 200a, 239a, 268a, 408d, 410a, 450c; vi. 552a–553

Tiberius, Emperor of Constantinople, iv. 444b, 458a–461, 462c, 482c

Tiberius, Roman Emperor, i. 49c, 73c, 81a, 102d, 131d–132; ii. 380c

Tigris, i. 199a, 201c; ii. 197c, 199a, 200b, 421c, 429c, 430a, 432c, 435a, 436b, 446b; iii. 288a

Timasius, iii. 113a, 292b–293

Timothy, St., iii. 140c; the Cat, v. 32c

Tiranes, King of Armenia, ii. 416c–417, 508b, 509d

Tiridates, i. 262c, 355c–360, 365b; ii. 157c, 158 n.[1], 416c

Titus, i. 73c–74, 335c–336; ii. 381a, 387 n.[2]; iii. 412a; iv. 415a; amphitheatre, ii. 191c; iv. 132c

Togrul Beg, vi. 1b, 8b, 9a, 11a, d

Tolbiac, iv. 50a, 51c, 387c–392

Toledo, iv. 85c, 86a, c; v. 366c, 368c–369

Tongres, ii. 203d, 211b; iii. 385b; iv. 47c

Torismond, iii. 266b, 393b, 415c

Totila, iv. 325c, 331b–342, 344a–351

Toulouse, iii. 263c, 271c, 378b, c–379, 393b, 414c; iv. 22b, 60c

Tours, iii. 142a; iv. 58c; v. 399d–401

Toxandria, ii. 204b, 211c; iii. 280a

Trajan, Count, ii. 512c; iii. 37a, 45a

Trajan, Emperor, i. 5b–7, 12c; ii. 22c–24, 406b, 429d; iii. 56a; iv. 386c; Forum, i. 47c; ii. 191c; iii. 212b

Trebizond, i. 256a, b; iv. 195c, 196a, 310c, 521b; v. 528a; vi. 25c, 457c

Trèves, ii. 174c, 203d, 258c, 295b, 490a, 500b, 502d, 503d, 519c, 522b; iii. 87b, 88d, 94a, 279a, 382a; iv. 79c

Tribigild, iii. 295b–297, 299c

Tribonian, iv. 396a–398, 399c

Tripoli (Africa), ii. 502*a*–503; iii. 331*c*, 408*a*, 440*b*, 443*c*; v. 353*a*, 578*d*

Tripoli (Syria), vi. 87*b*, 90*a*

Troy, i. 260*b*; ii. 75*b*; iv. 77*b*, 95*b*

Troyes, iii. 385*b*; iv. 46*c*

Tunis, iv. 223*d*; v. 359*a*, 579*b*

Turin, i. 406*b*; iii. 395*c*

Turkestan, vi. 7*a*, 8*c*, 18*d*, 20*c*, 284*d*, 314*a*

Turkmans, vi. 1*c*, 6*a*, 8*b*, 9*c*, 23*c*, 33*b*, 69*c*

Turks, iii. 11 n.[2], 148*a*, 287*a*; iv. 278*b*, 287 n.[3], 288*a*–296, 373*b*, 482*a*, 485*d*; v. 76*c*, 121*d*–127, 307*c*, 429*b*–430, 506*a*, 512*a*, 516*c*, 518*b*, 570*b*; vi. 1*a*, 12*b*, 14*c*, 32*a*, 80*a*, 218*a*, 240*a*, 253*d*, 264*b*, 273*a*

Tuscan haruspices, ii. 439*c*, 478*c*; iii. 240*c*

Tuscany, iii. 127 n.[1], 165*c*, 186*b*, 196*c*, 199*a*, 242*c*, 256*c*, 267*a*, 433*a*, 461*c*

Tyrants, the thirty, i. 267*c*–271

Tyre, iv. 98*a*, 170*c*, 179*b*; vi. 117*a*; council, ii. 293*a*, 299*d*

Ukraine, i. 239*c*, 254*a*; vi. 268*c*

Uldin, King of Huns, iii. 302*a*, 312*c*

Ulphilas, iii. 27 n.[1], 271*c*, *d*; iv. 20*c*–22, 25*c*–26

Ulpian, i. 147*a*, *c*, 148*b*, 150*b*; iv. 382*a*, 385*b*, 386*b*, 390*a*, 395*a*

Ulster, iii. 496*a*, 497*c*

Urban II., Pope, vi. 34*c*, 35*c*–39

Urban V., Pope, vi. 352*b*–353, 529*b*

Urban VI., Pope, vi. 530*c*–531, 532*b*

Ursacius, ii. 290*a*, 487*a*

Ursicinus, general, ii. 190*b*, 202*a*

Ursini, vi. 461*a*, 498*c*–501, 512*a*–513, 519*b*, 523*b*, 533*a*, 542*a*, 544*b*

Ursinus, ii. 484*c*–486

Utica, i. 36 n.[4]; iv. 30*c*

Uzbecks, iii. 4 n.[3]; iv. 108*a*

Vadomir, ii. 334*a*, 489*a*, 510*a*

Valens, Bishop of Mursa, ii. 287*b*,

290*a*; general, iii. 244*a*, 249*a*, *b*; pretender, i. 268*b*

Valens, Cæsar, i. 419*d*–420

Valens, Emperor, ii. 469*b*–523; iii. 1*c*, 2*c*, 15*a*, 27*b*–32*c*, 35*b*, 36*c*, 40*c*–44, 293*a*

Valentia, ii. 501*b*; iii. 273*d*

Valentinian I., Emperor, ii. 461*c*–522; II., iii. 1*c*, 71*c*, 73*b*, 90*a*–96, 108*c*–111, 122*c*; III., iii. 233*b*, 322*c*–326, 333*b*, 373*a*–374, 398*d*–399, 403*c*–406

Valentinians, ii. 260*d*, 400*a*; iii. 108*d*

Valeria, Empress, i. 415*c*–417; ii. 518*a*

Valerian, Emperor, i. 242*b*–243, 247*b*, 252*c*, 262*d*–266, 271*c*, 275*a*, 355*c*, 496*c*; ii. 43*c*–44

Vandals, i. 237*a*, 238*c*, 302*b*, 323*c*; ii. 148*b*, 151*a*, 491*a*; iii. 156*a*, 192*d*, 193*a*, 198*a*–205, 322*c*–443; iv. 22*c*, 27*b*, 32*b*, 220*d*, 234*c*–235, 326*a*, 330*b*

Varanes, i. 330*a*; iii. 215*a*, 319*b*; iv. 486*a*–487

Varangians, v. 522*d*–524, 566*b*–568; vi. 161*b*, 223*a*, 224*d*

Varro, iii. 406*b*; iv. 367*c*

Varus, i. 3 n.[1]; iii. 356 n.[2]

Vataces, John, vi. 195*b*, 197*a*, 201*b*–202, 216*d*; Theodore, vi. 219*a*–220, 224*a*

Vatican, ii. 16*a*, 296*a*; iii. 125*c*, 140*c*, 221 n.[3], 252*c*–254, 450*c*; iv. 5*b*, 254*c*, 479*a*; v. 171*b*; vi. 389*c*

Venedi, i. 238*d*, 239*a*; ii. 513*d*

Venetia, iii. 94*d*, 179*b*, 243*c*, 396*b*–398, 433*a*

Venetians, vi. 134*a*, 147*b*–151, 161*d*, 172*c*, 178*a*, 180*c*, 270*d*–272

Venice, iii. 190*b*, 396*b*–398; iv. 453*c*, 465*a*; vi. 147*c*–165, 272*c*, 368*c*–369

Venus, ii. 320*d*, 364*d*, 365*c*, 382*a*; iii. 129*c*, 169*a*; iv. 155*a*, 367*c*, 368*b*; v. 88*c*

Verina, Empress, iii. 452*a*; iv. 115*c*–116, 455*d*

Verona, i. 48*d*, 407*b*–408; iii. 180*b*, 186*d*, 187*a*, 205*a*, 211*b*, 395*b*; iv. 120*c*, 121*a*, 133*c*, 138*c*

Vespasian, Emperor, i. 47 n.², 49b, 73c–74, 79c; ii. 455 n.¹; iii. 217 n.¹

Vesta, i. 142 n.²; iii. 211c

Vetranio, ii. 165b–169

Victor, ii. 516b; iii. 43c, 45c, 46b, 51c; bishop, iv. 35c

Victory (goddess), iii. 121c, 122c, 124b, 137d

Vienna, ii. 206a, 338c; iii. 203c, 402d; iv. 113a

Vienne, iii. 327c, 333d; iii. 110c, 270a; iv. 55a, b, 59a

Vigilius, iii. 362d, 366d, 369d–370; iv. 33c

Vigilius, Pope, iv. 336b, 345c; v. 43a

Virgin Mary, iii. 317d; iv. 188b, 189a, 351d; v. 6c, 55d, 144a, 146c, 235c, 528b

Visigoths, i. 237a; ii. 513b, 514d, 516b; iii. 26c–63, 178c, 265 n.², 275b, 278b, 387a–446; iv. 22b, 42c

Vistula, iii. 129c, d; iv. 22d

Vitalian, iv. 148d–149, 183b, 262a; v. 36d

Vitiges (Goth), iv. 249c–271, 303d, 331a

Volga, iii. 4b, 20d, 22a, c, 23b, 69b, 192c, 343c, 348d; iv. 108a

Vortigern, iv. 88a, c, d, 94a

Walamir, iii. 349a; iv. 113a, 114b

Wales, iv. 93b, 94c, 96c, 99c

Walid, v. 308a, 374a, 388c–389

Wallachia, iii. 26d; iv. 285c; vi. 142c

Wallia, iii. 277b–279, 377b

Walter the Penniless, vi. 47c, 50a

West, the, ii. 517c, 523a; iii. 2d, 19a

William I. of Sicily, v. 585d–586

William II. of Sicily, v. 585d–586

Witiza, iv. 85c; v. 364b, 367d, 375a

Woden, iii. 195 n.²; iv. 21c, 92c

Wolodomir, v. 111a, 468c, 524a, 534b–535

Xenophon, ii. 177 n.¹, 420b; iii. 390c; iv. 202a

Xerxes, i. 190a; ii. 75a; iii. 30a, 268a

Yemen, ii. 156d; iv. 481a; v. 210a, 217b, 228a, 229b

Yermuk, battle of, v. 326b–328

Yezdegerd, v. 300a, 304a, 306a–307

York, i. 388b; ii. 134c, 258c

Zabergan the Bulgarian, iv. 360b–362

Zara, vi. 152d–153

Zemzem, v. 213b, 224b

Zendavestz, i. 192a, 193 n.¹, 194 n.¹, 195c

Zenghi, Sultan, vi. 106a

Zeno, Emperor, iii. 456c–457, iv. 35c, 112b, 115b–116, 194c; v. 33b

Zeno, philosopher, i. 77c; iv. 203a, 391c

Zenobia, i. 268b, 270d, 279d, 281a, 284a, 293c–301, 302b, 303b; ii. 45 n.³, 46a

Zingis Khan, iii. 3 n.², 10c, 11 n.¹, 346c, d, 354c–355, 366 n.¹; v. 76b; vi. 273a–281

Zobeir the Saracen, v. 354a–355

Zoe, wife of Romanus III., v. 106, 115c–117

Zoroaster, i. 191c–198, 264b, 443a; iv. 42a, 289d; v. 227c, 300a, 378c, 489c, 501c–502

Zosimus, ii. 130d; iii. 56b, 96a, 117b, 138c, 175a, 197a, 283a; iv. 14a